The Questions on the Octateuch

VOLUME 2
On Leviticus, Numbers, Deuteronomy,
Joshua, Judges, and Ruth

THE LIBRARY OF EARLY CHRISTIANITY

THE LIBRARY OF EARLY CHRISTIANITY

VOLUME 2

Theodoret of Cyrus
The Questions on the Octateuch

VOLUME 2
On Leviticus, Numbers, Deuteronomy,
Joshua, Judges, and Ruth

Greek text revised by
JOHN F. PETRUCCIONE

English translation with
introduction and commentary by
†ROBERT C. HILL

The Catholic University of America Press
Washington, D.C.

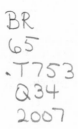
Designed and typeset by Kachergis Book Design;
printed by Edwards Brothers

LIBRARY OF CONGRESS CATALOGING-IN-PUBLICATION DATA
Theodoret, Bishop of Cyrrhus.
[Quaestiones in Octateuchum. English & Greek.]
The questions on the Octateuch. On Genesis and Exodus /
Theodoret of Cyrus ; Greek text revised by John F. Petruccione ;
English translation with introduction and commentary by Robert
C. Hill.
p. cm. — (The library of early Christianity ; v. 1)
Includes bibliographical references and index.
ISBN 978-0-8132-1498-6 (cloth-vol 1 : alk. paper) — ISBN 978-0-
8132-1499-3 (paper-vol 1 : alk. paper) — ISBN 978-0-8132-1500-6
(cloth-vol 2 : alk. paper) — ISBN 978-0-8132-1501-3 (paper-vol 2 :
alk. paper)   1. Bible. O.T. Genesis—Criticism, interpretation, etc.
2. Bible. O.T. Exodus—Criticism, interpretation, etc.   I. Petruccione, John, 1950–   II. Hill, Robert C. (Robert Charles), 1931–
III. Title.   IV. Title: On Genesis and Exodus.   V. Series.
BR65.T753Q34 2007
222′.07—dc22   2007001312

CONTENTS OF VOLUME 2

ABBREVIATIONS

Abbreviations

Abbreviations

Col   The Epistle to the Colossians

1–2Thes   The first and second Epistles to the Thessalonians

1–2Tm   The first and second Epistles to Timothy

Ti   The Epistle to Titus

Phlm   The Epistle to Philemon

Heb   The Epistle to the Hebrews

Jas   The Epistle of St. James

1–2Pt   The first and second Epistles of St. Peter

1–3Jn   The first through third Epistles of St. John

Jude   The Epistle of St. Jude

Rv   Apocalypse, Revelation

ANCIENT AUTHORS AND WORKS

Ador.   Cyr., *De adoratione et cultu in spiritu et ueritate*

Affect.   Thdt., *Graecarum affectionum curatio*

A.I.   Jos., *Antiquitates iudaicae*

Apoc.   Areth., *Commentarius in Apocalypsin*

Apol.   Iust., *Apologiae* 1–2

Areth.   Arethas Caesariensis Cappadociae

Aug.   Augustine

Bas.   Basilius Caesariensis Cappadociae

Bibl.   Phot., *Bibliotheca*

Cant. cant.   Thdt., *Commentarius in Canticum canticorum*

Cels.   Or., *Contra Celsum*

Chrys.   Johannes Chrysostomus

Civ.   Caesar, *De bello ciuili*

Clem.   Clemens Alexandrinus

Col.   Thdt., *Commentarius in Ep. ad colossenses*

Cor.   Thdt., *Commentarius in Epp. ad corinthios*

Cyr.   Cyrillus Alexandrinus

Dan.   Thdt., *Commentarius in Danielem*

D. e.   Eus., *Demonstratio euangelica*

Abbreviations

Dial.	*Dialogus*
Didym.	Didymus Alexandrinus
Diod.	Diodorus Tarsensis
Enarr. in Ps.	Aug., *Enarrationes in Psalmos*
ep(p).	*epistula(e)*
Epiph.	Epiphanius Constantiensis
Epp. Paul.	Thdt., *Interpretatio in xiv epistulas sancti Pauli*
Eran.	Thdt., *Eranistes*
Et. gud.	*Etymologicum gudianum*
Eus.	Eusebius Caesariensis
Exp. in Ps.	Chrys., *Expositiones in Psalmos quosdam*
Expl. apol. in hex.	Gr. Nyss., *Explicatio apolgetica in hexaemeron*
Ezech.	Thdt., *Commentarius in Ezechielem*
frag(g).	*fragmentum (-ta)*
Gal.	Thdt., *Commentarius in Ep. ad galatas*
Glaph. Gen.-Dt.	Cyr., *Glaphyra in Pentateuchum*
Gr. Naz.	Gregorius Nazianzenus
Gr. Nyss.	Gregorius Nyssenus
Haer.	Epiph., *Panarion seu Aduersus lxxx haereses* or Iren., *Aduersus haereses*
Haer. com.	Thdt., *Haereticarum fabularum compendium*
H. e.	Eus., *Historia ecclesiastica*
Heb.	Thdt., *Commentarius in Ep. ad hebraeos*
Her.	Herodotus
Hex.	Bas., *Homiliae in hexaemeron*
hom.	*homiliae, homilias*
Hom. 1–67 in Gen.	Chrys., *Homiliae in Genesim*
Hom. in Coloss.	Chrys, *Homiliae in epistulam ad colossenses*
Hom. in Ioh.	Chrys., *Homiliae in Iohannem*
Hom. in Ios.	Or., *Homiliae in Iosuam*
Hom. 1–6 in Is. 6.1	Chrys., *Homiliae in Isaiam (in illud, Vidi dominum)*
Hom. opif.	Gr. Nyss., *De hominis opificio*

Abbreviations

H. rel.	Thdt., *Historia religiosa*
Ier.	Thdt., *Commentarius in Ieremiam*
Ios.	Joshua
Iren.	Irenaeus Lugdunensis
Is.	Thdt., *Commentarius in Isaiam*
Iud.	Chrys., *Aduersus Iudaeos*
Iuln.	Cyr., *Contra Iulianum*
Iust.	Iustinus Martyr
Ios.	Josephus
Marc.	Tert., *Aduersus Marcionem*
Mi.	Thdt., *Commentarius in Michaeam*
Migr.	Ph., *De migratione Abrahami*
Or.	Origenes
or.	*oratio*
patm.	Thdt., *Epistulae, collectio patmensis*
pf.	*praefatio*
Ph.	Philo Iudaeus
Phot.	Photius Constantinopolitanus
Pl.	Plato
Placill.	Gr. Nyss., *Oratio funebris de Placilla*
Princ.	Or., *De principiis*
proem.	*proemium*
Proph. obscurit.	Chrys. *De prophetiarum obscuritate hom. 1–2*
Prouid.	Thdt., *Orationes de prouidentia*
Ps.	Thdt., *Commentarii in Psalmos*
Q. in Gen. (Ex., Leu., Num., Deut., Ios., Iud., Ruth)	Thdt., *Quaestiones in Genesin (Exodum, Leuiticum, Numeros, Deuteronomium, Iosuam, Iudices, Ruth)*
Quaest. et resp.	Thdt., *Quaestiones et responsiones ad orthodoxos*
Quaest. in oct.	Thdt., *Quaestiones in octateuchum*
Quaest. in Reg. et Par.	Diod. or Thdt., *Quaestiones in Reges et Paralipomena*
1–2 Reg.	libri 1–2 Regum = 1–2Kgs

Abbreviations

Abbreviations

Abbreviations

ThRes   Theological Resources

TLG   *Thesaurus linguae graecae* (stephanus.tlg.uci.edu)

TRE   *Theologische Realenzyklopädie*

VSen   Verba seniorum

OTHER ABBREVIATIONS

ad loc.   *ad locum* = on the aforementioned passage

ap. crit.   *apparatus criticus* = the critical notes on the Greek text

ap. font.   *apparatus fontium* = the apparatus of ancient sources

BIBLIOGRAPHY

SECONDARY WORKS: DICTIONARIES, MONOGRAPHS, ESSAYS, ARTICLES, *ETC.*

Bardy, G., "Interprétation chez les pères," *DBS* 4 (1949), pp. 569–91

———, "La littérature patristique des '*Quaestiones et Responsiones*' sur l'écriture sainte," *RB* 41 (1932), pp. 210–36, 341–69, 515–37; 42 (1933), pp. 14–30, 211–29, 328–52

———, "Théodoret," *DThC,* vol. 15 (Paris 1946), pp. 299–325

Bindley, T.H., and F.W. Green, *The Oecumenical Documents of the Faith,* 4th ed. (London 1950)

Brown, F., S.R. Driver, and C.A. Briggs, *A Hebrew and English Lexicon of the Old Testament,* rev. ed. (Oxford 1951)

Brown, R.E., and R. North, "Biblical Geography," *NJBC,* pp. 1175–95

Canivet, P., *Histoire d'une entreprise apologétique au Ve siècle* (Paris 1957)

Chadwick, H., "The Relativity of Moral Codes: Rome and Persia in Late Antiquity," pp. 135–53 of *Early Christian Literature and the Classical Intellectual Tradition, in honorem Robert M. Grant,* ed. W.R. Schoedel and R.L. Wilken, ThH, vol. 53 (Paris 1979)

Crouzel, H., *Origen,* trans. A.S. Worrall (San Francisco 1989)

Dahood, M., "Ebla, Ugarit and the Old Testament," *Month* 239 (1978), pp. 271–76, 341–45

Denniston, J.D., *The Greek Particles,* 2nd ed. K.J. Dover (London, *etc.* 1950)

Devreesse, R., *Les anciens commentateurs grecs de l'Octateuch et des Rois, StT,* vol. 201 (Vatican City 1959)

———, "Chaînes exégétiques grecques," *DBS,* ed. L. Pirot, vol. 1: *Abdeh-Chronologie* (Paris 1928), coll. 1083–1233

Eissfeldt, O., *The Old Testament: An Introduction,* trans. P.R. Ackroyd (Oxford 1965)

Ellis, E.E., "A Note on First Corinthians 10 4," *JBL* 76 (1957), pp. 53–56

Fernández Marcos, N., "La edición de las *Quaestiones in Reges et Paralipomena* de Teodoreto," *Sef.* 40 (1980), pp. 235–53

———, *The Septuagint in Context: Introduction to the Greek Versions of the Bible,* trans. W.G.E. Watson (Boston, *etc.* 2000)

———, "Some Reflections on the Antiochian Text of the Septuagint," in *Studien zur Septuagint Robert Hanhart zu Ehren,* ed. D. Fraenkel, U. Quast, J.W. Wevers, *MSU* 20 (1990), pp. 219–29

Bibliography

Gignac, F.T., *A Grammar of the Greek Papyri of the Roman and Byzantine Periods*, vol. 2: *Morphology* = TDSA, vol. 55-2 (Milan 1981)

Guinot, J.N., *L'Exégèse de Théodoret de Cyr*, ThH, vol. 100 (Paris 1995)

———, "Theodoret von Kyrrhos," *TRE*, vol. 33 (Berlin/New York 2002), pp. 250–54

Hill, R.C., "*Akribeia*: A Principle of Chrysostom's Exegesis," *Colloquium* 14 (1981), pp. 32–36

———, "Chrysostom on the Obscurity of the Old Testament," *OCP* 67 (2001), pp. 371–83

———, "His Master's Voice: Theodore of Mopsuestia on the Psalms," *HeyJ* 45 (2004), pp. 40–53

———, "On Looking Again at *Synkatabasis*," *Prudentia* 13 (1981), pp. 3–11

———, "Orientale lumen: Western Biblical Scholarship's Unacknowledged Debt," in *Orientale Lumen Australasia-Oceania 2000: Proceedings*, ed. L. Cross (Melbourne 2001), pp. 157–72

———, "Psalm 41 (42): A Classic Text for Antiochene Spirituality," *IThQ* 68 (2003), pp. 9–33

———, *Reading the Old Testament in Antioch*, Bible in Ancient Christianity, vol. 5 (Leiden/Boston 2005)

———, "Theodore of Mopsuestia, Interpreter of the Prophets," *SE* 40 (2001), pp. 107–29

———, "Theodoret Wrestling with Romans," *StudP* 34 (2001), pp. 347–52

Kahle, P.E., *The Cairo Genizah*, 2nd ed. (Oxford 1959)

Keith, A.B., "Some Uses of the Future in Greek," *CQ* 6 (1912), pp. 121–26

Kelly, J.N.D., *Early Christian Doctrines*, 5th ed. (New York 1978)

———, *Golden Mouth: The Story of John Chrysostom, Ascetic, Preacher, Bishop* (Ithaca, N.Y. 1995)

Kühner, R., and B. Gerth, *Ausführliche Grammatik der griechischen Sprache*, part 2: *Satzlehre*, vol. 1 (Hannover/Leipzig 1898)

Lampe, G.H.W., *The Cambridge History of the Bible*, vol. 2: *The West from the Fathers to the Reformation* (Cambridge 1969)

———, *Patristic Greek Lexicon* (Oxford 1961)

Liddell, H.G., R. Scott, H.S. Jones, and R. McKenzie, *A Greek-English Lexicon*, 9th ed., *With a Supplement* (Oxford 1968)

Mandilaris, B.G., *The Verb in the Greek Non-Literary Papyri* (Athens 1973)

Martini, E., *Indici e Cataloghi*, part 19: *Catalogo di Manoscritti greci esistenti nelle biblioteche italiane*, vol. 2: *Catalogus codicum graecorum qui in bibliotheca vallicelliana Romae adseruantur* (Milan 1902)

McKenzie, J.L., *Dictionary of the Bible* (London/Dublin 1965)

O'Connell, K.G., "Greek Versions of the Old Testament," *NJBC*, pp. 1091–96

———, "Hebrew Text of the Old Testament," *NJBC*, pp. 1085–91

Pásztori-Kupán, I., "Quotations of Theodoret's *De sancta et vivifica trinitate* in Euthymius Zigabenus' *Panoplia dogmatica*," *Aug* 42 (2002), pp. 481–89

Quasten, J., *Patrology*, 3 voll. (Utrecht 1950)

Bibliography

Rahlfs, A., *Verzeichnis der griechischen Handschriften des Alten Testaments* (Berlin 1914)

Schäublin, C., "Diodor von Tarsus," *TRE*, vol. 8 (Berlin/New York 1981), pp. 763–67

————, *Untersuchungen zu Methode und Herkunft der antiochenischen Exegese*, Theoph., vol. 23 (Cologne/Bonn 1974)

Schwyzer, E., and A. Debrunner, *Griechische Grammatik*, vol. 2: *Syntax und syntaktische Stilistik* (Munich 1950)

Senior, D., "Aspects of NT Thought: The Miracles of Jesus," *NJBC*, pp. 1369–73

Stefani, A. de, *Etymologicum gudianum* (Leipzig 1909)

Ternant, P., "La Θεωρία d'Antioche dans le cadre des sens de l'Écriture," *Bib.* 34 (1953), pp. 135–58, 354–83, 456–86

Trible, P., *Texts of Terror: Literary-Feminist Readings of Biblical Narratives*, Overtures to Biblical Theology, vol. 13 (Philadelphia 1984)

Groningen, B.A. van, *Short Manual of Greek Palaeography*, 2nd ed. (Leiden 1955)

Vaux, R. de, *Ancient Israel: Its Life and Institutions*, trans. J. McHugh (London 1961)

Vawter, B., *Biblical Inspiration*, ThRes (London/Philadelphia 1972)

Weitzman, M.P., *The Syriac Version of the Old Testament* (Cambridge 1999)

Wellhausen, J., *Prolegomena zur Geschichte Israels*, 5th ed. (Berlin 1899)

Yadin, Y., *Hazor: The Rediscovery of a Great Citadel of the Bible* (New York 1975)

Yarnold, E., *The Awe-Inspiring Rites of Initiation: Baptismal Homilies of the Fourth Century* (Slough 1972)

Young, F.M., *Biblical Exegesis and the Formation of Christian Culture* (Cambridge 1997)

————, *From Nicaea to Chalcedon: A Guide to the Literature and Its Background* (Philadelphia 1983)

Zorell, F., *Lexicon hebraicum et aramaicum ueteris testamenti* (Rome 1963)

BIBLE: ANCIENT TEXTS, VERSIONS, CONCORDANCE, AND CATENAE

I. Ancient Texts and Versions

Masoretic Text (MT)

Kittel, R., K. Elliger, W. Rudolph, *et al.*, *Biblia hebraica stuttgartensia* (Stuttgart 1967–77)

Septuagint (LXX)

Brenton, L.C.L., *The Septuagint with Apocrypha: Greek and English* (London 1851; rpt. Peabody, Mass. 1986)

Bibliography

Rahlfs, A., *Septuaginta: Id est Vetus Testamentum graece iuxta LXX inter-pretes* (Stuttgart 1935)

Wevers, J.W., *Genesis, Septuaginta*, vol. 1 (Göttingen 1974)

Wevers, J.W., and U. Quast, *Exodus, Septuaginta*, vol. 2.1 (Göttingen 1991)

Wevers, J.W., and U. Quast, *Leviticus, Septuaginta*, vol. 2.2 (Göttingen 1986)

Wevers, J.W., and U. Quast, *Numeri, Septuaginta*, vol. 3.1 (Göttingen 1982)

Wevers, J.W., and U. Quast, *Deuteronomium, Septuaginta*, vol. 3.2 (Göttingen 1977)

New Testament

Aland, B., *et al.*, *The Greek New Testament*, 4th ed. (Stuttgart 1994)

Vulgate

Weber, R., and R. Gryson, *Biblia sacra iuxta vulgatam versionem*, 4th ed. (Stuttgart 1994)

II. Concordance

Hatch, E., and H.A. Redpath, *A Concordance to the Septuagint and the Other Greek Versions of the Old Testament*, 2 voll. (Oxford 1897)

III. Catenae

Nikephoros Hieromonachos Theotokes, Σειρὰ ἑνὸς καὶ πεντήκοντα ὑπομνηματιστῶν εἰς τὴν ὀκτάτευχον καὶ τὰ τῶν βασιλειῶν, 2 voll. (Leipzig 1772–73)

Petit, F., *Catenae graecae in Genesim et in Exodum*, vol. 1: *Catena sinaitica*, CChr.SG, vol. 2 (Brepols/Turnhout 1977)

————, *Catenae graecae in Genesim et in Exodum*, vol. 2: *Collectio Coisliniana in Genesim*, CChr.SG, vol. 15 (Brepols/Turnhout 1986)

————, *La chaîne sur la Genèse: Édition intégrale*, TEG, voll. 1–4 (Louvain 1991–1996)

————, *La chaîne sur l'Exode: Édition intégrale*, voll. 2: *Collectio coisliniana* and 3: *Fonds caténique ancien (Exode 1,1–15,21)*, TEG, vol. 10 (Louvain, etc. 2000)

BIBLE: MODERN TRANSLATION AND COMMENTARIES

I. Translation

Metzger, B.M., and R.E. Murphy, *The New Oxford Annotated Bible with the Apocryphal / Deuterocanonical Books* (New York 1991)

Bibliography

II. Commentaries

Entire Bible

Brown, R.E., *et al.*, *New Jerome Biblical Commentary* (Englewood Cliffs, NJ 1990) = *NJBC*

Genesis

Clifford, R.J. and R.E. Murphy, "Genesis," *NJBC*, pp. 8–43
Rad, G. von, *Genesis*, trans. J.H. Marks, rev. ed., OTL (London 1972)
Speiser, E.A., *Genesis*, AncB, vol. 1 (Garden City, N.Y. 1964)

Exodus

Clifford, R.J., "Exodus," *NJBC*, pp. 44–60

Leviticus

Faley, R.J., "Leviticus," *NJBC*, pp. 61–79

Numbers

L'Heureux, C.E., "Numbers," *NJBC*, pp. 80–93

Deuteronomy

Blenkinsopp, J., "Deuteronomy," *NJBC*, pp. 94–109
Rad, G. von, *Deuteronomy, A Commentary*, trans. D. Barton (Philadelphia 1966)

Joshua, Judges, Ruth

Coogan, M.D., "Joshua," *NJBC*, pp. 110–31
Gray, J., *Joshua, Judges and Ruth*, NCBC (London 1967)
Laffey, A., "Ruth," *NJBC*, pp. 553–57
O'Connor, M., "Judges," *NJBC*, pp. 132–44

1–2 Samuel

Hertzberg, H.W., *I & II Samuel: A Commentary*, trans. J.S. Bowden (Philadelphia 1964)

Daniel

Hartman, L.F., and A.A. Di Lella, "Daniel," *NJBC*, pp. 406–20

Tobit

Nowell, I., "Tobit," *NJBC*, pp. 568–71

Psalms

Dahood, M., *Psalms*, 3 voll., AncB, voll. 16–17A (Garden City, N.Y. 1966–70)

Bibliography

Amos

Barré, M.L., "Amos," *NJBC*, pp. 209–16

Zechariah

Cody, A., "Haggai, Zecariah, Malachi," *NJBC*, pp. 349–59

Matthew

Albright, W.F., and C.S. Mann, *Matthew*, AncB, vol. 26 (Garden City, N.Y. 1971)

Viviano, B.T., "The Gospel According to St. Matthew," *NJBC*, pp. 630–74

Mark

Harrington, D.J., "Mark," *NJBC*, pp. 596–629

Luke

Fitzmyer, J., *The Gospel According to Luke I-IX*, AncB, vol. 28 (Garden City, N.Y. 1981)

John

Brown, R.E., *The Gospel According to John I-XII*, AncB, vol. 29 (Garden City, N.Y. 1966)

Perkins, P., "The Gospel According to John," *NJBC*, pp. 942–83

Galatians

Fitzmyer, J.A., "The Letter to the Galatians," *NJBC*, pp. 780–90

ANCIENT AUTHORS AND WORKS: TEXTS, TRANSLATION, COMMENTARIES

Augustine

Dekkers, E., and J. Fraipont, *Sancti Aurelii Augustini Enarrationes in Psalmos, Aurelii Augustini Opera*, part 10, vol. 1: *I-L*, CChr.SL, vol. 38 (Turnhout 1956)

Basil of Caesarea

Homilia in diuites

Courtonne, Y., *Saint Basile, Homélies sur la richesse* (Paris 1935)

Homiliae in hexaemeron

Giet, S., *Basile de Césarée, Homélies sur l'hexaéméron*, SC, vol. 26 bis (Paris 1968)

Bibliography

Clement of Alexandria

Le Boulluec, A., *Clément D'Alexandrie, Les Stromates, Stromate VII*, SC, vol. 428 (Paris 1997)

Didymus the Blind

Nautin, P., and L. Doutreleau, *Didyme L'Aveugle sur la Genèse*, SC, voll. 233 and 244 (Paris 1976–78)

Diodore of Tarsus

Quaestiones in octateuchum

Deconinck, J., *Essai sur la chaîne de l'Octateuch avec une édition des commentaires de Diodore de Tarse qui s'y trouvent contenus* (Paris 1912)

In Psalmos

Hill, R.C., *Diodore of Tarsus, Commentary on Psalms 1–51*, Writings of the Greco-Roman World, vol. 9 (Atlanta 2005)

Olivier, J.-M., *Diodori tarsensis Commentarii in psalmos*, vol. 1: *Commentarii in psalmos I-L*, CChr.SG, vol. 6 (Brepols/Turnhout 1980)

Eusebius of Caesarea

Heikel, I.A., *Eusebius Werke*, vol. 6: *Demonstratio euangelica*, GCS, vol. 23 (Leipzig 1913)

Gregory of Nyssa

Oratio funebris in Placillam imperatricem

Spira, A., *Gregorii Nysseni Opera*, vol. 9.1 (Leiden 1967)

Herodotus

Hude, C., *Herodoti Historiae*, vol. 2, 3rd ed. (Oxford 1927)

Hippolytus

Bonwetsch, G.N., and H. Achelis, *Hippolytus Werke*, vol. 1, pt. 2: *Hippolyt's kleinere exegetische und homiletische schriften*, GCS, vol. 1.2 (Leipzig 1897)

Jerome

Labourt, J., *Saint Jérôme, Lettres*, vol. 5: *Sancti Hieronymi Epistulae XCVI-CIX* (Paris 1955)

John Chrysostom

Opera omnia

Montfaucon, B. de, *Τοῦ ἐν ἁγίοις πατρὸς ἡμῶν Ἰωάννου ἀρχιεπ. Κωνσταντίνου πόλεως τοῦ Χρυσοστόμου τὰ εὑρισκόμενα πάντα.*

Bibliography

Sancti patris nostri Joannis Chrysostomi archiepiscopi Constantinopolitani opera omnia, 13 voll. (Paris 1718–38) = PG, voll. 47–64

Homiliae in Isaiam (*in illud, Vidi dominum*)
Dumortier, J., *Jean Chysostome, Homélies sur Ozias,* SC, vol. 277 (Paris 1981)

Josephus
Naber, S.A., *Flauii Iosephi Opera omnia,* voll. 1–4: *Antiquitates iudaeorum* (Leipzig 1888–93)

Origen
De Principiis
Crouzel, H., and M. Simonetti, *Origène, Traité des Principes,* vol. 4: (*Livres III et IV) Commentaire et fragments,* SC, vol. 269 (Paris 1980)

Homiliae in Ezechielem
Borret, M., *Origène, Homélies sur Ézéchiel,* SC, vol. 352 (Paris 1989)

Philo
Quaestiones et solutiones in Genesin
Marcus, R., *Philo, Questions and Answers on Genesis* (London/Cambridge, Mass. 1953)

De migratione Abrahami
Wendland, P., *Philonis alexandrini Opera quae supersunt,* vol. 2 (Berlin 1897)

The Suda
Adler, A., *Suidae Lexicon,* 5 voll. (Leipzig 1928–38) = *Lexicographi graeci,* vol. 1

Tertullian
Braun, R., *Tertullien, Contre Marcion,* vol. 2: *Livre II,* SC, vol. 368 (Paris 1991)

Theodore of Mopsuestia
Fragmenta in Genesin et Exodum
Devreesse, R., *Essai sur Théodore de Mopsueste,* StT, 141 (Vatican City 1948)
V. above (under *Catenae*) Nikephoros Hieromonachos Theotokes, Σειρὰ ἑνὸς, *etc.;* excerpted fragg. reprinted in PG, vol. 66, coll. 635–48

Bibliography

Commentarii in XII prophetas

Hill, R.C., *Theodore of Mopsuestia, Commentary on the Twelve Prophets,*
FOTC, vol. 108 (Washington 2004)

Commentarii in Epistolas S. Pauli

Swete, H.B., *Theodori episcopi mopsuesteni in epistolas S. Pauli Commentarii,* vol. 1 (Cambridge 1880)

Theodoret

Opera omnia

Schulze, J.L., Θεοδωρήτου ἐπισκόπου Κύρου Ἅπαντα. *Theodoreti cyrensis episcopi opera omnia* (Halle 1769ff.) = PG, voll. 80–84

Sirmond, J., *Theodoreti episcopi Cyri Opera omnia in quatuor tomos distributa* (Paris 1642)

Quaestiones in octateuchum

Fernández Marcos, N., and A. Sáenz-Badillos, *Theodoreti Cyrensis Quaestiones in octateuchum,* TECC, vol. 17 (Madrid 1979)

Siquans, A., *Der Deuteronomiumkommentar des Theodorets von Kyros,* OBS, vol. 19 (Frankfurt am Main, *etc.* 2002)

Quaestiones in Reges et Paralipomena

Fernández Marcos, N., and J.R. Busto Saiz, *Theodoreti Cyrensis Quaestiones in Reges et Paralipomena,* TECC, vol. 32 (Madrid 1984)

Commentarii in Psalmos

Hill, R.C., *Theodoret of Cyrus, Commentary on the Psalms,* FOTC, voll. 101f.
(Washington 2000–01)

Commentarii in Canticum canticorum

Hill, R.C., *Theodoret of Cyrus, Commentary on the Song of Songs,* Early Christian Studies, vol. 2 (Brisbane 2001)

[*Commentarii in Jeremiam*][1]

Hill, R.C., *Theodoret of Cyrus, Commentary on Jeremiah* (Boston 2004)

Commentarii in Epistolas S. Pauli

Hill, R.C., *Theodoret of Cyrus, Commentary on the Letters of St Paul* (Brookline, Mass. 2001)

---

1. This work is of dubious attribution.

Bibliography

Epistulae

Azéma, Y., *Théodoret de Cyr, Correspondance*, vol. 1: *Collectio patmensis, Epp. 1–52*, SC, vol. 40 (Paris 1955)

———, *Théodoret de Cyr, Correspondance*, vol. 2: *Collectio sirmondiana, Epp. 1–95*, SC, vol. 98 (Paris 1964)

———, *Théodoret de Cyr, Correspondance*, vol. 3: *Collectio sirmondiana, Epp. 96–147*, SC, vol. 111 (Paris 1965)

Eranistes

Ettlinger, G.H., *Theodoret of Cyrus, Eranistes* (Oxford 1975)

Graecarum affectionum curatio

Canivet, P., *Théodoret de Cyr, Thérapeutique des maladies helléniques*, SC, voll. 57, 57.2 (Paris 1958)

Historia religiosa

Canivet, P., and A. Leroy-Molinghen, *Théodoret de Cyr: Histoire des moines de Syrie*, SC, voll. 234 and 257 (Paris 1977, 1979)

Quaestiones et responsiones ad orthodoxos

Papadopoulos-Kerameus, A., Θεοδωρήτου ἐπισκόπου πόλεως Κύρρου πρὸς τὰς ἐπενεχθείσας αὐτῷ ἐπερωτήσεις παρά τινος τῶν ἐξ Αἰγύπτου ἐπισκόπων ἀποκρίσεις (St. Petersburg 1895)

CONSPECTUS SIGLORUM

J. F. P.

1. THE MANUSCRIPTS AND THEIR CONTENTS[1]

Abbreviations

1. Numbers accompanying abbreviated names of books of the Bible refer to the *Quaest. in oct.* Thus, "Gn 4–18" would indicate that a manuscript contains Theodoret's *Qq.* 4–18 on Gn, not chapters 4–18 of the biblical book.

2. An annotation of the form "38 (first line)" = the ms. contains the question of question 38 and the first line of the answer (*v., e.g.,* on *2a*)

3. An annotation of the form "Ex 2–54 (except question)" = the ms. contains the questions and answers of Ex 2–53, but only the answer of Ex 54 (*v., e.g.,* on *14*)

Class a

2: Rome, Biblioteca Apostolica Vaticana, *Vat. gr. 631* (11th c.)[2]

A composite of three different manuscripts united by one binding. Only the first contains the *Quaest. in oct.,* but, as this is in itself composite, each section is given its own *siglum:*

2a: Gn 4 (second half), 5–17, 18 (except last few lines of answer), 37 (except question, 37.1 and first third of 37.2), 38 (first line)

2c: Gn 67 (except question and first third of answer), 68–112; Ex; Lv; Nm; Dt; Jos; Jgs 1–19, 20 (first third)

These two, now separated from each other by the interposition of *2b* (*v.*

---

1. This list is based on information drawn from the introduction (pp. xi–xxvi), the marginal notes, and the *ap. crit.* of the edition of N. Fernández Marcos and A. Sáenz-Badillos, and further clarifications generously and patiently provided by Fr. Fernández Marcos in correspondence. It represents an attempt to specify which questions are available in a given manuscript, not the order in which they are actually found.

2. *Ibid.,* p. xiii and F. Petit, *Catenae,* vol. 2, pp. xxxiii–xxxvi.

class *c* below), are parts of the same book and were copied by the same hand.

6: Venice, Biblioteca Marciana, *Ms. gr. I. 33 = 977* (11th c.)

Ex 41 (except question and first line of answer), 42–72; Lv; Nm 1–26, 27 (except last couple of lines), 34 (except question and first third of answer), 35–51; Dt 1 (first third of 1.1 and last third of answer), 2–46; Jos; Jgs; Ruth

32: Munich, Bayerische Staatsbibliothek, *Cod. gr. 351* (16th c.)[3]

Gn 2–112; Ex; Lv; Nm; Dt; Jos; Jgs 1 (except question), 2–19, 20 (first third)

As the sections of this manuscript that contain the *Quaest. in oct.* are copied from other extant manuscripts, it has no value as a witness to the text; nonetheless it will be cited in this edition to illustrate its influence on Schulze's selection of readings.[4] It becomes representative of this group from Gn 71 on.

Class a₁

5: Florence, Biblioteca Medicea Laurenziana, *Plut. VI. 8* (13th–14th c.)

Gn 1–18, 19.1 (first quarter), 20 (except question and first half of answer), 21–45, 47–64, 66–112; Ex; Lv; Nm; Dt; Jos; Jgs; Ruth

Class a₂

11: Patmos, Ἰωάννου τοῦ Θεολόγου, *10* (11th c.)

Gn 62 (except question and first third of answer), 63–112; Ex; Lv; Nm; Dt; Jos; Jgs 5 (question only), 7 (except first half of 7.1), 8–19

12: Patmos, Ἰωάννου τοῦ Θεολόγου, *114* (10th–11th c.)

Gn 19–112; Ex; Lv; Nm; Dt; Jos; Jgs; Ruth

Class B

14: Paris, Bibliothèque Nationale, *Ancien fonds grec 5* (13th–14th c.)

Pf.; Gn 1–76; Ex 2–53, 54 (except question), 55–72; Lv; Nm 1–18, 19 (first half), 22 (last quarter), 23–32, 33 (twice), 34–51; Dt 1.2 (last few lines)–end, 2–31, 32 (last two lines), 33, 34 (except question, 34.1, and first third of 34.2), 35–46; Jos; Jgs 1–5, 6 (except last few lines), 7 (last fifth of 7.2), 8–28; Ruth

3. For the date, a century later than that indicated by Fernández Marcos and Sáenz-Badillos, *v.* F. Petit, *Catenae,* vol. 2, p. xxxiii, note 15.
4. *V.* F. Petit, *Catenae,* vol. 2, pp. xxxviif., li–liii. For the edition of J.L. Schulze, *v.* sec. 1.D of the "Introduction to the Greek Text."

The Manuscripts and Their Contents

17: Oxford, Bodleian Library, *Baroccianus 123* (13th c.)

Gn 58 (except question and first line and a half of answer), 59–76; Ex 2–53, 54 (except question), 55–72; Lv; Nm; Dt; Jos 16 (last third of answer), 17–20; Jgs 1–12, 13 (last third of answer), 17 (last couple of lines), 18–28; Ruth

This ms. will be cited with this group only from Lv on.

26a: Oxford, Bodleian Library, *Baroccianus 216* (12th–13th c.)

Jgs 13 (last third), 14–16, 17 (except last couple of lines of answer)

This is a leaf of *17* (f. 22) that has been bound with another portion of the *Quaest. in oct.* taken from a different book; *v.* the remarks on ms. *26b* listed among the unaffiliated mss.[5] As *17* and *26a* constitute just one source, I have not noted the spot in *Q.* 13 on Jgs, where *17* breaks off and *26a* begins nor that in *Q.* 17, where *26a* breaks off and *17* recommences. None of the text has been lost in the division of the codex.

24: Patmos, Ἰωάννου τοῦ Θεολόγου, *767* (14th c.)

Pf.; Gn 1–76; Ex 2–53, 54 (except question), 55–72; Lv 1–34, 35 (except question), 36–38; Nm 1–24, 31–51; Dt; Jos *pf.*–16, 17 (except question), 18–20; Jgs 1–17, 18 (first two thirds)

30: Florence, Biblioteca Medicea Laurenziana, *Plut. VI. 5* (12th c.)

Gn 13 (last few lines), 14–58, 59f. (both only partially legible), 61 (except question), 62–97, 98 (first third)

Class c

1: Florence, Biblioteca Medicea Laurenziana, *Plut. VI. 19* (11th c.)

Nm 3 (last quarter), 4–8, 12–22, 24–35; Dt 45f.; Jos; Jgs; Ruth

2b: Rome, Biblioteca Apostolica Vaticana, *Vat. gr. 631*

Pf. Gn 1–46 (question only), 47–66, 67 (question and first quarter of answer)

This section of the manuscript (*v.* on *2a* and *2c* in class *a* above) contains two texts both copied from Madrid, Biblioteca Nacional *4710*. The first, a transcription of Gn 2–67 was intercalated between *2a* and *2c* to supply the lacuna in the *Quaest. in Gn* in *2c*.[6] The second completed this supplement with the preface and *Q.* 1. As both sections are apographs of a surviving manuscript, *2b* will not be cited in this edition.[7]

---

5. N. Fernández Marcos and A. Sáenz-Badillos, p. xviii.
6. F. Petit, *Catenae*, vol. 2, p. xxxiv, note 20.
7. *Ibid.*, pp. xlviiif., lif., liv.

3: Florence, Biblioteca Medicea Laurenziana, *S. Marco 725* (9th c.)[8]

> *Pf.;* Gn 1–10, 11 (first few lines), 12–14, 15 (first sixth), 16–112; Ex 1–4, 6–72; Lv; Nm; Dt; Jos; Jgs; Ruth

8: Munich, Bayerische Staatsbibliothek, *Cod. gr. 209* (10th c.)

> *Pf.;* Gn; Ex 1–4, 6–72; Lv; Nm; Dt; Jos; Jgs; Ruth

15: Paris, Bibliothèque Nationale, *Coislinianus 113* (9th–10th c.)[9]

> *Pf.;* Gn; Ex 1–4, 6–72; Lv; Nm; Dt; Jos; Jgs; Ruth

Class c_1

50: Munich, Bayerische Staatsbibliothek, *Cod. gr. 9* (11th c.)

> *Pf.;* Gn 1–5, 6 (except question), 7–19, 20 (except question), 21–37, 39–54, 56–61, 63–69, 71–79, 81–101, 103–112; Ex 1–71, 72 (except question)

51: Rome, Biblioteca Apostolica Vaticana, *Vat. gr. 746* (11th-12th c.)

> *Pf.;* Gn 1 (except question), 2–14, 15 (first half), 18 (except first half of 18.1), 19–33, 37–69, 71–74, 75 (except question), 77–79, 81–102, 104–112; Ex 1f., 4, 6–18, 20–34, 37–46, 50, 52–54, 56, 61–63, 65, 67, 69–72; Lv 1, 3–5, 7–13, 16–18, 20, 22f., 26–31, 36–38; Nm 1f., 4f., 7, 10, 12–14, 18–51; Dt 1–28, 30–39, 41–46; Jos; Jgs 1–18, 21–28; Ruth

52: Rome, Biblioteca Apostolica Vaticana, *Vat. gr. 747* (11th c.)

> *Pf.;* Gn 1, 2 (except question), 3 (except question), 4 (except question), 5–33, 37–41, 43–69, 71–73, 75 (except question), 77–79, 81–102, 104–112; Ex 1–4, 6–18, 20–26, 28–38, 40–42, 44–46, 48–50, 52–67, 69–72; Lv 1, 3–32; Nm 5–49; Dt 2–6, 7.1 (first third), 9–46; Jos; Jgs; Ruth

53: Rome, Biblioteca Apostolica Vaticana, *Palat. gr. 203* (11th c.)

> *Pf.;* Gn 1–69, 71–75, 77–79, 81–103, 105–112; Ex 1–4, 6–18, 20–67, 69–72

Unaffiliated manuscripts

4: Rome, Biblioteca Angelica, *Gr. 41* (late 10th c.)

> *Pf.;* Gn 1–68, 69 (except last few lines of answer); Ex 40 (last fifth), 41–72; Lv; Nm; Dt 1–45, 46 (except last few lines of answer)

7: Vienna, Österreichische Nationalbibliothek, *Theol. gr. 153* (13th c.)

> *Pf.;* Gn 1–3 (except question), 4–112; Ex; Lv; Nm; Dt 1–44, 45 (except last couple of lines of answer); Jos; Jgs

---

8. For this date, which is different from that given by Fernández Marcos and Sáenz-Badillos, *v.* F. Petit, *Catenae*, vol. 2, p. xxiii, note 16.

9. *Ibid.*, p. xxi.

The Manuscripts and Their Contents

9: Rome, Biblioteca Vallicelliana, *B 25.1* (11th or 12th c.)

Complete

10: Rome, Biblioteca Vallicelliana, *E 63* (12th c. with later supplements)

In this ms., which has suffered the loss of the first two quaternios and of individual folios throughout, a hand of the 16th c. has replaced missing portions of the first fifteen questions on Gn.[10] Though the Madrid edition cites both the earlier and later portions by the same *siglum* (*10*), I have introduced the following distinction:

10 (12th c.): Gn. 3, 4 (question and first few lines of answer), 7.2–10, 11 (question only), 15 (last third), 16–32, 34–111, 112.1 (first sixth), 112.3 (last three fifths)–end; Ex; Lv 1–31, 32 (first half), 35 (except question and first 40 percent of answer), 36–38; Nm 1–14, 15 (except last couple of lines of answer), 19 (except question and first couple of lines of answer), 20–29 (twice), 30–51; Dt; Jos *pf.*–9, 10 (first half), 16 (except question and first half of answer), 17–20; Jgs; Ruth

10a (16th c.): Gn. 1f., 4 (except the question and first few lines of answer), 5f., 7 (question and first two lines of 7.1), 11 (answer only), 12–14, 15 (question and first two thirds of answer)

13: Patmos, ᾽Ιωάννου τοῦ Θεολόγου, *264* (12th c.)

Pf.; Gn 1, 2 (except the question and first few lines and last third of answer), 3, 6–11, 15–20, 23–28, 30, 33, 48 (incomplete),[11] 49–66, 67 (first half), 69 (except question and first third of answer), 70–85, 87

17: *V.* the description of this ms. in class *B* above.

18: Vienna, Österreichische Nationalbibliothek, *Theol. gr. 173* (15th c.)

Pf.; Gn 1–19

19: Vienna, Österreichische Nationalbibliothek, *Theol. gr. 178* (15th c.)

Gn 2–5,[12] 19 (except question), 20–29

20: Venice, Biblioteca Marciana, *Ms. gr. I. 37 = 1341* (10th c.?)

Pf.; Gn 1–17, 19–30, 51, 56–62, 68, 70, 71 (except last few lines of answer)

---

10. E. Martini (#76) tentatively identifies the later hand as that of Andreas Darmarius.

11. Fr. Fernández Marcos informs me that this ms. recommences in the midst of Q. 48, somewhere in the area corresponding to PG, vol. 80, col. 152 B, thus somewhere between οὖτος ἐκ τῶν ῥαφαῖν and ἀλαζονείαν, its alternative spelling of which is noted in the Madrid edition (l. 3, p. 48).

12. I assume that the references to ms. *19* in the notes on l. 14, p. 13 (*Q.* 11 on Gn) of the Madrid edition must be mistakes, perhaps for "*9.*"

26b: Oxford, Bodleian Library, *Baroccianus 216* (12th–13th c.)

Pf.; Gn 1, 2 (first few lines), 3 (last few lines), 4, 5 (first couple of lines), 11 (second half), 12f., 14 (first couple of lines), 18 (except question and last two thirds of 18.2)[13]

Though these pages are bound with others containing questions on Jgs, the two portions of this ms. are drawn from different books; *v.* the remarks on *26a* in class *B* above.

31: Munich, Bayerische Staatsbibliothek, *Cod. gr. 47* (16th c.)

Ex 1 (except question), 2f., 5 (last few lines), 6–10, 11 (except question), 12 (through first half of 12.2 + one line in 12.4), 13f., 15 (except question), 16–26, 27 (except question), 28–33, 35f., 37 (except question), 38f., 41–62, 63 (except question), 64–68, 69 (except question), 70f., 72 (except question); Lv 1–4, 5 (except question), 6,[14] 9, 10 (except question), 11–16, 18–35, 36 (except question), 37f.; Nm 1–6, 8–16, 18–26, 27 (except question), 28–47; Dt 1–13, 14 (except question), 15f., 17 (except question), 18–23, 25, 27, 28 (except question), 29 (except question), 34, 35 (except question), 37 (except question), 38 (except question), 39, 41 (except question), 42–46; Jos *pf.*–1, 2 (except question and one fifth of 2.2), 5–10, 12–14, 16–18, 20; Jgs 1, 5–7, 8 (except question), 9, 12, 15f., 20–22, 27 (first three quarters); Ruth 1

32: *V.* the description of this ms. in class *a* above.

35: Paris, Bibliothèque Nationale, *Ancien fonds grec 841* (10th c.)

Gn 13 (except question), 14–112; Ex; Lv; Nm 1–28, 29 (first few lines), 34 (last 60 percent), 35–51; Dt; Jos; Jgs; Ruth

37: Paris, Bibliothèque Nationale, *Ancien fonds grec 842* (12th c.)

Gn 2–17, 18 (first third of 18.1), 19 (except question and first line of answer), 20–112; Ex 1–4, 6–28, 29 (except part of question and first couple of lines of answer), 30–72; Lv; Nm; Dt; Jos; Jgs; Ruth

41: Dublin, Trinity College, *D.1. 28* (15th–16th c.)

Gn 67 (except last five lines of answer)

---

13. This manuscript does not carry any of *Qq. 6f.* In the Madrid edition, the marginal sign of a lacuna in the middle of the second sentence of *Q. 7* (p. 10) is a mistake. The lacuna at that point occurs in *10a*, not *26b*.

14. I assume that the references to ms. *31* in the notes on ll. 8 and 15, p. 162 (*Qq. 7f.* on Lv) of the Madrid edition must be mistakes.

Signs and Abbreviations

2. SIGNS AND ABBREVIATIONS USED IN THE GREEK TEXT AND THE CRITICAL NOTES

Manuscript Classes

a	in *Qq on* Gn		not used
	in *Qq. on* Ex–Jgs	=	the agreement of 2c and 6
	in *Qq. on* Ruth		not used
a_1	in *Qq. on* Gn–Ruth		replaced by "5"
a_2	in *Qq. on* Gn–Jgs	=	the agreement of 11 and 12
	in *Qq. on* Ruth		not used
A	in *Qq on* Gn	=	the agreement of 2c, 5, and a_2
	in *Qq. on* Ex–Jgs	=	the agreement of a, 5, and a_2
	in *Qq. on* Ruth		not used
B	in *Qq. on* Gn	=	the agreement of 14, 24, 30
	in *Qq. on* Ex	=	the agreement of 14 and 24
	in *Qq. on* Lv–Jgs.	=	the agreement of 14, 17 (or 26a), and 24
	in *Qq. on* Ruth	=	the agreement of 14 and 17
c	in *Qq. on* Gn–Lv	=	the agreement of 3, 8, and 15
	in *Qq. on* Nm–Ruth	=	the agreement of 1, 3, 8, and 15
c_1	in *Qq. on* Gn–Ex	=	the agreement of 50, 51, 52, and 53
	in *Qq. on* Lv–Ruth	=	the agreement of 51 and 52
C	in *Qq. on* Gn–Ruth	=	the agreement of c and c_1

Other Signs and Abbreviations

cod. A	*codex alexandrinus* (*V.* note 1 to *Q.* 4 on Jgs.)
cod. B	*codex vaticanus* (*V.* note 1 to *Q.* 4 on Jgs.)
codd.	*codices* = the reading of all the manuscripts
F.M.	N. Fernández Marcos and A. Sáenz-Badillos
F.P.	Françoise Petit
inc.	Marks manuscripts that are lacking something other than or more than just the initial query of a *Q.*
J.P.	conjectured by John Petruccione
om.	omit

Pic.	J. Picot
Q.	*Quaestio, i.e.* both the initial query and Theodoret's response
Sch.	J.L. Schulze[15]
Sir.	J. Sirmond
[32]	Citation within brackets indicates that a manuscript has no value as an independent witness.
‖	where a manuscript breaks off
		where a manuscript begins after a lacuna
=	in the body of a textual note, introduces the translation of a rejected variant
*	marks manuscripts lacking the query that introduces the *Q.*
(Sch.)	An abbreviated name enclosed in parentheses indicates the scholar, other than Fernández Marcos and Sáenz-Badillos, who attests to a reading of a manuscript or an edition.[16]

15. *N.B.* in reff. to Schulze's edition, there are two different forms of citation: (1) "n. 28 to col. 277" indicates that the call-out number 28 appears next to the word or phrase of col. 277 that is illustrated or supplemented by reference to the *Catena Nikephori;* (2) "n. 99, col. 201" directs the reader to note 99, which stands below the excerpts from the *Catena Nikephori* in col. 201.

16. These parentheses are used repeatedly to attribute to Schulze reports of readings adopted by Picot. As I am informed by Mr. P. Goodman, a cataloguer at the Library of Congress, the national databases list only two copies of Picot's edition in the United States: one at Harvard and the other at the University of Chicago.

The Questions on the Octateuch

VOLUME 2
*On Leviticus, Numbers, Deuteronomy,
Joshua, Judges, and Ruth*

QUAESTIONES IN LEVITICUM

I

Τίνος ἕνεκα τὰς θυσίας προσφέρεσθαι προσέταξεν ὁ
Θεός;

(1) Πολλαχοῦ μὲν ἡμῖν εἴρηται περὶ τούτων· κἂν τοῖς πρὸς
ἕλληνας συγγεγραμμένοις, κἂν τοῖς πρὸς τὰς αἱρέσεις, καὶ
5 μέντοι κἂν τοῖς πρὸς τοὺς μάγους, πρὸς δὲ τούτοις κἂν ταῖς
τῶν προφητῶν ἑρμηνείαις, καὶ τοῖς τῶν ἀποστολικῶν
ἐπιστολῶν ὑπομνήμασιν· ἐρῶ δὲ ὅμως κἀνταῦθα ἐν κεφαλαίῳ.

Ὅτι μὲν ἀνενδεὴς ὁ Θεός, οὐκ οἶμαι οὐδὲ τοὺς ἄγαν
ἀντερεῖν ἀνοήτους· ὅτι δὲ καὶ τὰς τοιαύτας οὐ προσίεται
10 θυσίας διὰ τῶν πλείστων ἐδίδαξε προφητῶν. ἐπειδὴ δέ, χρόνον
συχνὸν ἐν Αἰγύπτῳ διατετελεκώς, ὁ λαὸς θύειν δαίμοσιν
ἐδιδάχθη, συνεχώρησε τὰς θυσίας ἵνα τῆς δεισιδαιμονίας
ἐλευθερώσῃ. ὅτι γὰρ ταύταις ἔχαιρον μαρτυρεῖ τὰ περὶ τὸν
μόσχον γεγενημένα·[a] τοῦτο καὶ διὰ Ἰεζεκιὴλ τοῦ προφήτου
15 δεδήλωκεν· εἶδόν σε, γάρ φησι, πεφυρμένην ἐν τῷ αἵματί σου
καὶ εἶπόν σοι, ἐν τῷ αἵματί σου ζωή, πληθύνου·[b] λέγει δὲ ὅτι,

---

1 A [32], B, C, 4 7 9 10 31 35 37 = 20 mss.

ll. 6f. ἀποστολικῶν ἐπιστολῶν C, 10 35 37, Sir. Sch. : ἀποστολικῶν 5, B, 4
7 31 : ἀποστόλων ἐπιστολῶν 12, 9 = "in the commentaries on the epistles of
apostles" : ἀποστόλων F.M. = "in the commentaries on the apostles." Thdt.
composed commentaries on the epistles of St. Paul alone, not on those of all the
apostles; v. Quasten, vol. 3, p. 542. For the use of the adj., ἀποστολικός, with
particular reference to the works of St. Paul, v. Lampe, PGL, sub voce, II.B.4.b.

a. Ex 32.5f.   b. Ezek 16.6f.

ON LEVITICUS

I

Why did God command the offering of sacrifices?

(1) I have already said much about sacrifice in my writings against the Greeks and the heretics, and, especially in my work against the Persian magi, as well as in my expositions of the Old Testament prophets, and in my commentaries on the epistles of the apostle.[1] Nevertheless, I shall provide a brief treatment of this subject here as well.

I suppose not even a fool would deny that God is without need. Indeed, through the majority of the Old Testament prophets, he taught that he does not approve of these sacrifices. Since, however, the people in their long sojourn in Egypt had learned to sacrifice to demons, he allowed the sacrifices so that they might be freed from superstition. Proof of their delight in sacrifice appears in the episode of the calf.[a] He indicated this also through the prophet Ezekiel: "I saw you sullied with your blood and said to you, 'There is life in your blood; increase'"[b] —his meaning being, "I observed you

1. Theodoret composed the *Questions* towards the end of his life when he had already completed the last of the Christian apologies comparing Greek and Christian philosophy, a lost work against the Persian magi, a compendium of heresies from Simon Magus to Nestorius and Eutyches, and all his exegetical works on the Old Testament (προφητῶν) and the New Testament letters (ἀποστόλων); v. Guinot, pp. 43–63, esp. 62f.

θεασάμενός σε τῷ τῶν θυσιῶν αἵματι χαίρουσαν, συνεχώρησά
σοι τῆς τοιαύτης ἀπολαύειν ἐπιθυμίας.

Πρὸς δὲ τούτοις καὶ ἕτερον αὐτοῖς ἀλεξίκακον διὰ τούτου
20 κατεσκεύασε φάρμακον· θύεσθαι γὰρ αὐτῷ προσέταξε τὰ παρ'
αἰγυπτίων θεοποιούμενα· ἀπὸ μὲν τῶν τετραπόδων, μόσχον,[c]
καὶ τράγον,[d] καὶ πρόβατον,[e] ἀπὸ δὲ τῶν πτηνῶν, τρυγόνα καὶ
περιστερῶν νεοττούς.[f] οὐκ ἀγνοοῦμεν οὖν ὅτι καὶ ἄλλα
πάμπολλα ἐθεοποίουν αἰγύπτιοι, ἀλλὰ τῶν θεοποιουμένων τὰ
25 ἡμερώτερα ταῖς θυσίαις ἀπένειμε, τὰ ἄλλα δὲ ἀκάθαρτα
προσηγόρευσεν ἵνα, τὰ μέν ὡς ἀκάθαρτα βδελυττόμενοι, μὴ
θεοποιήσωσι, τὰ δέ, ὡς θύοντες, μὴ θεοὺς ὑπολάβωσιν ἀλλὰ
μόνον προσκυνῶσι τὸν ᾧ ταῦτα προσφέρεται. ἐπειδὴ δὲ οἱ μὲν
ἦσαν ἐν εὐπορίᾳ χρημάτων, οἱ δὲ πενίᾳ συζῶντες, τοῖς μὲν
30 μόσχον προσφέρειν, ἢ ἀρνίον, ἢ αἶγα προσέταξε, τοῖς δὲ δύο
τρυγόνας ἢ δύο νεοττοὺς περιστερῶν,[g] τοῖς δέ γε
πενεστάτοις σεμίδαλιν ὀλίγην ἀναμεμιγμένην ἐλαίῳ·[h]
σύμμετρα γὰρ τῇ δυνάμει νομοθετεῖ.

(2) Τούτων τὰ μὲν *δῶρα* προσηγόρευσεν ὡς, οὐκ ἐκ νομικῆς
35 ἀνάγκης, ἀλλ' ἐκ φιλοθέου προσφερόμενα γνώμης,[i] τὰς δὲ
θυσίας σωτηρίου[j] δηλοῖ δὲ τοὔνομα ἀρρωστίας ἢ χαλεπῶν
τινων ἑτέρων ἀπαλλαγήν. προσεφέροντο δὲ καὶ ὑπὲρ
ἁμαρτίας,[k] καὶ πλημμελείας, καὶ ἀγνοίας ἱερουργίαι.[l] δηλοῖ δὲ
ἡ μὲν *ἁμαρτία* νόμου τινὸς παράβασιν ἐθελούσιον, ἡ δὲ
40 *πλημμέλεια* τὴν ἐκ περιστάσεώς τινος γεγενημένην
παρανομίαν· συνέβαινε γάρ τινα παρὰ γνώμην ἢ λεπρῷ
πελάσαι, ἢ νεκρῷ, ἢ γονορρυεῖ. ἡ δὲ *ἄγνοια* σαφῆ τὴν
ἑρμηνείαν ἔχει· οὐ γὰρ πάντες ἅπαντας τοὺς νόμους
ἠπίσταντο· τὰ μὲν γὰρ τῆς ψυχῆς ἁμαρτήματα καὶ ἡ φύσις
45 ἐδίδασκε, ταῦτα δέ γε, ἃ μόνοις ἥρμοττεν ἰουδαίοις,
διδασκάλων ἐδεῖτο.

Καὶ τούτων δὲ τῶν θυμάτων τὰ μὲν ὁλοτελῆ κατεκαίετο,[m]

c. Lv 4.4   d. Lv 4.23   e. Lv 4.32   f. Lv 1.14; 5.7   g. Lv 5.7
h. Lv 2.1–10   i. Cf., e.g., Lv 1.3, 10, 14; 2.1.   j. Lv 3.1; 7.11   k. Lv 4.1–6.7
l. Lv 7.1–6   m. Lv 1

rejoicing in the blood of the sacrifices and allowed you to enjoy the object of your desire."

Furthermore, by permitting sacrifice, he devised yet another means of safeguarding them from evil, for he enjoined the offering of animals that the Egyptians considered gods: of the quadrupeds, the calf,[c] goat,[d] and sheep;[e] of the birds, the turtle-dove and young pigeons.[f] As we are well aware, the Egyptians deified many other animals as well. Of those deified he assigned the tamest to sacrifice and declared the others unclean, his purpose being to prevent them from deifying those they abhorred as unclean and from taking as gods those they sacrificed, so that they would adore only the one to whom they sacrificed the animals. Now, because some were affluent while others were living in poverty, he bade the former offer a calf, a lamb, or a goat, the latter two turtle-doves or two young pigeons,[g] and the poorest a little fine flour mixed with oil.[h] As you can see, he required offerings commensurate with one's wealth.

(2) He called some sacrifices "gifts" because not imposed as a legal obligation but offered in a spirit of devotion,[i] and others "sacrifices of salvation,"[j] a name suggesting liberation from sickness or some other affliction. Sacrifices were also offered for sins,[k] error, and ignorance.[l] "Sin" suggests deliberate transgression of a law, "error" the offense that arises from force of circumstance—for instance, unwittingly approaching a leper, a corpse, or a person suffering a discharge—while "ignorance" has an obvious explanation, since not everyone knew all the laws. They learned of the sins of the soul from nature but needed the instruction of teachers regarding those that applied only to the Jews.

In some sacrifices the victim was burned entire,[m] in others only

τῶν δὲ σμικρά τινα μόρια· ὁ τῆς κοιλίας ἐπίπλους, καὶ οἱ
νεφροί, καὶ τὸ ἐπικείμενον αὐτοῖς στέαρ, καὶ τοῦ ἥπατος ὁ
50 λοβός.[n] εἴρηται δὲ ἡμῖν τίνων ταῦτα δηλωτικά. ἡ δὲ ὑπὲρ
ἁμαρτίας προσφερομένη θυσία δίχα ἐλαίου καὶ λιβανωτοῦ
προσεφέρετο·[o] οὐ γὰρ ἔχουσι τοῦ φωτὸς τὴν τροφὴν οἱ ἐν
σκότει τῆς ἁμαρτίας καθήμενοι,[p] οὐδὲ τὸ ἱλαρὸν οἱ στένειν
ὀφείλοντες· κατὰ γὰρ τὸν προφήτην, τὸ πρόσωπον ἱλαρύνει τὸ
55 ἔλαιον·[q] οὐδὲ τὸ εὐῶδες οἱ τῆς πονηρίας μὴ ἀφιέντες τὴν
δυσοσμίαν.

(3) Ἐπειδὴ δὲ σκιὰν εἶχε *τῶν μελλόντων ὁ νόμος καὶ οὐκ*
αὐτὴν τὴν εἰκόνα τῶν πραγμάτων,[r] κατὰ τὸν θεῖον ἀπόστολον,
καὶ ὑποδείγματι καὶ σκιᾷ τῶν ἐπουρανίων λατρεύειν ἔφη τοὺς
60 ἐν τῷ νόμῳ,[s] οὐκ ἀπὸ τρόπου νομίζω τι δρᾶν, ταῖς τῶν ἀλόγων
ἱερείων διαφοραῖς ἐοικέναι λέγων τοὺς ἑαυτοὺς τῷ Θεῷ
προσφέροντας· οἱ μὲν γὰρ τὸν ἀκτήμονα καὶ ἀφρόντιδα
ἀσπαζόμενοι βίον ὅλους ἑαυτοὺς ἀφιεροῦσι τῷ τῶν ὅλων Θεῷ
καὶ σφᾶς αὐτοὺς ἀποφαίνουσιν ὁλοκαύτωμά τε καὶ
65 ὁλοκάρπωμα, οὐδὲν τῷ παρόντι καταλείποντες βίῳ ἀλλ' εἰς τὴν
ἀγήρω πάντα μετατιθέντες ζωήν. οἱ δὲ τούτων ἐλάττους τὰ
μὲν τῷ θυσιαστηρίῳ, τὰ δὲ τοῖς ἱερεῦσι, τὰ δὲ λοιπὰ τῇ τοῦ
σώματος ἀπονέμουσι χρείᾳ. καὶ οἱ μὲν προσφέρουσι τῶν
προβάτων τὴν ἐπιείκειαν, οἱ δέ, τοῖς εὐπειθέσι μόσχοις
70 παραπλησίως, φέρουσιν ἀσπασίως τὸν χρηστὸν τοῦ Κυρίου
ζυγόν, ἄλλοι δέ τινες, τὰς αἶγας μιμούμενοι, οἷόν τι γάλα
τοῖς δεομένοις παρέχουσι τῆς χρείας τὰ περιττὰ κατὰ τὴν
ἀποστολικὴν νομοθεσίαν, τὴν λέγουσαν, *τὸ ὑμῶν περίσσευμα*
εἰς τὸ ἐκείνων ὑστέρημα,[t] οἱ δὲ προσκομίζουσι τῶν τρυγόνων
75 τὸ σῶφρον καὶ φεύγουσιν ὡσαύτως τοῦ δευτέρου γάμου τὴν
ζεύγλην, οἱ δὲ ἁπλότητι καὶ ἀκακίᾳ κοσμοῦσι τὴν γνώμην,

---

l. 55 μὴ 8, 4 10 (F.M.), Sir. Sch. : <μὴ> F.M. : om. A [32], B, C⁻⁸, 7 9 31 35
37 (F.M.) = "and those who have cast off the stench of wickedness [have] no
pleasant fragrance."

n. Lv 3.4, 15   o. Lv 5.11   p. Mt 4.16; Lk 1.79   q. Ps 104.15   r. Heb 10.1
s. Heb 9.23   t. 2Cor 8.14

small parts of the victim: the membrane enclosing the belly, the kidneys, the fat on top of them, and the lobe of the liver.[n] I have explained elsewhere the symbolism of each of these.[2] The sacrifice for sin was offered without oil and incense,[o] for those seated in the darkness of sin have no nurturing light,[p] and those who ought to groan no joy—As the prophet says, oil makes the face joyful[q]—and those who have not yet cast off the stench of wickedness no pleasant fragrance.

(3) Yet, as the holy apostle declared that "the Law contained the shadow of things to come, not the true form of the realities,"[r] and those under the Law served a shadowy sketch of the heavenly things,[3s] I do not think I am out of order in remarking that those who offer themselves to God resemble the various animal victims. Those embracing a life free of possessions and worries devote themselves wholly to the God of the universe and turn themselves into holocausts and whole victims; they put aside nothing for this life but transfer everything to the life eternal. Those who are inferior to these apportion some of their possessions to the altar, others to the priests, and the rest to their own bodily needs. Some offer the gentleness of sheep; others, in the manner of obedient calves, gladly bear the easy yoke of the Lord; still others following the apostolic law, "Your abundance meeting their need,"[t] imitate goats and, from their budgetary surplus, provide milk, as it were, for the poor. Some offer the continence of the turtle-doves and, like doves, shun the

---

2. *V. Q.* 61 on Ex.
3. *Cf.* Theodoret's comment on Zec 8.23, where he again draws on Heb 10.1 for the terminology of typological exegesis.

μιμούμενοι τοὺς τῶν περιστερῶν νεοττούς· οὐδὲ γὰρ τελείας
θύεσθαι ταύτας ἐνομοθέτησεν, ἐπειδὴ τόδε τὸ ζῷον περὶ τὰς
μίξεις θερμότατον, ἀλλὰ τούτων τοὺς νεοττούς, ἀκακίᾳ μὲν
80 χρωμένους, συμπλοκῆς δὲ οὐ γεγευμένους. τὰ μέντοι πτηνὰ
οὔτε ὁ πατριάρχης διεῖλεν,ᵘ οὔτε ὁ νομοθέτης διαιρεθῆναι
κελεύει·ᵛ οἱ γὰρ πτηνοὶ τὴν διάνοιαν ἐξ ὅλης καρδίας
ἀγαπῶντες τὸν Θεόν, οὐ διαιροῦσιν αὐτὴν εἰς τὰ γήϊνα καὶ
οὐράνια ἀλλ' ὅλην ἀναπέμπουσιν ἄνω.

85 (4) Οὕτω τὰ περὶ τῶν θυσιῶν νοοῦντες, εὑρήσομεν καὶ τῇ
τῶν ἰουδαίων ἀσθενείᾳ τὸν περὶ τούτων νόμον ἁρμόδιον καὶ τῇ
εὐαγγελικῇ τελειότητι τὴν τοιαύτην νομοθεσίαν οὐ περιττήν.
οὕτω δὲ ταῦτα νοεῖν καὶ ὁ θεῖος ἡμᾶς ἐξεπαίδευσε Παῦλος·
τεθεικὼς γὰρ τὸν περὶ τῶν βοῶν νόμον, ὃς ἀπαγορεύει τοὺς
90 βοῦς ἀλοῶντας κημοῦν,ʷ ἐπήγαγε, μὴ τῶν βοῶν μέλει τῷ Θεῷ;
ἢ δι' ἡμᾶς πάντως λέγει; δι' ἡμᾶς γὰρ ἐγράφη, ὅτι ἐπ' ἐλπίδι
ὀφείλει ὁ ἀροτριῶν ἀροτριᾶν καὶ ὁ ἀλοῶν τῆς ἐλπίδος αὐτοῦ
μετέχειν ἐπ' ἐλπίδι.ˣ οὐκοῦν τοῦ νόμου τὸ μὲν αἰσθητὸν καὶ
ἐπιπόλαιον ἰουδαίοις κατάλληλον, τὸ δὲ πνευματικὸν τοῖς τὴν
95 εὐαγγελικὴν πολιτείαν ἀσπαζομένοις.

Ἰστέον δὲ καὶ τοῦτο, ὡς τὰ μὲν ὁλοκαυτούμενα ἄρσενα
ἦν·ʸ ἀνδρῶν γὰρ ἡ τελειότης· τὰ δὲ περὶ ἁμαρτίας θυόμενα
θήλεα·ᶻ ἀσθενοῦντος γὰρ τοῦ ἐν ἡμῖν ἡγεμονικοῦ, τὰ πάθη
κρατεῖ. ἐπισημήνασθαι δὲ καὶ τοῦτο δεῖ, ὡς ὑπὲρ ἁμαρτίας
100 οὐκ ἀμνοί, ἀλλὰ χίμαροι προσεφέροντο.ᵃᵃ δηλοῖ δὲ τοῦτο καὶ ὁ
δεσπότης Χριστὸς ἐν τοῖς ἱεροῖς εὐαγγελίοις, τοὺς μὲν
δικαίους ἀμνοῖς, τοὺς δὲ ἁμαρτωλοὺς ἐρίφοις ἀπεικάσας.ᵇᵇ

Προσεφέρετο δὲ καὶ ἀπὸ τῶν πετεινῶν ὁλοκαυτώματα·ᶜᶜ
πρόκειται γὰρ καὶ τοῖς πενομένοις ὁ τέλειος καὶ φιλόσοφος
105 βίος. ὥσπερ δὲ τῶν τετραπόδων οὔτε τὸ δέρμα οὔτε ἡ κόπρος
τῷ Θεῷ προσεφέρετο, οὕτω καὶ τῶν πτηνῶν ὁ πρόλοβος καὶ τὰ

---

u. Gn 15.10   v. Lv 1.17   w. Dt 25.4   x. 1Cor 9.9f. (NT var.)   y. Lv 1.3, 10
z. Lv 4.27f., 32   aa. Lv 4.22f., 27f.   bb. Mt 25.31–33   cc. Lv 1.14

yoke of a second marriage; others adorn their mind with simplicity and innocence in imitation of young pigeons, who live in innocence and have not tasted intercourse. Note, he required the sacrifice, not of mature pigeons, since this creature is avid for mating, but of the young. The patriarch did not divide the winged creatures,[u] nor did the lawgiver order their division;[v] those with winged mind love God with their whole heart and do not divide it between earth and heaven but direct all of it upwards.[4]

(4) If we follow this line of interpretation, we shall find that the law regarding sacrifices is appropriate to the weakness of the Jews, and that such legislation is not irrelevant even to evangelical perfection. This is how the divinely inspired Paul taught us to understand these passages. After citing the law which forbids the muzzling of oxen that tread the grain,[w] he went on, "Is God really concerned about the oxen? Or does he speak entirely for our sake? Indeed, it was written for our sake, since the ploughman should plough in hope, and the thresher should thresh in hope of partaking in his hope."[x] The materialistic and superficial in the Law is relevant to the Jews, the spiritual to those who have embraced the evangelical way of life.

Now, we should note that the whole burnt offerings were male,[y] perfection belonging to men, whereas the offerings for sin were female,[z] since the passions take over when our controlling intellect is weak. We should also point out that it was not lambs but goats that were offered for sin;[aa] Christ the Lord referred to this in the sacred Gospels when he likened the righteous to lambs but sinners to kids.[bb]

Even birds were offered in holocausts,[cc] since a life of perfection and wisdom is possible also for the poor. As neither the pelt nor the dung of the four-footed animals was offered to God, so the crop and

---

4. Theodoret must have suspected that Christian readers would regard the details of OT sacrificial ritual as irrelevant unless they were interpreted allegorically with reference to their own states of life and religious practices.

πτίλα πόρρω τῆς παρεμβολῆς ἐξεβάλλετο,[dd] καὶ οὐδὲ ταῦτα, ὡς
ἔτυχεν, ἐρρίπτετο, ἀλλ' ἐν καθαρῷ τινι χωρίῳ, ᾧ καὶ τοῦ βωμοῦ
τὴν κόνιν ἐνέβαλλον. *πρόλοβον* δὲ ὁ Θεοδοτίων *τὴν φύσαν*
110 ἐκάλεσεν, Ἀκύλας δὲ *τὴν σιτίζουσαν·* ἐκείνη γάρ, τὴν τροφὴν
δεχομένη, τῷ λοιπῷ σώματι χορηγεῖ. ὅθεν καὶ οἱ ἑβδομήκοντα
πρόλοβον αὐτὴν προσηγόρευσαν,[ee] ἅτε δὴ προσλαμβάνουσαν
τὴν τροφήν.

Ἐπισημήνασθαι δὲ προσήκει ὡς καὶ τὴν προσφερομένην
115 σεμίδαλιν, καὶ τοὺς κλιβανίτας ἄρτους, καὶ τοὺς ἐσχαρίτας,
καὶ τὰ ἀπὸ τηγάνου λάγανα *θυσίαν* καλεῖ,[ff] ψυχαγωγῶν τῷ
ὀνόματι τοὺς πενίᾳ συζῶντας ἵνα μὴ δυσχεραίνωσιν, ὡς ζῴων
σπανίζοντες.

Ἐπισημαντέον δὲ καὶ τοῦτο, ὡς τὸν προσφέροντα ζῷον
120 *ἄνθρωπον* ὀνομάζει· *ἄνθρωπος,* γάρ φησιν, *ἐξ ὑμῶν, ὃς ἐὰν*
προσφέρῃ δῶρον τῷ Κυρίῳ, ἀπὸ τῶν πτηνῶν, ἀπὸ τῶν βοῶν, ἢ
ἀπὸ τῶν προβάτων προσοίσεται αὐτό[gg] τὸν δὲ σεμίδαλιν
προσκομίζοντα *ψυχὴν* καλεῖ· *ἐὰν . . .* γὰρ *ψυχή,* φησί, *προσφέρῃ*
δῶρον θυσίαν τῷ Κυρίῳ, σεμίδαλις ἔσται τὸ δῶρον αὐτοῦ[hh] ὁ
125 λογικὸς γὰρ τὸ ἄλογον προσφέρει· ἡ δὲ ψυχὴ τὸ ἄψυχον.

(5) Ἀπαγορεύει δὲ *ζυμίτας ἄρτους* προσφέρεσθαι,[ii] δι' ἣν
ἔφην αἰτίαν· οὐδὲν γὰρ ἔχειν δεῖ τῆς αἰγυπτιακῆς πολιτείας.
ἀπαγορεύει καὶ *μέλι* προσφέρεσθαι τῷ βωμῷ.[jj] καί τινες μέν
φασιν ὡς τῆς μελίττης καὶ ἀκαθάρτοις τόποις ἐφιζανούσης
130 καὶ πάντοθεν ἀθροιζούσης τῆς μελιτουργίας τὰς ἀφορμάς,
τινὲς δὲ διδάσκεσθαι ἡμᾶς εἰρήκασιν ἐξ οἰκείων πόνων τὰς
θυσίας ἐπιτελεῖν, κατὰ τὴν τοῦ Σολομῶντος παραίνεσιν, τὴν
λέγουσαν, *τίμα τὸν Κύριον ἀπὸ σῶν δικαίων πόνων καὶ*
ἀπάρχου αὐτῷ ἀπὸ σῶν καρπῶν δικαιοσύνης[kk] ὁ δὲ τῆς
135 μελίττης καρπὸς οὐχ ἡμέτερος, φασίν, πόνος. ἀλλ' οὗτος ὁ

l. 135 φασίν A⁻¹² [32], 10 37, Sir. (-σι) Sch. (-σι) : φησίν F.M. = "According to
his (i.e. Solomon's) argument." Cf. τινὲς δὲ . . . εἰρήκασιν in the clause just preceding the quotation of Prv 3.9.

dd. Lv 1.16   ee. Lv 1.16   ff. Lv 2.1–9   gg. Lv 1.2 (LXX var.)   hh. Lv 2.1
ii. Ex 23.18   jj. Lv 2.11   kk. Prv 3.9

feathers of the birds were thrown out far away from the camp[dd]—and not just anywhere but in a clean place where the ashes from the altar were also dumped. Now, for "crop" Theodotion put "gullet" and Aquila "feeder." It receives the food and conveys it to the rest of the body; hence, the Septuagint calls it "crop" (πρόλοβον)[ee] as it takes in (προσλαμβάνουσαν) the food.

We should also point out that the offering of fine grain, the pan-baked loaves, the hearth-baked loaves, and the cakes from the frying pan were also termed a "sacrifice"[ff] to console the poor so they would not be upset at their lack of stock.

We should also point out that he used the term "man" of the one offering an animal: "If a man among you offers a gift to the Lord, he shall offer from the cattle, from the oxen, or from the sheep."[gg] On the other hand, he referred as "soul" to the one who offered the fine flour, "If a soul makes a gift of a sacrifice to the Lord, his gift will be of fine flour."[hh] It is the rational being that offers the irrational beast, the animate soul that offers the inanimate object.

(5) He forbade the offering of leavened bread[ii] for the reason I have already given, namely that they should retain nothing of the Egyptian way of life.[5] He also forbade the offering of honey on the altar.[jj] Some commentators have claimed that this is because bees rest even on unclean places and gather material to make honey from anywhere at all. But others have said that this teaches us to offer sacrifices from the products of our own hard work in keeping with the exhortation of Solomon, which goes, "Honor the Lord from your righteous labors and give him the first-fruits of your righteousness."[kk] According to this argument, honey is the produce of the bees, not of our own work. But this explanation overlooks an im-

---

5. *V. Q.* 55 on Ex.

The Questions on Leviticus

λόγος οὐκ ἔχει τὸ ἀκριβές. καὶ γὰρ ἡ μελιτουργία τῶν
ἀνθρώπων φιλοπονία· οἱ μὲν γὰρ γηπονίας, οἱ δὲ προβατείας
φροντίζουσι, καὶ οἱ μὲν ἐμπορίας, οἱ δὲ μελιτουργίας. οἶμαι
τοίνυν, διὰ μὲν τῆς ζύμης τὴν παλαιότητα τῆς πονηρίας
140 αἰνίττεσθαι, διὰ δὲ τοῦ μέλιτος τὴν ἡδονὴν ἀπαγορεύεσθαι.
τοῖς μέντοι ἱερεῦσι καὶ τὰς τούτων ἐκέλευσε προσφέρειν
ἀπαρχάς·[ll] οὗτοι γὰρ τὰς ὑπὲρ τῶν ἡμετέρων ἁμαρτημάτων
πρεσβείας προσφέρουσιν. ὅθεν διὰ τοῦ προφήτου ἔφη περὶ
αὐτῶν, ἁμαρτίας λαοῦ μου φάγονται.[mm]
145 Τοὺς δὲ ἅλας ἐπιβάλλεσθαι τοῖς ἱερείοις κελεύει,[nn] τὸ
διακριτικὸν τῆς ψυχῆς διὰ τούτων σημαίνων. τούτου ἐστέρητο
ἡ τοῦ Κάϊν θυσία·[oo] διὸ ἤκουσε παρὰ τοῦ τῶν ὅλων Θεοῦ, οὐκ,
ἂν ὀρθῶς προσενέγκῃς, ὀρθῶς δὲ μὴ διέλῃς;[pp] καὶ ὁ θεῖος
ἀπόστολος νομοθετεῖ λέγων, ὁ λόγος ὑμῶν ἔστω
150 πάντοτε ... ἅλατι ἠρτυμένος.[qq] καὶ ὁ Κύριος τοῖς ἀποστόλοις
ἔφη, ὑμεῖς ἐστε τὸ ἅλας τῆς γῆς· ἐὰν δὲ τὸ ἅλας μωρανθῇ, ἐν
τίνι ἁλισθήσεται;[rr]

(6) Ἀσινῆ δὲ καὶ ἄμωμα προσφέρειν ἅπαντα κελεύει τὰ
θύματα[ss] καίτοι διάφορα ὄντα καὶ κατὰ διαφόρους
155 προσφερόμενα τρόπους. διδάσκει δὲ διὰ τούτων τοὺς ἐν
ἑκάστῃ πολιτείᾳ τὸ ἄμωμον ἔχειν· καὶ τοὺς παρθενίαν
ἀσπαζομένους κατὰ τοὺς ταύτης πολιτεύεσθαι νόμους, τοὺς
τοῦ γάμου τὸν ζυγὸν αἱρουμένους τῇ πρὸς ἀλλήλους κοινωνίᾳ
μὴ διαφθεῖραι τούτου τὴν ζεύγλην, τοὺς τὴν ἀσκητικὴν
160 βιοτὴν προτιμῶντας τὸν τῆς τελειότητος διαφυλάττειν
κανόνα, καί, συλλήβδην εἰπεῖν, τοὺς ἐν πλούτῳ τοὺς ἐν πενίᾳ,
τοὺς ἐν δουλείᾳ τοὺς ἐν δυναστείᾳ ἐν τοῖς οἰκείοις τάγμασι
τὸ ἀλώβητον ἔχειν καὶ ἄμωμον.

ll. Lv 2.12   mm. Hos 4.8   nn. Lv 2.13   oo. Gn 4.3   pp. Gn 4.7 (LXX)
qq. Col 4.6 (NT var.)   rr. Mt 5.13   ss. Lv 1.3, 10; 3.1, 6; 4.3, 14 (LXX), 22f., 28, 32

portant point; after all, honey-making is a human labor. Some are engaged in the cultivation of the earth, others in the tending of sheep, others in commerce, others in honey-making. So my view is that in the case of the leaven there is an obscure reference to ancient wickedness, and in the case of the honey, a prohibition of pleasure.[6] Furthermore, he commanded that the first-fruits, even of leaven and honey, be offered to the priests,[ll] since they offer intercession for our sins. As he said of them through the prophet, "They will feed on the sins of my people."[mm]

He ordered that salt be thrown on the victims,[nn] in this signifying the soul's faculty of discernment. Cain's sacrifice had no salt;[oo] hence, he heard from the God of the universe: "[Have you] not [sinned] if you sacrifice correctly, but divide incorrectly?"[pp] And the holy apostle stated the law in these words: "Let your speech always be seasoned with salt";[qq] and the Lord said to the apostles, "You are the salt of the earth. If the salt lose its taste, how can its saltiness be restored?"[7rr]

(6) He commanded that all victims be without fault or blemish,[ss] different though they be and offered in different ways. Thus, he instructs people in every walk of life to keep free of fault: those embracing virginity to live according to its norms, those choosing the yoke of marriage to avoid impairing the conjugal bond in their intercourse, and those opting for the ascetical life to observe the norms of perfection—in a word, that people of wealth, people of poverty, people in servitude, people in power live an unblemished and unstained life in whatever position they have been stationed.

6. As Guinot points out (p. 771), the surviving patristic exegesis of Lv 2.11 is concerned solely with the prohibition against the offering of leaven and does not deal with that against the offering of honey. Nonetheless, we lack the discussions of Diodore and of Theodore of Mopsuestia, from whom Theodoret may here be drawing. The Jewish author Philo (*Spec.* 1.291) had explained this rejection of honey as due to the reputed genesis of bees from the decomposing carcasses of cattle; *cf.* Virgil's account of the *bougonia* in *Geo.* 4.281–314.

7. In the *Questions on Genesis,* Theodoret offered no interpretation of the baffling reproach of Cain attributed to the Lord in the septuagintal version of Gn 4.7.

Τῶν δὲ θυομένων, πλὴν τῶν ὁλοκαυτωμάτων, τὰ μὲν τῷ
165 βωμῷ προσεφέρετο, τὰ δὲ τοῖς ἱερεῦσιν ἐδίδοτο·ᵗᵗ διὸ
συμμερίζεσθαι αὐτοὺς τῷ θυσιαστηρίῳ ὁ θεῖος εἶπεν
ἀπόστολος·ᵘᵘ τὰ δὲ λοιπὰ τῶν κρεῶν τῇ τῶν προσφερόντων
ἀπενέμετο χρείᾳ. τοῖς μέντοι ὁλοκαυτώμασιν ἐπετίθετο τὰ
μερικῶς προσφερόμενα οἷον οἱ νεφροί, καὶ ἡ πιμελή, καὶ ὁ
170 τοῦ ἥπατος λοβός,ᵛᵛ ἐξ ἐνίων δὲ ἱερείων καὶ ἡ ὀσφύς ἤ, κατὰ
τοὺς ἄλλους ἑρμηνευτάς, ἡ κέρκος,ʷʷ ἐπειδὴ τοῖς ἐν ἀρετῇ
τελείοις οἱ ἀτελεῖς χρώμεθα πρεσβευταῖς καὶ δι' ἐκείνων τὰς
|26b ἡμετέρας προσφέρομεν προσευχάς. ἐπετίθει δὲ ὁ προσφέρων
τῷ ἱερείῳ τὰς χεῖρας οἱονεὶ τὰς ἑαυτοῦ πράξεις·ˣˣ τῶν γὰρ
175 πράξεων αἱ χεῖρες δηλωτικαί, ὑπὲρ δὲ τούτων τὸ θῦμα
προσέφερεν. αἵματος δὲ καὶ στέατος ἀπέχεσθαι κελεύει, καὶ
ἀμφότερα τῷ θυσιαστηρίῳ διαγορεύει προσφέρεσθαι·ʸʸ τὸ μὲν
γὰρ ζωῆς αἴτιον, τὸ δὲ ἀρετῆς δηλωτικόν, ἀμφότερα δὲ
ἀνατιθέναι τῷ Θεῷ δικαιότατον.

180 Τὸν δὲ ἀρχιερέα, νόμον τινὰ παραβεβηκότα, μόσχον
ἄμωμον ἱερεύειν κελεύειᶻᶻ καὶ τῷ μὲν θυσιαστηρίῳ προσφέρειν
ἃ προειρήκαμεν, τὰ δὲ κρέα καὶ τὸ δέρμα σὺν τῇ κόπρῳ ἔξω
τῆς παρεμβολῆς κατακαίειν.ᵃᵃᵃ τοῦτο δὲ δηλοῖ τὸ τὴν
ἁμαρτίαν ἀλλοτρίαν εἶναι τῶν ἱερῶν περιβόλων. καὶ παντὸς δὲ
185 τοῦ λαοῦ τοιαύτην τινὰ παρανομίαν τετολμηκότος, τὴν ἴσην
προσενεχθῆναι θυσίαν νενομοθέτηκε,ᵇᵇᵇ διδάσκων ἡλίκον τῆς
ἱερωσύνης τὸ γέρας· ἀντίρροπον γὰρ αὐτὸ παντὸς τέθεικε
τοῦ λαοῦ. τὸν δὲ ἄρχοντα παραβάντα τινὰ νόμον, οὐ μόσχον,
ἀλλὰ χίμαρον, τουτέστιν, ἔριφον ἐνιαυσιαῖον προσενεγκεῖν
190 διηγόρευσε·ᶜᶜᶜ τοσοῦτον ἀποδεῖ τῆς ἀρχιερατικῆς ἀξίας ὁ τὴν
σωματικὴν πεπιστευμένος ἀρχήν. τὸν δὲ μήτε ἱερέα ὄντα
μήτε ἄρχοντα, ἡμαρτηκότα δέ, χίμαιραν θῦσαι προσέταξε·ᵈᵈᵈ

---

tt. Lv 2.3, 10; 6.16–18, 26–29; 7.6–10, 14, 31–36   uu. 1Cor 9.13
vv. Lv 3.3–5   ww. Lv 3.9   xx. Lv 1.4; 3.2, 8, 13; 4.4, 15, 24, 29, 33
yy. Lv 3.17; 7.22–27   zz. Lv 4.3   aaa. Lv 4.11f.   bbb. Lv 4.13f.
ccc. Lv 4.22f.   ddd. Lv 4.27f.

Question 1

Of the things sacrificed, except the holocausts, a part was offered on the altar, and part was given to the priests;[tt] hence, the holy apostle said that they had a share at the altar.[uu] The part of the meat left over was devoted to the use of those who made the offering. They placed on top of the holocausts the partial offerings, such as the kidneys, the fat, and the lobe of the liver,[vv] and the loins of some victims—or, as the other translators say, "the tail"[ww]—since we who are imperfect depend on the intercession of those who are perfect in virtue and offer our prayers through them. On the victim the offerer placed his hands[xx]—his actions, as it were, since hands are suggestive of actions, and he was making the sacrifice on account of his actions. He bade them abstain from blood and fat and prescribed that both be offered on the altar,[yy] the former being the source of life, the latter indicative of virtue, and both very properly dedicated to God.

He commanded that if the high priest broke any law, he was to sacrifice an unblemished calf[zz] and offer on the altar the parts we have just mentioned but burn the meat, skin, and excrement outside the camp.[aaa] This indicates that sin is foreign to the sacred precincts. He legislated that an equivalent sacrifice be offered whenever the whole people were guilty of such a transgression,[bbb] his purpose being to bring out the dignity of the priesthood, which he had made of importance equal to the people as a whole. He proclaimed that when the ruler broke a law, he should offer, not a calf, but a he-goat, that is, a yearling goat[ccc]—so far removed from the dignity of the high priest is the ruler entrusted with worldly governance. On the other hand, he ordered the sacrifice of a female goat when the offender is not a priest or a ruler,[ddd] since the male is fitting

----

Here, drawing a connection between the verb διαιρέω, whose literal meaning is "cleave" or "divide" but which may also signify "determine" or "decide" and διακρίνω = "separate" or "discern," the root of the substantive διακριτικόν (the faculty of discernment), Theodoret suggests that the Lord was reproving Cain not simply, or even primarily, for the improper division of the sacrificial victim but for a lack of discernment.

πρόσφορον γὰρ τῷ μὲν ἄρχοντι τὸ ἄρρεν, τῷ δὲ ἀρχομένῳ τὸ
θῆλυ ὡς ἐν τοῖς πρόσθεν εἰρήκαμεν.

195 (7) Τὸν δέ γε ἢ ἀκαθάρτου τινὸς τῶν ἀπειρημένων
ἁψάμενον, ἤ τινος ὀμωμοκότος ἀκούσαντα καὶ τὸν
παραβεβηκότα τὸν ὅρκον μὴ διελέγξαντα, ἢ αὐτὸν
ὑποσχόμενον τὶ πράξειν ἢ τῷ Θεῷ τι προσοίσειν καὶ ὅρκῳ τὴν
ὑπόσχεσιν βεβαιώσαντα, τὸ δὲ ἔργον μὴ ἐπιθέντα τῷ λόγῳ
200 πρῶτον ἐξαγορεῦσαι τὴν ἁμαρτίαν κελεύει, ἔπειτα
προσενεγκεῖν ἢ ἀμνάδα ἢ χίμαιραν, καὶ τούτῳ τῷ τρόπῳ τὸν
Θεὸν ἱλεώσασθαι. εἰ δὲ πένης ᾖ, ἢ δύο τρυγόνας κελεύει
προσενεγκεῖν ἢ δύο νεοττοὺς περιστερῶν,ᵉᵉᵉ εἰ δὲ μηδὲ τούτων
εὐποροίη, μικρὰν σεμίδαλιν ἐλαίου δίχα καὶ λιβανωτοῦ
205 προσκομίσαι·ᶠᶠᶠ τὸ γὰρ ἔλαιον ἱλαρότητος δηλωτικόν, ὁ δὲ
λιβανωτὸς εὐωδίας· ἀμφοτέρων δὲ ἡ ἁμαρτία γεγύμνωται.
μάλα δὲ ἁρμοδίως τὸ ἅψασθαι ἀκαθάρτου καὶ τὸ κρύψαι τοῦ
ὀμωμοκότος καὶ ψευσαμένου τὴν ἁμαρτίαν συνέζευξεν· καὶ
γὰρ ὁ καθαρὸς ἁπτόμενος ἀκαθάρτων μολύνεται, καὶ ὁ μὴ
210 ὀμόσας ψευσαμένῳ κοινωνεῖ τῆς ἁμαρτίας, μὴ διελέγχων τὸ
ψεῦδος.ᵍᵍᵍ ἄξιον δὲ θαυμάσαι τοῦ δεσπότου τὴν ἀγαθότητα,
ὅτι τὸν ἐπαγγειλάμενόν τι προσενεγκεῖν, καὶ ὅρκῳ τὴν
ἐπαγγελίαν κυρώσαντα, τῷ ἔργῳ δὲ μὴ πληρώσαντα οὔτε ὡς
ἀχάριστον οὔτε ὡς ἐπίορκον τιμωρεῖται ἀλλὰ μικρᾷ θεραπεύει
215 ζημίᾳ.ʰʰʰ

II

Τί ἐστι *ψυχὴ ἐὰν λάθῃ αὐτὴν λήθῃ καὶ ἁμάρτῃ ἀκουσίως
ἀπὸ τῶν ἁγίων Κυρίου;*ᵃ
Συνέβαινε πολλάκις ἀσχολίᾳ τινὰ περιπεσόντα μὴ

eee. Lv 5.7   fff. Lv 5.11   ggg. Lv 5.1–3   hhh. Lv 5.4–13

11 A [32], B, C, 4 7 9 10 31 35 37 = 18 mss.
a. Lv 5.15

for the ruler, and the female for the ruled, as we have already remarked.[8]

(7) Whoever had touched any unclean forbidden thing, or heard someone take an oath and failed to censure him when he broke that oath, or himself promised to do something or offer something to God and failed to put his word into effect, although he had confirmed it with an oath, was commanded first to confess his sin and then to offer a lamb or a she-goat in appeasement of God. The poor man was commanded to offer two turtle-doves or two young pigeons;[eee] but if he lacked even these, he was to bring a small portion of fine flour without oil or incense,[fff] for oil is indicative of joy and incense of sweet odor, but sin has no trace of either. Now, it was very fitting that he should link touching something unclean and concealing the sin of one who took a false oath; the clean person is defiled by touching what is unclean, and the person who did not swear an oath shares the sin of the oath-breaker by not denouncing the perjury.[ggg] We ought to admire the kindliness of the Lord, who healed with a slight fine, rather than punishing as an ingrate or perjurer, the person who promised to make an offering and then failed to fulfil his promise, although he had confirmed it with an oath.[hhh]

II

What is the meaning of "If someone is truly unaware and sins unwittingly in any of the holy things of the Lord"?[a]

It often happened that busy people did not offer in due time

---

8. *Cf.* Lv 4 for the various sacrifices for transgressions and *Q.* 61 on Ex for the same explanation of the different use of the male and female victims.

προσενεγκεῖν εἰς καιρὸν τὰ τῷ Θεῷ ἀφιερωμένα οἷον τὰ
5 πρωτότοκα, ἢ τὰς ἀπαρχάς, ἢ τὰς ἐπαγγελίας. τὸν ταύτῃ
τοίνυν περιπεπτωκότα τῇ πλημμελείᾳ μείζονι ὑποβάλλει
ζημίᾳ· κελεύει γὰρ αὐτὸν πρότερον ἐκτίσαι τὸ θεῖον ὄφλημα,
τῆς ἀξίας τιμῆς τὸ πέμπτον προστεθεικότα, εἶθ' οὕτως ὑπὲρ
τῆς πλημμελείας κριὸν πεντήκοντα σίκλων ἄξιον
10 προσενεγκεῖν εἰς ἱερουργίαν, καὶ οὕτως λαβεῖν τῆς ἁμαρτίας
τὴν ἄφεσιν.[b]

Ταῦτα καὶ τὰ τούτοις ὅμοια περὶ τῶν ἀκουσίως
ἡμαρτηκότων νομοθετήσας, κελεύει καὶ τοὺς ἑκόντας
ἡμαρτηκότας καὶ ἢ παρακαταθήκην δεξαμένους καὶ
15 ψευσαμένους ἢ ἀδικίᾳ τινὶ χρησαμένους καὶ ὅρκῳ ψευδεῖ τὴν
ἁμαρτίαν αὐξήσαντας πρῶτον ἀποδοῦναι τοῖς ἠδικημένοις ἃ
παρανόμως ἀφείλαντο, καὶ προσθεῖναι τῷ κεφαλαίῳ τὸ
πέμπτον, εἶθ' οὕτω κριὸν προσενεγκεῖν, καὶ τὸν Θεὸν
ἱλεώσασθαι.[c] τοῦτο καὶ ὁ μακάριος Ζακχαῖος πεποίηκεν·
20 ἀπέδωκε γὰρ πρότερον ἅπερ ἠδίκησε τετραπλάσια· εἶθ' οὕτως
τὰ ἡμίση τῶν οἰκείων τοῖς πενομένοις διένειμεν.[d]

III

Διὰ τί τοῦ ἱερέως τὴν θυσίαν ὁλοκαυτοῦσθαι προσέταξεν;[a]
Τέλειον εἶναι διδάσκων τὸν ἱερέα καί, μὴ μερικῶς, ἀλλ'
ὅλον ἑαυτὸν ἀναθεῖναι τῷ τῶν ὅλων Θεῷ.

---

b. Lv 5.16   c. Lv 6.1–7   d. Lk 19.8f.

III A [32], B, C, 4 7 9 10 31 35 37 = 20 mss.
a. Lv 6.23

something consecrated to God, like the firstborn, first-fruits, or something they had vowed. So he subjected anyone guilty of this inadvertence to a heavier loss. He commanded him first to pay his debt to God and to add a fifth to the amount due; next, for his inadvertence, to offer in sacrifice a ram worth fifty shekels and only then receive forgiveness for his sin.[b]

Requiring this and similar things of involuntary sinners,[1] he commanded the deliberate sinners, those who had taken a deposit and broken their pledge or committed an injustice and aggravated the sin with a false oath, first to restore to the wronged whatever they had taken illegally and to add a fifth to the sum; then to offer a ram and thus appease God.[c] This is what the blessed Zacchaeus did. First, he made fourfold restitution of what he had wrongfully taken and then, apportioned a half of his possessions to the poor.[d]

III

Why did he prescribe that the priest's sacrifice be burned entire?[a]

To teach the priest to be perfect and to devote himself, not partially, but entirely, to the God of the universe.[1]

1. Theodoret deals first with the penalties for involuntary (Lv 5.14–19), and then for deliberate, offenses (6.1–7). His valuation of the ram is drawn from 5.15, in which his Bible may have read the word "fifty" before or after the noun shekels"; in the *ap. crit.* to this verse, Wevers and Quast, making no mention of Theodoret, cite only a couple of the LXX manuscripts and the Armenian version for the insertion of this figure.

1. This is Theodoret's own interpretation of the requirement in Lv 6.23; he does not provide his readers with a Christian parallel.

IV

Διὰ τί ἐν τῷ τόπῳ τῶν ὁλοκαυτωμάτων καὶ τὰς περὶ
ἁμαρτίας θυσίας ἱέρευον;[a]

Εἰς ψυχαγωγίαν τῶν προσφερόντων, ἵνα γνῶσιν ὡς οὐκ εἰσὶ
τῶν ἁγίων ἀλλότριοι, διὰ μετανοίας ἰατρευόμενοι. διὰ τοῦτο
5 καὶ ἅγια ἁγίων αὐτὰ προσηγόρευσεν.[b]

V

Τί ἐστι πᾶς ὁ ἁπτόμενος τῶν κρεῶν αὐτῆς ἁγιασθήσεται;[a]

Εὐλάβειαν αὐτοὺς διδάσκει, καὶ μετὰ δέους προσιέναι τοῖς
θείοις κελεύει, καὶ πόρρω τῶν ἱερῶν ἑστάναι διαγορεύει. τὸν
δὲ πελάζειν τολμῶντα, εἶτα τοῦ αἵματος ῥανίδα δεχόμενον τῷ
5 ναῷ προσεδρεύειν κελεύει ὡς οὐκέτι ἑαυτοῦ κύριον ὄντα·
προσεδρεύειν δέ, οὐχ ἱερουργοῦντα, ἀλλὰ τὴν ἄλλην
λειτουργίαν ἐπιτελοῦντα. διὰ τοῦτο καὶ τὰ ἱμάτια, τὰ τοῦ
αἵματος ἐκείνου τὰς ῥανίδας δεχόμενα, πλύνεσθαι κελεύει,[b]
τὰ δὲ σκεύη, εἰ μὲν χαλκᾶ εἴη, ἐπιμελῶς ἀποσμήχεσθαι, εἰ δὲ
10 κεράμεα, συντρίβεσθαι.[c]

iv A [32], B, C, 4 7 9 10 31 35 37 = 20 mss.
a. Lv 6.25   b. Lv 6.17f., 25

v A [32], B, C, 4 7 9 10 31* 35 37 = 20 mss.
a. Lv 6.27   b. Lv 6.27   c. Lv 6.28

IV

Why did they slay the sacrifices for sin in the same place they slew those for holocausts?[a]

As encouragement to the offerers, so they would know that they were not forbidden access to the holy when they were being healed through repentance. Hence, he called these sacrifices "most holy."[b]

V

What is the meaning of "Whoever touches its meat will be sanctified"?[a]

This teaches them reverence, bids them take part in divine service with respect, and requires them to stand at a distance from the sacred sacrifices. It prescribes that the one who presumes to approach and then is spattered with blood serve in the temple as someone no longer his own master; though by "serving" I mean not the celebration of sacred rites but the performance of some other duty. Hence, he also commands the washing of garments spattered with drops of that blood,[b] the careful scouring of bronze vessels, and the smashing of the earthenware.[c]

VI

Διὰ τί μετὰ τρίτην ἡμέραν οὐ κελεύει τῶν ἱερείων ἐσθίειν,
τῷ δὲ παραβαίνοντι τὸν νόμον ἐπιφέρει ζημίαν, ἄθυτον εἶναι
λέγων τὴν θυσίαν ἐκείνην;[a]

Βούλεται, μὴ μόνους αὐτοὺς εὐωχεῖσθαι, ἀλλὰ καὶ τοῖς
5 ἐνδεέσι τῶν κρεῶν μεταδιδόναι. τούτου χάριν τῇ πρώτῃ καὶ τῇ
δευτέρᾳ ἡμέρᾳ, τῶν κρεῶν ἐκείνων μεταλαμβάνειν κελεύει, τὰ
δὲ περιττεύοντα κατακαίεσθαι ἵν', ὑπὸ τῆς ἀνάγκης ταύτης
ὠθούμενοι, κοινωνοὺς ἔχωσι τοὺς τῆς εὐωχίας πένητας.

VII

Διὰ τί τὸν γονορρυοῦς, ἢ λεπροῦ, ἢ θνησιμαίου, ἢ ἄλλου
τινὸς τῶν καλουμένων ἀκαθάρτων ἁψάμενον ἀπαγορεύει τῶν
τῆς θυσίας μεταλαμβάνειν κρεῶν;[a]

Διὰ τῶν σμικρῶν τούτων τὰ μεγάλα θεραπεύει παθήματα. εἰ
5 γὰρ τὰ φυσικὰ μιαίνει κατὰ τὸν νόμον, πολλῷ μᾶλλον τὰ
γνωμικά, ἃ κυρίως καλεῖται παράνομα. ὅτι δὲ ταῦτα τοῦτον
ἔχει τὸν τρόπον τὰ ἑξῆς μαρτυρεῖ. κελεύσας γὰρ πᾶν στέαρ
τῷ θυσιαστηρίῳ προσφέρεσθαι, τῇ τῶν ἀνθρώπων χρείᾳ τὸ τῶν
θνησιμαίων καὶ θηριαλώτων ἀφώρισε στέαρ.[b] ἀκάθαρτα δὲ τὰ
10 τοιαῦτα ὠνόμασεν·[c] ἀκάθαρτος οὖν ἄρα ἦν καὶ ὁ τοιούτου γε
ἁπτόμενος. δῆλον τοίνυν κἀντεῦθεν ὡς ἄλλα δι' ἄλλων
νομοθετεῖ.

---

vi A *[32]*, B, C⁻⁵¹, *4 7 9 10 31 35 37* = 19 mss.

a. Lv 7.16–18

---

vii A *[32]*, B, C, *4 7 9 10 35 37* = 19 mss.

a. Lv 7.20f.   b. Lv 7.22–24   c. V., *e.g.*, Ex 22.31.

Question VII

VI

Why did he forbid the consumption of the sacrificial flesh after three days and impose a penalty for transgression of the law by declaring the sacrifice invalid?[a]

So they would not feast alone but share the meat with the needy. Therefore, he commanded them to partake of the meat on the first and second days but burn the leftovers, so that, under pressure of this obligation, they would invite the poor to share in the feast.[1]

VII

Why did he forbid a share of the sacrificial meat to anyone who had touched someone suffering a discharge, a leper, an animal carcass, or anything else declared unclean?[a]

He used these slight ailments to cure the serious. If in the eyes of the Law natural things cause defilement, this is much more the case with matters of intention, which are properly referred to as "transgressions." The following verses confirm the truth of this. After commanding that all fat be offered on the altar, he allotted to human usage the fat from animals that had died or been killed by others.[b] Yet as he declared all such things unclean,[c] anyone touching one of these was also unclean. We gather from this passage as well that he legislates some things through others.[1]

---

1. Theodoret feels free to develop a rationale of his own. R.J. Faley suggests (on 7.11–21, 28–34) that the intention of the law of Lv 7.16–18 was rather "to avoid the abuses that could easily arise in a sacrificial repast permitting a rather extensive lay participation."

---

1. Again, this Antiochene commentator has difficulty accepting that involuntary actions such as those mentioned in Lv 7.21 could be penalized; so he cites vv. 23–25, in which the fat from animals that have died on their own or been killed by others is allotted to secular use. The implication is that if God allows the use of this

VIII

Διὰ τί αἵματι καὶ ἐλαίῳ καὶ τὴν ἀκοὴν τοῦ ἱερέως τὴν
δεξιὰν ἔχρισε, καὶ τὴν χεῖρα τὴν δεξιάν, καὶ τὸν πόδα
ὡσαύτως;[a]

Τύπος ταῦτα τῶν ἡμετέρων ἀγαθῶν· τὸ μὲν αἷμα τοῦ
5 σωτηρίου αἵματος, τὸ δὲ ἔλαιον τοῦ παναγίου χρίσματος. ἡ δὲ
δεξιὰ ἀκοὴ σύμβολον τῆς ἐπαινουμένης ὑπακοῆς, ἡ δὲ χεὶρ
καὶ ὁ πούς, τῶν ἀγαθῶν πράξεων. διὰ γάρ τοι τοῦτο ἡ δεξιὰ
καὶ ὁ δεξιὸς ἐχρίσθη· εἰσὶ γὰρ καὶ εὐώνυμοι πράξεις καὶ
ὑπακοὴ βλαβερά.

IX

Πῶς νοητέον τὸ πῦρ, τὸ ἀλλότριον;[a]

Ἐδίδαξεν ἡμᾶς ἡ ἱστορία ὡς, τῆς πρώτης ἐπιτελουμένης
θυσίας, τῷ θείῳ πυρὶ κατηναλώθη τὰ ἱερεῖα. τοῦτο ἄσβεστον
διαφυλαχθῆναι προσέταξεν ὁ δεσπότης Θεός, καὶ νύκτωρ καὶ
5 μεθ' ἡμέραν ξύλα τῷ πυρὶ χορηγεῖσθαι ἵνα μὴ χειροποίητον
πῦρ ἀναμιγῇ τῷ θείῳ πυρί. ἐπειδὴ τοίνυν τοῦτον παρέβησαν
τὸν νόμον Ναδὰβ καὶ Ἀβιούδ, τοῦ Ἀαρὼν οἱ παῖδες, καὶ πῦρ
εἰσήνεγκαν χειροποίητον, τὸ θεῖον αὐτοὺς κατηνάλωσε πῦρ.[b]
ἡμεῖς δὲ παιδευόμεθα διὰ τούτων μὴ σβεννύναι τὸ πνεῦμα
10 ἀλλ' ἀναζωπυρεῖν ἣν ἐλάβομεν χάριν, καὶ μηδὲν ἀλλότριον
ἐπεισάγειν τῇ θείᾳ γραφῇ ἀλλ' ἀρκεῖσθαι τῇ διδασκαλίᾳ τοῦ

---

viii A [32], B, C, 4 7 9 10 35 37 = 19 mss.
a. Lv 8.23

---

ix A [32], B, C, 4 7 9 10 31 35 37 = 20 mss.
a. Lv 10.1   b. Lv 9.24–10.2

Question IX

VIII

Why did he anoint the priest's right ear, right hand, and foot with blood and oil?[a]

These are a type of our good things: the blood of the Savior's blood, and the oil of the most holy chrism. The right ear is a symbol of praiseworthy obedience, and the hand and foot of good actions—hence the anointing of the right hand and right foot. There is, after all, such a thing as sinister action and a harmful obedience.[1]

IX

How is "the unholy fire" to be understood?[a]

The biblical narrative informs us that, at the celebration of the first sacrifice, the victims were consumed by fire from God. The Lord God ordered them not to allow this fire to die out but to feed it with wood night and day, so that man-made fire would never be mixed with the divine. Since Aaron's sons Nadab and Abihu broke this law and introduced a man-made fire, they were consumed by the divine fire.[b] These events teach us not to quench the Spirit but to rekindle the grace we have received, not to introduce anything foreign into holy Scripture but to be content with the teaching of the Spirit, and to abhor heretics, some of whom have combined their

----

fat, even though anyone who touches it must become unclean, the issue of ritual purity or impurity cannot be of any real significance. *V.* also *Qq.* 20 (on the uncleanness of gonorrhea) and 27 (on the adulterated garment), in which Theodoret develops the same line of argument against the reality of uncleanness that is derived from anything but an act of the will.

1. Theodoret first offers a typological, and then a simpler ethical, interpretation of this anointing of the priest: *cf.* Lv 14.14–18, where oil and blood are used in the anointing of a leper.

The Questions on Leviticus

πνεύματος, καὶ μυσάττεσθαι τὰς αἱρέσεις, ὧν οἱ μὲν μύθους τοῖς θείοις λογίοις προσέθεσαν, οἱ δὲ τοὺς δυσσεβεῖς αὐτῶν λογισμοὺς τῆς γραφικῆς προετίμησαν διανοίας.

X

Διὰ τί τοὺς ἱερέας οἴνου κωλύει μεταλαμβάνειν;[a]

Οὐ παντάπασιν ἀπηγόρευσε τοῦτο, ἀλλὰ κατὰ τὸν τῆς λειτουργίας καιρόν· κατὰ γὰρ διαδοχὰς ἐλειτούργουν· οἱ μὲν ἐν ταύταις ταῖς ἡμέραις, οἱ δὲ ἐν ἄλλαις. νηφάλαιον[b] δὲ καὶ
5 ὁ ἀπόστολος τὸν ἱερέα εἶναι κελεύει, καὶ τοὺς διακόνους μὴ οἴνῳ πολλῷ προσέχοντας·[c] καί, τῷ Τιμοθέῳ γράφων, οἴνῳ ὀλίγῳ κεχρῆσθαι προσέταξε διὰ τὰς συχνὰς ἀσθενείας·[d] τέλειον γὰρ εἶναι τὸν ἱερέα προσήκει, ὡς τὴν ὑπὲρ τοῦ λαοῦ πρεσβείαν πεπιστευμένον. αὐτίκα γοῦν Μωϋσῆς ὁ νομοθέτης, θεασάμενος
10 τὸν περὶ τῆς ἁμαρτίας προσενεχθέντα χίμαρον ὁλοκαυτωθέντα παρὰ τὸν θεῖον νόμον, ὠργίσθη τῷ τε Ἐλεαζὰρ καὶ τῷ Ἰθαμάρ, λέγων, διὰ τί οὐκ ἐφάγετε τὰ περὶ τῆς ἁμαρτίας ἐν τόπῳ ἁγίῳ, ὅτι ἅγια ἁγίων ἐστίν; τοῦτο ἔδωκεν ὑμῖν Κύριος φαγεῖν ἵν' ἀφέλητε τὴν ἁμαρτίαν τῆς συναγωγῆς καὶ ἐξιλάσησθε περὶ
15 αὐτῶν ἔναντι Κυρίου.[e]

Διδασκόμεθα δὲ πάλιν ἐντεῦθεν ὡς, τὰ παρὰ τοῦ λαοῦ προσφερόμενα ἐσθίοντες, καὶ μὴ ἐννόμως ζῶντες, μηδὲ σπουδαίως τὰς ὑπὲρ τούτων προσφέροντες προσευχάς, δίκας ὑπέχομεν τῷ Θεῷ. τοῦτο αἰνιττόμενος ὁ δεσπότης Θεός, διὰ
20 τοῦ προφήτου ἔφη· ἁμαρτίας λαοῦ μου φάγονται.[f]

---

x A [32], B, C, 4 7 9 10 31* 35 37 = 20 mss.

l. 13 τοῦτο F.M. : οὐ τοῦτο A⁻¹² [32], 7 10 35, Sir. Sch. = "'Has not the Lord given it to you so . . . ?'"

a. Lv 10.9   b. 1Tm 3.2   c. 1Tm 3.8   d. 1Tm 5.23
e. Lv 10.17 (LXX var.)   f. Hos 4.8

26

mythological fables with the divine oracles, while others have preferred their own unholy notions to the sense of Scripture.[1]

X

Why did he forbid the priests to partake of wine?[a]

He did not forbid it absolutely, but only at the time of service. First one, then another group, served in consecutive shifts of a determined number of days. The apostle also enjoined that the priest be "sober"[b] and the deacons "not given to much drinking,"[c] but in a letter to Timothy, bade him take a little wine for his chronic infirmities.[d] Indeed, the priest must be perfect because entrusted with intercession for the people. Thus, as soon as Moses the lawgiver observed that the goat offered for sin had been burned in defiance of the divine Law, he was enraged with Eleazar and Ithamar, and said, "Why did you not eat the sin offering in the holy place, as it is most holy? The Lord has given it to you so you may remove the sin of the congregation and make atonement for them before the Lord."[e]

Now, this passage also teaches us that if we eat the offerings of the people but fail to live in accordance with the law and offer zealous prayers on their behalf, we become liable to God's punishment. Hinting at this, the Lord God declared through the prophet, "They will feed off my people's sin."[1f]

1. Theodoret draws a parallel between the offense of Aaron's sons against the holy fire and the misuse of the Scripture by Christian heretics, some of whom contest the limits of the canon while others offer interpretations at variance with what he regards as the clear sense of the text.

1. It is in the intercessory role of the priesthood that Theodoret sees the connection between Paul's injunctions to the Christian clergy regarding the consumption of alcohol and Moses' criticism of Aaron's sons for mishandling the sacrificial

The Questions on Leviticus

Τί σημαίνει τὸ διχηλοῦν καὶ μηρυκώμενον;[a]

(1) Τὸ μὲν διχηλοῦν οἶμαι δηλοῦν τὴν τῶν ἀγαθῶν πράξεων καὶ τὴν τῶν ἐναντίων διάκρισιν· πρὸς δὲ τούτῳ, τὸ μὴ μόνον τῷ παρόντι βίῳ ζῆν, ἀλλὰ καὶ τῷ μέλλοντι, καὶ τούτῳ μὲν
5 ἀπονέμειν τὰ ἀναγκαῖα, ἐκείνῳ δὲ πάντα, τουτέστι, καὶ τὴν ψυχὴν καὶ τὸ σῶμα καὶ τὰ περὶ τὸ σῶμα. τὸ δὲ μηρυκώμενον τὴν τῶν θείων λογίων σημαίνει μελέτην· ὥσπερ γὰρ τὸ πρόβατον καὶ τὰ τούτῳ προσόμοια διηνεκῶς ἀναπεμπάζεται τὴν τροφήν, οὕτως ὁ ἐμμελὴς καὶ φιλόθεος πρὸς τὸν τῶν ὅλων
10 βοᾷ Θεόν, ὡς ἠγάπησα τὸν νόμον σου, Κύριε· ὅλην τὴν ἡμέραν μελέτη μού ἐστιν.[b] καθάπερ δὲ τῶν ζῴων τὰ μὲν διχηλεῖ καὶ τὴν τροφὴν ἀναπεμπάζεται, τὰ δὲ οὐδέτερον αὐτῶν ποιεῖ ὡς ὄνος, καὶ ἡμίονος, καὶ ἵππος, καὶ τὰ θηρία, ἄλλα δὲ διχηλεῖ μὲν οὐκ ἀναπεμπάζεται δὲ τὴν τροφὴν ὥσπερ ὗς,[c] ἕτερα δὲ
15 μηρυκᾶται μὲν οὐ διχηλεῖ δὲ ὡς κάμηλος καὶ λαγωός,[d] οὕτως ἔστι καὶ παρὰ τοῖς ἀνθρώποις εὑρεῖν τοὺς μὲν τελείους καὶ τῶν θείων λογίων τὴν μελέτην ἀσπαζομένους καὶ τὴν ἀρετὴν ἐπιμελῶς μετιόντας, τοὺς δὲ ἀτελεῖς, τὰ μὲν θεῖα λόγια διὰ τῆς γλώττης προσφέροντας, διχηλεῖν δὲ οὐκ ἀνεχομένους, καὶ
20 τῇ καμήλῳ προσεοικότας, τινὰς δὲ τῶν τῆς εὐσεβείας οὐδέπω γεγευμένους, τὰ μὲν θεῖα λόγια μὴ προσιεμένους ἔργων δὲ ἀξιεπαίνων φροντίζοντας, ἄλλους δὲ καὶ πίστεως ἐρήμους καὶ πράξεως ἀγαθῆς παντελῶς γεγυμνωμένους.

Τῶν δὲ ἐνύδρων καθαρὰ εἶναι λέγει τὰ λεπίδας ἔχοντα καὶ
25 πτερύγια·[e] ταῦτα γὰρ ἄνω τοῖς ὕδασιν ἐπινήχεται. τὰ γὰρ οὐ

XI A [32], B, C, 4 7 9 10 31 35 37 = 20 mss.

a. Lv 11.3   b. Ps 119.97   c. Lv 11.7   d. Lv 11.4f.   e. Lv 11.9

XI

What is the significance of "cleft-footed and chewing the cud"?[a]

(1) I think "cleft-footed" suggests the discernment of good works from bad, and in addition to this, living not only for the present life but also for the future as one devotes only what is necessary to the former and everything—soul and body and things to do with the body—to the latter. "Chewing the cud," signifies study of the word of God. Just as the sheep and other creatures like it constantly regurgitate their food, so the devout and God-loving person cries out to the God of the universe, "How I have loved your Law, O Lord; it is my concern all day long."[b] Some animals are cleft-footed and regurgitate their food, whereas others, such as the ass, the mule, the horse, and the wild animals, have neither characteristic; others, like swine, are cleft-footed but do not regurgitate their food;[c] and others, like the camel and the hare, chew the cud but are not cleft-footed.[d] So also with human beings you can find some who are perfect, who devote themselves to the eager study of God's word and the assiduous practice of virtue; others who are imperfect and mouth the word of God but, resembling the camel, are reluctant "to divide the hoof"; others who have not yet so much as tasted religion, who do not accept the word of God yet give attention to commendable deeds; and others who are both devoid of faith and completely lacking in good works.

Of the creatures that live in the water he declares clean those that have scales and fins,[e] because they swim on top of the water, unlike

----

meat. The Christian priests must be above reproach to win God's forgiveness for their people, a task in which Eleazar and Ithamar failed when they neglected to consume the sin offering (Lv 10.16f.). Through the use of the first person plural, Theodoret gives the impression of addressing the contemporary clergy, though, unlike Chrysostom in the second Hannah homily (*De Anna* 2.4; *CPG* #4411), he does not imply that they were given to excessive drinking.

τοιαῦτα κάτω περὶ τὴν ἰλὺν καλινδεῖται. καθαροὶ τοίνυν κἂν
τοῖς λογικοῖς οἱ, μὴ τοῖς γηΐνοις προστετηκότες, ἀλλὰ τὰ
πτερὰ τῆς πίστεως ἔχοντες καὶ τῇ τῆς ἀρετῆς πεφραγμένοι
σκέπῃ. ὅπερ γάρ ἐστιν ἡ λεπὶς τοῖς ἰχθύσι, τοῦτο τοῖς
30 ἀνθρώποις ἡ τῆς ἀρετῆς πανοπλία· καὶ ὅπερ ἐκείνοις τὰ
πτερύγια, τοῦτο τοῖς ἀνθρώποις ἡ πίστις. ταῦτα δὲ ἡμῖν ὁ
μακάριος περιτίθησι Παῦλος, τὰ πτερὰ λέγων τῆς χάριτος καὶ
τὰ ὅπλα τοῦ πνεύματος.[f] τῶν δὲ πτηνῶν ἀκάθαρτα εἶναί φησι
τὰ ἁρπακτικὰ καὶ νεκροβόρα καὶ τὰ τῷ σκότει χαίροντα,[g]
35 διδάσκων ἡμᾶς καὶ πλεονεξίας ἀπέχεσθαι, καὶ τὴν δυσώδη τῆς
ἁμαρτίας τροφὴν ἀποστρέφεσθαι, καὶ τὸ σκότος μισεῖν.

(2) Ὅτι δὲ οὐκ ἀπὸ τρόπου ταῦθ' οὕτως ἔχειν νενοήκαμεν
μαρτυρεῖ τῶν πράξεων ἡ ἱστορία· εἶδε, γάρ φησιν, ὁ μακάριος
Πέτρος σινδόνα *τέσσαρσιν ἀρχαῖς καθιεμένην, ἐν ᾗ ἦν πάντα*
40 *τὰ τετράποδα . . . τῆς γῆς καὶ τὰ πετεινὰ τοῦ οὐρανοῦ,*[h] καὶ
ἤκουσε φωνῆς λεγούσης, *ἀναστάς, Πέτρε, θῦσον καὶ φάγε.*[i]
εἶτα εἰρηκότος ἐκείνου, *μηδαμῶς, Κύριε, ὅτι οὐδέποτε ἔφαγον*
πᾶν κοινὸν ἢ ἀκάθαρτον,[j] ἔφη ὁ δεσπότης Θεός, *ἃ ὁ Θεὸς*
ἐκαθάρισε σὺ μὴ κοίνου.[k] ὅτι δὲ τοῦ Κορνηλίου χάριν ταῦτα
45 ἐρρήθη, ἐθνικοῦ γε ὄντος καὶ σωτηρίας ἐφιεμένου, δηλοῖ τὰ
ἑξῆς. καὶ ὁ Κύριος δὲ τοῖς ἀποστόλοις ἔφη, πολλοὶ ἐλεύσονται
πρὸς ὑμᾶς ἐν ἐνδύμασι προβάτων, ἔσωθεν δέ εἰσι λύκοι
ἅρπαγες[l] καὶ τοῖς ἰουδαίοις, *γεννήματα ἐχιδνῶν·*[m] καὶ ὁ
ἀπόστολος, *βλέπετε τοὺς κύνας·*[n] καὶ τοῖς ἐφεσίων
50 πρεσβυτέροις, *οἶδα ὅτι μετὰ τὴν ἄφιξίν μου εἰσελεύσονται*
λύκοι βαρεῖς εἰς ὑμᾶς·[o] καὶ οἱ προφῆται τοὺς μὲν ἵππους
θηλυμανεῖς ὀνομάζουσι,[p] τοὺς δὲ *ὄφεις καὶ ἔκγονα ἀσπίδων*
πετομένων·[q] καὶ πάλιν ὁ Κύριος, ὡμοιώθη ἡ βασιλεία τῶν
οὐρανῶν *σαγήνῃ βληθείσῃ εἰς τὴν θάλασσαν καὶ ἐκ παντὸς*
55 *γένους συναγαγούσῃ·*[r] καὶ ὅπου . . . τὸ πτῶμα, ἐκεῖ

---

f. Eph 6.16f.　　g. Lv 11.13–19　　h. Acts 10.11f.　　i. Acts 10.13　　j. Acts 10.14
k. Acts 10.15　　l. Mt 7.15　　m. Mt 12.34; 23.33　　n. Phil 3.2　　o. Acts 20.29
p. Jer 5.8　　q. Is 30.6　　r. Mt 13.47

those that wallow in the mud below. In the case of rational creatures, the clean do not cling to earthly things but have the wings of
faith and are protected by the covering of virtue. As the panoply of
faith is to man so the scale to the fish, and as faith is to man so fins
to the fish. This is how St. Paul clothes us when he speaks of the
wings of grace and the weapons of the Spirit.[f] Of the birds he declares unclean those that prey upon others, feed on corpses, and delight in the dark,[g] his purpose being to teach us to abstain from
avarice, avoid the stinking food of sin, and hate the darkness.

(2) Now, the book of Acts confirms that our interpretation is not
out of order: St. Peter had a vision of a sheet "let down by its four
corners and containing all the four-footed creatures of the earth and
the birds of the sky,"[h] and he heard a voice saying, "Get up, Peter, kill,
and eat."[i] Then when he replied, "Far be it from me, Lord, for I have
never eaten anything profane or unclean,"[j] the Lord God said,
"What God has declared clean do not you call profane."[k] Now, the
sequel indicates that this was said with regard to Cornelius, who,
though a gentile, longed for salvation. And the Lord said to the
apostles, "Many will come to you in sheep's clothing, though within
they are ravenous wolves";[l] and to the Jews, "Brood of vipers."[m] The
apostle said, "Beware of the dogs";[n] and to the Ephesian elders, "I
know that after my departure savage wolves will come upon you."[o]
The prophets also called some men "stallions mad for females,"[p]
others "snakes and offspring of asps."[q] Furthermore, the Lord declared that "The Kingdom of Heaven is like a net cast into the sea,
which brings in a haul from every species of fish";[r] and "Where the

συναχθήσονται οἱ ἀετοί.ˢ συνᾴδει τοίνυν ἡ ἑρμηνεία τῇ τῆς
θείας γραφῆς διανοίᾳ.

Ἡμεῖς μὲν οὖν ταύτην λαμβάνομεν ἐκ τούτων τὴν ὄνησιν.
ἰουδαίοις δὲ διὰ τούτων αὐτῶν ἕτερον ὠφελείας προσενήνοχεν
60 εἶδος· διχῇ γὰρ διελὼν καὶ τὰ χερσαῖα ζῷα, καὶ τὰ πτηνά, καὶ
τὰ ἔνυδρα καὶ τὰ μὲν ἀκάθαρτα, τὰ δὲ καθαρὰ προσειπών,
πείθει μηδὲν τούτων ἡγεῖσθαι Θεόν· πῶς γὰρ ἄν τις σωφρονῶν
ἢ τὸ ἀκάθαρτον ὀνομάσοι *Θεόν,* ὃ μυσαττόμενος
ἀποστρέφεται, ἢ τὸ τῷ ἀληθινῷ Θεῷ προσφερόμενον καὶ παρ'
65 αὐτοῦ ἐσθιόμενον;

XII

Τί δή ποτε ἐὰν μὲν εἰς ὀστράκινον σκεῦος ἐμπέσοι τι τῶν
ἀκαθάρτων, συντρίβεσθαι τοῦτο κελεύει, ἂν δὲ εἰς χαλκοῦν, ἢ
ξύλινον, ἢ σάκκον, ἢ ἱμάτιον, ὕδατι πλύνεσθαι;[a]

Καὶ ἐντεῦθεν δῆλον ὡς οὐδὲν φύσει ἀκάθαρτον, ἀλλὰ διά
5 τινα αἰτίαν, τὰ μὲν εἶπεν ἀκάθαρτα, τὰ δὲ καθαρά. εἰ δὲ
φύσει ἀκάθαρτα ἦν, ἔδει καὶ τὰ χαλκᾶ συντρίβεσθαι καὶ τὰ
ξύλινα. ἀλλ', ἐπειδὴ δι' ἑτέραν αἰτίαν ἀκάθαρτα αὐτὰ
προσηγόρευσε, τὰ μὲν πλείονος ἄξια ὄντα τιμῆς πλύνεσθαι
κελεύει, τὰ δὲ εὔωνα συντρίβεσθαι· ταύτῃ μὲν τὸν περὶ τοῦ
10 ἀκαθάρτου νόμον κρατύνων, ἐκείνῃ δὲ παραδηλῶν τὸν τοῦ
νόμου σκοπόν. διά τοι τοῦτο καὶ κλιβάνους καὶ χυτρόποδας
καθαιρεῖσθαι κελεύει εἴ τι τούτων αὐτοῖς ἐμπέσοι τῶν ζῴων.
καὶ τὸ ἐν τοῖς ἀγγείοις ὕδωρ ὀνομάζει ἀκάθαρτον,
|30 ἐμπεσόντος αὐτοῖς θνησιμαίου,[b] τὸ δὲ πηγαῖον ὕδωρ οὐκέτι,
15 οὐδὲ τὸ λάκκιον·[c] μικραῖς γὰρ ζημίαις τὰ τοιαῦτα περιορίζει.

s. Mt 24.28

———

XII A [32], B, C, 4 7 9 10 31 35 37 = 20 mss.
a. Lv 11.32f.   b. Lv 11.34f.   c. Lv 11.36

corpse is, there the eagles will gather."[s] So our interpretation is in keeping with the sense of holy Scripture.[1]

While this is the useful teaching that we get from these passages, the Jews have derived from them a different sort of benefit. Dividing into two classes land animals, birds, and sea creatures, and declaring some unclean and others clean, Scripture convinces them to regard none as divine. After all, how could anyone in his right mind give the name "god" to an unclean thing, from which he turns away in loathing, or to that which he offers to the true God and then eats?

XII

Why did he order that an earthenware vessel be smashed if any of the unclean creatures should fall on it, but that a bronze or wooden vessel, or a bag, or garment be washed in water?[a]

We infer from this also that nothing is unclean by nature; God had a reason of his own when he declared some things unclean, others clean. If unclean by nature, the bronze and wooden vessels would have had to be smashed as well. Since, however, he declared them unclean for a different reason, he ordered that more expensive objects be washed, and cheap ones smashed. In the latter case, he confirmed the law about uncleanness, and in the former, intimated the purpose of the Law. This was why he also commanded that pans and foot-basins be destroyed if any of these animals fell on them and called the water in jars unclean if a carcass fell into them,[b] but not water from a spring or lake,[c] for which only slight penalties were

---

1. Theodoret demonstrates that he has scriptural support—a necessary criterion for an Antiochene—for understanding in a spiritual sense OT references to animals.

μανθάνομεν δὲ πάλιν ἡμεῖς ἡλίκον ἡ ἁμαρτία κακόν· τὸν γὰρ ἀληθῆ μολυσμὸν ἐκείνη προστρίβεται.

XIII

Διὰ τί ἂν μὲν δίχα ὕδατος σπέρματι ἐμπέσοι τὸ θνησιμαῖον οὐ μιαίνει, ἂν δὲ μετὰ ὕδατος ἀκάθαρτον ἀποφαίνει;[a]

'Επειδὴ ἡ ὑγρότης τοῦ ἰχῶρος μεταλαβεῖν παρασκευάζει τὸ
||26b 5 σπέρμα.

Διαφερόντως δὲ τὰ ἐπὶ τῆς κοιλίας ἰλυσπώμενα ἀκάθαρτα εἶναί φησιν·[b] ἀρχέκακος γὰρ ὁ ὄφις καὶ τῆς διαβολικῆς ἐπιβουλῆς ὑπουργός.[c]

XIV

Διὰ τί τὴν τεκοῦσαν ἄρρεν τεσσαράκοντα ἡμέρας ἀκάθαρτον εἶναί φησι, τὴν δὲ θῆλυ δὶς τοσαύτας;[a]

Δεῖ τοῦ νόμου τὸν σκοπὸν ἐξετάζειν· πολλάκις γὰρ ἕτερα δι' ἑτέρων διδάσκει. καὶ τοῦτο ῥάδιον ἐντεῦθεν καταμαθεῖν· εἰ
5 γὰρ ἡ τεκοῦσα ἀκάθαρτος, καὶ ἡ ἐγκύμων ἀκάθαρτος. οἶμαι τοίνυν τὸν νόμον διαναπαύεσθαι κελεύειν αὐτήν, ὡς σφόδρα πεπονηκυῖαν καὶ τῶν πικρῶν ὠδίνων ἀνασχομένην. ἀλλ' εἰ τοῦτο ἁπλῶς οὕτως διηγόρευσεν, οὐκ ἂν ἐκράτησαν τῆς ἐπιθυμίας οἱ ἄνδρες· ἀκάθαρτον δὲ αὐτὴν διδασκόμενοι,
10 φεύγουσι τὴν κοινωνίαν ἵνα μὴ τῆς ἀκαθαρσίας μετάσχωσιν. οὐκοῦν ὁ νόμος τῷ τῆς ἀκαθαρσίας λόγῳ τὴν ὄρεξιν σβέννυσι.

xiii A [32], B, C, 4 7 9 10 31 35 37 = 20 mss.

a. Lv 11.37f. b. Lv 11.29–32 c. 2Cor 11.3

xiv A [32], B, C⁻⁵¹, 4 7 9 10 31 35 37 = 19 mss.

a. Lv 12.1–5

assigned. Once again, we learn from this what a great evil sin is, since it is sin that causes real defilement.[1]

XIII

Why is it that if a carcass fell on unmoistened seed, it did not defile it, but if the seed had been moistened, it did render it unclean?[a]

Because the moisture causes the seed to come into contact with liquid discharged from the carcass.

He declares animals that wriggle on their stomach especially unclean,[b] since the serpent is the author of evil and minister to the devil's scheming.[c]

XIV

Why is it that, according to the Law, a woman bearing a male was unclean for forty days, but for twice as long if she bore a female?[a]

We must examine the purpose of the Law, which often teaches one thing by means of another, as we can easily learn from this passage as well. If the woman giving birth was unclean, so also was the pregnant woman. I think the Law intended her to rest after having undergone such tough work and suffered such severe pain. If it had spelled this out in so many words, the husbands would not have controlled their desires, whereas when they were told she was unclean, they shunned intercourse to avoid contracting the uncleanness. Thus, the Law quenched libido by the rule of uncleanness.

1. As in the preceding discussion of the distinction between clean and unclean animals (Q. 11), Theodoret attempts to find a spiritual application of lasting value in the laws dealing with contamination (Lv 11.29–38).

τὴν δὲ διαφορὰν τῶν ἡμερῶν τινὲς οὕτως ἡρμήνευσαν· ὅτι πλείονα πόνον ὑπομένουσιν αἱ γυναῖκες γεννῶσαι τὰ θήλεα, διὸ διπλάσιον αὐταῖς εἰς ἀνάπαυλαν ἀπένειμε χρόνον.

XV

Τί βούλεται ὁ περὶ τῆς λέπρας νόμος;[a]

Διὰ τῶν σωματικῶν παθημάτων τῆς ψυχῆς ἐπιδείκνυσι τὰ νοσήματα καὶ διὰ τῶν ἀκουσίων τῶν ἑκουσίων κατηγορεῖ. εἰ γὰρ τὰ φυσικὰ δοκεῖ πως εἶναι ἀκάθαρτα, πολλῷ μᾶλλον τὰ
5 γνωμικά. λέγει δὲ καὶ λέπρας διαφοράν,[b] ἐπειδὴ καὶ ἁμαρτημάτων ἐστὶ διαφορά· καὶ ἀρχὴ λέπρας, ἐπειδὴ καὶ ἀρχὴ ἁμαρτίας. ἀλλ' ὥσπερ τὴν λέπραν ὁ ἱερεὺς διακρίνει,[c] οὕτως χρὴ καὶ τῶν τῆς ψυχῆς ἁμαρτημάτων αὐτὸν εἶναι κριτήν. λεπρὸν δὲ καλεῖται τὸ ποικίλον τοῦ χρώματος· οὕτω κακία
10 προσγενομένη ψυχῇ, λέπραν αὐτὴν ἀπεργάζεται.

xv A *[32]*, B, C⁻⁵¹, 4 7 9 10 31 35 37 = 19 mss.

a. Lv 13f.   b. Lv 14.54–57   c. Lv 13.3, 10f., 19f., 24f., 30, 42–44

Some commentators have explained the difference in the numbers of days as due to the greater labor women suffer in giving birth to females; hence, the Law apportioned them a doubly long rest.[1]

XV

What is the meaning of the law regarding leprosy?[a]

Through bodily ailments it points to diseases of the soul, and through involuntary faults it censures the voluntary. After all, if natural weaknesses are thought to be unclean, the deliberate are much more so. It also mentions different kinds of leprosy,[b] since there are also different kinds of sin. Furthermore, leprosy has a beginning since sin does too. As it is the priest who makes the decision on leprosy,[c] so he must also be judge of the sins of the soul. Leprosy is a term for blotchy skin; likewise when evil infects the soul, it disfigures it with blotches.[1]

---

1. Theodoret addresses the provision establishing the period of uncleanness for a woman who has given birth. This he specifies as forty or eighty days, the sum of the initial period of one or two weeks (Lv. 12.2, 5) plus the subsequent period of thirty-three or sixty-six days (vv. 4f.; *cf.* Lk 2.22). As Guinot points out (p. 772), he draws this interpretation from Diodore (Deconinck, frag. 72), who tried to discern behind the provision a humane concern for the health of the mother. Diodore accounted for the greater labor of giving birth to a girl by quoting a current physiological opinion that the formation of the female fetus required eighty days, and that of the male only half as long. In contrast, the modern interpreter, R.J. Faley, explains (on 12.1–8) this provision as based upon the ancient Hebrew association of blood with life and both with "Yahweh, the source of life." The loss of blood in childbirth diminished the mother's vitality and thus separated her from the Lord. The uncleanness was of shorter duration in the birth of a boy "probably because of the greater strength and vitality connected with the male."

---

1. By contrast with the legislation regarding natal uncleanness, that for detection of leprosy (Lv 13f.) receives only a spiritual interpretation; *cf.* the closely similar discussion of the cases of uncleanness described in Q. 7.

XVI

Διὰ τί τὸν ὅλον λεπρὸν γενόμενον καθαρὸν ὀνομάζει;[a]

Φιλανθρωπίας καὶ οὗτος ὁ νόμος μεστός. ὥσπερ γὰρ ἐπὶ
τοῦ θνησιμαίου διηγόρευσεν, εἰ μὲν εἰς ἀγγεῖον ἐμπέσοι,
ἀκάθαρτον εἶναι, εἰ δὲ εἰς πηγὴν ἢ λάκκον, οὐκέτι, οὕτω τὸν
5 ποικίλον δεξάμενον χρῶμα τῶν ἄλλων ἀποκρίνει, ὡς ἐλπίδα
καθάρσεως ἔχοντα, τὸν δὲ ὁλόλευκον γενόμενον ἀναμίγνυσθαι
κελεύει τοῖς ἄλλοις ἵνα μὴ παρὰ πάντα τὸν βίον τῶν ἄλλων
ἀνθρώπων κεχωρισμένος διάγῃ.

Καὶ τοῦτο δὲ τῶν πνευματικῶν ἐστι τύπος. τοῖς μὲν γὰρ
10 πιστοῖς ἁμαρτάνουσιν οὐδὲ συνεσθίειν ὁ θεῖος κελεύει νόμος,
τοῖς δέ γε ἀπίστοις εἰς ἑστίασιν καλοῦσιν οὐ κωλύει
συνεστιᾶσθαι. λέγει δὲ οὕτως ὁ θεῖος ἀπόστολος· *ἐάν τις*
καλῇ ὑμᾶς τῶν ἀπίστων, καὶ θέλετε πορεύεσθαι, πᾶν τὸ
παρατιθέμενον ὑμῖν ἐσθίετε, μηδὲν ἀνακρίνοντες, καὶ τὰ
15 ἑξῆς.[b] περὶ δὲ τῶν ἁμαρτανόντων πιστῶν οὕτως ἔφη· *ἐάν τις*
ἀδελφὸς ὀνομαζόμενος ᾖ πόρνος, ἢ πλεονέκτης, ἢ
εἰδωλολάτρης, ἢ μέθυσος, ἢ λοίδορος, ἢ ἅρπαξ, τῷ τοιούτῳ
μηδὲ συνεσθίειν·[c] καὶ πάλιν, *στέλλεσθε ὑμᾶς ἀπὸ παντὸς*
ἀδελφοῦ ἀτάκτως περιπατοῦντος.[d] οὗτος τοίνυν ἔοικε τῷ ἐκ
20 μέρους λεπρῷ, ὁ δὲ ἄπιστος τῷ πᾶσαν τὴν φυσικὴν
ἀπολέσαντι χροιάν. ἀλλὰ τούτοις καὶ προσδιαλεγόμεθα καὶ
συναναστρεφόμεθα, ἐκείνοις δὲ οὐκέτι. καὶ τούτου μάρτυς ὁ
θεῖος ἀπόστολος· *ἔγραψα γὰρ ὑμῖν,* φησί, . . . *μὴ*

---

xvi A *[32]*, B, C, 4 7 9 10 31 35 37 = 20 mss.

ll. 12f. *ἐάν* . . . *καλῇ* . . . *θέλετε* Sir. Sch. F.M. : *εἰ* . . . *καλεῖ* . . . *θέλετε*
(?) J.P. I do not print this, the reading offered by Thdt. in his comment on 1Cor.
10.27, since F.M. reports no disagreement among the mss. on *ἐάν*; cf. *The Greek*
New Testament, ad loc.

a. Lv 13.12f.   b. 1Cor 10.27   c. 1Cor 5.11   d. 2Thes 3.6

XVI

Why did the Law pronounce clean a person who was entirely covered with leprosy?[a]

This law was also replete with loving-kindness. As in the case of the carcass that fell into a jar, the jar was declared unclean, but not a spring or lake into which it had fallen, so a man with blotchy skin was set apart from others, since he had hope of becoming clean. But the one who was completely white was commanded to mingle with others so as not to spend his whole life cut off from other people.

Now, this is a type of spiritual matters. While the divine Law forbids us even to eat with believers who sin, it does not forbid us to dine with unbelievers who invite us to a banquet. Thus, according to the holy apostle, "If an unbeliever invite you, and you want to go, eat everything set before you without quibble" and so on.[b] But about believers who are sinners he said, "If someone bearing the name of "brother" is sexually immoral, greedy, an idolater, a drunkard, a reviler, or a robber, do not eat with him";[c] and again, "Keep away from every brother whose life is disorderly."[d] Such a brother, then, resembles the one who is partly leprous, whereas the unbeliever is like the one who has lost all his natural color. We converse and associate with the latter, but not with the former. The holy apostle confirms this: "I wrote you not to mingle with the sexually immoral—not meaning all the sexually immoral people of this world, or the greedy, the robbers, and idolaters—but only anyone bearing the

συναναμίγνυσθαι πόρνοις καὶ οὐ πάντως τοῖς πόρνοις τοῦ
25 κόσμου τούτου, ἢ τοῖς πλεονέκταις, ἢ ἅρπαξιν, ἢ
εἰδωλολάτραις, ἀλλ'... ἐάν τις ἀδελφὸς ὀνομαζόμενος, καὶ τὰ
ἑξῆς.ᵉ καθαρὸν μέντοι κέκληκε τὸν ὅλον γεγενημένον λευκόν,
οὐχ ὡς ὑγιὲς ἔχοντα τὸ σῶμα, ἀλλ' ὡς μηκέτι τοὺς
πελάζοντας κατὰ τὸν νόμον μολύνοντα.

XVII

Διὰ τί τοῦ λεπροῦ ἀκάλυπτον εἶναι κελεύει τὴν κεφαλὴν
καὶ τὰ ἱμάτια παραλελυμένα;ᵃ
῞Ινα γνώριμος ᾖ, καὶ μὴ μεταλαγχάνωσι τῆς ἀκαθαρσίας οἱ
πελάζοντες. οὕτως ὁ ἀπόστολος περὶ τῶν ἁμαρτανόντων ἔφη·
5 στέλλεσθε ὑμᾶς ἀπὸ παντὸς ἀδελφοῦ ἀτάκτως περιπατοῦντος
καὶ μὴ κατὰ τὴν παράδοσιν, ἣν παρελάβετε παρ' ἡμῶν·ᵇ καί,
ἐάν τις ἀδελφὸς ὀνομαζόμενος ᾖ πόρνος, ἢ πλεονέκτης, ἢ
εἰδωλολάτρης, ἢ μέθυσος, ἢ λοίδορος, ἢ ἅρπαξ, τῷ τοιούτῳ
μηδὲ συνεσθίειν.ᶜ

XVIII

Πῶς ἐν τοῖς ἱματίοις λέπρα ἐγίνετο;ᵃ
Πολλὰς ὁ Θεὸς αὐτοῖς παιδείας τοιαύτας ἐπήγαγεν.
αὐτίκα γοῦν καὶ περὶ λεπρῶν οἴκων οὕτως ἔφη· ὡς ἂν
εἰσέλθητε εἰς τὴν γῆν τῶν χαναναίων, ἣν ἐγὼ δίδωμι

e. 1Cor 5.9–11

---

xvii A *[32]*, B, C, 4 7 9 10 35 37 = 19 mss.

a. Lv 13.45   b. 2Thes 3.6   c. 1Cor 5.11

---

xviii A *[32]*, B, C, 4 7 9 10 31 35 37 = 20 mss.

a. Lv 13.47–59

name of brother" and so on.[1e] Of course, when the Law used the term "clean" of the one who had turned completely white, it did not mean that he was enjoying bodily health, but that he no longer imparted legal impurity to those who approached him.

XVII

Why did the Law enjoin that the leper's head be uncovered and his clothes undone?[a]

So he would be known and those approaching him would not contract his uncleanness. Likewise, the apostle said of sinners, "Keep away from every brother whose life is disorderly and not in keeping with the tradition you have received from us;"[b] and "If someone bearing the name of "brother" is sexually immoral, greedy, an idolater, a drunkard, a reviler, or a robber, do not eat with him."[c]

XVIII

How could leprosy occur on clothing?[a]

God subjected the Israelites to many such chastisements. For example, he spoke also of leprous houses: "When you come into the land of the Canaanites, which I am giving you, and I put a plague of

---

1. In an effort to discover a spiritual meaning in the law of Lv 13.12f., which, with apparent inconsistency, clears of leprosy a person more generally afflicted than one declared leprous in the preceding provision (vv. 9–11), Theodoret quotes Paul's (1Cor 5.9–11 and 2Thes 3.6) rulings on associations acceptable for a Christian.

5 ὑμῖν, . . . καὶ δώσω ἀφὴν λέπρας ἐν ταῖς οἰκίαις τῆς γῆς τῆς
ἐγκτήτου ὑμῶν, καὶ τὰ ἑξῆς.[b] διδάσκει δὲ διὰ τούτων ὅτι
θεήλατοι ἦσαν πληγαί, ποτὲ μὲν κατὰ ἱματίων, ποτὲ δὲ κατὰ
οἰκιῶν φερόμεναι.

Ταῦτα δὲ τὴν ἄφατον τοῦ Θεοῦ φιλανθρωπίαν δηλοῖ· τῶν
10 γὰρ ἀνθρώπων ἁμαρτανόντων, ἱματίοις καὶ οἰκίαις ἐπέφερε
τὰς πληγάς, διὰ τούτων τοῖς ταῦτα κεκτημένοις τὴν
θεραπείαν προσφέρων. ἔοικε δὲ τῷ λεπρῶντι οἴκῳ ὁ οἶκος τοῦ
Ἰσραήλ, οὗ πολλάκις μὲν ἐξηρέθησαν, καθάπερ λίθοι τινὲς
λεπρῶντες,[c] οἱ πλημμελήσαντες, ποτὲ μὲν δι' ἀσσυρίων,[d] ποτὲ
15 δὲ διὰ βαβυλωνίων,[e] ἄλλοτε δὲ διὰ μακεδόνων.[f] ἐπειδὴ δὲ
παγίαν ἔσχον τὴν λέπραν, ἄρδην καταλυθῆναι τὴν οἰκίαν ὁ
νομοθέτης ἐκέλευσεν.[g] ἀκάθαρτοι οὖν οἱ εἰς τὰς τούτων
συναγωγὰς εἰσιόντες, ὡς εἰς λεπρῶσαν οἰκίαν εἰσιόντες.

XIX

Τί σημαίνει τὰ δύο ὀρνίθια, τὰ ὑπὲρ τοῦ καθαριζομένου
λεπροῦ προσφερόμενα;[a]

Τοῦ σωτηρίου πάθους περιέχει τὸν τύπον. ὥσπερ γὰρ
τούτων τὸ μὲν ἐθύετο, τὸ δέ, εἰς τὸ τοῦ τυθέντος αἷμα
5 βαπτόμενον, ἀπελύετο, οὕτως ὑπὲρ τῆς λεπρώσης
ἀνθρωπότητος ὁ δεσπότης ἐσταυρώθη Χριστός, τῆς μὲν
σαρκὸς δεξαμένης τὸν θάνατον, τῆς δὲ θεότητος
οἰκειωσαμένης τὸ τῆς ἀνθρωπότητος πάθος. καὶ καθάπερ
ὕδατι καθαρῷ τοῦ σφαγέντος ὀρνιθίου τὸ αἷμα μιγνύμενον διὰ
10 κεδρίνου ξύλου, καὶ ὑσσώπου, καὶ κοκκίνου κεκλωσμένου
περιραινόμενος, ὁ λεπρὸς λαμπρός τε καὶ καθαρὸς

---

b. Lv 14.34   c. Lv 14.40   d. V., *e.g.*, 2Kgs 18.9–12.   e. V., *e.g.*, 2Kgs 24.10–16.
f. V., *e.g.*, 2Mc 4.37f.   g. Lv 14.45

XIX   A [32], B, C⁻⁵¹, 4 7 9 10 31 35 37 = 19 mss.
a. Lv 14.4–7

leprosy in the houses of the land of your possession" and so on.[b] In this way, he taught that plagues were heaven-sent, sometimes affecting clothing, at others houses.

All of this demonstrates God's ineffable loving-kindness; though it was the people who sinned, he brought the plague on their clothing and houses to use them as a means of healing their owners. The house of Israel was like a leprous house, whose sinful members were often removed like leprous stones,[c] sometimes by the Assyrians,[d] at others by the Babylonians,[e] and at others by the Macedonians.[f] And when their leprosy had become incurable, the Lawgiver ordered the whole house destroyed.[g] As a result, those who enter the synagogues of these people are unclean, since they are entering a leprous house.[1]

XIX

What is the significance of the two small birds offered for the purification of the leper?[a]

They present a type of the saving passion. As one was sacrificed, while the other was dipped in the blood of the sacrifice and released, so Christ the Lord was crucified for leprous humanity: the flesh undergoing death, the divinity appropriating the suffering of the humanity. And as the leper emerges glowing and cleansed when sprinkled with the blood of the slain bird mixed with pure water on a branch of cedar with hyssop and crimson yarn, so whoever believes in Christ the Savior and is purified in the water of most holy baptism casts off the stain of his sins. Now, cedar, an incorruptible

---

1. Here Theodoret develops a metaphor for which there is no biblical precedent: the leprous house of Israel and its punishment. On the basis of Lv 14.46 he proceeds to depict Jewish synagogues (συναγωγάς) as places of moral or spiritual contamination for Christians.

ἀπεδείκνυτο, οὕτως ὁ τῷ σωτῆρι πιστεύων Χριστῷ καὶ τῷ τοῦ
παναγίου βαπτίσματος ὕδατι καθαιρόμενος, τὰς τῶν
ἁμαρτημάτων ἀποβάλλει κηλῖδας. σύμβολον δὲ τὸ μὲν κέδρινον
15 ξύλον τῆς ἀπαθοῦς θεότητος· ἄσηπτον γὰρ τόδε τὸ ξύλον· τὸ
δὲ κόκκινον τὸ κλωστὸν τῆς ἐκ ψυχῆς καὶ σώματος
ἀνθρωπότητος, τὸ δὲ ὕσσωπον τῆς τοῦ παναγίου πνεύματος
θερμότητός τε καὶ εὐοσμίας· διὰ τούτων γὰρ οἱ βαπτιζόμενοι
τῆς ψυχικῆς ἀπαλλάτονται λέπρας.
20 Καὶ ἡ κοτύλη δὲ τοῦ ἐλαίου[b] τοῦ πνευματικοῦ μύρου
σημαντική. δηλοῖ δὲ τὸ ἐπιχριόμενον ἔλαιον τῷ ὠτίῳ τῷ δεξιῷ,
καὶ τῇ δεξιᾷ χειρί, καὶ τῷ δεξιῷ ποδὶ[c] τὸ τὴν μὲν ἀκοὴν τοῖς
δεξιοῖς ἀφορίζεσθαι λόγοις, τὴν δὲ χεῖρα καὶ τὸν πόδα ταῖς
δεξιαῖς πράξεσιν. ἐπιβαλλόμενον δὲ καὶ τῇ κεφαλῇ,[d] δηλοῖ τὴν
25 ἀφιέρωσιν τοῦ λογικοῦ. ὁ μέντοι διαμείνας λεπρὸς ἔξω διῆγε
τῆς παρεμβολῆς[e] ὡς ὁ ἀμεταμέλητα πταίων τῆς ἐκκλησίας
ἐκβάλλεται.

XX

Διὰ τί τὸν γονορρυῆ ἀκάθαρτον ὀνομάζει;[a]

Καὶ ἤδη ἔφην ὅτι διὰ τῶν φυσικῶν παιδεύει τὰ γνωμικὰ
καὶ διδάσκει διὰ τούτων ὅπως ἐκεῖνα παγχάλεπα. εἰ γὰρ ἡ
κατὰ φύσιν γινομένη ῥύσις ἀκάθαρτος, πολλῷ μᾶλλον ἡ
5 λαγνεία παράνομος. διδάσκει δὲ πάλιν ἡμᾶς φεύγειν τῶν
τοιούτων τὰς συνουσίας· ἔφη γὰρ ἀκάθαρτον εἶναι τὸν τῷ
γονορρυεῖ προσπελάζοντα.[b] ὅτι δὲ τῶν κατὰ φύσιν γινομένων
οὐδὲν ἀληθῶς ἀκάθαρτον αὐτὸς ὁ νόμος δηλοῖ. εἰ γὰρ
ὀστρακίνου σκεύους ἅψαιτο ὁ γονορρυής, συντρίβεσθαι τοῦτο
10 κελεύει, εἰ δὲ χαλκοῦ ἢ ξυλίνου, ὕδατι ἀποσμήχεσθαι·[c] ἔδει δὲ

b. Lv 14.12, 15–18   c. Lv 14.17   d. Lv 14.18   e. Lv 13.46

xx A [32], B, C, 4 7 9 10 31 35 37 = 20 mss.

a. Lv 15.2   b. Lv 15.7   c. Lv 15.12

wood, is symbolic of the impassible divinity; the crimson twine, of the humanity, composed of soul and body; and the hyssop, of the ardor and sweet fragrance of the most Holy Spirit. It is through these that the baptized are rid of the leprosy of the soul.

Furthermore, the cup of oil[b] signifies spiritual ointment. The application of the oil to the right ear, hand, and foot[c] suggests confining one's hearing to right words and one's hand and foot to right actions. The application to the head suggests the dedication of one's reason.[d] But the person who remained leprous continued to dwell outside the camp,[e] just as the sinner who remains unrepentant is expelled from the Church.

XX

Why does the Law pronounce unclean anyone with gonorrhea?[a]

I have already said that, through the physical, it gives instruction in moral, defects and conveys through the former the gravity of the latter. If a naturally occurring discharge is unclean, lust must be all the more unlawful. Furthermore, this law teaches us to avoid associating with the immoral, for it pronounces unclean whoever approaches anyone with gonorrhea.[b] Now, this law actually implies that no natural condition is really unclean, for if the person with gonorrhea touches an earthenware vessel, it enjoins that the vessel be smashed, whereas a bronze or wooden one is to be scoured with water.[c] But these would also have to be smashed, just like the earth-

καὶ ταῦτα παραπλησίως τοῖς ὀστρακίνοις συντρίβεσθαι εἴπερ
ἄρα τῷ ὄντι ἀκάθαρτος ἦν ᾧ τόδε τὸ πάθος συνέβαινεν.

Οὕτω καὶ τὸν ὀνειρώττοντα ἀκάθαρτον εἶναί φησι,[d] καὶ
τοὺς νόμῳ γάμου συναπτομένους[e] καίτοι αὐτοῦ τὸν περὶ τοῦ
15 γάμου τεθεικότος νόμον καὶ πρῶτον νόμον· *ἀντὶ τούτου, γάρ*
φησιν, καταλείψει ἄνθρωπος τὸν πατέρα αὐτοῦ καὶ τὴν
μητέρα αὐτοῦ καὶ προσκολληθήσεται πρὸς τὴν γυναῖκα αὐτοῦ,
καὶ ἔσονται οἱ δύο εἰς σάρκα μίαν.[f] πῶς οὖν ἀκάθαρτον καλεῖ
τὸν κατὰ νόμον μιγνύμενον; ἀλλὰ δῆλόν ἐστιν ὡς καὶ τῆς
20 κατὰ νόμον μίξεως τὴν συμμετρίαν διδάσκει καὶ κελεύει
παιδογονίας χάριν, ἀλλ' οὐ φιληδονίας, γίνεσθαι τὴν
συνάφειαν. διὰ τοῦτο τοὺς μιγνυμένους ἀκαθάρτους καλεῖ καὶ
κελεύει καθαίρεσθαι ἵνα κωλύῃ τῆς συνουσίας τὸ συνεχὲς ἡ
περὶ τὴν κάθαρσιν ἀσχολία. ὁ δὲ θεῖος ἀπόστολος τοῖς
25 τελείοις γράφει, *τίμιος ὁ γάμος* . . . *καὶ ἡ κοίτη ἀμίαντος·*
πόρνους δὲ καὶ μοιχοὺς κρινεῖ ὁ Θεός.[g]

XXI

Διὰ τί τὴν τὸ περιττὸν τοῦ αἵματος κατὰ φύσιν
ἐκκρίνουσαν ἀκάθαρτον ὀνομάζει;[a]

Περὶ τοῦ γονορρυοῦς εἰρήκαμεν· ταὐτὰ καὶ περὶ ταύτης
φαμέν. πρὸς δὲ τούτοις, ἵνα μηδεὶς ταῖς τοιαύταις
5 συνάπτηται· φασὶ γάρ τινες ἐκ τῆς τοιαύτης συναφείας καὶ
λώβην καὶ λέπραν ἀπογεννᾶσθαι, τοῦ περιττώματος ἐκείνου τὰ

---

d. Lv 15.16   e. Lv 15.18   f. Gn 2.24   g. Heb 13.4

xxi A [32], B, C⁻⁵¹, 4 7 9 10 31 35 37 = 19 mss.

l. 3 Περὶ . . . ταὐτά *J.P.* : ῍Α περὶ . . . ταῦτα *Sir. Sch.* : Περὶ . . . ταῦτα
F.M. In support of my conjecture, *cf.,* e.g., Q. 101 on Gn (καὶ ὁ Δαβὶδ ταῦτά
φησι), and in support of the text offered by Sir. and Sch., *cf.,* e.g., Q. 78 on Gn
(ταῦτα παρασχεῖν οἷός τε ἦν, ἃ καὶ αὐτῷ ἔδωκε).

a. Lv 15.19–24

enware, if the person affected with this complaint were really unclean.[1]

Similarly, anyone who has an emission in his sleep is declared unclean,[d] as also those lawfully wedded,[e] although God himself gave the law about marriage, which was, in fact, the very first law: "For this reason a man shall leave his father and mother and cling to his wife, and the two shall become one flesh."[f] So how is it that a person having lawful intercourse is declared unclean? It is our conclusion that he was teaching continence in lawful intercourse and commanding that intercourse be directed to the production of children rather than pleasure. The Law declared the partners unclean and commanded them to be cleansed so that the trouble of cleansing would impede the frequency of intercourse.[2] In writing to spiritually mature people, the apostle says, "Marriage is to be held in honor, and the marriage bed kept undefiled; God will judge fornicators and adulterers."[g]

XXI

Why is the woman who naturally expels her excess blood pronounced unclean?[a]

What we said about gonorrhea applies here as well. Further, the purpose was to prevent anyone having intercourse with women in this condition. In fact, some commentators have claimed that a type of leprosy can develop from such intercourse, the flow of the exces-

---

1. As Theodoret attempts to find a spiritual meaning in these provisions, he interprets the law regarding gonorrhea (Lv 15) in a moral sense, though its main concerns were probably cultic and hygienic; v. R.J. Faley, on 15.1–33.

2. A pastor would need to eliminate confusion about the morality of sexual relations. Thus, Theodoret accounts for the apparent contradiction in Scripture by suggesting that the lawgiver has effected a pragmatic ruse directed to limiting sexual expression. The following quotation from St. Paul may be meant to counter a rigid encratism.

διαπλαττόμενα πημαίνοντος σώματα. τούτου χάριν ἀκάθαρτον
εἶναί φησι τὸν τῇ τοιαύτῃ συναπτόμενον. συντόμως δὲ τῶν
τοιούτων νόμων τὰς αἰτίας ἐδίδαξεν, εἰρηκώς, καὶ εὐλαβεῖς
10 ποιήσετε τοὺς υἱοὺς Ἰσραὴλ ἀπὸ τῶν ἀκαθαρσιῶν αὐτῶν, καὶ
οὐκ ἀποθανοῦνται διὰ τὴν ἀκαθαρσίαν αὐτῶν ἐν τῷ μιαίνειν
αὐτοὺς τὴν σκηνήν μου τὴν ἐν αὐτοῖς.[b] εἰ δὲ τὰ ἀκούσια
μιαίνειν ἔφη, δῆλον ὅτι πολλῷ μᾶλλον ἐναγῆ τὰ ἑκούσια. καὶ
ταῦτα δὲ μάλα ἥρμοττεν ἐκείνοις λαγνιστάτοις οὖσι καὶ
15 κακομάχλοις· τό τε γὰρ παραβαινόμενον οὐ μέγα καὶ
τηρούμενον ἐπιτηδειοτέρους εἰργάζετο πρὸς τὰ τέλεια.

XXII

Πότε ὁ ἀρχιερεὺς εἰς τὰ ἅγια τῶν ἁγίων εἰσήει;

(1) Ἐν τῇ τοῦ ἱλασμοῦ ἡμέρᾳ, ἣν ἐπιτελεῖσθαι προσέταξεν
ὁ Θεὸς τῇ δεκάτῃ τοῦ ἑβδόμου μηνός·[a] εἶπε, γάρ φησι, Κύριος
πρὸς Μωϋσῆν, λάλησον πρὸς Ἀαρὼν τὸν ἀδελφόν σου, καὶ μὴ
5 εἰσπορευέσθω πᾶσαν ὥραν εἰς τὸ ἅγιον ἐσώτερον τοῦ
καταπετάσματος εἰς πρόσωπον τοῦ ἱλαστηρίου, ὅ ἐστιν ἐπὶ
τῆς κιβωτοῦ τοῦ μαρτυρίου, καὶ οὐκ ἀποθανεῖται· ἐν γὰρ
νεφέλῃ ὀφθήσομαι ἐπὶ τοῦ ἱλαστηρίου.[b] ἐντεῦθεν δῆλον ὡς ἐν
τῷ ἱλαστηρίῳ τὴν οἰκείαν ἐπιφάνειαν ὁ δεσπότης ἐποιεῖτο

b. Lv 15.31

XXII A [32], B, C, 4 7 9 10 31 35 37 = 20 mss.
a. Lv 16.29   b. Lv 16.2

sive blood causing damage to bodies in the process of formation. This is the reason the Law pronounces unclean anyone who has intercourse with a woman in this condition. He briefly conveyed the reason for such laws when he said, "You will make the children of Israel beware their uncleanness, and they will not die because of their uncleanness by defiling my tabernacle that is among them."[1b] Now, if he said that involuntary actions cause defilement, we conclude that voluntary actions are much more sinful. These provisions were especially appropriate for the ancient Hebrews, among whom the men were lustful and the women wanton. As transgression was restricted to only slight matters and narrowly observed, they were the better prepared for perfection.

XXII

When did the high priest enter the Holy of Holies?[1]

(1) On the Day of Atonement, which God ordered to be celebrated on the tenth day of the seventh month.[a] As Scripture says, "The Lord said to Moses, 'Tell your brother Aaron not to come just at any time into the holy place beyond the veil before the mercy seat on the ark of witness, and he will not die; for I shall appear in the cloud upon the mercy seat.'"[b] We conclude from this passage that the Lord God made his appearance on the mercy seat, and that to manifest

---

1. Citing Lv 15.31, Theodoret finally acknowledges a cultic reason for rulings on matters such as the excessive flow of blood in vv. 19–30. As Guinot points out (p. 773), Theodoret likely derived his physiological lore from Diodore, who may in turn have drawn upon Eusebius of Emesa. According to Diodore (Deconinck, frag. 73), one current theory held that if, as a consequence of intercourse, any menstrual blood should be prevented from escaping the woman's body and redirected into the formation of a fetus, it would have deleterious effects in the long term. If the child survived infancy, it would be prone to develop leprosy, especially if exposed to severe heat and the air of certain climes.

---

1. This simple question provides an opportunity for Theodoret to explain the entire rite of the Day of Atonement. For his development of the christological sig-

10 Θεὸς καί, τὴν οἰκείαν ἐμφαίνων ἀγαθότητα, οὐκ ἐν γνόφῳ, καὶ
καπνῷ, καὶ πυρί, καθάπερ τῷ Ἰσραήλ,ᶜ ἀλλ' ἐν νεφέλῃ
φωτοειδεῖ ἑωρᾶτο.

Ἐδίδαξε δὲ καὶ τῶν θυσιῶν τὸν τρόπον, αἷς ἔδει τὸν
ἀρχιερέα χρησάμενον, τῶν ἀδύτων κατατολμῆσαι. ἐκέλευσε
15 γὰρ μόσχον μὲν ἱερεῦσαι περὶ ἁμαρτίας, κριὸν δὲ
ὁλοκαυτῶσαι,ᵈ καὶ ταῦτα μὲν ὑπὲρ ἑαυτοῦ προσενεγκεῖν, ὑπὲρ
δὲ παντὸς τοῦ λαοῦ, δύο τράγους περὶ ἁμαρτίας λαβεῖν καὶ
ἕνα κριὸν εἰς ὁλοκαύτωμα.ᵉ προσέταξε δὲ καὶ κλήρῳ διελεῖν
τοὺς τράγους, καὶ τὸν μὲν ἱερεῦσαι, τὸν δὲ εἰς τὴν ἔρημον
20 ἀποστεῖλαι.ᶠ

(2) Τοῦτο δέ τινες ἀνοήτως νενοηκότες, δαίμονά τινα τὸν
ἀποπομπαῖον ἐνόμισαν, ἐπειδὴ ἔφη, ἕνα τῷ Κυρίῳ καὶ ... ἕνα
τῷ ἀποπομπαίῳ.ᵍ τοῦτο δέ γε ἐκ πολλῆς ὑπέλαβον εὐηθείας·
πῶς γὰρ οἷόν τε ἦν τὸν εἰρηκότα, οὐκ ἔσονταί σοι θεοὶ ἕτεροι
25 πλὴν ἐμοῦ,ʰ καὶ οὐ προσκυνήσεις ... οὐδὲ ... λατρεύσεις Θεῷ
ἑτέρῳ,ⁱ δαίμονί τινι τὴν ἴσην ἀπονεῖμαι θυσίαν; ἔδει δὲ
αὐτοὺς ἐπιστῆσαι τὸν νοῦν ὅτι καὶ τὸν ἀπολυόμενον τράγον
ἑαυτῷ προσενεχθῆναι προσέταξε· λήψῃ, γάρ φησι, τὸν τράγον
τὸν ζῶντα ἔναντι Κυρίου τοῦ ἐξιλάσασθαι ἐπ' αὐτοῦ, τοῦ
30 ἐξαποστεῖλαι αὐτὸν εἰς τὴν ἀποπομπὴν ... εἰς τὴν ἔρημον.ʲ
τοῦτο δὲ δηλοῖ ὡς αὐτὸς ὁ τράγος ἀποπομπαῖος ἐκλήθη, ὡς
ἀποπεμπόμενος εἰς τὴν ἔρημον· τοῦτο γὰρ καὶ τὰ ἑξῆς δηλοῖ·
καὶ λήψεται ὁ τράγος ἐφ' ἑαυτῷ τὰς ἀνομίας αὐτῶν εἰς τὴν
ἄβατον.ᵏ καὶ ὁ Σύμμαχος δὲ τὸν ἀποπομπαῖον οὕτως
35 ἡρμήνευσεν· εἰς τράγον ἀπερχόμενον ὥστε ἀποστεῖλαι αὐτὸν
εἰς τὴν ἀποπομπήν· ὁ δὲ Ἀκύλας, εἰς τράγον ἀπολυόμενον εἰς
τὴν ἔρημον. οὐ τοίνυν θεῷ τινι ἢ δαίμονι ἀπεστέλλετο, ἀλλ'
ἀμφότεροι μὲν τῷ Θεῷ προσεφέροντο· τοῦ δὲ ἑνὸς θυομένου, ὁ
ἕτερος, τὰς ἁμαρτίας τοῦ λαοῦ λαμβάνων, εἰς τὴν ἔρημον
40 ἀπεπέμπετο. ὥσπερ γὰρ ἐπὶ τοῦ καθαιρομένου λεπροῦ, τοῦ

---

c. Ex 19.16–18   d. Lv 16.3   e. Lv 16.5   f. Lv 16.8–10   g. Lv 16.8
h. Ex 20.3   i. Ex 20.5   j. Lv 16.10   k. Lv 16.22

his goodness, he appeared not in darkness, smoke, and fire, as to Israel,[c] but in a luminous cloud.

He also gave instructions on the manner in which the high priest was to perform sacrifices when he dared to enter these precincts. He commanded him to sacrifice a calf as a sin offering and a ram as a holocaust[d]—these being offerings for himself—and to take two goats as a sin offering and one ram as a holocaust on behalf of the whole people.[e] He also ordered him to cast lots to separate the two goats and then sacrifice one and drive the other into the desert.[f]

(2) Now, some commentators have foolishly misunderstood this and imagined that the "dispatch" was a demon of some kind, since the text reads, "One for the Lord and one for the dispatch."[g] What a silly notion! How could the one who said, "You shall have no other gods but me,"[h] and "You shall not adore or worship any other god,"[i] assign an equal sacrifice to a demon? They ought to have paid attention to his command that the released goat was also to be offered to himself: "You shall bring the live goat before the Lord to make atonement over it so that it may be sent off as a dispatch into the desert."[j] This indicates that it is the goat itself that is called "dispatch," since it was dispatched into the desert. The sequel confirms this: "The goat will bear your sins on itself into the wilderness."[k] Symmachus rendered "dispatch" as "on a departing goat so as to send it away for the dispatch," and Aquila "on a goat released into the desert." So it was not sent off to some god or demon. Rather both were offered to God; one was sacrificed while the other took on the sins of the people and was dispatched into the desert. As, in the

---

nificance of the mercy seat *v.* his commentary on Romans (3.25) and R.C. Hill, "Theodoret Wrestling with Romans," p. 349.

ἑνὸς ὀρνέου θυομένου, τὸ ἕτερον εἰς τὸ τούτου αἷμα
βαπτόμενον ἀπελύετο,[l] οὕτως ὑπὲρ τῶν τοῦ λαοῦ ἁμαρτημάτων
δύο τράγων προσφερομένων, ὁ μὲν ἐθύετο, ὁ δὲ ἀπεπέμπετο.
Τύποι πάλιν ταῦτα τοῦ δεσπότου Χριστοῦ, τῶν δύο τούτων

45 ζῴων, οὐκ εἰς δύο πρόσωπα, ἀλλ' εἰς δύο φύσεις
λαμβανομένων. ἐπειδὴ γὰρ οὐχ οἷόν τε ἦν ἐν ἑνὶ τράγῳ
σκιογραφηθῆναι καὶ τὸ θνητὸν καὶ τὸ ἀθάνατον τοῦ δεσπότου
Χριστοῦ· θνητὸς γὰρ μόνον ὁ τράγος· ἀναγκαίως δύο
προσαχθῆναι προσέταξεν ἵνα ὁ μὲν θυόμενος τῆς σαρκὸς τὸ

50 παθητὸν προτυπώσῃ, ὁ δὲ ἀπολυόμενος δηλώσῃ τὸ ἀπαθὲς τῆς
θεότητος. οὕτως καὶ ὁ μακάριος Δαβὶδ τοῦ δεσπότου Χριστοῦ
τὸ πάθος, καὶ τὴν ἀνάστασιν, καὶ τὴν εἰς οὐρανοὺς ἀνάβασιν
προθεσπίζων, ἔφη, *ὁ Θεός, ἐν τῷ ἐκπορεύεσθαί σε ἐνώπιον τοῦ
λαοῦ σου, ἐν τῷ διαβαίνειν σε ἐν τῇ ἐρήμῳ, . . . γῆ ἐσείσθη·*

55 *καὶ γὰρ οἱ οὐρανοὶ ἔσταξαν.*[m] ἐδιδάχθημεν δὲ ὡς, τοῦ
δεσπότου σταυρουμένου Χριστοῦ, καὶ γῆ ἐσείσθη, καὶ αἱ
πέτραι ἐρράγησαν,[n] ὁ δὲ οὐρανὸς διὰ τοῦ σκοτισθέντος ἡλίου[o]
ἐμήνυσε τὴν τῆς ἀσεβείας ὑπερβολήν. ἡ δέ γε ἔρημος τοῦ
θανάτου τύπος· τούτου χάριν ἔφη, *ἐν τῷ διαβαίνειν σε ἐν τῇ*

60 *ἐρήμῳ.*

(3) Ἀλλὰ μηδεὶς ἀνάρμοστον ὑπολάβοι τὸ τράγους
προτυποῦν τοῦ σωτῆρος τὸ πάθος, ἐπειδήπερ *ἀμνὸν* αὐτὸν ὁ
μέγας προσηγόρευσεν Ἰωάννης.[p] σκοπησάτω δὲ ὡς, οὐ μόνον
ὑπὲρ δικαίων, ἀλλὰ καὶ ὑπὲρ ἁμαρτωλῶν ἑαυτὸν προσενήνοχεν.

65 ἐρίφοις δὲ τὴν τῶν ἁμαρτωλῶν συμμορίαν αὐτὸς ἀπείκασεν ὁ
δεσπότης· *στήσει,* γὰρ ἔφη, *τοὺς μὲν ἀμνοὺς ἐκ δεξιῶν, τοὺς
δὲ ἐρίφους ἐξ εὐωνύμων.*[q] καὶ ἐν τῷ νόμῳ δὲ περὶ ἁμαρτίας
ἔριφος προσεφέρετο.[r] αὐτὸς δέ γε ὁ Κύριος τὸν χαλκοῦν ὄφιν[s]
τύπον ἑαυτοῦ κέκληκεν· *καθώς,* γάρ φησι, *Μωϋσῆς ὕψωσε τὸν*

70 *ὄφιν ἐν τῇ ἐρήμῳ, οὕτως ὑψωθῆναι δεῖ τὸν υἱὸν τοῦ ἀνθρώπου*

l. Lv 14.4–7   m. Ps 68.7f.   n. Mt 27.51   o. Mt 27.45   p. Jn 1.29
q. Mt 25.33   r. Lv 4.22f., 27f.   s. Nm 21.8f.

cleansing of a leper, one little bird was killed, and the other was dipped in its blood and let go,[1] so for the people's sins, there was an offering of two goats: one sacrificed, the other dispatched.[2]

These two animals are also types of Christ the Lord, if they are taken, not as referring to two persons, but to two natures. Since it was impossible for Christ the Lord's mortality and immortality to be foreshadowed in one goat (the goat being only mortal), he necessarily ordered that both be offered so that the one sacrificed would prefigure the passibility of the flesh, and the one set free would manifest the impassibility of the divinity. Likewise, the blessed David, predicting the passion, resurrection, and ascension into heaven of the Lord Christ, declared, "When you went forth in the midst of your people, O God, when you passed through the desert, the earth shook, and the heavens dripped water."[m] Now, we have been informed that at the crucifixion of Christ the earth shook, rocks split open,[n] and, in the darkening of the sun,[o] the sky proclaimed the enormity of the outrage. The desert, in any case, is a type of death—hence his saying, "when you passed through the desert."

(3) No one should imagine that it is inappropriate for goats to prefigure the passion of Christ, since the mighty John called him a "lamb."[p] Rather you should consider that he offered himself not only for the righteous but also for sinners. The Lord himself likened the company of sinners to goats when he said, "He will set the lambs on his right, and the goats on his left."[q] And in the Law a goat was offered for sin.[r] Furthermore, the Lord himself called the bronze serpent[s] a type of himself: "Just as Moses lifted up the serpent in the desert, so must the Son of Man be lifted up so that everyone who

2. In Lv. 16.8, 10, our term "scapegoat" (for "escape goat") renders the Vulgate's *caper emissarius,* itself a translation of the term ἀποπομπαῖος used by the LXX. The Hebrew (as also the *NRSV*) has "Azazel." R. de Vaux believes (pp. 508f.) that "Azazel" is to be understood as a proper noun, the name of a demon parallel to Yahweh. Cyril of Alexandria informs us that Julian the Apostate (Cyr., *Iuln.* 9, PG, vol. 76, coll. 957D–960B) and others, perhaps Manicheans (*Glaph. Lv.,* περὶ τοῦ μὴ εἰσέρχεσθαι τὸν Ἀαρὼν διὰ παντὸς εἰς τὰ Ἅγια τῶν ἁγίων, secc. 2f.,

ἵνα πᾶς ὁ πιστεύων εἰς αὐτὸν μὴ ἀπόληται ἀλλ' ἔχῃ ζωὴν
αἰώνιον.ᵗ εἰ τοίνυν ἀνάρμοστος τῶν τράγων ὁ τύπος, πολλῷ
μᾶλλον ὁ τοῦ ὄφεως. ταῦτα μὲν οὖν προεδίδασκε τῆς
οἰκουμένης τὴν σωτηρίαν, ἰουδαίοις δέ, οἷα δὴ νηπίους,
75 ἐψυχαγώγει τὸ τὸν τράγον εἰς τὴν ἔρημον ἀπαγαγεῖν τὴν
ἁμαρτίαν. ἀνεμίμνησκε γὰρ αὐτοὺς τῆς πολλάκις τολμηθείσης
ἐν τῇ ἐρήμῳ παρανομίας καὶ τῆς ἀρρήτου τοῦ δεσπότου
φιλανθρωπίας, δι' ἥν, τὰς ἐνδίκους τιμωρίας διαφυγόντες, εἰς
τὴν ἐπηγγελμένην εἰσεληλύθασι γῆν.

80   Οὕτω ταῦτα γενέσθαι κελεύσας, διδάσκει καὶ ὅπως
εἰσελθεῖν εἰς τὰ ἅγια τῶν ἁγίων τὸν ἀρχιερέα προσήκει·
προσάξει, γάρ φησιν, *Ἀαρὼν τὸν μόσχον, τὸν περὶ ἁμαρτίας
τὸν ἑαυτοῦ, καὶ ἐξιλάσεται περὶ ἑαυτοῦ καὶ τοῦ οἴκου αὐτοῦ,
καὶ σφάξει τὸν μόσχον, τὸν περι . . . ἁμαρτίας τὸν ἑαυτοῦ. καὶ*
85 *λήψεται πλῆρες τὸ πυρεῖον ἀνθράκων πυρὸς ἀπὸ τοῦ
θυσιαστηρίου, τοῦ ἀπέναντι Κυρίου, καὶ πλήσει τὰς χεῖρας
αὐτοῦ θυμιάματος συνθέσεως λεπτῆς, καὶ εἰσοίσει ἐσώτερον
τοῦ καταπετάσματος, καὶ ἐπιθήσει τὸ θυμίαμα ἐπὶ τὸ πῦρ
ἔναντι Κυρίου, καὶ καλύψει ἡ ἀτμὶς τοῦ θυμιάματος τὸ*
90 *ἱλαστήριον, τὸ ἐπὶ τῶν μαρτυρίων, καὶ οὐκ ἀποθανεῖται.*ᵘ
δῆλον καὶ ἐντεῦθεν ὡς ἐκτὸς τοῦ καταπετάσματος τὸ
θυσιαστήριον τοῦ θυμιάματος ἔκειτο· οὐ γὰρ ἄν, εἴπερ ἔνδον
ἦν, εἰς τὸ πυρεῖον τοὺς ἄνθρακας λαβεῖν ἐκελεύσθη καὶ τοῦτο
εἴσω τοῦ καταπετάσματος ἐμβαλεῖν τὸ θυμίαμα. ἐδίδαξε δὲ
95 τοῦτο ἡμᾶς καὶ ὁ μακάριος Λουκᾶς, τὰ κατὰ τὸν Ζαχαρίαν
διηγούμενος, τὸν Ἰωάννου τοῦ βαπτιστοῦ πατέρα· κατὰ
τοῦτον γὰρ κἀκεῖνος τὸν καιρὸν εἰς τὰ ἅγια τῶν ἁγίων
εἰσελήλυθε καὶ τῆς ἀγγελικῆς ὀπτασίας ἀπήλαυσε.ᵛ

---

l. 98 ἀπήλαυσε *C, 37, Sir. Sch.* : ἀπολελαύκει *F.M.* : ἀπελελαύκει *a⁻⁶*. The
pluperfect would indicate that Zechariah had received the angelic vision, before,
not after, he entered the holy of holies.

t. Jn 3.14f.   u. Lv 16.11–13   v. Lk. 1.8–11

believes in him may not perish but have eternal life."[3t] So if the type from the goats is inappropriate, that from the snake is even worse. While these things forecast the salvation of the world, the goat taking their sin away into the desert was a means of instructing the simple-minded Jews, as it reminded them of the frequency with which they had dared to commit transgressions while in the desert and of God's ineffable loving-kindness, which permitted them to escape the retribution they deserved and to enter the promised land.

After giving these instructions, he also informed them of the way the high priest was to enter the Holy of Holies. "Aaron shall present his calf as a sin offering for himself and make atonement for himself and his household; he shall slaughter his calf as a sin offering for himself. Then he shall take a censer full of glowing coals from the altar before the Lord, fill his hands with fine compound incense, bring it inside the curtain, and place the incense on the fire before the Lord, and the smoke of the incense will cover the mercy seat on the testimonies, and he will not die."[u] We can also infer from this passage that the altar of incense was located outside the curtain. If it had been inside, he would not have been ordered to take the coals in a censor and toss the incense once inside the curtain. St. Luke also informed us of this in the story of Zechariah, the father of John the Baptist. At that time he, too, entered the Holy of Holies and was granted the angelic vision.[4v]

PG, vol. 69, coll. 585C–590 and *Ep.* 41, PG, vol. 77, coll. 204C–208A), had argued that one goat was to be set aside for the Lord and the other for a demon opposed to him. Theodoret, like Cyril, rejects this dualistic interpretation and interprets both goats as types of Christ.

3. Theodoret marshals disparate scriptural passages to support the notion of Jesus as scapegoat.

4. Not being a high priest, Zechariah (Lk 1.9–11) would not have entered the Holy of Holies, only the outer area where, as Theodoret has just demonstrated, the altar of incense was located. Yet Theodoret again refers to him as a high priest in *Q.* 2.4 on Jos.

(4) Ἐκελεύσθη δὲ καὶ διαρράναι τῷ δακτύλῳ ἑπτάκις πρὸ
100 τοῦ ἱλαστηρίου τοῦ αἵματος τοῦ τε μόσχου καὶ τοῦ τράγου.ʷ
ἐπειδὴ γὰρ ἐν ἑπτὰ ἡμέραις ὁ βίος ἀνακυκλεῖται, καθ'
ἑκάστην δέ, ὡς ἔπος εἰπεῖν, ἡμέραν, ἢ σμικρὰ ἢ μεγάλα
πλημμελοῦμεν, ἰσάριθμος προσεφέρετο ταῖς ἡμέραις ὁ τοῦ
αἵματος ῥαντισμὸς ὑπὲρ τῶν ἐν ταύταις γινομένων
105 πλημμελημάτων. λέγει δὲ τοῦτο, μὴ μόνον αὐτούς, ἀλλὰ καὶ
τὴν σκηνὴν καθαίρειν· ἐξιλάσεται, γάρ φησι, περὶ τῶν ἁγίων
ἀπὸ τῶν ἀκαθαρσιῶν τῶν υἱῶν Ἰσραὴλ καὶ ἀπὸ τῶν
ἀδικημάτων αὐτῶν περὶ πασῶν τῶν ἁμαρτιῶν αὐτῶν· καὶ οὕτω
ποιήσεις τῇ σκηνῇ τοῦ μαρτυρίου, τῇ ἐκτισμένῃ ἐν αὐτοῖς ἐν
110 μέσῳ τῆς ἀκαθαρσίας αὐτῶν.ˣ ἐκέλευσε δὲ μηδένα παρεῖναι,
ταύτης ὑπὸ τοῦ ἀρχιερέως γινομένης τῆς λειτουργίας.ʸ

Λέγει δὲ καὶ τὸν καιρὸν καθ' ὃν προσήκει ταῦτα γενέσθαι·
δεκάτῃ, γάρ φησι, τοῦ μηνὸς κακώσετε τὰς ψυχὰς ὑμῶν· καὶ
πᾶν ἔργον οὐ ποιήσετε ὁ αὐτόχθων καὶ ὁ προσήλυτος, ὁ
115 προσκείμενος ... ὑμῖν. ἐν γὰρ τῇ ἡμέρᾳ ταύτῃ ἐξιλάσεται
περὶ ὑμῶν καθαρίσαι ὑμᾶς ἀπὸ πασῶν τῶν ἁμαρτιῶν ὑμῶν
ἔναντι Κυρίου, καὶ καθαρισθήσεσθε. σάββατα σαββάτων
ἀνάπαυσις ... ἔσται ὑμῖν, καὶ κακώσετε τὰς ψυχὰς ὑμῶν·
νόμιμον αἰώνιον.ᶻ σάββατα δὲ σαββάτων ὡς ἅγια ἁγίων
120 ἐκάλεσε· πολλῷ γὰρ τῶν σαββάτων αὕτη σεβασμιωτέρα ἡ
ἑορτή. κάκωσιν δὲ τὴν νηστείαν ὠνόμασεν. εἶτα ἐπάγει, ἅπαξ
τοῦ ἐνιαυτοῦ ποιηθήσεται, καθάπερ συνέταξε Κύριος τῷ
Μωϋσῇ.ᵃᵃ καὶ τοῦτο δὲ προτυποῖ τὴν κατὰ σάρκα τοῦ σωτῆρος
ἡμῶν οἰκονομίαν. ὥσπερ γὰρ ἅπαξ τοῦ ἐνιαυτοῦ ὁ ἀρχιερεύς,
125 εἰς τὰ ἅγια τῶν ἁγίων εἰσιών, ταύτην ἐπετέλει τὴν
λειτουργίαν, οὕτως ὁ δεσπότης Χριστός, ἅπαξ τὸ σωτήριον
ὑπομείνας πάθος, εἰς τὸν οὐρανὸν ἀνελήλυθεν, αἰωνίαν
λύτρωσιν εὑράμενος, ἥ φησιν ὁ θεῖος ἀπόστολος.ᵇᵇ

l. 109 *ποιήσεις* F.M. : *ποιήσει* 6, 5, C, 4 35 37, Sir. Sch. = "'and thus he
shall do.'" Cf. Wevers and Quast, Lv 16.16.

w. Lv 16.14   x. Lv 16.16   y. Lv 16.17   z. Lv 16.29–31   aa. Lv 16.34
bb. Heb 9.12

(4) The high priest was also commanded to sprinkle with his finger some of the blood of the calf and the goat seven times before the mercy seat.[w] Since life runs in cycles of seven days, and every day, more or less, we sin in great or small matters, the blood was sprinkled as many times as there are days for the sins committed on those days. He said that they were to cleanse not only the people but also the tabernacle: "He will make atonement for the sanctuary because of the uncleanness of the children of Israel and because of their transgressions in all their sins; and thus shall you do for the tabernacle of the testimony that has been built among them in the midst of their uncleanness."[x] He forbade anyone to be present when this rite was being performed by the high priest.[y]

He also stated the time when this was to be done: "On the tenth day of the month, you shall afflict yourselves and do no work, both the native and the alien who resides among you. For on this day, he shall make atonement for you to cleanse you from all your sins before the Lord, and you will be cleansed. This rest will be a Sabbath of Sabbaths for you, and you shall afflict yourselves: an everlasting law."[z] Now, he used the term "Sabbath of Sabbaths" like "Holy of Holies," since this feast is much more solemn than any Sabbath; and by "affliction" he meant fasting. Then Scripture continues, "This is to be done once a year as the Lord bade Moses."[aa] This also prefigures the Incarnation of our Savior; as the high priest entered the Holy of Holies and performed this rite once a year, so Christ the Lord endured the saving passion and ascended to heaven once, "thus effecting eternal redemption," as the holy apostle says.[bb]

XXIII

Διὰ τί ἀπαγορεύει πόρρω τῆς σκηνῆς θύεσθαι τὰ ἐσθιόμενα θρέμματα;[a]

Ἤδει τὴν ἐνίων ἀσέβειαν καὶ ὅτι τοῖς δαίμοσι θυσίας προσοίσουσι. προσέταξε τοίνυν πάντα θῦσαι βουλόμενον ἢ
5 μόσχον, ἢ πρόβατον, ἢ αἶγα παρὰ τὴν θύραν τῆς σκηνῆς ἀγαγεῖν, καὶ τὸ αἷμα ἐκχέαι, καὶ μεταλαβεῖν οἴκαδε τῶν κρεῶν. τὸν δὲ τοῦτο μὴ δρῶντα ὡς φόνου ἔνοχον κατηγορεῖσθαι ἐκέλευσεν· αἷμα, γάρ φησι, λογισθήσεται τῷ ἀνθρώπῳ ἐκείνῳ· αἷμα ἐξέχεεν, ἐξολοθρευθήσεται ἡ ψυχὴ
10 ἐκείνη ἐκ τοῦ λαοῦ αὐτῆς.[b] καὶ ὅτι τοῦτον ἔχει τὸν σκοπὸν ὃν ἔφην ὁ νόμος διδάξει τὰ ἑξῆς· ἀνοίσει, γάρ φησιν, ὁ ἱερεὺς τὸ στέαρ εἰς ὀσμὴν εὐωδίας τῷ Κυρίῳ. καὶ οὐ θύσουσιν ἔτι τὰς θυσίας αὐτῶν τοῖς ματαίοις, ὧν αὐτοὶ ἐκπορνεύουσιν ὀπίσω αὐτῶν. νόμιμον αἰώνιον ἔσται ὑμῖν εἰς τὰς γενεὰς
15 ὑμῶν.[c] οὗτος ὁ νόμος μέχρι τοῦ παρόντος παρὰ ἰουδαίοις κρατεῖ· ὁ γὰρ ἱερεὺς θύει τὰ ἐσθιόμενα ζῷα.

Ἀπηγόρευσε δὲ καὶ τὸ ἐσθίειν αἷμα καὶ τὴν αἰτίαν ἐδίδαξεν· ἡ γὰρ ψυχή, φησί, πάσης σαρκὸς αἷμα αὐτοῦ ἐστιν, καὶ ἐγὼ δέδωκα ὑμῖν αὐτὸ ἐπὶ τοῦ θυσιαστηρίου ἐξιλάσκεσθαι
20 περὶ τῶν ψυχῶν ὑμῶν· τὸ γὰρ αἷμα αὐτοῦ ἀντὶ τῆς ψυχῆς αὐτοῦ ἐξιλάσεται. διὰ τοῦτο εἴρηκα τοῖς υἱοῖς Ἰσραήλ, πᾶσα ψυχὴ ἐξ ὑμῶν οὐ φάγεται αἷμα, καὶ ὁ προσήλυτος, ὁ προσκείμενος ὑμῖν οὐ φάγεται.[d] ὥσπερ, φησί, σὺ ψυχὴν ἀθάνατον ἔχεις, οὕτω τὸ ἄλογον ζῷον ἀντὶ ψυχῆς ἔχει τὸ
25 αἷμα. οὗ δὴ χάριν κελεύει τὴν τοῦ ἀλόγου ψυχήν, τουτέστι τὸ αἷμα, ἀντὶ τῆς σῆς προσενεχθῆναι ψυχῆς, τῆς ἀθανάτου καὶ λογικῆς. ἐὰν δὲ τοῦτο φάγῃς, ψυχὴν ἐσθίεις· λογικῆς γὰρ ψυχῆς τοῦτο τάξιν πληροῖ· διὸ καὶ φόνον τὴν βρῶσιν ὠνόμασε.

xxiii A [32], B, C, 4 7 9 10 31 35 37 = 20 mss.

a. Lv 17.3f.   b. Lv 17.4   c. Lv 17.6f.   d. Lv 17.11f.

XXIII

Why did he forbid that animals raised for their flesh be slaughtered away from the tabernacle?[a]

He was aware that some people were idolaters and knew they would offer sacrifices to demons. So he ordered anyone who wished to slay a calf, sheep, or goat to bring it to the door of the tabernacle, pour out the blood, and consume the meat at home. Whoever did not do this was to be regarded as guilty of murder: "That person will be considered guilty of bloodshed; he has shed blood, and his soul will be cut off from his people."[b] The following passage confirms that the law had the purpose I have alleged: "The priest will offer the fat as a sweet-smelling sacrifice to the Lord. They will no longer offer their sacrifices to the empty things to which they prostitute themselves. It will be an everlasting law for you for your generations."[c] This law is in force among Jews to the present day; the priest slaughters the animals that are to be eaten.[1]

He also forbade the consumption of blood and gave the reason: "For the life of all flesh is its blood, and I have given it to you to make atonement for your lives on the altar; its blood will make atonement for its life. Hence, I have said to the children of Israel, 'No person among you nor any alien resident among you shall consume the blood.'"[d] In other words, "as you have an immortal soul, so the brute beast has blood for a soul; thus, he commands that the brute beast's soul—that is, its blood—be offered for your immortal and rational soul. If you eat the blood, you eat its soul, since the blood takes the place of a rational soul." Thus, he went so far as to call its consumption "murder." Therefore, he also forbade the eating

---

1. Here, as in Q. 61 on Gn and Q. 15 on Ex, Theodoret shows his familiarity with contemporary Jewish life and worship.

τούτου ἕνεκα καὶ τὰ τεθνηκότα τῶν ζῴων ἐσθίειν ἀπαγορεύει,
30 ὡς τοῦ αἵματος μὴ χωρισθέντος τοῦ σώματος.

XXIV

Τινὲς μέμφονται ταῖς περὶ τῶν γάμων νομοθεσίαις,
λέγοντες ἀπαγορεῦσαι τὸν Θεὸν τὰ μηδαμῆ μηδαμῶς
γεγενημένα. τίς, γάρ φασιν, ἠνέσχετο τῇ ἑαυτοῦ μιγῆναι
μητρί;[a] ἢ τίς πώποτε συνεγένετο κτήνει;[b]
5 Οὐκ ἂν ὁ Θεὸς τὸ παρ' οὐδενὸς τολμηθὲν ἀπηγόρευσε. καὶ
ὅτι ταῦθ' οὕτως ἔχει μαρτυρεῖ τὸ τοῦδε τοῦ νόμου προοίμιον·
ἔφη γὰρ οὕτως· *κατὰ τὰ ἐπιτηδεύματα τῆς Αἰγύπτου, ἐν ᾗ
παρῳκήσατε ἐν αὐτῇ, οὐ ποιήσετε, καὶ κατὰ τὰ ἐπιτηδεύματα
τῆς γῆς Χαναάν, εἰς ἣν ἐγὼ εἰσάγω ὑμᾶς ἐκεῖ, οὐ ποιήσετε,
10 καὶ τοῖς νομίμοις αὐτῶν οὐ πορεύσεσθε.*[c] οὕτω ταῦτα εἰπών,
διδάσκει τὰ ὑπ' ἐκείνων τολμηθέντα καὶ τὴν τοιαύτην
ἀπαγορεύει πρᾶξιν. ὅτι δὲ πολλὰ τοιαῦτα τολμᾶται
μαρτυροῦσι καὶ πέρσαι μέχρι τοῦ παρόντος, οὐ μόνον
ἀδελφαῖς, ἀλλὰ καὶ μητράσι καὶ θυγατράσι νόμῳ γάμου
15 μιγνύμενοι. καὶ τὰς ἄλλας δὲ παρανομίας τολμῶσι πολλοί.

xxiv A *[32]*, B, C⁻⁵¹, *4 7 9 10 31 35 37* = 19 mss.

l. 3 φασιν *J.P.* : φησίν *Sir. Sch. F.M.* = "'Who,' he asks . . . ?" *Cf.* Τινὲς in the previous sentence. The change of the originally plural, to the singular, form is likely due to the mistaken notion that τίς was the subject of the parenthetical verb indicating quotation.

a. Lv 18.7   b. Lv 18.23   c. Lv 18.3

of animals that had died a natural death, since the blood had not been drained from the body.

XXIV

There are those who have found fault with the legislation regarding marriage, since, as they claim, God forbids acts that have never been done. "Who," they ask, "could engage in intercourse with his own mother?[a] Or who ever lay with a beast?"[b]

God would not have forbidden an act that no one had dared to commit, and the introduction of the law confirms this. It states the following: "You shall not act according to the practices of Egypt, where you dwelt, or according to the practices of the land of Canaan, to which I am bringing you, and you shall not walk according to their laws."[c] After this introduction, he set out the crimes committed by these people and forbade such behavior. The Persians provide confirmation that many such crimes are committed even to this day, for by their law of marriage they have relations not only with their sisters but even with their mothers and daughters.[1] There are many people who commit the other transgressions.

---

1. *V.* also Thdt., *ep.* 8, where the bishop of Cyrus again cites the example of the incestuous practices of the Persians, and *cf.* Guinot, who points out (p. 774) that the immorality of the Persians was a commonplace among the Greeks. Herodotus had described their polygamy (1.135) and presented a story regarding the origins of their incestuous marriages (3.31). For more references in Greek and Roman authors, *v.* H. Chadwick, "The Relativity of Moral Codes," pp. 146–53. Theodoret does not suggest that Jews were also guilty of such practices and, with his usual delicacy, abstains from comment on the forms of deviant behavior listed in this chapter; *cf.* note 1 to *Q.* 27 on Jgs.

XXV

Τί ἐστιν ἀπὸ τοῦ σπέρματός σου οὐ δώσεις λατρεύειν
ἄρχοντι καὶ οὐ βεβηλώσεις τὸ ὄνομά μου τὸ ἅγιον· ἐγὼ
Κύριος;[a]

Τὸ ἑβραϊκὸν τὸ Μόλοχ ἔχει, καὶ οἱ λοιποὶ δὲ ἑρμηνευταὶ
5 τοῦτο τεθείκασιν. εἴδωλον δὲ τοῦτο ἦν. διὸ καὶ διὰ τοῦ
προφήτου φησὶν ὁ Θεός, μὴ σφάγια καὶ θυσίας προσηνέγκατέ
μοι ἐν τῇ ἐρήμῳ ἔτη τεσσαράκοντα, υἱοὶ Ἰσραήλ; καὶ
ἀνελάβετε τὴν σκηνὴν τοῦ Μόλοχ καὶ τὸ ἄστρον τοῦ θεοῦ
ὑμῶν Ῥεφάν, τοὺς τύπους οὓς ἐποιήσατε προσκυνεῖν αὐτοῖς.[b]
10 ἀπαγορεύει τοίνυν τὸ τοὺς παῖδας ἱεροδούλους τοῖς εἰδώλοις
προσφέρειν· ὡς δέ τινές φασι, τὸ τοῖς ἀλλοφύλοις ἄρχουσι μὴ
διδόναι τοὺς παῖδας ὥστε εἶναι αὐτῶν οἰκέτας ἢ δορυφόρους
ἵνα μὴ τῆς ἐκείνων μεταλάχωσιν ἀσεβείας.

XXVI

Τί ἐστιν ἵνα μὴ προσοχθίσῃ ὑμῖν ἡ γῆ ἐν τῷ μιαίνειν ὑμᾶς
αὐτήν, ὃν τρόπον προσώχθισε τοῖς ἔθνεσι τοῖς πρὸ ὑμῶν;[a]

Μὴ βδελύξηται ὑμᾶς, φησίν, ὡς ἐβδελύξατο τοὺς
χαναναίους ἀντὶ τοῦ· ὥσπερ ἐκείνους διὰ τὰς πολλὰς αὐτῶν
5 παρανομίας πανωλεθρίᾳ παραδούς, ὑμῖν τὴν γῆν παραδέδωκα,
οὕτως ὑμᾶς τὰ ὅμοια δράσαντας τιμωρήσομαι.

---

xxv A *[32]*, B, C⁻⁵¹, 4 7 9 10 31 35 37 = 19 mss.
a. Lv 18.21 (LXX)   b. Am 5.25f. (LXX var.)

---

xxvi A *[32]*, B, C, 4 7 9 10 31 35 37 = 20 mss.
a. Lv 18.28

XXV

What is the meaning of "You shall not give any of your offspring in worship of a ruler and shall not profane my holy name: I am the Lord"?[a]

The Hebrew has "Moloch," which the other translators have also used. This was an idol. Hence, God also said through the prophet, "Surely you did not offer victims and sacrifices to me in the desert for forty years, sons of Israel? You took up the tent of Moloch and the star of your god Rephan, the images you made to worship."[1b] So he forbade the offering of their children as attendants on idols. On the other hand, some commentators have claimed that the purpose of this law was to prohibit the assignment of children as servants or bodyguards to foreign rulers, to prevent them from participating in their idolatry.

XXVI

What is the meaning of "So the land will not abhor you for defiling it as it abhorred the nations before you"?[a]

"So it will not abominate you as it abominated the Canaanites." In other words, "as I destroyed them for their repeated transgression and gave their land to you, so I shall punish you if you behave as they did."

---

1. Theodoret clarifies the meaning of Lv 18.21 by reference to Am 5.25f. He may also have checked Theodore of Mopsuestia's commentary on Amos, where (5.24–27), Theodore states "He mentions Moloch, an idol they worshipped." The LXX's ῾ρεφάν "Rephan" represents a Hebrew word that would be transliterated "Kaiwan," probably an intentionally distorted name of a deity derived from "an Akkadian name for the planet Saturn"; *v.* M.L. Barré, "Amos," on 5.26. The law of Lv 18.21 is now generally understood to refer to child sacrifice; *v.* R.J. Faley, on Lv. 18.1–30 and *cf.* the translation of the *NRSV*: "You shall not give any of your offspring to sacrifice them to Molech" *etc.*

The Questions on Leviticus

XXVII

Πῶς νοητέον τὰ κτήνη σου οὐ κατοχεύσεις ἑτέρῳ ζυγῷ καὶ τὸν ἀμπελῶνά σου οὐ κατασπερεῖς διάφορον καὶ ἱμάτιον ἐκ δύο ὑφασμένον κίβδηλον οὐκ ἐπιβαλεῖς σεαυτῷ;[a]

Πολλάκις ἔφην ὅτι διὰ τῶν αἰσθητῶν διδάσκει τὰ νοητά.
5 ἀπαγορεύει τοίνυν τῶν ἑτερογενῶν τὴν ὀχείαν, οἷον ἵππου καὶ ὄνου, ἵνα μὴ διαβῇ ἀπὸ τῶν ἀλόγων εἰς τοὺς λογικοὺς ἡ παράνομος μίξις. τούτου χάριν καὶ τὸ ἐξ ἐρίου καὶ λίνου ὑφασμένον ἱμάτιον κίβδηλον ὀνομάζει, διδάσκων πράξεις ἐναντίας μηδαμῶς ἐπιτηδεύειν. ὅτι γάρ, οὐ τὸ ἱμάτιον
10 κίβδηλον λέγει, ἀλλὰ τὴν πρᾶξιν διὰ τούτου δηλοῖ μαρτυρεῖ τῆς σκηνῆς τὰ καλύμματα ἐκ διαφόρων κατασκευασθέντα νημάτων.[b] οὕτω νοητέον καὶ τὰ περὶ τοῦ ἀμπελῶνος. καὶ ὁ ἀπόστολος δὲ τὴν πρὸς τοὺς ἀπίστους κοινωνίαν ἀπαγορεύει, λέγων, μὴ γίνεσθε ἑτεροζυγοῦντες ἀπίστοις.[c]

XXVIII

Τί ἐστιν οὐ ποιήσετε σισόην ἐκ τῆς κόμης τῆς κεφαλῆς ὑμῶν, οὐδὲ φθερεῖτε τὴν ὄψιν τοῦ πώγωνος ὑμῶν, καὶ ἐντομίδας ἐπὶ ψυχῇ οὐ ποιήσετε τῷ σώματι ὑμῶν, καὶ γράμματα στικτὰ οὐ ποιήσετε ἐν ὑμῖν;[a]

5 Τινὲς τὸ σισόην τὰς ἐξ ἐπιτηδεύσεως οὔλας γινομένας τρίχας ἡρμήνευσαν, ἐγὼ δὲ ἄλλο οἶμαι τὸν νόμον ἀπαγορεύειν.

xxvii A [32], B, C, 4 7 9 10 31 35 37 = 20 mss.

l. 1 ἑτέρῳ ζυγῷ Sir. Sch. F.M. : ἑτεροζύγῳ Wevers and Quast, Lv 19.19; cf. ap. crit. ad loc.

a. Lv 19.19   b. Ex 26.1   c. 2Cor 6.14

xxviii A [32], B, C, 4 7 9 10 31 35 37 = 20 mss.

a. Lv 19.27f.

XXVII

How are we to understand, "You shall not let your cattle breed with a different kind or sow your vineyard with different seed" and "You shall not put on an adulterated garment woven of two fabrics"?[a]

As I have often said, the Law teaches spiritual, through material, realities. Thus, it forbids the coupling of different species, like horse and ass, so that the unlawful intercourse will not pass from brute to rational creatures. And it calls the garment woven of wool and linen "adulterated" to teach us not to engage in contrary practices. The fact that the veils of the tabernacle were made of different yarns proves that the Law did not really regard the garment as adulterated but used it as a metaphor for behavior.[b] The reference to the vineyard is to be understood similarly. Likewise, the apostle forbids association with non-believers when he says, "Do not be mismatched with non-believers."[1c]

XXVIII

What is the meaning of "You shall not put a curl in your hair or spoil the appearance of your beard. You shall not make any gashes on your body for a soul or tattoo yourself"?[a]

Some commentators have understood "curl" to mean hair foppishly styled. But I think the Law forbids something else. Among the

1. Theodoret here applies allegorical interpretation to laws that were probably cultic in origin. According to Faley (on 19.1–37) these regulations, possibly of pre-Israelite origin, prohibit mixings regarded as "a perversion of the divinely established order."

εἰώθασιν ἕλληνες μὴ ἀποκείρειν τῶν παίδων τὰς κορυφάς,
ἀλλὰ μαλλοὺς ἐᾶν, καὶ τούτους μετὰ χρόνον ἀνατιθέναι τοῖς
δαίμοσιν. εἰώθασι δὲ καὶ τὰ γένεια ξυρᾶσθαι ἡνίκα ἐπένθουν
10 καὶ τέμνεσθαι τὰς παρειὰς εἰς τὴν τῶν τετελευτηκότων
τιμήν. καί τινα δὲ τοῦ σώματος μόρια βελόναις ἐκέντουν καὶ
μέλαν ἐπέβαλλον εἰς θεραπείαν δαιμόνων. ταῦτα οὖν ὁ θεῖος
νόμος ἀπαγορεύει.

XXIX

Τί ἐστιν ἐγγαστρίμυθος;[a]

Τινές, ὑπὸ δαιμόνων τινῶν ἐνεργούμενοι, ἐξηπάτουν
πολλοὺς τῶν ἀνοήτων, ὡς δῆθεν προαγορεύοντες.[b] οὓς
ἐντερομάντεις οἱ ἕλληνες προσηγόρευον, ὡς ἔνδοθεν
5 δοκοῦντος τοῦ δαίμονος φθέγγεσθαι.

XXX

Τίνος χάριν τοῖς ἱερεῦσι διαφερόντως περὶ τῶν γάμων
νομοθετεῖ;[a]

Ὅτι δεῖ τύπον εἶναι σωφροσύνης τὸν ἱερέα καί, ἵνα τὸ
γένος ἀκραιφνὲς διαμείνῃ, μηδεμίαν ὕβρεως ἀφορμὴν τοῖς
5 λοιδορεῖσθαι βουλομένοις παρέχον. διὸ καὶ ὁ θεῖος ἀπόστολος
ἀγαθὴν ἔχειν μαρτυρίαν καὶ παρὰ τῶν ἔξωθεν τὸν τῷ Θεῷ
λειτουργοῦντα διαγορεύει· *ἵνα μὴ εἰς ὀνειδισμόν*, φησίν,
ἐμπέσῃ καὶ παγίδα τοῦ διαβόλου.[b] τούτου χάριν τὴν μὲν

xxix A [32], B, C, 4 7 9 10 31 35 37 = 20 mss.

a. Lv 19.31; 20.6   b. Cf. Acts 16.16.

xxx A [32], B, C, 4 7 9 10 31 35 37 = 20 mss.

a. Lv 21.13–15   b. 1Tm 3.7

Greeks it is customary not to trim children's hair but to let it grow long and, after a while, to dedicate it to demons. It was their practice to shave their beards when they mourned and cut their cheeks in honor of the deceased. In fact, to honor their demons, they would pierce their limbs with needles and tattoo themselves with black ink. These are the practices forbidden by the Law of God.[1]

XXIX

What is a "person possessed by a divining spirit"?[a]

These were people who were possessed by demons and who could deceive many a simpleton into believing they really foretold the future.[b] The Greeks called them "ventriloquists," since the demon seemed to speak from inside them.

XXX

Why did he lay down special marriage laws for the priests?[a]

Because the priest had to be a model of temperance and his clan beyond reproach, one providing no grounds for criticism to those inclined to abuse. Hence, the holy apostle also says that the minister of God should have a good reputation even among outsiders "to avoid becoming a victim of disgrace and a snare of the devil."[1b] For

---

1. Theodoret identifies Greek practices analogous to the Canaanite customs forbidden in Lv 19.27f. The cutting of the hair and the laceration and tattooing of the body were "probably viewed as a means of warding off the departed spirit by changing the appearance to avoid recognition"; *v.* Faley (on 19.1–37).

---

1. Theodoret finds the Pauline prescription foreshadowed in the priestly requirements of Lv 21.

ἰσραηλῖτιν πορνεύουσαν ἀναιρεῖσθαι κελεύει, τὴν δὲ τοῦ
10 ἱερέως θυγατέρα παραπλήσια τολμῶσαν ἐμπίπρασθαι.ᶜ

Διὰ δὲ τὸ ἰουδαίων μεμψίμοιρον οὐδὲ τοὺς ἔχοντάς τινα
μῶμον σωματικὸν λειτουργεῖν συγχωρεῖ, διὰ τῶν ἀκουσίων
παθημάτων ἀπαγορεύων τὰ γνωμικά. τυφλότης μὲν γὰρ
ὀφθαλμῶν τὴν τῆς γνώσεως αἰνίττεται στέρησιν, ἐκτομὴ δὲ
15 ὠτὸς τὴν παρακοήν, ῥινὸς δὲ ἀφαίρεσις τοῦ διακριτικοῦ τὴν
ἀφαίρεσιν, ἀποκοπὴ δὲ χειρὸς τὴν ἀργίαν τοῦ πρακτικοῦ·ᵈ
οὕτω καὶ τὰ ἄλλα νοητέον.

Τούτου χάριν ἀρτιμελῆ κελεύει καὶ τὰ ἱερεῖα προσφέρειν,
τοὺς προσφέροντας διὰ τῶν προσφερομένων παιδεύων ὑγιεῖς
20 ἔχειν τὰς τῆς ψυχῆς ἐνεργείας.ᵉ ἀπαγορεύει δὲ μετὰ τῶν
ἄλλων καὶ τὸν ἐκτομίαν καὶ τὸν θλαδίαν·ᶠ γόνιμον μὲν γὰρ
εἶναι δεῖ, τῶν ἀγαθῶν πλήρη, τὸν τῆς θείας θεραπείας
φροντίζοντα.

XXXI

Διὰ τί τὰ πρωτότοκα τῶν θρεμμάτων μετὰ τὴν ὀγδόην
ἡμέραν προσφέρεσθαι διηγόρευσεν;ᵃ

Ἤδει τὴν ἐνίων γαστριμαργίαν καὶ ὅτι, τυχὸν εὐτραφὲς
αὐτὸ καὶ εὐειδὲς θεασάμενοι, τοῦτο μὲν καθέξουσιν, ἕτερον δὲ
5 προσοίσουσι. τούτου χάριν εὐθυγενῆ προσενεχθῆναι
προσέταξεν.

---

c. Lv 21.9   d. Lv 21.17–24   e. Lv 22.17–25   f. Lv 22.24

xxxi A [32], B, C, 4 7 9 10 31 35 37 = 20 mss.

a. Lv 22.27

this reason, he ordained the killing of an Israelite woman who engaged in prostitution but the burning of a priest's daughter guilty of the same offense.[c]

On account of the censoriousness of the Jews he did not allow men with any bodily disability to conduct the worship, thus prohibiting deliberate faults through the unintentional. For example, the blindness of the eyes suggests lack of knowledge, the loss of an ear disobedience, the loss of a nose lack of sound judgment, and the cutting off of a hand slothful behavior;[d] the rest should be understood in a similar manner.

For this reason he also commanded that only perfect specimens be offered and, through the sacrifices, instructed those making sacrifice to maintain the operations of the soul in good health.[e] He rejected, along with the others, geldings and victims whose testicles had been crushed,[f] for he who conducts the divine service ought to be fertile in good works.[2]

XXXI

Why did he ordain the sacrifice of the firstborn cattle after the seventh day?[a]

He knew that some people were gluttonous, and that if they saw a large, good-looking animal, they would hold on to it and offer another. Hence, he ordered the sacrifice of the newborn.[1]

---

2. *Cf.* the similar allegorical interpretation of the prohibition against a eunuch or a castrated male participating in the cultic levy in Q. 25 on Dt.

---

1. As Faley points out (on 22.1–33), it is in Ex 22.30 that this law is applied to the firstborn cattle. In Lv 22.27 the regulation concerns the fitness of the offering; the newborn is to remain with its mother until the eighth day, before which it is not ready to be eaten by men, let alone sacrificed to the Lord.

XXXII

Τί ἐστι πεφρυγμένα νέα χίδρα οὐ φάγεσθε . . . ἕως ἂν
προσενέγκητε ὑμεῖς τὰ δῶρα τῷ Θεῷ ὑμῶν;[a]

(1) Τῆς Παλαιστίνης ἡ γῆ θερμοτέρα οὖσα, πρωΐμους φέρει
καρπούς. κελεύει τοίνυν, μὴ πρότερόν τινα νέους ἀστάχυς
5 ἀφεῦσαι, καὶ φρύξαι, καὶ φαγεῖν, ἕως ἂν ἐκ τούτων τῷ Θεῷ
προσενέγκωσι δράγμα. κελεύει δὲ τοῦτο προσενεχθῆναι τῇ τοῦ
Πάσχα ἡμέρᾳ,[b] εἶτα ἐκ ταύτης ἑπτὰ ἑβδομάδας ἀριθμῆσαι,
καὶ τῆς Πεντηκοστῆς ἐπιτελέσαι τὴν ἑορτήν· οὕτω γὰρ ἔφη·
καὶ ἀριθμήσετε ὑμῖν ἀπὸ τῆς ἐπαύριον τῶν σαββάτων, ἀπὸ τῆς
10 ἡμέρας ἧς ἂν προσενέγκητε τὸ δράγμα τοῦ ἀφορίσματος, ἑπτὰ
ἑβδομάδας ὁλοκλήρους.[c] ἡ δὲ τῆς Πεντηκοστῆς ἑορτὴ μνήμη
τῆς εἰς τὴν γῆν τῆς ἐπαγγελίας εἰσόδου· τότε γὰρ καὶ
ἔσπειρον καὶ ἐθέριζον· ἐν γὰρ τῇ ἐρήμῳ τὸ μάννα ἤσθιον
οὐρανόθεν φερόμενον.

15 (2) Οὕτω διδάξας ὅπως χρὴ καὶ τοῦ Πάσχα καὶ τῆς
Πεντηκοστῆς ἐπιτελέσαι τὴν ἑορτήν, διδάσκει καὶ τίνα χρὴ
πρᾶξαι τῷ ἑβδόμῳ μηνί. καὶ τῇ μὲν νουμηνίᾳ τῶν σαλπίγγων
τὴν ἑορτὴν ἐπιτελέσαι κελεύει.[d] ἀνεμίμνησκον δὲ αὗται τῶν
ἐν τῷ Σινᾷ ὄρει γεγενημένων σαλπίγγων ἡνίκα τὸν νόμον ὁ
20 τῶν ὅλων ἐδεδώκει Θεός· φωνή, γάρ φησι, τῆς σάλπιγγος ἤχει
μέγα.[e] τῇ δεκάτῃ δὲ τοῦ μηνὸς νηστεῦσαι κελεύει· ταύτην
γὰρ τὴν ἡμέραν ἱλασμοῦ ἡμέραν καλεῖ· ταπεινώσετε, γάρ
φησι, τὰς ψυχὰς ὑμῶ‖ ἀπὸ ἐννάτης τοῦ μηνὸς . . . ἑσπέρας·[f]
καί, πᾶσα ψυχή, ἥτις μὴ ταπεινωθήσεται ἐν αὐτῇ,
25 ἐξολοθρευθήσεται ἡ ψυχὴ ἐκείνη ἐκ τοῦ λαοῦ αὐτῆς.[g] ἀλλ'
ἰουδαῖοι κατ' αὐτὴν τὴν ἡμέραν οὔτε σκυθρωπάζουσιν, ἀλλὰ

‖10

---

xxxii A [32], B, C⁻⁵¹, 4 7 9 10(inc.) 31 35 37 = 19 mss.

l. 4 τινα 5, C⁻⁵¹, 37, Sir. Sch. : τινι Pic. (Sch.) F.M.

a. Lv 23.14   b. Lv 23.11   c. Lv 23.15   d. Lv 23.23   e. Ex 19.16
f. Lv 23.32   g. Lv 23.29

XXXII

What is the meaning of "You shall not eat new grains roasted until you offer the gifts to your God"?[1a]

(1) The land of Palestine with its warm climate produces early crops. So the Law forbids the singeing, roasting, and eating of new ears of wheat before a sheaf is offered to God. It commands them to make this offering on Passover day,[b] then count seven weeks from this feast and celebrate Pentecost. Thus, it says, "You shall count off seven whole weeks from the day after the Sabbath, from the day you offer the sheaf of dedication."[c] The feast of Pentecost is a memorial of their entry into the promised land, that being the time they began to sow and harvest crops. In the desert, remember, they ate the manna that came from heaven.

(2) After giving these instructions on how to celebrate the feasts of Passover and Pentecost, it also teaches the rites of the seventh month. It commands them to celebrate on the first the Feast of the Trumpets.[d] This recalls the trumpet blasts on Mount Sinai when the God of the universe gave the Law, for as Scripture says, "There was a loud blast of the trumpet."[e] They are commanded to fast on the tenth, which is referred to as "the Day of Atonement." "You shall humble yourselves," the text says, "from the evening of the ninth";[f] and "anyone who does not humble himself on that day will be cut off from his people."[g] On that day, however, the Jews do not keep a long face; instead, they laugh, play, dance, and, in direct defiance of

1. As in answer to the simple Q. 22 Theodoret had provided a lengthy explanation of the feast of Atonement, he makes this question a pretext for a compendious review of the Jewish holidays and festivals prescribed in ch. 23: Passover, Pentecost, the Day of Trumpets (*i.e.,* New Year's; *v.* Faley on 23.23–25), the Day of Atonement, and Tabernacles. From cases such as these, it seems evident that his responses are crafted rather to set out a preconceived program of instruction than to reply to the queries of any individual or specific audience.

γελῶσι, καὶ παίζουσι, καὶ χορεύουσι, καὶ ἀκολάστοις ῥήμασι
καὶ πράγμασι κέχρηνται, ἄντικρυς τῷ νόμῳ μαχόμενοι. τῇ δὲ
πεντεκαιδεκάτῃ τὴν ἑορτὴν τῶν Σκηνῶν ἑορτάσαι νομοθετεῖ,
30 οὐ μέχρι τῆς ἑβδόμης, καθάπερ ἐπὶ τῶν ἄλλων ἑορτῶν, ἀλλὰ
καὶ τὴν ὀγδόην ταῖς ἑπτὰ προσθεῖναι κελεύει·[h] *καὶ ἡ ἡμέρα,*
γάρ φησιν, ἡ ὀγδόη κλητὴ ἁγία ἔσται ὑμῖν, καὶ προσάξετε
ὁλοκαυτώματα τῷ Κυρίῳ· ἐξόδιόν ἐστι· πᾶν ἔργον λατρευτὸν
οὐ ποιήσετε.[i] *τὸ δὲ ἐξόδιον* τὸ τέλος σημαίνει τῶν ἑορτῶν. ἡ
35 δὲ τῶν Σκηνῶν ἑορτὴ τῆς ἐν ἐρήμῳ διαγωγῆς ἀνεμίμνησκεν·
τοῦτο γὰρ καὶ νομοθετῶν ἔφη, ὅτι *ἐν σκηναῖς κατῴκισα τοὺς*
υἱοὺς Ἰσραὴλ ἐν τῷ ἐξαγαγεῖν με αὐτοὺς ἐκ γῆς Αἰγύπτου.[j]
τούτου χάριν κλάδοις δένδρων τὰς οἰκίας κοσμεῖν διηγόρευσε.
συνηρίθμησε δὲ τοῖς ἄλλοις κλάδοις καὶ τὸν ἄγνον, ὡς
40 σωφροσύνης δηλωτικὸν καὶ ἡδονῆς σβεστικόν·[k] φασὶ γὰρ
αὐτόν, καὶ ἐσθιόμενον καὶ ὑποστρωννύμενον, σβεννύναι τὴν
φλόγα τῶν ἡδονῶν. ἀλλὰ τούτοις, οὐκ ἰατρικῶς, χρήσασθαι
τοῖς τοῦ ἄγνου προσέταξε κλάδοις ἀλλὰ διὰ τοῦ ὀνόματος
ἐνιεὶς τῆς σωφροσύνης τὴν μνήμην.

XXXIII

Πῶς νοητέον τὸ *ὃς ἂν καταράσηται Θεόν, ἁμαρτίαν*
λήψεται, ὀνομάζων δὲ τὸ ὄνομα Κυρίου, θανάτῳ θανατούσθω;[a]

Ἤλω τις βλασφημήσας τὸν τῶν ὅλων Θεόν, οὐδέπω δὲ περὶ
βλασφημίας ἐγέγραπτο νόμος. τούτου χάριν ὁ νομοθέτης
5 τοῦτον μὲν φυλαχθῆναι προσέταξεν· ἤρετο δὲ τῇ ὑστεραίᾳ

---

h. Lv 23.39   i. Lv 23.36   j. Lv 23.43   k. Lv 23.40

XXXIII A [32], B, c, 4 7 9 31 35 37 = 17 mss.
a. Lv 24.15f.

the Law, engage in lewd talk and behavior.[2] The Law enjoins the celebration of the Feast of Tabernacles on the fifteenth, not for a week like the other feasts, but with the addition to the seven days of an eighth:[h] "The eighth day you will hold a convocation, and you will present holocausts to the Lord; it is the finale. You shall do no servile work."[i] By "finale" it means the end of the feasts. The Feast of Tabernacles recalls their sojourn in the desert. Indeed, as he was laying down this law, he declared, "Because I made the children of Israel live in tabernacles when I led them out of the land of Egypt."[j] Hence, he required them to festoon their houses with tree branches and included with the others willow branches as a symbol of sobriety and the curbing of pleasure.[k] It is said that when eaten or strewn on a bed, willow quenches the flame of lust. Yet it was not the purpose of this regulation to enjoin the medical use of the willow but to implant the thought of sobriety by the mention of the name.[3]

XXXIII

How are we to understand, "Anyone who curses God shall bear his sin; anyone who names the name of the Lord shall be put to death"?[a]

A man who blasphemed the God of the universe was arrested when no law regarding blasphemy had yet been written. Hence, Moses, the lawgiver, ordered him to be kept in custody and on the

---

2. After respectfully describing the rites of OT Judaism, Theodoret attacks the Jews of his own day; cf. the conclusion of Q. 18.

3. The Greek name for "willow" ἄγνος is very similar in spelling and sound to ἁγνός "pure," "chaste." As appears from 2Mc 10.6–8, the branches were originally gathered for use in "joyful processions" rather than to construct booths; v. Faley, on 23.33–36, 39–43. Theodoret, unconcerned with, or unaware of, its cultic significance, offers a moral interpretation of this law.

The Questions on Leviticus

Μωϋσῆς τὸν δεσπότην Θεὸν τί χρὴ παθεῖν τὸν ἀλάστορα. ὁ δὲ
τὸν μὲν καταλευσθῆναι προσέταξε, τῶν ἀκηκοότων τῆς
βλασφημίας πρώτων ἀφιέντων τοὺς λίθους.ᵇ ἔθηκε δὲ τὸν περὶ
τῆς βλασφημίας νόμον· καὶ θεὸν μὲν ὁμωνύμως ἐκάλεσε τὸν
10 ψευδώνυμον, τὸν δὲ τούτῳ λοιδορούμενον ἁμαρτάνειν μὲν ἔφη,
κολάσεως δὲ οὐκ ἔκρινεν ἄξιον. ἁμαρτάνει μέν, οὐχ ὁ εὐσεβὴς
τὸν ψευδώνυμον βλασφημῶν θεόν, ἀλλ' ὁ ἐκείνῳ πιστεύων μέν,
λοιδορούμενος δέ· βλασφημεῖ γὰρ ὃ σέβει. ἁμαρτίαν τοίνυν
τὴν τοιαύτην ἐκάλεσε βλασφημίαν, οὐ διὰ τὴν τοῦ
15 βλασφημουμένου ἀξίαν, ἀλλὰ διὰ τὴν τοῦ βλασφημοῦντος
ὑπόληψιν· οὐ γάρ, ὡς ψευδώνυμον, ἀλλ' ὡς ἀληθῆ Θεὸν
βλασφημεῖ. τὸν μέντοι τὸν ἀληθινὸν βλασφημοῦντα Θεὸν
λίθοις ἀναιρεῖσθαι προσέταξε.ᶜ μάλα δὲ εἰκότως τοῖς περὶ τῆς
βλασφημίας νόμοις καὶ τὸν περὶ τοῦ φόνου συνῆψεν,ᵈ ἐπειδὴ
20 καὶ ὁ βλασφημῶν, ἀνελεῖν μὴ δυνάμενος, τῇ γλώττῃ βάλλει
τὸν ποιητήν.

XXXIV

Διὰ τί *ὀφθαλμὸν ἀντὶ ὀφθαλμοῦ* ἐκκόπτεσθαι, καὶ *ὀδόντα
ἀντὶ ὀδόντος,* καὶ ὅσα τοιαῦτα προσέταξεν;ᵃ

Οὐχ ἵνα πάσχωσι ταῦτα νενομοθέτηκεν, ἀλλ' ἵνα μὴ
πράττωσι· τοῦ γὰρ πάθους τὸ δέος τὴν πρᾶξιν ἐκώλυσεν.

---

b. Lv 24.10–16   c. Lv 24.15f.   d. Lv 24.17

xxxiv A [32], B, c, 4 7 9 31 35 37 = 17 mss.
a. Lv 24.20

74

next day asked the Lord God what penalty the culprit should suffer. God ordered him to be stoned—all within hearing of the blasphemy being the first to cast stones.[b] In setting down the law on blasphemy, he used the word "God" to refer also to what is falsely called "God." He said that he who reviles a false god commits a sin, but he did not judge him worthy of punishment. It is not the man of right belief who commits sin when he blasphemes a false god, but the one who believes in it and reviles it, for he blasphemes what he reverences. So he called such a sin blasphemy, not because of the innate worth of what is blasphemed, but because of the belief of the one who commits the blasphemy, for he blasphemes the god, not as a false god, but as though it were the true God. It was the man who blasphemed the true God whom he ordered to be stoned to death.[c] Now, it was logical to link the law about murder with the law on blasphemy.[d] Since the blasphemer cannot do away with the Creator, he strikes at him with his tongue.

XXXIV

Why did he order "an eye to be cut out for an eye, a tooth for a tooth," and so on?[a]

He set down this law, not so that they would suffer such things, but to prevent them from committing them; fear of suffering deterred them from criminal behavior.[1]

---

1. Theodoret does not realize that the *lex talionis* was actually a relatively humane provision "limiting retaliation to the seriousness of the crime"; *v.* Faley, on 24.1–23. He does not quote the dominical mitigation in Mt 5.38–41.

XXXV

Διὰ τί τῷ ἑβδόμῳ ἔτει σπεῖραι τὴν γῆν ἀπαγορεύει;[a]

Τὸ ἄπληστον αὐτῶν κολάζει τῷ νόμῳ. ἐπειδὴ γάρ, τοῦ
πλείονος ἐφιέμενοι, διηνεκῶς ἔσπειρον, μὴ διαναπαυομένη δέ,
ἡ γῆ ἐξιτήλους ἔφερε τοὺς καρπούς, τῷ ἑβδόμῳ ἔτει ἄσπαρτον
5 ἐᾶσαι τὴν γῆν διηγόρευσε. τὰ δὲ αὐτομάτως φυόμενα τρυγᾶν
ἢ θερίζειν ἐκώλυσε, φιλανθρωπίαν ἐκπαιδεύων αὐτούς·[b]
ἐκέλευσε γὰρ σὺν αὐτοῖς καὶ χήρας, καὶ ὀρφανούς, καὶ
προσηλύτους ἐξ αὐτῶν μεταλαβεῖν τῶν καρπῶν.[c]

Πρὸς δὲ τούτοις καὶ ἕτερον πραγματεύεται· καὶ γὰρ
10 ἄφεσις ὀφλημάτων κατὰ τόδε τὸ ἔτος ἐγίνετο,[d] καὶ τῶν
δουλευόντων ἑβραίων ἐλευθερία.[e] διά τοι τοῦτο καὶ τὸν
ἰοβηλαῖον ἀργεῖν ἐνομοθέτησεν. ἐλευθερίαν δὲ καὶ ἄφεσιν
σημαίνει τὸ ὄνομα, *ἰοβηλαῖον* δὲ τὸ πεντηκοστὸν
προσαγορεύουσιν ἔτος· *ἑπτά, γάρ φησιν, ἑβδομάδας ἐτῶν*
15 *ἀριθμήσεις καὶ διαγγελεῖτε σάλπιγγος φωνῇ ἐν πάσῃ τῇ γῇ*
ὑμῶν ... τῇ δεκάτῃ τοῦ μηνός, τῇ ἡμέρᾳ τοῦ ἐξιλασμοῦ.[f] *ἐν ᾗ,*
φησίν, ἡμέρᾳ ἱλεοῦμαι ὑμῖν καὶ τὰ πεπλημμελημένα ὑμῖν
ἀφίημι, ἐν ταύτῃ μηνύσατε τὸ τῆς ἀφέσεως ἔτος. εἶτα
κελεύει ἐν τούτῳ τῷ ἔτει καὶ τὸν ἀγρὸν ἀναλαμβάνειν τὸν
20 πεπρακότα[g] καὶ τὰς ἐν τοῖς ἀγροῖς οἰκίας[h] καὶ χρεῶν
ἀποκοπὰς γενέσθαι καὶ παίδων ἑβραίων ἐλευθερίας.[i] ἐπειδὴ δὲ
εἰκὸς ἦν τινας ἐνοχλεῖν τοῖς ὀφείλουσιν, ὡς τοῦ τῆς ἀφέσεως
ἔτους πελάζοντος, ἀπηγόρευσε καὶ τοῦτο γίνεσθαι παρ'
αὐτῶν.[j] ὥστε δὲ περὶ τῆς ἀναγκαίας μὴ ἐνδοιάζειν τροφῆς,
25 ἅτε δὴ μὴ γεωργοῦντας τὴν γῆν ἐν τοῖς τῆς ἀφέσεως ἔτεσι,
ταῖς φιλοτίμοις ἐψυχαγώγησεν ὑποσχέσεσιν· ἐπηγγείλατο γὰρ
ἐν τῷ ἕκτῳ ἔτει, οὐ διπλασίαν πρόσοδον χορηγήσειν μόνην,

|10

---

xxxv A *[32]*, 14 17 24*, c, 4 7 9 10(*inc.*) 31 35 37 = 18 mss.

a. Lv 25.1–4   b. Lv 25.5   c. Dt 24.19–21   d. Lv 25.25–28
e. Lv 25.39–41   f. Lv 25.8f.   g. Lv 25.28   h. Lv 25.31   i. Lv 25.39f.
j. Lv 25.14–17

XXXV

Why did he forbid the sowing of the soil in the seventh year?[a]

He employed this law to chasten their avarice. Since in their hankering after greater yield they kept sowing, and the soil, which never lay fallow, began to produce denatured crops, he required them to leave the soil unsown in the seventh year, and, to teach them liberality, he did not allow them to pick or harvest crops that grew spontaneously.[b] Indeed, he ordered that widows, orphans, and aliens should share the produce with them.[1c]

Furthermore, he had another purpose: the cancellation of debts[d] and the release of Hebrews in servitude,[e] which also took place in this year. This is why he legislated for the Jubilee rest, the name signifying release and cancellation. They gave the name "Jubilee" to the fiftieth year: "You shall count off seven weeks of years and announce the Jubilee with a blast of the trumpet throughout all your land on the tenth day of the month, the Day of Atonement."[f] That is, "proclaim the year of cancellation on the day I am propitious to you and forgive your offenses."[2] He next commanded that, in this year, both property[g] and country houses[h] be restored to the seller, debts cancelled, and Hebrew slaves set free.[i] But as it was likely that some people would make trouble for their debtors as the year of cancellation approached, he also forbade that.[j] And to prevent them from worrying about not having enough food, since they were not to farm the land in the years of cancellation, he comforted them with generous promises. He guaranteed that in the sixth year he would supply them, not with a double, but with a triple, yield sufficient to feed them in the sixth and seventh years and last even until the eighth: "Sow in the eighth year, and you will eat from the old crop. Until the

---

1. It is in Dt 24.19–21, not this passage, that the Law enjoins sharing with widows, orphans, and aliens.

2. Theodoret's etymology is mistaken. The term "Jubilee" is derived from the Hebrew *yobel*, "trumpet" or "ram's horn."

ἀλλὰ καὶ τριπλασίαν αὐτοῖς, ἀποχρῶσαν καὶ ἐν τῷ ἕκτῳ καὶ
ἐν τῷ ἑβδόμῳ διαθρέψαι ἔτει, ἀλλὰ καὶ μέχρι τοῦ ὀγδόου
30 διαρκοῦσαν· *σπερεῖτε, γάρ φησιν, τὸ ἔτος τὸ ὄγδοον καὶ*
φάγεσθε ἀπὸ τῶν γενημάτων παλαιά· ἕως τοῦ ἔτους τοῦ
ἐννάτου, ἕως ἂν ἔλθῃ τὰ γενήματα αὐτῆς, φάγεσθε παλαιὰ
παλαιῶν.[k] εἶτα τῇ μνήμῃ τῆς δεσποτείας κρατύνει τὸν νόμον·
ἐμὴ γάρ ἐστι, φησίν, ἡ γῆ, διότι προσήλυτοι καὶ πάροικοι
35 *ὑμεῖς ἐστε ἐναντίον μου.*[l] ἐγώ, φησί, ταύτην ὑμῖν ἐδωρησάμην·
τοιγάρτοι ὡς δεσπότης νομοθετῶ.

XXXVI

Τί ἐστι *πέψουσι δέκα γυναῖκες τοὺς ἄρτους αὐτῶν ἐν*
κλιβάνῳ ἑνί;[a]

Ὡς περὶ τὴν γῆν κεχηνόσι καὶ νομοθετεῖ καὶ ἀπειλεῖ· καὶ
γὰρ ἐννόμως πολιτευομένοις τῆς γῆς αὐτοῖς ἐπαγγέλλεται
5 τὴν εὐκαρπίαν, καὶ αὖ πάλιν παραβαίνουσι καὶ γῆς ἀκαρπίαν,
καὶ πολεμίων ἔφοδον ἀπειλεῖ, καὶ πενίαν ἐσχάτην. τοῦτο καὶ
ἐνταῦθα δηλοῖ· ὅτι τοσαύτη ὑμᾶς καταλήψεται πενία ὡς δέκα
γυναῖκας ἐν ἑνὶ κλιβάνῳ τοὺς ἄρτους ποιεῖν διὰ τὴν σπάνιν
τῶν ἀναγκαίων· τοῦτο γὰρ ἐπήγαγε· *καὶ φάγεσθε καὶ οὐ μὴ*
10 *ἐμπλησθῆτε.*[b]

---

k. Lv 25.22   l. Lv 25.23

xxxvi A [32], B, C⁻⁵², 4 7 9 10 31* 35 37 = 19 mss.
a. Lv 26.26   b. Lv 26.26

ninth year, when the produce of the earth comes in, you will be eating the old of the old."[k] He then confirmed the law with a reference to his lordship: "The land is mine, and, therefore, you are aliens and tenants in my sight."[l] By this he meant, "I gave you the land as a gift; hence, it is as your master that I lay down the law."

XXXVI

What is the meaning of "Ten women will bake their loaves in one pan"?[a]

He set down laws and threats as though for a people gaping in anticipation for the land. He promised them fertility of the soil provided they lived in fidelity to the Law but threatened them with extremes of poverty if they disobeyed it. This passage makes the same point: "You will be in the grip of such awful want that ten women will bake your loaves in one pan because of the scarcity of provisions. He added, "You will eat and not be filled."[b]

XXXVII

Τί ἐστι τότε εὐδοκήσει ἡ γῆ τὰ σάββατα . . . πάσας τὰς
ἡμέρας τῆς ἐρημώσεως αὐτῆς;ᵃ

(1) Τὸ ἐπαγόμενον ἑρμηνεία τούτου ἐστίν· ἔφη γάρ, καὶ
ὑμεῖς ἔσεσθε ἐν τῇ γῇ τῶν ἐχθρῶν ὑμῶν·ᵇ ἐν Βαβυλῶνι γὰρ
5 ἑβδομήκοντα ἔτη δουλεύοντες διετέλεσαν.ᶜ ἀπὸ δὲ τῆς τοῦ
Σαοὺλ βασιλείας μέχρι τῆς αἰχμαλωσίας, τετρακόσια καὶ
ἐνενήκοντα συνάγεται ἔτη, τούτων δὲ τὸ ἕβδομον
ἑβδομήκοντα. τοῦτο τοίνυν φησίν· ὅτι ἄσπαρτος ἡ γῆ μενεῖ
καὶ ἀνήροτος ἑβδομήκοντα ἔτη, ὑμῶν τὴν ἀλλοτρίαν
10 οἰκούντων, ἐπειδή, μετὰ τῶν ἄλλων νόμων, παρέβητε καὶ τοῦ
σαββάτου τὴν ἐντολήν·ᵈ τοῦτο γὰρ ἐπήγαγε· καὶ σαββατιεῖ ἡ
γῆ . . . ἃ οὐκ ἐσαββάτισεν . . . ἡνίκα κατῳκεῖτε αὐτήν.ᵉ
προστέθεικε δὲ καὶ ἑτέραν ἀπειλήν· καὶ τοῖς καταλειφθεῖσιν
ἐξ ὑμῶν ἐπάξω δειλίαν εἰς τὴν καρδίαν αὐτῶν ἐν τῇ γῇ τῶν
15 ἐχθρῶν αὐτῶν· καὶ διώξεται αὐτοὺς φωνὴ φύλλου φερομένου,
καὶ φεύξονται ὡς φεύγοντες ἀπὸ πολέμου, καὶ τὰ ἑξῆς.ᶠ καὶ
αὕτη δὲ ἡ πρόρρησις πέρας ἔλαβεν· ἐν γὰρ τῇ τῶν χαλδαίων
πολιορκίᾳ πολλῶν μὲν ἐν ταῖς συμπλοκαῖς ἀναιρεθέντων,
πολλῶν δὲ λιμῷ διαφθαρέντων, τῶν ἀνδραποδισθέντων δὲ εἰς
20 Βαβυλῶνα μετοικισθέντων, οἱ τὰς τῶν πολεμίων χεῖρας
διαφυγόντες εἰς τὴν Αἴγυπτον ἔφυγον, δείσαντες τῶν
χαλδαίων τὴν ἔφοδον. καὶ τοῦτο σαφῶς ἡμᾶς ἡ τοῦ θειοτάτου
Ἱερεμίου προφητεία διδάσκει.ᵍ

|2a
(2) Μετὰ μέντοι τὰς ἀπειλὰς ὑπέσχετο καὶ χρηστὰ καὶ τὴν
25 ἀπὸ τῆς αἰχμαλωσίας ἐπάνοδον ἐπηγγείλατο, οὐ διὰ τὴν
αὐτῶν ἀξίαν, ἀλλὰ διὰ τὴν τῶν προγόνων εὐσέβειαν· τοῦτο
γὰρ ἔφη· καὶ μνησθήσομαι τῆς διαθήκης Ἰακώβ, καὶ τῆς
διαθήκης Ἰσαάκ, καὶ τῆς διαθήκης Ἀβραάμ.ʰ . . . καὶ

xxxvii A [32], B, C⁻⁵², 4 7 9 10 31 35 37 = 19 mss.

a. Lv 26.34   b. Lv 26.34   c. 2Chr 36.21   d. Lv 25.2–7   e. Lv 26.34f.
f. Lv 26.36   g. Jer 52.1–31; 44   h. Lv 26.42

Question XXXVII

XXXVII

What is the meaning of "Then the land shall enjoy its Sabbaths all the days of its desolation"?[a]

(1) What follows provides the interpretation, for he said, "You will be in the land of your enemies."[b] As you recall, they spent seventy years in Babylon.[1c] From the reign of Saul to the captivity was a total of four hundred and ninety years, and a seventh of this is seventy. So his meaning is: "The land will remain unsown and uncultivated for seventy years while you dwell in a foreign land, since, along with the other laws, you also broke the sabbath commandment."[d] In fact, after adding, "The land shall have its sabbath rest, which it did not have when you were living in it,"[e] he proceeded to deliver yet another threat: "I shall bring fear upon the heart of those of you who survive in the land of their foes; the sound of a falling leaf will pursue them, and they will take to flight as though fleeing from war" and so on.[f] Now, this prophecy was fulfilled; during the siege of the Chaldeans many were slain in battle, many perished through starvation, captives were deported to Babylon, and those who evaded the grasp of the enemy fled to Egypt in fear of the invading Chaldeans. We have detailed knowledge of this from the prophecy of the divinely inspired Jeremiah.[g]

(2) After these threats, however, he also promised blessings and guaranteed the return from captivity, not because of their worthiness, but in light of the piety of their forbears. As he said, "I shall remember my covenant with Jacob, my covenant with Isaac, and my covenant with Abraham,[h] and I shall remember my former

1. Theodoret grasps this element of prophecy appearing in a largely liturgical book and demonstrates its fulfilment. As Frances Young says, "The Antiochenes were fascinated by prophecy"; v. Biblical Exegesis, p. 168.

μνησθήσομαι αὐτῶν τῆς διαθήκης τῆς προτέρας, ὅτε ἐξήγαγον
30 αὐτοὺς ἐκ γῆς Αἰγύπτου, ἐξ οἴκου δουλείας, ἐναντίον πάντων
τῶν ἐθνῶν τοῦ εἶναι αὐτῶν Θεός· ἐγώ εἰμι Κύριος.[i] ἐδίδαξε δὲ
διὰ τούτων τὰς τῆς φιλανθρωπίας αἰτίας· διὰ γὰρ τὰς πρὸς
πατέρας αὐτῶν ἐπαγγελίας, φησί, τῆς τούτων ἀνέχομαι
παρανομίας, καὶ ἐπειδὴ ἔγνω πάντα τὰ ἔθνη διὰ τῶν
35 παραδόξων θαυμάτων ὅτι διαφερόντως τούτων ἐπιμελοῦμαι,
καὶ λαὸς ἐμὸς χρηματίζουσι.[j] τοῦ μέντοι Ἰακὼβ ἐμνημόνευσε
πρώτου, ἐπειδὴ τούτων ἁπάντων μόνος ἦν πρόγονος· ὁ γὰρ
Ἰσαὰκ καὶ τῶν ἰδουμαίων,[k] ὁ δὲ Ἀβραὰμ καὶ τῶν ἰσμαηλιτῶν
καὶ τῶν ἀπὸ Χεττούρας.[l] κάτωθεν τοίνυν ἀρξάμενος, κατὰ
40 τάξιν ἐπὶ τὸν Ἀβραὰμ ἀνελήλυθε, πρὸς ὃν ἐξ ἀρχῆς ἐπεποίητο
τὰς συνθήκας.

XXXVIII

Τί ἐστιν ὃς ἂν εὔξηται εὐχὴν ὥστε δοῦναι τιμὴν τῆς εὐχῆς
αὐτοῦ τῷ Κυρίῳ;[a]

Εὐχὴν καλεῖ τὴν ὑπόσχεσιν, ὃ πολλοὶ *τάγμα*
προσαγορεύουσι. τοῦτον δὲ τὸν νόμον ἔστι καὶ νῦν παρ' ἐνίοις
5 βαρβάροις εὑρεῖν φυλαττόμενον· οἱ γὰρ πιστοὶ τῶν νομάδων·
λέγω δὲ τοὺς ἀπογόνους τοῦ Ἰσμαήλ· ἀντιταλαντεύουσι τοῖς
εὐθυγενέσι βρέφεσιν ἄργυρον καὶ τοῦτον προσκομίζουσι τῷ
Θεῷ. περὶ τούτου νενομοθέτηκεν ὁ Θεός, καὶ γινώσκων, ὡς
Θεός, ὅτι τῶν ὑπισχνουμένων τινὲς δώσειν ὑπὲρ ἑαυτῶν τιμὴν
10 τῷ Θεῷ παραβήσονται τὴν ὑπόσχεσιν, σμικρύνοντες τὴν
τιμήν, ἐκέλευσε πεντήκοντα εἶναι δίδραχμα τοῦ ἄρρενος τὴν

---

l. 38 ἰσμαηλιτῶν *a₂*, B, *c⁻³*, 51, 7 9 31 37, Sir. : ἰσραηλιτῶν Sch. F.M. = "and
Abraham also of the Israelites and the offspring of Keturah."

i. Lv 26.45   j. Cf. Jos 2.8–11.   k. Gn 36.1–8   l. Gn 25.1–4

---

xxxviii A [32], B, C⁻⁵², 4 7 9 10 31 35 37 = 19 mss.

a. Lv 27.2 (LXX var.)

covenant with them when I led them out of the land of Egypt, out of the house of slavery in the sight of all the nations to be their God; I am the Lord."[i] Here, he taught the reason for his loving-kindness, for this means, "I put up with the lawlessness of this later generation because of my promises to their ancestors, and because all the nations learned through my amazing miracles that they are the object of my special care, and that they are called my people."[j] He mentioned Jacob first, since he was the progenitor of all their race and only their race, while Isaac was the ancestor also of the Idumeans,[k] and Abraham also of the Ishmaelites and the offspring of Keturah.[l] So beginning from a later generation he went back in time to Abraham, with whom he had initially made his covenant.[2]

XXXVIII

What is the meaning of "Whoever makes a vow to pay the price of his vow to the Lord"?[a]

By "vow" he means a promise, what many people call a "payment." Even today there are still some foreign peoples that observe this law. For instance, the Christian nomads—I mean, the descendants of Ishmael—pay money in gratitude for their newborn babes and offer it to God. God legislated for this practice. Furthermore, since God knew that some who promised to pay him a price for themselves would break the promise by setting a low price, he set

2. An Antiochene attentive to details of chronology, Theodoret takes note of, and tries to account for, the reversal of the usual order of the patriarchs.

τιμήν, τῆς δὲ θηλείας τριάκοντα, καὶ τῶν ἀκμαζόντων καὶ τῶν
γεγηρακότων ὑπεξῃρημένων. τὴν γὰρ μέσην περιώρισεν
ἡλικίαν, ἀπὸ εἰκοσαετοῦς εἰρηκὼς ἕως ἑξηκονταετοῦς·[b] τοῖς
15 γὰρ τούτων νεωτέροις καὶ πρεσβυτέροις ἄλλην ὥρισε τιμήν.[c]
τοὺς δὲ πένητας ὑπὸ τὴν τῶν ἱερέων καταλέλοιπε κρίσιν ἵν'
ἐκεῖνοι πρὸς τὰς δυνάμεις ὁρίζωσι τὰς τιμάς.[d]

Τὰ δὲ ἀφιερούμενα ἄλογα ἐναλλάττεσθαι παρὰ τῶν
προσφερόντων ἀπαγορεύει καί, ὥστε μὴ τοῦτο δρᾶν, τὴν τῆς
20 ζημίας αὐτοῖς ἐπιτίθησιν ἀνάγκην· *ἐὰν* . . . , *γάρ φησιν,*
ἀλλάσσων ἀλλάξῃ αὐτό, . . . *ἔσται αὐτὸ καὶ τὸ ἄλλαγμα αὐτοῦ*
ἅγιον.[e] τῶν μέντοι ἀκαθάρτων κτηνῶν ὁρίσαι τὴν τιμὴν τὸν
ἱερέα ἐκέλευσε.[f] τοῦτο καὶ ἐπὶ οἰκίας καὶ ἀγροῦ γενέσθαι
ἐκέλευσεν.[g] ὥρισε δὲ καὶ τὴν τοῦ διδράχμου ποσότητα· εἴκοσι
25 γὰρ ἐκέλευσεν ἕλκειν ὀβολούς.[h] τὸ δὲ *δίδραχμόν* τινες τῶν
ἑρμηνευτῶν στατῆρα ἐκάλεσαν. τὰ μέντοι ἀνατιθέμενα τῷ
Θεῷ προσέταξε μὴ λυτροῦσθαι.[i]

b. Lv 27.1–4   c. Lv 27.5–7   d. Lv 27.8   e. Lv 27.10   f. Lv 27.11–13
g. Lv 27.14–24   h. Lv 27.25   i. Lv 27.28f.

the price for a male at fifty didrachmas and that for a female at thirty, with the exception of the young and old. He defined the middle age as that from twenty to sixty;[b] for those younger and older he set a different price.[c] The poor he left to the judgment of the priests, who were to set the price according to their ability to pay.[d]

He forbade those who wished to make an offering to exchange one animal for another, and, to prevent this practice, imposed the following penalty: "If anyone should change a beast, both that one and its replacement will be holy."[e] Further, he commanded the priest to determine the price of the unclean beasts[f] and ordered the same to be done in the case of houses and property.[g] He also determined the value of the didrachma, whose worth he set at twenty obols.[h] Some translators have rendered the term "stater" rather than "didrachma." Moreover, he enjoined that dedications made to God would not be redeemable.[i]

QUAESTIONES IN NUMEROS

I

Διὰ τί προσέταξεν ἀριθμηθῆναι τὸν λαὸν ὁ Θεός;[a]

Ἵνα τῆς οἰκείας ἐπαγγελίας δείξῃ τὸ ἀληθές·
ὑπισχνούμενος γὰρ τῷ Ἀβραάμ, ἔφη, πληθύνων πληθυνῶ τὸ
σπέρμα σου ὡς τοὺς ἀστέρας τοῦ οὐρανοῦ καὶ ὡς τὴν ἄμμον,
5 τὴν παρὰ τὸ χεῖλος τῆς θαλάσσης.[b] ἔδειξε δὲ τὴν τῆς
ἐπαγγελίας ἀλήθειαν· ἐκ πέντε γὰρ καὶ ἑβδομήκοντα τῶν εἰς
Αἴγυπτον κατεληλυθότων[c] ἑξακόσιαι χιλιάδες καὶ τρισχίλιοι
καὶ ἑξακόσιοι καὶ πεντήκοντα ἠριθμήθησαν ἄνδρες δυνάμενοι
πολεμεῖν,[d] καὶ τῆς ἐξώρου ἡλικίας, καὶ τῆς ἀώρου
10 κεχωρισμένης, καὶ μέντοι καὶ τοῦ θήλεως γένους, καὶ τῆς
λευιτικῆς φυλῆς· οὐδὲ γὰρ αὕτη ταῖς λοιπαῖς συνηριθμήθη.[e]
ταύτην αὐτοῦ διδάσκων τὴν δύναμιν, ὁ δεσπότης Θεὸς καὶ διὰ
τοῦ προφήτου Ἡσαΐου ἔφη, ἐμβλέψατε εἰς Ἀβραὰμ τὸν
πατέρα ὑμῶν καὶ εἰς Σάρραν, τὴν ὠδίνουσαν ὑμᾶς, ὅτι εἷς ἦν,
15 καὶ ἐκάλεσα αὐτόν, καὶ εὐλόγησα αὐτόν, και ... ἐπλήθυνα
αὐτόν.[f]

---

1 A [32], B, c⁻¹, 51, 4 7 9 10 22(= Rome, Bibl. Apost. Vat., Ottob. gr. 16) 31 35 37 = 20 mss.

l. 6 ἐπαγγελίας B⁻¹⁷, 15, 51, 22 31, Sir. Sch. : ἀπαγγελίας F.M. = "And he gave proof of the truth of his report." Cf. the critical note on Q. 3 on Jos (ἐπαγγελίαν).

l. 12 αὐτοῦ Sir. Sch. : ἑαυτοῦ B 4 7 9 31 35 : αυτου F.M.

a. Nm 1.1–3   b. Gn 22.17   c. Gn 46.27   d. Nm 1.46   e. Nm 1.47–49
f. Is 51.2

ON NUMBERS

I

Why did God order a census of the nation?[a]

To demonstrate the realization of his promise. He had promised Abraham: "Indeed, I shall make your offspring as numerous as the stars of heaven and the sand on the seashore."[b] And he gave proof of the realization of his promise, since, though only seventy-five had gone down into Egypt,[c] they were numbered at 603,650 men of combat age,[d] not to mention those who were too young or too old, as well as the women and the tribe of Levi, which was not numbered with the others.[1e] Setting forth his power, the Lord God also declared through the prophet Isaiah, "Look to Abraham your father and to Sarah who bore you; he was but a single man, and I called him, blessed him, and made him many."[f]

---

1. Theodoret's sum exceeds that of the majority text of the LXX by 100. According to C.E. L'Heureux (on 1.1–47) such figures are generally agreed to be too high even for a census dating from the Davidic period. The total may have been excogitated by an author of the priestly tradition, who doubled the 301,775 shekels required to pay for the bases and hooks supporting the tabernacle curtains (Ex 38.26–28); such a calculation would reflect the post-exilic rate of one-half shekel tax per each adult male.

II

Διὰ τί ἐλάττων ἐστὶν ὁ τῶν λευιτῶν ἀριθμός;[a]

'Ως ἀρχόντων· δεῖ γὰρ τοὺς ἄρχοντας ἐλάττους εἶναι τῶν ἀρχομένων. ἄλλως τε καὶ τοῦ πολεμεῖν ἦσαν ἀπηλλαγμένοι καὶ μόνῃ τῇ θείᾳ λατρείᾳ προσήδρευον.

III

Πῶς οὖν ἡ τοῦ Ἰούδα φυλὴ ὑπερέβαλε πάσας τῷ ἀριθμῷ καίτοι οὖσα βασιλική;

'Εκ τῆς βασιλικῆς εἷς ἀνὴρ ἐβασίλευσεν, οἱ δὲ τῆς λευιτικῆς ἅπαντες ἐλειτούργουν· οἱ μὲν ἱερατεύοντες,[a] οἱ δὲ
5 τούτοις διακονοῦντες.[b] ἐδεῖ δὲ καὶ τὴν βασιλικὴν ὑπερέχειν τῷ ἀριθμῷ καὶ διὰ τὴν εὐλογίαν τοῦ δεσπότου Χριστοῦ· ἐξ αὐτῶν γὰρ ἔμελλεν κατὰ σάρκα βλαστάνειν·[c] καὶ ὥστε τοὺς ἐξ αὐτῆς χειροτονουμένους βασιλέας ἀρκοῦσαν ἔχειν τῶν φυλετῶν τὴν ἐπικουρίαν. συνέταξε δὲ κἀνταῦθα τῇ βασιλικῇ
10 φυλῇ τοὺς ἱερέας· πρὸς ἥλιον γὰρ ἀνίσχοντα τὴν Ἰούδα τάξας φυλήν, συνῆψεν αὐτοῖς τοὺς ἱερέας μετὰ τῆς κιβωτοῦ.[d]

Τῷ μέντοι Δὰν τὸ βόρειον ἀπεκλήρωσε τμῆμα·[e] *ἀπὸ προσώπου*, γάρ φησι, *βορρᾶ ἐκκαυθήσεται τὰ κακὰ ἐπὶ πάντας τοὺς κατοικοῦντας τὴν γῆν.*[f] εἴρηται δὲ ἡμῖν ἐν ταῖς τοῦ
15 Ἰακὼβ εὐλογίαις ὡς ἐκ τῆς Δὰν φυλῆς ὁ ἀλάστωρ τεχθήσεται, ὁ Χριστὸν μὲν ἑαυτὸν ὀνομάζων, τἀναντία δὲ τῇ προσηγορίᾳ

II A *[32]*, B, *c⁻¹*, 51, 4 7 9 10 31 35 37 = 19 mss.

a. Nm 3.39

III A *[32]*, B, 1*(inc.)* 3 8 15, 4 7 9 10 31 35 37 = 19 mss.

a. Nm 3.1–4   b. Nm 3.5–10   c. *Cf.* Mt 2.6.   d. Nm 1.52f.; 2.2f.
e. Nm 2.25   f. Jer 1.14

II

Why were there fewer Levites?[1a]

Because they were the leaders, and there must be fewer leaders than led. Moreover, they were exempt from fighting and concerned only with the divine service.

III

So why was the tribe of Judah, though the royal tribe, more numerous than all the others?

One man from the royal tribe occupied the throne, whereas everyone from the tribe of Levi performed the religious service, some in a priestly capacity,[a] others ministering to them.[b] The population of the royal tribe had to surpass that of the others, both because of the blessing conferred by Christ the Lord, who was to draw his bodily descent from that tribe,[c] and to ensure that those of its number appointed king would have sufficient assistance from their fellow tribesmen. He ranged the priests alongside the royal tribe, for he placed the tribe of Judah to the east and associated with them the priests and the ark.[1d]

He allotted Dan the north:[e] "From the direction of the north the troubles will blaze forth against all the inhabitants of the earth."[f] As we noted in the blessings of Jacob, the destroyer will be born from

1. Theodoret does not cite the actual number: 22,000 from one month old and upwards.

1. Judah occupied the position of honor, due east of the tabernacle, around which the Levites encamped.

διαπραττόμενος, καὶ σφετεριζόμενος τὰ μηδαμόθεν προσήκοντα.

|1   Καὶ τῷ Ἰούδᾳ δὲ μάλα εἰκότως τὸ ἑῷον ἀπένειμεν, ἐπειδὴ
20   καὶ περὶ τοῦ δεσπότου Χριστοῦ οἱ θεῖοι βοῶσι προφῆται, *ἰδοὺ*
ἀνήρ, Ἀνατολὴ ὄνομα αὐτῷ[g] *καί, τοῖς φοβουμένοις με ἀνατελεῖ*
ἥλιος δικαιοσύνης, καὶ ἴασις ἐν ταῖς πτέρυξιν αὐτοῦ[h] *καί, τοῖς*
ἐν σκότει καὶ σκιᾷ θανάτου καθημένοις φῶς ἀνέτειλεν αὐτοῖς.[i]

IV

Τίνα ἦν τὰ ἔργα τῶν ἱερέων, καὶ τίνα τὰ τῶν λευιτῶν;

Αὐτὸς ὁ τῶν ὅλων διδάσκει Θεός. *εἶπε*, γάρ φησι, *Κύριος*
πρὸς Μωϋσῆν, λάβε τὴν φυλὴν τοῦ Λευὶ καὶ στήσεις αὐτοὺς
ἐναντίον Ἀαρὼν τοῦ ἱερέως· καὶ λειτουργήσουσιν αὐτῷ, καὶ
5   *φυλάξουσιν τὰς φυλακὰς αὐτοῦ καὶ τὰς φυλακὰς τῶν υἱῶν*
Ἰσραὴλ ἐναντίον τῆς σκηνῆς τοῦ μαρτυρίου ἐργάζεσθαι τὰ
ἔργα τῆς σκηνῆς, καὶ φυλάξουσι πάντα τὰ σκεύη τῆς σκηνῆς
τοῦ μαρτυρίου, καὶ τὰς φυλακὰς τῶν υἱῶν Ἰσραήλ, καὶ πάντα
τὰ ἔργα τῆς σκηνῆς. καὶ δώσεις τοὺς λευίτας Ἀαρὼν τῷ
10 *ἀδελφῷ σου καὶ τοῖς υἱοῖς αὐτοῦ τοῖς ἱερεῦσι· δόμα δεδομένον*
εἰσὶν οὗτοι ἀπὸ τῶν υἱῶν Ἰσραήλ. καὶ Ἀαρὼν καὶ τοὺς υἱοὺς
αὐτοῦ καταστήσεις ἐπὶ τῆς σκηνῆς τοῦ μαρτυρίου, καὶ
φυλάξουσι τὴν ἱερατείαν αὐτῶν, καὶ πάντα τὰ κατὰ τὸν
βωμόν, καὶ τὰ ἔσω τοῦ καταπετάσματος· καὶ ὁ ἀλλογενὴς ὁ
15 *ἁπτόμενος ἀποθανεῖται.*[a] Μεμαθήκαμεν οὖν ἐντεῦθεν ὡς οἱ μὲν
ἱερεῖς τὰς θυσίας προσέφερον, οἱ δὲ λευῖται, τῶν μὲν ἱερέων
ὑπουργοί, τῆς δὲ σκηνῆς κατέστησαν φύλακες. διδάσκει δὲ ἐν
τοῖς ἑξῆς τίνα μὲν ἔδει φέρειν τοῦ Καὰθ τὸν δῆμον,[b] τίνα δὲ
τὸν Γεδεών,[c] τίνα δὲ τὸν Μεραρί.[d]

---

g. Zec 6.12   h. Mal 4.2 (LXX var.)   i. Mt 4.16; Is 9.1

iv   A *[32]*, B, C⁻⁵², *4 7 9 10 31 35 37* = 20 mss.

a. Nm 3.5–10 (LXX var.)   b. Nm 3.31f.   c. Nm 3.25f.   d. Nm 3.36f.

the tribe of Dan. Though calling himself the Christ, he will act in a way contrary to that name and usurp what does not belong to him.[2]

The allotment of the east to Judah was entirely appropriate, since, with regard to Christ the Lord, the holy prophets cry out, "Lo, a man, 'Dawn' is his name";[g] and "The Sun of Righteousness will rise on those who fear me, with healing in his wings";[h] and "A light has dawned on those sitting in darkness and the shadow of death."[3i]

IV

Which duties belonged to the priests, and which to the Levites?

The God of the universe himself informs us. As Scripture says, "The Lord said to Moses, 'Bring the tribe of Levi and set them before the priest Aaron. They shall minister to him and keep his charges and the charges of the children of Israel before the tabernacle of witness and perform the duties of the tabernacle. They shall take charge of all the vessels of the tabernacle of witness, the charges of the children of Israel, and all the duties of the tabernacle. You shall give the Levites to your brother Aaron and to his sons the priests; they are a gift from the children of Israel. But you shall place Aaron and his sons over the tabernacle of witness; they will have charge of the priestly service, and of everything to do with the altar, and of everything inside the curtain. Any outsider who touches these things will die.'"[a] So we learn from this that, while the priests offered the sacrifices, the Levites were appointed the attendants of the priests and the guardians of the tabernacle. In what follows he teaches the services that were to be performed by the families of Kohath,[b] Gershon,[c] and Merari.[d]

2. V. Q. 112.4 on Gn.

3. In his commentary on Zec 3.8 and 6.12, Theodoret follows Theodore of Mopsuestia in applying the title "Dawn" to Zerubbabel. Here, however, he offers a christological interpretation. In these verses, the reading of the LXX ἀνατολή ("Dawn") rests on a misinterpretation of the Hebrew term *semah* "Shoot" [of Babylon]; *v.* the remarks of A. Cody *ad locc.*

V

Τίνος ἕνεκεν προσέταξεν ὁ Θεὸς ἀριθμηθῆναι τοῦ λαοῦ τὰ πρωτότοκα;[a]

Ἐπειδὴ πᾶσαν τοῦ Λευὶ τὴν φυλὴν ταῖς θείαις ἀφιέρωσε λειτουργίαις καὶ τοῦ πολεμεῖν ἠλευθέρωσεν, εἰκὸς δὲ ἦν
5 δυσχεραίνειν τῶν ἄλλων τινάς, ὡς τούτων προτιμηθέντων, πείθει τοὺς δυσχεραίνοντας ὁ δεσπότης Θεὸς ὡς οὐδὲν προσέταξεν ἄδικον. ἡνίκα, γάρ φησιν, ὑμῶν χάριν ἀνῃρέθη τὰ τῶν αἰγυπτίων πρωτότοκα, τὰ ὑμέτερα διεσώθη πρωτότοκα· ἀντὶ τούτων τοίνυν, τὴν λευιτικὴν φυλὴν ταῖς ἐμαῖς
10 ἀπεκλήρωσα λειτουργίαις[b] καί, ἀντὶ τῶν πρωτοτόκων τῶν ὑμετέρων κτηνῶν, τῶν λευιτῶν τὰ πρωτότοκα.[c]

Ἐπειδὴ δὲ πλείους ὤφθησαν τῶν λευιτῶν τῶν ἄλλων φυλῶν οἱ πρωτότοκοι,[d] προσέταξεν ἕκαστον τῶν μετὰ τὸν ἴσον ἀριθμὸν πέντε δοῦναι σίκλους τοῖς ἱερεῦσιν, εἴκοσι ὀβολοὺς
15 ὁρίσας ἔχειν τὸν σίκλον καὶ τὸν τοιοῦτον ἀριθμὸν ἅγιον ὀνομάσας, ὡς τοῖς θείοις ἀφωρισμένον καὶ οὐ παρὰ πᾶσι πολιτευόμενον.[e] ἀλλαχοῦ μέντοι δίδραχμον ὀνομάζει τοὺς εἴκοσι ὀβολούς.[f] τοῦτο τὸ δίδραχμον καὶ ὁ Κύριος, ὡς πρωτότοκος, ἀπῃτήθη.[g]

VI

Τί δή ποτε τισὶ μὲν τῶν ἱερῶν σκευῶν ὑακίνθινα προσέταξεν ἐπιβληθῆναι καλύμματα, τισὶ δὲ πορφυρᾶ;[a]

---

v A [32], B, C, 4 7 9 10 31 35 37 = 21 mss.

a. Nm 3.40   b. Nm 3.12f.   c. Nm 3.41   d. Nm 3.39, 43   e. Nm 3.46f.
f. Lv 27.25   g. Mt 17.24–27

---

vi A [32], B, C⁻⁵¹, 4 7 9 10 31 35 37 = 20 mss.

a. Nm 4.12–14

V

Why did God order a census of the firstborn of the people?[a]

Some of the others were probably disgruntled at the special treatment accorded to the tribe of Levi whom he had assigned to the divine service and exempted from fighting. Therefore, the Lord God convinced the disgruntled that there was nothing unjust in his orders. "When the firstborn of the Egyptians were slain for your sake," he said, "your firstborn were spared, so in place of them, I have assigned to my service the tribe of Levi[b] and, in place of the firstborn of your cattle, the firstborn of the Levites.'"[c]

But because the firstborn of the other tribes proved to be more numerous than all the Levites,[d] he ordered each of the firstborn in excess of the number of the Levites to give five shekels to the priests. He determined the value of the shekel at twenty obols and called this number "holy" as dedicated to the divine service and not available for each and every use.[e] Elsewhere, however, Scripture gives the name "didrachma" to twenty obols.[f] Even the Lord, as firstborn, was taxed this didrachma.[1g]

VI

Why did he order some of the sacred vessels to be wrapped in a blue, and the others in a purple, cover?[a]

1. Modern scholars dispute the nature of the tax paid by Jesus and Peter; v. B.T. Viviano, "The Gospel according to Matthew," on 17.24–27.

Τῶν τιμιωτέρων ὑακίνθινα μόνα τὰ καλύμματα ἦν·
αἰνίττεται δὲ ἡ χρόα τὸν οὐρανόν. τούτου χάριν τὰ μὲν ἐντὸς
5 τοῦ σκεπάσματος τούτοις τοῖς ἐπιβλήμασιν καλυφθῆναι
προσέταξε, τὰ δὲ ἐκτὸς καὶ πορφυροῖς καὶ τοιούτοις.[b] ὁ μὲν
γὰρ οὐρανὸς τιμωρίας οὐκ ἔχει, ἡ δὲ γῆ διὰ τὰς τῶν νόμων
παραβάσεις δέχεται καὶ κολάσεις. τῆς δὲ βασιλείας ἡ
πορφύρα δηλωτική, θεία δέ, καὶ ἄναρχος, καὶ ἀνώλεθρος ἡ τοῦ
10 Θεοῦ βασιλεία. τούτου χάριν τὰ ἔξω τῆς σκηνῆς καὶ
πορφυροῖς καὶ ὑακινθίνοις ἐπιβλήμασιν ἐκαλύπτετο.
προμηθούμενος δὲ τοῦ δήμου τοῦ Καάθ, προσέταξε πρότερον
τοὺς ἱερέας, εἴσω τῶν ἀδύτων γενομένους, καλύπτειν τὴν
κιβωτὸν καὶ τὰ ἄλλα σκεύη τοῖς προειρημένοις καλύμμασιν,
15 εἶθ' οὕτω τοῦ Καάθ τὸν δῆμον ταῦτα μετακομίζειν ἵνα μή, τὰ
ἄψαυστα καὶ ἀθέατα θεασάμενοι, ἐκ τῆς παραδόξου θέας
ὑπομείνωσιν ὄλεθρον.[c]

VII

Τίνα καλεῖ *ἀκάθαρτον ἐπὶ ψυχῇ;*[a]
Τὸν τοῦ τεθνηκότος ἁψάμενον ἢ ὀστέοις νεκροῦ
πελάσαντα.

VIII

Καὶ τί δή ποτε καὶ τούτους, καὶ τοὺς λεπρούς, καὶ τοὺς
γονορρυεῖς ἔξω τῆς παρεμβολῆς διάγειν ἐκέλευσεν;[a]

b. Nm 4.5–15   c. Nm 4.15

---

vii A [32], B, C, 4 7 9 10 35 37 = 20 mss.

a. Nm 5.2

---

viii A [32], B, c, 52, 4 7 9 10 31 35 37 = 20 mss.

a. Nm 5.1–3

Only the covers of the more precious vessels were blue, a color that suggests heaven. Hence, he ordered the vessels inside the sanctuary covered with these drapes, and those outside with purple and something similar.[1b] Heaven, you see, does not have any punishments, whereas earth admits sanctions because of transgressions of the Law. Purple suggests royalty while the kingdom of God is divine, without beginning or end. Hence, what was outside the tabernacle was covered with both purple and blue drapes. In his concern for the family of Kohath he gave orders that the priests were first to enter the inmost shrine and cover the ark and the other furnishings with the aforementioned coverings; only then were the family of Kohath to carry them away, so they would not see what is not to be touched or seen and suffer destruction for setting eyes on these objects of wonder.[c]

VII

Whom does he call "unclean from a body"?[a]
The one who has touched a dead body or approached the bones of a corpse.

VIII

Why did he command these people, the lepers, and those with a discharge to dwell outside the camp?[1a]

1. The spiritual interpretation of the colors is Theodoret's.

---

1. Again Theodoret sees a moral, rather than a pragmatic, reason for exclusion from proximity to the tabernacle. As an Antiochene, he insists on human responsibility and on accountability, a theme absent from the text on which he is commenting.

Ἀπὸ τῶν σμικρῶν τὰ μεγάλα παιδεύων· εἰ γὰρ ὁ ἁπτόμενος
νεκροῦ ἀκάθαρτος, πολλῷ μᾶλλον ὁ νεκρὸν εἰργασάμενος διὰ
5 μιαιφονίας. καὶ εἰ ὁ λεπρὸς ἀκάθαρτος, πολλῷ μᾶλλον ὁ τὰ
ποικίλα τῆς κακίας ἐργαζόμενος εἴδη. οὕτω διὰ τοῦ
γονορρυοῦς ἡ μοιχεία κατηγορεῖται· εἰ γὰρ τὸ ἀκούσιον
μυσαρόν, πολλῷ δήπουθεν τὸ κατὰ γνώμην τολμώμενον.

IX

Τί ἐστιν *ἀνὴρ ἢ γυνὴ εἴ τις ποιήσει ἀπὸ πασῶν τῶν
ἁμαρτιῶν τῶν ἀνθρωπίνων;*[a]

Τὰ σμικρότερα τῶν ἁμαρτημάτων *ἀνθρώπινα* κέκληκεν,
ἐπειδή, τρεπτὴν οὖσαν τῶν ἀνθρώπων τὴν φύσιν, πάντων
5 ἀπηλλάχθαι τῶν ἁμαρτημάτων οὐχ οἷόν τε· *οὐδείς,* γάρ φησι,
καθαρὸς ἀπὸ ῥύπου, . . . οὐδ' ἂν μία ἡμέρα ἡ ζωὴ αὐτοῦ.[b]
τούτου χάριν καὶ ὁ θεῖος βοᾷ Δαβίδ, *μὴ εἰσέλθῃς εἰς κρίσιν
μετὰ τοῦ δούλου σου, ὅτι οὐ δικαιωθήσεται ἐνώπιόν σου πᾶς
ζῶν.*[c] μόνος γὰρ ὁ δεσπότης Χριστός, καὶ ὡς ἄνθρωπος, τὸ
10 ἄμωμον ἔχει,[d] καὶ τοῦτο προορῶν, ὁ προφήτης Ἡσαΐας ἐβόα,
*ὃς ἁμαρτίαν οὐκ ἐποίησεν, οὐδὲ εὑρέθη δόλος ἐν τῷ στόματι
αὐτοῦ.*[e] τούτου χάριν καὶ τὰς ἄλλων ἁμαρτίας ἀνέλαβεν,
οἰκείας οὐκ ἔχων· οὗτος γάρ φησι, *τὰς ἁμαρτίας ἡμῶν φέρει
καὶ περὶ ἡμῶν ὀδυνᾶται*[f] καὶ ὁ μέγας Ἰωάννης, *ἴδε ὁ ἀμνὸς
15 τοῦ Θεοῦ, ὁ αἴρων τὴν ἁμαρτίαν τοῦ κόσμου.*[g] διὰ τοῦτο καὶ
ἐν νεκροῖς ἐλεύθερος,[h] ὡς ἀδίκως ὑπομείνας τὸν θάνατον.

Διδάσκει τοίνυν ὁ θεῖος νόμος πῶς θεραπευτέον τοὺς τὰ
μέτρια πλημμελήσαντας. κελεύει γὰρ τὸν ἔν τισι συμβολαίοις
ἠδικηκότα πρῶτον ἐξαγορεῦσαι τὴν ἁμαρτίαν, εἶτα τῷ

ιχ A *[32]*, B, c⁻¹, 52, 4 7 9 10 31 35 37 = 19 mss.

a. Nm 5.6   b. Jb 14.4f.   c. Ps 143.2   d. Cf. 2Cor 5.21; 1Pt 2.22; 1Jn 3.5.
e. 1Pt 2.22; Is 53.9   f. Is 53.4   g. Jn 1.29   h. Ps 88.5

He was using issues of little importance to give instruction in the truly significant. If whoever touches a dead body is unclean, much more so is the one who has caused death by committing murder. And if the leper is unclean, much more so is whoever commits evil in all its various shades. Likewise, he indicated the blameworthiness of adultery by mention of the discharge; if the involuntary defiles, presumably a deliberate crime defiles much more.

IX

What is the meaning of "If any man or woman commits one of the human sins"?[a]

By "human" he referred to the lesser sins, since it is not possible for human nature, unstable as it is, to be exempt from all sins. "No one is clear of stain," remember, "not even if his life last but a single day."[b] Hence, the divinely inspired David also cried out, "Do not enter into judgment with your servant, because no one alive will be justified in your sight."[c] As you know, Christ the Lord alone was guiltless, even as man.[d] Foreseeing this, the prophet Isaiah cried out, "He committed no sin, nor was deceit found in his mouth."[e] And so he took on the sins of others, since he had none of his own. As Isaiah declared, "He bears our sins and suffers for us";[f] and the great John, "Behold, the lamb of God, who takes away the sins of the world."[g] Hence, he is also "free among the dead"[h] since he suffered death unjustly.

Therefore, the divine Law teaches how those guilty of moderate transgressions are to be cured. It commands anyone who has broken an agreement first to admit the sin, then to restore what he has

20 ἠδικημένῳ τὸ ληφθὲν ἀποδοῦναι, προστεθεικότα τῷ κεφαλαίῳ
τὸ πέμπτον·ⁱ εἰ δὲ συμβαίη τὸν ἠδικημένον πρὸ τῆς τοῦ
ἠδικηκότος μεταμελείας καταλῦσαι τὸν βίον, ἐκτῖσαι ταῦτα
τῷ ἀγχιστεύοντι. ἀγχιστεύοντα δὲ καλεῖ τὸν τῷ γένει
προσήκοντα. ἡ δὲ τάξις τοῦ γένους αὕτη· πρῶτος υἱός, εἶτα
25 θυγάτηρ, εἶτα ὁ τοῦ πατρὸς ἀδελφός, ἔπειτα ὁ τοῦ πάππου· εἰ
δὲ τούτων μηδεὶς εἴη, ὁ πλησιέστερος συγγενής. εἰ δὲ μὴ
εὑρίσκοιτο συγγενής, τῷ Θεῷ τὰ προρρηθέντα προσενεγκεῖν
διηγόρευσε· τοῦτο γὰρ εἶπεν· *ἐὰν δὲ μὴ ᾖ τῷ ἀνθρώπῳ*
ἀγχιστεύων ὥστε ἀποδοῦναι αὐτῷ τὸ πλημμέλημα τὸ πρὸς
30 *αὐτόν, τὸ πλημμέλημα τὸ ἀποδιδόμενον τῷ Κυρίῳ τῷ ἱερεῖ*
ἔσται, πλὴν τοῦ κριοῦ τοῦ ἱλασμοῦ, δι' οὗ ἐξιλάσεται περὶ
*αὐτοῦ ἐν αὐτῷ.*ʲ

Προσέταξε δὲ καὶ τὰς προσφερομένας ἀπαρχὰς τοὺς
ἱερέας ἐσθίειν· ἀπαρχαὶ γὰρ ἦσαν τοῦ μὲν λαοῦ οἱ λευῖται,
35 τῶν δὲ λευιτῶν οἱ ἱερεῖς. ὡς ἀπαρχαὶ τοίνυν, τὰς ἀπαρχὰς
ἐκομίζοντο.ᵏ

X

Διὰ τί ἄλευρον κρίθινον ὑπὸ τῆς ὑποπτευομένης
μοιχευθῆναι προσεκομίζετο;

(1) Αὐτὸς ὁ δεσπότης ἡρμήνευσεν· *ἔστιν γάρ, ἔφη, θυσία*
ζηλοτυπίας, θυσία μνημοσύνου, θυσία ἀναμιμνήσκουσα
5 *ἁμαρτίαν.*ᵃ ὅθεν οὐδὲ ἔλαιον αὐτὴν οὐδὲ λίβανον ἔχειν
προσέταξεν· ἐστέρητο γὰρ καὶ τῆς εὐωδίας καὶ τοῦ τῆς
δικαιοσύνης φωτός.

Τοῦτο μέντοι γίνεσθαι νενομοθέτηκεν ὁ δεσπότης Θεός,

---

i. Nm 5.6f.   j. Nm 5.8   k. Nm 5.9f.

---

x A *[32]*, B, C⁻¹, 4 7 9 10 31 35 37 = 20 mss.

a. Nm 5.15

stolen plus one-fifth to the party he has wronged.[i] If the wronged party happens to have departed from this life before the repentance of the wrongdoer, restitution is to be made to the next of kin. By "next of kin" the Law refers to a member of his family. Now, this is the order of precedence in the family: first a son, then a daughter, then the father's brother, then the grandfather's brother, and in the absence of these, the closest relative. But in cases where no relative is to be found, he ordained that the aforementioned restitution be offered to God: "If the person has no next of kin to whom restitution may be made for the sin against him, the reparation made to the Lord will be for the priest in addition to the ram of atonement through which atonement is made for him."[j]

He also ordered the priests to eat the offerings of first-fruits. The Levites, you see, were the first-fruits of the people, and the priests the first-fruits of the Levites. Thus, as first-fruits, they received the first-fruits.[k]

X

Why did women who were under suspicion of adultery offer barley meal?

(1) The Lord himself gave the explanation: "It is a sacrifice of jealousy, a sacrifice of remembrance, a sacrifice to recall sin."[a] Hence, he ordered that it contain neither oil nor incense; it was to be devoid of sweet odor and the light of righteousness.[1]

The Lord God set down this law with full knowledge of their

1. Theodoret again supplies a spiritualizing gloss. Here he does not proceed to comment unfavorably on the bias in favor of men as he had in his commentary on 1Cor 7.3f.: "Human laws, you know, enjoin continence on wives and prescribe punishment for those who transgress, though they do not require the same continence of husbands; men, the makers of the law, with no concern for equality, granted themselves license."

τὴν μιαιφόνον αὐτῶν ἐπιστάμενος γνώμην. ἵνα γὰρ μὴ ἐξ
10 ὑποψίας κατακτείνωσι τὰς ὁμοζύγας, ἐκέλευσε τὴν
ὑποπτευομένην αὐτῷ προσενεχθῆναι, ἅτε δὴ πάντα σαφῶς
ἐπισταμένῳ καὶ τὰ λάθρα γινόμενα· *προσάξει . . ., γάρ φησιν,
ὁ ἱερεύς, καὶ στήσει τὴν γυναῖκα ἔναντι Κυρίου, καὶ λήψεται
ὁ ἱερεὺς ὕδωρ καθαρὸν ζῶν ἔναντι Κυρίου ἐν ἀγγείῳ ὀστρακίνῳ*
15 *καὶ τῆς γῆς τῆς οὔσης ἐπὶ τοῦ ἐδάφους τῆς σκηνῆς τοῦ*
μαρτυρίου, καὶ λαβὼν ὁ ἱερεὺς ἐμβαλεῖ εἰς τὸ ὕδωρ· καὶ
στήσει ὁ ἱερεὺς τὴν γυναῖκα ἔναντι Κυρίου, καὶ ἀποκαλύψει
τὴν κεφαλὴν τῆς γυναικός, καὶ δώσει ἐπὶ τῶν χειρῶν αὐτῆς
τὴν θυσίαν τοῦ μνημοσύνου, τὴν θυσίαν τῆς ζηλοτυπίας. ἐν
20 *δὲ τῇ χειρὶ τοῦ ἱερέως ἔσται τὸ ὕδωρ τοῦ ἐλεγμοῦ τοῦ*
ἐπικαταρωμένου τούτου.[b]

(2) Ταῦτα δὲ πάντα γενέσθαι προσέταξε, τὴν γυναῖκα τὴν
ὑποπτευομένην ἐκδειματῶν ἵν', εἰ ἐξήμαρτεν, ὁμολογήσῃ καὶ
διὰ μετανοίας λάβῃ τὴν ἄφεσιν. τούτου χάριν ἀκάλυπτον
25 αὐτὴν τῷ Θεῷ προσενεχθῆναι κελεύει, διδάσκων ὅτι γυμνὰ
πάντα καὶ τετραχηλισμένα ἐνώπιον αὐτοῦ,[c] καὶ οὐδὲν αὐτὸν
λέληθε τῶν παρ' ἡμῶν γιγνομένων. ὅτι δὲ ταῦτα δεδιττόμενος
αὐτὴν γενέσθαι κεκέλευκε τὰ ἑξῆς δηλοῖ· *καὶ ὁρκιεῖ αὐτὴν ὁ*
ἱερεὺς καὶ ἐρεῖ τῇ γυναικί, εἰ μὴ κεκοίμηταί τις μετὰ σοῦ, εἰ
30 *μὴ παραβέβηκας μιανθῆναι ὑπὸ τὸν ἄνδρα τὸν σεαυτῆς, ἀθῷος*
ἴσθι ἀπὸ τοῦ ὕδατος τοῦ ἐλεγμοῦ τοῦ ἐπικαταρωμένου τούτου.
εἰ δὲ σὺ παραβέβηκας, ὕπανδρος οὖσα, ἢ σὺ μεμίανσαι, ἢ
ἔδωκέ τις τὴν κοίτην ἐν σοὶ πλὴν τοῦ ἀνδρός σου, . . . δῴη σε
Κύριος ἐν ἀρᾷ καὶ ἐνόρκιον ἐν μέσῳ τοῦ λαοῦ σου, ἐν τῷ
35 *δοῦναι Κύριον τὸν μηρόν σου διαπεπτωκότα, καὶ τὴν κοιλίαν*
σου πεπρησμένην.[d] ἐκέλευσε δὲ καὶ τὴν γυναῖκα συντίθεσθαι

l. 23 ὁμολογήσῃ C⁻¹⁵, 4 9 10 31 35 : ὁμολογήσει Sir. Sch. F.M. Cf. the
coördinated λάβῃ. In the *Quaest. in oct.* there are 149 occurences of ἵνα + a
clause that are Thdt.'s own words, rather than a quotation of Scripture. Only in
this one does the Madrid ed. print the future indicative rather than a
subjunctive or optative; it thus seems more consistent to suppose an error of
etacism.

b. Nm 5.16–18 (LXX var.)   c. Heb 4.13   d. Nm 5.19f., 21

murderous character. To prevent them from killing their partners on mere suspicion, he bade women under suspicion be brought to him, as he has precise knowledge of everything, even of what happens in secret. As Scripture says, "The priest will bring the woman forward and set her before the Lord. Then the priest will bring fresh running water before the Lord in an earthenware jar and take some of the dust on the floor of the tabernacle of witness and put it into the water. Then the priest will set the woman before the Lord, uncover the woman's head, and put in her hands the sacrifice of remembrance, the sacrifice of jealousy, and the priest will hold in his hand the water of accusation that brings a curse."[b]

(2) He ordered the performance of this rite to frighten the woman under suspicion so that, if guilty, she would confess and, through repentance, gain forgiveness. She was to be brought unveiled to the Lord to teach us that everything is naked and open before God,[c] and that nothing we do escapes his notice. The sequel shows that this command was meant to frighten her: "The priest will adjure her and say to the woman, 'If no one has slept with you, if you have not transgressed so as to be defiled while subject to your own husband, be unharmed by the water of accusation that brings a curse. But if, while subject to your husband, you have transgressed and become defiled, or someone other than your husband has slept with you, may the Lord make you accursed and an oath among your people when the Lord makes your thigh rot and your belly swell.'"[d] Furthermore, he

τῇ ἀρᾷ καὶ λεγείν, *γένοιτο γένοιτο·* καὶ γραφῆναι δὲ τὴν ἀρὰν
προσέταξε, καὶ ἐξαλειφθῆναι ὕδατι, καὶ πιεῖν τὴν γυναῖκα τὸ
ὕδωρ· πρότερον δὲ τὴν θυσίαν προσενεχθῆναι, τουτέστι, τὸ
40 κρίθινον ἄλευρον. εἶτα διδάσκει ὡς, ἀθῷος μὲν οὖσα, ὑγιὴς
φυλαχθήσεται· ἔνοχος δὲ οὖσα καὶ κρύπτουσα, τῇ πείρᾳ
μαθήσεται τῆς ἀρᾶς τὴν ἰσχύν, καὶ τῆς κοιλίας
διαρρηγνυμένης, καὶ τοῦ μηροῦ διαπίπτοντος.[e] δι' ὧν γὰρ ἡ
ἁμαρτία, διὰ τούτων ἡ τιμωρία.

45 Τὸ δὲ ἐνόρκιον οὕτω νοητέον· ὅταν τις δεινὰ καὶ ἀνήκεστα
πάθῃ, εἰώθασί τινες ὀμνύοντες λέγειν, μὴ πάθοιμι ἃ ὁ δεῖνα
πέπονθεν.

XI

Τί ἐστιν ὃς ἂν μεγάλως εὔξηται εὐχὴν ἀφαγνίσασθαι
ἀγνείαν τῷ Κυρίῳ;[a]

(1) Πολλὰ τῆς ἐπαγγελίας εἴδη. οἱ μὲν γὰρ θυσίας
ἐπηγγέλλοντο, οἱ δὲ χρήματα, οἱ δὲ ἑαυτούς· οἱ δὲ ῥητῶν
5 ἡμερῶν ἀριθμὸν μὴ πιεῖν οἶνον, μὴ κείρασθαι τὴν κεφαλήν.
τοιοῦτοι ἦσαν περὶ ὧν ὁ θεῖος εἶπεν Ἰάκωβος τῷ θεσπεσίῳ
Παύλῳ, *εἰσί τινες εὐχὴν ἔχοντες ἐφ' ἑαυτοῖς· τούτους
παραλαβών, ἁγνίσθητι σὺν αὐτοῖς καὶ δαπάνησον ἐπ' αὐτούς,*[b]
τουτέστι, τὰς ὑπὲρ αὐτῶν προσφερομένας κατὰ νόμον θυσίας
10 σὺ πάρασχε ἵνα λύσῃς τὴν ὑποψίαν. περὶ τούτων ἐνταῦθα ὁ
νόμος διαγορεύει καὶ κελεύει τοὺς ταύτην ὑπισχνουμένους
τὴν ἐπαγγελίαν καὶ ὄξους ἀπέχεσθαι, καὶ σταφυλῆς, καὶ
στεμφύλων πάσας τῆς εὐχῆς τὰς ἡμέρας·[c] εὐχὴν δὲ καλεῖ τὴν
ὑπόσχεσιν· καὶ τὴν κεφαλὴν μὴ κείρασθαι ἕως ἂν πληρωθῶσιν

---

e. Nm 5.23–28

xi A *[32]*, B, c⁻¹, 52, 4 7 9 10 31 35 37 = 19 mss.

a. Nm 6.2   b. Acts 21.23f.   c. Nm 6.1–4

commanded the woman to endorse the curse and say, "So be it, So be it." Then he ordered the curse to be written down and washed off with water and that the woman drink the water after offering her sacrifice, that is to say, the barley flour. He explained that if she was innocent, she would be kept safe and sound, but if she was guilty and denied it, she would learn by experience the force of the curse when her belly split open and her thigh rotted.[e] The punishment was to fall on those members by which she had sinned.

Now, this is what it means "to be an oath." When someone suffers a dire, intolerable fate, people often say when swearing, "May I not suffer what so-and-so has suffered."

XI

What is the meaning of "whoever makes a great vow to consecrate holiness to the Lord"?[a]

(1) There are many kinds of promises. Some people promised sacrifices, others money, others even themselves, and still others not to drink wine or cut their hair for a specified number of days. St. James was speaking of the latter when he said to the divinely inspired Paul, "There are some people who have taken a vow upon themselves; join them, and go through the rite of purification with them, and meet their expenses";[b] that is, "eliminate suspicion by providing the sacrifices prescribed for them by the Law." The law regarding these people commanded those making this promise to abstain from alcoholic drink made from grapes or the residue of pressed grapes all the days of the vow[c] (the word "vow" refers to the promise) and not to cut their hair until the completion of all the

15 αἱ ἡμέραι ὅσας ηὔξατο τῷ Κυρίῳ. ἅγιον δὲ καλεῖ τὸν
τρέφοντα κόμην, ὡς τῷ Θεῷ τὴν κόμην ἀφιερώσαντα· τοῦτο
γὰρ εἶπεν· ἅγιος ἔσται, τρέφων κόμην τρίχα κεφαλῆς πάσας
τὰς ἡμέρας τῆς εὐχῆς αὐτοῦ τῷ Κυρίῳ,ᵈ ἀντὶ τοῦ· ἃς
ἀφιέρωσας τῷ Θεῷ μὴ κείρῃς ἕως ἂν δῷς τῇ ὑποσχέσει τὸ
20 πέρας.

Κελεύει δὲ αὐτὸν μὴ πατρὶ τετελευτηκότι πελάζειν, μὴ
ἀδελφῷ, μὴ ἑτέρῳ τινί·ᵉ κἂν γὰρ ἐξαπίνης, φησί, τελευτήσαντός
τινος, παρεῖναι τοῦτον συμβῇ, ἀνάγκη πᾶσαν ἀφελεῖν τὴν
τρίχα, καὶ οὐ τῇ πρώτῃ μόνον ἡμέρᾳ, ἀλλὰ καὶ τῇ ἑβδόμῃ ἵνα
25 καὶ αἱ διαφυγοῦσαι τὸν ξυρὸν τρίχες, ἐν ταῖς ἑπτὰ αὐξηθεῖσαι
ἡμέραις, περιαιρεθῶσιν·ᶠ ἔπειτα τῇ ὀγδόῃ, δύο τρυγόνας
προσενεγκεῖν, τὴν μὲν περὶ ἁμαρτίας, τὴν δὲ εἰς ὁλοκαύτωσιν,
καὶ ἀμνὸν ἕνα περὶ πλημμελείας.ᵍ ἐντεῦθεν δὲ μανθάνομεν
ἀκριβέστερον ὡς περὶ πλημμελείας τὴν τῶν ἀκουσίων
30 ἁμαρτημάτων καλεῖ· ἀκούσιον γὰρ καὶ τὸ τούτῳ συμβάν·
ἐξαπίνης γάρ τινος τελευτήσαντος, ὑπέμεινε μολυσμόν. ἄνωθεν
δὲ αὐτὸν ἀριθμῆσαι κελεύει τὸν τῶν ἐπηγγελμένων ἡμερῶν
ἀριθμόν· ἀλόγιστοι, γάρ φησιν, ἔσονται αὐτῶν αἱ πρότεραι
ἡμέραι, ὅτι ἐμιάνθη ἡ κεφαλὴ τῆς εὐχῆς αὐτοῦ.ʰ

35 (2) Ἐδίδαξε δὲ καὶ τίνας προσήκει θυσίας προσενεγκεῖν
τὸν τοῦ ἁγνισμοῦ τὴν ἐπαγγελίαν πεπληρωκότα· ἀμνὸν μὲν
εἰς ὁλοκαύτωσιν, ἀμνάδα δὲ ὑπὲρ ἁμαρτίας· θήλεα γὰρ τὰ
ὑπὲρ ἁμαρτίας ἱερεῖα, ἐπειδὴ χαυνουμένου τοῦ λογικοῦ, ἡ
ἁμαρτία τολμᾶται. καὶ μέντοι καὶ κριὸν ἄμωμον εἰς σωτηρίαν
40 καὶ κανοῦν ἀζύμων προσενεγκεῖν διηγόρευσεν, εἶτα, τῆς
θυσίας ἐπιτελουμένης, τὰς τρίχας ἐπιθεῖναι τῇ θυσίᾳ τοῦ
σωτηρίου. ὁ δὲ βραχίων ὁ ἑφθός, ὁ ἐπιτιθέμενος ταῖς τοῦ
εὐξαμένου χερσὶ καὶ παρὰ τοῦ ἱερέως λαμβανόμενος, δηλοῖ
τελεσθεῖσαν τὴν ἐπηγγελμένην πρᾶξιν· πράξεως γὰρ
45 γεγενημένης ὁ ἑφθὸς βραχίων δηλωτικός.ⁱ

---

d. Nm 6.5f. e. Nm 6.6f. f. Nm 6.9 g. Nm 6.10–12 h. Nm 6.12
i. Nm 6.14–20

days vowed to the Lord. It referred to the man who was growing his hair long as "holy," since he had dedicated his hair to God. As Scripture says, "Holy will be the man who lets the locks of hair on his head grow long all the days of his vow to the Lord";[d] that is, "Do not cut the hair you have dedicated to God until you have fulfilled your promise."

It forbade him to go near a dead father, brother, or anyone else who had died.[e] If someone died suddenly, and he happened to be present, he must shear all his hair, not only on the first day but also on the seventh, so that even the hairs that had escaped the razor and grown in those seven days would also be removed.[f] Then, on the eighth day, he was to offer two turtle-doves, one as a sin offering, the other as a holocaust, and a lamb as a guilt offering.[g] This provides very explicit evidence that by "guilt offering" the Law referred to the sacrifice offered for voluntary sins, since the event was quite involuntary, as he had incurred defilement through someone's sudden death.[1] It commanded him to begin the promised number of days all over again: "Their former days will not count because the consecrated head has been defiled."[h]

(2) It also gave instructions regarding the victims to be offered by a person who had fulfilled the promise of consecration: a male lamb as a holocaust and a ewe-lamb as a sin offering—a female victim as a sin offering because the commission of sin presupposes a weakness of the rational faculty. Further, it prescribed the offering of a flawless ram as a peace offering and a basket of unleavened bread. As this sacrifice was being performed, the hair was to be placed on the peace offering. The limb that was cooked, then placed in the hands of the man who had made the vow, and then taken by the priest signified the completion of the promised action, since the cooked limb was symbolic of the fulfillment of the undertaking.[i]

---

1. Again, we note Theodoret's concern that his readers grasp their greater accountability for voluntary faults.

The Questions on Numbers

Ταῦτα δέ, οὐ μάτην νενομοθέτηκεν, ἀλλ' ἀκριβείας
ἐπιμελεῖσθαι διδάσκων, καὶ μήτε, ὡς ἔτυχεν, ἐπαγγέλλεσθαι
καί, ὑπισχνουμένους, τὰ ἐπηγγελμένα πληροῦν. παιδεύει δὲ
καὶ ἡμᾶς διὰ τούτων καὶ τὸν ἁγιασμὸν φυλάττειν ἀμόλυντον·
50 ὁ γὰρ κηλῖδα δεχόμενος, τῆς ἄνωθεν δεῖται καθάρσεως καὶ
τῆς διὰ μετανοίας τῶν μολυσμῶν ἀφαιρέσεως. τοῦτο γὰρ καὶ
γαλάταις ἐπιστέλλων, ὁ μακάριος ἔλεγε Παῦλος· τεκνία μου,
οὓς πάλιν ὠδίνω ἄχρις οὗ μορφωθῇ Χριστὸς ἐν ὑμῖν.ʲ

(3) Μετὰ ταῦτα διδάσκει πῶς εὐλογεῖν προσήκει τοὺς
55 ἱερέας, καὶ ὡς τὸ θεῖον ὄνομα χορηγεῖ τοῖς προσιοῦσιν
εὐλογίαν· ἐπιθήσουσι, γάρ φησι, τὸ ὄνομά μου ἐπὶ τοὺς υἱοὺς
Ἰσραήλ, καὶ ἐγὼ Κύριος εὐλογήσω αὐτούς.ᵏ λέγει δὲ καὶ αὐτὰ
τῆς εὐλογίας τὰ ῥήματα· εὐλογήσαι σε Κύριος καὶ φυλάξαι
σε· ἐπιφάναι Κύριος τὸ πρόσωπον αὐτοῦ ἐπὶ σὲ καὶ ἐλεήσαι
60 σε· ἐπάραι Κύριος τὸ πρόσωπον αὐτοῦ ἐπὶ σοὶ καὶ δῴη σοι
εἰρήνην.ˡ διδασκόμεθα δὲ διὰ τούτων ὡς χρὴ πρότερον τοῖς
εὐλογημένοις τὰς θείας αἰτεῖν δωρεάς· τοῦτο γὰρ σημαίνει τὸ
εὐλογῆσαι σε· εἶτα τὰ διδόμενα φυλαχθῆναι· ἐπήγαγε γάρ,
καὶ φυλάξαι σε. ἡ δὲ δευτέρα εὐλογία τὴν τοῦ Θεοῦ καὶ
65 σωτῆρος ἡμῶν ἐπιφάνειαν προθεσπίζει· ἐπιφάναι, γάρ φησιν,
τὸ πρόσωπον αὐτοῦ ἐπὶ σὲ καὶ ἐλεήσαι σε· ἐλέου γὰρ μεστὴ ἡ
κατὰ σάρκα τοῦ Θεοῦ καὶ σωτῆρος ἡμῶν οἰκονομία. διὸ καὶ
τὰς πρὸς Θεὸν ἡμῖν καταλλαγὰς ἐδωρήσατο· τοῦτο γὰρ ἡ
ἑξῆς εὐλογία διδάσκει· ἐπάραι Κύριος τὸ πρόσωπον αὐτοῦ ἐπὶ
70 σοὶ καὶ δῴη σοι εἰρήνην. περὶ ταύτης τῆς εἰρήνης καὶ ὁ
μακάριος ἔφη Παῦλος, αὐτὸς γάρ ἐστιν ἡ εἰρήνη ἡμῶν, ὁ
ποιήσας τὰ ἀμφότερα ἓν καὶ τὸ μεσότοιχον τοῦ φραγμοῦ
λύσας τὴν ἔχθραν ἐν τῇ σαρκὶ αὐτοῦ.ᵐ

Ταῦτα περὶ τῆς εὐλογίας διαλεχθεὶς ὁ προφήτης καὶ
75 διηγησάμενος ὅπως καὶ τὴν σκηνὴν ἔχρισεⁿ καὶ τίνα οἱ
φύλαρχοι προσεκόμισαν,ᵒ ἐδίδαξεν ὅπως θείαν φωνὴν τοῖς
ὠσὶν εἰσεδέξατο ἐκ τοῦ ἱλαστηρίου φερομένην, ὃ ἐπέκειτο μὲν

j. Gal 4.19   k. Nm 6.27   l. Nm 6.24–26   m. Eph 2.14   n. Nm 7.1
o. Nm 7.2–88

It was not without purpose that he ordained these laws. Indeed, he was instructing people to be precise in their accounting: to avoid making rash promises and to fulfil their vows whenever they did make a promise. With this law, he instructs us as well to keep holiness undefiled, since the person receiving a blemish must be purified from above and freed from defilement through repentance. St. Paul said as much in his letter to the Galatians: "My children, for whom I am suffering birth pangs again until Christ be formed in you."[j]

(3) Next he teaches how the priests are to bless the people, and how the divine name confers a blessing on those who draw near: "They shall put my name on the children of Israel, and I the Lord shall bless them."[k] He also speaks the precise words of the blessing: "The Lord bless you and keep you; the Lord make his face shine on you and be gracious to you; the Lord lift up his countenance upon you and give you peace."[l] Now, we learn from this that one must first beg the divine gifts for those who have been blessed (this is the sense of "bless you"); then beg that what has been given be preserved (hence, his addition of "keep you"). The second blessing foretells the manifestation of our God and Savior: "The Lord make his face shine on you and be gracious to you." As you know, the Incarnation of our God and Savior according to the flesh is replete with grace, as he granted us reconciliation with God. In fact, we learn this from the following blessing, "The Lord lift up his countenance upon you and give you peace." Of this peace St. Paul said, "For he is our peace, making the two one and in his flesh breaking down the dividing wall of hostility."[m]

After discoursing on the blessing and recounting his consecration of the tabernacle[n] and the offerings brought by the tribal leaders,[o] the prophet disclosed how he had heard with his own ears the divine voice issuing from the mercy seat, which was placed on the

τῇ κιβωτῷ, ταῖς δὲ τῶν χερουβὶμ συνεκαλύπτετο πτέρυξι.[p]
ταῦτα δέ, οὐ φιλοτιμούμενος γέγραφεν, ἀλλὰ διδάσκων ὡς
80 ἐκεῖθεν τοῖς ἀρχιερεῦσιν, ἅπαξ τοῦ ἐνιαυτοῦ εἰσιοῦσι,[q] τὴν
οἰκείαν ἐπιδείξει δόξαν ὁ δεσπότης Θεὸς ὅπως ἦν ἰδεῖν οἷά
τε τῶν ἀνθρώπων ἡ φύσις.

XII

Τί δή ποτε τοὺς λευίτας ἁγιασθῆναι κελεύσας, ἅπαν τὸ
σῶμα τῶν τριχῶν γυμνωθῆναι προσέταξεν;[a]
Αἱ τρίχες τῆς νεκρώσεως σύμβολον· νεκραὶ γὰρ αὗται καὶ
ὀδύνης αἴσθησιν οὐ δεχόμεναι. τὴν ἀληθῆ τοίνυν ζωὴν ἔχειν
5 κελεύει τοὺς τῷ Θεῷ λειτουργοῦντας καὶ μηδὲν νεκρὸν ἔχειν
μηδὲ δυσῶδες. τοῦτο καὶ ὁ θεσπέσιος ἡμᾶς διδάσκει Παῦλος·
Χριστῷ, γάρ φησι, *συνεσταύρωμαι· ζῶ δὲ οὐκέτι ἐγώ, ζῇ δὲ ἐν
ἐμοὶ Χριστός*.[b] ταῖς γὰρ θείαις, φησί, ἐνεργείαις ἐμαυτὸν
ἀφιέρωσα.

XIII

Διὰ τί μετὰ πέμπτον καὶ εἰκοστὸν ἔτος μέχρι τοῦ
πεντηκοστοῦ λειτουργεῖν τοὺς λευίτας κελεύει;[a]
Ἐπειδὴ ἡ μὲν πρώτη ἡλικία τελείαν οὐκ ἔχει τῶν ἀγαθῶν
καὶ κακῶν τὴν διάκρισιν, ἡ τελευταία δὲ ἀσθενέστερον ἔχει
5 τὸ σῶμα. ἀποκρίνει τοίνυν καὶ τὴν νεότητα καὶ τὸ γῆρας· τὴν

---

p. Nm 7.89   q. Lv 16.34

---

xii A [32], B, C, 4 7 9 10 31 35 37 = 21 mss.

a. Nm 8.7   b. Gal 2.19f.

---

xiii A [32], B, C, 4 7 9 10 31 35 37 = 21 mss.

a. Nm 8.24–26

ark and covered by the wings of the cherubim.[p] He wrote this, not out of self-glorification, but rather to indicate that it was there that, when they entered the Holy of Holies once a year,[q] the Lord God would reveal his glory to the high priests—at least, so far as human nature was capable of seeing it.

XII

Why, after commanding the sanctification of the Levites, did he order them to be stripped of all the hair on their bodies?[a]

Hair is a symbol of death, as hair is lifeless, with no sense of pain. But he commands those serving God to have true life and keep nothing lifeless or evil-smelling. The divinely inspired Paul also teaches us this: "I have been crucified with Christ. It is no longer I that live, but Christ lives in me";[b] that is, "I have consecrated myself to the power that comes from God."

XIII

Why did he enjoin that the service of the Levites begin at age twenty-five and end at age fifty?[a]

Because at the beginning of life, one does not yet possess a mature discernment of good and evil, and at the end, the body is weaker. So he disqualified both youth and old age, the former because of

μὲν διὰ τὸ ἀτελὲς τῆς ψυχῆς, τὸ δὲ διὰ τὸ τοῦ σώματος ἀσθενές.

XIV

Τίνος χάριν οὐκ ἠδύναντο ἐπιτελέσαι τὸ Πάσχα οἱ ἀκάθαρτοι ἐπὶ ψυχῇ;[a]

Συνῆπται ἡ αἰτία τῇ παραιτήσει· ὡς γὰρ ἀπὸ κήδους ὄντες καί τινας τῶν οἰκείων ταφῇ παραδεδωκότες, ἀκάθαρτοι κατὰ
5 τὴν τοῦ νόμου διαγόρευσιν ἦσαν. δεδιότες τοίνυν μή, τοῦ Πάσχα πληροῦντες τὴν ἐντολήν, παραβῶσι τὴν περὶ τῶν ἀκαθάρτων κειμένην καὶ ἀντινομίᾳ περιπέσωσι, τὴν αἰτίαν τὸν νομοθέτην ἐδίδαξαν. ἀλλ' οὐδὲ οὗτος ἐτόλμησεν ἀποκρίνασθαι ἕως τὸν δεσπότην ἠρώτησε. ταύτῃ γὰρ τῇ πλημμελείᾳ Ἰησοῦς
10 ὁ τοῦ Ναυῆ περιπέπτωκε, πρὸ τῆς ἐρωτήσεως τοὺς γαβαωνίτας δεξάμενος.[b] προσέταξε τοίνυν ὁ δεσπότης Θεὸς τοὺς τῷ μιασμῷ τούτῳ περιπίπτοντας ἢ πόρρωθεν οἰκοῦντας καὶ τούτου χάριν τῇ τεσσαρεσκαιδεκάτῃ τοῦ πρώτου μηνὸς ἐπιτελέσαι τὸ Πάσχα μὴ δυναμένους τῇ τεσσαρεσκαιδεκάτῃ
15 τοῦ δευτέρου μηνὸς ἐπιτελέσαι τὸ Πάσχα·[c]

Ἐκέλευσε δὲ καὶ τοὺς προσηλύτους τῶν ἴσων μεταλαχεῖν· νόμος, γάρ φησιν, εἷς ἔσται ὑμῖν· καὶ τῷ προσηλύτῳ καὶ τῷ αὐτόχθονι τῆς γῆς.[d] διὰ δὲ τούτων, τῶν ἐθνῶν προμηνύει τὴν κλῆσιν.

---

xiv A *[32]*, B, C, 4 7 9 10 31 35 37 = 21 mss.

a. Nm 9.6–11   b. Jos 9.3–15   c. Nm 9.10f.   d. Nm 9.14

the immaturity of the soul, the latter because of the weakness of the body.

XIV

Why were those who were unclean because of contact with a corpse unable to celebrate the Passover?[a]

The reason is attached to their request for exemption. They were unclean by declaration of the Law, as they were just coming out of mourning after consigning family members to the grave. Since they were afraid that, in carrying out the command regarding Passover, they would transgress the law about the unclean and become ensnared in a conflict between two laws, they explained their case to the lawgiver. Not even he, however, presumed to give a reply until he had consulted the Lord. As you recall, that was precisely the fault committed by Joshua son of Nun, who made a pact with the Gibeonites without asking for guidance.[1b] The Lord God, then, gave orders that Passover be celebrated on the fourteenth day of the second month by those who had incurred this defilement and those who lived at a distance and were therefore unable to celebrate Passover on the fourteenth day of the first month.[c]

He also commanded that aliens have an equal share in the celebration: "There is to be one law for you, both alien and native."[d] In this he foreshadowed the calling of the nations.

1. Jos 9.3–15 recounts how the Gibeonites deceived Joshua into granting them an ill-considered exemption from the ban. Theodoret uses Joshua's haste as a foil for Moses' exemplary prudence in pausing to request divine guidance on a difficult legal question.

XV

Πῶς νοητέον τὸ σημασίᾳ σαλπιεῖτε ἐν τῇ ἐξάρσει ὑμῶν·
καὶ ὅταν συναγάγητε τὴν συναγωγήν, σαλπιεῖτε καὶ οὐ
σημασίᾳ;[a]

Ὁ πάνσοφος λέγει Παῦλος, ἐὰν μὴ εὔσημον σάλπιγξ φωνὴν
5 δῷ, τίς παρασκευάσεται εἰς πόλεμον;[b] διαφοραὶ τοίνυν ἦσαν
ἠχῆς, καὶ ἡ μὲν τὴν ἀνάπαυλαν, ἡ δὲ τὴν ὁδοιπορίαν ἐδήλουν·
καὶ μία μὲν ἠχοῦσα σάλπιγξ ἐκάλει τοὺς ἄρχοντας, αἱ δὲ δύο
τὸν λαὸν καὶ τοὺς ἄρχοντας.[c] τὸ μέντοι σαλπίζειν μόνοις
ἀπενεμήθη τοῖς ἱερεῦσιν, ἐπειδὴ τοῦ Θεοῦ τὴν κλῆσιν ἡ
10 σάλπιγξ ἐμήνυε·[d] τοῦτο γὰρ ἐπήγαγε· ἐάν... ἐξέλθητε εἰς
πόλεμον ἐν τῇ γῇ ὑμῶν πρὸς τοὺς ὑπεναντίους, τοὺς
ἀνθεστηκότας ὑμῖν, καὶ σημανεῖτε ταῖς σάλπιγξιν, καὶ
ἀναμνησθήσεσθε ἔναντι Κυρίου, καὶ διασωθήσεσθε ἀπὸ τῶν
ἐχθρῶν ὑμῶν. καὶ ἐν ταῖς ἡμέραις τῆς εὐφροσύνης ὑμῶν, καὶ
15 ἐν ταῖς ἑορταῖς ὑμῶν, καὶ ἐν ταῖς νεομηνίαις ὑμῶν, σαλπιεῖτε
ταῖς σάλπιγξιν ἐπὶ τοῖς ὁλοκαυτώμασι καὶ ἐπὶ ταῖς θυσίαις
τῶν σωτηρίων ὑμῶν, καὶ ἔσται ὑμῖν ἀνάμνησις ἐναντίον τοῦ
Θεοῦ ὑμῶν· ἐγὼ Κύριος ὁ Θεὸς ὑμῶν.[e] ἐπειδὴ γάρ, νομοθετῶν ὁ
Θεὸς ἐν τῷ Σινᾷ ὄρει, μεγίστη σαλπίγγων ἠχῇ τὰς ἀκοὰς
20 αὐτῶν κατεκτύπησε,[f] τῆς ἐπιφανείας αὐτοὺς ἐκείνης
ἀναμιμνήσκει διὰ τῆς τῶν σαλπίγγων ἠχῆς· ὅθεν ὁ μακάριος
Δαβὶδ μελῳδῶν ἔφη, σαλπίσατε ἐν νεομηνίᾳ σάλπιγγι, ἐν
εὐσήμῳ ἡμέρᾳ ἑορτῆς ὑμῶν.[g]

Διὰ δὲ τούτων καὶ ἡμεῖς διδασκόμεθα, πᾶσαν ἀθροίζοντες
||10 25 τοῦ λαοῦ τὴν συναγωγήν, σαλπίζειν καὶ οὐ|| σημασίᾳ· ἀσήμως
γὰρ διὰ τοὺς ἀμυήτους περὶ τῶν θείων διαλεγόμεθα
μυστηρίων. τούτων δὲ χωριζομένων, σαφῶς τοὺς μεμυημένους
διδάσκομεν.

---

xv A [32], B, C⁻⁵¹, 4 7 9 10(inc.) 31 35 37 = 20 mss.

a. Nm 10.6f.   b. 1Cor 14.8   c. Nm 10.3f.   d. Nm 10.8   e. Nm 10.9f.
f. Ex 19.16   g. Ps 81.3

Question xv

XV

How are we to understand the verse, "You shall sound an alarm on the trumpet when you move out; when you summon an assembly, you shall sound the trumpet but no alarm"?[a]

Paul in his great wisdom declares, "Unless the trumpet give a clear signal, who will prepare for battle?"[b] So there were different sounds, one that signaled resting, another traveling. The blast of a single trumpet summoned the leaders, two trumpets the people and the leaders.[c] The sounding of the trumpet was assigned to the priests alone, because the trumpet blast revealed the call of God.[d] In fact, he went on, "If you go out to war in your land against adversaries who have risen against you, you shall sound the trumpet, and you will be remembered before the Lord, and you will be saved from your foes. Also on your days of rejoicing, your feasts, and your new moons, you shall sound the trumpets over your holocausts and over your peace-offerings, and they will be for you a reminder before your God. I am the Lord your God."[e] Since, in giving the Law on Mount Sinai, God had made a mighty sound of trumpets ring in their ears,[f] he reminded them of that manifestation through trumpet blasts. Hence, the blessed David sang, "Sound the trumpet on the new moon, on your glorious feast day."[g]

Now, from this we gather that we should use a trumpet, but no alarms, when we assemble the whole congregation of the people. When the uninitiated are present, we offer only muted teaching on the holy sacraments, whereas when they have been sent out, we impart explicit instruction to the initiated.[1]

1. In a significant pun, Theodoret plays on two words derived from the root "to signal," "to signify": σημασίᾳ = "with a sign," "with an alarm," and ἀσήμως = "indistinctly," "obscurely." Though far-fetched, this application of Ps 80.4 to contem-

XVI

Διὰ τί τὸν κηδεστὴν ὁ θεῖος Μωϋσῆς, Ἰοθὼρ ὀνομάσας ἐν τῇ Ἐξόδῳ,[a] νῦν αὐτὸν ἐκάλεσε Ῥαγουήλ;[b]

Διώνυμος ἦν, ὡς Ἰακὼβ καὶ Ἰσραήλ,[c] ὡς Σίμων Πέτρος,[d] ὡς Θωμᾶς ὁ λεγόμενος Δίδυμος,[e] ὡς Θαδδαῖος ὁ καὶ Λεββαῖος.[f]
5 τούτου υἱὸς ἦν ὁ Ἰωβάβ.

XVII

Τίς ἦν ὁ τοῦ λαοῦ γογγυσμός;[a]
Τὸν τῆς ὁδοιπορίας ἐδυσχέραινον πόνον.

XVIII

Τίνος ἕνεκεν ἁμαρτάνουσιν εὐθὺς ἐπάγει τὰς τιμωρίας;[a]
(1) Ἀρχὴν εἶχεν ὁ νόμος. ἔδει τοίνυν τῇ τῶν παραβαινόντων

---

xvi A *[32]*, B, C⁻⁵¹, 4 7 9 31 35 37 = 19 mss.

a. Ex 3.1; 4.18   b. Nm 10.29   c. Gn 32.28   d. Mt 10.2   e. Jn 20.24
f. Mt 10.3 (NT var.)

---

xvii A *[32]*, B, C⁻⁵¹, 4 7 9 35 37 = 18 mss.

a. Nm 11.1

---

xviii A *[32]*, B, C, 4 7 9 31 35 37 = 20 mss.

a. Nm 11.1

XVI

Why is it that in Exodus the divinely inspired Moses referred to his father-in-law by the name Jethro[a] but in this passage called him Reuel?[b]

He had two names, like Jacob and Israel,[c] Simon Peter,[d] Thomas known as Didymus,[e] and Thaddeus also called Lebbaeus.[f] Hobab was Reuel's son.[1]

XVII

What was the people's complaint?[a]

They could not put up with the hardship of travelling.

XVIII

Why did he immediately impose punishment on the sinners?[a]

(1) The Law held sway, and the rest had to be brought to their

----

porary Christian life reflects the exclusion, routine in the fourth and fifth centuries, of the catechumens from full knowledge of doctrine and participation in worship; *cf.* E. Yarnold, pp. 50–54.

---

1. Both the Hebrew and the LXX present both Jethro and Reuel for the name of Moses' father-in-law. The former appears in Ex 3.1 and 4.18, the latter in Ex 2.18 and Nm 10.29, the passage that prompts this question. In Theodoret's text of Mt 10.3, Thaddeus must have been coupled with the alternative name Lebbaeus. In Lk 6.16 we find the further variation of "Judas, son of James." From this inconsistency in the list of the disciples, J. Fitzmyer draws a conclusion (*v.* on Lk 6.16) that would be the opposite of Theodoret's: "it is unlikely that the same person had all three names. It is rather an indication that the names of the Twelve were no longer accurately preserved in the early church by the time that Luke and Matthew were writing, and that the group of the Twelve, though important at the outset, gradually lost its significance, even to the extent that people no longer could recall who once constituted the Twelve."

τιμωρίᾳ σωφρονίζεσθαι τοὺς λοιπούς· ἁρμόδιος γὰρ τοῖς
ἀρχομένοις ὁ φόβος. συνέζευκτο μέντοι τῇ τιμωρίᾳ
5 φιλανθρωπία· μεταμελούμενοι γάρ, εὐμενείας ἀπήλαυον.
αὐτίκα γοῦν τοῦ θηλάτου πυρὸς μέρος τι τῆς παρεμβολῆς
ἀναλώσαντος, εἶτα πάντων συνδεδραμηκότων εἰς δέησιν,
ᾔτησε μὲν ὁ νομοθέτης τὴν ἄφεσιν, παρέσχε δὲ ταύτην ὁ
φιλάνθρωπος Κύριος.[b]

10 Ὅτι δὲ ἀναγκαίως αὐτοῖς αἱ τιμωρίαι προσήγοντο τὰ ἑξῆς
μαρτυρεῖ· εὐθὺς γάρ, μετὰ τὴν παῦλαν τῆς τιμωρίας, τῆς
Αἰγύπτου τὴν μνήμην ἀνενεώσαντο, καὶ τῶν κρομμύων, καὶ
τῶν σκορόδων, καὶ τῶν ἄλλων, ὧν τὴν ἐπιθυμίαν τῆς
γαστριμαργίας τὸ πάθος ἐπύρσευσε.[c] μάλα τοίνυν εἰκότως
15 τῇ ἐκείνων ἀχαριστίᾳ τὴν θείαν συνῆψε φιλοτιμίαν ὁ
συγγραφεύς, τὰ περὶ τοῦ μάννα διηγησάμενος καὶ ὅτι, οὐ
μόνον ἄρτου χρείαν, ἀλλὰ καὶ ὄψου ἐπλήρου·[d] ἤλεθον..., γάρ
φησιν, ἐν τῷ μύλῳ, καὶ ἔτριβον ἐν τῇ θυείᾳ, καὶ ἥψουν... ἐν
τῇ χύτρᾳ, καὶ ἐποίουν... ἐγκρυφίας.[e]

20 Ἐκείνων δὲ ὀλοφυρομένων, χαλεπαίνει μὲν ὁ δεσπότης
Θεός, δυσχεραίνει δὲ ὁ προφήτης καὶ βοᾷ λέγων, ἵνα τί
ἐκάκωσας τὸν θεράποντά σου, καὶ διὰ τί οὐχ εὕρηκα χάριν
ἐναντίον σου, ἐπιθεῖναί μοι τὴν ὁρμὴν τοῦ λαοῦ τούτου ἐπ᾽
ἐμέ; μὴ ἐγὼ ἐν γαστρὶ ἔλαβον τὸν λαὸν τοῦτον ἢ ἐγὼ ἔτεκον
25 αὐτόν, ὅτι λέγεις μοι, ὅτι λάβε αὐτὸν εἰς τὸν κόλπον σου,
ὡσεὶ λάβοι τιθηνὸς τὸν θηλάζοντα, εἰς τὴν γῆν ἣν ὤμοσας
τοῖς πατράσιν αὐτῶν;[f] δεδήλωκε δὲ διὰ τούτων τὸ ἀτελὲς
αὐτῶν καὶ νηπιῶδες· θηλάζοντι γὰρ αὐτοὺς ἀπείκασεν, ἄλλο
μὲν οὐδὲν ἐργάσασθαι δυναμένῳ, ἐκμυζᾶν δὲ μόνον βουλομένῳ

---

l. 17 ἤλεθον Sir. Sch. F.M. : ἤληθον (?) J.P. : ἤλιθον a, a₂, 31. The form
adopted by earlier editors is, like ἤλι—an orthographical mistake; nevertheless,
I have thought it best to leave ἤλεθον as F.M. reports no attestation of the more
standard ἤληθον, and Wevers and Quast (*ap. crit.* on Nm 11.8), indicate that the
form with -ε- is attested also by some mss. of the LXX.

b. Nm 11.2   c. Nm 11.4–6   d. Nm 11.31f.   e. Nm 11.8   f. Nm 11.11f.

senses by the punishment of the transgressors; after all, fear is appropriate for those who are ruled. Nevertheless, kindness was linked with the punishment; on their repenting they enjoyed benevolence. As soon as fire from heaven consumed part of the camp, and everyone ran to beseech him, the lawgiver begged forgiveness, and the kindly Lord granted his request.[b]

As the following events show, there was good reason for the punishments inflicted on them. Right after the punishment had ceased, they recalled Egypt and the onions, garlic, and the rest, for which they longed, their desire inflamed by gluttony.[c] In fact, the historian quite properly juxtaposed God's generosity to their ingratitude as he went on to describe the manna and how God met their need not only for bread but also for meat.[d] As he reports, "They ground it in the mill, crushed it in the mortar, boiled it in the pot, and made cakes."[e]

But when they lamented their lot, the Lord God became angry, and the prophet so distressed that he cried out, "Why have you treated your servant so badly, and why have I not found grace in your sight, so you impose the burden of this people on me? Did I conceive this people, or did I bear them, that you should say to me, 'As a wet-nurse takes a suckling child, take them to your bosom, to the land you swore to their ancestors?'"[f] Now, in this comparison of the people to a nursing child incapable of doing anything else and wanting only to suck milk, he indicated their childish immaturity. As these words were indicative of deep distress—and what follows

30 τὸ γάλα. ἐπειδὴ δὲ σφόδρα ἦν τὰ ῥήματα δυσχεραίνοντος· καὶ
τὰ ἑξῆς γὰρ τοῦτον ἔχει τὸν νοῦν· διδάσκεται παρὰ τοῦ
δεσπότου Θεοῦ ὡς, οὐκ ἀνθρωπίνῃ δυνάμει, θείᾳ δὲ χάριτι τὸν
λαὸν κυβερνᾷ· ἔφη γὰρ πρὸς αὐτόν, *συνάγαγέ μοι*
ἑβδομήκοντα ἄνδρας ἀπὸ τῶν πρεσβυτέρων Ἰσραήλ, οὓς αὐτὸς
35 *οἶδας ὅτι αὐτοί εἰσι πρεσβύτεροι τοῦ λαοῦ καὶ γραμματεῖς*
αὐτῶν, καὶ ἄξεις αὐτοὺς εἰς τὴν σκηνὴν τοῦ μαρτυρίου, καὶ
στήσονται ἐκεῖ μετὰ σοῦ. καὶ καταβήσομαι, καὶ λαλήσω ἐκεῖ
μετὰ σοῦ, καὶ ἀφελῶ ἀπὸ τοῦ πνεύματος τοῦ ἐπὶ σοὶ καὶ
ἐπιθήσω ἐπ' αὐτούς. καὶ συναντιλήψονται μετὰ σοῦ τὴν ὁρμὴν
40 *τοῦ λαοῦ τούτου, καὶ οὐκ οἴσεις αὐτοὺς σὺ μόνος.*[g]

(2) Μεμάθηκε δὲ διὰ τούτων τῶν λόγων ὁ νομοθέτης ὡς
ἀποχρῶσαν ἔλαβε τῇ οἰκονομίᾳ τὴν χάριν. διὰ τοῦτο εἶπεν,
ἀφελῶ ἀπὸ τοῦ πνεύματος, τοῦ ἐπὶ σοί· οὐ γάρ, σπανίζων
ἑτέρας δυνάμεως ἢ χάριτος, τοῦτο ἔφη, ἀλλ' ἐκεῖνον διδάσκων
45 ὡς εἰλήφει δύναμιν ἀρκοῦσαν τῇ χρείᾳ. ὅτι δέ, καὶ τοῖς
ἑβδομήκοντα δούς, οὐκ ἐμείωσε τούτου τὴν χάριν τὰ
πράγματα μαρτυρεῖ· τὰ αὐτὰ γὰρ καὶ οἰκονομῶν καὶ
θαυματουργῶν διετέλει ἃ καὶ πρότερον ἐπετέλει.[h] ὥσπερ γὰρ
ἐκ μιᾶς θρυαλλίδος μυρίας τις ἐξάπτων, οὔτε ταύτην μειοῖ,
50 κἀκείναις μεταδίδωσι τοῦ φωτός, οὕτως ὁ τῶν ὅλων Θεὸς τῆς
τούτου χάριτος τοῖς ἑβδομήκοντα μεταδιδούς, τὴν τούτῳ
δοθεῖσαν οὐκ ἠλάττωσε χάριν. τοῦτο καὶ νῦν ὁρῶμεν
γινόμενον· πολλαὶ γὰρ ἀνθρώπων μυριάδες, ὑπὸ ἱερέως ἑνὸς
βαπτιζόμεναι καὶ τὴν θείαν δεχόμεναι δωρεάν, οὐ σμικρύνουσι
55 τοῦ ἱερέως τὴν χάριν, καὶ πάμπολλοι παρὰ τῶν ἀρχιερέων
χειροτονούμενοι καὶ τὴν ἱερατικὴν ἀξίαν δεχόμενοι, τοῦ
χειροτονοῦντος οὐκ ἐλαττοῦσι τὴν δωρεάν. μεμαρτύρηκε
μέντοι ὁ δεσπότης τῇ τοῦ θεράποντος ψήφῳ· ἔφη γὰρ αὐτῷ,
ἔκλεξαι οὓς οἶδας.

---

g. Nm 11.16f.   h. V., e.g., Nm 12.9–15.

has the same sense—he learned from the Lord God that it was not by human ability but by divine grace that he governed the people. Indeed, God said to him, "Assemble for me seventy men from the elders of Israel, whom you know to be elders of the people and their scribes, and bring them into the tabernacle of witness. They will stand there with you, and I shall come down and talk with you there, and I shall take some of the spirit that is on you and put it on them. They will bear some of the burden of this people along with you, and you will not have to bear them alone."[g]

(2) From these words the lawgiver learned that he had received grace sufficient for his task. This is why God had said, "I shall take some of the spirit that is on you." God spoke thus not because he lacked more might or grace, but to let Moses know that he had received as much power as he needed. Now, the sequence of events confirms that, by giving some to the seventy, God had not diminished Moses' grace, for he continued to perform the same functions and work wonders as he had done before.[h] Just as, from a single taper, one can light countless others and, without diminishing it, share its light with the rest, so the God of the universe shared Moses' grace with the seventy without lessening the grace that had already been granted to him. We see this happening even today when countless people are baptized by one priest and receive the divine gift without diminishing the priest's grace, and great numbers are appointed by the high priests and receive priestly office without lessening the gift of the man who appointed them.[i] Note that the Lord endorsed his servant's choice when he told him to choose "those you know."

1. *V.* the discussion of this passage in sec. 4 of the "Introduction to Theodoret's Life and Works."

XIX

Τί δή ποτε, τοῦ Θεοῦ δώσειν ὑποσχομένου κρέα, ὁ
προφήτης ἀμφέβαλλεν;[a]

Ἐπειδή, οὐ μόνον προφήτης, ἀλλὰ καὶ ἄνθρωπος ἦν.
ἐδιδάχθη δὲ παρὰ τοῦ δεσπότου Θεοῦ μὴ ἐνδοιάζειν,

|10 5 ὑπισχνου|μένου Θεοῦ· ἔφη γὰρ πρὸς αὐτόν, μὴ ἡ χεὶρ Κυρίου
οὐκ ἐξαρκέσει; ἤδη γνώσῃ εἰ ἐπικαταλήψεταί σε ὁ λόγος μου ἢ
οὔ.[b] ὑπισχνούμενος μέντοι δώσειν, τῇ φιλοτιμίᾳ τιμωρίαν

||14 συνῆψεν· εἰπὼν γὰρ ὅτι ἕως μηνὸς . . . φάγεσθε κρέα‖ ἕως ἂν
ἐξέλθῃ ἐκ τῶν μυκτήρων ὑμῶν, ἐπήγαγε, καὶ ἔσται ὑμῖν εἰς

10 χολέραν[c] ἤ, ὡς ὁ Σύμμαχος, εἰς ἀπεψίαν· ἡ γὰρ ἀδηφαγία τὴν
νόσον ἐπήγαγε, καὶ πολλοῖς τὸν θάνατον ἡ θεήλατος πληγή.[d]
διὸ καὶ ὁ θεῖος ἐπήγαγε Δαβίδ, ἔτι τῆς βρώσεως οὔσης ἐν τῷ
στόματι αὐτῶν, καὶ ὀργὴ τοῦ Θεοῦ ἀνέβη ἐπ' αὐτοὺς καὶ
ἀπέκτεινεν ἐν τοῖς πλείοσιν αὐτῶν.[e] εἰκότως τοίνυν ὁ

15 πάνσοφος παραινεῖ Παῦλος, μὴ ποιεῖσθε τῆς σαρκὸς πρόνοιαν
εἰς ἐπιθυμίαν.[f]

XX

Τίνος χάριν, εὐθὺς μὲν προβληθέντες, οἱ ἑβδομήκοντα
προεφήτευσαν, μετὰ δὲ ταῦτα, οὐκέτι;[a]

Ὅτι, οὐ προφητείας χάριν, ἀλλ' οἰκονομίας αὐτοὺς
προὐβάλετο. τῶν δὲ τοῦ πνεύματος χαρισμάτων καὶ τοῦτο·

5 ὅθεν ὁ μακάριος Παῦλος τοῖς ἀποστόλοις, καὶ τοῖς προφήταις,

---

xix A [32], 14(inc.) 17 24, C, 4 7 9 10(inc.) 31 35 37 = 21 mss.

a. Nm 11.21f.   b. Nm 11.23   c. Nm 11.20   d. Nm 11.33   e. Ps 78.30f.
f. Rom 13.14

---

xx A [32], B⁻¹⁴, C, 4 7 9 10 31 35 37 = 20 mss.

a. Nm 11.25

XIX

Why did the prophet express doubt when God promised to provide meat?[a]

Because he was not only a prophet but also a human being. But he was taught by the Lord God not to waver when God made a promise. In fact, God said to him, "Surely the Lord's hand will not fail to provide enough? Now you will know whether my word will or will not overtake you."[b] Yet after promising to give the meat, God joined punishment to generosity. Having said, "You will eat meat for a month until it comes out of your nostrils," he added, "It will nauseate you,"[c] or, as Symmachus puts it, "it will make you sick to your stomach." Overindulgence, in fact, brought on illness, and the heaven-sent disease killed many.[d] Hence, in his account, the divinely inspired David added, "While the food was still in their mouths, God's wrath arose against them and killed great numbers of them."[e] So Paul, in his great wisdom, rightly advised, "Make no provision for the flesh, to gratify its desires."[f]

XX

Why did the seventy prophesy immediately after being appointed but never again?[a]

Because he appointed them not for prophecy but for administration, which is another of the Spirit's charisms. Thus, along with apostleship, prophecy, teaching, and gifts of healing, St. Paul includ-

καὶ τοῖς διδασκάλοις, καὶ τοῖς χαρίσμασι τῶν ἰαμάτων τὰς
ἀντιλήψεις καὶ κυβερνήσεις συνέταξε.[b] τούτου οἱ ἑβδομήκοντα
τοῦ χαρίσματος ἠξιώθησαν. ἵνα δὲ δῆλοι γένωνται τῷ λαῷ ὅτι
δὴ τῆς θείας ἀπήλαυσαν δωρεᾶς, εὐθύς τινα προηγόρευσαν.

XXI

Ἐλδὰδ καὶ Μωδὰδ τί δή ποτε προεφήτευσαν, μὴ
συναριθμηθέντες τοῖς ἑβδομήκοντα;[a]

Εἰκὸς αὐτοὺς ἴσους εἶναι τὴν ἀξίαν τοῖς ἑβδομήκοντα καὶ
τούτου χάριν ἀπολαῦσαι τῆς δωρεᾶς. αἰνίττεται δὲ ὁ λόγος
5 ὅτι πολλάκις τοὺς ἀδοκίμους παρὰ ἀνθρώποις νομιζομένους
δοκίμους οἶδεν ὁ τὰ κεκρυμμένα γινώσκων.[b] οὕτως ἐπὶ τοῦ
Κορνηλίου προὔλαβε τὴν τῶν ἀνθρώπων διακονίαν ἡ θεία
φιλοτιμία· πρὸ γὰρ τοῦ βαπτίσματος ἔδωκεν αὐτῷ τὴν χάριν
τοῦ πνεύματος.[c]

10 Ἐδείχθη δὲ κἀνταῦθα τοῦ νομοθέτου τὸ ἄφθονον. τοῦ γὰρ
Ἰησοῦ εἰρηκότος, *Κύριε Μωϋσῆ, κώλυσον αὐτούς,* ὑπολαβὼν
ἔφη, *μὴ ζηλοῖς σύ μοι; καὶ τίς ἂν δῴη πάντα τὸν λαὸν Κυρίου
προφήτας, ὅταν δῷ Κύριος τὸ πνεῦμα αὐτοῦ ἐπ' αὐτούς;*[d] καὶ ὁ
πανεύφημος δὲ Ἰησοῦς, οὐ τοῦ φθόνου τὸ πάθος ἐδέξατο, ἀλλ'
15 αὐθάδειαν καὶ τυραννίδα τὸ πρᾶγμα νομίσας, τοῖσδε τοῖς
λόγοις ἐχρήσατο. ὅτι γὰρ τούτου τοῦ πάθους ἐλεύθερος ἦν ὁ
ἔπαινος μαρτυρεῖ· οὕτω γὰρ ἔφη· *καὶ ἀποκριθεὶς Ἰησοῦς ὁ τοῦ
Ναυῆ, ὁ παρεστηκὼς Μωϋσῆ, ὁ ἐκλεκτός, εἶπεν, Κύριε Μωϋσῆ,
κώλυσον αὐτούς.*[e]

b. 1Cor 12.28

---

xxi A *[32]*, B⁻¹⁴, C, 4 7 9 10 31 35 37 = 20 mss.

a. Nm 11.26f.   b. *Cf.* Mt 13.11, 35.   c. Acts 10.44–48   d. Nm 11.28f.
e. Nm 11.28

ed assistance and leadership.[b] This is the charism that was accorded to the seventy. It was only so that the people would realize that they had received the divine gift that they immediately spoke in prophecy.

XXI

Why did Eldad and Medad prophesy though they were not numbered among the seventy?[a]

They were probably just as worthy as the seventy and therefore received the gift. This story hints that he who knows what is hidden often esteems those disesteemed among men.[b] Similarly, in the case of Cornelius, divine generosity anticipated human intervention and conferred the grace of the Spirit before baptism.[c]

Here as well, the ungrudging attitude of the lawgiver was revealed. When Joshua said, "My lord Moses, stop them," he replied, "Surely you are not jealous for me? I wish someone would make all the Lord's people prophets when the Lord puts his spirit on them."[d] Not that the admirable Joshua had contracted the vice of envy. He spoke these words in the belief that Eldad and Medad were boldly plotting rebellion. In fact, the complimentary description confirms that he was free of this vice. It reads as follows: "Joshua son of Nun, chosen to assist Moses, said, 'My lord Moses, stop them.'"[e]

The Questions on Numbers

XXII

Τίνα χρὴ νοῆσαι τὴν αἰθιόπισσαν γυναῖκα, ἣν ἔλαβε
Μωϋσῆς;[a]

(1) Ἰώσηπος μὲν εἶπεν ὡς, ἡνίκα ἐν τοῖς βασιλείοις
ἐτρέφετο, στρατηγὸς εἰς τὸν κατὰ αἰθιόπων χειροτονηθεὶς
5 πόλεμον, εἶτα νικήσας, ἠγάγετο τοῦ βασιλέως ἐκείνου τὴν
θυγατέρα. Ἀπολινάριος δὲ μῦθον ἀνέπλασε πολλῷ μυθωδέστερον
τούτου· ἔφη γάρ, μετὰ τὴν Σεπφώραν, ἄλλην αὐτὸν αἰθιόπισσαν
γῆμαι ἵνα, φησί, γένηται τύπος τοῦ δεσπότου Χριστοῦ, ὅς,
μετὰ τὴν ἰσραηλῖτιν, τὴν ἐξ ἐθνῶν ἐκκλησίαν ἐμνήστευσεν.
10 ἀλλὰ καὶ ἡ Σεπφώρα ἀλλόφυλος ἦν. τὸ τοίνυν πλάττειν μύθους,
οὐ τοῦ θείου πνεύματος, ἀλλὰ τοῦ ἐναντίου.

Τοσαύτης γὰρ ἁγνείας μετὰ τὴν κλῆσιν ὁ νομοθέτης
ἐφρόντισεν ὅτι καὶ τὴν Σεπφώραν κατέλιπεν, εἰς Αἴγυπτον
εἰσιών. μετὰ δὲ τὴν ἐκεῖθεν ἔξοδον, ἀφίκετο πρὸς αὐτὸν ὁ
15 κηδεστής, ἄγων ἐκείνην μετὰ τῶν παιδίων, καὶ προστέθεικεν
ὅτι μετὰ τὴν ἄφεσιν ἤγαγεν αὐτήν.[b] τὴν Σεπφώραν τοίνυν
ὠνόμασεν αἰθιόπισσαν· τὸ γὰρ Σαβὰ ἔθνος αἰθιοπικόν ἐστιν· ὁ
γὰρ εὐαγγελιστής φησιν, βασίλισσα αἰθιόπων ἀναστήσεται
καὶ κατακρινεῖ τὴν γενεὰν ταύτην,[c] ἀλλ' ἡ τῶν βασιλειῶν
20 ἱστορία βασίλισσαν Σαβὰ προσηγόρευσε ταύτην.[d] Σαβὰ δὲ
καλεῖται τῶν ὁμηριτῶν τὸ ἔθνος· τούτοις οἱ μαδιηναῖοι
πελάζουσιν.[e]

(2) Ἐπειδὴ τοίνυν ὁ Ἀαρὼν ἰσραηλῖτιν ἠγάγετο,[f] ἀλλόφυλον
δὲ ὁ Μωϋσῆς, μικροψυχίας γενομένης, ταύτην αὐτῷ τὴν
25 λοιδορίαν προσήνεγκαν. καὶ μαρτυρεῖ δὲ τῇ τελειοτάτῃ ἀρετῇ
τοῦ νομοθέτου τῶν ἀδελφῶν ἡ παροινία· ἀπορήσαντες γὰρ
δηλονότι κατηγορίας ἑτέρας, τῆς γυναικὸς αὐτῷ τὸν ψόγον
ἐπήνεγκαν. μαρτυρεῖ δέ μου τῷ λόγῳ καὶ ἡ ψῆφος τοῦ

xxii A [32], 14(inc.) 17 24, C, 4 7 9 10 31 35 37 = 21 mss.

a. Nm 12.1   b. Ex 18.2   c. Mt 12.42; Lk 11.31   d. 1Kgs 10.1   e. Hab 3.7
f. Ex 6.23

XXII

With whom should we identify the Ethiopian woman that Moses married?[a]

(1) According to Josephus, while Moses was dwelling in the palace, he was appointed commander in a war against the Ethiopians and, after defeating them, married the daughter of their king. Apollinaris concocted an even more implausible tale, claiming that, after Zipporah, he married another woman, an Ethiopian, so as to become a type of Christ the Lord, who, after the Israelite church, espoused the church of the nations. But Zipporah, too, was a foreigner. As you can see, the spinning of mythological tales shows the influence not of the divine Spirit but of the Enemy.

In fact, after his calling, the lawgiver was so concerned for his purity that he left Zipporah behind when he went into Egypt. After the Exodus, however, his father-in-law came to him with her and the children, and as Scripture adds, "He brought her after her dismissal."[b] So it was Zipporah who is referred to as the Ethiopian woman, for Sheba is an Ethiopian nation. As the evangelist says, "The queen of Ethiopia will rise up and condemn this generation."[c] In the narrative of Kings, however, she is called "the queen of Sheba."[d] And the name "Sheba" is applied to the Homeritae, whose land borders on that of the Midianites.[1e]

(2) Since Aaron had married an Israelite,[f] but Moses a foreigner, they brought this reproach against Moses out of sheer pettiness. Now, the folly of his family confirms the lawgiver's perfect virtue. Obviously lacking other grounds for criticism, they blamed him for his wife. This explanation of mine can claim the backing of the judge of perfect righteousness: "If there is a prophet among you, I

---

1. Perhaps on the basis of Is 43.3, Josephus (*AJ* 2.249) had identified Sheba as "the royal city," *i.e.*, capital, of Ethiopia; *v.* J.L. McKenzie ("Sheba," *Dict.*, p. 796) for the general modern opinion identifying Sheba with a region "in the SW corner of

δικαιοτάτου κριτοῦ· ἔφη γάρ, ἐὰν γένηται προφήτης ὑμῖν . . . ἐν

30 ὁράματι αὐτῷ γνωσθήσομαι καὶ ἐν ὕπνῳ αὐτῷ λαλήσω. οὐχ οὕτως
ὡς ὁ θεράπων μου Μωϋσῆς· ἐν ὅλῳ τῷ οἴκῳ μου πιστός ἐστι·
στόμα κατὰ στόμα λαλήσω αὐτῷ, ἐν εἴδει καὶ οὐ δι' αἰνιγμάτων,

|14 καὶ Ιτὴν δόξαν Κυρίου εἶδε. καὶ διὰ τί οὐκ ἐφοβήθητε
καταλαλῆσαι κατὰ τοῦ θεράποντός μου Μωϋσῆ;[g]

35 Ἀληθὴς ἄρα ὁ λόγος ἐκεῖνος, ὁ φάσκων, ἐμοὶ ἐκδίκησις,
ἐγὼ ἀνταποδώσω, λέγει Κύριος.[h] διδασκόμεθα γάρ, καὶ διὰ
τούτων καὶ δι' ἐκείνων, μὴ ἀμύνεσθαι τοὺς ἀδικοῦντας, ἀλλὰ
τὴν θείαν ψῆφον προσμένειν, μάλα τῶν ἀδικουμένων
προμηθουμένην ὥσπερ ἀμέλει καὶ τότε, Μωϋσῆ σιγῶντος, τῇ

40 Μαριὰμ τὴν λέπραν ἐπήνεγκεν.

XXIII

Τί δή ποτε, τῶν δύο λελοιδορηκότων, ἐκείνη δίκας ἔτισε
μόνη;[a]

Πρῶτον ἐπειδὴ μεῖζον ἦν τῆς γυναικὸς τὸ πλημμέλημα· τῷ
ἄρρενι γὰρ καὶ ἡ φύσις καὶ ὁ νόμος ὑποτάττει τὸ θῆλυ.

5 ἔπειτα εἶχέ τινα μετρίαν συγγνώμην ὁ Ἀαρών, καὶ ὡς τῷ
χρόνῳ πρεσβύτερος καὶ ὡς ἀρχιερωσύνης ἠξιωμένος. πρὸς δὲ
τούτοις, ἐπειδὴ ἀκάθαρτος ὁ λεπρὸς ἐδόκει εἶναι κατὰ τὸν
νόμον, ῥίζα δὲ τῶν ἱερέων καὶ κρηπὶς ἦν ὁ Ἀαρών, ἵνα μὴ εἰς
ἅπαν διαβῇ τὸ γένος τὸ ὄνειδος, τὴν ἴσην οὐκ ἐπήγαγεν αὐτῷ

10 τιμωρίαν, ἀλλὰ διὰ τῆς ἀδελφῆς ἐφόβησεν ὁμοῦ καὶ
ἐπαίδευσεν. οὕτω γὰρ αὐτὸν τὸ πάθος ἠνίασεν ὅτι πρὸ τῆς
τοῦτο δεξαμένης αὐτὸς τὸν ἠδικημένον ἱκέτευσε λῦσαι τῇ
πρεσβείᾳ τὴν συμφοράν. ὁ δὲ οὐκ ἠμέλησεν ἀλλ' αὐτίκα τὴν
ἱκετηρίαν προσήνεγκεν. εἶτα ὁ φιλάνθρωπος ἐδίδαξε Κύριος

g. Nm 12.6–8   h. Rom 12.19; Heb 10.30; Dt 32.35

xxiii A [32], B, C⁻¹, 4 7 9 10 31 35 37 = 20 mss.

a. Nm 12.10

shall make myself known to him in a vision and shall speak to him in a dream. Not so is my servant Moses, who is faithful in all my house. With him I shall speak face to face, directly, and not in riddles; he has seen the glory of God. So why were you not afraid to malign my servant Moses?"[g]

Indeed that verse is true, which says, "Vengeance is mine; I shall repay, says the Lord."[h] We learn from this and from the passage cited above not to take vengeance on those who wrong us but to await the divine verdict, which takes good care of the wronged, just as in the case in point when it inflicted leprosy on Miriam while Moses kept silence.

XXIII

Why is it that, though both Aaron and Miriam had reviled him, Miriam alone paid the penalty?[a]

First, because the woman's trespass was greater. After all, both nature and the Law subject the female to the male. Second, Aaron had some measure of excuse, since he was both the elder and the one who had been honored with the office of high priest. In addition, since the leper was reckoned unclean by the Law, and Aaron was the root and foundation of the priests, God did not exact equal retribution from him to prevent the shame from passing to the whole race; instead he frightened and, at the same time, admonished him through his sister. In fact, her affliction so distressed Aaron that, on behalf of the woman who had received the punishment, he personally begged the man they had wronged to intercede for a remedy for this calamity. And Moses did not ignore him but

----

the Arabian peninsula," *i.e.* in present-day Yemen. Theodoret, who realizes that Sheba is a region, rather than a city, probably draws on Habakkuk (3.7), a text on which he had already commented, for the erroneous information that Midian and Ethiopia were neighbors. Theodoret here defends the exemplarity of Moses by denying that he could have contracted a second marriage.

15 ὡς, οὐ δικαστικῶς αὐτήν, ἀλλὰ πατρικῶς ἐπαίδευσεν· ἔφη γάρ,
εἰ ὁ πατὴρ αὐτῆς ἐμπτύων ἐνέπτυσεν εἰς τὸ πρόσωπον αὐτῆς,
οὐκ ἐντραπήσεται; ἑπτὰ ἡμέρας ἀφορισθήσεται ἔξω τῆς
παρεμβολῆς καὶ μετὰ ταῦτα εἰσελεύσεται.[b] συνέζευκται δὲ καὶ
τιμὴ τῇ ἀτιμίᾳ· οὐκ ἀπῆρε γὰρ ὁ λαὸς ἕως ἀπηλλάγη τοῦ
20 πάθους.

XXIV

Τίνος χάριν κατασκόπους ἀποσταλῆναι προσέταξεν;[a]
Ἵνα προμαθόντες τῆς γῆς τὴν εὐκαρπίαν, ἐπιθυμήσωσι
μεταλαχεῖν τῶν ἐπαινουμένων καρπῶν· ὀκνοῦντες δὲ καὶ
ὀκλάζοντες, μηδεμίαν ἔχωσι παραίτησιν, κολαζόμενοι.

XXV

Τί δή ποτε τὸν Αὐσήν, ἡνίκα κατάσκοπον ἔπεμπεν,
ἐκάλεσεν Ἰησοῦν;[a]
Ὅτι τύπος ἦν τοῦ ἀληθινοῦ Ἰησοῦ, ὃς τὸ τῶν κατασκόπων
ἐμιμήσατο σχῆμα, τὴν ἡμετέραν οἰκονομῶν σωτηρίαν. καθάπερ
5 γὰρ οἱ κατάσκοποι τῷ τῶν ἐθνῶν ἐκείνων ἃ κατασκοποῦσι καὶ
σχήματι κέχρηνται καὶ φωνῇ, οὕτως ὁ Θεὸς λόγος, τὴν
ἀνθρωπείαν περιθέμενος φύσιν καὶ τῇ ταύτης γλώττῃ
χρησάμενος, τὴν ἡμετέραν ᾠκονόμησε σωτηρίαν.

b. Nm 12.14

xxiv A [32], B, C, 4 7 9 10 31 35 37 = 21 mss.
a. Nm 13.1–20

xxv A [32], B⁻²⁴, C, 4 7 9 10 31 35 37 = 20 mss.
a. Nm 13.16

immediately offered supplication. Then the loving Lord explained that he had chastised her, not as a judge, but as a father, saying, "If her father had spat in her face, would she not be covered in confusion? She is to be barred from the camp for seven days, and after that she will return."[b] Respect was mingled with disrepute; the people did not move on until she was rid of her affliction.

XXIV

Why did God order the sending of spies?[a]

So that when the people had learned of the fertility of the land and heard the praises of its fruits, they would desire to have a share in them. Or, if they hung back in hesitation, so they would have no grounds of excuse when they were punished.

XXV

Why did Moses call Hosea "Joshua" when he sent him out to spy?[a]

Because he was a type of the true Joshua, who, to secure our salvation, imitated the disguise of the spies. As spies adopt the dress and language of the nations on which they are spying, so God the Word clad himself in human nature and adopted human language to secure our salvation.[1]

---

1. Theodoret was not aware that the Hebrew name, represented in Greek as Ἰη-σοῦς (= both "Joshua" and "Jesus" in English), appears in the variant forms *Yehoshua, Yeshua,* and *Hoshea.* The figurative analogy of this passage fails to give adequate expression to the true humanity of Christ.

XXVI

Τίνα λέγει γενεὰν Ἐνάκ;[a]
Ὀνομαστότατος οὗτος ἦν καὶ πολυθρύλλητος, ὡς εἰκός, διὰ τὸ τοῦ σώματος μέγεθος. καὶ τὸ γένος δὲ πάντως τῷ προγόνῳ ἐῴκει.

XXVII

Τί ἐστιν ἐμπλήσει ἡ δόξα Κυρίου πᾶσαν τὴν γῆν;[a]

Προλέγει τὴν ἰουδαίων ἀποβολὴν καὶ τῆς οἰκουμένης τὴν σωτηρίαν καὶ ὅρκον τῇ προρρήσει προστίθησι· *ζῶ, γάρ φησιν, ἐγώ, καὶ ζῇ τὸ ὄνομά μου, καὶ ἐμπλήσει ἡ δόξα Κυρίου πᾶσαν*
5 *τὴν γῆν,*[b] κατὰ δὲ τοὺς ἄλλους ἑρμηνευτάς, ὅτι *ἐμπλήσει πᾶσαν τὴν γῆν ἡ δόξα Κυρίου.* εἶτα ἐκφέρει τὴν ψῆφον κατὰ τῶν ἀριθμηθέντων ἁπάντων, πλὴν Χαλὲβ υἱοῦ Ἰεφωνῆ καὶ Ἰησοῦ υἱοῦ Ναυῆ, οἳ πρὸς τῇ ἀληθείᾳ τῶν μηνυμάτων τὴν εὐσεβῆ παραίνεσιν προσήνεγκαν τῷ λαῷ. ταύτῃ μέντοι
10 παραβαλεῖν προσήκει τῇ ἀποφάσει τὴν ἐν τοῖς εὐαγγελίοις εἰρημένην· *ἀρθήσεται ἀφ' ὑμῶν ἡ βασιλεία... καὶ δοθήσεται ἔθνει ποιοῦντι τοὺς καρποὺς αὐτῆς·*[c] τύπος γὰρ τῶν μὲν ‖6 ἠπιστηκότων ἰουδαίων οἱ ἐν τῇ ἐρήμῳ πεπ‖τωκότες δι' ἀπιστίαν, τῶν δὲ πεπιστευκότων ἐθνῶν οἱ ἀπερίτμητοι παῖδες,
15 οἱ ἀντ' ἐκείνων διὰ Ἰησοῦ τὴν γῆν ἀπειληφότες, τὴν τοῖς προγόνοις ἐπηγγελμένην.

---

xxvi A [32], B⁻²⁴, C, 4 7 9 10 31 35 37 = 20 mss.
a. Nm 13.22

---

xxvii 2c 6(inc.) [32], 5, a₂, B⁻²⁴, C, 4 7 9 10 31* 35 37 = 20 mss.
a. Nm 14.21   b. Nm 14.21   c. Mt 21.43

XXVI

Who are meant by "the descendants of Anak"?[a]

This Anak was a very famous man and, so it seems, renowned for his great stature. His descendants were just like their ancestor.[1]

XXVII

What is the meaning of "The glory of the Lord will fill the whole earth"?[a]

Foretelling the rejection of the Jews and the salvation of the world, he complemented his prophecy with an oath, "As I live, and my name lives, the glory of the Lord will fill the whole earth."[b] The other translators offer: "There will fill the whole earth the glory of the Lord." He then delivered his sentence on all who were counted, except Caleb son of Jephunneh and Joshua son of Nun, who not only reported the truth but also urged the people to dutiful obedience. Of course, we should, compare with this the verdict stated in the Gospels: "The kingdom will be taken away from you and given to a nation that produces its fruits."[c] Those who died in the desert because of their unbelief were a type of the Jews who have refused to believe, whereas their uncircumcised children, who in their place under Joshua's leadership reached the land promised to their forbears, were a type of the gentiles who have believed.

1. The LXX version of Nm 13.23 (= 22 MT) only mentions, but does not describe, the sons of Anak, and v. 34 (= v. 33 MT) contains nothing to represent the Hebrew clause relating the Anakites to the gigantic Nephilim of Gn 6.4. Since Theodoret characterizes the Anakim as giants, his Greek translation may have offered a more complete rendition of Nm 13.33 MT.

XXVIII

Τί δή ποτε περὶ τῶν αὐτῶν θυσιῶν πολλὰ νενομοθέτηκεν;[a]
Ἵνα τῇ συνεχείᾳ τῆς νομοθεσίας παγίαν τῶν νόμων τὴν
μνήμην ἐργάσηται.

XXIX

Τί ἐστι ψυχὴ ἥτις ποιήσει ἐν χειρὶ ὑπερηφανίαν;[a]

Περὶ τῶν ἀκουσίως ἡμαρτηκότων νομοθετήσας ὁποίαν χρὴ
θυσίαν προσενεγκεῖν, καὶ περὶ τῶν ἑκουσίως ἡμαρτηκότων
νομοθετεῖ. διάφορα δὲ τὰ ἁμαρτήματα· οἱ μὲν γὰρ οὐ
φέρουσι‖ διὰ τὴν τῆς ψυχῆς ἀσθένειαν τὴν τῶν παθῶν
ἐπανάστασιν καὶ ἐνδιδόντες ἡττῶνται· οἱ δὲ καὶ ἐξ ἑτέρας
περιστάσεως ἁμαρτήμασι περιπίπτουσιν. εἰσὶ δὲ οἳ καὶ
καταφρονητικῶς περὶ τοὺς θείους διάκεινται νόμους· τούτους
ἐξ ὑπερηφανίας ἁμαρτάνειν ἔφη, ὡς ἑκόντας τῶν νόμων
καταφρονοῦντας. τὸν τοιοῦτον ἐξαλειφθήσεσθαι ἔφη καὶ τὴν
αἰτίαν ἐπήγαγεν· ὅτι τὸ ῥῆμα Κυρίου ἐφαύλισε καὶ τὰς
ἐντολὰς αὐτοῦ διεσκέδασεν, ἐκτρίψει ἐκτριβήσεται ἡ ψυχὴ
ἐκείνη· ... ἁμαρτία γὰρ αὐτῆς ἐν αὐτῇ.[b] ὁ μὲν γάρ, δι'
ἀσθένειαν ἡττώμενος τῶν παθῶν, εἶτα στένων καὶ ὀδυρόμενος,
ἔχει τινὰ γοῦν σμικρὰν συγγνώμην· ὁ δέ, τὰ πονηρὰ
ἀσπαζόμενος καὶ τῶν θείων καταφρονῶν ἐντολῶν, πάσης
ἀπολογίας ἐστέρηται.

||35   5

10

15

xxviii A⁻⁶ [32], B⁻²⁴, C, 4 7 9 10 31 35 37 = 20 mss.
a. Nm 15.1–13; v., e.g., Ezek 46.4–7, 11, 13–15; Ex 29.38–41; Lv 7.11–14

xxvix A⁻⁶ [32], B⁻²⁴, C, 4 7 9 10(twice) 31 35(inc.) 37 = 19 mss.
a. Nm 15.30   b. Nm 15.31

XXVIII

Why did he legislate so many times regarding the same sacrifices?[a]

To establish a firm memory of the laws through the repetition of the legislation.[1]

XXIX

What is the meaning of "Whoever acts high-handedly"?[a]

After laying down the law regarding the kind of sacrifice to be offered for involuntary sins, he legislated also for voluntary sinners. Sins are of different kinds. There are weak-willed people, who yield and are overcome, because they cannot withstand the rebellion of their passions; others fall into sin as a result of different circumstances. But there are also people who adopt an attitude of scorn toward God's laws. These are said to sin through high-handedness, since they deliberately scorn his laws. He ordained that such a person be exterminated and gave the reason as well: "Because he despised the word of the Lord and disregarded his commandments, he shall be utterly crushed; his sin is upon him."[b] While someone who has succumbed to his passions through weakness and then heaves sighs of compunction has at least some slight ground for pardon, anyone who embraces wickedness and scorns the commandments of God is stripped of all defense.[1]

---

1. To account for the repetition in Nm 15 of cultic regulations given elsewhere, Theodoret propounds the idea of God's gradual education of the chosen people. In contrast, the modern commentator C.E. L'Heureux (15.1–41) regards this repetition as a sign of a later priestly redaction.

---

1. Again Theodoret seizes the opportunity to distinguish indeliberate faults from those for which one is really accountable.

XXX

Διὰ τί τὸν ἐν τῷ σαββάτῳ συλλέξαντα ξύλα καταλευσθῆναι προσέταξεν;[a]

Ὡς πρῶτον τοῦτον παραβεβηκότα τὸν νόμον ἵνα μὴ γένηται παρανομίας ἀρχέτυπον· ἡ γὰρ τούτου τιμωρία δέος ἐνέθηκεν
5 ἅπασιν.

XXXI

Τί δή ποτε προσέταξεν αὐτοῖς ὁ Θεὸς τοῖς κρασπέδοις τῶν ἱματίων κλῶσμα ὑακίνθινον ἐπιθεῖναι;[a]

Τὸ ὑακίνθινον κλῶσμα τοῦ οὐρανοῦ μιμεῖται τὴν χρόαν. ἀνεμίμνησκε τοίνυν αὐτοὺς τοῦ νομοθέτου, ὃς πληροῖ μὲν τὰ
5 πάντα, οἰκεῖν δὲ δοκεῖ τὸν οὐρανόν· ὁ οὐρανός, γάρ φησι, *τοῦ οὐρανοῦ τῷ Κυρίῳ*[b] καί, *ὁ κατοικῶν ἐν οὐρανοῖς ἐκγελάσεται αὐτούς.*[c] τοῦτο δὲ καὶ ὁ νόμος διδάσκει· *ὄψεσθε,* γάρ φησι, *τὰ κράσπεδα καὶ ἀναμνησθήσεσθε πάσας τὰς ἐντολὰς Κυρίου ποιῆσαι αὐτὰς καὶ οὐ διαστραφήσεσθε ὀπίσω τῶν διανοιῶν*
10 *ὑμῶν καὶ . . . τῶν ὀφθαλμῶν . . ., ἐν οἷς ὑμεῖς ἐκπορνεύετε ὀπίσω αὐτῶν.*[d]

---

xxx A^{-6} *[32]*, B^{-24}, C, *4 7 9 10 31 35 37* = 19 mss.

a. Nm 15.32–36

---

xxxi A^{-6} *[32]*, B, C, *4 7 9 10 31 37* = 19 mss.

a. Nm 15.38   b. Ps 115.16   c. Ps 2.4   d. Nm 15.39

XXX

Why did he ordain the stoning of the man who was gathering wood on the Sabbath?[a]

To prevent him from becoming a model of lawlessness, as he was the first to transgress the law. His punishment instilled fear in everyone else.

XXXI

Why did God order them to put blue tassels on the hems of their garments?[a]

The blue tassel reproduces the color of the sky, so it reminded them of the Lawgiver, who, though he fills all things, seems to dwell in heaven. As Scripture says, "The heaven of heaven is the Lord's";[b] and "He who dwells in the heavens will mock them."[c] Now, this law teaches the same thing: "You will see the hem and remember all the commandments of the Lord so as to do them and will not turn to follow your thoughts and eyes, with which you play the whore."[d]

XXXII

Τὸ μέντοι Κορὲ στασιάσαι κατὰ τοῦ νομοθέτου ἔχει τινὰ
λόγον· ἐκ γὰρ τῆς λευιτικῆς ὑπῆρχε φυλῆς· Δαθὰν δέ, καὶ
Ἀβειρών, καὶ Ἐλιάβ, ἐκ τοῦ Ῥουβὴν τὸ γένος κατάγοντες,
ποίαν ἔχουσι τῆς στάσεως ἀφορμήν;[a]

5   Πρωτότοκος ἦν ὁ Ῥουβήν, καὶ ᾠήθησαν πρωτοτόκοις τὴν
ἱερωσύνην ἁρμόττειν καὶ οὐκ ἐσκόπησαν ὡς ὁ πρόγονος αὐτῶν
τῶν πρωτοτοκίων διὰ τὴν παρανομίαν ἐξέπεσεν.[b]

XXXIII

Τί ἐστι μὴ πρόσχῃς εἰς τὴν θυσίαν αὐτῶν;[a]

Ἀγὼν περὶ τῆς ἱερωσύνης ἐγίνετο, καὶ ἔμελλον καὶ οὗτοι
κἀκεῖνοι προσφέρειν θυμίαμα· κριτῇ δὲ ἐχρῶντο τῷ δεσπότῃ
Θεῷ.[b] ἀθυμήσας τοίνυν ὁ προφήτης διὰ τοὺς τῆς στάσεως
5 ἀρχηγούς, ἱκέτευε τὸν κριτὴν μὴ δέξασθαι τὸ παρανόμως ὑπὸ
τῶν στασιαστῶν προσφερόμενον καὶ εἰς μαρτυρίαν αὐτὸν τῆς
οἰκείας ἐπιεικείας καλεῖ· *μὴ πρόσχῃς*, γάρ φησιν, *εἰς θυσίαν
αὐτῶν· οὐκ ἐπιθύμημα οὐδενὸς αὐτῶν εἴληφα οὐδὲ ἐκάκωσα
οὐδένα αὐτῶν.*[c] ἔργῳ δὲ τὴν μαρτυρίαν ἐβεβαίωσεν ὁ κριτής·
10 *ἀποσχίσθητε*, γάρ φησιν, *ἐκ μέσου τῆς συναγωγῆς ταύτης, καὶ
ἐξαναλώσω αὐτοὺς εἰς ἅπαξ.*[d] δεδήλωκε δὲ πάλιν ὁ πανεύφημος
Μωϋσῆς τὴν οἰκείαν πραότητα.[e] προκυλινδούμενος γὰρ τοῦ
κριτοῦ ἐβόα, *ὁ Θεὸς τῶν πνευμάτων καὶ πάσης σαρκός, εἰ
ἄνθρωπος εἷς ἥμαρτεν, ἐπὶ πᾶσαν τὴν συναγωγὴν ἡ ὀργὴ*

---

xxxii A⁻⁶ [32], B, C, 4 7 9 10 35 37 = 19 mss.

a. Nm 16.1f.   b. Gn 49.3f.

---

xxxiii A⁻⁶ [32], 14(twice) 17 24, C, 4 7 9 10 35 37 = 19 mss.

a. Nm 16.15   b. Nm 16.4–7   c. Nm 16.15   d. Nm 16.21
e. *Cf.*, e.g., Nm 14.11–19.

XXXII

Though Korah, being a member of the levitical tribe, had some reasonable grounds to revolt against the lawgiver, what pretext for revolt did Dathan, Abiram, and Eliab have, descended as they were, from Reuben?[a]

Reuben was the firstborn, and they thought that the priesthood belonged to the firstborn. They did not consider that their ancestor had forfeited his rights by his lawlessness.[1b]

XXXIII

What is the meaning of "Pay no attention to their sacrifice"?[a]

There was a contest for the priesthood: both sides would offer incense and invoke the Lord God as judge.[b] Losing heart at the leaders' revolt, the prophet implored the judge not to accept the rebels' unlawful offering and called on him as a witness of his own fairness: "Pay no attention to their sacrifice; I have taken nothing they desired nor harmed any of them."[c] The Judge confirmed his witness with action: "Separate yourselves from the midst of this congregation, and I shall consume them once and for all."[d] Then Moses, excellent man that he was, yet again gave proof of that gentleness for which he was known;[e] throwing himself down before the Judge he cried out, "God of the spirits and of all flesh, if a single person has sinned, will the wrath of the Lord fall on the whole congregation?"[f]

1. With the precision typical of an Antiochene exegete, Theodoret notes a discrepancy in this story, which interweaves into one two originally distinct narratives: the first concerning the Levite Korah and the second the Reubenites Dathan and Abiram, who are said to have contested the priestly authority of Moses and Aaron; *cf.* C.E. L'Heureux on 16.1–35.

15 Κυρίου·^f δεξάμενος δὲ ὁ φιλάνθρωπος Κύριος τὴν τοῦ
θεράποντος ἱκετείαν, τῶν μὲν στασιαστῶν ἀποκριθῆναι
κελεύει τοὺς ἄλλους,^g χῆναι δὲ νεύσας τῇ γῇ, αὐτάνδρους τὰς
σκηνὰς ὑποβρυχίους ἀπέφηνε,^h καὶ οἱ διὰ μέσης θαλάττης
ὁδεύσαντες ἐν τῇ γῇ κατεπόθησαν. ῥάδιον γὰρ τῷ ποιητῇ καὶ
20 ξηρὰν ὁδὸν ἐν τῇ θαλάττῃ δημιουργεῖν καὶ τῇ γῇ πάλιν εἰς
τιμωρίαν ἀντὶ θαλάττης κεχρῆσθαι· τοῖς μὲν γὰρ αἰγυπτίοις
τὸν δι' ὕδατος ἐπήγαγεν ὄλεθρον, τὸν δὲ Δαθάν, καὶ Ἀβειρών,
καὶ τοὺς ἄλλους τοῖς τῆς γῆς συνεκάλυψε κύμασι. τούτους
μὲν οὖν ζῶντας τῷ ᾅδῃ παρέπεμψε, τοῦ δὲ Κορὲ τὴν
25 συναγωγὴν πυρὶ κατηνάλωσεν.ⁱ

XXXIV

Διὰ τί προσέταξεν ὁ Θεὸς τὰ τῶν στασιαστῶν πυρεῖα τῷ
θυσιαστηρίῳ γενέσθαι περίθεμα;^a

(1) Εἰς ἔλεγχον τῶν κατὰ τῆς ἱερωσύνης θρασυνομένων καὶ
βεβαίωσιν τῶν ἱερουργεῖν προστεταγμένων· τοῦτο γὰρ ἐπήγαγε·
5 *μνημόσυνον τοῖς υἱοῖς Ἰσραὴλ ὅπως ἂν μὴ προσέλθῃ μηδεὶς*
ἀλλογενὴς ὃς οὐκ ἔστιν ἐκ τοῦ σπέρματος Ἀαρὼν ἐπιθεῖναι
θυμίαμα ἔναντι Κυρίου.^b τούτου χάριν καὶ τὴν βλαστήσασαν
ῥάβδον ἐντεθῆναι προσέταξεν τῇ κιβωτῷ^c καὶ πάλιν ἐνομοθέτησε
τοὺς μὲν ἱερέας ἱερουργεῖν, τοὺς δὲ λευίτας ὑπουργεῖν, μήτε
10 τῷ θυσιαστηρίῳ μήτε τοῖς ἱεροῖς πελάζοντας σκεύεσιν.^d

Εἶτα διδάσκει καὶ τίνα χρὴ τοὺς ἱερέας λαμβάνειν. τὰς
γὰρ αὐτῷ προσφερομένας ἀπαρχὰς οἴνου, καὶ σίτου, καὶ
ἐλαίου, καὶ ἄρτων αὐτοὺς ἐσθίειν ἐκέλευσε.^e καὶ μέντοι καὶ τὰ
ἀναθήματα καὶ τὰ πρωτότοκα αὐτοὺς πάλιν λαμβάνειν

---

f. Nm 16.22   g. Nm 16.26f.   h. Nm 16.31–33   i. Nm 16.35

XXXIV *2c 6(inc.) [32], 5, a₂, B, C, 4 7 9 10 31 35(inc.) 37* = 21 mss.

a. Nm 16.37f.   b. Nm 16.40   c. Nm 17.10   d. Nm 18.3   e. Nm 18.12f.

Accepting his servant's supplication, the loving Lord commanded the others to separate themselves from the rebels.[g] Then, bidding the ground open, he caused their tents along with all their households to disappear,[h] and those who had traveled through the sea were swallowed up by the land. Indeed, for the Creator it is an easy matter to fashion dry land in the sea or to punish with land, rather than sea. While he used water to destroy the Egyptians, he immersed Dathan, Abiram, and the others in the waves of the land. Having dispatched these to Hell while still alive, he consumed in fire the congregation of Korah.[i]

XXXIV

Why did God order that the rebels' censers be made into a covering for the altar?[a]

(1) As a reproof to those who had shown presumption in regard to the priesthood and as an endorsement of those appointed to serve. In fact, he added, "to be a reminder to the children of Israel that no outsider, no one who is not a descendant of Aaron, should approach to offer incense before the Lord."[b] For this reason, he also ordered that the blossoming rod be deposited in the ark[c] and once more laid down the law that the priests were to conduct the divine service and the Levites to minister to them but keep away from the altar and the sacred vessels.[d]

He then explained what the priests should receive and commanded them to eat the first-fruits of wine, grain, oil, and bread that were offered to him.[e] In addition, he stated that they should

|6   15   διηγό|ρευσε·^f τῶν μὲν ἀκαθάρτων κτηνῶν ὁρίσας τὰ λύτρα· ἡ
|35   λύτρωσις γὰρ *αὐτοῦ*, φησίν, |*ἀπὸ μηνιαίου, ἡ συντίμησις*
            πέντε σίκλων· κατὰ τὸν σίκλον τὸν ἅγιον, εἴκοσι ὀβολοί εἰσι.^g
            τῶν δὲ καθαρῶν πρωτοτόκων ζῴων τὸ μὲν αἷμα ἐκχεθῆναι
            προσέταξε παρὰ τὴν τοῦ θυσιαστηρίου βάσιν, τὸ δὲ στέαρ
    20   προσενεχθῆναι, τὰ δὲ κρέα αὐτοὺς λαμβάνειν ὥσπερ δὴ τὸ
            στηθύνιον καὶ τὸν βραχίονα ἀπὸ τῶν ἄλλων θυμάτων
            κομίζονται.^h *διαθήκην δὲ ἁλὸς* τὴν κοινωνίαν ἐκάλεσεν,ⁱ
            ἐπειδή, κατὰ τὸν θεῖον ἀπόστολον, *οἱ τῷ θυσιαστηρίῳ*
            προσεδρεύοντες τῷ θυσιαστηρίῳ συμμερίζονται.^j τινὲς δέ
    25   φασιν ἐπειδὴ ταῖς θυσίαις ἐπιβάλλεσθαι τοὺς ἅλας
            προσέταξεν.

            (2) Εἶτα διδάσκει καὶ τοὺς ἱερέας καὶ τοὺς λευίτας ὡς, οὐ
            βούλεται αὐτοὺς κλῆρον λαβεῖν ὡς τὰς ἄλλας φυλάς, ἀλλὰ
            παρὰ παντὸς κομίζεσθαι τοῦ λαοῦ τοὺς λευίτας καὶ τῶν ἀπὸ
    30   γῆς φυομένων τὰς δεκάτας, καὶ τῶν ἐκ ποιμνίων καὶ βουκολίων
            προσγινομένων κερδῶν, καὶ τῶν ἐξ ἐμπορίας, ἢ ἑτέρας τινὸς
            χρείας·^k τοὺς δὲ λευίτας τῶν δεκατῶν τὰς δεκάτας προσφέρειν
            τοῖς ἱερεῦσι. καὶ τούτων μὲν ἐν παντὶ τόπῳ κελεύει
            μεταλαγχάνειν,^l τὰ δέ γε ἐκ τῶν θυσιῶν ἀφωρισμένα αὐτοῖς
    35   ἔνδον ἐσθίειν ἐν τῷ ναῷ.^m καλεῖ δὲ καὶ τὰς δεκάτας *μισθὸν* εἰς
            τὴν τοῦ λαοῦ ὠφέλειαν· ὑμῶν, γάρ φησιν, γεωργούντων, ἢ ἐμ-
            πορευομένων, ἢ οἴκοι διαγόντων, οὗτοι ἀντὶ πάντων ὑμῶν τῇ
            ἐμῇ προσεδρεύουσι λειτουργίᾳ· τοῦτο γὰρ ἔφη· *ὅτι μισθὸς ὑμῶν*
            οὗτός ἐστιν ἀντὶ τῶν λειτουργιῶν ὑμῶν, τῶν ἐν τῇ σκηνῇ τοῦ
    40   *μαρτυρίου.*ⁿ

---

f. Nm 18.14f.   g. Nm 18.16   h. Nm 18.17f.   i. Nm 18.19   j. 1Cor 9.13
k. Nm 18.20–24   l. Nm 18.31   m. Cf., e.g., Lv 10.16–18.   n. Nm 18.31

also receive votive offerings and firstborn animals.[f] He set the price of redemption for unclean animals: "Its price of redemption from the age of one month will be five shekels according to the shekel of the sanctuary, which is worth twenty obols."[g] But he ordered that the blood of clean firstborn animals be poured out at the base of the altar—the fat offered to him, but the meat taken by the priests, just as they took the breast and the shoulder of the other victims.[h] He referred to their share as a "covenant of salt,"[i] since according to the holy apostle, "Those attending on the altar have a share in the altar."[j] Some commentators claim that the name is derived from his command to sprinkle salt on the sacrifices.[1]

(2) Next, he informed the priests and Levites that he did not want them to receive an inheritance like the other tribes. Instead, the Levites were to be maintained by the whole people with tithes of the produce of the earth and of the profits accruing from flocks and herds, trading, and any other commerce.[k] He instructed the Levites to offer a tenth of the tithes to the priests, who were to partake of the tithes in every place,[l] but to eat inside the temple whatever was set aside for them from the sacrifices.[m] He called the tithes a "payment" for their service to the people. In effect, he declared, "While you are farming, trading, or living at home, the Levites devote themselves to my service in place of you all." That is the sense of "This is your payment for services conducted in the tabernacle of witness."[n]

1. The sealing of a covenant with a meal recalls Gn 31.51–54; the term "covenant of salt" occurs also at 2Chr 13.5.

XXXV

Πῶς νοητέον τὰ περὶ τῆς πυρρᾶς δαμάλεως διηγορευμένα;[a]

Προσενεχθῆναι μὲν ταύτην ὑπὲρ τῆς τοῦ λαοῦ ἁμαρτίας νενομοθέτηκε· προτυποῖ δὲ τὸ σωτήριον πάθος, ὃ τοῦ κόσμου παντὸς ἦρε τὴν ἁμαρτίαν. πυρρὰν δὲ προσκομισθῆναι κελεύει
5 δάμαλιν[b] ἵνα προτυπώσῃ τὸ γήϊνον σῶμα· καὶ γὰρ τοῦ Ἀδὰμ ἡ προσηγορία τὴν ἐρυθρὰν αἰνίττεται γῆν, ἐξ ἧς αὐτοῦ διεπλάσθη τὸ σῶμα.[c] καὶ τὸ ἄμωμον δὲ τῆς δαμάλεως τὸ ἀναμάρτητον προδηλοῖ τοῦ δεσπότου Χριστοῦ.[d] καὶ τὸ ἄζυγα εἶναι τὴν δάμαλιν[e] τὴν τοῦ σωτῆρος ἡμῶν ἐλευθερίαν
10 αἰνίττεται· ὁ γὰρ ζυγὸς τὴν δουλείαν δηλοῖ, ὁ δὲ Κύριος, τὸ δίδραχμον ἀπαιτούμενος, ἔφη, *ἄρα γε ἐλεύθεροί εἰσιν οἱ υἱοί.*[f] ἡ δὲ ἔξω τῆς παρεμβολῆς σφαγὴ τῆς δαμάλεως[g] τὸ ἔξω τῆς πύλης γενόμενον τοῦ σωτῆρος πάθος. ταῦτα δὲ σαφέστερον διδάσκει ὁ θεῖος ἀπόστολος ἐν τῇ πρὸς ἑβραίους ἐπιστολῇ.[h]
15 πᾶσαν δὲ τὴν δάμαλιν σὺν τῷ δέρματι καὶ τοῖς ἄλλοις κατακαυθῆναι προσέταξεν,[i] ἐπειδὴ πάντα καθαρὰ τοῦ δεσπότου Χριστοῦ. τὸ δὲ ξύλον τὸ κέδρινον τοῦ σταυροῦ σύμβολον ἦν· ὥσπερ γὰρ τοῦτο ἄσηπτον, οὕτως ἐκεῖνο ζωοποιόν· τὸ δὲ κόκκινον τοῦ δεσποτικοῦ αἵματος, τὸ δέ γε
20 ὕσσωπον ὅτι ἡ ζωτικὴ θερμότης διέλυσε τοῦ θανάτου τὴν ψυχρότητα.[j] τὸν μέντοι κατακαίοντα τὴν δάμαλιν ἀκάθαρτον μέχρις ἑσπέρας φησὶν εἶναι εἰς τύπον τῶν τὸν δεσπότην ἐσταυρωκότων Χριστόν.[k]

Ταύτῃ δὲ τῇ σποδῷ μεθ' ὕδατος χρωμένους ἐκέλευσε
25 περιρραίνεσθαι τοὺς τῷ τεθνηκότι πελάζοντας, ἢ ὀστῶν ἁπτομένους, ἢ ἄλλῳ τινὶ τοιούτῳ μολυνομένους.[l] *καὶ ἄνθρωπος,*

---

xxxv A *[32]*, B, C, 4 7 9 10 31 35 37 = 21 mss.

a. Nm 19   b. Nm 19.2   c. Gn 2.7   d. *Cf.*, e.g., 2Cor 5.21; 1Pt 2.22; 1Jn 3.5.
e. Nm 19.2   f. Mt 17.26   g. Nm 19.3   h. Heb 9.11–14; 13.12   i. Nm 19.5
j. Nm 19.6   k. Nm 19.7   l. Nm 19.11–19

XXXV

How are we to understand the prescriptions regarding the red heifer?[a]

God prescribed the offering of this animal for the sin of the people, and this prefigured the saving passion, which took away the sin of the whole world. He commanded them to bring him a red heifer[b] so as to prefigure the earthly body, since the name "Adam" suggests the red earth from which his body was formed.[1c] Furthermore, the heifer's freedom from blemish gave a prior indication of the sinlessness of Christ the Lord.[d] Its being unyoked hinted at our Savior's freedom, for the yoke signifies slavery,[e] but when the Lord was asked to pay the didrachma, he said, "Surely the sons are free."[f] The slaying of the heifer took place outside the camp,[g] the passion of the Savior outside the gate as the holy apostle teaches quite explicitly in his letter to the Hebrews.[h] God ordered the whole heifer to be burned with its skin and everything else,[i] since everything pertaining to Christ the Lord is pure. The cedar wood was a symbol of the cross: as cedar is incorruptible, so the cross is life-giving. The crimson was symbolic of the Lord's blood, the hyssop of the fact that the warmth of life melted the frigidity of death.[j] Whoever burned the heifer was declared unclean till evening as a type of those who crucified Christ the Lord.[k]

He ordered them to combine this dust with water to sprinkle anyone who had come near a dead person, touched the bones of the dead, or been defiled by something similar.[l] "Whoever is not puri-

1. Nm 19.1–13 is the only biblical text setting out this ritual for purifying the unclean. Here Theodoret confuses two separate Hebrew stems, one the source of the words "man" and "earth," the other of "red" (cf. *in Cant. cant.* 5.10 and *in Is.* 63.1).

φησίν, ὃς ἐὰν ... μὴ ἀφαγνισθῇ, ἐξολοθρευθήσεται ἡ ψυχὴ
ἐκείνη ἐκ μέσου τῆς συναγωγῆς ... ὅτι ὕδωρ ῥαντισμοῦ οὐ
περιερραντίσθη ἐπ' αὐτόν.[m] οὕτω καὶ ὁ Κύριος ἐν τοῖς ἱεροῖς
30 εὐαγγελίοις ἔφη, ἐὰν μή τις γεννηθῇ ἐξ ὕδατος καὶ
πνεύματος, οὐ μὴ εἰσέλθῃ εἰς τὴν βασιλείαν τῶν οὐρανῶν.[n]

XXXVI

Διὰ τί ἀκάθαρτον εἶναι λέγει μέχρις ἑσπέρας καὶ τὸν
περιρραίνοντα καὶ τὸν περιρραινόμενον;[a]

Ἐπειδὴ κατὰ τὸν νόμον ἀκάθαρτος ἦν ὁ ἁπτόμενος ὀστέου
νεκροῦ.[b] οὐκοῦν ἡ κάθαρσις τῇ ἀληθείᾳ συμβαίνει· διὰ Χριστοῦ
5 γὰρ ἡ κάθαρσις· τὸ δὲ ἀκάθαρτον εἶναι τῷ νόμῳ· ὁ δὲ νόμος
προετύπου τὴν χάριν. καὶ οὗτοι δὲ ἀκάθαρτοι ἦσαν μέχρις
ἑσπέρας, τουτέστι, μέχρι τοῦ τέλους τοῦ νόμου· ὄρθρῳ γὰρ
ἔοικεν ἡ δεσποτικὴ παρουσία· τοῖς γὰρ ἐν σκότῳ καὶ σκιᾷ
θανάτου καθημένοις φῶς ἀνέτειλεν,[c] ἤ φησιν ὁ προφήτης
10 Ἡσαΐας· καὶ ἀλλαχοῦ δὲ αὐτὸς εἴρηκεν ὁ Θεός, τοῖς δὲ
φοβουμένοις με ἀνατελεῖ ἥλιος δικαιοσύνης, καὶ ἴασις ἐν ταῖς
πτέρυξιν αὐτοῦ·[d] καὶ πάλιν, ἰδοὺ ἀνήρ, Ἀνατολὴ ὄνομα αὐτῷ.[e]

XXXVII

Τί δή ποτε ὠργίσθη τῷ Μωϋσῇ καὶ τῷ Ἀαρὼν ὁ δεσπότης
Θεὸς ἡνίκα τὸ ὕδωρ ἐκ τῆς πέτρας ἐξήγαγον;[a]

m. Nm 19.20   n. Jn 3.5

---

xxxvi A *[32]*, B, C⁻¹, 4 7 9 10 31 35 37 = 20 mss.

a. Nm 19.19, 21   b. Nm 19.16   c. Mt 4.16; Is 9.2   d. Mal 4.2 (LXX var.)
e. Zec 6.12

---

xxxvii A *[32]*, B, C⁻¹, 4 7 9 10 31 35 37 = 20 mss.

a. Nm 20.9–12

fied, that person will be cut off from the midst of the assembly, because the water of sprinkling was not sprinkled on him."[m] Just so, the Lord himself said in the sacred Gospels, "No one who is not born again of water and Spirit will enter into the Kingdom of Heaven."[n]

XXXVI

Why did the Law declare unclean till evening both the person who sprinkled and the person who received the sprinkling?[a]

Because, according to the Law, the person touching the bones of a corpse was unclean.[b] Now, cleansing is consequent on the fulfillment, since cleansing is accomplished through Christ. Uncleanness, on the other hand, was consequent on the Law, but the Law prefigured grace. And they were unclean till evening, that is, till the end of the Law, for the Lord's coming was like a dawn. As the prophet Isaiah says, "A light has dawned on those dwelling in darkness and the shadow of death."[c] And elsewhere God himself said, "The Sun of Righteousness will rise on those who fear me, with healing in his wings";[d] and again, "Lo, a man, 'Dawn' is his name."[1e]

XXXVII

Why was the Lord God angry with Moses and Aaron when they brought water out of the rock?[a]

1. *Cf.* Q. 3 on Nm (and note 3) where this series of texts has already been cited.

Ἀθυμοῦσιν αὐτοῖς διὰ τὴν τῆς ἀδελφῆς τελευτὴν
ἐπέκειντο,[b] διὰ τὴν τοῦ ὕδατος στασιάζοντες σπάνιν.[c]
5 δυσχεραίνοντες οὖν τὴν πολλὴν αὐτῶν ἀκρασίαν, ἀμφιβόλοις
ἐχρήσαντο ῥήμασιν, τὸ ὕδωρ ἐξαγαγόντες· ἔφη γὰρ οὕτως ὁ
νομοθέτης· ἀκούσατέ μου, οἱ ἀπειθεῖς· μὴ ἐκ τῆς πέτρας
ταύτης ἐξάξω ὑμῖν ὕδωρ;[d] τούτου χάριν ὁ δεσπότης Θεὸς τὴν
κατ' αὐτῶν ἐξενήνοχε ψῆφον· ἔφη δὲ οὕτως· ὅτι οὐκ
10 ἐπιστεύσατέ μοι ἁγιάσαι με ἐναντίον τῶν υἱῶν Ἰσραήλ, διὰ
τοῦτο οὐκ εἰσάξετε ὑμεῖς τὴν συναγωγὴν ταύτην εἰς τὴν γῆν
ἣν ἔδωκα αὐτοῖς.[e] τοῦτο καὶ μελῳδῶν, ὁ θεῖος εἶπε Δαβίδ· καὶ
ἐκακώθη Μωϋσῆς δι' αὐτούς, ὅτι παρεπίκραναν τὸ πνεῦμα
αὐτοῦ, καὶ διέστειλεν ἐν τοῖς χείλεσιν αὐτοῦ[f] ὀργιζόμενος
15 γὰρ ἐκείνοις, ἀμφιβόλως τὸν λόγον προήνεγκε. καὶ ἦν, οὐ τῆς
ψυχῆς, ἀλλὰ τῆς γλώττης ἡ ἀμφιβολία· τοῦτο γὰρ ἔφη·
διέστειλεν ἐν τοῖς χείλεσιν αὐτοῦ. ἰστέον μέντοι ὡς, ἕτερον
οἰκονομῶν, ὁ Θεὸς ταύτην ἐξενήνοχε τὴν ἀπόφασιν· ὅπερ εἰς
καιρὸν δηλώσομεν.

XXXVIII

Τί δή ποτε διὰ τοῦ χαλκοῦ ὄφεως θεραπεύεσθαι προσέταξεν
ὁ Θεὸς τὰ τῶν ὄφεων δήγματα;[a]

Προτυποῖ καὶ τοῦτο τὸ σωτήριον πάθος. διὰ γὰρ τοῦ ὄφεως
ἡ ἁμαρτία ἐβλάστησεν, ὅθεν καὶ τὴν κατάραν παρὰ τοῦ Θεοῦ
5 τῶν ὅλων ἐδέξατο.[b] τύπος τοίνυν καὶ τῆς ἁμαρτίας καὶ τῆς
κατάρας ὁ ὄφις. ἐπειδὴ τοίνυν ὁ δεσπότης Χριστὸς ἐν
ὁμοιώματι σαρκὸς ἁμαρτίας,[c] ἥ φησιν ὁ θεῖος ἀπόστολος,
ἐπεφάνη· σῶμα μὲν γὰρ ἀληθῶς ἔλαβεν, ἁμαρτίαν δὲ οὐκ
ἐποίησεν, οὐδὲ εὑρέθη δόλος ἐν τῷ στόματι αὐτοῦ[d]

b. Nm 20.1   c. Nm 20.2–5   d. Nm 20.10   e. Nm 20.12   f. Ps 106.32f.

xxxviii A [32], B, C⁻¹, 4 7 9 10 31 35 37 = 20 mss.

a. Nm 21.4–9   b. Gn 3.1–5, 13–15   c. Rom 8.3   d. 1Pt 2.22; Is 53.9

Suffering from a shortage of water,[c] the people importuned
Moses and Aaron while they were grieving for the death of their sister.[b] And in their annoyance at this display of petulance, they used
ambiguous words when they drew forth the water. Indeed, the lawgiver put it like this: "Listen to me, you unbelievers; surely I am not
going to bring water out of this rock for you, am I?"[d] Therefore, the
Lord God delivered this sentence upon them: "Because you did not
trust me and show my holiness before the children of Israel, you
shall not lead this congregation into the land I have given them."[e]
This is what the divinely inspired David said in song: "Moses suffered harm on their account, because they provoked his spirit, and
he gave command with his lips."[f] That is to say, in his anger against
them, he spoke ambiguously, but this was an ambiguity of language,
not of soul; hence the statement, "He gave command with his lips."
Yet you should realize that, when God delivered this verdict, he had
in mind another purpose, which we shall point out in due course.[1]

XXXVIII

Why did God ordain the cure of the snakebites by means of a
bronze serpent?[a]

This, too, prefigures the saving passion. Sin came into being
through the serpent, which, therefore, received a curse from the God
of the universe.[b] So the serpent is a type of both sin and curse. Now
because, as the holy apostle says, Christ the Lord "appeared in the
likeness of sinful flesh"[c] and took a real body but committed no sin,
"nor was guile found in his mouth,"[d] the saving passion is prefig-

1. C.E. L'Heureux provides (on 20.1–13) an overview of the discussion of the
precise nature of Moses' offense in Nm 20. Some have argued that, though instructed by God simply to speak to the rock (20.8), Moses struck it with the rod,
and not just once, but twice. Others, including Theodoret, who interpret this passage in light of Ps 106.32f., have identified the fault in Moses' response to the people in v. 10. Note that in his *Questions on Exodus,* Theodoret had offered no com-

10 προτυποῦται τὸ σωτήριον πάθος ἐν τῷ ὄφει τῷ χαλκῷ. ὥσπερ
γὰρ ὁ χαλκοῦς ὄφις ἴνδαλμα μὲν τῶν ὄφεων ἦν, οὐκ εἶχε δὲ
τῶν ὄφεων τὸν ἰόν, οὕτως ὁ μονογενὴς υἱὸς σῶμα μὲν εἶχεν
ἀνθρώπινον, κηλῖδα δὲ ἁμαρτημάτων οὐκ εἶχε.[e] καὶ καθάπερ οἱ
ὑπὸ τῶν ὄφεων δακνόμενοι, εἰς τὸν χαλκοῦν ἀποβλέποντες
15 ὄφιν, σωτηρίας ἀπήλαυον, οὕτως οἱ ὑπὸ τῆς ἁμαρτίας
πληττόμενοι, τῷ πάθει τοῦ σωτῆρος ἡμῶν ἀνενδοιάστως
πιστεύοντες, κρείττους ἀποφαίνονται τοῦ θανάτου καὶ τῆς
αἰωνίου ζωῆς ἀπολαύουσιν.

XXXIX

Εἰ μάντις ἦν ὁ Βαλαάμ, τί δή ποτε τὸν Κύριον ἠρώτα;[a]
Ἐκεῖνος μὲν οὐ τὸν ἀληθινὸν ἠρώτα Θεόν· ἀπεκρίνατο δὲ
αὐτῷ, οὐχ ὁ παρ' αὐτοῦ καλούμενος, ἀλλ' ὁ παρ' αὐτοῦ
ἀγνοούμενος· *ἦλθε, γάρ φησιν, ὁ Θεὸς πρὸς Βαλαὰμ καὶ εἶπεν*
5 *αὐτῷ, τί οἱ ἄνθρωποι οὗτοι παρὰ σοί;*[b] οὐκ ἐπειδὴ τὴν αἰτίαν
τῆς ἐκείνων παρουσίας ἠγνόει, ἀλλ' ἵνα, παρὰ τοῦ μάντεως
λαβὼν ἀφορμήν, τὸ πρακτέον κελεύσῃ.

XL

Τίνος χάριν, κελεύσας αὐτῷ μὴ ἀπελθεῖν, πάλιν ἐκέλευσεν
ἀπελθεῖν;[a]

---

e. 2Cor 5.21

---

xxxix A *[32]*, B, C⁻¹, 4 7 9 10 31 35 37 = 20 mss.

a. Nm 22.8   b. Nm 22.9

---

xl A *[32]*, B, C⁻¹, 4 7 9 10 31 35 37 = 20 mss.

a. Nm 22.12, 20

ured in the bronze serpent.[1] That is, as the bronze serpent was an image of real serpents but lacked their venom, so the only-begotten Son had a human body but no stain of sin.[e] And as those bitten by the snakes were delivered from death by gazing on the bronze serpent, so those stricken by sin prove superior to death and receive eternal life by placing unquestioning faith in the passion of our Savior.

XXXIX

If Balaam was a seer, why did he enquire of the Lord?[a]

Balaam did not direct his question to the true God, but he received his response, not from the god on whom he had called, but from the One he did not know. As Scripture says, "God came to Balaam, and said to him, 'Why are these men with you?'"[b] Not that God was ignorant of the reason for their presence; rather, he desired to use the seer's response as an opportunity to issue his commands.

XL

Why was it that, after forbidding Balaam to go, God then commanded him to go?[a]

----

ment on a different version of this story in Ex 17, where no punishment is imposed on Moses, a story which he ignores in the present question as he had in his earlier *Commentary on the Psalms.* In both his comment on Ps 105.33 (LXX) and in Q. 43 on Dt, Theodoret tries to explain why it was better, in the larger scheme of things, that Moses not enter the promised land.

---

1. Chrysostom offers a similar, though more extensive, development of this typology in *hom. in Ioh.* 27.2, a discussion of Jn 3.12–14, where Jesus himself draws the parallel between the lifting up of the serpent and the lifting up of the "Son of Man."

Ἐπειδή, τῶν ἀπαγγελθέντων χρημάτων ὁ Βαλαὰμ ἐρασθείς,
ἤρετο πάλιν εἰ χρὴ τοῖς ἀποσταλεῖσιν συναπελθεῖν, νομίσας
5 μεταμελείᾳ κεχρῆσθαι τὸν δεσπότην Θεόν, ἐπέτρεψεν
ἀπελθεῖν, μονονουχὶ λέγων, ἄπελθε μέν, ἐπειδὴ τοῦτο πρᾶξαι
ποθεῖς. ἴσθι μέντοι ὡς ἅπερ ἂν ἐθελήσω λαλήσεις.

XLI

Διὰ τί, κελεύσας ἀπελθεῖν, διὰ ἀγγέλου τὴν πορείαν
κωλύει;[a]
Δεδίττεται αὐτὸν καὶ τῇ τῆς ὄνου φωνῇ παρὰ φύσιν
γεγενημένῃ καὶ τῇ τοῦ ἀγγέλου θεωρίᾳ[b] ἵνα γνῷ πόσην ὁ
5 Θεὸς τοῦ λαοῦ ποιεῖται κηδεμονίαν. φασὶ δέ τινες τὸν
ἄγγελον τὸν Μιχαὴλ εἶναι, τὸν τοῦ λαοῦ προστατεύοντα.[c]

XLII

Καὶ ποίαν ἰσχὺν εἶχεν ἡ τοῦ μάντεως ἀρά, μὴ βουλομένου
Θεοῦ;[a]
Ἰσχὺν μὲν εἶχεν οὐδεμίαν· ψευδὴς γὰρ ἦν ἡ περὶ αὐτοῦ
κατέχουσα δόξα· ἐπειδὴ δέ, συνεχῶς παρανομῶν, ὁ λαὸς
5 ὑπέμενεν θεηλάτους πληγάς, πρὸς τὴν ἐκείνων ἀσθένειαν τὰ
κατὰ τὸν Βαλαὰμ ᾠκονόμησεν ὁ δεσπότης Θεός. ἵνα γὰρ μὴ
νομίσωσι, παρὰ τοῦ Θεοῦ παιδευόμενοι, διὰ τὰς τοῦ μάντεως
ἀρὰς συμφοραῖς περιπίπτειν, οὐκ εἴασε τὸν μάντιν χρήσασθαι
ταῖς ἀραῖς, τὰς τῶν ἀνοήτων ἀφορμὰς περικόπτων. ὅτι γάρ, εἰ
10 καὶ ἰσχύν τινα εἶχον αἱ τοῦ μάντεως ἀραί, ῥάδιον ἦν τῷ τὰ

XLI A [32], B, C⁻¹, 4 7 9 10 31 35 37 = 20 mss.
a. Nm 22.22f.   b. Nm 22.24–35   c. Dn 12.1

XLII A [32], B, C⁻¹, 4 7 9 10 31 35 37 = 20 mss.
a. Nm 24.10–13

Question XLII

In his desire for the money promised him, Balaam, imagining that the Lord God could change his mind, again asked whether he should accompany the men sent to him, so God allowed him to go. It was as if he said, "Since you want to do it, go, but be sure to say whatever I choose."

XLI

Why did God command him to go and then block his way with the angel?[a]

God frightened him with the donkey's preternatural speech and the vision of the angel[b] to let him know the extent of his care for his people. Some commentators assert that the angel was Michael, the protector of the people.[1c]

XLII

What power did the curse of the seer have against the will of God?[a]

It had no power at all, for his reputation, though widespread, was false. Since, as a result of their constant lawlessness, the people kept suffering heaven-sent afflictions, it was with a view to their frailty that the Lord God arranged the events regarding Balaam. You see, in case they might imagine they were suffering disasters caused by the seer's curse when they were really being chastised by God, he did not allow the seer to pronounce curses; he thus cut short any ground of argument that fools might latch onto. In fact, anyone schooled in

---

1. *Cf.* Theodoret's remarks on Michael in his comment on Dn 10.13, a passage presupposing that God had given each nation a guardian angel of its own (*cf.* Dt 32.8); *v.* also Orig., *hom.* 13.7 and 14.3 *in Num.* In his *Commentary on Colossians* (on 2.18), Theodoret had mentioned the contemporary cult of the angels and reported the erection of chapels to Michael.

πάντα τεκτηναμένῳ ταύτας ἀποφῆναι ματαίας δῆλον τοῖς τὰ
θεῖα πεπαιδευμένοις· *Κύριος, γάρ φησι, διασκεδάζει βουλὰς*
ἐθνῶν, ἀθετεῖ δὲ λογισμοὺς λαῶν, καὶ ἀθετεῖ βουλὰς ἀρχόντων·
ἡ δὲ βουλὴ τοῦ Κυρίου μένει εἰς τὸν αἰῶνα.[b]

15   Ὁ μέντοι Βαλαάμ, καὶ τοῦ Θεοῦ τὴν κηδεμονίαν
μεμαθηκώς, ταῖς θυσίαις μεταπεῖσαι πειρᾶται, ἕνα τῶν
ψευδωνύμων εἶναι τοπάζων, οὓς καὶ *τρεπτοὺς* ὀνομάζουσιν οἱ
τούτων θεραπευταί.[c] τὸ δὲ *ἐπορεύθη ἐπ' εὐθεῖαν*[d] δηλοῖ ὅτι τὸ
πρακτέον ἀληθῶς ἠβουλήθη μαθεῖν. τούτου χάριν τὸ ἀκάθαρτον
20   στόμα τοῦ παναγίου πνεύματος ἐδέξατο τὴν ἐνέργειαν, καὶ
φθέγγεται ἃ μὴ βούλεται, καὶ βοᾷ, *τί ἀράσομαι ὃν μὴ ἀρᾶται*
Κύριος; καὶ τί καταράσομαι ὃν μὴ καταρᾶται Θεός;[e] καὶ
προαγορεύει τὰ ἐσόμενα· *ἰδοὺ λαὸς μόνος κατοικήσει καὶ ἐν*
ἔθνεσιν οὐ συλλογισθήσεται. τίς ἐξηκριβώσατο σπέρμα Ἰακώβ,
25   *καὶ τίς ἐξαριθμήσεται δήμους Ἰσραήλ;*[f] εἶτα αἰτεῖ τῆς ἐκείνων
μετασχεῖν κοινωνίας· *ἀποθάνοι ἡ ψυχή μου ἐν ψυχαῖς δικαίων,*
καὶ γένοιτο τὸ σπέρμα μου ὡς τὸ σπέρμα τούτων.[g]
      Ἐπειδὴ δέ, δυσχεράνας ὁ Βαλὰκ καὶ τοπάσας ὅτι, τῶν
ἑβραίων τὸ πλῆθος ἰδών, τὴν εὐλογίαν προσήνεγκεν, εἰς
30   ἕτερον αὐτὸν ἀπήγαγε τόπον, ἐξ οὗ μέρος οἷόν τε ἦν ἰδεῖν
τοῦ λαοῦ,[h] εἰκότως πάλιν τὸ πανάγιον πνεῦμα δι' ἐκείνου
φησίν, *οὐχ ὡς ἄνθρωπος ὁ Θεὸς διαρτηθῆναι, οὐδὲ ὡς υἱὸς*
ἀνθρώπου ἀπειληθῆναι· αὐτὸς εἰπών, οὐχὶ ποιήσει; λαλήσει καὶ
οὐκ ἐμμενεῖ;[i] ἄτρεπτος, φησίν, ὦ Βαλάκ, καὶ ἀναλλοίωτος, ἡ
35   τοῦ Θεοῦ φύσις οὐκ ἔχει γνώμην τρεπτὴν τοῖς ἀνθρώποις
παραπλησίως· *ἰδού, εὐλογεῖν παρείλημμαι· εὐλογήσω, καὶ οὐ*
μὴ ἀποστραφῶ.[j]

---

b. Ps 33.10f.   c. Nm 23.14, 29f.   d. Nm 23.3   e. Nm 23.8
f. Nm 23.9f.   g. Nm 23.10   h. Nm 23.13   i. Nm 23.19   j. Nm 23.20

Scripture knows that he who has fashioned everything could have easily voided the seer's curses even if they had had any force: "The Lord scatters the counsels of nations, brings to naught the schemes of peoples, and brings to naught the counsels of their leaders, but the Lord's counsel abides forever."[b]

Even after Balaam had recognized God's love for Israel, he tried to win him over with sacrifices, as he took him to be one of the false gods that their worshippers called "changeable."[c] Yet the words "he went straight forward"[1d] suggest that he really wanted to know the right thing to do. Therefore, his unclean mouth received the power of the most Holy Spirit and uttered what he had not intended. He cried out, "Why shall I curse whom God does not curse and denounce whom God does not denounce?"[e] He also foretold the future: "Lo, a people will dwell in solitude and will not be reckoned among the nations. Who has tallied the offspring of Jacob, or who will count the people of Israel?"[f] He then asked to share their company: "May my soul die among the souls of the righteous, and my offspring be like their offspring."[g]

Then Balak was angered and suspected he had offered the blessing because he had seen the vast number of the Hebrews, so he took Balaam to a different spot, from which he would be able to see only part of the people.[h] Yet, as one might expect, the most Holy Spirit declared through him, "God is not like a man, that he should have doubts or like a son of man, that he should succumb to threats. Has he promised and will not deliver? If he says something, will it not abide?"[i] It is as if he had said, "Balak, God's nature is unchanging and without alteration; he does not change his mind like human beings: 'Lo, I have been appointed to give a blessing; blessing I shall give nor be diverted.'"[j]

---

1. This phrase, appearing at the end of Nm 23.3 in the LXX, has no equivalent in the MT.

XLIII

Τί ἐστιν ὡς δόξα μονοκέρωτος αὐτῷ;[a]

Ὁ μονόκερως ζῷόν ἐστιν ἓν ἔχων κέρας ἐν τῇ κεφαλῇ. περὶ
τούτου καὶ πρὸς τὸν Ἰὼβ ὁ δεσπότης ἔφη Θεός, βουλήσεται
δέ σοι μονόκερως δουλεῦσαι;[b] διὰ τούτου διδάσκων καὶ τὴν
5 δύναμιν τοῦ ζῴου καὶ τὸ ἀδούλωτον. τινὲς μὲν οὖν τούτῳ
ἀπείκασαν τὸν δεσπότην Θεόν. ἐγὼ δὲ οἶμαι περὶ τοῦ λαοῦ
τοῦτο εἰρῆσθαι, ὅτι, καθάπερ ὁ μονόκερως ἓν ἔχει κέρας,
οὕτως ὁ εὐσεβὴς λαὸς ἕνα προσκυνεῖ Θεόν. διὸ καὶ Δαβὶδ ὁ
μακάριος λέγει, ἐν σοὶ τοὺς ἐχθροὺς ἡμῶν κερατιοῦμεν.[c] πῶς
10 δὲ νοητέον τὸν ἕνα Θεὸν πολλάκις εἰρήκαμεν.

Τὸ δὲ οὐκ... ἔσται οἰωνισμὸς ἐν Ἰακώβ, οὐδὲ μαντεία ἐν
Ἰσραήλ· κατὰ καιρὸν ῥηθήσεται τῷ Ἰακὼβ καὶ τῷ Ἰσραὴλ τί
ἐπιτελέσει ὁ Θεὸς[d] οὕτω νοητέον· ὅτι κατὰ τοῦ Ἰσραὴλ οὔτε
μαντεία ἰσχύει, οὔτε οἰωνῶν παρατήρησις· ὁ γὰρ δεσπότης
15 Θεὸς διὰ τῶν οἰκείων προφητῶν καὶ τὰ ἐσόμενα αὐτῷ
προλέγει καὶ ὑποτίθεται τὸ πρακτέον.

XLIV

Τί ἐστιν οὐκ ἐπορεύθη Βαλαὰμ κατὰ τὸ εἰωθὸς εἰς
συνάντησιν τοῖς οἰωνοῖς;[a]

(1) Τῇ πείρᾳ μαθὼν ὡς οὐδὲν ὀνίνησι τῇ ματαίᾳ χρώμενος
τέχνῃ· ἀπείρῳ γὰρ τῷ μέτρῳ δυνατώτερος ὁ μεταφέρων αὐτοῦ
5 τὴν γλῶτταν εἰς ἅπερ ἐθέλει· οὐκέτι τοῖς συνήθεσι συμβόλοις
ἐχρήσατο, ἀλλ' εἰς ὑπουργίαν τοῦ Θεοῦ τὴν γλῶτταν ἀφώρισεν.

XLIII A [32], B, C[-1], 4 7 9 10 31 35 37 = 20 mss.

a. Nm 23.22   b. Jb 39.9   c. Ps 44.5   d. Nm 23.23

XLIV A [32], B, C[-1], 4 7 9 10 31 35 37 = 20 mss.

a. Nm 24.1

XLIII

What is the meaning of "His glory is like the unicorn's"?[a]

The unicorn is an animal that has a single horn on its head. The Lord God was again referring to this animal when he said to Job, "Will a unicorn wish to serve you?"[b]—in this conveying this animal's power and unwillingness to serve. Though some commentators have thought the comparison here is between the Lord God and this creature, I believe the reference is to the people; as the unicorn has one horn, so the pious adore one God. Hence, the blessed David says, "Through you we shall gore our foes."[1c] Now, I have often explained how the unity of God is to be understood.[2]

The verse, "There will be no augury in Jacob nor divination in Israel; in due time it will be revealed to Jacob and to Israel what God will perform"[d] is to be taken as follows: "Neither divination nor augury prevails against Israel, but, through his prophets, the Lord God foretells the future to Israel and sets out his commands."

XLIV

What is the meaning of "Balaam did not go as usual to meet the birds of omen"?[a]

(1) He had learned by experience that there was nothing to gain from this futile art, as he who diverted his speech for his own purposes was infinitely more powerful. So without recourse to the usual portents, he directed his tongue to the service of God.

1. Origen, who had also adduced Job 39.9 as a parallel to Nm 23.22, saw the unicorn as a symbol of Christ (*hom. 16.6 in Num.*). In fact, the Hebrew term *rem*, which appears in both passages, refers to an animal with two horns.
2. *Cf. Q.* 19 on Gn and *Q.* 2 on Dt.

Ἰστέον μέντοι ὥς τισιν ἔδοξε μηδὲν αὐτὸν περὶ τοῦ σωτῆρος ἡμῶν προειρηκέναι. οὓς ἐχρῆν συνιδεῖν ὅτι καὶ τῷ Ναβουχοδονόσορ, ἄγαν ὄντι δυσσεβεῖ, τὴν τοῦ Θεοῦ καὶ
10 σωτῆρος ἡμῶν ἀπεκάλυψε παρουσίαν· εἶδε γὰρ λίθον τμηθέντα *ἄνευ χειρῶν, καὶ πατάξαντα τὴν εἰκόνα, καὶ συντρίψαντα τὸν χρυσόν, τὸν ἄργυρον, τὸν χαλκόν, τὸν σίδηρον, τὸ ὄστρακον, καὶ γενόμενον ὄρος μέγα, καὶ καλύψαντα πᾶσαν τὴν γῆν.*[b] ὁ τοίνυν ἐκεῖνα δι' ἐκείνου προαγορεύσας καὶ διὰ τούτου
15 προείρηκε τῆς οἰκουμένης τὴν σωτηρίαν ἵνα καὶ παρὰ τοῖς ἔθνεσιν αἱ τοιαῦται προρρήσεις φυλάττωνται.

Μαρτυρεῖ δὲ τῇ προρρήσει τῶν πραγμάτων τὸ τέλος· ὁ γὰρ ἐξ Ἰούδα κατὰ σάρκα βλαστήσας, οὐ μόνον τοὺς ἀρχηγοὺς Μωάβ, ἀλλὰ καὶ πάντας τοὺς υἱοὺς Σὴθ προενόμευσεν.[c] υἱοὶ δὲ
20 τοῦ Σὴθ ἅπαντες ἄνθρωποι· ἀπόγονος γὰρ ὁ Νῶε τοῦ Σήθ,[d] ἐκ δὲ τοῦ Νῶε ἅπασα τῶν ἀνθρώπων ἡ φύσις. προεῖπε δὲ καὶ τὴν μακεδόνων κατὰ περσῶν νίκην· *ἐξελεύσεται, γάρ φησιν, ἐκ χειρὸς Χετιήμ, καὶ κακώσουσιν Ἀσσούρ, καὶ κακώσουσιν ἑβραίους.*[e] Ἀλέξανδρος μὲν γὰρ τὴν περσῶν κατέλυσε
25 βασιλείαν, Ἀντίοχος δέ, ἰουδαίοις ἐπιστρατεύσας, καὶ τὴν μητρόπολιν αὐτῶν εἷλε καὶ τὸν θεῖον νεὼν ἀπέφηνεν ἔρημον. αἱ μέντοι προρρήσεις αὗται, οὐ τῆς ψευδοῦς ἦσαν μαντείας, ἀλλὰ τῆς τοῦ παναγίου πνεύματος ἐνεργείας. ὁ γὰρ τὴν ὄνον ἀνθρωπείᾳ χρήσασθαι φωνῇ παρὰ φύσιν κελεύσας, οὗτος καὶ
30 διὰ τῆς γλώττης τοῦ μάντεως τὰ ἐσόμενα προηγόρευσεν·[f] *ἐγένετο, γάρ φησι, πνεῦμα Θεοῦ ἐν αὐτῷ.*[g] τοῦτο γέγονε καὶ ἐν τῷ παρανόμῳ Σαούλ, ὅθεν διὰ τὸ παράδοξον καὶ ἡ παροιμία ἐγένετο· *εἰ καὶ Σαοὺλ ἐν προφήταις;*[h]

(2) Τοσαύτην μέντοι πεῖραν τοῦ Θεοῦ λαβών, ὁ ψευδόμαντις
35 ἑτέρας ἐτεκτήνατο κατὰ τοῦ Θεοῦ μηχανάς· συννοήσας γὰρ ὡς ἄμαχον ἔχουσι δύναμιν, ὑπὸ τοῦ Θεοῦ τειχιζόμενοι, τὴν διὰ τῆς ἀκολασίας αὐτοῖς ἀσέβειαν ἐπενόησεν ἵνα, διὰ τὴν

b. Dn 2.34f.   c. Nm 24.17   d. Gn 5.28f.   e. Nm 24.24
f. Nm 22.28–30   g. Nm 24.2   h. 1Sm 10.11

You should know that some commentators have concluded that he made no prophecy regarding our Savior, but they should have understood that the coming of our God and Savior was revealed even to Nebuchadnezzar, despite his wickedness: "He saw a stone that, cut without human hands, struck the image and crushed the gold, silver, bronze, iron, and clay and then became a mighty mountain, which covered the whole earth."[b] He who predicted these things through Nebuchadnezzar also foretold the salvation of the world through Balaam so that prophecies such as these would be remembered among the gentiles.[1]

Now, the historical events confirmed this prophecy. He who was born of Judah according to the flesh plundered not only the princes of Moab but all the children of Seth.[c] All human beings are children of Seth, since Noah was a descendant of Seth,[d] and all the human race comes from Noah. He foretold also the Macedonians' victory against the Persians: "He will come forth from the hand of the Kittim, and they will oppress Assur, and they will oppress the Hebrews."[e] Now, Alexander overthrew the Persian empire, and Antiochus attacked the Jews, captured their capital, and left the Temple of God in desolation.[2] Indeed, these prophecies issued, not from false divination, but from the power of the most Holy Spirit. He who bade the donkey preternaturally adopt a human voice also used the seer's tongue to foretell the future.[f] Remember, Scripture says, "The spirit of God was in him."[g] The same thing happened in the case of that criminal Saul; hence, the proverb that arose from that unexpected event: "Is Saul also among the prophets?"[h]

(2) Even after so much experience of God, the false prophet continued his machinations against him. Since he had realized that those protected by God enjoy invincible power, he plotted to draw them into a sin of lust so that they would become vulnerable when

1. Here, as in his earlier commentary on the book of Daniel, Theodoret interprets the stone of Dn 2.34f. in a christological sense.
2. In this interpretation of the oracle (24.24), Theodoret apparently takes "As-

The Questions on Numbers

ἀσέβειαν τῆς θείας γυμνωθέντες ἐπικουρίας, εὐάλωτοι
γένωνται. καὶ τοῖς μαδιανίταις ὑπέθετο, μὴ τοὺς ἄνδρας κατ'
40 αὐτῶν, ἀλλὰ τὰς γυναῖκας ὁπλίσαι, γενέσθαι δὲ αὐτοῖς ὅπλον
τὴν τοῦ σώματος ὥραν καὶ τῶν λόγων τὸ δέλεαρ ἵνα,
δελεασθέντες ὑπὸ τοῦ κάλλους καὶ τοῖς λόγοις
καταθελχθέντες, τοῖς ἐκείνων εἰδώλοις λατρεύσωσι. καὶ τοῦτο
ἡμᾶς ὁ μακάριος ἐδίδαξε Μωϋσῆς, μετὰ τὴν κατὰ τῶν
45 μαδιανιτῶν νίκην ἐπιμεμψάμενος τοῖς τὰς γυναῖκας
ζωγρήσασιν· ἔφη γὰρ οὕτως· ἵνα τί ἐζωγρήσατε πᾶν θῆλυ;
αὗται γὰρ ἦσαν τοῖς υἱοῖς Ἰσραὴλ κατὰ τὸ ῥῆμα Βαλαὰμ τοῦ
ἀποστῆναι καὶ ὑπεριδεῖν τὸ ῥῆμα Κυρίου ἕνεκεν Φογώρ, καὶ
ἐγένετο... πληγὴ ἐν τῇ συναγωγῇ Κυρίου.[i] Φογὼρ δὲ τοῦ
50 εἰδώλου τὸ ὄνομα. ταύτης τῆς ἀσεβείας καὶ ὁ θεῖος ἐμνήσθη
Δαβίδ· καὶ ἐτελέσθησαν τῷ Βεελφεγὼρ καὶ ἔφαγον θυσίας
νεκρῶν.[j] τούτου χάριν καὶ ἐχθραίνειν τοῖς μαδιηναίοις
προσέταξεν ὁ Θεός, ὅτι ἐχθραίνουσιν αὐτοί, φησίν, ὑμῖν ἐν
δολιότητι... διὰ Φογώρ.[k] τοῦ μέντοι λαοῦ ἡμαρτηκότος, οἱ
55 ἄρχοντες ἐκρεμάσθησαν,[l] ὡς ὁ Σύμμαχος ἔφη, ὡς μὴ
ἐξάραντες τὸ πονηρὸν ἐξ αὐτῶν.

Τὸ δὲ ὑψωθήσεται ἢ Γὼγ βασιλεία αὐτοῦ,[m] ὁ Σύμμαχος
οὕτως ἡρμήνευσεν· καὶ ὑψωθήσεται ὑπὲρ Ὢγ βασιλεὺς αὐτοῦ.
δηλοῖ δὲ ὁ λόγος ὅτι, καὶ του Ὢγ ἐπιστρατεύσαντος,
60 περιέσονται διὰ τὸν ἐξ αὐτῶν κατὰ σάρκα βλαστήσαντα
βασιλέα.

i. Nm 31.15f.   j. Ps 106.28   k. Nm 25.18   l. Nm 25.4   m. Nm 24.7

divested of divine assistance because of their impiety. He advised the Midianites to arm, not their men, but their women against Israel and to use as weapons the bodily charms and enticing words of their women so that Israel, enticed by their beauty and charmed by their words, would serve their idols. This is what blessed Moses taught us when, after the victory over the Midianites, he upbraided the men who had taken the women alive. He said, "Why have you taken every female alive? On Balaam's advice, they were bent on making the sons of Israel rebel and neglect the word of the Lord in favor of Peor, and so a plague has befallen the assembly of the Lord."[i] "Peor" was the name of the idol. The divinely inspired David also mentioned their idolatry: "They were initiated into the rites of Baal Peor and ate sacrifices to the dead."[j] Therefore, God ordered them to regard the Midianites as their enemies: "Because they were your enemies and deceived you through Peor."[3k] According to the translation of Symmachus, when the people sinned, their rulers were hanged[l] for failing to root out the wickedness from among them.

Furthermore, Symmachus rendered the verse, "The kingdom of Gog will be exalted,"[m] as "Its king will be exalted over Og." This verse indicates that they will prevail even against the attack of Og, thanks to the King who drew his bodily descent from them.[4]

----

sur" to refer to the Assyrian empire and thus, by extension, to Persia, and "Kittim" to signify Greece. According to C.E. L'Heureux (on 24.20-25), the first should probably be identified with a tribe mentioned in Gn 25.3, 18, and 2Sm 2.9, and the second with the Philistines.

3. The author of chapter 31 has introduced into the wanderings of the tribes a war against the Midianites, who are said to have encouraged, on the advice of Balaam, the Israelites' idolatry with the Baal of Peor (25.16–18). For a discussion of the constitution of this narrative from various strands of biblical tradition, v. C.E. L'Heureux on 31.1–54. "Peor" is actually the name of the place, not the idol, as Theodoret had correctly pointed out in his comment on Ps 106.28 = 105.28 (LXX).

4. Theodoret apparently identifies the Gog of 24.7 (LXX) with one of the evil kings of the eschatological conflict envisioned in Rv 20.7–10. Christ, the king who draws his bodily descent from Israel, will prevail against him.

The Questions on Numbers

XLV

Τίνος ἕνεκα πάλιν ἀριθμηθῆναι προσέταξε ὁ Θεὸς τὸν λαόν;[a]

Ἐπειδὴ κατὰ τῶν ἀριθμηθέντων ἤδη τὴν ψῆφον ἐξήνεγκεν, ἔμελλεν δὲ τοὺς ἐκείνων παῖδας εἰς τὴν ἐπηγγελμένην
5 εἰσαγαγεῖν γῆν, περὶ ὧν εἶπον ἐκεῖνοι ὅτι αἰχμάλωτοι ἔσονται,[b] ἐκέλευσεν ἀριθμηθῆναι καὶ τούτους ἵνα δείξῃ τῆς οἰκείας εὐλογίας τὴν δύναμιν, ὅτι, καὶ τῶν πατέρων ἀναιρεθέντων, ὁ αὐτὸς διέμεινεν ἀριθμός.[c]

XLVI

Τί δή ποτε κλήρῳ μερισθῆναι τὴν γῆν προσέταξεν ὁ Θεός;[a]

Ὥστε πᾶσαν ἔριν καὶ φιλονεικίαν σβέσαι, ὡς τοῦ Θεοῦ διὰ τοῦ κλήρου τὴν γῆν διανέμοντος· οὕτως γὰρ ψήφῳ τινὶ τὸ πρᾶγμα πιστεῦσαι προσέταξε. τοῦτο πεποιήκασι καὶ οἱ θεῖοι
5 ἀπόστολοι πρὶν ἐπιφοιτῆσαι τὸ πανάγιον πνεῦμα· κλήρους γὰρ βαλόντες, ἱκέτευσαν τὸν ἅπαντα σαφῶς ἐπιστάμενον δεῖξαι τὸν ἀξιώτερον.[b] οὕτω καὶ ὁ θεῖος Παῦλος περὶ ἡμῶν ἔφη, *ἐν ᾧ... ἐκληρώθημεν, προορισθέντες κατὰ πρόθεσιν τοῦ... πάντα ἐνεργοῦντος κατὰ τὴν βουλὴν τοῦ θελήματος αὐτοῦ.*[c]

---

xlv A [32], B, C⁻¹, 4 7 9 10 31 35 37 = 20 mss.

a. Nm 26.1f.   b. Nm 14.3   c. Nm 1.46; 26.51

---

xlvi A [32], B, C⁻¹, 4 7 9 10 31 35 37 = 20 mss.

a. Nm 26.55   b. Acts 1.23–26   c. Eph 1.11

XLV

Why did God order a second census of the people?[a]

He had delivered sentence against those who had already been counted, and instead of them, intended to bring into the promised land their children, whom their parents had expected to be led off as prisoners of war.[b] He commanded a census of this generation as well to bring out the force of his blessing in that, despite the loss of their parents, the number remained the same.[c]

XLVI

Why did God order the use of the lot in the division of the land?[a]

This quenched any rivalry or dispute, since God was assigning the land by lot; thus, he ordered them to entrust this decision to a pebble. The holy apostles also did this before the coming of the most Holy Spirit. Casting lots, they implored the Omniscient to indicate who was the worthier of the two.[b] Likewise St. Paul said of us, "In him have we been allotted our portion, we who have been predestined according to the purpose of him who performs everything according to the decision of his will."[1c]

1. Nm. 26 presents two different methods of apportioning the land, the first according to the size of the tribe, the second by lot. The lot reappears in 33.54 and 34.13. As C.E. L'Heureux notes (on 26.52–56), it is unclear how the two principles could be reconciled.

XLVII

Τί δή ποτε, μαρτυρήσας ὁ δεσπότης Θεὸς τῷ Ἰησοῦ ὅτι ἔχει πνεῦμα Θεοῦ ἐν αὐτῷ, προσέταξε τῷ Μωϋσῇ ἐπιθεῖναι αὐτῷ τὰς χεῖρας;[a]

Τοῦτο καὶ ἐπὶ τοῦ Κορνηλίου ἐγένετο· μετὰ γὰρ τὸ λαβεῖν
5 τὴν χάριν τοῦ πνεύματος, τότε τοῦ βαπτίσματος ἠξιώθησαν.[b] καὶ μέντοι καὶ ὁ δεσπότης Χριστός, πάντα τοῦ πνεύματος τὰ χαρίσματα κατὰ τὸ ἀνθρώπειον πρὸ ὠδίνων δεξάμενος, τῷ Ἰωάννου βαπτίσματι προσελήλυθε, καὶ ἐπιτεθῆναι αὐτοῦ τῇ κεφαλῇ τὴν τοῦ θεράποντος προσέταξε χεῖρα,[c] καὶ ἔδειξε τὸ
10 πανάγιον πνεῦμα ἐν εἴδει περιστερᾶς ἐρχόμενον ἐπ' αὐτόν.[d] καὶ οἱ ἀπόστολοι, πνεῦμα ἅγιον διὰ τοῦ δεσποτικοῦ λαβόντες ἐμφυσήματος,[e] ἐδέξαντο τὴν οὐρανόθεν ἐπιφοιτήσασαν χάριν.[f] τοῦτο καὶ ἐπὶ Ἰησοῦ τοῦ Ναυῆ γεγένηται· εἶχε μὲν γὰρ τὴν χάριν τοῦ πνεύματος· ἵνα δὲ καὶ ὁ λαὸς πιστεύσῃ θεόθεν
15 αὐτὸν τῆς ἡγεμονίας τὴν χειροτονίαν δεδέχθαι, ἐπετέθησαν αὐτῷ τοῦ νομοθέτου αἱ χεῖρες. καὶ τοῦτο δέδρακεν ὁ θεῖος Μωϋσῆς, ὑπὸ τοῦ Θεοῦ προσταχθείς· ἐπιθήσεις, γάρ φησι, τὰς χεῖράς σου ἐπ' αὐτόν, καὶ στήσεις... ἐναντίον Ἐλεαζὰρ τοῦ ἱερέως, καὶ ἐντελῇ αὐτῷ ἐναντίον πάσης τῆς
20 συναγωγῆς,... καὶ δώσεις τῆς δόξης σου ἐπ' αὐτὸν ὅπως... εἰσακούσωσιν αὐτοῦ οἱ υἱοὶ Ἰσραήλ· καὶ ἐναντίον Ἐλεαζὰρ τοῦ ἱερέως στήσεται[g] ἀντὶ τοῦ· τὴν ἴσην ἐκείνῳ σχήσει τιμὴν καὶ διὰ τοῦ λογίου τῆς κρίσεως, ὃ τοῖς ἐκείνου στέρνοις ἐπέκειτο, τὸ πρακτέον μαθήσεται. μανθάνομεν δὲ
25 ἐντεῦθεν ὅπως οἱ παρὰ τῶν ἀρχιερέων τὴν χειροτονίαν δεχόμενοι τῆς πνευματικῆς μεταλαγχάνουσι χάριτος· καὶ γὰρ ἐνταῦθα ὁ δεσπότης ἔφη Θεός, δώσεις τῆς δόξης σου ἐπ' αὐτόν. θαυμάσαι δὲ ἄξιον τὸν προφήτην, ὅτι, καὶ παῖδας ἔχων

---

xlvii A [32], B, C[-1], 4 7 9 10 31 35 37 = 20 mss.

a. Nm 27.18   b. Acts 10.44–48   c. Mt 3.13–15   d. Mt 3.16   e. Jn 20.22
f. Acts 2.1–4   g. Nm 27.18–21

XLVII

Why did the Lord God order Moses to place his hands on Joshua after he had already testified that Joshua had the Spirit of God in him?[a]

This happened also in the case of Cornelius; it was after receiving the grace of the Spirit that he was granted baptism.[b] Furthermore, Christ the Lord had received all the charisms of the Spirit in his humanity before birth, though he presented himself for John's baptism and ordered the servant to place his hand on his head[c] and showed the most Holy Spirit "coming upon him" in the form of a dove.[d] Also, the apostles, who had already received the Holy Spirit through the breath of the Lord,[e] obtained the grace that descended on them from heaven.[f] The same thing happened also in the case of Joshua son of Nun. Though he already had the grace of the Spirit, the hands of the lawgiver were laid on him to ensure that the people would believe that God had chosen him to command. In this the divinely inspired Moses acted at God's command: "You shall place your hands on him and set him before Eleazar the priest, and lay your command upon him before the whole congregation and bestow upon him some of your glory so that the children of Israel will hearken to him. And he shall stand before Eleazar the priest."[g] In other words, "He will be as important as the priest, and through the oracle of judgment on Eleazar's chest, Joshua will learn what he must do."[1] Now, we learn from this that those who receive a commission from the high priests are allotted a share of the grace of the Spirit; hence, the Lord God said, "You will bestow upon him some of your glory." It is worthy of remark that the prophet, though hav-

---

1. *Cf.* note 10 to Q. 60 on Exodus. As in Ex 28, the LXX here speaks of the urim and thummim, or the breastplate on which they rest, as a λογεῖον, *i.e.,* "oracle."

καὶ ἀδελφόν, καὶ ἀδελφιδοῦν, οὐδένα τούτων ἡγεμόνα
30 προὐβάλλετο, ἀλλὰ τὸν Θεὸν ᾔρετο, καὶ τὸν ὑπ' αὐτοῦ
ψηφισθέντα κεχειροτόνηκε.[h]

Μετὰ ταῦτα, τῶν ἑορτῶν καὶ τῶν θυσιῶν ἀναμνήσας,[i]
νομοθετεῖ περὶ τῶν ὑπισχνουμένων τι προσφέρειν τῷ δεσπότῃ
Θεῷ. καὶ πρῶτον μὲν διηγόρευσε πάντα ὑπισχνούμενον ἔργῳ
35 τὴν ὑπόσχεσιν ἐμπεδοῦν.[j] τῆς δὲ ὑπὸ τὴν τοῦ πατρὸς
τελούσης ἐξουσίαν ὑπισχνουμένης, τὸν πατέρα βεβαιοῦν τὴν
ὑπόσχεσιν, καὶ ἐὰν ἐκεῖνος, ταύτης ὑπισχνουμένης, ἀνανεύσῃ,
μὴ ὑποκεῖσθαι τὴν ὑποσχομένην ἐγκλήματι· ἐὰν δέ, ταύτης
ἐπαγγελλομένης, ἢ συγκατάθηται ὁ πατὴρ ἢ σιγήσῃ, τὰ
40 ἐπηγγελμένα πληροῦσθαι.[k] τοῦτο δὲ καὶ ἐπὶ τῆς ἀνδρὶ
συνημμένης νενομοθέτηκε καὶ τὴν τοῦ ἀνδρὸς συγκατάθεσιν
βεβαιοῦν ἐκέλευσε τὴν ὑπόσχεσιν.[l]

XLVIII

Διὰ τί τῶν μαδιανιτῶν τὰς ἀνδρὶ συνημμένας ὁ νομοθέτης
ἀναιρεθῆναι προσέταξεν;[a]

Ὡς πεπαιδευμένας τῆς ἀσεβείας τὰ δόγματα καὶ
διαφθείρειν τοὺς ἐξανδραποδίσαντας δυναμένας.

h. Nm 27.15–23   i. Nm 28f.   j. Nm 30.1f.   k. Nm 30.3–5   l. Nm 30.6–15

xlviii A *[32]*, B, C⁻¹, 4 7 9 10 35 37 = 19 mss.
a. Nm 31.17

ing children, a brother, and a nephew, promoted none of these to the leadership, but consulted God and appointed the man chosen by him.[h]

Next, having recalled the feasts and the sacrifices,[i] he legislated regarding those who made vows of sacrifice to the Lord God. First, he declared that whoever made a vow should put it into effect.[j] In the case of a vow made by a woman still under the authority of her father, the father should confirm the vow. If he expressed his disagreement when she was making her vow, the woman who had made the vow would be free from any claim, whereas if her father expressed agreement or kept silent while she was making her vow, she was to fulfil her promise.[k] He set down the same law also for married women and commanded that the agreement of the husband should confirm the vow.[l]

XLVIII

Why did the lawgiver order the slaying of all the Midianite women who had had intercourse with a man?[a]

Because they were schooled in the teachings of idolatry and apt to corrupt their captors.

The Questions on Numbers

XLIX

Διὰ τί τοὺς σταθμοὺς ἀναγράπτους ὁ νομοθέτης πεποίηκεν;[a]

Ὥστε τοὺς εἰς ὕστερον ἐσομένους γνῶναι τὴν τοῦ Θεοῦ κηδεμονίαν· δι' ἀβάτων γὰρ αὐτοὺς καὶ ἀνύδρων ὁδηγήσας
5 χωρίων, ἀφθόνως αὐτοῖς τὴν τῶν ἀναγκαίων ἐχορήγησε χρείαν.

L

Τί δή ποτε τῷ ἀκουσίως πεφονευκότι μετὰ τὴν τοῦ ἀρχιερέως τελευτὴν ὁρίζει τὴν κάθοδον;[a]

Ὅτι τοῦ *κατὰ τὴν τάξιν τοῦ Μελχισεδὲκ*[b] ἀρχιερέως ὁ θάνατος λύσις τῆς τῶν ἀνθρώπων ἁμαρτίας ἐγένετο· οὗτος
5 εἰς τὸν παράδεισον ἐπανήγαγε τὸν ἐκεῖθεν ἐξορισθέντα. καὶ κατ' ἐκεῖνον δὲ τὸν καιρὸν ἐμάλαττεν ἡ φυγὴ τοῦ πεφονευκότος τὸν τῶν ἀγχιστευόντων θυμὸν καὶ τὴν φονικὴν αὐτῶν ὁρμὴν ἐχαλίνου. τὸ δὲ μετὰ τὴν τελευτὴν τοῦ ἀρχιερέως λυθῆναι τοῖς φεύγουσι τὴν τιμωρίαν ἱκανὸν ἦν
10 πεῖσαι τοὺς ἀγχιστεύοντας σβέσαι λοιπὸν τὴν ὀργήν, ὡς τοῦ ἀρχιερέως τετελευτηκότος ἐφ' οὗ τὸ πλημμέλημα γέγονε, καὶ τοῦ νομοθέτου ταύτην ὁρίσαντος καὶ τῇ πλημμελείᾳ καὶ τῇ τιμωρίᾳ τὴν λύσιν.

XLIX A [32], B, C⁻¹, 4 7 9 10 35 37 = 19 mss.
a. Nm 33.2

L A [32], B, c⁻¹, 51, 4 7 9 10 35 37 = 18 mss.
a. Nm 35.25–28, 32   b. Heb 7.11; Ps 110.4

Question L

XLIX

Why did the lawgiver make a record of the stages?[a]

So that later generations would know God's providence: how he had led them through trackless and waterless places and made abundant provision for their needs.

L

Why did he delay the return of the involuntary homicide until after the death of the high priest?[a]

Because the death of the high priest "according to the order of Melchizedek"[b] effected the removal of the sins of mankind. It was he who restored to paradise the man who had been cast out. Also, at that time, the homicide's flight mollified the anger of the next-of-kin and restrained their desire to kill. The cancellation of the penalty of banishment after the death of the high priest was sufficient to persuade the next-of-kin to extinguish their rage, as the high priest in whose time the fault had been committed was now dead, and the lawgiver had set this limit for release from both the offense and the penalty.[1]

---

1. Theodoret offers first a spiritual christological, then a pragmatic historical, interpretation of the amnesty prescribed at the death of a high priest (Nm 35.28, 32).

LI

Τίνος χάριν τὰς φυλὰς διακεκρῖσθαι προσέταξεν;[a]

"Ινα ἀκέραιον διαφυλαχθῇ τοῦ 'Ιούδα τὸ σπέρμα, δι' οὗ τὴν εὐλογίαν τοῖς ἔθνεσιν ὁ Θεὸς ἐπηγγείλατο.[b] ἐκοινώνησαν μέντοι ἀλλήλαις ἡ βασιλικὴ καὶ ἡ ἱερατικὴ φυλή, ἐπειδὴ καὶ
5 ἀρχιερεὺς κατὰ τὸ ἀνθρώπινον καὶ βασιλεὺς ὁ δεσπότης Χριστός.

ʟɪ A *[32]*, B, *c⁻¹*, *51, 4 7 9 10 35 37* = 18 mss.

a. Nm 36.5–9   b. Gn 49.10

LI

Why did he order that the tribes be kept separate?[a]

To maintain the purity of the seed of Judah, through which God had promised his blessing on the nations.[b] Nevertheless, the royal and priestly tribes intermarried with each other, since, according to his humanity, Christ the Lord was both high priest and king.[1]

1. In this interpretation of Nm 36.5–9, a ruling meant to keep marriage and, therefore, property within a tribe (*cf.* Tb 6.12; 7.9–13),Theodoret neglects the historical and pragmatic to concentrate entirely on the spiritual and christological; *cf.* note 1 to Q. 50 above. Theodoret develops the same christological typology in Q. 19.1 on Jos, where he cites examples of high priests who married women of Judah.

QUAESTIONES IN DEUTERONOMIUM

I

Διὰ τί τὸ πέμπτον βιβλίον τοῦ νομοθέτου Δευτερονόμιον ἐκλήθη;

(1) Ἐξαγαγὼν ἐξ Αἰγύπτου τὸν λαόν, ὁ δεσπότης Θεὸς ἔδωκεν ἐν τῷ Σινᾷ ὄρει τὸν νόμον, καθ' ὃν ἐχρῆν αὐτοὺς
5 πολιτεύεσθαι.[a] εἶτα τῷ δευτέρῳ ἔτει προσέταξε παραλαβεῖν τὴν γῆν, ἣν τοῖς προγόνοις αὐτῶν ἐπηγγείλατο δώσειν.[b] ἐκείνων δὲ ἀντειρηκότων καὶ τοῦτο δρᾶσαι μὴ βουληθέντων,[c] ὤμοσε μηδενὶ τῶν ἀριθμηθέντων ὑπὸ τοῦ νομοθέτου δώσειν ἐκείνην τὴν γῆν ἀλλὰ τούτους ἅπαντας ἐν τῇ ἐρήμῳ
10 καταναλώσειν.[d] τεσσαράκοντα τοίνυν διεληλυθότων ἐτῶν, κἀκείνων κατὰ τὴν θείαν ψῆφον διολωλότων, ἐκέλευσε τοὺς ἐκείνων ἀριθμηθῆναι παῖδας, τὴν αὐτὴν ἄγοντας ἡλικίαν,[e] ἥνπερ ἦγον ἐκεῖνοι καθ' ὃν ἠριθμήθησαν χρόνον.[f] τούτους μέλλων εἰσαγαγεῖν ὁ Θεὸς εἰς ἣν ἐπηγγείλατο γῆν, διδάσκει
15 διὰ τοῦ προφήτου τὸν νόμον, ὃν τοῖς παρανόμοις αὐτῶν‖ ἐδεδώκει πατράσι. τὸ τοίνυν Δευτερονόμιον ἀνακεφαλαίωσιν ἔχει τῶν ἐν τῇ Ἐξόδῳ, καὶ τῷ Λευιτικῷ, καὶ τοῖς Ἀριθμοῖς νενομοθετημένων τε καὶ πεπραγμένων. λέγει δὲ καὶ τὸν χρόνον καὶ τὸν τόπον, καθ' ὃν καὶ ἐν ᾧ τῇ νεολαίᾳ ταύτῃ τὴν
20 διδασκαλίαν προσήνεγκε· *πέραν, γάρ φησι, τοῦ Ἰορδάνου, ἐν τῇ ἐρήμῳ, πρὸς δυσμαῖς, ... ἐν τῷ τεσσαρακοστῷ ἔτει, ἐν τῷ*

‖6 (margin, line 15)

---

1 2c 6(inc.) [32], 5, a₂, 14(inc.) 17 24, c⁻¹, 51, 4 7 9 10 31 35 37 = 19 mss.
a. Ex 19.1–34.28   b. Nm 13   c. Nm 14.1–10   d. Nm 14.20–23
e. Nm 26.1f.   f. Nm 1.1–3

ON DEUTERONOMY

I

Why is the lawgiver's fifth book called "Deuteronomy"?

(1) When the Lord God had led the people out of Egypt, he gave them on Mt. Sinai the Law by which they were to live.[a] Then, in the second year, he ordered them to take possession of the land he had promised to give their ancestors.[b] But when they opposed him and were unwilling to do this,[c] he swore he would not give that land to any of those included in the census of the lawgiver but would destroy them all in the wilderness.[d] So, when forty years had passed, and all those people had died as God had decreed, he enjoined a census of their children, who were now of the same age[e] as their parents when they had been counted.[f] When he was about to bring them into the promised land, God taught these people, through the agency of the prophet, the Law that he had given to their lawbreaker parents. Therefore, Deuteronomy contains a summary of the legislation and the events of Exodus, Leviticus, and Numbers and mentions the time and place at which he offered this instruction to the youth of the nation: "Beyond the Jordan, in the wilderness, towards the west, in the fortieth year, in the tenth month, on the first day of the month, after he smote Sihon king of the Amorites and Og king

The Questions on Deuteronomy

δεκάτῳ μηνί, μιᾷ τοῦ μηνός, . . . μετὰ τὸ πατάξαι αὐτὸν τὸν
Σηὼν βασιλέα τῶν ἀμορραίων . . . καὶ τὸν ῍Ωγ βασιλέα τῆς
Βασάν.[g] καὶ ὅτι, οὐ δεύτερον νόμον ἔδωκεν, ἀλλὰ τῆς
25 προτέρας ἀναμιμνήσκει νομοθεσίας, αὐτὸ διδάσκει τοῦ βιβλίου
τὸ προοίμιον· ἤρξατο, γάρ φησι, Μωϋσῆς διασαφῆσαι τὸν
νόμον τοῦτον, λέγων, Κύριος ὁ Θεὸς ἡμῶν ἐλάλησεν ἡμῖν ἐν
Χωρήβ.[h]

(2) Εἶτα εἰρηκὼς καὶ ὡς προσέταξεν αὐτοὺς εἰσελθόντας
30 κληρονομῆσαι τὴν γῆν,[i] ἐπήγαγεν ὡς κατ' ἐκεῖνον εἰρήκει τὸν
καιρόν,[j] ὅτι μόνος ἐγὼ τοσούτων προστατεύειν οὐ δύναμαι
μυριάδων καὶ διὰ τοῦτο κατέστησα, φησί, χιλιάρχους καὶ
ἑκατοντάρχους ὥστε ἔχειν αὐτοὺς τῆς ἀρχῆς κοινωνούς.[k]
τούτων δὲ τῶν λόγων ἀνέμνησεν, ἐπειδήπερ Ἰησοῦν τὸν Ναυῆ
35 κατέστησε τῆς ἡγεμονίας διάδοχον,[l] διδάσκων ὡς, καὶ ἔτι
περιών, ἑτέροις τὴν προστασίαν ἐπίστευσε καὶ ὅτι χρὴ καὶ
τούτῳ προθύμως ὑπακούειν καὶ τὰ κελευόμενα δρᾶν.
ἀναμιμνήσκει δὲ αὐτοὺς ὅπως μὲν ὁ Θεὸς προσέταξε
παραλαβεῖν αὐτοὺς ἣν ἐπηγγείλατο γῆν,[m] ὅπως δὲ
40 κατασκόπους αὐτοὶ πεμφθῆναι προτέρους ἠξίωσαν, καὶ ὅτι,
ἐκείνων ἐπανελθόντων καὶ τὰ περὶ τῆς γῆς μεμηνυκότων,
ἠπίστησαν μὲν τῷ σεσωκότι Θεῷ, ἀπολαβεῖν δὲ τὴν γῆν οὐκ
ἠθέλησαν ὡς χαλεπῆναι μὲν τὸν δεσπότην Θεόν, ἀποφήνασθαι
δὲ κατὰ πασῶν ἐκείνων τῶν μυριάδων ὥστε μηδένα ἐκείνων εἰς
45 ἐκείνην τὴν γῆν εἰσελθεῖν, πλὴν Χαλὲβ υἱοῦ Ἰεφωνῆ·[n] οὗτος,
φησίν, ὄψεται αὐτήν, καὶ τούτῳ δώσω τὴν γῆν ἐφ' ἣν ἐπέβη
καὶ τοῖς υἱοῖς αὐτοῦ, διὰ τὸ προσκεῖσθαι αὐτὸν τὰ πρὸς
Κύριον.[o] τούτου μέντοι ἐμνημόνευσε μόνου. καὶ τὸν Ἰησοῦν
ἔταξεν ὡς ἄρχοντα, καὶ στρατηγόν, καὶ προφήτην· τοῦτο γὰρ

---

l. 22   δεκάτῳ F.M. : ἐνδεκάτῳ 2c [32], 12, 7 9 10, Sir. Sch. = "in the eleventh
month." Cf. Wevers and Quast, ap. crit. to Dt 1.3.
l. 40   αὐτοὶ . . . ἠξίωσαν 5, C[-52], 37, Sir. Sch. : αὐτοὶ . . . ἠξιώθησαν 12 :
αὐτοῖς . . . ἠξίωσαν 24 : αὐτοῖς . . . ἠξιώθησαν Pic. (Sch.) F.M.

g. Dt 1.1–4   h. Dt 1.5f.   i. Dt 1.6–8   j. Ex 18.18   k. Dt 1.9–15
l. Nm 27.18–23   m. Dt 1.19–21   n. Dt 1.22–36   o. Dt 1.36

Question 1

of Bashan."[g] We learn from the introduction to this book that he did not give a second Law but reminded them of the earlier legislation: "Moses began to clarify this Law, saying, 'The Lord our God spoke to us on Horeb.'"[1h]

(2) Then, after relating how he had ordered them to enter and take possession of the land,[i] Moses recalled how he had said back then[j] that he was unable to lead such a vast number by himself. "And that is why," he declared, "I appointed commanders of thousands and hundreds to have a share in government."[k] He reminded them of these words, since he had appointed Joshua son of Nun his successor[l] and wished to indicate that he had entrusted leadership to others while still alive and that the people should give Joshua their full obedience and do as he commanded. He reminded them of how God had ordered them to occupy the land he had promised;[m] how they had thought fit to send spies ahead; and how, when the spies returned and reported on the land, the people lost faith in the God who had saved them and refused to occupy the land, so that the Lord God was displeased and passed sentence on all that countless host, the sentence that none of them would enter the land except Caleb son of Jephunneh:[n] "He will see it, and, because of his devotion to the work of the Lord, I shall give him and his descendants the land on which he set foot."[o] He mentioned Caleb alone. Furthermore, he appointed Joshua ruler, general, and prophet, as he indicated in what

1. Our English title is taken from the Greek term δευτερονόμιον used in 17.18 (LXX). Though the Hebrew text of that verse clearly refers to a copy of this law, *i.e.* the law contained in this book, the Greek δευτερονόμιον could signify not only "copy" or "repetition of the Law" but also "a second law." Thus, both Jewish and early Christian exegetes discuss the question of the relationship of the law contained in this book with that promulgated on Sinai; *v.* A. Siquans, pp. 98–101. In fact, it is now widely believed that Dt reached its final form in the exilic period and was intended to replace the earlier Covenant Code of Ex 20.21–23.19; *v.* J. Blenkinsopp, "Deuteronomy," p. 94. The variation in the name of the holy mountain,

The Questions on Deuteronomy

50 δηλοῖ τὰ ἑξῆς· εἰπὼν γὰρ ὅτι, κἀμοὶ ὠργίσθη δι' ὑμᾶς ὁ
δεσπότης Θεός·ᵖ ὑμῶν γάρ με θορυβησάντων, οὐ κατὰ λόγον
τῷ θείῳ προστάγματι διηκόνησα καὶ τούτου χάριν εἰσαγαγεῖν
ὑμᾶς εἰς τὴν γῆν ἐκείνην κεκώλυμαι·�q ἀνέμνησε τῶν παρὰ τοῦ
Θεοῦ πρὸς αὐτὸν εἰρημένων·Ἰησοῦς υἱὸς Ναυῆ, ὁ παρεστηκώς
55 σοι, οὗτος εἰσελεύσεται ἐκεῖ· αὐτὸν κατίσχυσον, ὅτι αὐτὸς
κατακληρονομήσει αὐτὴν τῷ Ἰσραήλ.ʳ ταῦτα δὲ λέγει,
διδάσκων αὐτοὺς ὡς θεόθεν ὁ στρατηγὸς τὴν χειροτονίαν
ἐδέξατο ἵνα μὴ πάλιν περὶ τῆς ἀρχῆς στασιάσωσιν.

Διηγεῖται δὲ αὐτοῖς ὅπως μέν, ὕστερον μεταμεληθέντες,
60 ἐβουλήθησαν πολεμῆσαι τοῖς χαναναίοις, ὅπως δὲ αὐτοὺς ὁ
Θεὸς διεκώλυσε, καὶ ὅτι, θρασυνόμενοι καὶ παρὰ τὴν θείαν
ἐντολὴν ἀναβάντες, ἡττηθέντες ἐπανῆλθον,ˢ καὶ ὅσον ἐν τῇ
ἐρήμῳ κατηνάλωσαν χρόνον, τὴν ἄβατον γῆν ἐκείνην καὶ
ἄνυδρον περιϊόντες,ᵗ τίνα τε ἰδουμαίοις καὶ μωαβίταις
|14 65 Ιδεδηλωκότες, φιλικῶν οὐκ ἔτυχον ἀποκρίσεων,ᵘ καὶ ὅπως τὸν
Σηὼν καὶ τὸν Ὢγ, τοὺς βασιλεῖς τῶν ἀμορραίων, πανστρατιᾷ
μετὰ τῶν τὰς πόλεις καὶ τὰς κώμας οἰκούντων πανωλεθρίᾳ
παρέδοσαν.ᵛ εἶπεν δὲ αὐτοῦ καὶ τὸ τοῦ σώματος μέγεθος· ἡ
γὰρ κλίνη, φησίν,Ὢγ σιδηρᾶ... ἐννέα πήχεων τὸ μῆκος
70 αὐτῆς, καὶ τεσσάρων πήχεων τὸ εὖρος αὐτῆς.ʷ

(3) Ἔπειτα παρήνεσε καὶ συνεβούλευσε φυλάττειν
ἐπιμελῶς τοῦ δεσπότου τὰς ἐντολάς· ἄκουε, γάρ φησιν,
Ἰσραήλ, τῶν δικαιωμάτων καὶ τῶν κριμάτων, ὅσα ἐγὼ διδάσκω

---

l. 65 φιλικῶν 5, c⁻¹, 51, 37, Sir. Sch. : φιλονεικούντων F.M., ap. crit. (The
nonsensical φιλιονεικούντων appears in the text.) = "what they proposed to the
Idumeans and Moabites and received no hostile response." V. Nm 20.18–21 for
Edom's unfriendly reception of the Israelite ambassadors.

p. Dt 1.37   q. Dt 1.37   r. Dt 1.38   s. Dt 1.41–45   t. Dt 2.7
u. Dt 2.8–22   v. Dt 2.24–3.10   w. Dt 3.11

follows. After saying, "Because of you, the Lord God grew angry with me as well[p] when you upset me with your clamor and I failed to carry out God's command as instructed, and for this I am prevented from leading you into the land,"[q] he recalled what God had said to him: "Joshua son of Nun, your assistant, is the man who will enter there. Encourage him, for he is the one who will take possession of the land for Israel."[r] Now, he said this to let them know that the general had received his commission from God so they would not rebel against his governance as they had against that of Moses.

Then he recounted how they later had a change of heart and wanted to wage war on the Canaanites, and that, though God forbade them, they were emboldened to go up in defiance of the divine will, were defeated, and returned;[s] how long a time they spent in the wilderness as they traversed that trackless and waterless land;[t] what they proposed to the Idumeans and Moabites and yet received no friendly response;[u] how they wiped out Sihon and Og, the kings of the Amorites, along with their armies and the inhabitants of their cities and towns;[v] and even how enormous that king was: "Og's bed was of iron; nine cubits was its length and four cubits its breadth."[2w]

(3) Then he exhorted them, he counseled them to observe carefully all the commandments of the Lord: "Listen, Israel, to all the ordinances and judgments that I instruct you to keep today, so that

----
"Sinai" in Exodus (Yahwistic) and "Horeb" here (Deuteronomistic), reflects the different periods and contexts within which these texts arose; *v.* R.E. Brown and R. North, "Biblical Geography," p. 1179. Theodoret, however, does not entertain the idea of a difference of authorship but explains the term "Deuteronomy" as denoting a restatement or summary of the Law for the benefit of the younger generation, either still unborn or too young to understand when God first spoke to Moses on Sinai. His remarks regarding the educational value of the summary recapitulation of a previous narrative recall the similar argument adduced by John Chrysostom (*hom.* 12.1 *in Gen.*) to account for the appearance of a second, less detailed, story of creation in Gn 2 (Yahwistic) immediately after the fuller narrative of ch. 1 (Priestly).

2. Here Theodoret takes time to mention a fascinating detail from the defeat of

ὑμᾶς σήμερον ποιεῖν, ἵνα ζῆτε καὶ εἰσελθόντες κληρονομήσητε
75 τὴν γῆν, ἣν Κύριος ὁ Θεὸς τῶν πατέρων ὑμῶν δίδωσιν ὑμῖν.ˣ
εἶτα ἀναγκαίως τοῦ Βεελφεγὼρ εἰς μέσον φέρει τὴν μνήμην
καὶ τῶν δι' ἐκείνην τὴν ἀσέβειαν ἐν τῇ ἐρήμῳ διολωλότων.ʸ
ἔπειτα ἐκ παραλλήλου δείκνυσι τὰς θείας εὐεργεσίας· ποῖον,
γάρ φησιν, ἔθνος μέγα ᾧ ἐστιν αὐτῷ Θεὸς ἐγγίζων αὐτοῖς ὡς
80 Κύριος ὁ Θεὸς ἡμῶν ἐν ἅπασιν οἷς ἐὰν αὐτὸν ἐπικαλεσώμεθα;ᶻ
κελεύει δέ, μὴ μόνον αὐτοὺς φυλάττειν τοῦ Θεοῦ τοὺς νόμους,
ἀλλὰ καὶ τοὺς παῖδας καὶ τοὺς ἐγγόνους ἐν εὐσεβείᾳ
διατρέφειν καὶ παιδόθεν τὰς θείας ἐντολὰς ἐκπαιδεύειν.ᵃᵃ

Εἶτα πάλιν αὐτοὺς ἀνέμνησεν ὅπως αὐτοῖς ὁ τῶν ὅλων
85 ἐπέφανε Θεός, λόγους μὲν διὰ πυρὸς ἀφείς, οὐδὲν δὲ εἶδος
ἐπιδεικνύς· τοῦτο γὰρ ἔφη· ἐκ μέσου τοῦ πυρὸς φωνὴν
ῥημάτων ὑμεῖς ἠκούσατε καὶ ὁμοίωμα οὐκ ἴδετε ἀλλ' ἢ
φωνήν.ᵇᵇ ταῦτα δὲ λέγει, παιδεύων αὐτοὺς μηδὲν ἴνδαλμα
τεκτήνασθαι μηδὲ πειραθῆναί ποτε θείαν εἰκόνα
90 κατασκευάσαι, ἐπειδὴ τοῦ ἀρχετύπου τὸ εἶδος οὐχ ἑωράκασιν·
ὅθεν πάλιν ἐπήγαγε, μὴ ἀνομήσητε μηδὲ ποιήσητε ὑμῖν
αὐτοῖς γλυπτὸν ὁμοίωμα, πᾶσαν εἰκόνα, ὁμοίωμα ἀρσενικοῦ ἢ
θηλυκοῦ, ὁμοίωμα παντὸς κτήνους τῶν ὄντων ἐπὶ τῆς γῆς,
ὁμοίωμα παντὸς ὀρνέου πετομένου, ὃ πέταται ὑπὸ τὸν
95 οὐρανόν, ὁμοίωμα παντὸς ἑρπετοῦ, ὃ ἕρπει ἐπὶ τῆς γῆς,
ὁμοίωμα παντὸς ἰχθύος, ὅσα ἐστὶν ἐν τοῖς ὕδασιν ὑποκάτω τῆς
γῆς.ᶜᶜ ταῦτα πάντα, φησίν, εἰς χρείαν ὑμετέραν πεποίηκεν ὁ
Θεός· ἀνοίας τοίνυν ἐσχάτης τὸ εἰκόνας τῶν ὑπηκόων
θεοποιεῖν· προστέθεικε δὲ καὶ ταῦτα· μὴ ἀναβλέψας εἰς τὸν
100 οὐρανὸν καὶ ἰδὼν τὸν ἥλιον, καὶ τὴν σελήνην, ... καὶ πάντα
τὸν κόσμον τοῦ οὐρανοῦ, πλανηθεὶς προσκυνήσῃς αὐτοῖς, ... ἃ
ἀπένειμε Κύριος ὁ Θεός σου αὐτὰ πᾶσι τοῖς ἔθνεσι τοῖς
ὑποκάτω τοῦ οὐρανοῦ.ᵈᵈ ταῦτα, φησίν, εἰς τὴν τῶν ἀνθρώπων
|6   κατεσκεύασεν χρείαν ὁ ποιητής· μὴ Ιτοίνυν ὑπολάβῃς θεοὺς
105 τοὺς ὑπὸ τοῦ Θεοῦ τῶν ὅλων ἀφορισθέντας ὥστε ταῖς χρείαις

---

x. Dt 4.1   y. Dt 4.3   z. Dt 4.7   aa. Dt 4.9f.   bb. Dt 4.12
cc. Dt 4.16–18   dd. Dt 4.19

you may live and enter and occupy the land that the Lord, the God of your fathers, is giving you."[x] Next, he made apposite mention of the Baal of Peor and of those who perished in the wilderness because of that act of idolatry.[y] Then, by contrast, he brought out God's benefactions: "What great nation has its god so near to it as the Lord our God is to all who call upon him?"[z] He commanded them not only to observe God's laws themselves but to raise their children and their grandchildren in piety and to school them in God's commandments from childhood.[aa]

Then he reminded them how the God of the universe had manifested himself and delivered his words in the midst of the fire but showed them no form. As the text reads, "From the midst of the fire you heard the sound of words but perceived no form—only a voice."[bb] Now, Moses said this to instruct them not to shape any image or try to make any likeness of God, since they had not seen the form of the Archetype. Hence, he added, "Do not transgress by making yourselves a carved likeness, any image, a male or female likeness, a likeness of any animal on the earth, a likeness of any winged creature that flies under heaven, a likeness of any reptile that crawls on the ground, a likeness of any fish that is in the waters under the earth."[cc] "All these," he said, "God made for your use, so it is the height of folly to make gods of images of beings that are subject to you." He went on, "When you look up into the sky and see the sun, the moon, and all the array of heaven, do not be deceived and bow down to them, since the Lord your God has apportioned them to all the nations under heaven."[dd] He means, "The Creator made these for human use, so do not regard as gods those that the God of the universe has assigned to serve the needs of man." Thus, the oth-

----

Sihon and Og, an event he had passed over—perhaps so he could devote more attention to the subsequent saga of Balaam—in his commentary on Nm 21.

τῶν ἀνθρώπων διακονεῖν· οὕτω γὰρ καὶ οἱ λοιποὶ ἡρμήνευσαν· ἄτινα διεκόσμησεν ὁ Θεός σου εἰς τοὺς λαοὺς ὑφ' ὅλον τὸν οὐρανόν.

(4) Εἶτα δεδίττεται αὐτοὺς ταῖς ἀπειλαῖς ὡς, εἰ
110 τολμήσαιεν τὸν θεῖον παραβῆναι νόμον καί τινος τῶν ὄντων ὁμοίωμα κατασκευάσαι καὶ θεοποιῆσαι, εἰς πᾶσαν αὐτοὺς διασπερεῖ τὴν γῆν, καὶ ὡς δουλεύοντες τοὺς ψευδωνύμους θεοὺς προσκυνήσουσιν.[ee] ἔπειτα πάλιν ἀπὸ συγκρίσεως δείκνυσι τὸ παντοδύναμον τοῦ Θεοῦ· ἐπερωτήσατε, γάρ φησιν,
115 ἡμέρας τὰς προτέρας, γενομένας προτέρας σου, ἀπὸ τῆς ἡμέρας ἧς ἔκτισεν ὁ Θεὸς τὸν ἄνθρωπον ἐπὶ τῆς γῆς καὶ ἐπὶ τὸ ἄκρον τοῦ οὐρανοῦ..., εἰ γέγονε κατὰ τὸ ῥῆμα... τοῦτο, εἰ ἠκούσατε τοιοῦτον· εἰ ἀκήκοεν ἔθνος φωνὴν Θεοῦ ζῶντος λαλοῦντος ἐκ μέσου τοῦ πυρός, ὃν τρόπον ἀκήκοας σὺ καὶ
120 ἔζησας.[ff] ἔφη δὲ καὶ ὅπως αὐτοὺς ἠλευθέρωσε τῆς πικρᾶς τῶν αἰγυπτίων δουλείας. συνεχῶς μέντοι διδάσκει αὐτοὺς καὶ ὡς οὐρανόθεν αὐτοῖς ὁ τῶν ὅλων διελέχθη Θεὸς καί, ἐκ μέσου τοῦ πυρὸς φωνῇ κεχρημένος, νενομοθέτηκεν ἵνα μηδεμίαν εἰκόνα κατασκευάσωσι τοῦ ἀοράτου Θεοῦ.[gg] διδάσκει δὲ καὶ ὡς
125 πάμπαν ἀμήχανον θείαν εἰκόνα κατασκευάσαι· οὐ γὰρ μόνον ἀόρατον ἔχει τὴν φύσιν, ἀλλὰ καὶ πάμπαν ἀπερίγραφον· Κύριος, γάρ φησιν, ὁ Θεός σου, οὗτος Θεὸς ἐν τῷ οὐρανῷ ἄνω καὶ ἐπὶ τῆς γῆς κάτω, καὶ οὐκ ἔστι... πλὴν αὐτοῦ.[hh]

Ἰστέον μέντοι ὡς, οὐκ ἐν ἡμέρᾳ μιᾷ ταῦτα πάντα ὁ
130 προφήτης τῷ λαῷ διελέχθη, ἀλλ' ἐν πολλαῖς αὐτοῖς ἡμέραις τὴν διδασκαλίαν προσήνεγκεν. ὅθεν πολλάκις τοὺς αὐτοὺς λόγους ἀνακυκλοῖ ἵνα τῇ συνεχείᾳ παγίαν τὴν μνήμην ἐργάσηται. αὐτίκα γοῦν, μετὰ τὴν διάλεξιν ταύτην, τὰ περὶ τῶν πόλεων ἱστόρησεν, εἰς ἃς καταφεύγειν τοὺς ἀκουσίοις

---

ll. 116f. καὶ ἐπὶ τὸ ἄκρον τοῦ οὐρανοῦ Pic. (Sch.) F.M. : ἐπὶ τὸ ἄκρον τοῦ οὐρανοῦ ἕως ἄκρου τοῦ οὐρανοῦ 5 (ἀπὸ τοῦ -οῦ), 51, Sir. Sch. = "'from one end of heaven to the other'" : καὶ ἐπὶ τὸ ἄκρον τοῦ οὐρανοῦ ἕως ἄκρου τοῦ οὐρανοῦ [32], 9 = "'and from one end of heaven to the other.'"

ee. Dt 4.25–28   ff. Dt 4.32f.   gg. Dt 4.34–36   hh. Dt 4.39

er translators offer: "All that your God mustered in array for the peoples under the whole of heaven."[3]

(4) Next, he put fear into them with the threat that, if they presumed to transgress the Law of God by preparing a likeness of any creature and making a god of it, God would scatter them across the whole earth, and they would bow down to their false gods in slavery.[ee] And he demonstrated God's omnipotence by use of a comparison: "Ask about former times before your day, from the time when God created man on earth and to the end of heaven, whether anything like this has ever happened, whether you have heard of anything like it, whether any nation has heard a voice of the living God speaking from the midst of the fire as you have heard and lived."[ff] He also related how God had freed them from harsh slavery to the Egyptians. He taught them over and over again that the God of the universe had spoken from heaven and, with a voice issuing from the midst of the fire, had given them the Law so that they would make no image of the unseen God.[gg] And he taught them that it is utterly impossible to make an image of God, who by nature is not only invisible but also utterly uncircumscribed: "The Lord your God is God who is in heaven above and on earth below, and there is no other but him."[hh]

You should know that the prophet did not deliver all these discourses on just one day but taught the people over the space of many days. Hence, he often recurred to the same topics to strengthen their memory by repetition. In any case, immediately after this discourse, he gave an account of the cities to which those guilty of

3. Theodoret develops at length the prohibition of images. Antiochene commentators are generally wary also of linguistic anthropomorphisms that might seem to impugn the divine transcendence; *cf. Qq.* 19f. on Gn.

135 περιπεπτωκότας φόνοις ἐκέλευσεν.[ii] εἶτα ἐδίδαξεν ὅτι πάλιν
συνήθροισε τὸν λαὸν καὶ θεοσδότων ἀνέμνησε νόμων.[jj] καὶ ὅτι,
οὐχ ἕτερον δέδωκε νόμον, ἀλλὰ τὸν πρότερον ἐκπαιδεύει τοὺς
τῆς νομοθεσίας ἐκείνης διὰ τὸ τῆς ἡλικίας ἀτελὲς ἐπακοῦσαι
μὴ δυνηθέντας αὐτὰ διδάξει τοῦ προφήτου τὰ ῥήματα· *Κύριος,*
140 *γάρ φησιν, ὁ Θεὸς ἡμῶν διέθετο πρὸς ὑμᾶς διαθήκην ἐν*
Χωρήβ. οὐχὶ τοῖς πατράσιν ὑμῶν διέθετο Κύριος τὴν διαθήκην
ταύτην, ἀλλὰ πρὸς ὑμᾶς.[kk] ἐπειδὴ γὰρ ἐκεῖνοι παραβάντες
διώλοντο, τούτοις δὲ τὴν τοῖς πατράσιν ἐπηγγελμένην ἐδίδου
γῆν,[ll] τούτοις ἔφη τὸν νόμον δεδόσθαι. εἶτα λέγει τὰς
145 ἐντολάς, ὧν τὸν νοῦν ἀνεπτύξαμεν, τὴν Ἔξοδον
ἑρμηνεύοντες.[mm]

(5) Ἐδίδαξε δὲ κἀνταῦθα τὸν τῆς ἀργίας τοῦ σαββάτου
σκοπόν· ἔφη γάρ, *ἵνα ἀναπαύσηται ὁ παῖς σου, καὶ ἡ παιδίσκη*
σου, καὶ τὸ ὑποζύγιόν σου.[nn] καθάπερ, φησί, σὺ τούτων
150 ἀπολαύεις διαπαντός, οὕτως ἅπαξ γοῦν ἀπολαυσάτωσαν ἐν
ταῖς ἑπτὰ τῆς ἑβδομάδος ἡμέραις οἱ θεράποντες, καὶ αἱ
θεράπαιναι, καὶ τὰ ὑποζύγια. ἔπειτα τῇ μνήμῃ τῆς ἐν
Αἰγύπτῳ δουλείας τὴν συμπάθειαν πραγματεύεται· *ὅτι*
οἰκέτης, φησίν, ἦσθα ἐν τῇ Αἰγύπτῳ, καὶ ἐξήγαγέ σε
155 *Κύριος . . . ἐκεῖθεν ἐν χειρὶ κραταιᾷ καὶ ἐν βραχίονι ὑψηλῷ,*
διὰ τοῦτο συνέταξε . . . Κύριος ὁ Θεός σου ὥστε φυλάττεσθαί
σε τὴν ἡμέραν τῶν σαββάτων καὶ ἁγιάζειν αὐτήν.[oo] τῇ πείρᾳ
μεμάθηκας τὸ τῆς δουλείας πικρόν· ἐκείνων
ἀναμιμνησκόμενος, ἥμερος γενοῦ τοῖς ὑπηκόοις καὶ πρᾶος καὶ
160 ἧς ἀπολαύεις ἀναπαύλης διηνεκῶς μετάδος τούτοις ἐν τῇ
ἑβδόμῃ τῆς ἑβδομάδος ἡμέρᾳ. ἐν δὲ τοῖς μετὰ ταῦτα τὸ
πνευματικὸν οὐκ ἀπηγόρευσεν ἔργον· ἔφη γάρ, *πᾶν ἔργον*

---

l. 140 ἡμῶν . . . ὑμᾶς *Sir. F.M.* : ὑμῶν . . . ἡμᾶς *17 24* = "'The Lord your
God made a covenant with us'" : ἡμῶν . . . ἡμᾶς *14* = "'The Lord our God made
a covenant with us'" : ὑμῶν . . . ὑμᾶς *a [32], 12, 15, 10 31, Sch.* = "'The Lord your
God made a covenant with you.'" *Cf.* Wevers and Quast, *ap. crit.* to Dt 5.2.

ii. Dt 4.41–43   jj. Dt 5.1   kk. Dt 5.2f.   ll. Dt 2.14f.   mm. Dt 5.7–21
nn. Dt 5.14 (LXX var.)   oo. Dt 5.15

Question 1

involuntary homicide were to flee for refuge. [ii] Then Scripture recounts that he once again assembled the people and reminded them of their God-given laws.[jj] It will be clear from the prophet's own words that he was not giving them a different law but instructing in the earlier legislation those who had been too young to be able to pay heed to it: "The Lord our God made a covenant with you on Horeb. It was not with your parents that the Lord made this covenant, but with you."[4kk] Since those who had transgressed had died, and it was instead to the more recent generation that he gave the land promised to their fathers,[ll] he said that the Law had been given to them. He then recited the commandments, which we have already interpreted in our discussion of Exodus.[5mm]

(5) Here, too, he explained the purpose of the sabbath rest: "so that your male and female slave may rest and your beast of burden as well."[nn] In effect, this is to say, "Since you benefit from them all the time, let your male and female servants and your beasts of burden benefit from rest at least once in the seven days of the week." Next he excited compassion by recalling their slavery in Egypt: "Because you were a slave in Egypt, and the Lord brought you out with a strong hand and an uplifted arm, the Lord your God has commanded you to keep the day of the Sabbath and to hallow it."[oo] In other words, "You know from experience the harshness of slavery; mindful of that, be kind and gentle to the servants, and, on the seventh day of the week, share with them the rest you always enjoy." But in what follows he did not forbid spiritual work. The text says, "You shall do no servile work, the exception being what you do for the benefit of

---

4. In Dt 5.2f. Theodoret's version of the LXX read "our God," "with you," "with your parents," and "with you" while the Masoretic text has "our God," "with us," "with our parents," and "with us." The Göttingen edition of the Septuagint, which otherwise agrees with Theodoret, offers "your God."

5. V. Qq. 37–43, where, however, Theodoret comments only on the first three commandments; cf. note 1 to Q. 45 on Ex.

λατρευτὸν οὐ ποιήσετε ... πλὴν ὅσα ποιηθήσεται ἐπὶ ψυχῇ[pp]
οἷον ἀνάγνωσις, θείων λογίων ἀκρόασις, ψαλμῳδίαι,
165 ἱερουργίαι, καὶ τὰ τούτοις προσόμοια.

II

Πῶς νοητέον τὸ ἄκουε, Ἰσραήλ· Κύριος ὁ Θεός σου, Κύριος
εἷς ἐστιν;[a]

Πολλάκις εἰρήκαμεν ὅτι τὸ ὄνομα τὸ Κύριος καὶ Θεός, τῆς
θείας φύσεως, οὐ τῆς τῶν προσώπων διαιρέσεως δηλωτικά, ὁ
5 δὲ πατήρ, καὶ ὁ υἱός, καὶ τὸ ἅγιον πνεῦμα τῶν ἰδιοτήτων
σημαντικά. ἀλλὰ τοῖς ἀτελέσιν ἰουδαίοις τὴν ἀκριβῆ
θεολογίαν προσενεχθῆναι οὐχ οἷόν τε ἦν· ταύτην γὰρ ἂν
πολυθεΐας ἀφορμὴν ἐποιήσαντο. οὗ δὴ χάριν μοναδικῶς τὸ
θεῖον ἐν τῇ παλαιᾷ προφέρεται ὄνομα, ἔχει δὲ ὅμως τὰ τῆς
10 τριάδος αἰνίγματα. τὸ γὰρ Κύριος ὁ Θεός σου, Κύριος εἷς ἐστι
καὶ τὸ τῆς οὐσίας διδάσκει μοναδικὸν καὶ παραδηλοῖ τῶν
προσώπων τὸν ἀριθμόν· ἅπαξ γὰρ τὸ Θεός, δὶς δὲ τὸ Κύριος
τέθεικεν.

pp. Ex 12.16

II A [32], B, C⁻¹, 4 7 9 10 31 35 37 = 20 mss.

a. Dt 6.4

your soul,"[pp] such as reading and listening to the holy Scriptures, psalmody, the divine service, and the like.[6]

II

How are we to understand the verse "Listen, Israel, your God is the Lord; the Lord is one"?[a]

I have often remarked that the terms "Lord" and "God" refer to the divine nature, not to the distinction in persons, whereas "Father," "Son," and "Holy Spirit" refer to the individual persons.[1] But the precise doctrine of God could not be presented to the Jews, who, imperfect as they were, would have found it a pretext for polytheism. Hence, in the Old Testament, the the divine name is expressed in the singular but contains obscure hints of the Trinity. The verse, "Your God is the Lord; the Lord is one," as well as conveying the unity of being, also indicates the number of persons. Note that he used "God" once and "Lord" twice.[2]

---

6. Theodoret emphasizes what J. Blenkinsopp (on 5.12–15) terms the "humanitarian" motivation given in Dt for the law of the Sabbath. Theodoret's term "servile" (λατρευτὸν) is absent from the LXX both in Dt 5.14 and from the statement of the same commandment in Ex 20.10 and has no equivalent in the MT. He has drawn this from the regulations for the feast of Tabernacles (Lv 23.35). In his exposition of this law, Theodoret insists on the distinction between servile and spiritual work, rather than on attendance at a place of worship.

---

1. V., e.g., Q. 19 on Gn.
2. In Dt 6.4 Theodoret finds clues (αἰνίγματα), though not a clear statement, of the trinitarian doctrine of God (θεολογία).

III

Τί ἐστιν τὸ ἀγαπήσεις Κύριον τὸν Θεόν σου ἐξ ὅλης τῆς καρδίας σου, καὶ τὰ ἑξῆς;[a]

Σαφῶς ἡμᾶς ὁ Κύριος ἐδίδαξεν ὅτι οὐδεὶς δύναται δυσὶ κυρίοις δουλεύειν.[b] καὶ ἐνταῦθα τοίνυν διδασκόμεθα, μὴ
5 μερίζειν τὴν ἀγάπην εἰς Θεὸν καὶ χρυσόν, εἰς Θεὸν καὶ γυναῖκα, εἰς Θεὸν καὶ παῖδας, ἀλλὰ πᾶσαν τῆς ἀγάπης τὴν δύναμιν ἀφιεροῦν τῷ πεποιηκότι Θεῷ· μετὰ δέ γε τὸν ποιητήν, ἀπονέμειν ἑκάστῳ τὰ πρόσφορα· καὶ παισί, καὶ ἀδελφοῖς, καὶ φίλοις. τῆς γὰρ τοῦ Θεοῦ ἀγάπης καὶ τὸ ταῦτα
10 πληροῦν· ὁ ἀγαπῶν με, γάρ φησι, τὰς ἐντολάς μου πληρώσει.[c] αἱ δὲ τοῦ Θεοῦ ἐντολαὶ περὶ τούτων διαγορεύουσιν.

IV

Τί δή ποτε κατὰ τοῦ Θεοῦ ὀμνύναι διαγορεύει ὁ νόμος;[a]

Ἵνα μὴ κατὰ τῶν ψευδωνύμων ὀμνύωσι θεῶν· τοῦτο γὰρ καὶ διὰ τοῦ προφήτου ἔφη· ἐὰν ἐξάρῃς τὰ ὀνόματα τῶν βααλεὶμ ἐκ τοῦ στόματός σου[b] καὶ ὀμόσῃς, ζῇ Κύριος, μετὰ ἀληθείας.[c]
5 καὶ ἐνταῦθα δέ, εἰρηκώς, Κύριον τὸν Θεόν σου φοβηθήσῃ, καὶ αὐτῷ μόνῳ λατρεύσεις, καὶ πρὸς αὐτὸν κολληθήσῃ, καὶ τῷ ὀνόματι αὐτοῦ ὀμῇ, ἐπήγαγεν, οὐ πορεύσεσθε ὀπίσω θεῶν ἑτέρων ἀπὸ τῶν θεῶν τῶν ἐθνῶν, τῶν περικύκλῳ ὑμῶν.[d]

III A [32], B, C⁻¹, 4 7 9 10 31 35 37 = 20 mss.
a. Dt 6.5   b. Mt 6.24   c. Jn 14.15

IV A [32], B, C⁻¹, 4 7 9 10 31 35 37 = 20 mss.
a. Dt 6.13   b. Hos 2.17   c. Jer 4.2   d. Dt 6.13f.

III

What is the meaning of the verse "You shall love the Lord your God with all your heart" and so on?[a]

The Lord gave us explicit instruction that "no one can serve two masters."[b] Here, then, we are taught not to divide our love between God and gold, God and wife, or God and children, but to dedicate all the force of our love to the God who made us, and, after the Creator, to apportion to each—children, relatives, and friends—his due. In fact, the performance of this duty is also consequent upon the love for God, for as Scripture says, "He who loves me will carry out my commandments,"[c] and God's commandments refer explicitly to these people.

IV

Why does the Law require them to swear by God's name?[a]

So they will not swear by false gods. He delivered the same command through his prophet: "If you remove the names of the Baals from your mouth[b] and swear, 'As the Lord lives,' <you will swear> a truthful oath."[c] Here, too, after saying, "You shall fear the Lord your God, and serve him alone, and cling to him, and swear by his name," he added, "You shall not go after other gods, any of the gods of the nations who are round about you."[d]

V

Πῶς νοητέον τὸ οὐκ ἐκπειράσεις Κύριον τὸν Θεόν σου;[a]

Ὁ Κύριος αὐτὸ ἐν τοῖς ἱεροῖς εὐαγγελίοις ἡρμήνευσε· τοῦ
γὰρ διαβόλου εἰρηκότος, βάλε σεαυτὸν ἄνωθεν κάτω, εἶπεν,
οὐκ ἐκπειράσεις Κύριον τὸν Θεόν σου.[b] ἐκπειράζει δὲ τὸν
5 Θεὸν ὁ δίχα λογισμοῦ ῥιψοκινδύνως τι πράττων.

VI

Τί δή ποτε ἀπαγορεύει ὁ νόμος τὰς πρὸς τοὺς ὁμόρους
ἀλλοφύλους ἐπιγαμβρίας;[a]
Οὐ δεῖται σαφηνείας ὁ νόμος· ἑαυτὸν γὰρ ἑρμηνεύει· ἔφη
γὰρ ὅτι, ἀποστήσουσι τὸν υἱόν σου ἀπ' ἐμοῦ, καὶ λατρεύσει
5 θεοῖς ἑτέροις.[b] ἀναγκαίως μέντοι καὶ τὴν αἰτίαν αὐτοὺς τῆς
θείας διδάσκει κηδεμονίας· οὐ γὰρ διὰ τὸ πλείους εἶναι, φησί,
τῶν ἐθνῶν προέκρινεν ὑμᾶς ὁ Θεός, ἀλλὰ διὰ τὴν τῶν
προγόνων εὐσέβειαν καὶ τὴν γεγενημένην πρὸς ἐκείνους
ὑπόσχεσιν.[c] εἶτα τὸ ἀληθὲς αὐτοῦ δεικνύς, ἐπήγαγεν ὅτι ὁ
10 Θεὸς . . . πιστός, . . . φυλάσσων . . . διαθήκην καὶ . . . ἔλεον τοῖς
ἀγαπῶσιν αὐτὸν καὶ τοῖς φυλάσσουσι τὰς ἐντολὰς αὐτοῦ εἰς
χιλίας γενεάς.[d] καὶ ἐπειδὴ ἀτελεῖς ἦσαν, καὶ τροφῆς
γαλακτώδους ἐδέοντο,[e] καὶ ἀκούειν περὶ τῶν αἰωνίων ἀγαθῶν
οὐκ ἐδύναντο, ὑπισχνεῖται αὐτοῖς πολυγονίαν, καὶ γῆς
15 εὐκαρπίαν, καὶ ποιμνίων καὶ βουκολίων εὐεξίαν, καὶ σώματος
ὑγείαν, καὶ τὴν ἐν πολέμοις νίκην, καὶ ὅσα τοιαῦτα.[f]

v A [32], B, C⁻¹, 4 7 9 10 31 35 37 = 20 mss.

a. Dt 6.16   b. Mt 4.6f.

---

vi A [32], B, C⁻¹, 4 7 9 10 31 35 37 = 20 mss.

a. Dt 7.3   b. Dt 7.4   c. Dt 7.7f.   d. Dt 7.9   e. Cf. 1Cor 3.2; Heb 5.12.
f. Dt 7.11–16

Question VI

V

How are we to understand the verse "Do not put the Lord your God to the test"?[a]

The Lord provided the interpretation in the sacred Gospels. When the devil said, "Throw yourself down from on high," he replied, "You shall not put the Lord your God to the test."[1b] Thus, people who act thoughtlessly and recklessly put God to the test.

VI

Why does the Law forbid intermarriage with foreign neighbors?[a]

This law requires no clarification, as it comments on itself, declaring, "Because they will turn your son away from me, and he will serve other gods."[b] Thus, with good reason it goes on to teach them why God cared for them: "It was not that you were more numerous that God preferred you to the nations but because of the piety of your forbears and the promise he had made to them."[c] Then, to bring out his reliability, he added, "God is faithful in observing covenant and mercy with those who love him and keep his commandments—even to a thousand generations."[d] Since they were imperfect, needing to be fed milk[e] and unable to hear of eternal good things, he promised them an abundance of children, fertility of the soil, fecundity of flocks and herds, health of body, victory in war, and that sort of thing.[f]

---

1. This prohibition refers, as does Jesus' citation, to the people's provocation of God at Massah and Meribah; *v.* Blenkinsopp on Dt 6.16 and Albright and Mann on Mt 4.7. Theodoret, who had not commented on either version of this story (Ex 17 and Nm 20), here offers an interpretation that, neglecting the reference to the previous narrative, amounts to no more than a platitude.

Ἔπειτα πάλιν αὐτοὺς ἀνέμνησε τῆς ἐν τῇ ἐρήμῳ διαγωγῆς καὶ τὰς ταύτης αἰτίας ἐδίδαξεν· ἐκάκωσε..., *γάρ* φησι, *καὶ ἐλιμαγχόνησέ σε καὶ ἐψώμισέ σε τὸ μάννα... ἵνα ἀναγγείλῃ*

20 *σοι ὅτι, οὐκ ἐπ' ἄρτῳ μόνῳ ζήσεται... ἄνθρωπος, ἀλλ' ἐπὶ παντὶ ῥήματι... ἐκπορευομένῳ διὰ στόματος Θεοῦ.*[g] διὰ μέντοι τούτων καὶ ἡμεῖς παιδευόμεθα μὴ δυσχεραίνειν, δυσκολίαις τισὶ περιπεσόντες, ἀλλὰ στέργειν τὰς θείας οἰκονομίας καὶ προσμένειν τὴν λύσιν τῶν πειρασμῶν. ἐπιδείκνυσι δὲ καὶ τὰς

25 ἄλλας εὐεργεσίας· *τὰ ἱμάτιά σου οὐ κατετρίβη ἀπὸ σοῦ, οἱ πόδες σου οὐκ ἐτυλώθησαν, ἰδού, τεσσαράκοντα ἔτη. καὶ γνώσῃ τῇ καρδίᾳ σου ὅτι, ὡς εἴ τις παιδεύσαι ἄνθρωπος τὸν υἱὸν αὐτοῦ, οὕτως Κύριος ὁ Θεός σου παιδεύσει σε. καὶ φυλάξῃ τὰς ἐντολὰς Κυρίου, τοῦ Θεοῦ σου, πορεύεσθαι ἐν ταῖς ὁδοῖς αὐτοῦ*

30 *καὶ φοβεῖσθαι αὐτόν.*[h] μετὰ τὸν πειρασμὸν ἡ παράκλησις, μετὰ τῆς παιδείας ἡ ψυχαγωγία· λιμὸς καὶ τρυφή, ὁδοιπορίας πόνος καὶ σώματος εὐπάθεια, σπάνις ἀναγκαίων καὶ τῶν εὐφθάρτων ἱματίων καὶ ὑποδημάτων τὸ διαρκές. εἶτα παραινεῖ νικῶντας, μὴ τῇ οἰκείᾳ ῥώμῃ τὴν νίκην ἐπιγράφειν, ἀλλὰ τῷ ἐπικούρῳ καὶ

35 προμάχῳ Θεῷ.[i]

VII

Τίνας λέγει *υἱοὺς Ἐνάκ;*

(1) Ἀπόγονοι γιγάντων ἦσαν ὡς ἡ ἱστορία διδάσκει· τοῦτο γὰρ ἔφη· *λαὸν πολὺν καὶ εὐμήκη, υἱοὺς Ἐνάκ, οὓς σὺ οἶσθα καὶ σὺ ἀκήκοας· τίς ἀντιστήσεται κατὰ πρόσωπον υἱῶν Ἐνάκ;*[a]

5 τὸ δὲ *σὺ οἶσθα καὶ ἀκήκοας* τέθεικε, τῶν λόγων ἀναμιμνήσκων τῶν ἐκείνην κατασκοπησάντων τὴν γῆν· ἐκεῖνοι γὰρ ἔλεγον, ὅτι *ἦμεν ἐνώπιον αὐτῶν ὡσεὶ ἀκρίδες.*[b]‖

‖52

---

g. Dt 8.3   h. Dt 8.4–6   i. Dt 8.17f.

vii A [32], B, c⁻¹, 51 52(inc.), 4 7 9 10 31 35 37 = 20 mss.

a. Dt 9.2   b. Nm 13.33

He next reminded them of their life in the wilderness, and explained the reason for it: "He afflicted you, exposing you to hunger and feeding you with manna, to let you know that man shall not live by bread alone, but by every word that comes from the mouth of God."[g] This also teaches us not to become upset when we encounter difficulties, but to accept God's plan and look forward to the resolution of our trials.[1] He also set out God's other acts of favor: "Your garments were not worn out, nor your feet callused these forty years. Know in your heart that as a man disciplines his child, so the Lord your God will discipline you. You shall keep the commandments of the Lord your God to walk in all his ways and fear him."[h] After the testing, comes consolation, after the discipline, encouragement: hunger then abundance, the hardship of travelling then bodily pleasure, want of necessities then the durability of even their fragile clothing and footwear. He then warned the victors not to ascribe the victory to their own strength, but to God, their ally and champion.[i]

VII

Whom does he call "the sons of Anak"?

(1) As the sacred history explains, they were descendants of giants. This is what he said: "A numerous people, tall, sons of Anak, whom you know, and of whom you have heard it said, 'Who will resist in the face of the sons of Anak?'"[a] The statements "You know" and "You have heard it said" were meant to remind them of the report given by the men who had spied out the land. They had declared, "Compared to them we were like grasshoppers."[b]

---

1. As A. Siquans (pp. 140f.) points out, Theodoret both discusses this passage regarding the manna in its narrative context and applies it to the life of his audience. Moses, speaking to the Israelites, confirms the validity of the promise of the

Οὕτω τὸν ἐπὶ τῇ ῥώμῃ καταστείλας τῦφον, διδάσκει αὐτοὺς
μηδὲ ἐπὶ τοῖς τῆς ψυχῆς κατορθώμασι μέγα φρονεῖν· μὴ εἴπῃς,
10 γάρ φησιν, ἐν τῇ καρδίᾳ σου, ὅτι διὰ τὰς δικαιοσύνας μου
εἰσήγαγέ με Κύριος κληρονομῆσαι τὴν γῆν τὴν ἀγαθὴν ταύτην.
διὰ γὰρ τὴν ἀσέβειαν τῶν ἐθνῶν τούτων, Κύριος ἐξολοθρεύσει
αὐτοὺς ἀπὸ προσώπου σου· οὐχὶ διὰ τὴν δικαιοσύνην σου οὐδὲ
διὰ τὴν ὁσιότητα τῆς καρδίας σου σὺ εἰσπορεύῃ κληρονομῆσαι
15 τὴν γῆν.ᶜ ταῦτα δὲ ἔφη, δύο κατὰ ταὐτὸν πραγματευόμενος·
καὶ μετριάζειν διδάσκων αὐτοὺς καὶ τῇ τοῦ Θεοῦ βοηθείᾳ τὸ
πᾶν ἐπιγράφειν καὶ προλέγων ὡς τὰ παραπλήσια πείσονται
τοῖς ἔθνεσιν ἐκείνοις εἰ τὰ ὅμοια δράσαιεν.

(2) Εἰς καιρὸν δὲ καὶ τῶν ἐν τῇ ἐρήμῳ παρανομηθέντων
20 ἀνέμνησε, τὸν λόγον ἐκεῖνον κρατύνων ὡς οὐ διὰ τὰς
δικαιοσύνας αὐτῶν κληρονομήσουσι τὴν γῆν· μνήσθητι, γὰρ
ἔφη, καὶ μὴ ἐπιλάθῃ ὅσα παρώξυνας Κύριον τὸν Θεόν σου ἐν
τῇ ἐρήμῳ.ᵈ ἤγαγε δὲ εἰς μέσον καὶ τὴν τοῦ μόσχου λατρείαν,
καὶ ὅτι διὰ τὴν ἐκείνων ἀσέβειαν τὰς θεοσδότους συνέτριψε
25 πλάκας, καὶ ὡς, σπουδαίαν ἱκετείαν προσενεγκών, ἱλεώσατο
τὸν Θεὸν μάλα καὶ αὐτοῖς καὶ τῷ Ἀαρὼν ὀργιζόμενον·ᵉ καὶ
ἐπὶ Ἀαρών, γάρ φησιν, ἐθυμώθη Κύριος σφόδρα ἐξολοθρεῦσαι
αὐτόν, καὶ ηὐξάμην καὶ περὶ Ἀαρὼν ἐν τῷ καιρῷ ἐκείνῳ.ᶠ οὕτω
καὶ τὰ ἄλλα γεγενημένα διεξελθών, φησί, καὶ νῦν, Ἰσραήλ, τί
30 Κύριος ὁ Θεὸς . . . αἰτεῖ παρὰ σοῦ ἀλλ᾽ ἢ φοβεῖσθαι Κύριον τὸν
Θεόν σου, καὶ πορεύεσθαι ἐν πάσαις ταῖς ἐντολαῖς
αὐτοῦ, . . . λατρεύειν Κυρίῳ τῷ Θεῷ σου ἐξ ὅλης τῆς καρδίας
σοῦ·ᵍ καὶ ἵνα μὴ τοπάσωσι τὸν Θεὸν ταῦτα νομοθετεῖν, ὡς
θυμάτων δεόμενον, ἐπήγαγεν, ἰδοὺ Κυρίου τοῦ Θεοῦ σου ὁ
35 οὐρανός, καὶ ὁ οὐρανὸς τοῦ οὐρανοῦ, ἡ γῆ καὶ πάντα ὅσα
ἐστὶν ἐν αὐτοῖς· πλὴν τοὺς πατέρας ὑμῶν προείλετο Κύριος
ἀγαπᾶν αὐτοὺς καὶ ἐξελέξατο τὸ σπέρμα αὐτῶν μετ᾽ αὐτούς,
ὑμᾶς, παρὰ πάντα τὰ ἔθνη.ʰ διδασκόμεθα δὲ διὰ τούτων ὡς
ἀπολαύουσι παῖδες ἀγαθῶν διὰ τὴν τῶν προγόνων εὐσέβειαν.

c. Dt 9.4f.   d. Dt 9.7   e. Dt 9.16–20   f. Dt 9.20   g. Dt 10.12
h. Dt 10.14f.

Having repressed their boasts of physical strength, he taught them not to be conceited because of their spiritual achievements: "Do not say in your heart, 'It is because of my righteousness that the Lord has brought me in to occupy this good land'; it is because of the idolatry of these nations that the Lord will eliminate them from before you. It is not because of your righteousness or the holiness of your heart that you are entering to occupy the land."[c] This statement was meant to achieve two things at once: first, to teach them to be humble and to ascribe everything to God's help, and second, to predict that they would suffer the same punishments as the gentiles if they committed the same offenses.

(2) He then made an apposite reference to their transgressions in the wilderness to confirm the warning that it was not because of their righteousness that they would occupy the land: "Remember and do not forget all the provocation you gave the Lord your God in the wilderness."[d] He brought up their worship of the calf; that, due to their idolatry, he had smashed the God-given tablets; and that, through earnest entreaty, he had placated God, who was extremely angry with them and with Aaron:[e] "The Lord was so angry with Aaron as to destroy him, and I prayed for Aaron at that moment."[f] After recounting other events as well, he asked, "And now, Israel, what does the Lord God require of you but to fear the Lord your God, to walk in all his commandments, and to serve the Lord your God with all your heart?"[g] Moreover, so they would not suppose that God was laying down these laws because he needed their sacrifices, he added, "Lo, the heaven, and the heaven of heaven, the earth and everything in them belong to the Lord your God. Yet the Lord chose your ancestors to love them and selected you their offspring after them instead of all the nations."[h] From this we learn how much the offspring benefit from the piety of their forbears.

----

land by citing an earlier example of God's provision for Israel, and Christians should learn from this story patience in difficulties and hope in divine Providence; *cf.* the conclusion of Q. 26. In her discussion, Siquans cites as well other patristic remarks on Dt 8.3, most of which are preserved in the catena on the Octateuch published by Nikephoros; *cf.* note 1 to Q. 1 on Ex.

40   Ἐδίδαξε δὲ καὶ ποία περιτομὴ τῷ Θεῷ προσφιλής·
περιτεμεῖσθε, γὰρ ἔφη, τὴν σκληροκαρδίαν ὑμῶν καὶ τὸν
τράχηλον ὑμῶν οὐ σκληρυνεῖτε ἔτι,[i] καὶ ταῦτα ἐλέγετο τοῖς
μηδέπω τὴν ἀκροβυστίαν περιτμηθεῖσιν· Ἰησοῦς γὰρ ὁ τοῦ
Ναυῆ μετὰ τὸ διαβῆναι τὸν Ἰορδάνην ἐν Γαλγάλοις αὐτοὺς
45   περιέτεμεν.[j] ἀλλ' ὅμως, καὶ ἀπεριτμήτοις οὖσιν, οὐκ ἐκέλευσε
τὴν ἀκροβυστίαν περιτμηθῆναι, ἀλλὰ τὴν σκληροκαρδίαν καὶ
τὸν τράχηλον τὸν σκληρόν. τοιγάρτοι τιμιωτέρα ἡ τῆς
καρδίας περιτομή. ταύτην δὲ αὐτῶν τὴν κατηγορίαν καὶ διὰ
Ἱερεμίου τοῦ προφήτου ὁ δεσπότης Θεὸς ἐποιήσατο· *πάντα,*
50   γὰρ ἔφη, *τὰ ἔθνη ἀπερίτμητα σαρκί, ὁ δὲ οἶκος Ἰσραήλ,
ἀπερίτμητοι καρδίαις αὐτῶν.*[k]

VIII

    Πῶς νοητέον *ὁ γὰρ Κύριος, ὁ Θεὸς ὑμῶν, οὗτος Θεὸς τῶν
θεῶν καὶ Κύριος τῶν κυρίων;*[a]

    Θεοὺς τοὺς κριτὰς ὀνομάζει· *θεοὺς,* γάρ φησιν, *οὐ
κακολογήσεις καὶ ἄρχοντα τοῦ λαοῦ σου οὐκ ἐρεῖς κακῶς.*[b] καὶ
5   ἔνθα δὲ εἶπον οἱ ἑβδομήκοντα, *ἄξεις αὐτὸν . . . εἰς τὸ
κριτήριον,*[c] οἱ δὲ περὶ τὸν Ἀκύλαν καὶ τὸν Σύμμαχον *ἄξεις
αὐτὸν πρὸς τοὺς θεοὺς* ἡρμήνευσαν, θεοὺς τοὺς κριτὰς
ὀνομάσαντες. τούτων αὐτὸν εἶπε Θεὸν θεῶν, οὐ γάρ τοι τῶν
ψευδωνύμων. καὶ ἤδη δὲ διὰ πλειόνων ἡρμηνεύσαμεν ταῦτα.

---

i. Dt 10.16   j. Jos 5.2–7   k. Jer 9.26

VIII A [32], B, c⁻¹, 51, 4 7 9 10 31 35 37 = 20 mss.

a. Dt 10.17   b. Ex 22.28   c. Ex 21.6

Question VIII

He also explained what kind of circumcision is pleasing to God: "Circumcise your hardness of heart and no longer stiffen your necks."[i] He said this to those who had not yet received the circumcision of the foreskin, since Joshua, the son of Nun, circumcised them in Gilgal after they had crossed the Jordan.[j] Yet even when they were uncircumcised, his command was to circumcise, not their foreskin, but their hard hearts and stiff necks. Thus, greater value is ascribed to circumcision of the heart. Furthermore, the Lord God laid this accusation against them through the prophet Jeremiah: "The gentiles are uncircumcised in the flesh, but as for the house of Israel, they are uncircumcised in their hearts."[k]

VIII

How are we to understand "For the Lord your God is God of gods and Lord of lords"?[a]

By "gods" he meant judges. Elsewhere he said, "You shall not revile gods or malign a ruler of your people."[b] And where the Seventy have "You will bring him to judgment,"[c] Aquila and Symmachus and their followers render, "You will bring him to the gods,"—by "gods" referring to judges. Of course, he meant that God is God of these gods, not of the false gods. But I have already commented at length on these verses.[1]

1. *V. Q.* 51 on Ex.

IX

Πῶς νοητέον *οὐ ποιήσετε πάντα ἃ ἡμεῖς ποιοῦμεν ὧδε σήμερον, ἕκαστος τὸ ἀρεστὸν ἐναντίον αὐτοῦ;*[a]

Ἐν ἅπασιν οἷς κατεσκήνωσαν τόποις, θυσίας προσήνεγκαν τῷ δεσπότῃ Θεῷ, πρὶν μὲν τὴν σκηνὴν κατασκευάσαι ἐκ λίθων
5 αὐτοφυῶν οἰκοδομοῦντες θυσιαστήρια.[b] μετὰ δὲ τὴν ταύτης κατασκευὴν ἐν ταύτῃ τὰς θείας λειτουργίας ἐπιτελοῦντες, οὐκ ἐν ἑνὶ μέντοι τόπῳ ταύτας ἐπετέλουν, ἀλλ' ἐν ἑκάστῳ σταθμῷ· συνεχῶς γὰρ μετέβαινον, ἅτε δὴ τεσσαρακοντούτην χρόνον ἐν τῇ ἐρήμῳ καταναλώσαντες.[c] ἀπαγορεύει τοίνυν ἐν
10 τῇ γῇ τῆς ἐπαγγελίας τὰ παραπλήσια δρᾶν ἵνα μὴ πρόφασιν λάβωσι τοῖς ψευδωνύμοις θύειν θεοῖς. παρεγγυᾷ δὲ ἐν ἐκείνῳ μόνῳ τῷ τόπῳ τὰς θείας ἐπιτελεῖν λειτουργίας ὃν ἂν ἐκλέξηται Κύριος ὁ Θεός. ἐν ἐκείνῳ τῷ τόπῳ καὶ θύειν καὶ εὐωχεῖσθαι παρακελεύεται· *ἔσται, γάρ φησιν, ὁ τόπος ὃν ἂν*
15 *ἐκλέξηται Κύριος ὁ Θεὸς ὑμῶν ἐπικληθῆναι ἐκεῖ τὸ ὄνομα αὐτοῦ, ἐκεῖ οἴσετε πάντα ὅσα ἐγὼ ἐντέλλομαι ὑμῖν σήμερον· τὰ ὁλοκαυτώματα ὑμῶν, καὶ τὰ θυσιάσματα ὑμῶν, . . . τὰ ἐπιδέκατα ὑμῶν, καὶ τὰς ἀπαρχὰς τῶν χειρῶν ὑμῶν, καὶ τὰ ἑξῆς.*[d] τὰ δὲ *δόματα* οἱ λοιποὶ *τὰ ἑκούσια* ἡρμήνευσαν,
20 τουτέστιν, ὅσα ἂν ἑκόντες προσενεγκεῖν ἐθελήσητε.[e]

Εἶτα ἀπαγορεύσας τὸ ἐν παντὶ τόπῳ τὰς θυσίας προσφέρειν,[f] εἰ κρεῶν μεταλαβεῖν ἐπιθυμήσαιεν, μεταλαβεῖν συνεχώρησεν ἐν αἷς κατοικοῦσι πόλεσι, τοῦ μὲν ἱερέως θύοντος, τοῦ δὲ αἵματος εἰς τὴν γῆν ἐκχεομένου. ἐκέλευσε δὲ
25 καὶ τὸν ἀκάθαρτον σὺν τῷ καθαρῷ τῶν τοιούτων ἀδιαφόρως ἀπολαῦσαι κρεῶν, διδάσκων ὡς τὰ τοιαῦτα θύματα κοινά ἐστι

---

l. 18 καὶ τὰς ἀπαρχὰς τῶν χειρῶν ὑμῶν F.M. : καὶ τὰς ἀπαρχὰς τῶν χειρῶν ὑμῶν καὶ τὰ δόματα ὑμῶν 11, C⁻¹, 10 37, Sir. Sch. = "'the first-fruits of your hands and your gifts' and so on."

IX A [32], B, C⁻¹, 4 7 9 10 31 35 37 = 20 mss.

a. Dt 12.8   b. Ex 20.25   c. Cf. Nm 33.38.   d. Dt 12.11   e. Dt 12.11
f. Dt 12.13f.

IX

How are we to understand, "You shall not do all we are doing here today, each as is pleasing to himself"?[a]

Before the construction of the tabernacle, they would offer sacrifices to the Lord God wherever they encamped, building altars out of the local stone.[b] After constructing an altar, they performed there the divine service, though not in just one place, but at each stage along the way, since they were constantly on the move and spent forty years in the wilderness.[c] But when they were in the promised land, he forbade them to continue in this manner, as he wished to prevent them from finding a pretext to sacrifice to false gods. Instead, he commanded them to perform the divine service only in the place chosen by the Lord God. It was there, as he ordered, that they were to hold their sacrifices and feasts: "To the place that the Lord your God has chosen for his name to be invoked you shall bring all I command you today: your holocausts, your sacrifices, your tithes, and the first-fruits of your hands" and so on.[1d] The other translators render "gifts" as "voluntary offerings," that is, whatever you wish to offer of your own accord.[2e]

Then, after forbidding them to offer sacrifices without regard to place,[f] he granted them permission to partake of meat wherever they lived whenever they so desired, provided that a priest butcher the victim, and its blood be poured out on the ground. As an indication that such victims were available to all and not dedicated to

1. Choosing this verse for commentary, Theodoret rightly draws attention to the basic message of Dt: one God, one people, one sanctuary. Unaware that this chapter combines three different versions of the law centralizing the cult (*v.* Blenkinsopp on 12.1–27), Theodoret does not note that the singular verb and pronominal adjectives of verse 17 contrast with the plural forms of verses 4 and 8.

2. The word "gifts" probably refers to the phrase καὶ τὰ δόματα ὑμῶν, a phrase Theodoret most likely omitted from his citation of Dt 12.11; *cf.* the critical note.

καὶ οὐ θεῖα·^g τῶν γὰρ δὴ θυσιῶν οὐκ ἐξὸν ἦν τοῖς ἀκαθάρτοις μεταλαμβάνειν.^h ὅθεν εἰκότως ἐπήγαγεν, *φάγετε αὐτὸ ὡς δορκάδα ἢ ἔλαφον·*ⁱ ταῦτα δὲ καθαρὰ μὲν ἦν, εἰς δὲ θυσίαν οὐ
30 προσεφέρετο.

X

Τὰς δεκάτας τοῖς ἱερεῦσι προσφέρειν νομοθετήσας, πῶς ἔφη, *οὐ δυνήσῃ φαγεῖν ἐν ταῖς πόλεσί σου τὰ ἐπιδέκατα τοῦ σίτου σου, καὶ τοῦ οἴνου σου, καὶ τοῦ ἐλαίου σου;*^a

Δύο δεκάτας ἀφιεροῦσθαι τῶν ὄντων προσέταξε· καὶ τὴν
5 μὲν τοῖς λευΐταις προσφέρεσθαι,^b τὴν δὲ ἄλλην διαπιπράσκεσθαι καὶ τὴν ταύτης τιμὴν εἰς τὴν αὐτῶν εὐωχίαν^c καὶ τὴν τῶν χηρῶν, καὶ τῶν ὀρφανῶν, καὶ τῶν προσηλύτων ἀναλίσκεσθαι θεραπείαν.^d εὐωχεῖσθαι δὲ αὐτοὺς ἐκέλευσε παρὰ τὸν θεῖον νεών.^e
10 Ταῦτα δὲ ὁ πάνσοφος νενομοθέτηκε Κύριος, τῆς τῶν ψευδωνύμων αὐτοὺς θεῶν πλάνης ἐλευθερῶν. ἐπειδὴ γὰρ ὁ τῆς ἀσεβείας διδάσκαλος διὰ γαστριμαργίας καὶ φιληδονίας ἐξανδραποδίζων τῶν ἀνθρώπων τὸ γένος, ταῖς τῶν δαιμόνων ἑορταῖς πολλὰς ἀνέμιξε παιγνίας, ἐκείνης τὸν Ἰσραὴλ
15 ἀπαλλάττων τῆς πλάνης, ὁ εὐμήχανος Κύριος καὶ τὰ περὶ τῶν ἑορτῶν ἐνομοθέτησε, καὶ τὰς θυσίας συνεχώρησε, καὶ τῶν μουσικῶν ὀργάνων ἠνέσχετο, καὶ εὐωχεῖσθαι προσέταξε, ταῖς τοιαύταις ψυχαγωγίαις τὴν τῶν εἰδώλων ἐκκόπτων ἀσέβειαν.

---

g. Dt 12.20–25   h. V., e.g., Nm 9.6.   i. Dt 12.15

x A [32], B, C⁻¹, 4 7 9 10 31 35 37 = 20 mss.

a. Dt 12.17   b. Nm 18.21–24   c. Dt 14.24–26   d. Dt 26.12   e. Dt 12.18

God,[g] he commanded that such meat be available to both the unclean and the clean without distinction, for in the case of actual sacrifices, the unclean were forbidden all participation.[h] Hence, his logical addendum: "Eat it like a deer or a stag,"[i] these being clean but not offered as sacrificial victims.

X

How is it that, after requiring them to offer tithes to the priests, he said, "In your cities you shall not be able to eat the tithes of your grain, your wine, and your oil"?[a]

He ordered the dedication of two tithes of property: one to be offered to the Levites,[b] the other to be sold and the proceeds spent on feasting[c] and on the care of widows, orphans, and aliens.[d] He commanded them to conduct their feasting close to the Temple of God.[1e]

Now, it was to free them from the deceit of false gods that the Lord, in his great wisdom, required this. As the teacher of idolatry, intending to enslave the whole human race through gluttony and debauchery, had seasoned the festivals of the demons with great jollity, the Lord, desiring to free Israel from that error, ingeniously established laws for festivals, permitted sacrifices, conceded the use of musical instruments, and gave orders for feasting, his aim in such comforts being to undermine the sacrilegious worship of idols.

1. Convinced that the Levites must have been separately provided for, Theodoret reads a second tithe into Dt 12.17–19; he found further support for his interpretation in 14.22–29 and 26.12; *v.* Q.13 and note 3.

XI

Τί δή ποτε συνεχῶς ἀπαγορεύει τὴν τοῦ αἵματος βρῶσιν;[a]

Ἔφη μὲν καὶ αὐτὸς ὁ νομοθέτης ὅτι τὸ αἷμα αὐτοῦ ψυχὴ
αὐτοῦ ἐστι.[b] πλὴν οἶμαι τὸν νόμον καὶ ἕτερον
πραγματεύεσθαι· τὴν μιαιφόνον γὰρ αὐτῶν ἰατρεύει γνώμην.
5 εἰ γὰρ τὸ τῶν ἀλόγων αἷμα φαγεῖν ψυχήν ἐστι φαγεῖν, πολλῷ
μᾶλλον ἀνόσιον τὸ τὴν λογικὴν ψυχὴν χωρίσαι τοῦ σώματος.

XII

Ἐκ ποίας δυνάμεως ὁ τἀναντία διδάσκων προφήτης
θαυματουργεῖ;[a]
   Τοῦ Θεοῦ συγχωροῦντος, ἐνεργοῦσιν οἱ δαίμονες. οὕτω καὶ
τοῦ Φαραὼ οἱ φάρμακοι καὶ τὸ τῆς ῥάβδου,[b] καὶ τὸ τοῦ
5 ποταμοῦ,[c] καὶ τὸ τῶν βατράχων[d] εἰργάσαντο, ἐνδεδωκότος τοῦ
πανσόφου Θεοῦ διὰ τὴν τοῦ προστάττοντος ἄνοιαν· ἐπιτείνειν
γὰρ αὐτοῖς ἐκέλευσε τὰς θεηλάτους πληγάς. λύειν μέντοι τὰς
τιμωρίας οὐκ ἴσχυον οὔτε μὴν τὸν σκνῖπα ἐξαγαγεῖν
ἠδυνήθησαν·[e] ἃ γὰρ συνεχώρησεν ὁ Θεὸς εἰργάσαντο μόνα.
10 τοῦτο καὶ ἐνταῦθα δεδήλωκεν· εἰρηκὼς γάρ, ἐὰν... ἀναστῇ ἐν
σοὶ προφήτης... ἐνυπνιαζόμενος ἐνύπνιον καὶ δώσει σημεῖον ἢ

---

xi A [32], B, C⁻¹, 4 7 9 10 31 35 37 = 20 mss.

a. Dt 12.23–25   b. V., e.g., Gn 9.4; Lv 17.11.

---

xii A [32], B, C⁻¹, 4 7 9 10 31 35 37 = 20 mss.

l. 11 δώσει *Sir. Sch. F.M.* : δῷ σοι (?) *J.P.; Cf. Wevers and Quast, Dt 13.1
and ap. crit.* Shulze had signalled (n. 5 to col. 420) his doubts about the future
indicative. Though δώσει seems clearly an error of etacism, it entered the
tradition at an early date as witnessed by Washington Freer Gallery, *I* (fifth c.).
As F.M. reports no variants, I have not ventured to print the obviously
meaningful and grammatically correct aorist subjunctive + pronoun.

a. Dt 13.1f.   b. Ex 7.11f   c. Ex 7.22   d. Ex 8.7   e. Ex 8.18

XI

Why did he repeat so often the prohibition against the consumption of blood?[a]

Admittedly, it was the Lawgiver himself who declared that the beast's blood is its soul.[1b] My view, however, is that this law had also a secondary purpose: to cure their readiness to homicide. For if to consume the blood of brute beasts is to consume their soul, it must be much more wicked to sever the rational soul from its body.

XII

By what power can a prophet, though teaching against God, perform miracles?[a]

Demons operate only by God's permission. That was how Pharaoh's soothsayers worked the marvels of the rod,[b] the river,[c] and the frogs.[d] God, in his great wisdom, permitted them to act, because of the folly of the ruler, by whose orders they intensified the heaven-sent plagues, though they had no power to put an end to the punishments or even to produce the gnat.[e] In other words, they did only what God allowed, as Moses has indicated here as well, his words being: "If there arises among you a prophet who dreams a

1. *V.* also *Q.* 54 on Gn (9.4) and *Q.* 23 on Lv (17.10-14). In the former, Theodoret divines a hint of an eschatological event, the resurrection of the body, in God's statement that he will exact an account of human blood from the beasts. In this question, he sees God imparting ethical instruction to the Jews through the prohibition against human consumption of animal blood.

τέρας, καὶ ἔλθῃ τὸ σημεῖον ἢ τὸ τέρας, ὃ ἐλάλησε πρὸς σέ, καὶ
εἴπῃ· πορευθῶμεν καὶ λατρεύσωμεν θεοῖς ἑτέροις οἷς οὐκ
οἴδατε, οὐκ εἰσακούσεσθε … τοῦ προφήτου ἐκείνου ἢ τοῦ
15 ἐνυπνιαζομένου τὸ ἐνύπνιον ἐκεῖνο, ὅτι πειράζει Κύριος ὁ Θεὸς
ὑμῶν … εἰ ἀγαπᾶτε Κύριον τὸν Θεὸν ὑμῶν ἐξ ὅλης τῆς καρδίας
ὑμῶν καὶ ἐξ ὅλης τῆς διανοίας ὑμῶν.ᶠ τοιγάρτοι τοῦ Θεοῦ
συγχωροῦντος, ὁ ψευδοπροφήτης τερατουργεῖ. διδασκόμεθα δὲ
μὴ προσέχειν σημείοις ὅταν ὁ ταῦτα δρῶν ἐναντία τῇ εὐσεβείᾳ
20 διδάσκῃ. ἐκέλευσε δὲ καὶ τὸν ψευδοπροφήτην ἀποκτανθῆναι,
καὶ τὸν λαὸν τῆς πονηρᾶς διδασκαλίας ἀπαλλαγῆναι·
ἀφανιεῖτε, γάρ φησι, τὸν πονηρὸν ἐξ ὑμῶν αὐτῶν.ᵍ

Ἐπειδὴ δὲ συνέβαινεν ἢ ἀδελφόν, ἢ φίλον, ἢ συγγενῆ, τῇ
πλάνῃ δεδουλευκότα, πειραθῆναι φενακίσαι καὶ ἄλλους,
25 ἀναγκαίως καὶ περὶ τούτου νενομοθέτηκε καὶ προσέταξε δῆλον
ἀποφανθῆναι τὸν τῆς ἀσεβείας διδάσκαλον, καὶ πρῶτον
ἀφεῖναι λίθον τὸν τῶν τοιούτων ὑπακούσαντα λόγων, εἶθ'
οὕτως πάντα τὸν λαὸν καταλεῦσαι τὸν ἀλιτήριον, καὶ τῇ
τούτου τιμωρίᾳ σωφρονισθῆναι τοὺς ἄλλους.ʰ

XIII

Τί ἐστιν οὐ φοιβήσετε καὶ οὐκ ἐπιθήσετε φαλάκρωμα ἀνὰ
μέσον τῶν ὀφθαλμῶν ὑμῶν ἐπὶ νεκρῷ;ᵃ

(1) Τῶν δυσσεβῶν ἐθνῶν ἀπαγορεύει τὰ ἔθη. καὶ διὰ μὲν τοῦ
οὐ φοιβήσετε τὰς μαντείας ἐξέβαλε· Φοῖβον γὰρ τὸν
5 ψευδόμαντιν ἐκάλουν τὸν Πύθιον. διὰ δὲ τοῦ οὐ ποιήσετε
φαλάκρωμα ἀνὰ μέσον τῶν ὀφθαλμῶν ὑμῶν ἐπὶ νεκρῷ τὴν τοῦ
πένθους ἀπηγόρευσεν ἀμετρίαν· τινὲς μὲν γὰρ τῶν ἀλλοφύλων
ἐθνῶν τὰς τῆς κεφαλῆς ἀπεκείροντο τρίχας καὶ ταύτας

---

f. Dt 13.1–3   g. Dt 13.5   h. Dt 13.6–11

xiii A [32], B, C⁻¹, 4 7 9 10 31 35 37 = 20 mss.
a. Dt 14.1

dream and produces a sign or portent, and the sign or portent he spoke to you comes to pass, and he says, 'Let us go and serve other gods that you do not know,' you shall not hearken to that prophet or to the dreamer of that dream, because the Lord your God is testing you to see whether you love the Lord your God with your whole heart and your whole mind."[f] So the false prophet works portents only by God's permission, but we learn not to heed signs when the wonder worker teaches what is contrary to right religion. He also commanded that the false prophet should be put to death, and the people rid of his evil teaching: "You shall remove the evil one from among you."[g]

Now, since on occasion a brother or friend or relative in thrall to error tried to trick others as well, he had to establish an ordinance also for that kind of case. He ordered that the teacher of idolatry be exposed, that whoever had listened to such ideas cast the first stone, and that all the assembly then stone the offender so that, by his punishment, everyone else would be brought to his senses.[h]

XIII

What is the meaning of "You shall not enquire of Phoebus or make a bald patch between your eyes for the dead"?[a]

(1) He forbade the practices of the irreligious gentiles, and with "You shall not enquire of Phoebus" he rejected soothsaying, as "Phoebus" was the name given to the prophet of Delphi.[1] In the following "You shall not make a bald patch between your eyes for the dead" he forbade immoderate grief. Some foreign peoples cut the

---

1. The MT of 14.1 contains a prohibition against the mourning rites of self-laceration and shaving, practices reported in Jer 16.6 and 41.5. In place of the former, the Septuagint offers the prohibition, οὐ φοιβήσετε, a plural future from the verb φοιβᾶν, here used of divination. As Theodoret explains, this verb is derived from the epithet φοῖβος = "the bright," "the pure" applied to Apollo, the Greek god of prophecy.

προσέφερον τοῖς νεκροῖς, τινὲς δὲ τὰς τῶν γενείων, ἄλλοι τὰς
10 τῶν ὀφρύων. ταῦτα γίνεσθαι ὁ θεῖος ἀπηγόρευσε *νόμος*.

  Ὅτι δὲ δύο δεκάτας ἀφορίζεσθαι πάντων προσέταξε σαφῶς
ἐνταῦθα δεδήλωκε ὅτι δύο δεκάτας προσάγειν νενομοθέτηκε τῷ
λαῷ, μίαν τοῖς λευίταις καὶ μίαν εἰς λόγον δοχῆς καὶ εὐωχίας·
δεκάτην, γάρ φησιν, ἀποδεκατώσεις παντὸς γενήματος τοῦ
15 *σπέρματός σου, τὸ γένημα τοῦ ἀγροῦ σου ἐνιαυτὸν κατ' ἐνιαυτόν,*
καὶ φάγῃ αὐτὸ ἐναντίον Κυρίου τοῦ Θεοῦ σου ἐν τῷ τόπῳ ᾧ ἂν
ἐκλέξηται Κύριος ὁ Θεός σου ἐπικληθῆναι τὸ ὄνομα αὐτοῦ ἐκεῖ.[b]
εἰ δὲ μία δεκάτη ἦν, πῶς οἷόν τε καὶ τοὺς λευίτας λαμβάνειν,
καὶ τοὺς προσκομίζοντας εὐωχεῖσθαι; ἀλλὰ δῆλον ὡς τοῖς μὲν
20 λευίταις μίαν δεκάτην ἀπένειμεν, ταῖς δὲ τῶν προσφερόντων
εὐωχίαις ἑτέραν. τοῦτο δὲ δηλοῖ καὶ τὰ ἐπαγόμενα· *ἐάν, γάρ*
φησιν, ἡ ὁδὸς μακρὰν εἴη ἀπὸ σοῦ, διαπώλησον, καὶ λαβὼν τὴν
τιμήν, εἰς ἐκεῖνον ἴθι τὸν τόπον ὃν ἂν ἐκλέξηται Κύριος ὁ Θεός
σου . . . καὶ δὸς τὸ ἀργύριον εἰς πᾶν ὃ ἐπιθυμεῖ ἡ ψυχή σου· ἐπὶ
25 *βουσίν, ἢ ἐπὶ προβάτοις, ἢ ἐπὶ οἴνῳ, ἢ ἐπὶ σίκερα, ἢ ἐπὶ παντὸς*
οὗ ἂν ἐπιθυμῇ ἡ ψυχή σου· καὶ φάγῃ ἐκεῖ ἐναντίον Κυρίου τοῦ
Θεοῦ σου . . . σύ, καὶ ὁ οἶκός σου, καὶ ὁ λευίτης, ὁ ἐν ταῖς
πόλεσί σου, ὅτι οὐκ ἔστιν αὐτῷ μερὶς μετὰ σοῦ οὐδὲ κλῆρος.[c]

  (2) Εἶτα περὶ τῶν ὀφειλόντων δοθῆναι τοῖς λευίταις
30 νομοθετεῖ· *μετὰ τρία ἔτη ἐξοίσεις πᾶν τὸ ἐπιδέκατον τῶν*
γενημάτων σου ἐν τῷ ἐνιαυτῷ ἐκείνῳ καὶ θήσεις αὐτὸ ἐν ταῖς
πόλεσί σου, καὶ ἐλεύσεται ὁ λευίτης, ὅτι οὐκ ἔστιν αὐτῷ μερὶς
οὐδὲ κλῆρος μετὰ σοῦ, καὶ ὁ προσήλυτος, καὶ ὁ ὀρφανός, καὶ ἡ
χήρα, οἱ ἐν ταῖς πόλεσί σου, καὶ φάγονται καὶ ἐμπλησθήσονται
35 *ἵνα εὐλογήσῃ σε Κύριος ὁ Θεός σου ἐν πᾶσι τοῖς ἔργοις σου,*
οἷς ἂν ποιῇς.[d] ἰστέον δὲ ὡς Ἰώσηπος, ἐντεῦθεν λαβὼν ἀφορμήν,
μᾶλλον δὲ καὶ τὸ ἰουδαίων ἐπιστάμενος ἔθος ὡς ἰουδαῖος, τρεῖς
ἔφη δεκάτας προστετάχεναι τὸν νόμον προσφέρεσθαι· τὴν μὲν
τοῖς λευίταις, τὴν δὲ τοῖς ὀρφανοῖς καὶ ταῖς χήραις, τὴν δὲ
40 ἄλλην ταῖς τῶν προσφερόντων εὐωχίαις.

b. Dt 14.22f.　　c. Dt 14.24–27　　d. Dt 14.28f.

hair of their head, others their beard, others their eyebrows and offered the hair to the dead. The divine law forbade this practice.[2]

We can conclude that he ordered two tithes of all produce from the law in this passage in which he orders the people to offer two tithes, one for the Levites and one for entertaining and feasting. As Scripture says, "You shall offer a tithe of all the yield of your seed, the annual yield of the field, and you shall eat it in the presence of the Lord your God in whatever place the Lord your God choose for the invocation of his name."[b] If there was just a single tithe, how could the Levites have received it and worshippers feasted on it? No, he clearly apportioned one tithe to the Levites and a second for the feasting of those who were making the offerings. This is apparent also in what follows: "If the distance be too great for you, sell it and bring the money to the place which the Lord your God has chosen and spend the money on whatever your heart desires: oxen, sheep, wine, strong drink, or anything else your heart desires. You shall eat it there in the presence of the Lord your God, you and your household and the Levite resident in your cities, because he has no part or allotment with you."[c]

(2) The next law regards the gifts due to the Levites. "After three years you shall bring out the full tithe of your produce in that year and store it in your cities. The Levite shall come, because he has no part or allotment with you, and the alien, the orphan, and the widow who live in your cities; they shall eat and be filled so that the Lord your God may bless you in all your works."[d] Now, it is notable that, either basing himself on this passage or, more likely, as a Jew, who knew the custom of the Jews, Josephus claimed that the Law enjoined the offering of three tithes: one for the Levites, one for the orphans and widows, and a third for the feasting of those who were making the offering.[3]

2. Theodoret would agree with von Rad (*Deuteronomy,* on 14.1f.) that "Israel deprived the dead and the grave of every sacral quality. This was a great achievement!"
3. In his interpretation of 14.24–29, Theodoret continues to argue (*v. Q.* 10),

XIV

Διὰ τί τὸ πεπηρωμένον πρωτότοκον ἀπαγορεύει
προσφέρειν;[a]

Διὰ τῶν ἀλόγων παιδεύων τοὺς λογικοὺς ἄρτιον ἔχειν τὸ
φρόνημα, πρὸς πᾶν ἔργον ἀγαθὸν ἐξηρτισμένον.

XV

Τίς ὁ τῶν ἀζύμων λόγος;

Ὁ νόμος ἡμᾶς ἐδίδαξεν· ἔφη γάρ, *ἑπτὰ ἡμέρας*
φάγῃ . . . ἄρτον κακώσεως, ὅτι ἐν σπουδῇ ἐξήλθετε ἐξ
Αἰγύπτου.[a] ἀποχρώντως δὲ καὶ περὶ τούτου εἰρήκαμεν ἤδη,
5 τὴν Ἔξοδον ἑρμηνεύοντες.

XVI

Τί ἐστι *δικαίως τὸ δίκαιον διώξετε;*[a]

Κατὰ τὸν τοῦ δικαίου, φησί, σκοπόν, μὴ διὰ δόξαν κενήν,

---

xiv A *[32]*, B, C⁻¹, 4 7 9 10 31* 35 37 = 20 mss.
a. Dt 15.21

---

xv A *[32]*, B, C⁻¹, 4 7 9 10 31 35 37 = 20 mss.
a. Dt 16.3

---

xvi A *[32]*, B, C⁻¹, 4 7 9 10 31 35 37 = 20 mss.
a. Dt 16.20

XIV

Why did he forbid the offering of a maimed firstborn?[a]

He was using the irrational to teach the rational to have a perfect attitude, ready for every good work.[1]

XV

What is the reason for the unleavened bread?

The Law informs us in the words, "For seven days you shall eat the bread of affliction because you went out from Egypt in haste."[a] I have already given this matter adequate attention in my comments on Exodus.[1]

XVI

What is the meaning of "You shall pursue justice justly"?[a]

He meant with a just intention, not out of vainglory or to im-

----

that there must have been two tithes if provision was to be made for the Levites; he cites Josephus, who, though differing with him over the number of tithes, does agree that there was more than one. Both Josephus (*Antiq. Iud.* 4.240) and Tobit reflect the "postexilic interpretation of the pentateuchal texts on tithing . . . in which the law is taken to prescribe three tithes rather than three distributions of the one yearly tithe. In this interpretation, first-fruits and firstlings went to the priests (Lv 27.26f., 30-33), the first tithe to the Levites (Nm 18.21–24), the second tithe to the banquet (Dt 14.22–26), and the third tithe to the poor (Dt 14.28f.)"; *v.* I. Nowell, on Tobit 1.6–8. Theodoret does not quote Tobit, perhaps because this text did not figure in his biblical canon. Though J. Blenkinsopp does not subscribe to Theodoret's view of two tithes, he does express surprise that there is no mention of "support of the Temple personnel" in 14.24–26.

----

1. Theodoret rather surprisingly has recourse to a spiritual, rather than a more literal, interpretation; *cf. Q.* 31 on Lv.

----

1. *V. Q.* 24.1–3 on Ex.

μὴ διὰ θεραπείαν ἀνθρωπίνην, ἀλλὰ δι' αὐτὸ τὸ ἀγαθόν· εἰσὶ
γάρ τινες γνώμῃ μὲν οὐ τιμῶντες τὸ δίκαιον, διὰ δὲ τοὺς
5 ἀληθῶς τιμῶντας τὸ δίκαιον ὑποκρινόμενοι τιμᾶν τὸ δίκαιον.

XVII

Τί ἐστιν ἐάν... ἀδυνατήσῃ ἀπὸ σοῦ ῥῆμα ἐν κρίσει ἀνὰ
μέσον... αἵματος, καὶ ἀνὰ μέσον... κρίσεως, καὶ ἀνὰ
μέσον... ἀφῆς, καὶ τὰ ἑξῆς;[a]

'Εάν, φησί, μὴ δυνηθῇς εὑρεῖν τἀληθὲς δικάζων, ἢ τὸ σῶμα
5 τὸ λεπρὸν δοκιμάζων· τοῦτο γὰρ ἀφὴν καλεῖ· μηδὲ διαγνῷς
εἴτε ἀλφός ἐστιν εἴτε λέπρα, μήτε κρίνῃς μήτε δικάσῃς ἐξ
ὑποψίας, ἀλλ' εἰς τὸν θεῖον νεὼν ἄπιθι, καὶ δίδαξον αὐτὰ τὸν
ἱερέα ἢ τὸν κατ' ἐκεῖνον τὸν καιρὸν τὴν δημαγωγίαν
πεπιστευμένον, καὶ τὸ κελευόμενον πλήρωσον. εἰ δή τις, τύφῳ
10 χρώμενος, τοῖς ὑπὸ τοῦ ἀρχιερέως ἢ τοῦ κριτοῦ λεγομένοις
ἀντείποι, θανάτῳ ζημιούσθω καὶ γινέσθω τοῖς ἄλλοις ὠφελείας
ἀρχέτυπον.[b]

XVIII

Τί δή ποτε κελεύει τὸν ἄρχοντα ἵππους μὴ πληθύνειν;[a]
Βούλεται αὐτοὺς τῷ Θεῷ μόνῳ θαρρεῖν. διά τοι τοῦτο καὶ
Δαβὶδ ὁ μακάριος ἐβόα, οὐ σῴζεται βασιλεὺς διὰ πολλὴν
δύναμιν, καὶ γίγας οὐ σωθήσεται ἐν πλήθει ἰσχύος αὐτοῦ.
5 ψευδὴς ἵππος εἰς σωτηρίαν, ἐν δὲ πλήθει δυνάμεως αὐτοῦ οὐ
σωθήσεται.[b]

---

xvii A [32], B, C⁻¹, 4 7 9 10 31* 35 37 = 20 mss.
a. Dt 17.8f.   b. Dt 17.12f.

---

xviii A [32], B, C⁻¹, 4 7 9 10 31 35 37 = 20 mss.
a. Dt 17.16   b. Ps 33.16f.

press other people, but for goodness' sake. Indeed, there are some who, though devoid of any real respect for justice, make a pretense of honoring it solely in order to make a favorable impression on those who do truly honor justice.

XVII

What is the meaning of "If it is too hard for you to decide between blood and blood, one legal right and another, one infection and another" and so on?[a]

This means, "If in the course of judgment you cannot find the truth, or in the examination of an eruption of the skin (this is the sense of 'infection') you can not determine whether it is a tetter or leprosy, do not make a judgment or a determination on the basis of suspicion. Instead, go to the Temple of God, explain the case to the priest or the official duly constituted at that time, and abide by his direction. But, if someone arrogantly opposes the directions of the high priest or the judge, let him pay with his life and become a salutary example to the rest."[b]

XVIII

Why does he forbid the ruler to multiply horses?[a]

He wants them to trust in God alone. This is why the blessed David cries out, "A king is not saved by a mighty army, nor a giant by his vast strength. A false hope of salvation is the horse; he will not be saved by his great might."[b]

XIX

Διὰ τί τὴν αἰχμάλωτον θρηνεῖν τοὺς οἰκείους κελεύει
ῥητὸν ἡμερῶν ἀριθμὸν εἶθ' οὕτω συναφθῆναι τῷ ταύτην
ἀνδραποδίσαντι;[a]

Οὐ βούλεται ἀναμιγῆναι θρῆνον εὐφροσύνῃ, οὐδὲ μειδιάματι
5 δάκρυον. τούτου χάριν προσέταξε καιρὸν αὐτὴν τοῦ πένθους
λαβεῖν τριάκοντα ἡμέρας, εἶθ' οὕτω τοῦ πένθους
ἀπαλλαγεῖσαν, μεταλαχεῖν τῆς γαμικῆς ὁμιλίας. πρὸς δὲ
τούτῳ καὶ τὴν ἐπιθυμίαν τὴν ἐκείνου κολάζει, κελεύων, μὴ τῆς
ἡδονῆς τὸ πάθος, ἀλλὰ τὸν λογισμὸν τῆς κοινωνίας
10 ἡγήσασθαι. ἐὰν δὲ μετὰ τὴν κοινωνίαν παραιτήσαιτο τὸν
γάμον, ἀπολυθῆναι προσέταξε, μισθὸν τῆς κοινωνίας τὴν
ἐλευθερίαν λαβοῦσαν.[b]

XX

Διὰ τί κοινὴν εἶναι βούλεται τὴν τῶν γονέων κατηγορίαν
κατὰ παιδὸς γινομένην;[a]

Ἐπειδὴ μαρτυρεῖ τῇ τῆς κατηγορίας ἀληθείᾳ τῶν
κατηγορούντων ἡ συμφωνία· συμβαίνει γὰρ πολλάκις, μάτην
5 τοῦ πατρὸς κατηγοροῦντος, ἀντειπεῖν τὴν μητέρα ἤ, τῆς
μητρὸς αἰτιωμένης, ἀντειπεῖν τὸν πατέρα. τὰ αὐτὰ μέντοι
ἀμφοτέρων κατηγορούντων, δῆλον ἔσται τῆς κατηγορίας τὸ
ἀληθές. οὗ δὴ χάριν ἀναιρεῖσθαι κελεύει τὸν οὕτω
κατηγορούμενον.

---

xix A [32], B, C⁻¹, 4 7 9 10 31 35 37 = 20 mss.
a. Dt 21.10–13   b. Dt 21.14

---

xx A [32], B, C⁻¹, 4 7 9 10 31 35 37 = 20 mss.
a. Dt 21.18–21

XIX

Why did he command a captive woman to grieve for her family for a set number of days and then be joined to the man who had enslaved her?[a]

He did not want grieving to be mingled with happiness, or tears with smiles. Thus, he ordered her to mourn for a period of thirty days and only after her release from grieving to engage in marital relations. He also tempered the man's desires by commanding that reason, not the passion of pleasure, should direct their intercourse. Further he enjoined that, if after intercourse the man declined to marry her, she should be dismissed, receiving her freedom in return for the intercourse.[b]

XX

Why did he require that parents should agree in an accusation against a child?[a]

Because this agreement between the accusers confirms the truth of the indictment. It frequently happens that when a father makes idle accusations, the mother contradicts him, or, when the mother finds fault, the father contradicts her. When both make the same accusation, the truth of the indictment will be evident. Thus he commanded the death of a son under such an indictment.

XXI

Τί δή ποτε τὸν νεοττοὺς ὀρνίθων εὑρηκότα τούτους μὲν κελεύει λαβεῖν, τοὺς δὲ γεγεννηκότας ἀφεῖναι;[a]

Φιλανθρωπίαν παιδεύει· εἰ γὰρ τοὺς τεκόντας λάβοι καὶ καταλίποι τοὺς νεοττούς, ἀπολοῦνται πάντως, οὐκ ὄντος τοῦ τρέφοντος. εἰ δὲ καὶ τούτους κἀκείνους θηρεύσαι—διαφθαρήσεται δηλονότι τῶν ὀρνίθων τὸ γένος εἰ πάντες τὰ ὅμοια δράσαιεν.

XXII

Τίνος χάριν στεφάνην τῷ δώματι γενέσθαι παρεκελεύσατο;[a]

Ἐδίδαξε τὰ ἑξῆς· ἔφη γάρ, *καὶ οὐ ποιήσεις φόνον ἐν τῇ οἰκίᾳ σου ἐὰν πέσῃ ὁ πεσὼν ἀπ' αὐτοῦ.*[b] λόγῳ γὰρ ἡμᾶς τιμήσας, βούλεται τούτῳ εἰς δέον κεχρῆσθαι, καὶ πάντων προμηθεῖσθαι, καὶ μὴ ἀνοήτως πάντων παραχωρεῖν τῷ Θεῷ, ἀλλά, τὰ παρ' ἑαυτῶν συνεισφέροντας, ἀναμένειν τὴν ἐκεῖθεν βοήθειαν. οὕτω, σπείροντες, οὐ θαρροῦμεν τῇ γῇ, ἀλλὰ τὴν θείαν φιλανθρωπίαν προσμένομεν καί, χρώμενοι ἰατροῖς, ἴσμεν

---

xxi A [32], B, C⁻¹, 4 7 9 10 31 35 37 = 20 mss.

l. 5 θηρεύσαι J.P. : θηρεύσει 5, B⁻¹⁷, c, 4 31 : θηρεύσοι *Sir. Sch. F.M.* In the conditional sentences of the *Quaest. in oct.*, Thdt. combines a subordinate aorist optative with the future indicative both in this question (εἰ . . . καταλίποι . . . ἀπολοῦνται) and in *Qq.* 40 on Ex (εἰ . . . ζηλώσαιεν . . . ἐπάξω), 1 on Dt (εἰ τολμήσαιεν . . . διασπερεῖ), and 7 on Dt (πείσονται . . . εἰ δράσαιεν), but nowhere else in this work does he combine a subordinate future indicative with the future indicative or a subordinate future optative with the future indicative. In fact, the future optative is rarely used in direct discourse, even in classical literature; *v.* A. Keith, pp. 123–26.

a. Dt 22.6f.

---

xxii A [32], B, C⁻¹, 4 7 9 10 31 35 37 = 20 mss.

a. Dt 22.8   b. Dt 22.8

XXI

Why did he command anyone who came across a nest full of chicks to take them but let the parents go?[a]

This was a lesson in kindness. If one were to take the parents and leave the chicks with no one to feed them, they would certainly die. But if one were to hunt both chicks and parents—birds would obviously die out if everyone did that.

XXII

Why did he order the building of parapets around housetops?[a]

The explanation is in what follows: "You will not be responsible for bloodshed in your house if someone fall from it."[b] As he has favored us with an explanation, he wants us to apply this principle as necessary and use forethought in all circumstances, not thoughtlessly leave everything to God. Only after we have done what lies within our own power, should we await help from above.[1] So, when we sow crops, we do not trust in the earth but wait on God's loving-

---

1. Theodoret understands this as a pragmatic prescription consistent with the Antiochene insistence on the coöperation of the human, with the divine, will; cf. Q. 11 on Jos. Similarly, Chrysostom (on Ps 7.4), listing the conditions in which God is inclined to answer prayer, includes the worthiness of the asker and his willingness to offer his all to God.

ὅτι τοῦ Θεοῦ τὸ διὰ τούτων ἰάσασθαι· τοσαῦτα γὰρ ἡ τέχνη
10 δύναται, ὅσαπερ ὁ ταύτην δεδωκὼς βούλεται.

XXIII

Τί ἐστιν *οὐ κατασπερεῖς τὸν ἀμπελῶνά σου διάφορον ἵνα*
μὴ ἁγιασθῇ τὸ γένημα καὶ τὸ σπέρμα ὃ ἂν σπείρῃς μετὰ τοῦ
γενήματος τοῦ ἀμπελῶνός σου;[a]

Καὶ τὴν ἀπληστίαν ἐκκόπτει καὶ αὐτῶν προμηθεῖται τῶν
5 γεωργούντων· πλείονα γὰρ ἡ γῆ σπέρματα δεχομένη,
ἐξιτήλους δίδωσι τοὺς καρπούς. κελεύει τοίνυν μήτε
ἀναμεμιγμένα σπέρματα καταβάλλειν μήτε μὴν τὰς ἀμπέλους
σπείρειν. εἶτα τῷ παραβαίνοντι δίδωσιν ἐπιτίμιον, τὴν τοῦ
κέρδους κολάζων ἐπιθυμίαν· ἐκέλευσε γὰρ αὐτῷ τὰ τοιαῦτα
10 προσφέρεσθαι· τοῦτο γὰρ εἶπεν· *ἵνα μὴ ἁγιασθῇ τὸ γένημα.*

XXIV

Διὰ τί τῷ μοιχῷ παραπλησίως κολάζεσθαι κελεύει τὸν
φθείροντα τὴν ἄλλῳ μεμνηστευμένην;[a]

Ἐπειδὴ τὰ τῆς μνηστείας αὐτοὺς συνήρμοσεν σύμβολα.
ὅθεν καὶ *γυναῖκα* αὐτὴν προσηγόρευσεν· *ἐταπείνωσε,* γάρ
5 φησι, *τὴν γυναῖκα τοῦ πλησίον.*[b] οὕτω καὶ ἡ ἁγία παρθένος
γυνὴ τοῦ Ἰωσὴφ ἐχρημάτισεν· *μὴ φοβηθῇς,* γάρ φησι,
παραλαβεῖν Μαριὰμ τὴν γυναῖκά σου.[c]

XXIII A [32], B, C⁻¹, 4 7 9 10 31 35 37 = 20 mss.

a. Dt 22.9

XXIV A [32], B, C⁻¹, 4 7 9 10 35 37 = 19 mss.

a. Dt 22.23f.   b. Dt 22.24   c. Mt 1.20

kindness, and when we go to physicians, we are aware that God is responsible for the healing that comes through them. In short, technology can achieve only so much as God, who has granted us that technology, wills.

XXIII

What is the meaning of "You shall not sow your vineyard with different seed lest its produce be devoted as well as the seed you have sown along with the produce of your vineyard"?[a]

This ordinance restrained their greed and protected the farmers themselves. After all, when the soil receives many different kinds of seed, it produces fruit of poor quality. So he forbade them to sow a mixture of seed and to sow seed in their vineyards. Then, punishing the transgressor's lust for profit and assigning him a penalty, God ordered that the produce of mixed seed be offered to himself. That is the meaning of "lest the produce be devoted."

XXIV

Why did he command that a man guilty of seducing a woman betrothed to another endure the same punishment as an adulterer?[a]

Because they had been joined by the contract of betrothal. Hence, the reference to her as "wife": "He humiliated his neighbor's wife."[b] Similarly, the holy virgin was styled Joseph's "wife": "Do not be afraid to receive Mary your wife."[c]

XXV

Διὰ τί τὸν θλαδίαν καὶ τὸν ἐκτομίαν εἰσελθεῖν εἰς
ἐκκλησίαν ἀπαγορεύει;[a]

Τὸ ἄγονον τῆς ψυχῆς διὰ τούτων αἰνίττεται· ἀλλοτρία γὰρ
Θεοῦ ἡ τῶν ἀγαθῶν ἀκαρπία. ἄλλως δέ, οὐ μόνον ἐπὶ τῶν
5 ἀνθρώπων, ἀλλὰ καὶ ἐπὶ τῶν κτηνῶν ἀπαγορεύει τὰ τοιαῦτα
ποιεῖν·[b] εἰς γὰρ τὴν τοῦ γένους αὔξησιν τὰ γεννητικὰ
δεδημιούργηται μόρια. ὥσπερ δὲ τὴν ἀκαρπίαν ἀπαγορεύει,
οὕτως καὶ τὸν πονηρὸν ἐκβάλλει καρπόν· *οὐκ εἰσελεύσεται,*
γάρ φησιν, ἐκ πόρνης εἰς ἐκκλησίαν Κυρίου.[c]

XXVI

Τί δή ποτε τὴν πρὸς μωαβίτας καὶ ἀμμανίτας ἐπιμιξίαν
κωλύει, οὐ κατὰ ῥητόν τινα χρόνον, ἀλλ' ἕως εἰς τὸν αἰῶνα;[a]

Πρῶτον διὰ τὴν παράνομον αὐτῶν ῥίζαν· ἐκ παρανόμου γὰρ
γεγέννηνται συνουσίας.[b] ἔπειτα διὰ τὴν ἀσέβειαν ἧς καὶ τοὺς
5 ἰσραηλίτας μεταλαχεῖν παρεσκεύασαν, ὡραΐσαντες τὰς
γυναῖκας καὶ διὰ τούτων αὐτοὺς εἰς τὴν τῶν εἰδώλων λατρείαν
ἀγρεύσαντες.[c] τὸν μέντοι ἰδουμαῖον καὶ τὸν αἰγύπτιον μετὰ
τρίτην κελεύει προσίεσθαι γενεάν· τὸν μὲν ὡς ἀδελφόν, τὸν
δὲ ὡς εὐεργέτην ἐν καιρῷ γεγενημένον·[d] λιμοῦ γὰρ
10 προσπεσόντος, εἰς Αἴγυπτον εἰσελθόντες, οἱ πατέρες αὐτῶν
διετράφησαν.[e] διδάσκει τοίνυν ἡμᾶς ὁ νόμος μηδὲ παλαιᾶς
εὐεργεσίας ἀμνημονεῖν.

---

xxv A *[32]*, B, C⁻¹, 4 7 9 10 31 35 37 = 20 mss.

a. Dt 23.1   b. Lv 22.24   c. Dt 23.2

---

xxvi A *[32]*, B, C⁻¹, 4 7 9 10 35 37 = 19 mss.

a. Dt 23.3   b. Gn 19.36–38   c. Nm 25.1–3   d. Dt 23.7f.   e. Gn 46

XXV

Why did he deny access to the assembly to a man whose testicles had been crushed or removed?[a]

This was a riddling reference to spiritual sterility. Failure to produce good fruit separates one from God. Besides, he laid down this prohibition not only for men but for cattle as well,[b] since the genitals have been created for the increase of the race. Forbidding fruitlessness, he also rejected the bad crop: "He that is born of a prostitute shall not enter the assembly of the Lord."[c]

XXVI

Why did he prohibit intermingling with Moabites and Ammonites, not for a specified time, but forever?[a]

First, because of their sinful origin, since they were born of a sinful union.[b] Next, on account of their idolatry, in which they involved the Israelites as well, by adorning their women and using them to ensnare the Israelites in idol worship.[c] In contrast, he commanded the admission of the Idumean and the Egyptian after the third generation: the former as a brother, the latter as a benefactor in time of need.[d] Remember, when they were reduced to starvation, their ancestors migrated to Egypt and were fed.[e] The Law teaches us, therefore, not to forget even an ancient act of kindness.

XXVII

Τί ἐστιν ὅτι *Κύριος ὁ Θεός σου ἐμπεριπατεῖ ἐν τῇ*
παρεμβολῇ σου;[a]

Οἶδε πολλάκις, δυσοσμίας ὁ ἀὴρ ἐμπιπλάμενος, λοιμὸν
ἐμποιεῖν. ἐκέλευσε τοίνυν αὐτοῖς στρατοπεδευομένοις τὴν
5 ἐκκρινομένην καταχωννύναι κόπρον. ἵνα δὲ μὴ ἀπειθήσαντες
βλάβην εἰσδέξωνται, ἀναγκαίως ἐπήγαγεν, ὅτι *Κύριος ὁ Θεὸς*
ἐμπεριπατεῖ ἐν τῇ παρεμβολῇ σου, καὶ τὴν αἰτίαν διδάσκει·
ἐξελέσθαι σε καὶ παραδοῦναι τὸν ἐχθρόν σου πρὸ προσώπου
σου. διὰ δὲ τούτου παιδεύει μηδὲν πράττειν παράνομον· τοῦτο
10 γὰρ ἐπάγει· *καὶ ἔσται ἡ παρεμβολή σου ἁγία, καὶ οὐχ*
εὑρεθήσεται ἐν σοὶ ἀσχημοσύνη πράγματος.[b]

XXVIII

Τί ἐστι *τελεσφόρος,* καὶ *τελισκόμενος,* καὶ *τελισκομένη;*[a]

Ὥσπερ ἡμεῖς *πιστοὺς* ὀνομάζομεν τοὺς τῶν θείων
μυστηρίων μετέχοντας, οὕτως *τετελεσμένους* ἐκάλει τὰ ἔθνη
τοὺς δαιμόνων τινῶν διδασκομένους μυστήρια. *τελεσφόρον*
5 τοίνυν καλεῖ τὸν μυσταγωγοῦντα, *τελισκόμενον* δὲ τὸν
μυσταγωγούμενον.

---

xxvii A [32], B, C⁻¹, 4 7 9 10 31 35 37 = 20 mss.

a. Dt 23.14   b. Dt 23.14

---

xxviii A [32], B, C⁻¹, 4 7 9 10 31* 35 37 = 20 mss.

a. Dt 23.17 (LXX)

XXVII

What is the meaning of "because the Lord your God walks about in your camp"?[a]

Polluted air can often cause disease, so he commanded them, when in camp, to bury their excrement. And to prevent them from disobeying and coming to harm, he made the essential addition, "because the Lord your God walks about in your camp," and explained the reason, "to save you and to hand over your enemies before you." With this, he taught them to avoid all unlawful conduct as is evident from what follows: "Your camp shall be holy, and nothing shameful shall be found among you."[b]

XXVIII

What is the meaning of "initiator" and "initiated"?[a]

As we apply the name "faithful" to those who participate in the Eucharist, so pagans used the term "initiated" for those who had been schooled in the rites of demons. So by "initiator" he referred to one who provided introduction to the rites, and by "initiated" to one who was being inducted.[1]

1. The LXX of Dt 23.17 is longer than its Hebrew original (23.18). The latter, concerned to outlaw sacral prostitution, contains one term for a female, and one for a male, prostitute, which the LXX first translates by the terms "harlot" (πόρνη) and "fornicator" (πορνεύων) and then glosses with "initiator among the daughters of Israel" (τελεσφόρος ἀπὸ θυγατέρων Ἰσραὴλ) and "initiate among the sons of Israel" (τελισκόμενος ἀπὸ υἱῶν Ἰσραήλ). It may be that Theodoret regarded the first pair as part of a simple prohibition against prostitution and the second as part of a separate prohibition of foreign rites.

XXIX

Τίνα ἐστὶ τὰ ἐκπορευόμενα διὰ τῶν χειλέων σου φυλάξῃ;[a]

Ἐπαγγελλόμενος τῷ Θεῷ, χρέος νόμιζε τὴν ὑπόσχεσιν. σπούδασον τοίνυν ταύτην ἀποδοῦναι συντόμως· τοῦτο γὰρ ἔφη· οὐ χρονιεῖς ἀποδοῦναι τὴν εὐχήν σου, ὅτι ἐκζητῶν

5 ἐκζητήσει Κύριος ὁ Θεός σου παρὰ σοῦ, καὶ ἔσται σοι ἁμαρτία.[b] εἶτα διδάσκων ὅτι τῆς ἐξουσίας ἐστὶ τῆς γνώμης τὸ ὑποσχέσθαι ἢ μή, ἐπήγαγεν, ἐὰν δὲ μὴ θελήσῃς εὔξασθαι, οὐκ ἔσται σοι ἁμαρτία.[c] ὅθεν καὶ ὁ μακάριος Δαβίδ, ἀποδώσω σοι τὰς εὐχάς μου, ἃς διέστειλε τὰ χείλη μου, καὶ ἐλάλησε τὸ

10 στόμα μου ἐν τῇ θλίψει μου.[d]

Πάλιν μέντοι τὸν περὶ τῆς λέπρας τεθεικὼς νόμον, τῆς Μαρίας ἀνέμνησε, λέγων, μνήσθητι ὅσα ἐποίησε Κύριος ὁ Θεός σου τῇ Μαριὰμ ἐν τῇ ὁδῷ,[e] διδάσκων ὡς θεήλατος ἡ πληγή, καὶ ταύτην αὐτοῖς ἁμαρτάνουσιν ἐπέφερεν ὁ Θεὸς καὶ

15 αὖ πάλιν μεταμελουμένων ἔπαυσε.

Καὶ μέντοι καὶ περὶ τῆς τῶν παίδων ἀπειλῆς τὸ ἀμφίβολον ἔλυσεν·[f] ἔφη γάρ, οὐκ ἀποθανοῦνται πατέρες ὑπὲρ τέκνων, οὐδὲ τέκνα… ὑπὲρ πατέρων· ἕκαστος τῇ ἰδίᾳ ἁμαρτίᾳ ἀποθανεῖται·[g] εἰκὸς γὰρ καὶ πατέρας συμβουλεῦσαι μὲν παισὶ

20 τὰ συμφέροντα, μηδὲν δὲ διὰ τὴν ἐκείνων ἀπείθειαν ὀνῆσαι, καὶ παῖδας κρείττους τῶν πατέρων γενέσθαι.

xxix A *[32]*, B, c⁻¹, 52, 4 7 9 10 31* 35 37 = 19 mss.

a. Dt 23.23   b. Dt 23.21   c. Dt 23.22   d. Ps 66.13f.   e. Dt 24.9
f. Ex 20.5   g. Dt 24.16

XXIX

What is the meaning of "You shall observe what passes through your lips"?[a]

Whenever you make a promise to God, take the promise as a debt and make haste to pay it promptly: "Do not delay in fulfilling your vow, because the Lord your God will certainly require it of you, and it will be a sin for you."[b] Then, to bring out that the choice to make a promise is a matter of free will, he added, "If you do not wish to make a vow, it will be no sin for you."[c] Hence, the blessed David declared, "I shall fulfil my vows to you, which my lips uttered and my mouth spoke in my distress."[d]

Furthermore, having once again set down the law about leprosy, he reminded them of Miriam with the words "Remember what the Lord your God did to Miriam on the way."[e] This was to teach them that this affliction was heaven-sent, that God inflicted it on them when they sinned, but put a stop to it when they repented.

Moreover, he also removed the uncertainty regarding the threat against children[f] by saying, "Parents shall not die for their children, nor children for their parents; each will die for his own sin."[g] Indeed, it is quite likely that parents might give sound ethical advice to their children but fail to do them any good because of their children's disobedience, and, conversely, that children might turn out better than their parents.

XXX

Τί δή ποτε, τοῦ Θεοῦ κελεύσαντος τεσσαράκοντα
λαμβάνειν τὸν πλημμελήσαντα μάστιγας,[a] παρὰ μίαν πληγὴν
ἐπιφέρουσιν ἰουδαῖοι;

Ἐπειδὴ ὁ πλείων ἀριθμὸς τὸν αἰκιζόμενον ἀτιμοῖ· *ἐὰν . . .*
5 *γὰρ προσθῶσι μαστιγῶσαι αὐτόν, . . . ἀσχημονήσει ὁ ἀδελφός
σου ἐναντίον σου.*[b] παρὰ μίαν διδόασιν ἵνα μή, τὸν ἀκριβῆ
φυλάττοντες ἀριθμόν, καὶ ἄκοντες τὸν τυπτόμενον ἀτιμάσωσι,
τὸν περιττὸν ἐπιφέροντες.[c]

XXXI

Τί ἐστιν *οὐ φιμώσεις βοῦν ἀλοῶντα;*[a]

Τὸ μὲν τῆς ἀναγωγῆς νόημα σαφῶς ἡμᾶς ἐδίδαξεν ὁ θεῖος
ἀπόστολος. καὶ αὐτὸ δὲ τὸ πρόχειρον εὐσεβές· ἄδικον γὰρ τὸν
ἀρόσαντα τὴν γῆν καὶ τὰ δράγματα σὺν πόνῳ τέμνοντα μὴ
5 μεταλαγχάνειν τοῦ καρποῦ.

---

xxx A *[32]*, B, C⁻¹, 4 7 9 10 35 37 = 19 mss.

a. Dt 25.2f.   b. Dt 25.3   c. *Cf.* 2Cor 11.24.

---

xxxi A *[32]*, B, C⁻¹, 4 7 9 10 35 37 = 19 mss.

a. Dt 25.4

XXX

Why is it that, though God commanded forty lashes for the wrongdoer,[a] the Jews inflict thirty-nine?

Because any higher number dishonors the man being scourged: "If they add to his strokes, your brother will be degraded in your sight."[b] They give one fewer to avoid mistaking the number and unwittingly dishonoring the man who is being beaten by inflicting an extra blow.[c]

XXXI

What is the meaning of "You shall not muzzle an ox that is treading the grain"?[a]

The holy apostle has given us clear instruction in the spiritual sense. Yet even the immediately apparent sense is itself religious. It would be unjust if a man who works hard ploughing the earth and cutting the sheaves did not share in the crop.[1]

---

1. J. Blenkinsopp (on 25.4) interprets this law as evincing a "concern for animal welfare." Theodoret, perhaps under the influence of 1Tm 5.18, claims that his interpretation—that laborers must be paid in return for their work—still respects the obvious sense (τὸ πρόχειρον) of the verse and is itself in accord with religious principle. He presents Paul, who at 1Cor 9.9f. applies this precept to evangelical labor, as lifting the Law to a spiritual level (τὸ τῆς ἀναγωγῆς νόημα); for this terminology, cf. Q. 83 on Gn (κατὰ μὲν τὸ πρόχειρον καὶ ἐπιπόλαιον τοῦ γράμματος νόημα ... κατὰ δὲ τὴν ... ἑρμηνείαν) and Q. 2.3 on Ruth (κατὰ μὲν τὸ πρόχειρον νόημα ... κατὰ δὲ τὴν ἀλήθειαν).

XXXII

Τί δή ποτε ἐμπτύεσθαι κελεύει τὸν τοῦ ἄπαιδος ἀδελφοῦ
τὴν γυναῖκα μὴ βουλόμενον γῆμαι;[a]

Ἀνάγκην αὐτοῖς, διὰ τῆς ἀτιμίας, φιλαδελφίας ἐπιθείς·
ἄμεινον μὲν γὰρ ἦν διὰ τὴν φύσιν προμηθεῖσθαι τοῦ
τεθνηκότος. ἐπειδὴ δὲ Ιοὐχ ἅπαντες αἰδοῦνται τὸν τῆς
φύσεως νόμον, τὴν τῆς ἀτιμίας αὐτοῖς ἀνάγκην ἐπέθηκεν.

|14   5

XXXIII

Διὰ τί πανωλεθρίᾳ κελεύει παραδοῦναι τὸν Ἀμαλήκ;[a]

Καὶ δυσσεβεῖς ἦσαν καὶ μισάδελφοι. καὶ γὰρ ἐκ τοῦ Ἠσαῦ
τὸ γένος κατάγοντες,[b] πρῶτοι τὸν κατὰ τοῦ Ἰσραὴλ
ἀνεδέξαντο πόλεμον, καὶ ταῦτα πόρρωθεν ὄντος καὶ τοῖς
ὁρίοις αὐτῶν μὴ πελάσαντος.[c]

5

Ἐδίδαξε δὲ πάλιν σαφέστερον ὡς δύο ἀφορίζεσθαι δεκάτας
προσέταξεν· ἔφη δὲ οὕτως· *ἐὰν δὲ συντελέσῃς ἀποδεκατῶσαι*
πᾶν τὸ ἐπιδέκατον τῶν γενημάτων τῆς γῆς σου ἐν τῷ ἔτει τῷ
τρίτῳ, τὸ δεύτερον ἐπιδέκατον δώσεις τῷ λευίτῃ, καὶ τῷ
προσηλύτῳ, καὶ τῇ χήρᾳ, καὶ τῷ ὀρφανῷ, καὶ φάγονται ἐν ταῖς
πόλεσί σου καὶ ἐμπλησθήσονται.[d]

10

Ὅτι μέντοι οὐκ ἐν μιᾷ ἡμέρᾳ τῷ λαῷ ταύτην τὴν
διδασκαλίαν ὁ προφήτης προσήνεγκε καὶ ταῦτα δηλοῖ·
προσέταξε, γάρ φησι, Μωϋσῆς καὶ ἡ γερουσία Ἰσραήλ,
λέγοντες, φυλάσσεσθε ποιεῖν πάσας τὰς ἐντολὰς ταύτας, ὅσας
ἐγὼ ἐντέλλομαι ὑμῖν σήμερον.[e]

15

---

xxxii *A [32], B, C⁻¹, 4 7 9 10 35 37* = 19 mss.

a. Dt 25.9

---

xxxiii *A [32], 14(twice) 17 24, C⁻¹, 4 7 9 10 35 37* = 19 mss.

a. Dt 25.17–19   b. Gn 36.12   c. Ex 17.8–14   d. Dt 26.12   e. Dt 27.1

XXXII

Why did he command that anyone who refused to marry the widow of his childless brother be spat upon?[a]

To use public disgrace to compel them to practice brotherly love. Of course, it would have been better to rely on natural feeling to provide for the deceased, but since not everyone respected the law of nature, he also applied the pressure of disgrace.

XXXIII

Why did he command them to devote Amalek to destruction?[a]

The Amalekites were heathens and hated their brethren. Although descended from Esau,[b] they were the first to wage war on the Israelites, although they were still far off and had not approached their boundaries.[c]

Here again he brought out very clearly that he ordered the payment of two tithes. Scripture says, "If you have finished taking a complete tithe of the produce of your land in the third year, you shall give the second tithe to the Levite, the alien, the widow, and the orphan, and they will eat it in your cities and be filled."[1d]

Furthermore, the following passage proves that the prophet did not present all this teaching in just one day: "Moses and the elders of Israel instructed them saying, 'Be sure to carry out all these commandments I give you today.'"[e]

---

1. *V.* note 1 to *Q.* 10 and note 3 to *Q.* 13 for Theodoret's conviction that the Law required two tithes. As A. Siquans points out (p. 197), in Dt 26.12, the LXX's δεύτερον ("second") rests upon a pointing of the Hebrew consonantal text different from that of the MT, which correctly speaks of the "year of the tithe," rather than "the second tithe." While concentrating on this, for us, relatively minor point, Theodoret passes over the cultic credo of Dt 26.5–9 meant to accompany the offering of first-fruits, a formula like that at 6.20-25, on which he had likewise failed to

Εἶτα ἐκέλευσεν ὁ δεσπότης Θεός, μετὰ τὸ διαβῆναι τὸν
Ἰορδάνην, δύο στῆσαι λίθους μεγάλους, καὶ κονιάσαι αὐτούς,
καὶ ταύτας ἐπιγράψαι τὰς ἐντολάς·[f] ἔπειτα ἐκ λίθων αὐτοφυῶν
20 οἰκοδομῆσαι θυσιαστήριον ἐν τῷ ὄρει Γεβάλ, καὶ τὰς
νενομισμένας ἐπιτελέσαι θυσίας καὶ πρὸς ταῖς ἄλλαις, οἷόν
τινα χαριστήριον, τὴν τοῦ σωτηρίου, καὶ μετὰ ταῦτα
εὐωχηθῆναι, τὸν εὐεργέτην ἀνυμνοῦντας Θεόν.[g]

XXXIV

Τί δή ποτε κατάραις αὐτοὺς καὶ εὐλογίαις ὑπέβαλεν;[a]
(1) Ὁ δεσπότης Χριστός, τὰ τέλεια μαθήματα τοῖς
τελείοις προσενεγκών, βασιλείαν μὲν οὐρανῶν τοῖς ταῦτα
πληροῦσιν ὑπέσχετο, ἠπείλησε δὲ τοῖς παραβαίνουσι γέενναν.
5 ἰουδαίοις δέ, χαμαιπετὲς ἔχουσι καὶ χαμαίζηλον φρόνημα,
τὰς τῇ γῇ προσηκούσας ἀρὰς καὶ εὐλογίας ἀπένειμεν· οἱ γάρ,
μηδὲ τοῖς ὁρωμένοις πιστεύσαντες θαύμασι, πῶς ἂν ἐδέξαντο
τὰ τῷ μέλλοντι βίῳ προσήκοντα;

Ἐπισημήνασθαι δὲ χρὴ ὡς τὰς μὲν εὐλογίας ταῖς ἐκ τῶν
10 ἐλευθέρων βεβλαστηκυίαις φυλαῖς ἀπένειμε, καὶ τὴν ἱερατικὴν
ἐνταῦθα τῷ λαῷ συνηρίθμησε, καὶ τὴν τοῦ Ἰωσήφ, διπλῆν
οὖσαν, ὡς μίαν προσέταξεν εὐλογεῖν. τὰς δὲ κατάρας τοῖς
ἡμιδούλοις ἐκλήρωσε, συντάξας αὐτοῖς διὰ τὸν τῶν φυλῶν
ἀριθμὸν τὸν Ῥουβὴν καὶ τὸν Ζαβουλών·[b] τὸν μὲν ὡς ἁμαρτίᾳ
15 περιπεπτωκότα,[c] τὸν δὲ ὡς ἔσχατον τῶν τῆς Λείας υἱῶν.[d]

f. Dt 27.2–4   g. Dt 27.5–7

xxxiv A [32], 14(inc.) 17 24, C⁻¹, 4 7 9 10 31 35 37 = 20 mss.

a. Dt 27.11–28.68   b. Dt 27.12f.   c. Gn 35.22   d. Gn 35.23

Question xxxiv

Next, the Lord God gave orders that, after crossing the Jordan, they should set up two large stones, plaster them, and inscribe them with these commandments;[f] then build an altar of unwrought stone on Mount Ebal and perform the required sacrifices, including a peace offering in thanksgiving; then feast as they sang the praise of God their benefactor.[g]

XXXIV

Why did he subject them to curses and blessings?[a]

(1) Proposing teachings of perfection to the perfect, Christ the Lord promised the Kingdom of Heaven, if they did as they were taught, but threatened them with hell if they transgressed. In contrast, in accord with their earthly and groveling mentality, God gave the Jews curses and blessings related to the earth. How could they have grasped what relates to the future life when they would not even put trust in the miracles that were taking place right before their eyes?

Now, we should note first that he gave the task of blessing to the tribes descended from the free men; then that he here numbered the priestly tribe within the nation; and finally that he directed that Joseph, though a double tribe, bless as one.[1] In contrast, he assigned the task of cursing to the half-slaves, along with whom he set Reuben and Zebulun to fill up the number of the tribes:[b] the former because of his sin,[c] the latter because of his place as the last of Leah's sons.[d]

----

comment. Von Rad (on 26.1–11) regards these passages as "summaries of salvation history," which preserve "the earlier and more original form of an historical outline which we possess in a much more fully developed form in the sources of the Pentateuch," *i.e.* as providing the historical kernel of Israel's theology.

1. The tribes of Levi and Joseph here take the two places among the twelve usually accorded to the tribes descended from Joseph's sons Manasseh and Ephraim; *cf., e.g.,* Nm 34.13–29.

Ἐπαρᾶσθαι δὲ πρὸ τῶν ἄλλων ἁπάντων ἐκέλευσε τοῖς εἰς τὸ
θεῖον ἀσεβοῦσι καὶ τὰ χειροποίητα προσκυνοῦσιν ἀγάλματα,ᵉ
εἶτα τοῖς εἰς πατέρας παρανομοῦσι·ᶠ μετὰ γὰρ τὰ θεῖα,
δίκαιον θεραπεύειν τούτους δι' ὧν εἰς τὸ εἶναι παρήχθημεν·
20 ἔπειτα τοῖς ἐπικερτομοῦσι τοῖς τὸ βλέπειν ἀφῃρημένοις καὶ
τῆς εὐθείας αὐτοὺς ἐκτρέπειν ὁδοῦ πειρωμένοις,ᵍ καὶ
ἁπαξαπλῶς τοῖς τὰς προειρημένας παραβαίνουσιν ἐντολάς.
ταῦτα δὲ τῶν ἱερέων λεγόντων, ἐκέλευσε τὸν λαὸν ἐπιλέγειν,
γένοιτο,ʰ οἷον ὑπογραφήν τινα γραμματείου ταύτην παρ'
25 αὐτῶν κομιζόμενος τὴν φωνήν.

(2) Τοῖς δὲ τὰς θείας φυλάττουσιν ἐντολὰς τὰς
παντοδαπὰς δέδωκεν εὐλογίας· καὶ τοῖς τὰς πόλεις καὶ τὰς
κώμας οἰκοῦσιν εὐπαιδίαν, πολυπαιδίαν, ποιμνίων καὶ
βουκολίων πολυγονίαν, τὴν ἀπὸ γῆς εὐκαρπίαν, τὴν ἐν εἰρήνῃ
30 διαγωγήν, τὴν ἐν πολέμοις νίκην, καὶ τὰ τούτοις προσόμοια.ⁱ
ταῖς δὲ σωματικαῖς καὶ πνευματικὴν εὐλογίαν προστέθεικεν·
ἀναστῆσαι σε Κύριος ἑαυτῷ λαὸν ἅγιον, ὃν τρόπον ὤμοσε τοῖς
πατράσι σου. καὶ τοῦτον δὲ προστέθεικε τὸν διορισμόν· ἐὰν
εἰσακούσῃ τῆς φωνῆς Κυρίου τοῦ Θεοῦ σου καὶ πορευθῇς ἐν
35 ταῖς ὁδοῖς αὐτοῦ.ʲ ταῦτα γὰρ οἱ μὲν ὁρῶντες, οἱ δὲ ἀκούοντες,
φοβηθήσονται, λογιζόμενοι τὴν θείαν κηδεμονίαν ἧς
ἀπολαύετε. τὸ μέντοι γενέσθαι εἰς κεφαλὴν καὶ μὴ εἰς οὐρὰν
ἄρχοντα λέγει καὶ μὴ δουλεύοντα· τοῦτο γὰρ ἐπήγαγε· καὶ
ἔσῃ τότε ἐπάνω καὶ οὐχ… ὑποκάτω.ᵏ

|14 40 Εἶτα πάλιν ἐπιφέρει τὰς ἀράς, |τἀναντία τῶν προρρηθεισῶν
ἐχούσας εὐλογιῶν· ἀγονίαν, δυσκληρίαν, ἔνδειαν, νόσους,
ταλαιπωρίαν, λιμόν, λοιμόν, πόλεμον, ἧτταν, ἀνομβρίαν, γῆς
ἀκαρπίαν·ˡ τοῦτο γὰρ ἡ σιδηρᾶ γῆ δηλοῖ, καὶ ὁ χαλκοῦς
οὐρανός·ᵐ ἔπειτα τὰ ἐν πολιορκίᾳ γινόμενα· γυναῖκα λήψῃ,
45 καὶ ἀνὴρ ἕτερος ἕξει αὐτήν· οἰκίαν οἰκοδομήσεις καὶ οὐκ
ἐνοικήσεις ἐν αὐτῇ· ἀμπελῶνα φυτεύσεις καὶ οὐ τρυγήσεις
αὐτόν· ὁ μόσχος σου ἐσφαγμένος ἐναντίον σου, καὶ οὐ φάγῃ

---

e. Dt 27.15   f. Dt 27.16   g. Dt 27.18   h. Dt 27.15–26   i. Dt 28.1–8
j. Dt 28.9   k. Dt 28.13   l. Dt 28.15–29   m. Dt 28.23

He commanded that a curse be directed, first and foremost, at those who committed sacrilege against divinity by worshiping images made by human hands;[e] then at those who committed offenses against their parents,[f] for justice requires us to devote to them a care second only to that of religion, as we were brought into being through our parents; then at those who made mock of the blind and tried to misdirect them from the right way;[g] and, in short at all those who transgressed the aforementioned commandments. He commanded that, as the priests pronounced the curses, the people reply, "So be it,"[h] this response being like a signature to a contract.

(2) On the other hand, he bestowed all sorts of blessings on those who observed the divine commandments: on the residents of both cities and villages a sound and numerous progeny, abundant increase of flocks and herds, fertility of the soil, a peaceful life, victory in war, and the like.[i] To these corporal blessings he added as well a spiritual: "May the Lord raise you up as a people holy to himself, as he swore to your fathers." But he added this condition: "provided you hearken to the voice of the Lord your God and walk in his ways,[j] for those who see or hear of this will fear you, when they consider how you enjoy God's care." The phrase "to become the head, not the tail" means that they would rule rather than serve. As he went on to say, "At that time you will be on the top, not at the bottom."[k]

Next, he spoke the curses, which contained the opposite of the aforementioned blessings: sterility, misfortune, indigence, disease, hardship, starvation, pestilence, war, defeat, and drought, and infertility of the earth,[l] for that is the meaning of "the earth of iron" and "the sky of bronze."[m] Then the sufferings of a siege: "You will marry a woman, but another will possess her; you will build a house but not live in it; you will plant a vineyard but not harvest it; your calf

ἐξ αὐτοῦ.[n] καὶ τὰ ἑξῆς τὴν αὐτὴν τούτοις ἔχει διάνοιαν.
προστίθησι δὲ καὶ ἑλκῶν ἀπειλάς, καὶ παθημάτων διαφοράς,
50 καὶ ἀνδραποδισμούς,[o] καὶ τὸ πάντων χαλεπώτατον· ὁ
προσήλυτος, φησίν, ὅστις ἔστι ... σοι, ἀναβήσεται ἐπὶ σὲ ἄνω
..., σὺ δὲ καταβήσῃ κάτω.[p] αἰνίττεται δὲ διὰ τούτων τῶν
ἐθνῶν τὴν εὐσέβειαν καὶ τὴν αὐτῶν ἀπιστίαν. προεῖπεν αὐτοῖς
καὶ τὴν ὑπ' ἀσσυρίων, καὶ βαβυλωνίων, καὶ μακεδόνων, καὶ τὸ
55 τελευταῖον τὴν ὑπὸ ῥωμαίων γεγενημένην πολιορκίαν, καὶ τῆς
πολιορκίας τὰς συμφοράς· φάγῃ, γὰρ ἔφη, τὰ ἔγγονα τῆς
κοιλίας σου, κρέα υἱῶν σου καὶ θυγατέρων σου, ὅσα ἔδωκέ σοι
Κύριος ὁ Θεός σου, ἐν τῇ στενοχωρίᾳ σου καὶ ἐν τῇ θλίψει
σου, ᾗ θλίψει σε ὁ ἐχθρός σου.[q] καὶ τὰ ἄλλα ὅσα μετὰ τὴν
60 πεῖραν ὁ προφήτης Ἱερεμίας ἔφη, τοὺς θρήνους συγγράφων.
ἠπείλησε δέ, οὐ μόνον ταύτας, ἀλλὰ καὶ ἑτέρας πολλαπλασίας
ἐποίσειν αὐτοῖς τιμωρίας τὰς θείας παραβαίνουσιν ἐντολάς.
ἠπείλησεν αὐτοῖς καὶ τὴν αἰγυπτίων δουλείαν, ἧς πεῖραν
λαβόντες, ἔναυλον εἶχον τὴν μνήμην· οἱ γὰρ
65 ἐξανδραποδίζοντές σε, φησίν, ἐκεῖνοί σε ἀποδώσονται.[r]

XXXV

Ταύτας τὰς ἀρὰς καὶ τὰς εὐλογίας τοῖς τούτων οὐκ
ἐδεδώκει πατράσιν. ἔχει τοίνυν ἡ βίβλος αὕτη καινήν τινα
παρὰ τὰς ἄλλας διδασκαλίαν.

Ἐπεσημήνατο τοῦτο καὶ ὁ προφήτης. πεπληρωκὼς γὰρ τὸν
5 περὶ τῶν ἀρῶν καὶ τῶν εὐλογιῶν λόγον, ἐπήγαγεν, οὗτοι οἱ
λόγοι τῆς διαθήκης, ὅσα ἐνετείλατο Κύριος τῷ Μωϋσῇ στῆσαι
τοῖς υἱοῖς Ἰσραὴλ ἐν γῇ Μωάβ, πλὴν τῆς διαθήκης ἧς διέθετο
αὐτοῖς ἐν Χωρήβ.[a] ἐπειδὴ γὰρ ἔμελλεν αὐτοὺς εἰσάξειν εἰς ἣν

---

n. Dt 28.30f.   o. Dt 28.35f.   p. Dt 28.43   q. Dt 28.53 (LXX var.)
r. Dt 28.68

---

xxxv A *[32]*, B, C⁻¹, *4 7 9 10 31* 35 37* = 20 mss.
a. Dt 29.1

will be butchered before your eyes, but you will not eat any of it,"[n] and the rest with the same purport. He added threats of ulcers, various ailments, enslavement,[o] and, worst of all, "The alien in your midst will rise above you, and you will fall down low."[p] Now, in this he hinted at the belief of the nations and foretold their own unbelief as well as the sieges they were to endure at the hands of the Assyrians, Babylonians, Macedonians, and finally the Romans. Then he enumerated the calamities of siege, saying, "In your affliction, in the distress that your foe will impose on you, you will eat the offspring of your belly, the flesh of your sons and your daughters, whom the Lord your God has given you"[q] and everything else that the prophet Jeremiah mentioned when he composed his Lamentations after these predictions came true. This was not the sum of his threats, for he threatened them with all sorts of other punishments if they broke the divine commandments. He even threatened them with slavery to the Egyptians, something they had already experienced and of which they still had vivid memories. As he said, "Those who enslave you will put you up for sale."[r]

XXXV

He had not bestowed these curses and blessings on their ancestors, so this book contains some new teaching not in the others.

The prophet also noted this. After completing the list of curses and blessings, he went on, "These are the words of the covenant that the Lord commanded Moses to make with the children of Israel in the land of Moab besides the covenant he had made with them at Horeb."[1a] Since he was about to lead them into the promised land,

---

1. Theodoret recognizes that Dt 29.1 (= 28.69 MT) does not conclude what precedes but introduces what follows: a covenant in the land of Moab, not mentioned elsewhere in the OT. He does not note the distinction between the names Sinai and Horeb; *cf.* note 1 to *Q.* 1.

ἐπηγγείλατο γῆν, ἀναγκαίως καὶ ταῖς τῶν ἀγαθῶν
10 ἐπαγγελίαις προτρέπει, καὶ ταῖς τῶν τιμωριῶν ἀπειλαῖς
καταπλήττει, καὶ πάντα κινεῖ πόρον εἰς τὴν τῶν ψυχῶν αὐτῶν
ἰατρείαν.

XXXVI

Τί δή ποτε πλείους τῶν εὐλογιῶν[a] αἱ ἀραί;[b]
Τοὺς πονηροὺς οἰκέτας οὐ τοσοῦτον ὠφελοῦσιν αἱ τῆς
ἐλευθερίας ἐπαγγελίαι, ὅσον τῶν μαστίγων αἱ ἀπειλαί.

XXXVII

Πῶς νοητέον τὸ *οὐκ ἔδωκε Κύριος ὁ Θεὸς ὑμῖν καρδίαν
εἰδέναι, καὶ ὀφθαλμοὺς βλέπειν, καὶ ὦτα ἀκούειν ἕως τῆς
ἡμέρας ταύτης;*[a]
(1) Ὡς τὸ *παρέδωκεν αὐτοὺς εἰς ἀδόκιμον νοῦν*·[b] καί,
5 *παρέδωκεν αὐτοὺς . . . εἰς πάθη ἀτιμίας*·[c] καί,
ἐσκλήρυνε . . . Κύριος τὴν καρδίαν Φαραώ·[d] ἀγαθῶν γὰρ αἴτιος
ὁ Θεός, κακῶν δὲ ἀναίτιος. ἐπιδείκνυσι γὰρ τὸ πρακτέον,
ἀποτρέπει δὲ τῶν ἐναντίων· οὐ βιάζεται δὲ τῶν ἀνθρώπων τὴν
γνώμην ἀλλὰ τῷ αὐτεξουσίῳ παραχωρεῖ. ἐπειδὴ δὲ συγχωρεῖ
10 γενέσθαι τἀναντία, κωλῦσαι δυνάμενος, οὐκ ἀνέχεται δὲ
κωλύειν ἵνα μὴ βίᾳ καὶ ἀνάγκῃ γένηται τὸ πραττόμενον· τὸ
γὰρ ἐθελούσιον τῆς ἀρετῆς ἀξιέπαινον· τὴν συγχώρησιν
αἰτίαν ἐκάλεσε. τούτῳ ἔοικε τὸ ἐν τοῖς θείοις εἰρημένον

---

xxxvi A *[32]*, B, C⁻¹, 4 7 9 10 35 37 = 19 mss.

a. Dt 28.1–14   b. Dt 28.15–68

---

xxxvii A *[32]*, B, C⁻¹, 4 7 9 10 31* 35 37 = 20 mss.

a. Dt 29.4   b. Rom 1.28   c. Rom 1.26   d. Ex 9.12; 10.20, 27; 14.8

he, of course, encouraged them with promises of rewards, frightened them with threats of punishments, and tried every means of healing their souls.

XXXVI

Why were there more curses[b] than blessings?[a]

For wicked servants promises of freedom are not so beneficial as threats of punishment.[1]

XXXVII

How are we to understand the verse "To this day the Lord God has not given you a heart to understand, eyes to see, or ears to hear"?[a]

(1) In the same way as we interpret "He gave them up to a reprobate mentality";[b] "He gave them up to shameful passions";[c] and "The Lord hardened Pharaoh's heart."[1d] God is responsible for good, not for evil. He indicates what we should do, turns us away from sin, does not force our choices but yields to our free will. Since God permits sin and, though he might, refuses to prevent it to avoid compelling any act by overwhelming force (for it is the voluntary aspect of virtuous action that is praiseworthy), Moses spoke of God's permission as responsibility. Similar to this passage of

1. Theodoret here hits upon a difficulty that has long concerned commentators. Von Rad explains (p. 173 and on 28.1–46) that an original, more symmetrical, enumeration of blessings and curses has been disrupted by the interpolation of additional curses; these additions reflect the experience of the capture of Jerusalem in 587 and the subsequent exile. Theodoret, of course, regards the exile as an event long subsequent to the composition of this text; *cf. Q.* 34.2.

1. These verses all challenge Antiochene morality, which placed primary emphasis on human responsibility; Theodoret, however, did not raise the issue of di-

εὐαγγελίοις· τετύφλωκεν αὐτῶν τοὺς ὀφθαλμοὺς καὶ
15 πεπώρωκεν αὐτῶν τὴν καρδίαν.ᵉ καὶ μὴν πάντα πόρον
κεκίνηκεν ὥστε αὐτοὺς ἀπολαῦσαι τῆς σωτηρίας·
θαυματουργῶν, τὰ πεπηρωμένα μέλη θεραπεύων,ᶠ ἐν ἐρήμῳ
τρέφων,ᵍ τοῖς στοιχείοις κελεύων.ʰ οὐ τοίνυν αὐτὸς τῆς
ἐκείνων αἴτιος ἀπιστίας. τί δή ποτε τοίνυν ὁ εὐαγγελιστὴς
20 τὴν προφητικὴν τέθεικε μαρτυρίαν; ἵνα δείξῃ ὡς, οὐδὲν
τούτων ἠγνόησεν ὁ δεσπότης Θεός, ἀλλὰ πόρρωθεν αὐτὰ
προηγόρευσεν· ἀκοῇ, γάρ φησιν, ἀκούσετε καὶ οὐ μὴ συνῆτε
καὶ βλέποντες βλέψετε καὶ οὐ μὴ ἴδητε.ⁱ οὕτω νοητέον καὶ τὸ
ἐνταῦθα κείμενον· οὐκ ἔδωκε Κύριος ὑμῖν καρδίαν εἰδέναι, καὶ
25 ὀφθαλμοὺς βλέπειν, καὶ ὦτα ἀκούειν ἕως τῆς ἡμέρας ταύτης.ʲ

(2) Εἰ δὲ αὐτὸς οὐκ ἔδωκε τὸ βλέπειν, καὶ τὸ ἀκούειν, καὶ
τὸ λογίζεσθαι, τί δή ποτε καὶ ἐπαρᾶται καὶ τιμωρεῖται τοὺς
οὐχ ἑκόντας παρανομήσαντας; ἀλλὰ περιττὸν οἶμαι περὶ
τούτου μηκύνειν· δῆλον γὰρ καὶ τοῖς ἄγαν ἀνοήτοις ὡς ὁ
30 τοσαύτην διδασκαλίαν προσενεγκών, οὐκ ἀφαιρεῖται τὸ
βλέπειν, ἀλλὰ ποδηγεῖ, καὶ φωτίζει, καὶ τὴν εὐθεῖαν ὁδὸν
ἐπιδείκνυσι. διδάσκει δὲ τοῦτο καὶ τὰ ἑξῆς· οὐχ ὑμῖν, γάρ
φησιν, μόνοις ἐγὼ διατίθεμαι τὴν διαθήκην ταύτην καὶ τὴν
ἀρὰν ταύτην ἀλλὰ καὶ τοῖς ὁδεύουσι μεθ' ὑμῶν σήμερον ἔναντι
35 Κυρίου τοῦ Θεοῦ ὑμῶν καὶ τοῖς μὴ οὖσιν μεθ' ὑμῶν ὧδε
σήμερον.ᵏ ὁ δὲ καὶ τῶν μελλόντων ἔσεσθαι προμηθούμενος πῶς
ἂν τῶν παρόντων καὶ δεχομένων τὸν νόμον ἠμέλησε; τί δή
ποτε δὲ καὶ ἐνομοθέτει τοῖς συνιέναι μὴ δυναμένοις;

Ἰστέον δὲ καὶ τοῦτο· ὡς καὶ τοῖς ἀνθρωπίνοις πολλάκις οἱ
40 προφῆται κέχρηνται λόγοις, ὡς μᾶλλον γνωριμωτέροις.
εἰώθασι δέ τινες, καὶ οἰκέταις ἐγκαλοῦντες καὶ μαθηταῖς,
λέγειν, ἐτύφλωσεν ὁ Θεὸς τὴν καρδίαν σου, ἐκώφωσεν τὰ ὦτά

---

e. Jn 12.40   f. *V., e.g.,* Mt 12.9–14.   g. *V., e.g.,* Mt 14.13–21.   h. Mt 8.26f.
i. Mt 13.14; Is 6.9   j. Dt 29.4   k. Dt 29.14f.

Deuteronomy is that of the holy Gospels: "He has blinded their eyes and hardened their heart."ᵉ He actually did everything possible so that they would take advantage of salvation: working wonders, curing maimed limbs,ᶠ feeding them in the wilderness,ᵍ subjecting the elements to his command.ʰ So it was not he who was responsible for their unbelief. Why, then, did the evangelist cite the verse of the prophet? To show that the Lord God was not ignorant of this but had foretold it far in advance: "You will hear and hear but not understand, you will look and look but not see."ⁱ This is how we are to interpret the verse under consideration: "To this day the Lord has not given you a heart to understand, eyes to see, or ears to hear."ʲ

(2) Now, if he did not endow them with the capacity to see, hear, and think, why did he curse and punish people who transgressed involuntarily? I think it unnecessary to go into this at length. After all, even a great fool can see that, as he went to such effort to educate them, he hardly blinded them, but guided and enlightened them, and showed them the straight path. The following passage teaches the same thing: "I set this covenant and this curse not before you alone, but also before those who travel with you today in the presence of the Lord your God and before those who are not here with you today."²ᵏ Now, if he took care even for those yet unborn, how could God have neglected those who were present to receive the Law? Furthermore, why did he legislate also for those still incapable of understanding?

Now, you should also realize that the prophets often make use of human expressions in order to render their meaning more accessible. People often upbraid their servants and pupils with remarks like "God has blinded your heart" or "God has deafened your ears."

---

vine intervention versus human independence in either his commentary on Romans 1.26, 28 or his discussion of the plagues in the *Quaest. in Ex.* Chrysostom deals with this theme in his homilies on Is 45.7: *Ego dominus deus feci lumen* (= *CPG* #4418) and Jer 10.23: *Domine, non est in homine* (= *CPG* #4419).

2. In Dt. 29.15 Theodoret's version of the Septuagint reads τοῖς ὁδεύουσι (those who travel) in place of the more widely attested τοῖς ὧδε οὖσιν (those

σου. τοιοῦτόν τι καὶ ἐνταῦθα ὁ προφήτης πεποίηκε καὶ διὰ
τῶν συνήθων λόγων τῆς ἀνοίας αὐτῶν κατηγόρησε.

XXXVIII

Πῶς νοητέον ἐάν τις ἀκούσῃ τὰ ῥήματα τῆς ἀρᾶς ταύτης
καὶ ἐπιφημίσηται ἐν τῇ καρδίᾳ αὐτοῦ, λέγων, ὅσιά μοι
γένοιτο, ὅτι ἐν τῇ ἀποπλανήσει τῆς καρδίας μου πορεύσομαι;[a]

(1) Τὸν κατὰ τῶν θείων θρασυνόμενον ἐντολῶν ὁ λόγος
5 διέγραψε. πολλοὶ μὲν γὰρ διὰ ῥαθυμίαν τὸν θεῖον
παραβαίνουσι νόμον, πολλοὶ δὲ δι' αὐθάδειαν καὶ τῦφον
καταφρονοῦσι τῶν ἐντολῶν. τοῦτον ἐνταῦθα δεδήλωκεν, ὡς τὴν
ἐναντίαν ὁδὸν προαιρούμενον καὶ τὴν πλανῶσαν τῆς εὐθείας
προκρίνοντα. τούτῳ τὸν ἔσχατον ἠπείλησεν ὄλεθρον ὥστε καὶ
10 τοῖς ὁρῶσι καὶ τοῖς ἀκούουσιν εὐσεβείας γενέσθαι
παράδειγμα.[b] διδάσκων δὲ αὐτοὺς ὡς οὐδὲν ἀγνοεῖ τῶν λάθρα
γινομένων, ἐπήγαγε, τὰ κρυπτὰ Κυρίῳ τῷ Θεῷ ὑμῶν, τὰ δὲ
φανερὰ ὑμῖν καὶ τοῖς τέκνοις ὑμῶν.[c] ὥσπερ ὑμεῖς, φησί,
γιγνώσκετε τὰ προφανῶς γινόμενα, οὕτως ἐμοὶ δῆλα καὶ αὐτὰ
15 τῶν λογισμῶν τὰ κινήματα.

Εἰσάγει δὲ καὶ τὸν περὶ μετανοίας λόγον. ἐάν, γάρ φησι,
τὰς θείας παραβεβηκὼς ἐντολάς, ταῖς ἀραῖς περιπέσῃς, καί,
δορυάλωτος γενόμενος, τὸν τῆς δουλείας δέξῃ ζυγόν, εἶτα,
σώφρονι χρησάμενος λογισμῷ, τὰς τῆς δουλείας αἰτίας
20 ἐπιζητήσῃς, καὶ ἐξιλεώσῃ τὸν νομοθέτην, οἴκτῳ χρώμενος,
ἐπανάξει σε καὶ τὴν πατρῴαν ἀποδώσει σοι γῆν.[d] καὶ τοῦτο
πολλάκις γεγένηται καὶ διδάσκει σαφῶς καὶ τῶν Κριτῶν ἡ
βίβλος καὶ τῶν Βασιλειῶν καὶ τῶν Παραλειπομένων αἱ
ἱστορίαι. ὕστερον μέντοι, κατὰ τοῦ σωτῆρος λυττήσαντες, εἰς

---

xxxviii A [32], B, C⁻¹, 4 7 9 10 31* 35 37 = 20 mss.

a. Dt 29.19 b. Dt 29.20–28 c. Dt 29.29 d. Dt 30.1–5

That is just what the prophet did here: he censured their folly in everyday language.

XXXVIII

How are we to understand, "If anyone hear the words of this oath and promise himself in his heart, 'I shall walk wherever my heart lead me, and may I receive holy blessings'"?[a]

(1) This verse describes the person who adopts an attitude of insolence toward God's commandments. Many transgress the Law of God through indifference; many others, in their obstinate pride, contemptuously reject the commandments. This is the kind of person he pointed to here, the sort who deliberately chooses the way of evil and prefers the path of wrong to the straight and narrow. This is the man God threatened with such complete ruin that he would become an admonition to religious behavior for all who should see and hear of him.[b] To teach them that nothing done in secret escapes his knowledge, he added, "Secrets belong to the Lord your God, the manifest to you and your children."[c] This is tantamount to saying, "As you know whatever takes place in broad daylight, so I see clearly the very movements of thought."

He also introduced a word regarding repentance: "Should you break God's commandments and become subject to the curses, should you go into captivity and take on the yoke of slavery but then come to your senses and seek out the reasons for your slavery and appease the Lawgiver, he will show compassion, bring you back, and restore your ancestral land to you."[d] This happened many times, as we learn from the book of Judges and the narratives of Kings and Chronicles. Later, however, when they raged against the Savior, they

----
who are here); *v.* J.W. Wevers, *ad loc.* The commentator, now arguing on the basis of probability, is still struggling with the same moral conundrum. At the end of the question he will finally appeal to the freedom of everyday usage.

25 ἅπασαν μὲν γῆν καὶ θάλατταν διεσπάρησαν· τετρακοσίων δὲ
διεληλυθότων ἐτῶν, οὐκ ἔτυχον ἀνακλήσεως.

(2) Ἐπέδειξε δὲ καὶ τῆς τῶν νόμων φυλακῆς τὴν εὐκολίαν·
*ἡ ἐντολή, γάρ φησιν, αὕτη, ἣν ἐγὼ ἐντέλλομαί σοι σήμερον,
οὐχ ὑπέρογκος . . . οὐδὲ μακράν ἐστιν ἀπὸ σοῦ· οὐκ ἐν τῷ*
30 *οὐρανῷ ἐστι, λέγων, τίς ἀναβήσεται . . . εἰς τὸν οὐρανὸν καὶ
λήψεται ἡμῖν αὐτὴν καί, ἀκούσαντες αὐτήν, ποιήσομεν· οὐδὲ
πέραν τῆς θαλάσσης . . ., λέγων, τίς διαπεράσει . . . εἰς τὸ
πέραν τῆς θαλάσσης, καὶ λήψεται ἡμῖν αὐτήν, καὶ ἀκουστὴν
ἡμῖν ποιήσει αὐτήν, καὶ ποιήσομεν; οὔτε πτερῶν σοι, φησί,*
35 *χρεία εἰς πτῆσιν οὔτε πλοίων εἰς ἀποδημίαν ἵνα διδαχθῇς τὸ
πρακτέον, ἀλλ᾽ ἐγγύς σου . . . τὸ ῥῆμα σφόδρα ἐν τῷ στόματί
σου, καὶ ἐν τῇ καρδίᾳ σου, καὶ ἐν ταῖς χερσί σου, ποιεῖν
αὐτό.*[e] δηλοῖ δὲ διὰ μὲν τοῦ *στόματος* τὴν τῶν θείων λογίων
μελέτην, διὰ δὲ τῆς *καρδίας* τὴν τῆς ψυχῆς προθυμίαν, διὰ δὲ
40 τῶν *χειρῶν* τὴν πρᾶξιν τῶν ἐντολῶν. ταύτῃ τῇ μαρτυρίᾳ καὶ ὁ
θεῖος ἐχρήσατο Παῦλος· *ἐάν, γάρ φησιν, ὁμολογήσῃς ἐν τῷ
στόματί σου Κύριον Ἰησοῦν καὶ πιστεύσῃς ἐν τῇ καρδίᾳ σου
ὅτι ὁ Θεὸς αὐτὸν ἤγειρεν ἐκ νεκρῶν, σωθήσῃ· καρδίᾳ γὰρ
πιστεύεται εἰς δικαιοσύνην, στόματι δὲ ὁμολογεῖται εἰς*
45 *σωτηρίαν.*[f] τέθεικε δὲ καὶ τῆς τῶν *νόμων* φυλακῆς καὶ τῆς
παραβάσεως τὰ ἆθλα· *τὴν ζωὴν καὶ τὸν θάνατον.*[g]

XXXIX

Τί δή ποτε μετὰ ἑπτὰ ἔτη προσέταξεν ὁ νομοθέτης ταύτην
αὐτοῖς ἀναγνωσθῆναι τὴν βίβλον;[a]

Οὐκ ἦγον σχολήν, πολεμοῦντες, καὶ τὰς πόλεις
πολιορκοῦντες, καὶ μέντοι καὶ μετὰ τὴν νίκην κατὰ φυλὰς τὴν

---

e. Dt 30.11–14   f. Rom 10.9f.   g. Dt 30.15–18

xxxix A [32], B, C⁻¹, 4 7 9 10 31 35 37 = 20 mss.
a. Dt 31.10–13

were scattered across every land and sea, and, despite the passage of four hundred years, they have not been granted restoration.

(2) He also indicated how easy it was to observe the laws: "The commandment I command you today is neither burdensome nor far away. It is not in heaven that you should say, 'Who will go up to heaven and get it for us so that we may hear and perform it?' Nor is it beyond the sea that you should say, 'Who will travel across the sea and get it for us and bring it to our hearing so that we may perform it?'" He says, in effect, "You have no need of wings to fly, nor of ships to sail abroad to learn what you are to do. Rather, as Scripture says, "the word is very near you: in your mouth, and in your heart, and in your hands for you to do it."[e] By "mouth" he signifies attention to the divine oracles, by "heart" an eager spirit, and by "hands" the practice of the commandments. St. Paul also referred to this kind of witness when he said, "If you confess with your mouth that Jesus is Lord and believe in your heart that God raised him from the dead, you will be saved; for by the belief of the heart we are justified, and by the confession of the mouth we are saved."[f] He also set before them the rewards for observing and transgressing the laws: life and death.[1g]

XXXIX

Why did the lawgiver order that this book be read out to them seven years later?[a]

They were constantly busy fighting, besieging cities, and, after the conquest, dividing the land among the tribes, towns, families,

---

1. Theodoret hastily passes over the two ways leading to life and death (Dt 30.15–20), a form of words probably traditional in the making or renewing of covenants; v. von Rad, *ad loc.*

5 γῆν μεριζόμενοι, καὶ κατὰ δήμους, καὶ κατὰ πατριάς, καὶ καθ'
ἕνα, εἶτα οἰκοδομοῦντες, καὶ γεωργοῦντες, καὶ τἆλλα
ποιοῦντες, ὅσα πράττειν ἀνάγκη τοὺς ξένης γῆς τὴν
δεσποτείαν παρειληφότας. τούτου χάριν τῷ ἑβδόμῳ ἔτει μετὰ
τὴν τούτων ἀπαλλαγήν, γενέσθαι προσέταξε τὴν ἀνάγνωσιν.

XL

Διὰ τί τὸν οὐρανὸν καὶ τὴν γῆν διαμαρτύρασθαι
προσέταξεν;[a]

Οὐκ ἐπειδὴ ἔμψυχα ταῦτα καὶ λογικά, ἀλλ' ὅτι πάντων
ἐστὶ τῶν κτισμάτων περιεκτικά. τοῦτο καὶ Ἡσαΐας ὁ
5 προφήτης πεποίηκεν· *ἄκουε, γάρ φησιν, οὐρανέ, καὶ ἐνωτίζου,
γῆ, ὅτι Κύριος ἐλάλησε·*[b] τοῦτο καὶ ὁ θεῖος Ἱερεμίας· *ἐξέστη,
γάρ φησιν, ὁ οὐρανὸς ἐπὶ τούτῳ, καὶ ἔφριξεν ἐπιπλεῖον ἡ γῆ,
λέγει Κύριος.*[c] ἐπειδὴ γὰρ εἰς μαρτυρίαν αὐτὰ τῆς ἀπειλῆς ὁ
νομοθέτης ἐκάλεσεν, εἰκότως μετὰ τὴν τῶν νόμων παράβασιν
10 καὶ φρίξαι λέγεται καὶ ἐκστῆναι. οὕτω καὶ ὁ Ἰακὼβ καὶ ὁ
Λάβαν τὸν βουνὸν ὠνόμασαν *βουνὸν τῆς μαρτυρίας,*[d] καὶ
Ἀβραὰμ ὁ πατριάρχης καὶ Ἀβιμέλεχ τῶν γεράρων ὁ βασιλεὺς
φρέαρ τοῦ ὅρκου,[e] ὡς ἐκεῖ μεθ' ὅρκου ποιησάμενοι τὰς
συνθήκας.

---

xl A *[32]*, B, c⁻¹, 52, 4 7 9 10 35 37 = 18 mss.

a. Dt 31.28   b. Is 1.2   c. Jer 2.12 (LXX var.)   d. Gn 31.47   e. Gn 21.31

and individuals. Then, they were building, farming, and accomplishing all the other tasks that had to be done on taking possession of the foreign land. Therefore, he ordered this book to be read seven years later when they had gotten through all this.

XL

Why did Moses order heaven and earth to bear witness?[a]

Not that they have life and reason, but because they sum up all created things. The prophet Isaiah did the same thing: "Listen, heaven, and give ear, earth, because the Lord has spoken."[b] Likewise, the holy Jeremiah: "At this heaven was astonished, and earth shuddered deeply, says the Lord."[1c] As the lawgiver called them to witness the threat, it is appropriate that they should be said to shudder and be astonished at the transgression of the laws. Similarly, Jacob and Laban called a hill "the hill of witness,"[d] and the patriarch Abraham and Abimelech king of Gerar called a well "the well of the oath,"[e] since on that spot that they concluded their treaty with an oath.

1. Theodoret quotes Jer 2.12 in an Antiochene form of the LXX, which opposes heaven and earth; cf. also the paraphrase of this verse in the commentary on Jeremiah attributed to Theodoret. In the more widely attested text, "heaven" is the subject of ἔφριξεν = "shuddered" as well as ἐξέστη = "was astonished." Theodoret's answer to this question, though plausible, is contradicted by Blenkinsopp, who thinks rather that the appeal to heaven and earth is a faint reminiscence of the ancient practice of calling deities to witness treaty making; v. on 4.25–31; 30.19; and 32.1.

XLI

Πῶς νοητέον τὸ ἐγὼ παραζηλώσω ὑμᾶς ἐπ' οὐκ ἔθνει, ἐπ' ἔθνει ἀσυνέτῳ παροργιῶ ὑμᾶς;[a]

Οὐκ ἔθνος ἓν οἱ τῷ σωτῆρι Χριστῷ πεπιστευκότες, ἀλλὰ μυρία. καὶ ταῦτα δέ ποτε ἀσύνετα ἦν καὶ ἀνόητα, ᾗ φησιν ὁ
5 μακάριος Παῦλος· ἦμεν γάρ ποτε καὶ ἡμεῖς ἀνόητοι, ἀπειθεῖς, πλανώμενοι, δουλεύοντες ἐπιθυμίαις καὶ ἡδοναῖς ποικίλαις, καὶ τὰ ἑξῆς.[b] ὥσπερ τοίνυν, φησίν, ὑμεῖς, τὸν ἕνα καταλιπόντες Θεόν, πολλοὺς ψευδωνύμους προτετιμήκατε, οὕτως ἐγώ, τὸν ἕνα λαὸν ἀπορρίψας, πᾶσι τοῖς ἔθνεσι παρέξω τὴν σωτηρίαν.
10 ἀλλ' οἱ μὲν τοὺς οὐκ ὄντας τετιμηκότες θεοὺς οὐκ ἀπεφήνατε θεούς· ἐγὼ δὲ τὰ ἀσύνετα ἔθνη θείας ἐμπλήσω σοφίας· ὑμεῖς δὲ ὁρῶντες τῷ φθόνῳ τακήσεσθε.

XLII

Πῶς νοητέον τὸ εὐφράνθητε, ἔθνη, μετὰ τοῦ λαοῦ αὐτοῦ, καὶ ἐνισχυσάτωσαν αὐτοὺς πάντες ἄγγελοι Θεοῦ;[a]

(1) Καὶ ἐξ ἰουδαίων πολλαὶ μυριάδες ἐπίστευσαν τῷ δεσπότῃ Χριστῷ, καὶ τὸ πλεῖστον τῶν κατὰ τὴν οἰκουμένην ἐθνῶν, ἀλλὰ
5 τοῖς ἔθνεσι τὴν διδασκαλίαν οἱ ἐξ ἰουδαίων πεπιστευκότες προσήνεγκαν· ἐξ ἰουδαίων γὰρ οἱ θεῖοι ἀπόστολοι. ταῦτα τοίνυν προθεσπίζων, ὁ προφήτης ἔφη, εὐφράνθητε, ἔθνη, μετὰ

XLI A [32], B, C⁻¹, 4 7 9 10 31* 35 37 = 20 mss.

a. Dt 32.21   b. Ti 3.3

XLII A [32], B, C⁻¹, 4 7 9 10 31 35 37 = 20 mss.

l. 2 αὐτούς [32], 3, 7 37, Sir. Sch. : αὐτῷ F.M. = "'gain strength in him'" : αὐτόν 5, 15 = "'strengthen him'" : om. c_1

a. Dt 32.43 (LXX)

XLI

How are we to understand the verse "I shall make you jealous with a nation that is no nation, provoke you with a people that lacks understanding"?[a]

Those who believe in Christ the Savior are not one nation but countless nations. And these were once foolish and senseless, as St. Paul says, "We too were once foolish, unbelieving, straying, enslaved to all sorts of lusts and pleasures" and so on.[b] Thus his meaning is that "as you forsook the one God and preferred many false deities, so I shall cast off this one people and offer salvation to all the nations. You honored what were not real gods without making them into gods, but I shall fill the senseless nations with wisdom, and when you see this, you will melt with envy."[1]

XLII

How are we to understand the verse "Rejoice, nations, with his people, and let all God's angels strengthen them"?[1a]

(1) Most of the nations throughout the world and even countless Jews came to faith in Christ the Lord, but it was the Jewish believers who taught the gentiles. Indeed the holy apostles were Jews. Foretelling this, the prophet said, "Rejoice, nations, with his people"—that is, with those of the Jews who have believed—"and let all God's

---

1. Von Rad, who notes (on 32.19–25) that the nation mentioned in 32.21 is usually identified as the Babylonians, expresses reservations regarding the historical interpretations so far advanced by modern scholarship. Theodoret implicitly rejects a literal identification of this nation in order to interpret the reversal of Israel's election in an eschatological sense.

---

1. Theodoret cites the fourth member of Dt 32.43 in both the question and the subsequent response. Though Fernández Marcos and Sáenz-Badillos print

τοῦ λαοῦ αὐτοῦ· τουτέστι, τῶν ἐξ ἰουδαίων πεπιστευκότων· καὶ
ἐνισχυσάτωσαν αὐτοὺς πάντες ἄγγελοι Θεοῦ, τοὺς εἰς αὐτὸν
10 πεπιστευκότας. καὶ γὰρ τοῦ σωτῆρος ἡμῶν γεννηθέντος, χορὸς
ἀγγέλων ὑμνεῖ τὴν θείαν φιλανθρωπίαν, βοῶν, *δόξα ἐν ὑψίστοις*
Θεῷ, καὶ ἐπὶ γῆς εἰρήνη, ἐν ἀνθρώποις εὐδοκία.[b] καὶ τὰς
ἀσπάρτους δὲ καὶ ἀλοχεύτους ἐκείνας ὠδῖνας Γαβριὴλ
προείρηκεν ὁ ἀρχάγγελος·[c] κἂν τῷ πρὸς τὸν διάβολον ἀγῶνι
15 παρῆσαν τῶν ἀγγέλων οἱ δῆμοι· *προσελθόντες, γάρ φησιν,*
ἄγγελοι . . . διηκόνουν αὐτῷ·[d] καὶ τῷ πάθει παρῆσαν,[e] καὶ μετὰ
τὴν ἀνάστασιν τῷ τάφῳ προσήδρευον, καὶ ταῖς γυναιξὶν
ἔλεγον, *τί ζητεῖτε τὸν ζῶντα μετὰ τῶν νεκρῶν*;[f] καὶ μετὰ τὴν
εἰς οὐρανοὺς ἄνοδον τοῖς ἱεροῖς ἔφασαν ἀποστόλοις, *τί*
20 *ἐστήκατε ἐμβλέποντες εἰς τὸν οὐρανόν; οὗτος ὁ Ἰησοῦς, ὁ*
ἀναληφθεὶς ἀφ᾽ ὑμῶν εἰς τὸν οὐρανόν, οὕτως ἐλεύσεται ὃν
τρόπον ἐθεάσασθε αὐτὸν πορευόμενον εἰς τὸν οὐρανόν·[g] καὶ τῷ
Κορνηλίῳ ἄγγελος τὰ κατὰ τὸν μέγαν Πέτρον ἐμήνυσε·[h] καὶ ὁ
θεῖος ἀπόστολος ἐν τῷ πλοίῳ τοῖς συμπλέουσιν ἔφη, *ὤφθη μοι*
25 *ἄγγελος τοῦ Θεοῦ οὗ εἰμι*,[i] καὶ πολλὰ δὲ τοιαῦτα εὕροι τις ἂν
ἐθελήσας.

(2) Ταῦτα μέντοι περὶ τῶν πεπιστευκότων εἰπών, ὁ
προφήτης προλέγει καὶ τῶν ἀπίστων τὰς τιμωρίας καὶ δήλας
τούτων τὰς αἰτίας ποιεῖ· ἔφη γὰρ οὕτως· *ὅτι τὸ αἷμα τῶν*
30 *υἱῶν αὐτοῦ ἐκδικεῖται καὶ ἐκδικήσει, καὶ ἀνταποδώσει δίκην*
τοῖς ἐχθροῖς αὐτοῦ, καὶ τοῖς μισοῦσιν αὐτὸν ἀνταποδώσει, καὶ
ἐκκαθαριεῖ Κύριος τὴν γῆν τοῦ λαοῦ αὐτοῦ.[j] υἱοὺς δὲ τοῦ Θεοῦ
κέκληκε τοὺς ἁγίους, οὓς ἀνεῖλον οἱ μιαιφόνοι· ἵνα γὰρ τῶν
προφητῶν τὰς σφαγὰς καταλίπω[k] καὶ τοῦ δεσπότου τὸ
35 σωτήριον πάθος, τὸν μὲν καλλίνικον κατέλευσαν Στέφανον,[l]
ξύλῳ δὲ τὸν μέγαν ἀνεῖλον Ἰάκωβον,[m] εἰς θεραπείαν δὲ αὐτῶν

---

l. 9 αὐτούς Sir. Sch. F.M. : αὐτῷ a₂, B, 3, 9 31 35 : αὐτόν 8 15

b. Lk 2.14   c. Lk 1.26–38   d. Mt 4.11   e. Cf. Lk 22.43.   f. Lk 24.5
g. Acts 1.11   h. Acts 10.3–6   i. Acts 27.23   j. Dt 32.43
k. Cf. Mt 23.29–31; Acts 7.51f.; 1Thes 2.14f.   l. Acts 7.57–60
m. Cf. Eus. H.E. 2.23.3, 18; Jos. A.J. 20.200.

angels strengthen them"—those who have believed in him. Thus, for example, at the birth of our Savior, a choir of angels singing the praises of God's loving-kindness, cried out, "Glory to God in the highest, and peace on earth, God's good will among mankind."[b] Also, the archangel Gabriel foretold that birth, which happened without seed or normal delivery.[c] And in the contest with the devil, the choirs of angels stood by. As Scripture says, "Angels came forward and ministered to him."[d] They were also present at the passion[e] and, after the resurrection, they sat by the tomb and said to the women, "Why do you look among the dead for one who lives?"[f] And after the ascension into heaven, they said to the holy apostles, "Why do you stand looking up into heaven? This Jesus, who has been taken up from you into heaven, will come in the same way you have seen him going up to heaven."[g] An angel brought Cornelius the report regarding the mighty Peter.[h] And the holy apostle said to those who were sailing in the same ship with him, "An angel of the God to whom I belong has appeared to me."[i] Anyone who wishes could find many further examples.[2]

(2) After these words regarding the believers, the prophet also foretold the punishments of the unbelievers and explained the reasons for these. As he said, "He will exact vengeance for the blood of his children, he will avenge them, deliver retribution to his foes, and repay those who hate him, and the Lord will cleanse the land of his people."[j] Now, by "God's children" he refers to his holy ones, who were slain by murderers. Even if we pass over the killing of the prophets[k] and the saving passion of the Lord, the Jews stoned the victorious Stephen[l] and clubbed to death the mighty James.[m] To

---

ἐνισχυσάτωσαν αὐτῷ in the former and ἐνισχυσάτωσαν αὐτοὺς in the latter, it seems unlikely that Theodoret quoted the verse in one, and then went on to expound it in a significantly different, form. Given his argument that, throughout salvation history, the angels have helped humanity to perceive and respond to God's acts of grace, he must have read the accusative, αὐτοὺς ("strengthen them") rather than the more widely attested dative αὐτῷ ("gain strength in him"); v. the critical notes on these two places.

2. For Theodoret's interest in angels cf. Q. 41 on Nm and note 1.

καὶ τὸν ἕτερον Ἰάκωβον Ἡρώδης ἀπετυμπάνισε,[n] καὶ πολλὰς
δὲ ἄλλας μιαιφονίας ἐτόλμησαν. καὶ τῶν τῷ Κυρίῳ
πεπιστευκότων τὰς οἰκίας ἐξεπόρθησαν, καὶ τοῦτο δεδήλωκεν
40 ὁ θεῖος ἀπόστολος ἐν τῇ πρὸς Ἑβραίους ἐπιστολῇ· *καὶ τὴν*
ἁρπαγήν, φησίν, τῶν ὑπαρχόντων ὑμῶν μεθ' ἡδονῆς
προσεδέξασθε·[o] καὶ θεσσαλονικεῦσι δὲ ἐπιστέλλων, οὕτως
ἔφη· *μιμηταὶ γὰρ ἐγένεσθε . . . τῶν ἁγίων, τῶν . . . ἐν τῇ*
Ἰουδαίᾳ . . . · τὰ γὰρ αὐτὰ καὶ ὑμεῖς ἐπάθετε ὑπὸ τῶν ἰδίων
45 *συμφυλετῶν, καθάπερ ἐκεῖνοι ὑπὸ τῶν ἰουδαίων, τῶν καὶ τὸν*
Κύριον ἀποκτεινάντων Ἰησοῦν καὶ τοὺς ἰδίους προφήτας, καὶ
ἡμᾶς ἐκδιωξάντων, καὶ Θεῷ μὴ ἀρεσκόντων, καὶ πᾶσιν
ἀνθρώποις ἐναντίων.[p] ταῦτα καὶ ὁ Κύριος αὐτῶν κατηγόρησεν
ἐν τῇ τοῦ ἀμπελῶνος παραβολῇ· ὅτι τῶν δούλων ὃν μὲν
50 ἔδειραν, ὃν δὲ ἀπέκτειναν, ὃν δὲ ἐλιθοβόλησαν.[q] τούτου χάριν
αὐτοὺς εἰς πᾶσαν τὴν οἰκουμένην διέσπειρεν.

XLIII

Τί δή ποτε διὰ σμικρὰν πλημμέλειαν πόρρωθεν ἰδεῖν ὁ
Μωϋσῆς προσετάχθη τὴν γῆν, εἰσαγαγεῖν δὲ τὸν λαὸν
ἐκωλύθη;[a]

Διδάσκει διὰ τούτων ἡμᾶς ὁ δεσπότης ὡς τοὺς ἐν ἀρετῇ
5 τελείους τὴν ἄκραν ἀρετὴν ἀπαιτεῖ καί, τοῖς ἄλλοις ἀνθρώποις
μεγάλα παρανομοῦσι μακροθυμῶν, τοῖς ἁγίοις ταύτης οὐ
μεταδίδωσι τῆς συγγνώμης. τοῦτο καὶ σοφός τις ἔφη· *ὁ μὲν*
γὰρ ἐλάχιστος συγγνωστός ἐστιν ἐλέους, δυνατοὶ δὲ δυνατῶς
ἐτασθήσονται·[b] καὶ ὁ Κύριος ἐν τοῖς ἱεροῖς εὐαγγελίοις, ᾧ μὲν
10 γὰρ ὀλίγον δοθήσεται, ὀλίγον καὶ ἀπαιτήσουσι παρ' αὐτοῦ, ᾧ
δὲ πολὺ δοθήσεται, πολὺ ἀπαιτήσουσι παρ' αὐτοῦ.[c]

n. Acts 12.2   o. Heb 10.34   p. 1Thes 2.14f. (NT var.)   q. Mt 21.35

xliii A [32], B, C⁻¹, 4 7 9 10 31 35 37 = 20 mss.

a. Dt 32.48–52   b. Wis 6.6   c. Lk 12.48

gain their favor, Herod had the other James killed,[n] and they committed many other acts of murder. They also plundered the homes of those who had believed in the Lord as the holy apostle indicated in his Epistle to the Hebrews: "You cheerfully suffered the robbery of your possessions";[o] while in the letter to the Thessalonians he declared, "You became imitators of the saints in Judea, for you endured the same sufferings at the hands of your compatriots as they did from the Jews, who killed both the Lord Jesus and their own prophets and drove us out. Displeasing God, they oppose everyone."[p] The Lord laid the same charges against them in the parable of the vineyard: "Thrashing one of the servants, killing another, and stoning another."[q] This is why he scattered them all over the world.[3]

XLIII

Why was it that, for such a slight fault, Moses was commanded to view the land from afar and forbidden to lead in the people?[a]

In this the Lord teaches us that he requires the utmost virtue from those who are perfect; although showing long-suffering to others who are guilty of grave transgressions, he does not make any such allowance for the saints. A sage has also said as much: "While the weakest deserves pardon and mercy, the mighty will be mightily tested."[b] And the Lord declared in the holy Gospels: "Of him to whom little is given little will be required, but of him to whom much is given much will be required."[c]

---

3. Theodoret, like many of his contemporaries, believed that the Jews had brought upon themselves the destruction of the Temple and the subsequent diaspora. Here he cites several NT texts as evidence for the fulfilment of the threats of divine vengeance prophesied in Dt 32.43.

Ἰστέον μέντοι καὶ τοῦτο, ὡς ἕτερα δι' ἑτέρων ὁ δεσπότης
οἰκονομεῖ. ὥσπερ ἀμέλει καὶ τουτονὶ τὸν μέγαν προφήτην οὐκ
εἴασεν εἰς τὴν γῆν τῆς ἐπαγγελίας εἰσαγαγεῖν τὸν λαὸν ἵνα
15 μὴ ὡς Θεὸν αὐτὸν σεβασθῶσιν οἱ ἰσραηλῖται· οἱ γὰρ τὰ ἄψυχα
θεοποιήσαντες καὶ μόσχου εἰκόνα θεὸν ὀνομάσαντεςᵈ δῆλον
ὅτι πολλῷ μᾶλλον ὡς θεὸν ἂν ἐσεβάσθησαν τὸν τοσούτων
αὐτοῖς ἀγαθῶν γεγενημένον διάκονον· τούτου χάριν αὐτοῦ καὶ
τὸν τάφον ἄδηλον πεποίηκεν ὁ σοφῶς τὰ καθ' ἡμᾶς
20 πρυτανεύων Θεός.ᵉ

Εἰδέναι δὲ καὶ τοῦτο προσήκει, ὡς Μωϋσῆς τύπον ἐπέχει
τοῦ νόμου. διὸ καὶ *Μωϋσῆς* τὴν προσηγορίαν ὁ *νόμος ἔχει·*
ἔχουσι, γάρ φησι, *Μωϋσέα καὶ τοὺς προφήτας*ᶠ καί, *ἕως*
*σήμερον ἡνίκα ἀναγινώσκεται Μωϋσῆς*ᵍ καί, *ἐβασίλευσεν ὁ*
25 *θάνατος ἀπὸ Ἀδὰμ μέχρι Μωϋσέως.*ʰ ὥσπερ γὰρ Ἡσαΐαν
καλοῦμεν, οὐ τὸν προφήτην μόνον, ἀλλὰ καὶ τὸ ἐκείνου
βιβλίον, καὶ Ἰερεμίαν καὶ Ἰεζεκιήλ, οὐ τοὺς ἄνδρας μόνον,
ἀλλὰ καὶ τὰ ἐκείνων βιβλία, καὶ *τὸν ἀπόστολον,* οὐ μόνον
αὐτὸν τῆς ἀληθείας τὸν κήρυκα, ἀλλὰ καὶ τὸ ἐκείνου βιβλίον,
30 οὕτω καὶ *Μωϋσῆς* ὁ *νόμος* ὠνόμασται. Ἰησοῦς δὲ ὁ τοῦ Ναυῆ
τύπος τοῦ σωτῆρος τῆς οἰκουμένης. ὥσπερ τοίνυν Μωϋσῆς
μὲν ἐξήγαγε τὸν λαὸν ἐξ Αἰγύπτου, Ἰησοῦς δὲ αὐτὸν εἰς τὴν
ἐπηγγελμένην εἰσήγαγε γῆν, οὕτως ὁ νόμος μὲν τῆς ἀσεβείας
ἀπαλλάττει τοὺς πειθομένους, ἡ δὲ τῶν εὐαγγελίων χάρις εἰς
35 τὴν βασιλείαν εἰσάγει τῶν οὐρανῶν.

d. Ex 32.4   e. Dt 34.6   f. Lk 16.29   g. 2Cor 3.15   h. Rom 5.14

You should also realize that the Lord accomplishes one thing by means of another. As he forbade this mighty prophet to bring the people into the land of promise to prevent the Israelites from worshipping him as God—after all, those who had made a god of the inanimate and addressed the image of a calf as "God"[d] would have been much more likely to accord divinity to the man through whose agency they had received such wonderful blessings—so God, who makes wise provision in all things that concern us, hid even the place of his burial. [1e]

Now, you should also know that Moses was a type of the Law, and hence, the name "Moses" stands for the Law. As Scripture says, "They have Moses and the prophets";[f] and "To this day as Moses is read out";[g] and "Death exercised dominion from Adam to Moses."[h] Just as we use the name "Isaiah," not only for the prophet, but also for his book and "Jeremiah" and "Ezekiel" for both the men and their books, and "the apostle," not just for the herald of truth himself, but also for his book, so the Law is called "Moses," whereas Joshua son of Nun is a type of the Savior of the world. As Moses led the people out of Egypt, but Joshua led them into the promised land, so the Law frees its subjects from idolatry, whereas the grace of the Gospels leads to the Kingdom of Heaven.

1. For Theodoret's discussion of the "slight fault" which resulted in Moses' exclusion from the promised land *v.* Q. 37 on Nm 20 and note 1. Here he fulfils the promise he had made in that question to reveal a further divine purpose for the lawgiver's punishment: *viz.,* the danger of Moses' deification.

XLIV

Πῶς νοητέον τὰς τῶν φυλῶν εὐλογίας;[a]

(1) Πρῶτον ἀνέμνησεν ὁ προφήτης τῆς θείας ἐπιφανείας τῆς ἐν τῷ Σινᾷ ὄρει γεγενημένης· *Κύριος, γάρ φησιν, ἐκ Σινᾶ ἥξει, καὶ ἐπέφανεν ἡμῖν ἐκ Σιείρ, καὶ κατέπαυσεν ἐξ ὄρους*
5 *Φαρὰν σὺν μυριάσι Κάδης· ἐκ δεξιῶν αὐτοῦ ἄγγελοι μετ' αὐτοῦ.*[b] καὶ ἐν τῇ ἐρήμῳ τῇ Φαρὰν καὶ ἐν τῷ Σιεὶρ τῆς θείας κηδεμονίας ἀπήλαυσαν. Κάδης δὲ ἐνταῦθα, οὐ τὴν ἔρημον λέγει, ἀλλὰ τὴν τοῦ ὀνόματος ἑρμηνείαν· τὸ γὰρ *Κάδης* τῇ ἑβραίων φωνῇ *τὸν ἅγιον* δηλοῖ. ἔφη τοίνυν ὅτι πολλαὶ
10 μυριάδες ἁγίων ἀγγέλων τῷ δεσπότῃ συνῆσαν τῆς οἰκείας αὐτοὺς ἀξιοῦντι κηδεμονίας. ἀναγκαίως δὲ προστέθεικε, καὶ *πάντες... ἡγιασμένοι ὑπὸ τὰς χεῖρας αὐτοῦ, καὶ οὗτοι ὑπὸ σέ εἰσιν·*[c] εἰ γὰρ καὶ ἀόρατον ἔχουσι φύσιν, ἀλλ' ὑπὸ τὴν σὴν δεσποτείαν τελοῦσι· σὲ γὰρ ἔχουσι ποιητήν. προλέγει δὲ ὅτι
15 ὁ νῦν τὸν Ἰσραὴλ ἐκλεξάμενος μικρὸν ὕστερον καὶ πάντα καλέσει τὰ ἔθνη, καὶ τούτων κἀκείνων αὐτὸς ἔσται ἄρχων καὶ βασιλεύς· *ἔσται, γάρ φησιν, ἐν τῷ ἠγαπημένῳ ἄρχων, συναχθέντων... λαῶν ἅμα φυλαῖς Ἰσραήλ.*[d]

Ταῦτα εἰπών, πρῶτον εὐλογεῖ τὸν Ῥουβὴν καὶ λύει τὴν
20 πατρῴαν ἀράν,[e] ἀντιτάξας τὴν φιλαδελφίαν[f] τῇ περὶ τὸν πατέρα παρανομίᾳ·[g] ἐξῆν δὲ ὡς νομοθέτῃ εἰς εὐλογίαν τὴν ἀρὰν μεταθεῖναι· *ζήτω Ῥουβὴν καὶ μὴ ἀποθανέτω καὶ ἔσται πολὺς ἐν ἀριθμῷ.*[h] ἐπειδὴ γὰρ ὁ πατὴρ εἶπεν, *ὡς ὕδωρ μὴ ἐκζέσῃς,*[i] τουτέστι, μὴ θερμανθῇς εἰς πολυγονίαν, εἰκότως
25 αὐτῷ τῶν ἀπογόνων τὸ πλῆθος ἐπηύξατο.

xliv A [32], B, C⁻¹, 4 7 9 10 31 35 37 = 20 mss.

l. 4 κατέπαυσεν Sir. F.M.: κατέκαυσεν 6, 5, 11, B⁻¹⁴, 4 9 10 31 35, Sch. = "'consumed with fire.'" Cf. Wevers and Quast, Dt 33.2.

a. Dt 33.6–25   b. Dt 33.2   c. Dt 33.3   d. Dt 33.5   e. Gn 49.3f.
f. Gn 37.22   g. Gn 35.22   h. Dt 33.6   i. Gn 49.4

XLIV

How are we to understand the blessings of the tribes?[1a]

(1) The prophet first called to mind the appearance of God on Mount Sinai: "The Lord will come from Sinai and has appeared to us from Seir and has rested from Mount Paran[2] with countless numbers of Kadesh, his angels with him at his right hand."[b] They had enjoyed God's care in both the wilderness of Paran and in Seir. By "Kadesh" he here referred, not to the wilderness, but to the literal meaning of the word, which in Hebrew signifies "the holy one." So his meaning was that vast numbers of holy angels accompanied the Lord, who deemed Israel worthy of his personal attention. Then, he added the essential statement, "All those who have been sanctified are under his hands, and they are under you,"[c] which means, "Even if they possess an invisible nature, they serve under your lordship, for you are their Creator." He also foretold that he who had just chosen Israel would shortly afterwards call all nations and would be ruler and king of both the former and the latter: "He will be a ruler amongst the beloved when the peoples are gathered together with the tribes of Israel."[d]

After this, he conferred the first blessing on Reuben and, balancing the love he had shown to his brother[f] against the sin he had committed against his father,[g] canceled the ancestral curse,[e] for as lawgiver he was able to turn the curse into a blessing: "May Reuben live and not die; he will become many in number."[h] That is, while his father Jacob had said, "May you not bubble up like water,"[i] meaning "May you not grow warm to produce numerous children," Moses prayed that he would have an abundance of descendants.

---

1. The LXX version of the blessings of Moses (ch. 33) diverges at many points from the MT, which is itself often obscure. In choosing to comment on this difficult passage, Theodoret is influenced, at least in part, by the perceived eschatological significance of the tribal blessings. If we occasionally fault Theodoret's selection of material for commentary, it is not because he avoids the most challenging.

2. In Dt 33.2 Theodoret's LXX apparently read κατέπαυσεν = "he rested" (*cf.* the intransitive use of the same form in 33.12) or "he made an end of." This offers

The Questions on Deuteronomy

(2) Εἶτα τὴν τάξιν ὑπερβάς, τῷ Ἰούδᾳ τὴν εὐλογίαν προσφέρει διὰ τὸν ἐκεῖθεν κατὰ σάρκα βεβλαστηκότα δεσπότην· πρόδηλον, γάρ φησιν ὁ θεῖος ἀπόστολος, ὅτι ἐξ Ἰούδα ἀνατέταλκεν ὁ Κύριος ἡμῶν.[j] προλέγει δὲ καὶ τὴν
30 δαβιτικὴν βασιλείαν· εἰσάκουσον, γάρ φησι, Κύριε, φωνῆς Ἰούδα, καὶ εἰς τὸν λαὸν αὐτοῦ ἔλθοι. . . . αἱ χεῖρες αὐτοῦ διακρινοῦσιν αὐτῷ, καὶ βοηθὸς ἐκ τῶν ἐχθρῶν αὐτοῦ ἔσῃ.[k]

Οὕτω τὴν βασιλικὴν εὐλογήσας φυλήν, εἰς τὴν ἱερατικὴν μεταβαίνει· δότε Λευὶ δήλους αὐτῷ καὶ ἀλήθειαν αὐτοῦ τῷ
35 ἀνδρὶ τῷ ὁσίῳ.[l] τῷ στέρνῳ τοῦ ἱερέως τὸ λόγιον ἐπέκειτο, εἶχε δὲ τοῦτο τὴν δήλωσιν καὶ τὴν ἀλήθειαν·[m] πολλὰ γὰρ ἐκεῖθεν προεδηλοῦτο. συνῆπται δὲ τοῖς δήλοις ἡ ἀλήθεια διὰ τὸ ἀψευδὲς τῶν δηλουμένων. ὃν ἐπείρασαν αὐτὸν ἐν πείρᾳ ἐλοιδόρησαν αὐτὸν ἐφ' ὕδατος ἀντιλογίας[n] τῶν εἰς αὐτὸν καὶ
40 τὸν ἀδελφὸν γεγενημένων ἀνέμνησεν.[o] ὁ λέγων τῷ πατρὶ αὐτοῦ καὶ τῇ μητρὶ αὐτοῦ, οὐχ ἑώρακά σε, καὶ τοὺς ἀδελφοὺς αὐτοῦ οὐκ ἐπέγνω, καὶ τοὺς υἱοὺς αὐτοῦ ἀπέγνω· ἐφύλαξε τὰ λόγιά σου καὶ τὴν διαθήκην σου διετήρησεν[p] τὸ τέλειον τῶν ἱερέων ὁ λόγος διδάσκει· πάντων γὰρ τῶν κατὰ τὸν βίον
45 καταφρονεῖν προσήκει τὸν ἱερέα καὶ τῇ θείᾳ προσεδρεύειν ἱερουργίᾳ. τούτου χάριν, οὐδὲ κλῆρον αὐτοῖς ἀπένειμεν οὐδὲ κτῆσιν ἔχειν ἐνομοθέτησεν, ἀλλὰ τὰς ἀπαρχὰς καὶ τὰς δεκάτας παρὰ παντὸς κομίζεσθαι τοῦ λαοῦ ἵνα, τῶν βιωτικῶν ἀπηλλαγμένοι φροντίδων, ἁγίως τὴν ἐγκεχειρισμένην
50 ἁγιστείαν ἐπιτελῶσιν. αὐτίκα γοῦν Ἀαρὼν ὁ πρῶτος ἀρχιερεὺς οὔτε κηδεῦσαι τοὺς τεθνηκότας συνεχωρήθη παῖδας.[q] οὕτω δέ φησιν· ἑαυτοὺς τελειώσαντες, δηλώσουσι τὰ δικαιώματά σου τῷ Ἰακὼβ καὶ τὸν νόμον σου τῷ Ἰσραήλ· ἐπιθήσουσι θυμίαμα ἐν ὀργῇ σου διὰ παντὸς ἐπὶ τοῦ θυσιαστηρίου σου.[r] τοῦτο καὶ
55 τοῦ λαοῦ τιμωρουμένου γεγένηται· ὁ γὰρ Ἀαρών, προσενεγκὼν τὸ θυμίαμα, τὸν θεήλατον ἐκώλυσε θάνατον.[s] εἶτα τὴν θείαν

---

j. Heb 7.14   k. Dt 33.7   l. Dt 33.8   m. Ex 28.28–30   n. Dt 33.8
o. Nm 20.2f.   p. Dt 33.9   q. Lv 10.6   r. Dt 33.10   s. Nm 16.44–48

(2) Then, jumping ahead in the order, he offered the next blessing to Judah, since, the Lord drew his bodily descent from that tribe. Remember, as the holy apostle said, "Our Lord has arisen from Judah as foretold."[j] He also prophesied the Davidic kingdom: "Hearken, Lord, to the voice of Judah, and may he come to his people. His hands will decide in their favor, and you will be their ally against their foes."[k]

Having blessed the royal, he moved on to the priestly, tribe: "Give Levi his urim, and his thummim to the man who is holy."[l] The oracle on the priest's chest contained the urim and thummim,[m] by which future events were often foretold, and the thummim, or truth, was joined to the urim, or revelations, because the revelations were true.[3] The verse "He whom they tested at the testing, they reviled at the water of contradiction,"[n] recalled what happened to Moses and his brother.[o] The verse "He who said to father and mother, 'I do not recognize you,' who did not acknowledge his brothers, and rejected his sons kept your oracles and observed your covenant"[p] conveys the perfection of the priests, for the priest must scorn everything of this life to attend to the service of God. Thus, he assigned them no lot and provided them with no possession; instead, they were to receive the first-fruits and tithes from all the people so as to be free of earthly cares and discharge in holiness the holy task that had been committed to them. In fact, Aaron was the first high priest, and he was not even permitted to attend to his own dead sons.[q] As Moses said, "After perfecting themselves, they will reveal your ordinances to Jacob and your Law to Israel, and when you are angry, they will ever place incense on your altar."[r] This is just what happened when the people were being punished; by his offering of incense, Aaron stopped the deadly plague that had been sent from heaven.[s] Then

----

no really satisfying sense, for the intransitive use consorts ill with the following prepositional phrase, and the transitive requires a direct object that cannot be supplied from the context. Some manuscripts of the *Quaest. in oct.* present the variant, κατέκαυσεν = "he burned" or "consumed with fire," but this is also a transitive verb. In manuscripts of the LXX, the more widely attested reading is the obviously meaningful κατέσπευσεν = "he rushed." See the critical note.

3. *Cf.* Q. 60.5 on Ex (ch. 28) and notes 9f. for this terminology connected with

αὐτοῖς εὐλογίαν αἰτεῖ· εὐλόγησον, Κύριε, τὴν ἰσχὺν αὐτοῦ καὶ
τὰ ἔργα τῶν χειρῶν αὐτοῦ δέξαι· χρεία γὰρ καὶ σωματικῆς
δυνάμεως τοῖς λειτουργοῦσιν ἵνα μηδὲν ἐμποδὼν γένηται τῇ
60 προθυμίᾳ· κάταξον ὀσφῦν ἐπανεστηκότων ἐχθρῶν αὐτοῦ, καὶ οἱ
μισοῦντες αὐτὸν μὴ ἀναστήτωσαν.ᵗ διὰ δὲ τούτων χαλινοῖ τῶν
τυραννούντων τὸ θράσος· ἀναμιμνήσκει δὲ καὶ ὧν ἔπαθε Κορέ,
καὶ Δαθάν, καὶ Ἀβειρών, τὴν στάσιν κατὰ τῶν ἱερέων
κινήσαντες.ᵘ

XLV

Τίνος χάριν, ἔσχατον ὄντα,ᵃ τέταρτον ἔταξε τὸν Βενιαμίν;ᵇ

(1) Ταύτης ἦν τῆς φυλῆς ἡ μητρόπολις,ᶜ ἐν ἐκείνῃ δὲ ὁ
ναὸς ἐδομήθη.ᵈ τοιγάρτοι εἰκότως τῇ ἱερατικῇ φυλῇ τὸν ἱερὸν
συνέταξε τόπον. καὶ ἡ εὐλογία δὲ τοῦτο προαγορεύει·
5 ἠγαπημένος, γάρ φησιν, ὑπὸ Κυρίου κατασκηνώσει πεποιθώς.
ἔδειξε δὲ καὶ τὴν αἰτίαν τῆς πεποιθήσεως· καὶ ὁ Θεὸς
σκιάζει ἐπ' αὐτῷ πάσας τὰς ἡμέρας καὶ ἀνὰ μέσον τῶν ὤμων
αὐτοῦ κατέπαυσε.ᵉ πελάζων γὰρ τῷ θείῳ νεῷ, διηνεκῶς τῆς
θείας κηδεμονίας ἀπήλαυσε. τὸ δὲ ἐν μέσῳ τῶν ὤμων αὐτοῦ
10 κατέπαυσε περὶ τοῦ Θεοῦ ἔφη, ὅς, ἐν τῇ Ἰερουσαλὴμ τὸν
ναὸν οἰκοδομηθῆναι κελεύσας, ἐν ἐκείνῳ τὴν οἰκείαν
ἐπιφάνειαν ἐποιεῖτο.ᶠ

Μετὰ ταύτας τὰς φυλάς, τὸν Ἰωσὴφ εὐλόγησε καὶ ταῖς δύο
φυλαῖς κατὰ ταὐτὸν τὴν εὐλογίαν προσήνεγκεν· ἀπ' εὐλογίας
15 Κυρίου ἡ γῆ αὐτοῦ· ἀπὸ ὡρῶν οὐρανοῦ καὶ δρόσου, καὶ ἀπὸ

---

t. Dt 33.11   u. Nm 16

xlv A [32], B, C, 4 7(inc.) 9 10 31 35 37 = 21 mss.

a. Cf. Gn 42.13.   b. Dt 33.12   c. Jos 18.28   d. 1Kgs 6f.   e. Dt 33.12
f. 1Kgs 8.10f.

Question XLV

Moses entreated God's blessing on Israel: "Bless his strength, Lord, and accept the works of his hands." The priests who conduct the divine service also require bodily strength so that nothing will hinder their zeal. "Crush the loins of the foes who have risen against him, and may those who hate him not rise up."[t] With these words recalling the fate of Korah, Dathan, and Abiram, who had organized a revolt against the priests, he bridled the boldness of demagogues.[u]

XLV

Why did he put Benjamin in fourth place[b] though he was the youngest?[a]

(1) To this tribe belonged the capital city,[c] where the Temple was built,[d] so he quite logically set the sacred place alongside the priestly tribe. This blessing makes the following prediction: "The beloved of the Lord will dwell in confidence." To bring out the reason for this confidence, he declared, "And God overshadows him all his days and has rested between his shoulders."[e] Thus, thanks to his proximity to God's Temple, Benjamin enjoyed the benefit of God's constant attention. Now, in the clause, "he rested between his shoulders," he referred to God, who commanded the construction of his Temple in Jerusalem and then manifested himself there.[1f]

Next, he blessed Joseph. Indeed, he bestowed the blessing on both tribes at the same time: "His land is of the blessing of the Lord, of the seasons of heaven, of dew, of springs that well up from the

----

the high priest's oracular breastplate: τὸ λόγιον = "the declaration" or "oracle"; ἡ δήλωσις = "the demonstration" or "the urim"; and ἡ ἀλήθεια = "the truth" or "the thummim."

----

1. Theodoret correctly points out that Jebus/Jerusalem was originally in the territory of Benjamin; v. Jos 18.28 and McKenzie, *Dict.,* "Benjamin," p. 89.

ἀβύσσων πηγῶν κάτωθεν, καὶ καθ' ὥραν γενήματα ἡλίου
τροπῶν, καὶ ἀπὸ συνόδου μηνῶν, . . . καὶ ἀπὸ κορυφῆς βουνῶν
ἀεννάων.ᵍ ᾔτησεν αὐτῷ τὰ οὐρανόθεν δωρούμενα ἀγαθά, τοὺς
ἀπὸ τῆς γῆς παρεχομένους καρπούς, οὓς ἄρδουσι μὲν ὑετοί,
20 τρέφουσι δὲ δρόσοι, πεπαίνει δὲ ἥλιος κατὰ τὰς τῶν ὡρῶν καὶ
μηνῶν περιόδους. φέρει δὲ τούτους, οὐ μόνον ἡ ὑπτία γῆ,
ἀλλὰ καὶ ὄρειος. εἰς βεβαίωσιν δὲ τῆς εὐλογίας ἀνέμνησε τοῦ
ὀφθέντος ἐν τῇ βάτῳ Θεοῦ.ʰ λέγει δὲ αὐτὸν καὶ τῶν
πρωτοτοκίων τετυχηκέναι, καὶ τούτου χάριν διχῇ τὴν φυλὴν
25 μερισθῆναι, καὶ δύο τὴν μίαν γενέσθαι, ἐπειδὴ διπλῆν μοῖραν
ἐλάμβανον οἱ πρωτότοκοι. καὶ τὸ δυνατὸν δὲ τῶν φυλῶν
διδάσκων, μονοκέρωτι καὶ ταύρῳ ἀπείκασε. καὶ προτέταχε τοῦ
Μανασσῆ τὸν Ἐφραῒμ κατὰ τὴν τοῦ προπάτορος εὐλογίαν.ⁱ

(2) Τῷ δὲ Ζαβουλὼν καὶ τῷ Ἰσσαχάρ, τῷ μὲν ὡς τὴν
30 παραλίαν οἰκοῦντι, τῷ δὲ ὡς γειτονεύοντι καὶ τὴν ἐν πολέμοις
ἐπηύξατο *νίκην*, καὶ τὴν θείαν ἐπικουρίαν, καὶ τὰ ἀπὸ
θαλάττης ἀγαθά· *ἔθνη, γάρ φησι, ἐξολοθρεύσουσι, καὶ*
ἐπικαλέσονται ἐκεῖ, καὶ θύσουσι θυσίαν δικαιοσύνης, καὶ
πλοῦτον θαλάσσης θηλάσουσι καὶ ἐμπορίαν παραλίαν
35 *κατοικούντων·*ʲ οἱ γὰρ θαλάττῃ πελάζοντες, οὐ μόνον τῶν
οἰκείων καρπῶν, ἀλλὰ καὶ τῶν πάντοθεν φερομένων ἀγαθῶν
ἀπολαύουσι.

Τὸν δὲ Γὰδ ἀπείκασε λέοντι· οὕτω γὰρ καὶ ὁ πατριάρχης
Ἰακὼβ ἔφη· *Γὰδ πειρατήριον πειρατεύσει αὐτόν, καὶ αὐτὸς δὲ*
40 *πειρατεύσει αὐτὸν κατὰ πόδας.*ᵏ

Σκύμνον δὲ τὸν Δὰν ὠνόμασεν *ἐκπηδῶντα ἐκ τοῦ Βασάν,*ˡ
ἐπειδή, ἐξαπίνης τῇ Λαϊσσᾷ προσβαλόντες πόλει, καὶ αὐτὴν
εἷλον, καὶ τοὺς ἐνοικοῦντας ἀνεῖλον, καὶ οἰκεῖον ἀπέφηναν
οἰκητήριον.ᵐ

---

l. 16 γενήματα F.M. : γενημάτων Sir. Sch. The accusative γενήματα is, in
fact, meaningless in the context, and the translation presupposes the genitive
(*cf.* Wevers and Quast, Dt 33.14), yet γενήματα has some attestation also in the
mss. of the LXX (*v. ap. crit. ad loc.*).

g. Dt 33.13–15   h. Dt 33.16   i. Dt 33.17   j. Dt 33.19   k. Gn 49.19
l. Dt 33.22   m. Jgs 18.27–29

deep below, with the seasonal produce of the rotations of the sun and the assembly of the months, and of the crest of ancient mountains."[g] He besought for him those heaven-sent blessings, the fruits of the earth, watered by the rains, nourished by the dews, and ripened by the sun in the cycles of seasons and months. These are produced not only on the plains but also in the mountains. To confirm the blessing, he recalled God's appearance in the burning bush.[h] He declared as well that this tribe gained the right of the firstborn and was therefore divided, with the one tribe becoming two, since the firstborn was entitled to a double share. He brought out the power of these tribes by comparing their might to that of a unicorn and a bull. Finally, according to the blessing of Jacob, the founder of the family, he put Ephraim ahead of Manasseh.[i]

(2) For Zebulun and Issachar, the former a coast-dweller, the latter his neighbor, he besought victory in war, God's support, and blessings from the sea. "They will destroy nations, call on God's name there, sacrifice a sacrifice of righteousness, and batten on the wealth of the sea and the trade of those who dwell on the coast."[j] Those who live by the sea enjoy not only their own produce but also goods imported from all quarters.

Gad he likened to a lion. The patriarch Jacob had declared: "A nest of pirates will plunder him, but he will plunder him in close pursuit."[k]

He called Dan a cub leaping out from Bashan,[l] because they launched a sudden attack on the city of Leshem, captured it, slew its inhabitants, and made it their own dwelling-place.[2m]

2. Theodoret applies the same interpretation to two different oracles regarding Dan; *cf.* the present passage with his exposition of Gn 49.16f., one of the blessings of Jacob, in Q. 112.4 on Gn. and *v.* note 5 *ad loc.*

45   Καὶ τῷ Νεφθαλεὶμ δὲ τὴν ἀπὸ γῆς καὶ θαλάττης εὐπορίαν
      ἀπήγγειλεν·[n] πρόσοικος γὰρ καὶ οὗτος ἦν τῆς θαλάττης, ἔχων
      ἀπὸ νότου τὴν Γαλιλαίαν. τοῦτο δὲ καὶ ὁ προφήτης καὶ ὁ
      εὐαγγελιστὴς ἔφη· *γῆ Ζαβουλών, καὶ γῆ Νεφθαλείμ,*[o] *καὶ οἱ*
      λοιποί, οἱ τὴν παραλίαν κατοικοῦντες,[p] *Γαλιλαίαν τῶν ἐθνῶν,*[q]
50   *ὁ λαὸς ὁ καθήμενος ἐν σκότει εἶδε φῶς μέγα.*[r] τὸ μέντοι
      πλησμονὴ δεκτῶν,[s] πλησμονὴ εὐδοκίας ὁ Σύμμαχος ἡρμήνευσε.
      τὴν δὲ αὐτὴν ἔχει διάνοιαν· δεκτὰ γὰρ τὰ εὐδοκούμενα.

      Καὶ μέντοι καὶ τῷ Ἀσὴρ καὶ τῆς γῆς τὴν εὐκαρπίαν καὶ
||7   τὴν ἀπὸ θαλάττης εὐπορίαν αἰτεῖ·|| καὶ γὰρ τὸ *βάψει ἐν ἐλαίῳ*
55   *τὸν πόδα αὐτοῦ, καὶ σίδηρος καὶ χαλκὸς τὸ ὑπόδημα αὐτοῦ*[t]
      τὴν ἀφθονίαν τῶν ἀγαθῶν δηλοῖ.

XLVI

      Τί δή ποτε τὸν Συμεὼν οὐκ εὐλόγησεν;

      Ὁ Ῥουβὴν ἔσχε τὴν φιλαδελφίαν ἀφορμὴν εὐλογίας·[a] διὰ
      γὰρ ἐκείνης, τῆς ἀρᾶς ἀπηλλάγη, καὶ ὁ Λευὶ διὰ Μωϋσὴν τὸν
      μέγαν τῆς εὐλογίας τετύχηκεν· ἡ γὰρ τοῖς ἄλλοις λύουσα τὰς
5   ἀράς, πολλῷ μᾶλλον ἔλυσε τὴν οἰκείαν·[b] ὁ δὲ Συμεὼν οὐδεμίαν
      ἔσχε πρόφασιν ὥστε τῆς εὐλογίας τυχεῖν. οἶμαι δὲ αὐτὸν καὶ
      ἀρχηγὸν τῆς κατὰ τοῦ Ἰωσὴφ ἐπιβουλῆς γεγενῆσθαι, καὶ
      τούτου τεκμήριον τὸ τὸν ἀξιάγαστον ἄνδρα ἐκεῖνον τοὺς μὲν
      ἄλλους ἅπαντας ἀπολῦσαι, τοῦτον δὲ μόνον καὶ συλληφθῆναι,
10   καὶ δεθῆναι, καὶ καθειρχθῆναι κελεῦσαι.[c] μετέσχε δὲ ὅμως καὶ
      οὗτος τῆς εὐλογίας· οὐ γὰρ μόνον ἰδίᾳ ἑκάστῃ φυλῇ δέδωκεν
      εὐλογίαν, ἀλλὰ καὶ κοινὴν παντὶ τῷ λαῷ· *κατασκηνώσει,* γάρ
      φησιν, *Ἰσραὴλ πεποιθὼς μόνος ἐπὶ γῆς Ἰακώβ, ἐπὶ γῆς σίτου*

---

n. Dt 33.23   o. Is 9.1; Mt 4.15   p. Is 9.1   q. Is 9.1; Mt 4.15   r. Mt 4.16
s Dt 33.23   t Dt 33.24f.

---

xlvi A [32], B, C, 4(inc.) 9 10 31 35 37 = 20 mss.

a. Gn 37.22   b. Gn 49.5–7   c. Gn 42.24

For Naphtali as well he foretold trading on land and sea.[n] In fact, this tribe was also located along the sea, north of Galilee. As both the prophet and the evangelist said, "Land of Zebulun and land of Naphtali,[o] and the others inhabiting the coast[p] of Galilee of the gentiles,[q] the people dwelling in darkness has seen a great light."[r] Symmachus rendered the phrase "a plenitude of acceptable things"[s] as "a plenitude of approval," but there is no difference in meaning, for things that are received with approval are acceptable.

For Asher, too, he asked plentiful harvests of the land and rich commerce from the sea. The clause "He will dip his foot in oil, and he will be shod with iron and bronze"[t] indicates the abundance of those blessings.

XLVI

Why did he give no blessing to Simeon?

Reuben had grounds for a blessing thanks to the love he had shown his brother,[a] through which he escaped from the curse. As for Levi, he received a blessing through the mighty Moses; as his blessing canceled curses affecting others, it was more than capable of canceling one on his own tribe.[1b] But Simeon had no claim to a blessing. I am of the view that he was the ringleader in the plot against Joseph, and in support of this I note that, although that admirable man released the others, he gave orders that Simeon alone be arrested, bound, and imprisoned.[2c] Nevertheless, he too shared in the blessing, since Moses conferred not only a separate blessing on each tribe but also a general blessing on the nation as a whole: "Israel will dwell in confidence alone in the land of Jacob, in a land of

---

1. *Cf.* Theodoret's comment on the blessing of Reuben in *Q.* 44.1.

2. Neither Simeon's absence nor Levi's status as a clerical tribe suggests to Theodoret that Moses' blessing must date to a period subsequent to the invasion of Canaan. Von Rad (on 33.18f.) believes that the poem reflects the circumstances of the ninth or eighth century. By then Simeon had probably been absorbed into Judah; *v.* McKenzie, *Dict.,* "Simeon," p. 816.

καὶ οἴνου, καὶ ὁ οὐρανός σοι συννεφὴς δρόσῳ.[d] πολλὰ δὲ καὶ
15 ἄλλα τῇ κοινῇ εὐλογίᾳ προστέθεικε.

Μετὰ μέντοι τὰς εὐλογίας, ἔδειξεν ὁ δεσπότης Θεὸς τῷ
προφήτῃ τὴν γῆν ἅπασαν, εἰσελθεῖν δὲ αὐτὸν ἐκεῖ
διεκώλυσεν.[e] προτυποῖ δὲ τοῦτο τὸ παρὰ τοῦ σωτῆρος ἡμῶν
||4   εἰρημένον·|| *πολλοὶ προφῆται, καὶ βασιλεῖς, καὶ δίκαιοι*
20 *ἐπεθύμησαν ἰδεῖν ἃ βλέπετε καὶ οὐκ εἶδον, καὶ ἀκοῦσαι ἃ*
ἀκούετε καὶ οὐκ ἤκουσαν.[f]

d. Dt 33.28   e. Dt 34.1–4   f. Mt 13.17 (NT var.)

grain and wine, where heaven is cloudy with dew."[d] And he made many other additions to the general blessing.

Then, after the blessing, the Lord God showed the prophet the whole land but forbade him to enter it.[e] This prefigures the word of our Savior: "Many prophets and kings and righteous people longed to see what you are seeing but never saw it and to hear what you are hearing but never heard it."[3f]

---

3. With this abrupt conclusion to the commentary on Deuteronomy, Theodoret avoids dealing with the question of how Moses could have reported his own death and the mystery of his tomb (ch. 34). The immediate transition to the book of Joshua may suggest that Theodoret did not regard the Pentateuch/Torah as a separate literary and theological unit. In moving to Joshua, he says nothing about a change of authorship.

QUAESTIONES IN IOSUAM

PRAEFATIO IN QUAESTIONES IN IOSUAM

Καὶ ἐγένετο μετὰ τὴν τελευτὴν Μωϋσῆ δούλου Κυρίου,
εἶπε Κύριος τῷ Ἰησοῦ υἱῷ Ναυῆ, τῷ ὑπουργῷ Μωϋσῆ, λέγων,
Μωϋσῆς ὁ θεράπων μου τετελεύτηκε. νῦν οὖν ἀναστὰς διάβηθι
τὸν Ἰορδάνην, σὺ καὶ πᾶς ὁ λαὸς οὗτος, εἰς τὴν γῆν ἣν ἐγὼ
5 δίδωμι αὐτοῖς.ᵃ ὁ πάνσοφος ἡμᾶς ἐδίδαξε Παῦλος ὡς τύπος ἦν
ἡ παλαιὰ τῆς καινῆς· ταῦτα γὰρ πάντα, φησί, τύποι
συνέβαινον ἐκείνοις, ἐγράφη δὲ πρὸς νουθεσίαν ἡμῶν, εἰς οὓς
τὰ τέλη τῶν αἰώνων κατήντησεν.ᵇ καὶ γαλάταις δὲ
ἐπιστέλλων, οὕτως ἔφη· γέγραπται ... ὅτι Ἀβραὰμ δύο υἱοὺς
10 ἔσχεν· ἕνα ἐκ τῆς παιδίσκης καὶ ἕνα ἐκ τῆς ἐλευθέρας. ἀλλ' ὁ
μὲν ἐκ τῆς παιδίσκης κατὰ σάρκα γεγέννηται, ὁ δὲ ἐκ τῆς
ἐλευθέρας διὰ τῆς ἐπαγγελίας. ἄτινά ἐστιν ἀλληγορούμενα·
αὗται γάρ εἰσι δύο διαθῆκαι, καὶ τὰ ἑξῆς.ᶜ καὶ γέγραφεν, οὐ
τὴν ἱστορίαν ἐκβάλλων, ἀλλὰ τῇ ἀληθείᾳ παραβάλλων τὸν
15 τύπον· τὸν Ἀβραὰμ τῷ Θεῷ, τὰς γυναῖκας ταῖς δύο διαθήκαις,
τοὺς υἱοὺς τοῖς λαοῖς. οὕτω τοίνυν κἀνταῦθα Μωϋσέα νοητέον
τὸν νόμον, Ἰησοῦν τὸν ὁμώνυμον ἐκείνῳ σωτῆρα.

Ὅτι δὲ καὶ ὁ νόμος Μωϋσῆς ὠνόμασται ἀπεδείξαμεν ἤδη
ταῖς τῆς θείας γραφῆς μαρτυρίαις χρησάμενοι· ἔχουσι, γάρ
20 φησι, Μωϋσέα καὶ τοὺς προφήτας.ᵈ καί, μέχρι τῆς σήμερον,

PRAEFATIO A [32], B⁻¹⁷, C, 7 9 10 31 35 37 = 19 mss.

a. Jos 1.1f. (LXX var.)   b. 1Cor 10.11   c. Gal 4.22–24   d. Lk 16.29

ON JOSHUA

PREFACE TO *THE QUESTIONS ON JOSHUA*

"After the death of Moses, the servant of the Lord, the Lord said to Joshua, the son of Nun, assistant to Moses, 'Moses my servant is dead; so rise up now, you and all this people, and cross the Jordan into the land I am giving them.'"[a] Paul, the all wise, has taught us that the Old Testament was a type of the New: "All this" he declared, "happened to them in types and was written to instruct us, on whom the end of the ages has come."[b] And in his letter to the Galatians he said, "Scripture tells us that Abraham had two sons, one of the slave woman, the other of the free: the son of the slave woman was born according to the flesh, the son of the free through the promise. This is an allegory, in which the women stand for two covenants" and so on.[c] He wrote this, not to reject the historical facts, but to relate the type to the reality: Abraham to God, the women to the two covenants, the sons to the peoples.[1] Here too, therefore, we are to understand Moses as the Law and Joshua as the Savior of the same name.

On the evidence of holy Scripture, we have already demonstrated that the Law is referred to by the name "Moses": "They have Moses and the prophets";[d] and "To this day as Moses is read out, a veil lies

1. Theodoret insists that, while accepting the historical reality of the Old Testament narrative (τὴν ἱστορίαν), Paul pointed to its deeper meaning or fulfilment (τῇ ἀληθείᾳ). He here recalls a very similar statement that Diodore of Tarsus had made in the prologue to his commentary on the Psalms. There Diodore had argued that, though Paul had used a term signifying "allegory" (ἀλληγορούμενα, Gal 4.24), he had meant it only as a synonym for "spiritual interpretation" (τὴν θεωρίαν). Unlike the Alexandrian allegorists, who, wise in their own conceit, de-

ἡνίκα ἀναγινώσκεται Μωϋσῆς, κάλυμμα ἐπὶ τὴν καρδίαν
αὐτῶν κεῖται.ᵉ ὥσπερ τοίνυν κατὰ τὴν ἱστορίαν, Μωϋσῆ
τετελευτηκότος, Ἰησοῦς τὸν λαὸν εἰς τὴν ἐπηγγελμένην
εἰσήγαγε γῆν, οὕτω, μετὰ τὸ τοῦ νόμου τέλος, ὁ ἡμέτερος
25 ἐπιφανεὶς Ἰησοῦς ἀνέῳξε τῷ εὐσεβεῖ λαῷ τὴν βασιλείαν τῶν
οὐρανῶν· τέλος, γάρ φησι, νόμου Χριστὸς εἰς δικαιοσύνην
παντὶ τῷ πιστεύοντι ᶠ καί, ὁ νόμος καὶ οἱ προφῆται ἕως
Ἰωάννου προεφήτευσαν· ἀπὸ δὲ τῶν ἡμερῶν Ἰωάννου... ἡ
βασιλεία τῶν οὐρανῶν βιάζεται, καὶ βιασταὶ ἁρπάζουσιν
30 αὐτήν.ᵍ

I

Καὶ πῶς ἁρμόττει τῷ Κυρίῳ ἡμῶν Ἰησοῦ Χριστῷ τὸ τῆς
ὑπουργίας ὄνομα; περὶ γὰρ Ἰησοῦ τοῦ Ναυῆ ἔφη, εἶπε Κύριος
τῷ Ἰησοῦ υἱῷ Ναυῆ τῷ ὑπουργῷ Μωϋσῆ.ᵃ

Ἀκούομεν καὶ τοῦ ἀποστόλου λέγοντος, λέγω δὲ Χριστὸν
5 Ἰησοῦν διάκονον γεγενῆσθαι περιτομῆς ὑπὲρ ἀληθείας Θεοῦ,
εἰς τὸ βεβαιῶσαι τὰς ἐπαγγελίας τῶν πατέρων ᵇ καὶ πάλιν,
ὅτε δὲ ἦλθε τὸ πλήρωμα τοῦ χρόνου, ἐξαπέστειλεν ὁ Θεὸς τὸν
υἱὸν αὐτοῦ, γεννώμενον ἐκ γυναικός, γεννώμενον ὑπὸ νόμον,

---

e. 2Cor 3.15   f. Rom 10.4   g. Mt 11.12f.

1 A [32], B⁻¹⁷, C, 7 9 10 31 35 37 = 19 mss.

l. 8 γεννώμενον a, 12, B⁻¹⁷, 3 8, 52, 31 35, Sch. F.M. : γενόμενον 5, 11, 1 15,
51, 7 9 10 37, Sir.; cf. The Greek New Testament, Gal. 4.4 = "'born of a woman.'"
In his extant works, Thdt. quotes Gal. 4.4 in seven other places; v. his comments
on Ps 9.10 (LXX = 9.9 MT); Rom 5.8f.; Gal 4.4 (where he cites the participle
twice); Heb 5.2; and Haer. com. 5.2 and Prouid. 10. In four of these Sir. and Sch.
print γενο- and in three γεννω-. The latter may draw support from the
Quaest. et resp. 76, where, according to the edition of Papadopoulos-Kerameus,
Thdt. cites Lk 1.35 according to the form τὸ γεννώμενον ἐκ σοῦ (cf. the ap.
crit. of the New Testament ad loc.); for the authenticity of the Quaest. et resp.,
v. Quasten, pp. 548f.

a. Jos 1.1   b. Rom 15.8 (NT var.)

over their heart."[2e] So, as sacred history tells us that, after the death of Moses, Joshua led the people into the promised land, so, after the end of the Law, our Joshua came and opened the Kingdom of Heaven to his holy people.[3] Indeed, Scripture says, "Christ is the end of the Law for the justification of everyone who believes";[f] and "The Law and the prophets were in effect until John, but from the time of John, the Kingdom of Heaven has been suffering violence, and the violent have been taking it by force."[g]

I

How can the title "subordinate assistant" apply to our Lord Jesus Christ? With regard to Joshua, the son of Nun, Scripture says, "The Lord said to Joshua, the son of Nun, assistant to Moses."[a]

We hear the word of the apostle himself: "I say that Christ Jesus became a minister to the circumcision on behalf of God's truth to confirm the promises made to the fathers";[b] and again, "But when the fullness of time had come, God sent his Son, engendered of a woman, born subject to the Law, to redeem those subject to the Law,

---

parted from traditional interpretation of Scripture (οἱ καινοτόμοι τῆς θείας γραφῆς καὶ οἰησίσοφοι), Paul had explained the spiritual sense of the historical narrative without rejecting its literal meaning (ὁ Ἀπόστολος οὐδαμοῦ τὴν ἱστορίαν ἀνέτρεψεν, ἐπεισενεγκὼν τὴν θεωρίαν καὶ ταῦτα ἀλληγορίαν καλέσας τὴν θεωρίαν).

2. V. Q. 43 on Dt.

3. Theodoret's typology rests, in part, on the identity in Greek of the names "Joshua" and "Jesus," both represented by Ἰησοῦς; v. note 1 to Q. 25 on Nm.

ἵνα τοὺς ὑπὸ νόμον ἐξαγοράσῃ ἵνα τὴν υἱοθεσίαν ἀπολάβωμεν.[c]

10 ὡς ὑπὸ νόμον τοίνυν γενόμενος, οὕτω καὶ διάκονος ἐκλήθη
περιτομῆς. οὕτω καὶ τοῖς ἰουδαίοις ἔφη, εἰ ... ἐπιστεύετε
Μωϋσῇ, ἐπιστεύετε ἂν ἐμοί· περὶ γὰρ ἐμοῦ ἐκεῖνος ἐλάλησεν.[d]
καὶ γὰρ ἐκεῖνοι πρὸς Ἰησοῦν εἰρήκεισαν τὸν Ναυῆ, κατὰ
πάντα ὅσα ἠκούσαμεν Μωϋσῇ, ἀκουσόμεθα καὶ σοῦ.[e]

II

Τί δή ποτε, ὑποσχόμενος ὁ Θεὸς πάντα τόπον δώσειν
αὐτοῖς οὗ ἂν ἐπιβῶσι τῷ ἴχνει τῶν ποδῶν αὐτῶν· καὶ τὴν
ἔρημον καὶ τὸν Ἀντιλίβανον ἕως τοῦ ποταμοῦ τοῦ μεγάλου
Εὐφράτου·[a] οὐκ ἐπλήρωσε τὴν ὑπόσχεσιν;

5 (1) Σαφὴς ὁ λόγος καὶ οὐ πολλῆς ἑρμηνείας δεόμενος·
πρῶτον μὲν γὰρ εἴρηται, ὅτι πᾶς τόπος οὗ ἐὰν ἐπιβῆτε τῷ
ἴχνει τῶν ποδῶν ὑμῶν ὑμῖν δώσω αὐτόν. εἰκὸς οὖν αὐτοὺς μὴ
ἐπιβῆναι τῆς ἄλλης γῆς, Ἰησοῦ τοῦ Ναυῆ στρατηγοῦντος. ἡ
ἐπαγωγὴ δὲ τέλεον λύει τὸ ζήτημα· ἐπήγαγε γάρ, ὃν τρόπον
10 εἴρηκα τῷ Μωϋσῇ.[b] οὐκ ἀορίστως δὲ πρὸς ἐκεῖνον ἐποιήσατο
τὴν ὑπόσχεσιν, ἀλλ' ἐὰν φυλάξητε τὰς ἐντολάς μου καὶ τὰ
δικαιώματά μου.[c] ἐκεῖνοι μὲν οὖν, ὡς εὐθὺς παραβεβηκότες
τὸν νόμον, τῆς ἐπαγγελίας τελείας οὐκ ἔτυχον.

Οἱ δὲ θεῖοι ἀπόστολοι, οὐ μόνον ἐκείνων τῶν τόπων
15 ἐκράτησαν ὧν ἐπέβησαν, ἀλλὰ κἀκείνων ἐν οἷς αὐτῶν
ἀνεγνώσθη τὰ πάνσοφα γράμματα. καὶ τὴν πάλαι ἔρημον
παράδεισον ἀπέφηναν θεῖον· περὶ ταύτης τῆς ἐρήμου καὶ ὁ
προφήτης ἔλεγεν Ἡσαΐας, εὐφράνθητι, ἔρημος διψῶσα,[d] καὶ
εὐφράνθητι, ἔρημος καὶ αἱ κῶμαι αὐτῆς.[e] καὶ ὁ δεσπότης Θεὸς
20 διὰ τῆς ἐκείνου γλώττης ὑπέσχετο ποιήσειν τὴν ἔρημον εἰς

c. Gal 4.4f.   d. Jn 5.46   e. Jos 1.17

II A [32], B⁻¹⁷, C, 7 9 10 31(inc.) 35 37 = 19 mss.

a. Jos 1.3f.   b. Jos 1.3   c. Dt 11.22f.   d. Is 35.1   e. Is 42.11

so that we might receive adoption as children."[1c] As one born subject to the Law, he was styled "a minister to the circumcision." Thus, Christ also declared to the Jews, "If you believed Moses, you would also believe me, for he spoke of me."[d] Indeed, the ancients had said to Joshua, the son of Nun, "We shall obey you just as we obeyed Moses."[e]

11

Why did God promise to give them every place on which they set the sole of their feet—the wilderness and Anti-Lebanon as far as the mighty river Euphrates[a]—and then fail to fulfil his promise?

(1) The word is clear, requiring no lengthy interpretation. First, as it says, "I shall give you every place on which you set the sole of your feet," it is likely they did not set foot on the rest of the land while Joshua, the son of Nun, was in command. Then the sequel solves the problem completely, for the text continues, "As I said to Moses."[b] Yet God made him no unconditional promise, but a promise only "provided you keep my commandments and my ordinances."[c] Thus, as they immediately broke the Law, they did not attain the entirety of the promise.

In contrast, the holy apostles gained control not only of those places on which they trod but also of those where their writings, full of wisdom, were read out. Furthermore they transformed what had formerly been a wilderness into God's garden. Isaiah the prophet said of this wilderness, "Rejoice, parched wilderness,"[d] and "let the wilderness and its towns rejoice,"[e] and through the prophet's tongue, the Lord God promised to turn the wilderness into ponds and the

1. The Antiochene text of Gal 4.4 read γεννώμενον ("engendered") rather than the more widely attested γενόμενον ("born"). In his commentary on that passage, Theodoret had defended the former reading as referring to Mary's virginal conception, a position rejected by Fitzmyer (*ad loc.*) as an "anachronistic interpretation."

ἔλη καὶ τὴν διψῶσαν γῆν ἐν ὑδραγωγοῖς.ᶠ ταύτην πάλιν
γενήσεσθαι τὴν ἔρημον ὡς τὸν Κάρμηλον ἔφη.ᵍ ἐκληρονόμησαν
δὲ καὶ τὸν Ἀντιλίβανον τῆς ἀληθείας οἱ κήρυκες. αἰνίττεται
δὲ καὶ οὗτος τὴν τῶν ἐθνῶν σωτηρίαν, ἐπειδὴ καὶ Λίβανος ἡ
25 Ἰερουσαλὴμ ὠνομάσθη· ὁ ἀετός, γάρ φησιν, ὁ
μεγαλοπτέρυγος, . . . ὃς ἔχει τὸ ἥγημα εἰσελθεῖν εἰς τὸν
Λίβανον καὶ ἀπέκνισε τὰ ἀπαλὰ τῆς κέδρου καὶ τῆς
κυπαρίττου·ʰ ἀετὸν γὰρ τὸν βαβυλώνιον κέκληκε, Λίβανον δὲ
τὴν Ἰερουσαλήμ, τὰ ἀπαλὰ δὲ τῆς κέδρου καὶ τῆς κυπαρίττου
30 τὸν βασιλέα καὶ τοὺς ἄρχοντας.

Τούτους, οὐ μόνον κατασκόπους, ἀλλὰ καὶ στρατηγοὺς ὁ
ἡμέτερος ἀπέστειλεν Ἰησοῦς. καθάπερ δὲ οἱ παρὰ τοῦ Ἰησοῦ
τοῦ Ναυῆ πεμφθέντες κατάσκοποι τὴν πεπιστευκυῖαν
διέσωσαν πόρνην, σύμβολον αὐτῇ σωτηρίας δεδωκότες τὸ
35 σπαρτίον τὸ κόκκινον,ⁱ οὕτως οἱ τοῦ σωτῆρος ἡμῶν ἀπόστολοι
τὴν πάλαι πόρνην, τὴν διαφόροις εἰδώλοις ἀνακειμένην
ἐκκλησίαν, καὶ τῆς προτέρας ἀκολασίας ἀπέστησαν καὶ τῶν
αἰωνίων ἠξίωσαν ἀγαθῶν, οὐ σπαρτίῳ κοκκίνῳ χρησάμενοι
συμβόλῳ, ἀλλὰ τῷ παναγίῳ αἵματι τὴν σωτηρίαν
40 πραγματευσάμενοι.

(2) Μηδεὶς οὖν νομιζέτω ἀνάξιον εἶναι τῆς ἐκκλησίας τῆς
Ῥαὰβ τὸν τύπον· ἀκουσάτω δὲ τοῦ ἀποστόλου λέγοντος, ἦμεν
γάρ ποτε καὶ ἡμεῖς ἀνόητοι, ἀπειθεῖς, πλανώμενοι,
δουλεύοντες ἐπιθυμίαις καὶ ἡδοναῖς ποικίλαις, ἐν κακίᾳ καὶ
45 φθόνῳ διάγοντες, στυγητοί, μισοῦντες ἀλλήλους·ʲ καὶ πάλιν,
ἀλλὰ τότε μέν, ὡς οὐκ εἰδότες Θεόν, ἐδουλεύσατε τοῖς μὴ
οὖσι θεοῖς·ᵏ καὶ ἀλλαχοῦ, ἦτε γάρ ποτε σκότος, νῦν δὲ φῶς ἐν
Κυρίῳ·ˡ καὶ ἑτέρωθι, μὴ πλανᾶσθε· οὔτε πόρνοι, οὔτε μοιχοί,
οὔτε μαλακοί, οὔτε ἀρσενοκοῖται, οὔτε εἰδωλολάτραι, οὔτε
50 πλεονέκται, οὔτε κλέπται, οὐ λοίδοροι, οὐ μέθυσοι, οὐχ
ἅρπαγες βασιλείαν Θεοῦ κληρονομήσουσιν·ᵐ εἶτα ἐπήγαγε,

---

f. Is 35.6f.   g. Is 35.2   h. Ezek 17.3f. (LXX var.)
i. Jos 2.1–21   j. Ti 3.3   k. Gal 4.8   l. Eph 5.8   m. 1Cor 6.9f.

parched earth into irrigation channels.[f] He said that this wilderness would become like Carmel.[g] The heralds of the truth also took possession of the Anti-Lebanon. The name, "Anti-Lebanon" hints at the salvation of the nations, since "Lebanon" was a designation for Jerusalem: "The long-winged eagle which intends to enter Lebanon and nipped off the choice parts of the cedar and the cypress."[h] Here "the eagle" refers to Babylon, "Lebanon" to Jerusalem, and "the choice parts of the cedar and the cypress" to the king and the rulers.

Our Joshua dispatched the apostles not only as spies but also as generals. As the spies sent by Joshua, the son of Nun, saved the faithful prostitute by giving her the crimson cord as a token of salvation,[i] so the apostles of our Savior delivered from her former licentiousness her who had once been a prostitute, the Church devoted to competing idols, and accorded her eternal blessings. It was with no token of a crimson cord, but with the sacred blood, that they accomplished her salvation.

(2) No one should imagine that Rahab was unworthy of being a type of the Church. Instead, heed the words of the apostle: "For we too were once foolish, disobedient, straying, enslaved to lust and manifold passions, living in malice and envy, despicable, hating each other";[j] and again: "But at the time, ignorant of God, you served false gods";[k] and elsewhere: "For though once darkness, you are now light in the Lord";[l] and in another place: "Be in no doubt: No fornicators, no adulterers, no male prostitutes, no sodomites, no idolaters, no coveters, no thieves, or revilers, or drunkards, or robbers will inherit the Kingdom of Heaven."[m] And he continued, "This is

καὶ ταῦτά τινες ἦτε, ἀλλ' ἀπελούσασθε, ἀλλ' ἡγιάσθητε, ἀλλ'
ἐδικαιώθητε ἐν τῷ ὀνόματι τοῦ Κυρίου ἡμῶν Ἰησοῦ Χριστοῦ
καὶ ἐν τῷ πνεύματι τοῦ Θεοῦ ἡμῶν.[n] οὕτω καὶ Ῥαὰβ ἡ πόρνη
55 τὸ πρότερον ἦν, ὑπεδέξατο δὲ τοὺς κατασκόπους πιστῶς καί,
βασιλέως παραδοθῆναι τούτους προστεταχότος, οὐκ εἶξεν,
ἀλλὰ κατέκρυψεν·[o] ἐπίστευσε γὰρ τῷ τῶν ἑβραίων Θεῷ. καὶ
δηλοῖ τὴν πίστιν τὰ ῥήματα· ἐπίσταμαι, γὰρ ἔφη, ὅτι
παρέδωκε ... Κύριος ὁ Θεὸς ὑμῶν τὴν γῆν· ἐπιπέπτωκε γὰρ ὁ
||31 60 φόβος ὑμῶν ἐφ' ἡμᾶς· ἀκηκόαμεν·|| γὰρ ὅτι κατεξήρανε Κύριος
ὁ Θεὸς τὴν θάλασσαν τὴν Ἐρυθρὰν ἀπὸ προσώπου ὑμῶν ὅτε
ἐξεπορεύεσθε ἐξ ... Αἰγύπτου, καὶ ὅσα ἐποιήσατε τοῖς δυσὶ
βασιλεῦσι τῶν ἀμορραίων, οἳ ἦσαν πέραν τοῦ Ἰορδάνου, Σηὼν
καὶ Ὢγ, οὓς ἐξωλοθρεύσατε αὐτούς· καὶ ἀκούσαντες ἡμεῖς
65 ἐξέστημεν τῇ καρδίᾳ ἡμῶν, καὶ οὐκ ἔστι ... πνεῦμα ἐν οὐδενὶ
ἀπὸ προσώπου ὑμῶν, ὅτι Κύριος, ὁ Θεὸς ὑμῶν, Θεὸς ἐν οὐρανῷ
|31 ἄνω καὶ ἐπὶ ... |γῆς κάτω.[p] ἀληθὴς ἄρα ὁ λόγος ἐκεῖνος ὃν ὁ
δεσπότης Θεὸς περὶ τοῦ Φαραὼ ἔφη· εἰς αὐτὸ τοῦτο ἐξήγειρά
σε, ὅπως ἐνδείξωμαι ἐν σοὶ τὴν δύναμίν μου, καὶ ὅπως
70 διαγγελῇ τὸ ὄνομά μου ἐν πάσῃ τῇ γῇ·[q] διὰ γὰρ τῶν εἰς
ἐκεῖνον γεγενημένων δῆλος ἅπασι γέγονεν ὁ ἑβραίων Θεός.
καὶ αἱ συνθῆκαι δὲ τῶν κατασκόπων σφόδρα τῇ ἀληθείᾳ
συμβαίνουσι· πᾶς, γὰρ ἔφασαν, ὃς ἂν ἐξέλθῃ τὴν θύραν τῆς
οἰκίας σου ἔξω, ἔνοχος ἑαυτῷ ἔσται· ἡμεῖς δὲ ἀθῷοι τῷ λόγῳ
75 σου τούτῳ.[r] καὶ ἡμῖν δὲ ἡ σωτηρία διὰ τῆς ἐκκλησίας
προσγίνεται· οἱ δὲ ταύτης ἐκτὸς οὐκ ἀπολαύουσι τῆς αἰωνίου
ζωῆς.

(3) Καὶ τὰ λοιπὰ δὲ τῆς ἱστορίας προδιέγραψε τὴν
ἀλήθειαν. ἡνίκα γὰρ ἤμελλον διαβαίνειν τὸν Ἰορδάνην, εἶπεν
80 Κύριος πρὸς Ἰησοῦν, ἐν τῇ ἡμέρᾳ ταύτῃ ἄρχομαι ὑψῶσαί σε
κατενώπιον τῶν υἱῶν Ἰσραήλ.[s] τοῦτο καὶ ἐπὶ τῆς ἀληθείας
ἐγένετο· ὥσπερ γὰρ ὁ τοῦ Ναυῆ Ἰησοῦς ἐκ τοῦ κατὰ τὸν

n. 1Cor 6.11   o. Jos 2.3f.   p. Jos 2.9–11   q. Rom 9.17   r. Jos 2.19
s. Jos 3.7

what some of you were, but you were washed, you were sanctified, you were justified in the name of our Lord Jesus Christ and in the Spirit of our God."[n] Such also was once Rahab the prostitute, but she welcomed the spies in faith, and, though the king ordered her to hand them over, she did not give in but hid them.[o] For she believed in the God of the Hebrews, and her words revealed her faith: "I know that the Lord your God has handed over the land, for fear of you has fallen upon us. We have heard that the Lord God dried up the Red Sea before you when you came out of Egypt and of all you did to the two kings of the Amorites, who were beyond the Jordan, Sihon and Og, whom you destroyed. When we heard this, our hearts fell, and none of us had the spirit to face you, because the Lord your God is God in heaven above and on earth below."[p] Thus, the Lord God's statement regarding Pharaoh—"I prompted you to do this in order to manifest my power in you and to broadcast my name throughout the land"[q]—was proven true, since the God of the Hebrews became universally known through what happened to Pharaoh. Furthermore, the pact made by the spies was very much in keeping with the reality: "Whoever goes out of doors, will be responsible for his own fate, and, as you have agreed, we shall be guiltless."[r] Indeed, salvation comes to us through the Church, and those outside it do not enjoy eternal life.

(3) This prefiguration of reality continues throughout the rest of the narrative. When they were about to cross the Jordan, the Lord said to Joshua, "On this day I shall begin to exalt you in the sight of the children of Israel."[s] This also happened in reality. As God's love for Joshua, the son of Nun, was clearly revealed by the miracle at the

Ἰορδάνην θαύματος δῆλος γέγονε θεοφιλὴς ὢν ἀνήρ,ᵗ οὕτως
καὶ ὁ ἡμέτερος Ἰησοῦς μετὰ τὸν Ἰορδάνην καὶ τὸ Ἰωάννου
85 βάπτισμα τῆς διδασκαλίας καὶ τῶν θαυμάτων τὴν ἀρχὴν
ἐποιήσατο. ἀλλ' ἴσως τισὶν ἀνάρμοστον εἶναι δοκεῖ τὸ *ἐν τῇ*
ἡμέρᾳ ταύτῃ ἄρχομαι ὑψῶσαί σε ἐπὶ τοῦ Κυρίου καὶ σωτῆρος
ἡμῶν τιθέμενον. ἀλλ' ἀκουσάτωσαν αὐτοῦ πρὸς τὸν πατέρα
λέγοντος, *πάτερ, δόξασόν με . . . τῇ δόξῃ ᾗ εἶχον παρὰ σοὶ*
90 *πρὸ τοῦ τὸν κόσμον εἶναι·*ᵘ καὶ ὁ ἀπόστολος δέ φησι, *διὸ καὶ*
ὁ Θεὸς αὐτὸν ὑπερύψωσεν καὶ ἐχαρίσατο αὐτῷ . . . ὄνομα τὸ
*ὑπὲρ πᾶν ὄνομα.*ᵛ ὑψωθεὶς δέ, οὐκ ἔλαβεν ὃ μὴ εἶχεν, ἀλλ'
ἔδειξεν ὅπερ εἶχεν· ἀγνοούμενος γὰρ ὅτι υἱός ἐστι τοῦ τῶν
ὅλων Θεοῦ, ἐδείχθη τοῦτο ὤν, τοῦ πατρὸς παρὰ τὸν Ἰορδάνην
95 εἰρηκότος, *οὗτός ἐστιν ὁ υἱός μου ὁ ἀγαπητὸς ἐν ᾧ εὐδόκησα.*ʷ

(4) Προτυποῦσι δὲ καὶ οἱ ἱερεῖς, οἱ αἴροντες τὴν κιβωτὸν
τῆς διαθήκης Κυρίου, τὸν βαπτιστὴν Ἰωάννην·ˣ ἱερεὺς γὰρ
κἀκεῖνος καὶ ἀρχιερέως υἱός. ὥσπερ τοίνυν, τῶν ἱερέων τὴν
κιβωτὸν φερόντων καὶ πρῶτον εἰς τὸν Ἰορδάνην
100 εἰσεληλυθότων, καὶ μετὰ τοῦ Ἰησοῦ, τοῦ προφήτου καὶ
στρατηγοῦ, ἅπας διελήλυθεν ὁ λαός, οὕτως Ἰωάννου τοῦ πάνυ
βαπτίζειν ἀρξαμένου, καὶ Ἰησοῦ τοῦ σωτῆρος ἁγιάσαντος τῶν
ὑδάτων τὴν φύσιν, ὁ εὐσεβὴς λαὸς διὰ τοῦ παναγίου
βαπτίσματος εἰς τὴν τῶν οὐρανῶν εἴσεισι βασιλείαν. καὶ
105 μέντοι καὶ οἱ δώδεκα ἄνδρες καὶ οἱ ἰσάριθμοι λίθοι τὸν θεῖον
προετύπωσαν τῶν ἀποστόλων χορόν·ʸ οἱ γὰρ αὐτοὶ καὶ
οἰκοδόμοι καὶ θεμέλιοι· *οἰκοδομηθέντες, γάρ φησιν, ἐπὶ τῷ*
*θεμελίῳ τῶν ἀποστόλων καὶ προφητῶν·*ᶻ καὶ πάλιν ὁ αὐτὸς
ἀπόστολος ἔφη, *ἐγώ, ὡς σοφὸς ἀρχιτέκτων, θεμέλιον τέθεικα.*ᵃᵃ
110 Τὸ μέντοι *πῆγμα,*ᵇᵇ *ἄσκωμα* ὁ Σύμμαχος ἡρμήνευσεν·
ἐπεχομένη γὰρ τῶν ὑδάτων ἡ ῥύμη, οἷον ἠσκοῦτο καὶ
ἐκορυφοῦτο· παντὸς γὰρ ἀδαμαντίνου τείχους πλέον ἐπεῖχεν
αὐτὴν ὁ τοῦ δημιουργήσαντος ὅρος.

---

t. Jos 4.14   u. Jn 17.5   v. Phil 2.9   w. Mt 3.17   x. Jos 3.13
y. Jos 4.4–9   z. Eph 2.20   aa. 1Cor 3.10   bb. Jos 3.16

Jordan,[t] so too, our Joshua, after the Jordan and the baptism of John, began his career of teaching and miracles. Perhaps some people may think it inappropriate to apply to our Lord and Savior the verse: "On this day I shall begin to exalt you," but let them listen to him saying to the Father, "Father, glorify me with the glory I had with you before the world existed."[u] Moreover, the apostle says, "Hence, God has exalted him and bestowed on him a name above every name."[v] Yet, when he was exalted, he received nothing he did not already possess; rather, he revealed what he had, for though he had not been recognized as Son of the God of the universe, his identity was revealed when the Father declared at the Jordan, "This is my beloved Son, in whom I have been well pleased."[w]

(4) In addition, the priests who carried the ark of the Lord's covenant prefigured John the Baptist,[x] who was both a priest and the son of a high priest. Just as the priests carrying the ark were the first to enter the Jordan, and the whole people made the crossing with Joshua prophet and general, so, since the great John was the first to begin baptizing, and Jesus the Savior sanctified the waters, the Christian people enter the Kingdom of Heaven through most holy baptism. Furthermore, both the twelve men and the equal number of stones prefigured the holy band of apostles,[y] who were both builders and foundation, for as Scripture says, "Built on the foundation of the apostles and prophets."[z] Indeed, the same apostle said, "I laid the foundation like a skilled master builder."[aa]

Now, Symmachus rendered the term "heap"[bb] as "wine-skin." That is, as the rush of the waters was blocked, they swelled like a wine-skin and piled up, with the Creator's will checking them more firmly than any wall of steel.[1]

---

1. Theodoret commends Symmachus for this apposite imagery and proceeds to explicate it with a metaphor of his own; *cf. Q.* 86 on Gn.

Καὶ πρὸ τοῦ Πάσχα δὲ γέγονεν ἡ διάβασις· τῇ δεκάτῃ γὰρ
115 διαβάντες,^{cc} ἐπετέλεσαν τῇ τεσσαρεσκαιδεκάτῃ τοῦ Πάσχα
τὴν ἑορτήν,^{dd} ἐπειδὴ κἂν τῇ ἀληθείᾳ, μετὰ τὸ σωτήριον
βάπτισμα ἡ τοῦ ἀμώμου ἀμνοῦ μετάληψις γίνεται.

III

Πῶς νοητέον τὸ *περίτεμε τοὺς υἱοὺς Ἰσραὴλ ἐκ δευτέρου;*^a

Τὴν ἀλήθειαν μάλιστα οὗτος ὁ λόγος προδιαγράφει. τοῖς
γὰρ τὴν μωσαϊκὴν δεξαμένοις περιτομὴν τὴν πνευματικὴν
προσήνεγκαν περιτομὴν τῶν εὐαγγελίων οἱ κήρυκες·
5 πιστεύσατε, γὰρ ἔλεγον, *καὶ βαπτισθήτω ἕκαστος ὑμῶν εἰς τὸ
ὄνομα τοῦ Κυρίου ἡμῶν Ἰησοῦ Χριστοῦ, . . . καὶ λήψεσθε τὴν
ἐπαγγελίαν τοῦ ἁγίου πνεύματος.*^b ταύτην ὁ θεῖος ἀπόστολος
ἀχειροποίητον περιτομὴν προσηγόρευσε·^c καὶ ἀλλαχοῦ,
περιτομή, φησί, *καρδίας ἐν πνεύματι, οὐ γράμματι.*^d οἱ τοίνυν
10 ἐξ ἰουδαίων τῷ σωτῆρι πεπιστευκότες, τὴν μωσαϊκὴν
περιτομὴν ἔχοντες, προσέλαβον τὴν πνευματικήν. τὸ τοίνυν
ἐκ δευτέρου τὴν ἀλήθειαν προτυποῖ· τὴν γὰρ σάρκα δὶς
περιτμηθῆναι τῶν ἀδυνάτων.

Ἡ δὲ ἐξεπιπολῆς τοῦ γράμματος διάνοια τοῦτο δηλοῖ· ὅτι
15 καθάπερ τῷ Ἀβραὰμ τοῦτον ἐξ ἀρχῆς ὁ Θεὸς ἐδεδώκει τὸν
νόμον, οὕτως *ἐκ δευτέρου* προσέταξε τῷ Ἰησοῦ τοὺς

---

cc. Jos 4.19   dd. Jos 5.10

III A [32], B⁻¹⁷, C, 7 9 10 35 37 = 18 mss.

l. 1 *περίτεμε* C⁻¹⁵, 9; cf. Jos 5.2 (codd. A B) = "'Circumcise the children of
Israel'" : *περιέτεμε* Sir. Sch. F.M. = "'He circumcised the children of Israel'" :
περιτεμεῖν a₂ : *ἔτεμεν* B. Thdt.'s quotation follows the text of *cod. A*, but
both *codd. A* and *B* carry the imperative; this mood is also supported by Thdt.'s
subsequent statement, προσέταξε τῷ Ἰησοῦ τοὺς ἀπεριτμήτους
περιτεμεῖν.

a. Jos 5.2 (LXX var.)   b. Acts 2.38 (NT var.)   c. Col 2.11   d. Rom 2.29

Question III

The crossing took place before Passover; they crossed on the tenth day[cc] and celebrated the feast of Passover on the fourteenth.[dd] Just so, in the fulfilment of the type, saving baptism precedes the feast on the blameless lamb.[2]

III

How are we to understand the verse "Circumcise the children of Israel a second time"?[a]

This verse foreshadows the reality in a very important way. As you recall, the heralds of the Good News, offered the spiritual, to those who had already received the Mosaic, circumcision. They declared, "Believe, and let each of you be baptized in the name of our Lord Jesus Christ, and you will receive the promise of the Holy Spirit."[b] The holy apostle referred to this as "the circumcision not performed by hand."[c] Elsewhere he declared, "Circumcision of the heart is spiritual, not literal."[d] So those of the Jews who believed in the Savior, though already possessing the Mosaic circumcision, received as well the spiritual. The phrase "a second time," therefore, prefigures the reality, as it is impossible for the flesh to be circumcised twice.

In its superficial sense, the text literally signifies that, just as God, in the beginning, gave this law to Abraham, so, on a second occasion, he ordered Joshua to circumcise the uncircumcised. Pity the

2. Adopting a sacramental interpretation, Theodoret explains the crossing followed by the Passover as a type fulfilled ($\kappa\grave{\alpha}\nu$ $\tau\hat{\eta}$ $\dot{\alpha}\lambda\eta\theta\epsilon\acute{\iota}\alpha$) in the Easter liturgy, where baptism precedes communion.

ἀπεριτμήτους περιτεμεῖν. θρηνῆσαι δὲ ἄξιον ἰουδαίους
συνιδεῖν οὐ δυναμένους ὡς οἱ περιτετμημένοι μὲν ἀνῃρέθησαν
διαφόροις τιμωρίαις περιπεσόντες, οἱ δὲ ἀπερίτμητοι
20 διεσώθησαν· καὶ οἱ μὲν πατέρες διώλοντο, οἱ δὲ παῖδες τὴν
ἐπαγγελίαν ἐδέξαντο. οὕτω καὶ ἡμεῖς, παῖδες ὄντες, τὴν τῶν
οὐρανῶν προσδεχόμεθα βασιλείαν· ἰουδαῖοι δέ, τάξιν ἔχοντες
πατέρων, τῶν αἰωνίων ἐξέπεσον ἀγαθῶν καὶ τῆς τῶν
πατριαρχῶν ἐξεβλήθησαν συγγενείας.
25 Ἐχρῆν τοίνυν αὐτοὺς διὰ τούτων μαθεῖν ὡς οὐκ ἀεὶ τῆς
περιτομῆς ἀναγκαῖον τὸ χρῆμα. προμηνύσας γὰρ τῷ Ἀβραὰμ
τῆς παροικίας τὸν χρόνον, ὁ δεσπότης Θεὸς περιτμηθῆναι
προσέταξε, τῆς αἰγυπτίων δὲ δουλείας ἀπαλλαγέντας καὶ ἐν
ἐρήμῳ διάγοντας οὐκ ἀπήτησε τοῦδε τοῦ νόμου τὴν φυλακὴν
30 οὐδὲ τῆς παραβάσεως εἰσέπραξε δίκας, ἐπειδή, καθ' ἑαυτοὺς
ζῶντες καὶ τῆς τῶν ἀλλοφύλων ἐθνῶν ἐπιμιξίας ἀπηλλαγμένοι,
τοῦ σημείου τῆς περιτομῆς οὐκ ἐδέοντο. ὅτε δὲ λοιπὸν αὐτοὺς
εἰς τὴν ἐπηγγελμένην εἰσήγαγε γῆν, περιτμηθῆναι
προσέταξεν ἵνα μὴ ἡ ἐπιμιξία τῇ εὐσεβείᾳ λυμήνηται. εἰ γὰρ
35 καὶ συνέβαινε περιπεσεῖν ἀπάτῃ τινά, ῥάδιον ἦν τὸ σημεῖον
ἰδεῖν καὶ τὴν ἀγέλην καταλαβεῖν· τὰ γὰρ ἐσφραγισμένα
πρόβατα, κἂν ἀπόληται, ῥᾳδίως εὑρίσκεται.

IV

Διὰ τί μαχαίραις αὐτοὺς πετρίναις περιτμηθῆναι
προσέταξεν;[a]

Πάμπολυ πλῆθος ἦν τὸ περιτεμνόμενον, καὶ συντόμως ἔδει
περιτμηθῆναι καὶ ἐπιτελέσαι τοῦ Πάσχα τὴν ἑορτήν. εἰκὸς

---

l. 21 ἐπαγγελίαν 6, 12, 8 15, 7 37 : ἀπαγγελίαν Sir. Sch. F.M. = "the
children received the report." Cf. the critical note on Q. 1 on Nm.

IV A [32], B⁻¹⁷, C, 7 9 10 35 37 = 18 mss.

a. Jos 5.2

Question IV

Jews who can not understand that, while the circumcised encountered various punishments and were killed, the uncircumcised were saved; while the parents perished, the children received the promise! Likewise we, the children, receive the Kingdom of Heaven, whereas the Jews, in the role of the parents, have lost the eternal blessings and been excluded from kinship with the patriarchs.

Furthermore, they should have learned from this passage that the practice of circumcision was not always necessary. When the Lord God foretold to Abraham the period of their sojourn in Egypt, he ordered them to be circumcised. But, once they were freed from the captivity of Egypt and living in the wilderness, he did not require observance of this law or exact penalties for its transgression. Since they were living by themselves and exempt from intercourse with foreign nations, they had no need for the sign of circumcision. But, when he led them into the promised land, he ordered them to be circumcised to prevent the undermining of their religion through intercourse with the gentiles. Even if someone happened to be led astray, it was easy to see the sign and pull the flock together; sheep that have been branded, even if lost, are easily found.

IV

Why did he order them to be circumcised with flint knives?[a]

A vast number were to be circumcised and needed to be circumcised promptly to celebrate the feast of Passover. So it seems quite

5 οὖν ἦν τοὺς ἐν ἐρήμῳ τοσοῦτον διάγοντας χρόνον μὴ ἔχειν
πολλὰς ἐκ σιδήρου κατασκευασμένας μαχαίρας. ἄλλως τε καὶ
προτυποῦσιν αἱ πέτριναι μάχαιραι τὴν ἡμετέραν περιτομήν.
πέτρα γὰρ ὁ δεσπότης Χριστός· *ἔπινον γάρ, φησίν, ἐκ*
πνευματικῆς ἀκολουθούσης πέτρας· ἡ δὲ πέτρα ἦν ὁ Χριστός.[b]
10 ὁ δὲ αὐτὸς καὶ μάχαιρα κέκληται· *ζῶν . . ., γάρ φησιν, ὁ*
λόγος τοῦ Θεοῦ καὶ ἐνεργὴς καὶ τομώτερος ὑπὲρ πᾶσαν
μάχαιραν δίστομον.[c] ἡ δὲ σωτήριος αὐτοῦ διδασκαλία τὴν
πνευματικὴν ἡμῖν προσφέρει περιτομήν. ἡ μέντοι ἱστορία
ἐδίδαξεν ὅτι πολλοὶ καὶ τῶν ἐν Αἰγύπτῳ τεχθέντων τὴν
15 περιτομὴν οὐκ ἐδέξαντο, δεισάντων, ὡς εἰκός, τῶν ἐκείνους
γεγεννηκότων διὰ τὴν τῶν βρεφῶν ἀναίρεσιν προσενεγκεῖν
αὐτοῖς τὴν περιτομήν. ἅπαντες δέ, ὡς ἔπος εἰπεῖν, πλὴν
ὀλίγων, οἱ ἐν τῇ ἐρήμῳ φύντες ἀπερίτμητοι μεμενήκασι.

Γάλγαλα δὲ ὁ τόπος ὠνομάσθη, τοὔνομα δὲ τὴν ἐλευθερίαν
20 δηλοῖ. τότε ὁ τῶν ὅλων ἔφη Θεός, *ἐν τῇ σήμερον ἡμέρᾳ*
ἀφεῖλον τὸν ὀνειδισμὸν Αἰγύπτου ἀφ' ὑμῶν.[d] δηλοῖ δὲ ὁ λόγος
τὴν τῆς αἰγυπτιακῆς δουλείας καὶ δυσσεβείας ἀπαλλαγὴν καὶ
τῆς ἐπηγγελμένης γῆς τὴν ἀπόληψιν. καὶ ἡμεῖς δὲ
μανθάνομεν ὡς ὁ τοῦ παναγίου βαπτίσματος ἀξιούμενος καὶ
25 τὴν πνευματικὴν περιτομὴν δεχόμενος τὸ τῆς ἁμαρτίας
ὄνειδος ἀποτίθεται.

---

b. 1Cor 10.4   c. Heb 4.12   d. Jos 5.9

likely that, having lived for such a long time in the wilderness, they had few iron knives. More importantly, the knives of rock prefigure our circumcision, as Christ the Lord is a rock: "They drank from the spiritual rock that followed them, and the rock was Christ."[b] He is also called a knife: "The Word of God is living, active, and sharper than any two-edged knife."[1c] And it is his saving teaching that confers spiritual circumcision on us. Indeed, the narrative indicates that many, even of those born in Egypt, had not received circumcision; probably their parents had been afraid to circumcise them because of the slaughter of the infants. Broadly speaking, all but a few of those born in the desert remained uncircumcised.

Now, the place was called Gilgal, a name indicative of freedom. It was then that the God of the universe declared, "Today I have removed the disgrace of Egypt from you."[d] The term signifies their liberation from Egyptian slavery and idolatry and their reception of the promised land. As for us, we learn that whoever is accorded most holy baptism and receives the spiritual circumcision lays aside the disgrace of sin.[2]

1. The Greek word μάχαιρα, usually translated "sword" in Heb 4.12, may also mean "knife." Theodoret is less concerned with the literal sense of the word than with its figurative application to Christ.

2. Ignoring the toponym "Hill of Foreskins" given at 5.3, Theodoret focuses on the name "Gilgal." Unaware that "Gilgal," actually means "circle," he misses the implicit connection between the toponym and the process of circumcision. Instead, his etymology Gilgal = freedom, probably dependent on the popular derivation of the name from the Hebrew verb "to roll away" presented in 5.9, allows him to develop the typology connecting the circumcision that frees the adult Hebrews from the disgrace of idolatry with the baptism that effects the forgiveness of sins of adult Christians.

V

Τίνα νοητέον τὸν ἀρχιστράτηγον τῆς δυνάμεως Κυρίου;[a]

Τινές φασι τὸν Θεὸν λόγον ὀφθῆναι· ἐγὼ δὲ οἶμαι Μιχαὴλ
τὸν ἀρχάγγελον εἶναι. ἡνίκα γὰρ ἐπλημμέλησαν, ὁ τῶν ὅλων
ἔφη Θεός, οὐ ... μὴ συναναβῶ μετὰ σοῦ διὰ τὸ τὸν λαὸν
5 σκληροτράχηλον ... εἶναι[b] ἀλλ' ἀποστελῶ τὸν ἄγγελόν μου πρὸ
προσώπου σου πρότερόν σου.[c] τοῦτον οἶμαι νῦν ὀφθῆναι τῷ
Ἰησοῦ, παραθαρρύνοντα καὶ τὴν θείαν βοήθειαν
προσημαίνοντα.

VI

Πῶς τοίνυν τοῖς θείοις ἐχρήσατο ῥήμασι; λῦσον, γὰρ ἔφη,
τὸ ὑπόδημα ἐκ τῶν ποδῶν σου· ὁ γὰρ τόπος ἐφ' ᾧ ... ἕστηκας
ἅγιός ἐστιν.[a]
Ἐπειδὴ ἔφη πρὸς αὐτὸν ὁ τῶν ὅλων Θεός, ὡς ἐγενόμην
5 μετὰ Μωϋσῆ, ἔσομαι καὶ μετὰ σοῦ,[b] τούτου χάριν ὧν ἤκουσεν
ἐκεῖνος ἀκούει καὶ οὗτος ἵνα θαρσαλεώτερος γένηται, ὡς τῆς
αὐτῆς ἀξίας τετυχηκώς.

---

v A *[32]*, B⁻¹⁷, C, 7 9 10 31 35 37 = 19 mss.

a. Jos 5.14   b. Ex 33.3   c. Ex 33.2 (LXX var.)

---

vi A *[32]*, B⁻¹⁷, C, 7 9 10 31 35 37 = 19 mss.

a. Jos 5.15; Ex 3.5   b. Jos 1.5

V

How are we to identify "the commander-in-chief of the Lord's host"?[a]

Some commentators claim that it was God the Word who appeared, but I think it was Michael the archangel. As you remember, when they sinned, the God of the universe declared, "I shall not accompany you, because this is a stiff-necked people;[b] instead, I shall send my angel before you in advance of you."[1c] In my view, it was he who appeared to Joshua to encourage him and prophesy divine assistance.

VI

If that is the case, how is it that he employed God's own words: "Remove your sandals from your feet; the place on which you are standing is holy."[a]

Because the God of the universe had promised Joshua, "As I was with Moses, so I shall be with you."[b] Hence, he heard what Moses had also heard, so that, as the recipient of the same honor, he might gain in confidence.

---

1. Though Theodoret had not felt it necessary to refer to any of his predecessors throughout the commentary on Deuteronomy, he now cites an Alexandrian view. Both Origen (*hom.* 6.2 *in Ios.*) and Eusebius (*D. e.* 4.10.17; 7.1.5, 13; *H. e.* 1.2.3, 11; 10.4.15) had identified Joshua's visitant as the second Person of the Trinity; *v.* Guinot, p. 777.

The Questions on Joshua

VII

Διὰ τί τὴν Ἰεριχὼ πόλιν ἀναθεματισθῆναι προσέταξεν;[a]

Πρώτην ταύτην εἷλον πόλιν μετὰ τὸ διαβῆναι τὸν ποταμόν. ὥσπερ τοίνυν προσέταξεν αὐτοὺς τῶν καρπῶν προσφέρειν τὰς ἀπαρχάς,[b] οὕτως ἐκέλευσεν καὶ τὰ τῶν σκύλων προσενεγκεῖν
5 ἀκροθίνια.[c] πρὸς δὲ τούτοις καὶ γυμνάζει αὐτοὺς διὰ τούτων τῶν νόμων ὥστε τοὺς ἀναγκαίους νόμους διατηρεῖν. τὴν οἰκείαν δὲ αὐτοῖς ἐπιδεικνὺς δύναμιν, τὴν πρώτην πόλιν δίχα ὅπλων καὶ μηχανημάτων ἑλεῖν παρεσκεύασε καὶ μόνῃ κατέλυσε τῇ τῶν σαλπίγγων ἠχῇ ἵν', ὅταν ἡττηθῶσι
10 παραταττόμενοι, γνῶσιν ὡς αὐτοὶ παρέσχον τῆς ἥττης τὰς ἀφορμάς, τῶν θείων νόμων καταφρονήσαντες.

VIII

Τί δή ποτε, ἀλλόφυλος οὖσα, ἡ Ῥαὰβ κατῴκησεν ἐν τοῖς υἱοῖς Ἰσραὴλ ὡς ἡ ἱστορία διδάσκει;[a]

Καὶ τοῦτο προτυποῖ τὰ ἡμέτερα. ἔφη γὰρ ὁ δεσπότης· καὶ ἄλλα πρόβατα ἔχω, ἃ οὐκ ἔστιν ἐκ τῆς αὐλῆς ταύτης, κἀκεῖνά
5 με δεῖ ἀγαγεῖν, καὶ τῆς φωνῆς μου ἀκούσουσι, καὶ γενήσεται μία ποίμνη, εἰς ποιμήν.[b] τούτου χάριν καὶ νομοθετῶν, ἔφη, εἷς νόμος ἔσται ... τῷ προσηλύτῳ καὶ τῷ αὐτόχθονι.[c] διὰ τοῦτο οὐδὲ Μωϋσῆς ὁ νομοθέτης ἐκώλυσε τῶν αἰγυπτίων τοὺς

VII A [32], B⁻¹⁷, C, 7 9 10 31 35 37 = 19 mss.

a. Jos 6.17   b. V., e.g., Ex 23.19; 34.26.   c. Jos 6.17–19

VIII A [32], B⁻¹⁷, C, 7 9 10 31 35 37 = 19 mss.

a. Jos 6.25   b. Jn 10.16   c. Nm 9.14

VII

Why did he order the imposition of the ban on the city of Jericho?[a]

This was the first city they took after crossing the river. As he had ordered them to offer the first-fruits of their agricultural produce,[b] so he commanded them to offer the first of their spoils.[1c] Furthermore, with these instructions he trained them in the observation of the laws to which they were bound by covenant. In a demonstration of his own power, he arranged the capture of the first city without weapons or siege machinery and destroyed it with no more than the blast of trumpets, his purpose being that whenever they suffered defeat on the field of battle, they would know that they themselves, through their contempt of the divine laws, had provided occasion for the setback.

VIII

Why did Rahab, though a foreigner, live among the children of Israel, as the sacred history indicates?[a]

This also prefigures our present-day situation. As the Lord said, "I have other sheep as well that are not of this fold, and I must bring them in also; they will hear my voice, and there will be one flock and one shepherd."[b] Thus, even when he gave the Law, he declared, "There will be one law for the alien and for the native."[c] Hence, Moses the lawgiver put no obstacle in the way of those Egyptians

---

1. As M.D. Coogan points out (*ad loc.*), the LXX lacks the material in vv. 6.3b–4 of the MT, which employ verbs that may have a liturgical, as well as a military, application to describe the parading of the priests with the ark; *cf.* Ps. 48.12. Theodoret's recapitulation of the story does not permit us to decide if the Greek text used in Antioch here resembled more closely the MT or the form of the LXX attested by other early authors.

The Questions on Joshua

συναπᾶραι αὐτοῖς ἐθελήσαντας.[d] ἔδει δὲ καὶ ὡς ἀγριέλαιον
10 ἐγκεντρισθῆναι εἰς τὴν καλλιέλαιον, ἧ φησιν ὁ μακάριος
Παῦλος.[e]

IX

Τί ἐστιν ἐν τῷ πρωτοτόκῳ αὐτοῦ θεμελιώσει αὐτὴν καὶ ἐν
τῷ ἐλαχίστῳ... ἐπιστήσει τὰς πύλας αὐτῆς;[a]

Ἐπειδὴ τὴν πόλιν ἀνέθηκε τῷ Θεῷ, εἰκότως αὐτὴν
κατέσκαψεν, ἄτοπον ἡγησάμενος οἰκητήριον γενέσθαι κοινὸν
5 τὸ τῷ Θεῷ ἀπονεμηθέν. ἐπηράσατο δὲ τοῖς ταύτην
οἰκοδομοῦσιν ὥστε τὸν ἐπιχειροῦντα παραβῆναι τὸν ὅρον, τὰ
θεμέλια μὲν πηγνύντα, τῶν υἱέων ἀποβαλεῖν τὸν πρωτότοκον,
τὰς δὲ πύλας ἐπιτιθέντα, τὸν ἔσχατον. μέμνηται δὲ τῆς ἀρᾶς
καὶ ἡ τῶν Βασιλειῶν ἱστορία.[b]

X

Τί δή ποτε, τοῦ Ἄχαρ κεκλοφότος, ἅπας ὁ λαὸς
ἐπαιδεύθη;[a]

Ὑπέλαβεν ὁ κεκλοφώς, ὥσπερ τοὺς ἀνθρώπους, οὕτω δὴ
λήσειν καὶ τὸν Θεόν. ἠβουλήθη τοίνυν κἀκεῖνον διελέγξαι καὶ
5 πᾶσιν ἐνθεῖναι δέος ὅπως οἱ τοὺς θείους νόμους φυλάττοντες
||10 τοὺς παραβαίνοντας διελέγχωσιν, ὡς τῆς ἐπαχθησομένης||
μεθέξοντες τιμωρίας. τὴν δὲ ψιλὴν ὁ Ἀκύλας στολὴν
ἡρμήνευσεν, ὁ δὲ Ἰώσηπος χλανίδα· τὴν δὲ γλῶσσαν, μάζαν
χρυσῆν.[b] δῆλον δὲ καὶ ἐντεῦθεν ὡς ἡ ὑπὸ τῶν προφητῶν

---

d. Ex 12.38   e. Rom 11.17, 24

ιχ A [32], B⁻¹⁷, C, 7 9 10 31 35 37 = 19 mss.

a. Jos 6.26   b. 1Kgs 16.34

χ A [32], B⁻¹⁷, C, 7 9 10(inc.) 31 35 37 = 19 mss.

a. Jos 7.1–5   b. Jos 7.21

who wished to depart along with them.[d] Moreover, as St. Paul says, the wild olive had to be grafted onto the cultivated.[e]

IX

What is the meaning of "At the cost of his firstborn he will lay its foundations, and at the cost of his youngest he will set up its gates"?[a]

Since he had devoted the city to God, he was right to raze it, as he thought it wrong that what had been dedicated to God should become an ordinary place of habitation. He cursed any who should try to rebuild it, so that whoever dared transgress the law and lay the foundations would forfeit the firstborn of his sons, and whoever set up the gates his youngest. The narrative of Kings also mentions this curse.[b]

X

Why was the whole people chastised when it was just Achan who committed theft?[a]

The thief imagined he would escape God's notice as he had escaped that of men. So he wanted to censure Achan and to instill fear into everyone else, so that those who observed God's laws would censure those who broke them, to avoid sharing in the punishment that was bound to follow. Now, for "garment" Aquila put "robe" while Josephus used "mantle," and instead of "ingot," "lump of gold."[1b] Furthermore, this passage is explicit evidence that Achan

1. In this question and the next, Theodoret refers to a translator of the Hebrew Scriptures, Josephus, who is to be distinguished from the Jewish historian of the first century, whom Theodoret had cited in *Qq.* 24.1, 30, and 64 on Ex. N. Fernández Marcos (*Septuagint in Context*) suggests (pp. 169–72) that this Josephus must have been either contemporary with, or subsequent to, Jerome, since there are notable points of agreement between the Vulgate and fragments of Josephus' Greek translation.

10 καλουμένη *κοιλὰς Ἀχώρ* αὕτη ἐστὶν ἐν ᾗ ὁ Ἀχὰρ κατελεύσθη·[c]
καὶ γὰρ ἡ *Ἐμεκαχώρ, φάραγξ Ἀχώρ* ἑρμηνεύεται.

XI

Διὰ τί προσέταξεν ὁ Θεὸς προλοχῆσαι τὴν Γαΐ;[a]
Διδάσκει καὶ ταῖς ἀνθρωπίναις ἐπινοίαις κεχρῆσθαι,
πιστεύοντας δηλονότι τῇ θείᾳ ῥοπῇ. ἐπειδὴ γὰρ διὰ μόνης
τῆς τῶν σαλπίγγων ἠχῆς εἷλον τὴν πρώτην πόλιν,[b] μάλα
5 εἰκότως μανθάνουσιν ἀγωνίζεσθαι, καὶ πονεῖν, καὶ τὴν θείαν
προσμένειν ἐπικουρίαν. αὐτίκα γοῦν πολεμοῦσιν αὐτοῖς
ἐπεκούρησε καὶ τοὺς πεφευγότας σκηπτοῖς καὶ χαλάζῃ
κατηνάλωσεν ἅπαντας.[c] τὸ μέντοι *γαῖσον,*[d] ᾧ τοὺς λοχῶντας
διήγειρεν Ἰησοῦς, *ἀσπίδα* ἡρμήνευσεν ὁ Ἰώσηπος ὡσαύτως δὲ
10 καὶ ὁ Σύμμαχος.

XII

Τινὲς ὠμότητα τοῦ προφήτου κατηγοροῦσιν, ὅτι καὶ
πάντας ἄρδην ἀνῄρει καὶ τοὺς βασιλέας ἐσταύρου.[a]

c. Hos 2.15

---

xi A [32], B⁻¹⁷, C, 7 9 35 37 = 17 mss.

a. Jos 8.2   b. Jos 6.20   c. Cf. Jos 10.11.   d. Jos 8.18

---

xii A [32], B⁻¹⁷, C, 7 9 31 35 37 = 18 mss.

a. Jos 10.20f., 26f.

was stoned to death in what the prophets called the Valley of Achor:[c] "Emekachor" means "the ravine of Achor."[2]

XI

Why did God give orders for the ambush against Ai?[a]

His lesson is that while trusting in divine help they should also employ human initiative.[1] Since they had taken the first city with nothing more than trumpet blasts,[b] they learned, quite reasonably, to fight and make their own effort and then await divine assistance. Later, indeed, he did come to their aid in battle and, with a rain of thunderbolts and hail, slew all those who fled the field.[c] Now, Josephus, as also Symmachus, rendered the word for the "javelin"[d] with which Joshua roused the men in ambush as "shield."[2]

XII

There are those who accuse the prophet of cruelty for slaying everyone without exception and crucifying the kings.[a]

2. In his interpretation of "Emekachor," Theodoret wrongly derives the name of the valley from that of the culprit; Emekachor actually means "Valley of Trouble." Neither here nor in Q. 7 does he give the theological basis for the ban set out in Dt 7.1–6 and 20.15–18; cf. also Q. 59 on 1Kgs (= 3Kgs [LXX]).

1. Theodoret rightly observes that the capture of Ai differs markedly from that of Jericho; the latter was a miraculous event, which followed what was as much a religious ceremony as a siege, while the former was the result of military tactics. Oddly, he asserts that in the subsequent battle between Joshua and the five kings, God slew the fugitive Amorites with thunderbolts and hail, although there is no mention of thunderbolts in either the LXX or the MT of 10.11.

2. Theodoret perhaps displays an excess of Antiochene precision in his note on the various renderings of the Hebrew term denoting the implement raised by Joshua in 8.18. Modern lexicographers believe that this term refers, not to a javelin, but to a sicklesword; v. M.D. Coogan, ad loc.

Ὁ τοῦ προφήτου κατηγορῶν τοῦ ταῦτα προστεταχότος κατηγορεῖ. αὐτὸς γὰρ διὰ Μωϋσῆ τοῦ νομοθέτου προσέταξε

5 πάντας ἄρδην ἀναιρεθῆναι τοὺς τὴν γῆν ἐκείνην οἰκήσαντας, ἅτε δὴ πανωλεθρίας ἄξια πεπραχότας καὶ εἰς ἔσχατον παρανομίας ἐλάσαντας.ᵇ τούτου χάριν καὶ τὸν κατακλυσμὸν ἐπενήνοχε πάλαι καὶ τὰ Σόδομα καὶ τὰ Γόμορρα πυρὶ κατηνάλωσε.ᶜ

10 Καὶ τοῖς ἄρχουσι δὲ προσέταξεν ὁ προφήτης ἐπιθεῖναι τοὺς πόδας τοῖς τῶν βασιλέων τραχήλοις ἵνα θαρρήσαντες προθυμότερον παρατάξωνται.ᵈ τοῦτο καὶ ὁ Κύριος ἡμῶν προσέταξεν Ἰησοῦς· *ἰδού, γὰρ ἔφη, δέδωκα ὑμῖν . . . ἐξουσίαν . . . πατεῖν ἐπάνω ὄφεων, καὶ σκορπίων, καὶ*

15 *ἐπὶ πᾶσαν τὴν δύναμιν τοῦ ἐχθροῦ.*ᵉ εἴη τοίνυν καὶ ἡμᾶς ἐπιθεῖναι τοὺς πόδας ἡμῶν ἐπὶ τοὺς τραχήλους τῶν ἀντικειμένων πνευμάτων.

---

b. Dt 7.1–6; 20.15–18   c. Gn 19.24f.   d. Jos 10.24f.   e. Lk 10.19

Question XII

Whoever accuses the prophet accuses him who gave the order: It was he who, through Moses, the lawgiver, enjoined the slaying of every single inhabitant of that land for reaching the limit of lawlessness and committing crimes deserving of extermination.[1b] For this reason, in ancient times he brought on the flood and wiped out Sodom and Gomorrah with fire.[c]

The prophet also ordered the officers to place their feet on the necks of the kings so that they would grow in confidence and go into battle with greater enthusiasm.[d] And this is just what Jesus our Lord told us to do: "Lo, I have given you power to walk on snakes, and scorpions, and on all the might of the foe."[e] So, may we too put our feet on the necks of hostile spirits![2]

---

1. Though, in the preface to the *Quaest. in oct.,* Theodoret had promised to silence those who criticize the teaching of Scripture, he justifies Joshua's massacre of the Amorites and the execution of the five kings by a bare reference to the Lord's command. One cannot imagine that such an answer would have mollified those who accused Joshua and his Lord of cruelty. Theodoret and his peers, unappreciative of the concerns of the biblical authors, were not in a position to do justice to this crucial question of how Christian readers should view the morality sanctioned by the OT conquest narratives. Note that here Theodoret identifies Joshua as "prophet" (τοῦ προφήτου), a title probably meant rather to signify his divinely given knowledge and power than to imply his authorship of this book; *cf.* Q. 14, where Joshua the prophet (τοῦ προφήτου) is distinguished from the author (ὁ συγγραφεύς), and the first sentence of the introduction to the *Quaest. in Reg. et Par.,* where Joshua is called "the prophet" (τοῦ προφήτου) and Moses "the lawgiver" (τοῦ νομοθέτου).

2. After pursuing a literal reading of the narrative of ch. 10, Theodoret has recourse to a spiritual interpretation in which Israel's ancient defeat and massacre of enemy kings are taken to refer to the future defeat of evil powers by the apostles and the ordinary Christian. Guinot (p. 778) suggests that in this development Theodoret is dependent upon Or., *hom.* 8.7 *in Ios.*

XIII

Διὰ τί ξυλοκόπους καὶ ὑδροφόρους τοὺς γαβαωνίτας
ἀπέφηνεν;[a]

'Εξηπάτησαν καὶ τῷ σχήματι καὶ τῷ ψεύδει τῶν λόγων.[b]
καὶ δέον ἔρεσθαι τὸν δεσπότην Θεὸν εἶθ' οὕτως τὰς πρὸς
5 αὐτοὺς συνθήκας ποιήσασθαι, τοῖς ψευδέσι λόγοις αὐτῶν
πεπιστευκότες, ἐπείσαντο καὶ τὰς συνθήκας ἐκράτυναν ὅρκῳ.[c]
προσετετάχει δὲ ὁ τῶν ὅλων Θεὸς πάντας ἐκείνους
παραδοθῆναι θανάτῳ.[d] τῆς θείας τοίνυν ἐντολῆς καὶ τῶν ὅρκων
μέσος ἀποληφθείς, ὑπηρέτας αὐτοὺς τῆς ἱερᾶς λειτουργίας
10 ἀπέφηνεν. οὐκ ἀτιμία δὲ τὸ διακονεῖν τῷ Θεῷ, ἀλλὰ καὶ
μεγίστη τιμή.

῎Εδει δὲ καὶ τοῦ Νῶε τὴν πρόρρησιν πέρας λαβεῖν· ἔφη γάρ,
ἐπικατάρατος Χαναὰν παῖς· οἰκέτης ἔσται τοῖς ἀδελφοῖς
αὐτοῦ.[e] ἐν δὲ τοῖς γαβαωνίταις ἡ πρόρρησις τὸ πέρας
15 ἐδέξατο.

XIV

Τί ἐστι τὸ οὐχὶ αὐτὸ γέγραπται ἐπὶ βιβλίον τὸ εὑρεθέν;[a]

Διδάξας ἡμᾶς ὁ συγγραφεὺς τοῦ προφήτου τὴν δύναμιν,
ὅτι, λόγῳ μόνῳ χρησάμενος, προβῆναι τοὺς μεγάλους
φωστῆρας κεκώλυκεν ἕως κατὰ κράτος ἐνίκησεν,[b] ὑπειδόμενος

XIII A *[32]*, B⁻¹⁷, C, 7 9 31 35 37 = 18 mss.

a. Jos 9.21–27   b. Jos 9.3–13   c. Jos 9.14f.   d. Jos 9.24   e. Gn 9.25

XIV A *[32]*, B⁻¹⁷, C, 7 9 31 35 37 = 18 mss.

l. 1   τὸ εὑρεθέν Sir. Sch. F.M. : τοῦ ευθυς (i.e. a corrupt form of εὐθοῦς;
cf. Thdt., Q. 4 on 2Kgs (2Sm) and v. LSJ, sub uoce εὐθής) 5 = "'the book of the
upright'"

a. Jos 10.13 (LXX var.)   b. Jos 10.12f.

XIII

Why did he make the Gibeonites into hewers of wood and drawers of water?[a]

They had recourse to deception in both their appearance and their lying words.[b] The Israelites should have deferred making a treaty with them until they had consulted the Lord God, but they trusted the Gibeonites' lies and confirmed the treaty with an oath.[c] Now, the God of the universe had ordered that entire people to be consigned to death.[d] Thus, caught between God's command and his own oath, Joshua made them servants for the divine worship. In fact, the ministry of God is no dishonor, but a very great honor.

Furthermore, the prophecy of Noah had to take effect. Remember, he had declared, "Cursed be the son of Canaan; he shall be a servant to his brothers."[e] This prophecy received its fulfilment in the Gibeonites.[1]

XIV

What is the meaning of the verse "Is this not written in the book that was found"?[a]

After he had set out the mighty deed of the prophet, who with no more than a word prevented the great heavenly lights from advancing until he had won a complete victory,[b] the author, suspecting that

---

1 *V. Q.* 58 on Gn.

5 μή τις ἀπιστήσῃ τῷ λόγῳ, ἔφη τοῦτο ἐν τῷ παλαιῷ εὑρηκέναι
συγγράμματι. δῆλον τοίνυν κἀντεῦθεν ὡς ἄλλος τις τῶν
μεταγενεστέρων τὴν βίβλον ταύτην συνέγραψε, λαβὼν ἐξ
ἑτέρας βίβλου τὰς ἀφορμάς.

Καὶ τοῦτο δὲ προτυποῖ τὴν τοῦ σωτῆρος θαυματουργίαν.
10 ὥσπερ γὰρ τοῦ προφήτου πολεμοῦντος, ὁ ἥλιος ἔστη, οὕτω τοῦ
σωτῆρος ἡμῶν θανάτῳ τὸν θάνατον καταλύοντος, ἐπέσχε τὰς
ἀκτῖνας ὁ ἥλιος καὶ σκότους ἐν μεσημβρίᾳ τὴν οἰκουμένην
ἐπλήρωσε.[c]

XV

Πῶς νοητέον τὸ *παρὰ Κυρίου ἐγένετο κατισχῦσαι τὴν
καρδίαν αὐτῶν ὥστε συναντᾶν αὐτοὺς εἰς πόλεμον ἐπὶ Ἰσραὴλ
ἵνα ἐξολοθρευθῶσι καὶ ὅπως μὴ δοθῇ αὐτοῖς ἔλεος τοῦ
ἀφανισθῆναι αὐτούς... ὃν τρόπον εἶπε Κύριος πρὸς Μωϋσῆν;*[a]
5 Περὶ τῶν ἄλλων ἐθνῶν ἐνομοθέτησε τῷ Ἰσραὴλ ὁ Θεὸς
ὥστε, εἰ, πολιορκούντων αὐτῶν τὴν πόλιν, πρεσβεύσαιντο
ἐκεῖνοι καὶ φιλίαν ἀσπάσαιντο, δέξασθαι τὴν πρεσβείαν, καὶ
λῦσαι τὴν πολιορκίαν, καὶ σπείσασθαι τὴν εἰρήνην.[b] διδάσκει
τοίνυν ἡμᾶς ὁ λόγος ὡς, σταθμῷ καὶ μέτρῳ πάντα
10 πρυτανεύων, Θεὸς συνεχώρει τούτοις ἀντιπαρατάττεσθαι τῷ

---

c. Mt 27.45

xv A [32], B⁻¹⁷, C, 7 9 35 37 = 17 mss.

a. Jos 11.20 (LXX var.)   b. Dt 20.10f.

some people might not trust his account, declared that he had found this in an ancient text. From this we conclude that the author of the book of Joshua lived in a subsequent age and drew his source material from that other book.[1]

This event also prefigured the miracles of our Savior. Just as the sun stood still while the prophet was fighting his battle, so while our Savior was destroying Death with his own death, the sun withheld its rays and filled the whole world with darkness at noon.[2c]

XV

How are we to understand the verse "It was the Lord who emboldened their hearts to assemble for war on Israel so that they would be destroyed and receive no pity but be exterminated, as the Lord had commanded Moses"?[a]

Regarding the rest of the gentiles, God enjoined that, if Israel laid siege to a town, and its inhabitants entered into negotiations and agreed to an alliance, Israel was to accept the delegation, raise the siege, and make peace.[b] Now, this verse teaches us that God, who exercises a moderate restraint in his governance of the world, permitted these nations to take up arms against his people, so that, receiv-

---

1. In agreement with the MT but in contrast to all other forms of the LXX, Theodoret's text of Jos 10.13 contained a reference to an ancient source for the miraculous failure of the sun to set over Gibeon. The Hebrew refers to the book of "Jashar," or "the upright" both here and in 2Sm 1.18, and in the latter passage the LXX offers the entirely equivalent βιβλίου τοῦ εὐθοῦς. In Jos 10.13, Theodoret's version apparently contained the corrupt τὸ εὑρεθέν, "the book that was found," although one manuscript of the *Quaest.* does offer a form of the word "upright" found at 2Sm 1.18; *v.* the critical note. The LXX may contain a reference to this same work at 3Kgs 8.53, though there it is called "The Book of the Song" (βιβλίῳ τῆς ᾠδῆς). As Theodoret surmised, this must have been an ancient historical writing upon which the author of the book of Joshua drew; for a similar bit of source criticism, *cf.* his introduction to the *Quaest. in Reg. et Par.*

2. Theodoret dwells on this story, not to emphasize its sensational aspects, but to develop another typological connection between Joshua and Christ. Not inter-

The Questions on Joshua

λαῷ ἵνα μηδεμιᾶς ἀξιωθῶσι φειδοῦς ἀλλὰ κατὰ τὸν θεῖον ὅρον ἀναιρεθῶσιν.

XVI

Διὰ τί τοῖς μὲν Μωϋσῆς διανέμει τοὺς κλήρους τῆς γῆς,[a] τοῖς δὲ Ἰησοῦς;[b]

Καὶ τοῦτο πάλιν προτυποῖ τὴν ἀλήθειαν. τοῖς μὲν γὰρ ἐπέκεινα τοῦ Ἰορδάνου Μωϋσῆς διεῖλε τὴν γῆν, τοῖς δὲ μετὰ
5 τὸν Ἰορδάνην ὁ Ἰησοῦς. καὶ τῶν μὲν ἰουδαίων ἔχουσι τὸν τύπον οἱ διὰ Μωϋσέως εἰληφότες τοὺς κλήρους, οἱ δέ γε διὰ Ἰησοῦ τῶν πεπιστευκότων ἐθνῶν. καὶ ἐπειδὴ πρωτότοκος ὁ Ἰσραήλ, οἱ πρωτότοκοι διὰ Μωϋσέως τοὺς κλήρους ἐδέξαντο· Ῥουβήν,[c] καὶ Γάδ,[d] καὶ Μανασσῆς.[e] διαβαίνουσι μέντοι καὶ
|10 10 οὗτοι εὔζωνοι πρὸ τῶν ἄλλων·[f] οἱ γὰρ ἐξ ἰουδαίων πεπιστευκότες τοῖς ἔθνεσι τὴν σωτηρίαν προσήνεγκαν.

Ὑπελείφθησαν δὲ ὅμως καὶ ἰεβουσαῖοι,[g] καὶ χαναναῖοι,[h] καὶ ἔτερα ἔθνη τῶν ἀλλοφύλων καὶ συνῴκει τῷ Ἰσραήλ.[i] καὶ τούτου δὲ τοῦ τύπου τὴν ἀλήθειαν ἔστιν εὑρεῖν· οὐδὲ γὰρ ἄπαντες
15 τὸν σωτήριον ἐδέξαντο λόγον, ἀλλ' ἐπέμειναν ἀντιλέγοντες καὶ ἰουδαῖοι καὶ ἕλληνες, τὰς αὐτὰς ἡμῖν καὶ πόλεις καὶ
|17 κώμας οἰκοῦντες, οὓς οὐκ ἄν τις ἁμάρτοι, χαναναίους, καὶ χετταίους, καὶ ἰεβουσαίους ὀνομάζων. ταύτης δὲ ἄξιοι τῆς προσηγορίας καὶ οἱ τὰ μυσαρὰ τῶν αἱρέσεων θρησκεύοντες
20 δόγματα. διά τοι τοῦτο καὶ ὁ θεῖος ἀπόστολος ἔφη, νῦν δὲ οὔπω ὁρῶμεν αὐτῷ τὰ πάντα ὑποτεταγμένα·[j] καὶ πάλιν, δεῖ γὰρ αὐτὸν βασιλεύειν ἄχρις οὗ θῇ πάντας τοὺς ἐχθροὺς αὐτοῦ ὑπὸ τοὺς πόδας αὐτοῦ.[k]

---

xvi A [32], 14 17(inc.) 24, C, 7 9 10(inc.) 31 35 37 = 20 mss.

a. Nm 32.33   b. Jos 18.10–19.51   c. Gn 29.32   d. Gn 30.10f.
e. Gn 41.51   f. Jos 4.12   g. Jos 15.63   h. Jos 16.10; 17.12f.
i. Jos 19.47 (LXX)   j. Heb 2.8   k. 1Cor 15.25

ing no mercy, they would be destroyed according to the divine decree.

XVI

Why did Moses distribute their land allotments to some tribes,[a] and Joshua to others?[b]

This also prefigured the reality. Moses distributed land to those who dwelt on the far side, and Joshua to those who dwelt on the other side, of the Jordan. Those who received their allotments from Moses are a type of the Jews, and those who received theirs from Joshua a type of the gentiles who believed. Since Israel was the firstborn, Reuben,[c] Gad,[d] and Manasseh,[e] all firstborn, received their allotments from Moses. Nonetheless, they girt themselves and crossed before the others,[f] for it was the believers among the Jews who brought salvation to the gentiles.

The Jebusites,[g] Canaanites,[h] and some of the other foreign nations who were spared dwelled alongside Israel.[i] One can find the fulfilment of this type, too: not everyone accepted the saving word, but Jews and Greeks, living alongside us in the same cities and towns, persisted in their opposition. You would not be wrong to call them "Canaanites," "Hittites," and "Jebusites." Indeed, those devoted to foul heresies also deserve this name. Thus, the holy apostle said, "We do not yet see everything in subjection to him";[j] and again, "He must reign until he make all his enemies his footstool."[k]

---

ested in simply diverting his readers, he continues to pursue a significant theological point.

The Questions on Joshua

XVII

Τί δή ποτε τὴν Χεβρὼν ὁ Χαλὲβ ᾔτησεν;[a]

Εὐσεβείᾳ κοσμούμενος, πάντων προτέταχε τὴν πόλιν ἐν ᾗ παρῴκησαν οἱ παντάριστοι πατριάρχαι καὶ ταφῇ παρεδόθησαν.

Δηλοῖ δὲ ὁ τούτου λόγος ὡς, ἑπταετῆ πολεμήσαντες
5 χρόνον, τὴν γῆν διενείμαντο. ἔφη γὰρ οὕτως ὁ Χαλέβ· *τεσσαράκοντα ... ἐτῶν ἤμην ὅτε ἀπέστειλέ με Μωϋσῆς, ὁ παῖς Κυρίου, ... ἐκ Κάδης Βαρνῆ, κατασκοπεῦσαι τὴν γῆν,[b] ... καὶ νῦν διέθρεψέ με Κύριος ὃν τρόπον εἶπε. τοῦτο τεσσαρακοστὸν καὶ πέμπτον ἔτος ἀφ' οὗ ἐλάλησε*
10 *Κύριος ... πρὸς Μωϋσῆν.[c]* μετὰ δὲ τὴν κατὰ τῶν ἑξακοσίων χιλιάδων ἀπόφασιν τοῦ Θεοῦ,[d] τριάκοντα καὶ ὀκτὼ διετέλεσαν ἔτη ἐν τῇ ἐρήμῳ διάγοντες.[e] ἑπτὰ τοίνυν ἐστὶ τὰ λειπόμενα τοῖς πέντε καὶ ὀγδοήκοντα.[f] τοῦτο δὲ καὶ ὁ τῶν ὅλων δεσπότης διὰ τοῦ θειοτάτου προείρηκε Μωυσέως· *ἐὰν*
15 *εἰσαγάγῃ σε Κύριος ὁ Θεός σου εἰς τὴν γῆν[g] ἣν ἐπηγγείλατο τοῖς πατράσι σου,[h] μετὰ ἑπτὰ ἔτη ... ἀναγνώσῃ τὸν νόμον τοῦτον παντὶ τῷ λαῷ.[i]*

Ἐπισημήνασθαι δὲ προσήκει ὡς τὴν Ἰερουσαλὴμ Ἰεβοῦς ὀνομάζει[j] καὶ ταύτην λέγει τῷ Βενιαμὶν κληρωθῆναι.[k] ὁ δέ γε
20 Συμεὼν κατὰ τὴν τοῦ πατρὸς πρόρρησιν διεσπαρμένον ἔσχε τὸν κλῆρον·[l] *ἐγενήθη, γάρ φησιν, ἡ κληρονομία αὐτοῦ ἀνὰ μέσον κλήρου υἱῶν Ἰούδα.[m]* εἶτα τὰς πόλεις εἰπών,[n] ἐπήγαγεν, *αὕτη ἡ κληρονομία φυλῆς υἱῶν Συμεών ... ὅτι ἐγενήθη ἡ μερὶς τῆς κληρονομίας υἱῶν Ἰούδα μείζων ... αὐτῶν, καὶ*
25 *ἐκληρονόμησαν ... υἱοὶ Συμεὼν ἐν μέσῳ τοῦ κλήρου αὐτῶν.[o]*

XVII A [32], 14 17 24*, C, 7 9 10 31 35 37 = 20 mss.

a. Jos 14.12f.   b. Jos 14.7   c. Jos 14.10   d. Nm 1.45f.; 14.20–23
e. Dt 2.14   f. Jos 14.10   g. Dt 7.1   h. Dt 6.10   i. Dt 31.10f.
j. Jos 15.8   k. Jos 18.28   l. Gn 49.7   m. Jos 19.1   n. Jos 19.2–8
o. Jos 19.8f.

XVII

Why did Caleb ask for Hebron?[a]

Pious as he was, Caleb preferred to all others the city where those excellent men, the patriarchs, had sojourned, and in which they were interred.

Now, his words suggest that they distributed the land after seven years of fighting. As Caleb said, "I was forty years old when Moses, the servant of the Lord, sent me from Kadesh-barnea to spy out the land,[b] and now the Lord has kept me alive, as he promised. This is the forty-fifth year since the Lord spoke to Moses."[c] But after God delivered his sentence on the six hundred thousand,[d] they spent thirty-eight years in the desert.[e] Thus, we need seven to make up the total of eighty-five.[f] This was just what the Lord of the universe foretold through Moses, his inspired prophet: "Seven years after the Lord your God brings you into the land[g] promised to your ancestors,[h] you will recite this Law to all the people."[1i]

Furthermore, we should point out that Scripture here calls Jerusalem "Jebus,"[j] and says that it was assigned to Benjamin.[k] But Simeon, in keeping with his father's prophecy, received a scattered inheritance:[l] "His inheritance was within the lot of the children of Judah."[m] After enumerating his cities,[n] it adds, "This is the inheritance of the tribe of the children of Simeon; because the portion inherited by the children of Judah was too big for them, the children of Simeon had an inheritance in the middle of their lot."[o]

1. With typical Antiochene precision Theodoret uses Caleb's statement to compute the duration of the war of conquest. Comparing the forty-five years mentioned in Jos 14.10 with the thirty-eight years of wandering recalled by Moses in Dt 2.14, he arrives at the figure of seven years. For this he finds confirmation in the law of Dt 31.10, which actually provides for the septennial reading of the Law, but which the LXX misleadingly suggests was a one-time event occurring at the end of

XVIII

Τίνος ἕνεκα τοῖς ἄλλοις διανείμας τὴν γῆν, ὁ θειότατος
Ἰησοῦς οὐκ ἀπένειμεν ἑαυτῷ κλῆρον ἀλλὰ παρὰ τοῦ λαοῦ τὴν
Θαμνασαχὰρ ἐκομίσατο;[a]

Μιμεῖται κἂν τούτῳ τοῦ δεσπότου τὴν μετριότητα· *μάθετε,*
5 *γάρ φησιν, ἀπ' ἐμοῦ, ὅτι πρᾶός εἰμι καὶ ταπεινὸς τῇ καρδίᾳ,*
καὶ εὑρήσετε ἀνάπαυσιν ταῖς ψυχαῖς ὑμῶν.[b] καὶ τὴν ἐσχάτην
δὲ μετῆλθε πενίαν ὡς μηδὲ οἰκίας εὐπορῆσαι· *ὁ ... γὰρ υἱός,*
φησί, *τοῦ ἀνθρώπου οὐκ ἔχει ποῦ τὴν κεφαλὴν κλῖναι.*[c] ἐπειδὴ
τοίνυν τύπος ἦν αὐτοῦ, ὁ ὁμώνυμος Ἰησοῦς οὐκ ἀπένειμεν
10 ἑαυτῷ κλῆρον, τὸν δὲ προσενεχθέντα ἐδέξατο, διδάσκων τοὺς
ἀρχήν τινα πεπιστευμένους, μὴ τῆς οἰκείας θεραπείας, ἀλλὰ
τῆς τῶν ὑπηκόων ὠφελείας φροντίζειν.

XIX

Τί δή ποτε τοῖς ἱερεῦσιν ἐν τῇ Ἰούδα φυλῇ, καὶ τῇ
Βενιαμίν, καὶ τῇ Συμεὼν τὰς πόλεις ἀπένειμεν;[a]

(1) Κἂν τῇ ἐρήμῳ τὴν πορείαν ποιούμενοι, τῇ Ἰούδα φυλῇ
συνεζεύχθησαν· τὸ γὰρ ἑῷον ἔλαχον τμῆμα καὶ οἱ ἱερεῖς καὶ ἡ
5 Ἰούδα φυλή.[b] καὶ ἐνταῦθα πάλιν συνεκληρώθησαν τῇ Ἰούδα
φυλῇ, ἐπειδὴ καὶ ἐπιμιξία τούτων ἐγένετο τῶν φυλῶν. Ἀαρὼν
γάρ, ὁ πρῶτος ἀρχιερεύς, τὴν τοῦ Ἀμιναδὰβ ἠγάγετο
θυγατέρα,[c] καὶ Ἰωδαέ, ὁ πανεύφημος ἀρχιερεύς, τοῦ Ὀχοζίου
τὴν ἀδελφήν.[d] συνεχώρησε δὲ τὰς φυλὰς ταύτας ὁ δεσπότης
10 ἐπιμιγῆναι Θεός, ἐπειδὴ ἐκ τῆς Ἰούδα κατὰ σάρκα

---

xviii A *[32]*, B, C, 7 9 10 31 35 37 = 20 mss.

a. Jos 19.49f.; 21.42 (LXX)   b. Mt 11.29   c. Mt 8.20

---

xix A *[32]*, B, C, 7 9 10 35 37 = 19 mss.

a. Jos 21.4, 9–19   b. Nm 2.3   c. Ex 6.23; Nm 1.7   d. 2Chr 22.11

XVIII

Why is it that, after assigning land to others, Joshua, the inspired prophet, did not assign a lot to himself but accepted Timnath-serah from the people?[a]

In this as well he imitated the moderation of the Lord. As you recall, Christ declared, "Learn from me, for I am gentle and lowly of heart, and you will find rest for your souls."[b] In fact, he was so poor that he had no home of his own. As he said, "The Son of Man has nowhere to lay his head."[c] Now, as Joshua was a type of Christ as well as his namesake, he did not assign himself a lot but accepted what he was offered, his purpose being to teach those entrusted with public office to focus not on taking care of themselves but on doing what is best for those subject to them.[1]

XIX

Why did he assign the priests cities in the tribes of Judah, Benjamin, and Simeon?[a]

(1) Even while the people were traveling in the desert, the priests were linked to the tribe of Judah, for they had been allotted the eastern flank along with Judah.[b] At this time also they shared the lot of the tribe of Judah, as there was intermarriage between these tribes. Aaron, the first high priest, had married the daughter of Aminadab,[c] and Jehoiada, the renowned high priest, married the sister of Ahaziah.[d] The Lord God permitted the intermarriage of these tribes, since he who drew his bodily descent from Judah bore not only the title of

---

seven years (μετὰ ἑπτὰ ἔτη). Of course, Theodoret here overlooks the round figure of forty years for the wanderings prophesied in Nm 14.33.

---

1. Despite the parallels between Jesus and Moses developed in the fourth Gospel (*v.* P. Perkins on Jn 5.45–47; 6.1–71, 30f., 32f.; and D. Senior, "The Miracles of Jesus," p. 1373), Theodoret, because of the identity of name, focuses rather on Joshua as a type for Jesus.

βλαστήσας, οὐ βασιλεὺς μόνος, ἀλλὰ καὶ ἀρχιερεὺς
ἐχρημάτισεν. ἔδει δὲ αὐτοὺς καὶ ἐν τῇ Βενιαμίτιδι φυλῇ
κατοικεῖν, ἐπειδὴ καὶ ὁ θεῖος νεὼς ἐν τῇ ἐκείνων ἔμελλεν
οἰκοδομεῖσθαι φυλῇ. ἔλαβον δὲ καὶ ἐκ τῆς συμεωνίτιδος φυλῆς
15 ἐνίας πόλεις, ἐπειδὴ καὶ ὁ τούτων κλῆρος ἐπέλαζε τῷ νεῷ.
καθάπερ γὰρ τῶν ἀπὸ γῆς καρπῶν καὶ τῶν βοσκημάτων τὰς
δεκάτας τοῖς ἱερεῦσι καὶ τοῖς λευΐταις ἀπένειμεν,ᵉ οὕτω καὶ
τῶν πόλεων οἱονεὶ δεκάτας αὐτοῖς δοθῆναι προσέταξε. ταύτας
μέντοι δώσειν τῷ Θεῷ τὰς δεκάτας ὁ πατριάρχης Ἰακὼβ
20 ἐπηγγείλατο· πάντων, γὰρ ἔφη, ὧν ἐάν μοι δῷς, δεκάτην
ἀποδεκατώσω αὐτά σοι.ᶠ χρέος τοίνυν πατρῷον ἐξέτινεν ὁ
λαός, οὐ δῶρον προσέφερε· πρὸς δὲ τούτῳ κατεῖχεν αὐτῶν καὶ
τὸν κλῆρον τῆς γῆς.

(2) Παυσαμένου μέντοι τοῦ πολέμου, καὶ τῆς διαιρέσεως
25 γενομένης, ἀπελύθησαν μὲν οἱ πέραν τοῦ ποταμοῦ τοὺς
κλήρους εἰληφότες.ᵍ πρὶν δέ γε διαβῆναι τὸν ποταμόν, βωμὸν
ᾠκοδόμησαν μέγιστον.ʰ τὸν δὲ τῆς οἰκοδομίας ἠγνοηκότες
σκοπὸν οἱ τῶν ἐννέα φυλῶν, ἀσεβείας δὲ ἀρχὴν τὴν
οἰκοδομίαν τοπάσαντες, πανδημεὶ στρατεῦσαι κατ' αὐτῶν
30 ἠβουλήθησαν, τῆς συγγενείας προτιμήσαντες τὴν εὐσέβειαν.ⁱ
ἀλλ' οἱ πάνσοφοι Ἰησοῦς καὶ Ἐλεάζαρ τὸν Φινεὲς ἀπέστειλαν,
ὡς τῷ ζήλῳ κατὰ τῆς ἀσεβείας ἐν τῇ ἐρήμῳ χρησάμενον,ʲ
ὥστε καὶ τῶν προγόνων καὶ τῶν θεοσδότων ἀγαθῶν ἀναμνῆσαι
καὶ τὴν τολμηθεῖσαν παῦσαι παρανομίαν.ᵏ ἐπειδὴ δὲ
35 ἀπελθόντες ἔγνωσαν οὐ θρησκείας χάριν τολμηθεῖσαν τὴν
καινοτομίαν ἀλλὰ τῆς περὶ τὴν εὐσέβειαν κοινωνίας μνημεῖον
κληθῆναι τὸν γεγενημένον συνεῖδον βωμόν, ἵν' ἔχοιεν οἱ
ἀπόγονοι δεικνύναι τοῦτον εἰς ἔλεγχον τῶν ἀπείργειν αὐτοὺς
τῶν θείων πανηγύρεων πειρωμένων, ἀνέστρεψαν γεγηθότες καὶ

l. 21 ἐξέτινεν a [32], 5, 37, Sir. Sch. : ἐξέτισεν F.M. : ἐξήτησεν a₂, 8 = "the
people . . . demanded an ancestral debt." In favor of the past imperfect ἐξέτινεν,
cf. the subsequent προσέφερε.

e. Nm 18.21–32   f. Gn 28.22   g. Jos 22.1–6   h. Jos 22.10   i. Jos 22.11f.
j. Nm 25.6–8   k. Jos 22.13–20

"king" but also that of "high priest."[1] They had to dwell in the tribe of Benjamin as well, since the holy Temple was destined to be built in the territory of that tribe. And they had some cities in the tribe of Simeon, since the Simeonites' lot bordered on the Temple. As he had allotted the priests and the Levites tithes of the crops of the earth and the cattle,[e] so he ordered that they be given what we might term "tithes of the cities." Indeed, the patriarch Jacob had promised to give these tithes to God: "Of all you give me I shall give a tithe of one tenth to you."[f] So, in fact, the people were not giving anything away but repaying an ancestral debt. Furthermore, the people retained the possession of the land that was allotted to the priests.

(2) Once the fighting was over, and the land had been distributed, those who had received lots on the far side of the river were permitted to leave.[g] But before crossing the river, they built a huge altar.[h] The men of the other nine tribes, ignorant of the purpose of this structure and suspecting that it signalled a beginning of idolatry, put religion before kinship and formed a plan to attack them with all their armed might.[i] Then, Joshua and Eleazar, wise as they were, commissioned Phinehas, who had demonstrated zeal against idolatry in the wilderness,[j] to remind them of their forbears and all the gifts they had received from God and to desist from this attempted trespass.[k] But the envoys ascertained that this novel gesture had nothing to do with superstitious cult and found out that the altar had been built as a reminder of the tribes' participation in the common worship so that their descendants might be able to point to it to confound anyone who tried to exclude them from participation in God's festivals. So they returned rejoicing and singing the

---

1. *Cf.* note 1 to *Q.* 51 on Nm.

40 τὸν Θεὸν ἀνυμνοῦντες ἐπὶ τῇ τῶν ἀδελφῶν εὐσεβείᾳ καὶ τῇ
κοινῇ πάντων εἰρήνῃ.¹ τοῦτο ἐχρῆν καὶ τοὺς νῦν ἰουδαίους
εἰδέναι τε καὶ λέγειν, ὡς ὁ βωμὸς αὐτῶν, οὐ τὸ ἀληθινὸν ἦν
θυσιαστήριον, ἀλλὰ τὸ ἀληθινὸν προετύπου.

(3) Μέλλων μέντοι τὸν βίον ὁ προφήτης ὑπεξιέναι,
45 συνεκάλεσε ἄπαντας καὶ τὰ εἰκότα παρήνεσεν αὐτοῖς ὥστε
μηδεμίαν πρὸς ἐγχωρίους ἐπιγαμίαν ποιήσασθαι,ᵐ ὡς τῆς
τοιαύτης ἐπιμιξίας τὰς τῆς ἀσεβείας παρεχούσης προφάσεις.
προστέθεικε δὲ καὶ τῇ παραινέσει ἀπειλάς· ἐάν, γάρ φησι,
τοῦτο ποιήσητε, *γινώσκετε ὅτι οὐ μὴ προσθῇ*
50 *Κύριος . . . ἐξολοθρεῦσαι τὰ ἔθνη ταῦτα ἀπὸ προσώπου ὑμῶν,*
καὶ ἔσται ὑμῖν εἰς παγίδας καὶ εἰς σκάνδαλα . . . ἐν ταῖς
πλευραῖς ὑμῶν καὶ σκῶλα ἐν τοῖς ὀφθαλμοῖς ὑμῶν ἕως ἂν
ἀπόλησθε ἐκ τῆς γῆς τῆς ἀγαθῆς ταύτης, ἣν ἔδωκεν ὑμῖν
*Κύριος ὁ Θεὸς ὑμῶν.*ⁿ ταῦτα δὲ σαφέστερον ἡμᾶς ἐδίδαξεν ἡ
55 τῶν Κριτῶν ἱστορία. ἔγνωμεν δὲ καὶ τὴν αἰτίαν δι' ἣν κατὰ
τὴν θείαν ἐπαγγελίαν οὐχ ἁπάσης τῆς γῆς τὴν δεσποτείαν
παρέλαβον· ἀσπασάμενοι γὰρ τῶν δυσσεβῶν ἐθνῶν τὴν
συγγένειαν καὶ μιμησάμενοι τὴν ἀσέβειαν, τῆς θείας
ἐγυμνώθησαν προμηθείας καὶ δουλεύειν αὐτοῖς ἠναγκάζοντο.

60 Θαυμαστὸς δὲ αὐτοῦ καὶ φιλόσοφος καὶ ὁ περὶ τοῦ θανάτου
λόγος· *ἐγώ, γὰρ ἔφη, ἀποτρέχω τὴν ὁδὸν καθὰ καὶ πάντες οἱ*
ἐπὶ τῆς γῆς. δείκνυσι δὲ αὐτοῖς καὶ τὸ τῆς θείας προρρήσεως
ἀψευδές· *καὶ γνώσεσθε ἐν τῇ καρδίᾳ ὑμῶν καὶ ἐν τῇ ψυχῇ*
ὑμῶν διότι οὐ διέπεσε λόγος εἷς ἀπὸ πάντων τῶν λόγων τῶν
65 *καλῶν, ὧν εἶπε Κύριος ὁ Θεὸς ἡμῶν πρὸς ἡμᾶς· πάντα ἃ*
*εἴρηκεν ἡμῖν δέδωκεν ἡμῖν· οὐδὲν διαπεφώνηκεν ἐξ αὐτῶν.*ᵒ τὸ
ἀληθές, φησί, τῶν θείων ἐπαγγελιῶν ἐκ τῶν εὐεργεσιῶν
μεμαθήκατε· πεπλήρωκε ἅπερ ὑπέσχετο. τοιγαροῦν ἐντεῦθεν
μάθετε καὶ τὸ τῶν ἀπειλῶν ἀψευδές· τοῦτο γὰρ ἐπήγαγεν· καὶ
70 *ἔσται ὃν τρόπον ἦλθεν ἐφ' ὑμᾶς πάντα τὰ ῥήματα τὰ καλά,*
ὅσα ἐλάλησε . . . πρὸς ὑμᾶς, οὕτως ἐπάξει Κύριος ἐφ' ὑμᾶς

l. Jos 22.24–33   m. Jos 23.2   n. Jos 23.13   o. Jos 23.14

praises of God for the piety of their brethren and the concord of the whole nation.[l] Thus, present-day Jews should know and admit that their altar was not the true one but only a prefiguration of it.

(3) When he was about to leave this life, the prophet summoned the whole people and exhorted them not to contract marriage with the indigenous peoples,[m] since such intermarriage would provide the occasion for idolatry. And he reinforced his exhortation with threats: "If you do this, be aware that the Lord will no more eliminate these nations from your path; they will be snares for you, goads in your sides, and pointed stakes in your eyes, until you perish from this good land, which the Lord your God has given you."[n] Of this the Book of Judges has given us a more detailed account. We also know why they did not gain possession of all the land in keeping with the divine promise. Since they entered into kinship with the pagan nations and imitated their idolatry, they were deprived of God's care and forced to serve the gentiles.

What an admirable and virtuous statement he made concerning his own death! "I am departing by the same path as everyone on earth." And he set before them the reliability of the divine prophecy: "You will know in your heart and in your soul that not a word has failed of all the promises of blessing that the Lord our God made to us. He has given us everything he has spoken to us; not one thing has failed to occur."[o] He meant "you have learned the truth of the divine promises from his favors; he has fulfilled all he promised. So, learn from this as well the reliability of his threats." Indeed, he went on to say, "Just as all the promises of blessing that the Lord made to you came to pass for you, so he will inflict on you all his threats of woe until he eliminate you from this good land, which the Lord has

πάντα τὰ ῥήματα τὰ πονηρὰ ἕως ἂν ἐξολοθρεύσῃ ὑμᾶς ἀπὸ
τῆς γῆς τῆς ἀγαθῆς ταύτης, ἧς ἔδωκεν ὑμῖν Κύριος, ἐν τῷ
παραβῆναι ὑμᾶς τὴν διαθήκην Κυρίου τοῦ Θεοῦ ὑμῶν, ἣν
75 ἐνετείλατο ἡμῖν.ᵖ διδάσκων δὲ ὡς οὐκ ἀνθρώπινα ταῦτα τὰ
ῥήματα, ἐπήγαγεν ὅτι, τάδε λέγει Κύριος ὁ Θεὸς Ἰσραήλ.�q

(4) Καὶ ἀναμιμνήσκει Θάρρα τοῦ πατρὸς Ἀβραὰμ καὶ
Ναχώρ·ʳ τέθεικε δὲ τὸν Ναχὼρ διὰ τὸ μητρῷον γένος· ἐξ
ἐκείνου γὰρ ἡ Ῥεβέκκα,ˢ καὶ ἡ Λεία, καὶ ἡ Ῥαχήλ.ᵗ εἶτα
80 διδάσκει ὡς ὁ Θάρρα θεοῖς ἑτέροις ἐλάτρευσε καὶ ὡς, τούτου
χάριν ὁ δεσπότης Θεὸς χωρίσας τὸν Ἀβραάμ, εἰς τὴν γῆν
ἐκείνην μετέστησεν. προστέθεικε δὲ καὶ τὴν εἰς Αἴγυπτον
τοῦ Ἰακὼβ εἴσοδον, καὶ τὴν διὰ Μωϋσέως γεγενημένην
ἔξοδον, καὶ τῆς θαλάττης τὸ θαῦμα, καὶ τὴν ἐν τῇ ἐρήμῳ
85 διαγωγήν, καὶ τὴν τῶν ἀμορραίων πανωλεθρίαν, καὶ τὰς τοῦ
Βαλὰκ ἐπινοίας, καὶ τὰς παρὰ γνώμην τοῦ Βαλαὰμ εὐλογίας,
καὶ τοῦ ποταμοῦ τὴν ξένην διάβασιν, καὶ τὴν τῶν
ἐπαναστάντων πολεμίων ἀναίρεσιν, καὶ τῶν παντοδαπῶν
ἀγαθῶν ἀπόλαυσιν. καὶ παραινεῖ τῆς μὲν τῶν ἀλλοτρίων θεῶν
90 ἀπαλλαγῆναι δουλείας, μόνῳ δὲ λατρεύειν τῷ πεποιηκότι καὶ
σεσωκότι Θεῷ.ᵘ προστέθεικε δὲ αὐτοῖς καὶ αἵρεσιν· ἐκλέξασθε,
γάρ φησιν, ὑμῖν αὐτοῖς σήμερον τίνι λατρεύσητε· εἴτε τοῖς
θεοῖς τῶν πατέρων ὑμῶν, τοῖς ἐν τῷ πέραν τοῦ ποταμοῦ, εἴτε
τοῖς θεοῖς τῶν ἀμορραίων, ἐν οἷς ὑμεῖς κατοικεῖτε ἐν τῇ γῇ
95 αὐτῶν. οὕτω τοῖς ἄλλοις προστεθεικὼς τὴν αἵρεσιν, αὐτὸς τὸ
τῆς οἰκείας γνώμης ἐπέδειξεν εὐσεβές· ἔφη γάρ, ἐγὼ δὲ καὶ ἡ
οἰκία μου λατρεύσομεν Κυρίῳ, ὅτι ἅγιός ἐστιν.ᵛ εἶτα τοῦ λαοῦ
τῶν μὲν ψευδωνύμων ἀπαγορεύσαντος τὴν λατρείαν,
ὑποσχομένου δὲ μόνῳ δουλεύειν τῷ σεσωκότι Θεῷ,ʷ ὑπολαβὼν
100 ὁ θειότατος Ἰησοῦς ἔφη πρὸς αὐτούς, οὐ μὴ δυνήσεσθε
λατρεύειν Κυρίῳ, ὅτι Θεὸς ἅγιός ἐστι καί, ζηλώσας ὑμᾶς, οὐκ
ἀνήσει ὑμῶν τὰ ἀνομήματα καὶ τὰ ἁμαρτήματα ὑμῶν ἡνίκα ἂν
ἐγκαταλίπητε Κύριον καὶ λατρεύσητε θεοῖς ἑτέροις, καὶ

p. Jos 23.15f.   q. Jos 24.2   r. Jos 24.2   s. Gn 24.24   t. Gn 29.16
u. Jos 24.2–14   v. Jos 24.15   w. Jos 24.16–18

given you, if you transgress the covenant of the Lord your God, which he has laid upon you."[p] Then, to convey the fact that these were not just human promises, he added, "so says the Lord God of Israel."[q]

(4) Then he reminded them of Terah, the father of Abraham and Nahor[r] (He cited Nahor on account of the maternal line, that of Rebekah,[s] Leah, and Rachel),[t] recounting how Terah served other gods, and how, for this reason, the Lord God set Abraham apart and transferred him to that land. He proceeded to mention Jacob's entrance into Egypt, the exodus under Moses' leadership, the miracle of the sea, their life in the wilderness, the destruction of the Amorites, Balak's schemes, Balaam's involuntary blessings, the marvelous crossing of the Jordan, the slaughter of the enemies who rose against them, and their enjoyment of manifold blessings. He urged them to eschew slavery to foreign gods and to serve only the God who had created and saved them.[u] Then he offered them a choice: "Choose for yourselves today whom you will serve, either the gods of your fathers beyond the river or the gods of the Amorites, in whose land you are dwelling." Having offered this choice to the rest, he expressed his own belief in right religion: "My household and I will serve the Lord, because he is holy."[v] Then, though the people renounced the worship of the false gods and promised to serve only the God who had saved them,[w] Joshua, inspired prophet that he was, said in reply, "You will not be able to serve the Lord, because he is a holy God, and, in his jealousy for you, he will not put up with your transgressions and your sins when you forsake the Lord and

ἐπελθὼν κακώσει ὑμᾶς, καὶ ἐξαναλώσει ὑμᾶς, ἀνθ' ὧν εὖ
105 ἐποίησεν ὑμῖν.ˣ μὴ προσδοκήσητε, φησίν, καὶ παρανομοῦντες,
τῶν αὐτῶν ἀγαθῶν ἀπολαύσεσθαι· οἶδε γάρ, οὐ μόνον
εὐεργετεῖν, ἀλλὰ καὶ κολάζειν τοὺς παραβαίνοντας ὁ
δεσπότης Θεός. ἐκείνων δὲ καὶ ταύτην δεξαμένων τὴν
πρότασιν καὶ ὑποσχομένων τῷ Κυρίῳ δουλεύειν, ἀναγκαίως
110 ἐπήγαγε, μάρτυρες ὑμεῖς καθ' ὑμῶν ὅτι ὑμεῖς ἐξελέξασθε
Κύριον λατρεύειν αὐτῷ.ʸ ἐδίδαξε δὲ καὶ ταῦτα ἡ ἱστορία, ὡς,
παραινέσας αὐτοῖς τῆς τῶν ἀλλοτρίων θεῶν ἀπαλλαγῆναι
λατρείας καὶ τὰ περὶ τῆς εὐσεβείας νομοθετήσας, οὐκ ἄγραφα
ταῦτα κατέλιπεν, ἀλλ' ἀνάγραπτον αὐτῶν τὴν μνήμην
115 ἐφύλαξεν.ᶻ

XX

Τί δή ποτε, τὸν λίθον στήσας, εἴρηκεν, ὁ λίθος οὗτος ἔσται
ὑμῖν εἰς μαρτύριον, ὅτι οὗτος ἀκήκοε πάντα τὰ
λεχθέντα . . . παρὰ Κυρίου, ἃ ἐλάλησε πρὸς ὑμᾶς σήμερον;ᵃ
Ἄψυχος μὲν ὁ λίθος, εἰς ἔλεγχον δὲ τῶν ἐμψύχων καὶ
5 λογικῶν διὰ τῶν ἀψύχων μαρτύρεται. ἐχρήσατο δὲ καὶ τῷ ἔθει
τῷ παλαιῷ· καὶ γὰρ ὁ Ἰακὼβ καὶ ὁ Λάβαν, ποιησάμενοι τὰς

---

ll. 105f. μὴ προσδοκήσητε . . . ἀπολαύσεσθαι *J.P.* : μὴ προσδοκήσητε
. . . ὅτι . . . ἀπολαύσεσθε 6, C⁻¹⁵, 37, *Sir. Sch.* : μὴ προσδοκήσητε . . .
ἀπολαύσεσθε *F.M.* Thdt. uses a form of προσδοκῶ + another verb forty-two
times; in all of these it is followed by an infinitive, never by ὅτι + the
indicative. Cf. *ep.* 83 (διὰ μόνην δὲ πίστιν ἐν τῇ τῆς θείας ἐπιφανείας
ἡμέρᾳ φειδοῦς τινος ἀπολαύσεσθαι προσδοκῶ). Nonetheless, the
combination of προσδοκῶ + ὅτι + the indicative is used by Chrys. in *hom.* 8.2
in Coloss. (μὴ προσδοκήσητε, φησίν, ὅτι τὸ αὐτὸ πείσεται). The form of
expression printed by F.M. is a syntactical solecism unlikely in an author so
careful as Thdt.

x. Jos 24.19f.   y. Jos 24.22   z. Jos 24.26

---

xx A [32], B, C, 7 9 10 31 35 37 = 20 mss.

a. Jos 24.27

serve other gods. He will visit you, afflict you, and consume you because of the blessings he has bestowed on you."[x] In other words, "Do
not expect that, when you sin, you will enjoy the same blessings; the
Lord God knows not only how to confer favors but also how to punish transgressors." Once they had accepted that proposition and
promised to serve the Lord, he proceeded to draw the consequence:
"You are witnesses against yourselves that you have chosen the Lord
to serve him."[y] The sacred history also states that, after urging them
to eschew the service of foreign gods and giving laws regarding religion, he did not leave this unrecorded but preserved a written
record.[zz]

xx

Why did he set up the stone and say, "This stone will be as a witness amongst you, because it has heard everything said by the Lord
that he spoke to you today"?[a]

The stone was inanimate, but he used the witness of the inanimate to censure the animate and the rational. In this he was
following an ancient custom. As you recall, when Jacob and Laban

2. In this summary of chapters 21–24 Theodoret sidesteps the question of authorship by use of the periphrasis ἡ ἱστορία (*i.e.,* "the biblical narrative" or "sacred history"); *cf.* the same use of this word in the pf. to the *Qq.* on Jos and in *Qq.*
2.3, 4, 7, 9, and 20.

συνθήκας, τὸν βουνὸν ἐκάλεσαν μάρτυρα τῶν συνθηκῶν.[b]

Ὅσον μέντοι ὀνίνησιν ἄρχων εὐσεβὴς καὶ φιλόθεος ἡ
ἱστορία διδάσκει· ἐλάτρευσε, γάρ φησιν, Ἰσραὴλ τῷ Κυρίῳ
10 πάσας τὰς ἡμέρας Ἰησοῦ καὶ πάσας τὰς ἡμέρας τῶν
πρεσβυτέρων ὅσοι ἐφείλκυσαν τὸν χρόνον μετὰ Ἰησοῦν, καὶ
ὅσοι εἶδον πάντα τὰ ἔργα Κυρίου, ὅσα ἐποίησε μετὰ τοῦ
Ἰσραήλ.[c] μετὰ δὲ τὴν τούτων τελευτήν, ἀπέκλιναν εἰς
ἀσέβειαν· τοῦτο γὰρ καὶ τῆς ἱστορίας τὸ τέλος ἐδίδαξεν. ἀλλ'
15 ἔδοσαν δίκας τῆς ἀσεβείας· τῆς γὰρ θείας γυμνωθέντες
κηδεμονίας, ὑπεβλήθησαν τῷ τῆς δουλείας ζυγῷ καὶ δεσπότην
ἔσχον τὸν τῶν μωαβιτῶν βασιλέα. ἀλλ' ὁ φιλάνθρωπος Κύριος,
τῆς πρὸς τοὺς πατέρας μεμνημένος ἐπαγγελίας,
ὀκτωκαιδεκαετεῖ χρόνῳ περιώρισε τὴν δουλείαν.[d]

l. 11 μετὰ Ἰησοῦν C; cf. Jgs 2.7 (cod. A) : μετὰ Ἰησοῦ 9 37, Sir. Sch.; cf.
Jgs 2.7 (cod. B) : om. F.M. = "and all the days of the elders who drew out their
life"

b. Gn 31.46–48   c. Jos 24.31   d. Jos 24.33 (LXX); Jgs 3.12, 14

had concluded a pact, they called the hill a "witness" of their pact.[b]

Furthermore, the sacred history explains how beneficial a pious and God-loving ruler is: "Israel served the Lord all the days of Joshua and all the days of the elders who drew out their life after Joshua and had seen all the works of the Lord, which he had done with Israel."[c] After the death of those men, they turned aside to idolatry, as the end of this book reports. But they paid the penalty for their idolatry, for, deprived of God's care, they were subjected to the yoke of slavery, with the king of Moab as their master. Yet, the loving Lord, mindful of his promise to their ancestors, limited their subjection to a period of eighteen years. [1d]

1. There is another significant textual divergence between the MT and the LXX at the conclusion of the book of Joshua; while the former ends with the notice of the death and burial of Eleazar, the LXX adds several lines regarding the subsequent idolatry, punishment, and deliverance of Israel; *cf.* note 1 to *Q.* 7. It is notable that, throughout his commentary of this book, Theodoret has shown himself to be a theologian, rather than an annalist. Passing over some sections, such as the lists of kings defeated and allotments distributed, he has devoted extensive discussion to the covenant ceremony at Shechem.

QUAESTIONES IN IUDICES

Iᵃ

Διὰ τί Κριταὶ τὸ βιβλίον ὠνόμασται;

Ὥσπερ τῶν Βασιλειῶν ἡ βίβλος πολλὰ μὲν ἔχει καὶ διάφορα
διηγήματα, ὠνομάσθη δὲ Βασιλεῖαι, ἐπειδὴ τὰ τῷ λαῷ
συμβεβηκότα κατὰ τὸν τῶν βασιλέων καιρὸν ἱστορεῖ, οὕτω καὶ
5 τὸ προκείμενον βιβλίον προσηγορεύθη Κριτῶν, ἐπειδὴ τὰ κατὰ
τὸν τῆς δημαγωγίας καιρὸν γεγενημένα διδάσκει. τὴν μέντοι
τῆσδε τῆς ἱστορίας ἀρχὴν ἀνακεφαλαίωσιν οἶμαι εἶναι τῶν
ὑπὸ Ἰησοῦ τοῦ Ναυῆ κατωρθωμένων· μέμνηται γὰρ καὶ τοῦ
Ἀδωνιβεζὲκ καὶ τοῦ κατ' αὐτὸν πολέμου, καὶ τῆς ἥττης αὐτοῦ,
10 καὶ τῆς ἀναιρέσεως.ᵇ μέμνηται δὲ καὶ τῆς Χεβρών, ὡς
ἀπονεμηθείσης τῷ Χαλέβ, καὶ τῆς τῶν τριῶν γιγάντων
ἀναιρέσεως, τοῦ Ἐσσί, καὶ τοῦ Ἀχιμάν, καὶ τοῦ Θολόμ, οὓς
τοῦ Ἐνὰκ ἀπογόνους ὠνόμασεν. εἰκὸς δὲ τότε μὲν
προρρηθῆναι τὴν τούτων ἀναίρεσιν, ὕστερον δὲ λαβεῖν τὴν
15 πρόρρησιν τέλος.ᶜ

---

1 A⁻¹¹ [32*], B, C, 7 9 10 31 35 37 = 18 mss.

a. V. sec. 3 of the. "Introduction to Theodoret's Life and Works," esp. n. 20.

b. Jgs 1.4–7   c. Jos 15.13f.; Jgs 1.10, 20

ON JUDGES

Why is the book called "Judges"?

As the book of Kings contains many different narratives and yet is called "Kings," because it treats the history of the people at the time of the kings, so the present book is called "Judges," because it recounts what happened at the time of popular government. But, in my view, the beginning of this narrative is a summary of the achievements of Joshua, son of Nun. Indeed, it mentions Adoni-bezek and the war against him, his defeat, and death.[b] It mentions Hebron as an allotment to Caleb and the slaying of the three giants Sheshai, Ahiman, and Talmai, who are called descendants of Anak. Most likely, their death was foretold at that time, and the prophecy fulfilled at a later.[c]

II

1   Εἰ κάτ' ἐκεῖνον τὸν καιρὸν ἀνάστατος Ἰερουσαλὴμ
ἐγεγόνει,[a] πῶς ὕστερον αὐτὴν βασιλεύων ὁ Δαβὶδ εἷλε
πολιορκίᾳ;[b]

    Πολλὰς ἔσχε μεταβολὰς ὁ λαὸς ὡς ἡ τῶν Κριτῶν ἱστορία
5   διδάσκει· ποτὲ μὲν γὰρ ἐνίκων, ποτὲ δὲ ἡττῶντο καὶ ποτὲ μὲν
ἦρχον τῶν ἀλλοφύλων, ποτὲ δὲ ἐδούλευον. δῆλον τοίνυν ὡς
ἐμπρησθεῖσαν τὴν Ἰερουσαλὴμ πάλιν ἀνῳκοδόμησαν οἱ
ἰεβουσαῖοι, τῆς τοῦ λαοῦ δυσκληρίας ἐπιλαβόμενοι.[c]

    Καὶ ταύτην δὲ ὕστερον οἶμαι συγγραφῆναι τὴν βίβλον,
10   τεκμηρίῳ χρώμενος τῷ τήνδε τὴν πόλιν Ἰερουσαλὴμ ὀνομάζειν
τὴν ἱστορίαν· ὕστερον γὰρ ταύτην ἔσχε τὴν προσηγορίαν,
Ἰεβοῦς ὠνομασμένη.[d]

III

    Τί ἐστι *δός μοι . . . λύτρωσιν ὕδατος, καὶ λύτρωσιν*
μετεώρων, καὶ λύτρωσιν ταπεινῶν;[a]

    Οἱ περὶ τὸν Σύμμαχον *ἀρδείαν ὕδατος* καί, ἀντὶ τοῦ
ταπεινῶν, πεδινῶν, ἡρμήνευσαν. ὑπεβλήθη δὲ παρὰ τοῦ
5   Γοθονιήλ, τοῦ ἀνδρὸς αὐτῆς, Ἀσχὰ αἰτῆσαι ἀγρόν.[b] ᾔτησε
τοίνυν ἀρδείαν ὕδατος καὶ ἔλαβεν ὥσπερ ᾔτησεν, οὐ μόνον
πεδιάδα γῆν, ἀλλὰ καὶ ὄρειον· τὸ μὲν γὰρ *κατὰ τὴν καρδίαν*
αὐτῆς τὸ καταθύμιον σημαίνει. *μετέωρα* δὲ τὰ ὄρεια κέκληκε,
ταπεινὰ δὲ τὰ ὕπτια.

II A⁻¹¹ [32], B, C, 7 9 10 35 37 = 18 mss.

a. Jgs 1.8   b. 2Sm 5.6–9   c. Jos 15.63   d. Jos 15.8

III A⁻¹¹ [32], B, C, 7 9 10 35 37 = 18 mss.

l. 5 Ἀσχὰ J.P.; cf. Jgs 1.15 (codd. A B) : Ἀσχὰν F.M. : ἡ Ἀσχὰν 5, C⁻⁵¹, 37,
Sir. Sch.

a. Jgs 1.15 (LXX B)   b. Jgs 1.14

Question III

II

If Jerusalem was overthrown at that time,[a] how could David have besieged and captured it during his reign?[b]

As the book of Judges recounts, the people experienced many changes of fortune: at one time victorious, at another defeated, at one time ruling the gentiles, at another enslaved to them. So the Jebusites clearly took advantage of the people's misfortune and rebuilt Jerusalem after it had been burned.[c]

Now, I believe the composition of this book is to be dated to a later period. In support, I note that the narrative refers to this city as Jerusalem; previously named Jebus, it was only later that it received this name.[1d]

III

What is the meaning of "Give me a redemption of water," and "a redemption of higher parts, and a redemption of lower parts"?[a]

Symmachus and his followers rendered "redemption of water" as "irrigation of water," and "lower parts" as "plains." When her husband Othniel prompted her to ask for territory,[b] Achsah requested an irrigation of water. And in accordance with her request, she received both plain and hill country. Indeed, the phrase "after her heart" indicates that this was just what she desired. The text refers to the hill country as "the higher parts," and to the plain as the "lower."[1]

1. Here, as in Q. 14 on Jos, Theodoret engages in source criticism. Perceiving that the notice regarding the capture and burning of Jerusalem in Jgs 1.8 explicitly conflicts with the account of David's capture of Jebus in 2Sm 5.6–9 (v. also Jos 15.63), he is coming to see that Judges is a multi-layered text, to whose composition a later author must have contributed; cf. also his remarks on the structure of the book in Q. 27.2.

1. Dealing with Jgs 1.15, a verse that in his text makes nonsense, Theodoret shrewdly consults an alternative version; he lacks, however, sufficient linguistic ex-

IV

Πῶς ἐνταῦθα τοῦ νομοθέτου τὸν κηδεστὴν Ἰωβὰβ ὠνόμασεν,[a]
Ἰοθὼρ[b] καὶ Ῥαγουὴλ[c] ἐν ἐκείναις ταῖς ἱστορίαις ὠνομασμένον;
Καὶ ἤδη ἔφην ὡς ὁ Ἰωβὰβ ἐκείνου ἦν υἱός. πενθερὸν δὲ
αὐτὸν κέκληκεν ὡς τῆς γαμετῆς ἀδελφόν· καὶ γὰρ νῦν πολλοὶ
5 τοὺς τοιούτους *πενθερίδας* καλοῦσι. τοῦ Ἰωβὰβ τοίνυν οἱ
παῖδες ἔγγονοι τοῦ Ἰοθώρ εἰσιν.

V

||11

Πόλιν φοινίκων ποίαν καλεῖ;[a]||

Τὴν Ἱεριχώ. νομίζω δὲ οὕτως αὐτὴν προσαγορεύεσθαι διὰ
τὸν τῶν φοινίκων καρπόν· καὶ γὰρ ἐν τῇ πρὸ ταύτης βίβλῳ,
εὐθὺς τοῦ λαοῦ διαβάντος τὸν Ἰορδάνην, ὁ συγγραφεὺς ἔφη,
5 ὅτι *ἔφαγον ἀπὸ τοῦ καρποῦ τῆς γῆς ἄζυμα, καὶ ὅτι ἐν αὐτῇ
τῇ ἡμέρᾳ ἐξέλιπε τὸ μάννα μετὰ τὸ βεβρωκέναι αὐτοὺς ἀπὸ
τοῦ σίτου τῆς γῆς, καὶ οὐκ ἔτι ὑπῆρχε τοῖς υἱοῖς Ἰσραὴλ
μάννα·* ἐκαρπώσαντο γὰρ τὴν γῆν τῶν φοινίκων ἐν τῷ ἐνιαυτῷ
ἐκείνῳ.[b] καὶ ἡ δευτέρα δὲ τῶν Παραλειπομένων περὶ ὧν
10 ἠχμαλώτευσαν ἐκ τῆς Ἰούδα φυλῆς αἱ δέκα φυλαὶ διηγουμένη,

---

iv A[−11] [32], B, C, 7 9 10 35 37 = 18 mss.

a. Jgs 1.16   b. Ex 3.1; 4.18   c. Nm 10.29

---

v a, 5, 11(inc.) 12 [32], B, C, 7 9 10 31 35 37 = 20 mss.

a. Jgs 1.16   b. Jos 5.11f.

Question v

IV

Why is the lawgiver's father-in-law called Hobab in this passage,[a] but Jethro[b] and Reuel in the earlier narratives?[c]

I have already remarked that Hobab was Reuel's son. Nonetheless, he is called πενθερὸν (pentheron), an "in-law," since he was the brother of Moses' wife. Even today, many people call these relatives πενθερίδες (pentherides), or "brothers-in-law." So Hobab's children were Jethro's grandchildren.[1]

V

Which city is called "The City of Palms"?[a]

Jericho. My view is that it was so named because of the fruit of its palm trees. In the previous book, the author said that, as soon as the people crossed the Jordan, they ate unleavened bread from the crops of the land and that "the manna ceased on that day after they had eaten some of the grain of the land. There was no more manna for the children of Israel, as they harvested the land of the palms that year."[b] And in the second book of Chronicles, in the passage regard-

---

pertise to realize that the LXX has confused the two similar Hebrew terms for "redemption" and "irrigated land."

1. Throughout this book, Theodoret's text of the LXX agrees with the recension of the *codex alexandrinus* (*A*: early fifth century), against the *vaticanus* (*B*: fourth century). In this passage, both Theodoret's Antiochene text and *codex A* read the name Ιωβαβ (Hobab) while *codex B* reads Ιοθορ (Jethro). On the relationships between each of the recensions witnessed by *A*, *B*, and Theodoret to the original form of the LXX, *v.* sec. 3 of the "Introduction to Theodoret's Life and Works" and N. Fernández Marcos, *The Septuagint in Context*, p. 94. Both Greek terms κηδεστής and πενθερός can signify "brother-in-law" as well as "father-in-law." Theodoret has already dealt with this complicated issue in Q. 16 on Nm (10.29), where, instead of the Jethro of Ex, Reuel appears as Moses' father-in-law. Neither there nor here does he engage in the source criticism that would point to more than one author.

οὕτως ἔφη· καὶ κατέστησαν αὐτοὺς εἰς Ἱεριχώ, τὴν πόλιν τῶν φοινίκων, πρὸς τοὺς ἀδελφοὺς αὐτῶν.ᶜ

VI

Πῶς νοητέον καὶ ἦν Κύριος μετὰ Ἰούδα, καὶ ἐκληρονόμησε τὸ ὄρος, ὅτι οὐκ ἐδύνατο κληρονομῆσαι τοὺς κατοικοῦντας τὴν κοιλάδα, ὅτι Ῥηχὰβ διεστείλατο αὐτοῖς;ᵃ

Τοῦ Ῥηχάβ, ὡς εὐσεβοῦς ἄγαν, πολλαχοῦ ἡ θεία μνημονεύει
5 γραφὴ καὶ ὅτι μέχρι τῶν ἀπογόνων αὐτοῦ διέδραμεν ἡ εὐσέβεια.ᵇ τοῦτον εἰσηγήσασθαι λέγει τῇ Ἰούδα φυλῇ τὴν κοιλάδα καταλιπεῖν καὶ τὸ ὄρος οἰκῆσαι. ἦν δὲ καὶ αὐτὸς τῆς Ἰούδα φυλῆς ὡς ἡ τῶν Παραλιπομένων διδάσκει βίβλος.ᶜ

Οἶμαι δὲ αὐτὸν συμβεβουλευκέναι τὴν κοιλάδα φυγεῖν διὰ
||14 10 τὴν τῶν πεⲒⲒριοίκων ἀσέβειαν καὶ μέντοι καὶ διὰ τὸ τῆς θαλάττης γειτόνημα. οἱ γὰρ θαλάττῃ πελάζοντες καὶ τοὺς πόρρωθεν καταπλέοντας δέχονται, καὶ αὐτοὶ ναυτιλίας ὀρέγονται. ἡ δὲ τῶν ἀλλογενῶν ἐπιμιξία τὴν νομικὴν ἐλυμαίνετο πολιτείαν.

---

c. 2Chr 28.15

---

vɪ A⁻¹¹ [32], 14(inc.) 17 24, C, 7 9 10 31 35 37 = 19 mss.

a. Jgs 1.19 (LXX)   b. V., e.g., Jer 35; 2Kgs 10.15, 23.   c. 1Chr 2.55

ing the captives taken from the tribe of Judah by the ten tribes, we read "They brought them to their brethren at Jericho, the city of palms."[1c]

VI

How are we to understand "And the Lord was with Judah, and he took possession of the hill country, because he could not supplant the inhabitants of the valley, as Rechab instructed them"?[a]

Holy Scripture often mentions the exemplary piety of Rechab and that his piety passed to his descendants.[b] It relates that he proposed to the tribe of Judah that they leave the valley and occupy the mountains. He was a member of the tribe of Judah, as the book of Chronicles mentions.[1c]

Now, it is my belief that he advised them to shun the valley not only because of the idolatry of the neighboring peoples but principally because of its closeness to the sea. Those who dwell near the sea receive voyagers from afar and take an interest in sailing themselves, and association with foreigners undermines life according to the Law.

---

1. Theodoret's careful comparison of parallel places is only partly successful. Like Jgs 1.16, 2Chr 18.15 does indeed identify Jericho as the city of palm trees (Πόλιν φοινίκων). Yet the noun φοῖνιξ may mean "Phoenician" as well as "palm," as it probably does in Jos 5.12 (τὴν γῆν τῶν φοινίκων). Though Theodoret quotes the latter to throw light on our passage in Jgs, the Hebrew there speaks of "the land of Canaan."

---

1. The LXX of Jgs 1.19, confusing two Hebrew words spelled with the same three consonants, mistranslates the common noun for "chariot" as the personal name "Rechab." Thus the *NRSV* offers: "Judah . . . took possession of the hill country, but could not drive out the inhabitants of the plain, because they had chariots of iron." Despite what might seem an odd occurrence of the name in this context, Theodoret follows the reading of the LXX without even consulting an alternative version; *cf.* the ardent endorsement of the Rechabites in the commentary on Jer (ch. 35) attributed to Theodoret.

The Questions on Judges

VII

Τί δή ποτε, μὴ πάσας εἷλον τὰς πόλεις, ἀλλὰ πλῆθος αὐτοῖς συνῴκει τῶν ἀλλοφύλων ἐθνῶν;

(1) Πρῶτον διὰ νωθείαν πάσης τῆς γῆς οὐκ ἐκράτησαν, ἔπειτα καὶ διὰ πλεονεξίαν· ἔθεντο, γάρ φησι, τὸν χαναναῖον
5 εἰς φόρον καὶ ἐξαίρων οὐκ ἐξῆρεν αὐτόν,[a] καὶ τοῦτο περὶ ἑκάστης ὁ συγγραφεὺς εἶπε φυλῆς. πρὸς δὲ τούτοις, τὸν θεῖον παραβάντες νόμον καὶ τοῖς τῶν ἀλλοφύλων δεδουλευκότες θεοῖς, τῆς θείας ἐγυμνώθησαν προμηθείας. οὗ δὴ χάριν ὁ πάνσοφος Κύριος, οὐκ ἄρδην τὸ τῶν χαναναίων ἐθνῶν
10 διέφθειρε γένος, ἀλλ' εἴασε πολλοὺς γειτονεύειν αὐτοῖς ἵνα, πολεμούμενοι καὶ δουλεύειν ἀναγκαζόμενοι, αἰσθάνωνται μὲν τῆς ἀπὸ τῆς πλάνης γεγενημένης βλάβης, προστεθῶσι δὲ τῷ σεσωκότι Θεῷ καὶ τῆς παρ' αὐτοῦ ῥοπῆς ἀπολαύσωσι.

Καὶ ὅτι ταῦτα, οὐ λογισμοῖς ἀνθρωπίνοις κεχρημένος, λέγω
15 ἀλλὰ παρ' αὐτῆς διδαχθεὶς τῆς ἱστορίας αὐτίκα δηλώσω· ἀνέβη, γάρ φησιν, ἄγγελος Κυρίου ἀπὸ Γαλγὰλ ἐπὶ τὸν Κλαυθμῶνα, καὶ ἐπὶ Βαιθήλ, καὶ ἐπὶ τὸν οἶκον Ἰσραὴλ ἀπὸ Γαλγάλων.[b] Γάλγαλα δὲ ὁ τῶν ἀκροβυστιῶν ὠνομάσθη τόπος,[c] δηλοῖ δὲ τοὔνομα κατὰ τὴν ἑβραίων φωνὴν τὴν ἐλευθερίαν.
20 ἐκεῖθεν πέμπει τὸν ἄγγελον, ἀναμιμνήσκων αὐτοὺς τῆς τε τοῦ ποταμοῦ διαβάσεως καὶ τῆς γεγενημένης περιτομῆς. εἶτα λέγει καὶ τίνα τὰ ῥηθέντα ὑπὸ τοῦ ἀγγέλου· |Κύριος ἀνήγαγεν ὑμᾶς ἐξ Αἰγύπτου, καὶ εἰσήγαγεν ὑμᾶς εἰς τὴν γῆν ἣν ὤμοσε τοῖς πατράσιν ὑμῶν ... δοῦναι ὑμῖν, καὶ εἶπεν ὑμῖν, οὐ μὴ
25 διασκεδάσω τὴν διαθήκην μου, τὴν μεθ' ὑμῶν εἰς τὸν αἰῶνα, καὶ ὑμεῖς οὐ διαθήσεσθε διαθήκην τοῖς ἐγκαθημένοις ἐν τῇ γῇ ταύτῃ, οὐδὲ τοῖς θεοῖς αὐτῶν οὐ μὴ προσκυνήσετε, ἀλλὰ τὰ γλυπτὰ αὐτῶν συντρίψετε, καὶ τὰ θυσιαστήρια αὐτῶν

|11

VII a [32], 5, 11(inc.) 12, 14(inc.) 17 24, C, 7 9 10 31 35 37 = 20 mss.

a. Jgs 1.28   b. Jgs 2.1   c. Jos 5.3

VII

Why did they fail to take all the cities, and why did they allow a multitude of gentiles to live among them?

(1) They failed to take control of the whole land for several reasons. First, their laziness. Second, their greed: "They reduced the Canaanites to tributaries and did not utterly wipe them out,"[a] a statement the author makes regarding each tribe. Third, when they broke the divine Law and enthralled themselves to foreign gods, they were deprived of God's care. Thus, the Lord, in his great wisdom, did not completely destroy the Canaanite nations but allowed many of them to live close by, so that when the people were attacked and forced into slavery, they would appreciate the harm caused by their infidelity, have recourse to God their Savior, and benefit from his intervention.

This is the proof that my argument is not based on human reasoning but informed by the sacred history: "An angel of the Lord went up from Gilgal to Weeping, and to Bethel, and to the house of Israel from Gilgal."[b] Now, Gilgal was the name given to the place of the foreskins;[c] in Hebrew the name indicates freedom.[1] He sent the angel from there to remind them of the crossing of the river and the act of circumcision. Next we are told what the angel said: "The Lord brought you out of Egypt and led you into the land, which he swore to your fathers he would give you, and he said to you, 'I shall not annul my eternal covenant with you. And you are not to make a covenant with the inhabitants of this land or worship their gods. Instead, smash their statues and overthrow their altars.' You did not heed his voice when you did these things. And he declared, 'I shall not continue to dislodge the people I promised to drive out before your face; they will afflict you, and their gods will be a stumbling

---

1. In Jgs 2.1, the LXX rightly renders the Hebrew "Bochim" as τὸν κλαυθμῶνα or "place of mourning." As we have pointed out, however, Theodoret's explanation of the name "Gilgal" is mistaken; v. note 2 to Q. 4 on Jos.

κατασκάψετε· καὶ οὐκ εἰσηκούσατε τῆς φωνῆς αὐτοῦ ὅτε
30 ταῦτα ἐποιήσατε. καὶ ἐγώ, φησίν, οὐ προσθήσω τοῦ μετοικίσαι
τὸν λαὸν ὃν εἶπον, τοῦ ἐξῶσαι αὐτὸν ἀπὸ προσώπου ὑμῶν, καὶ
ἔσονται ὑμῖν εἰς συνοχάς, καὶ οἱ θεοὶ αὐτῶν ἔσονται ὑμῖν εἰς
σκάνδαλον.ᵈ παρέβητέ μου, φησί, τὸν νόμον, οὐκ ἐφυλάξατε
τὰς ἐντολάς μου· εἰρήνην ἐσπείσασθε πρὸς τοὺς τῆς
35 ἀσεβείας διδασκάλους καὶ τοῖς τούτων θεοῖς ἐδουλεύσατε.
ἀπολαύετε τοιγαροῦν ὧν ἐποθήσατε καὶ ἀμήσατε τῶν
σπερμάτων ὑμῶν τὰ δράγματα· οἵ τε γὰρ διαφυγόντες τὸν ἐκ
πολέμου θάνατον πολεμοῦντες ὑμῖν διατελέσουσι, καὶ οἱ
τούτων θεοὶ τὰς ὑμετέρας ἐξανδραποδιοῦσι ψυχάς. τούτων
40 ὑπὸ τοῦ ἀγγέλου ῥηθέντων, ἐθρήνησεν ὁ λαός, ὅθεν καὶ ὁ
τόπος ὠνομάσθη Κλαυθμῶν.

(2) Ἐντεῦθεν ὑπέλαβον τὰ πλείονα τῶν εἰρημένων
ἀνακεφαλαίωσιν εἶναι τῶν ἐπὶ τοῦ Ἰησοῦ πεπραγμένων· ἔφη
γὰρ ὁ συγγραφεύς, καὶ ἐξαπέστειλεν Ἰησοῦς τὸν λαόν, καὶ
45 ἀπῆλθον οἱ υἱοὶ Ἰσραήλ, ἕκαστος εἰς τὸν τόπον αὐτοῦ, καὶ
ἕκαστος εἰς τὴν κληρονομίαν αὐτοῦ... κατακληρονομῆσαι τὴν
γῆν. καὶ ἐδούλευσεν ὁ λαὸς τῷ Κυρίῳ πάσας τὰς ἡμέρας Ἰησοῦ
καὶ πάσας τὰς ἡμέρας τῶν πρεσβυτέρων, ὅσοι
ἐμακροημέρευσαν μετὰ Ἰησοῦν, ὅσοι ἔγνωσαν πᾶν τὸ ἔργον
50 Κυρίου τὸ μέγα ὃ ἐποίησε τῷ Ἰσραήλ.ᵉ λέγει δὲ καὶ ὅσων ἐτῶν
ἐτελεύτησε καὶ ἔνθα ἐτάφηᶠ καὶ προστέθεικεν ὅτι, ἀνέστη
γενεὰ ἑτέρα μετ' αὐτοὺς καὶ οὐκ ἔγνωσαν... Κύριον καὶ τὸ
ἔργον ὃ ἐποίησε τῷ Ἰσραὴλᵍ καὶ ὅτι, τοῖς χαναναίοις, καὶ
τοῖς φερεζαίοις, καὶ τοῖς ἄλλοις συνοικοῦντες ἀλλοφύλοις,
55 τάς τε πρὸς αὐτοὺς ἐπιγαμίας ἐποιήσαντο καὶ διὰ τῆς
ἐπιγαμίας τῆς ἀσεβείας μετέλαχον· ἐλάτρευσαν γὰρ τοῖς
Βααλεὶμ καὶ τοῖς Ἀσταρώθ.ʰ

Διδασκόμεθα δὲ διὰ τούτων ὅσον τοὺς ὑπηκόους ὀνίνησιν ἡ
τῶν ἀρχόντων εὐσέβεια, καὶ ὅσον ἡ ἀναρχία λυμαίνεται, καὶ
60 αὖ πάλιν ἡ τῶν πονηρῶν ἡγεμονία. τοῦτο γὰρ καὶ ἥδε ἡ

d. Jgs 2.1–3   e. Jgs 2.6f.   f. Jgs 2.8f.   g. Jgs 2.10   h. Jgs 2.11–13

block to you."[d] This is tantamount to saying, "You broke my Law and did not keep my commandments; you made peace with the teachers of idolatry and served their gods. So enjoy what you longed for, and reap what you have sown. Whoever escapes death in battle will go on making war against you, and their gods will enslave your souls." When the angel had said this, the people lamented—hence, the place was named Weeping.

(2) From this I deduce that most of the angel's speech is a summary of events that occurred during the time of Joshua's leadership. Indeed, the historian remarks, "Joshua dismissed the people, and the children of Israel went off, each to his place and each to his inheritance, to take possession of the land. The people served the Lord all the days of Joshua and all the days of the elders, who outlived Joshua and knew all the great work of the Lord that he had done for Israel."[e] He also mentions how old Joshua was when he died and where he was buried.[f] Then he added that, "after that generation, there arose another that did not know the Lord and the work he had done for Israel,"[g] and these intermarried with the Canaanites, the Perizzites, and the other gentiles, among whom they were living, and, as a result of the intermarriage, participated in their idolatry and worshiped their Baals and Astartes.[h]

We can learn from this the great benefit conferred on their subjects by the piety of the rulers and the great harm caused by anarchy and government by the wicked. Indeed, this is the lesson of the sub-

ἱστορία διδάσκει· ἤγειρε γὰρ αὐτοῖς, φησί, *Κύριος κριτὰς καὶ*
ἔσωσεν αὐτοὺς ἐκ χειρὸς τῶν προνομευσάντων αὐτούς.[i] *καὶ*
ὅτε ἤγειρεν αὐτοῖς . . . τοὺς κριτάς, καὶ ἦν Κύριος μετὰ τοῦ
κριτοῦ καὶ ἔσωζεν αὐτοὺς ἐκ χειρὸς τῶν ἐχθρῶν αὐτῶν πάσας
65 *τὰς ἡμέρας τοῦ κριτοῦ·*[j] καὶ μετ' ὀλίγα, *καὶ ἐγένετο ὡς*
ἀπέθνησκεν ὁ κριτής, καὶ ἀπέστρεφον καὶ διέφθειρον πάλιν
ὑπὲρ τοὺς πατέρας αὐτῶν τοῦ πορευθῆναι ὀπίσω θεῶν ἑτέρων,
|14 *τοῦ λατρεύειν αὐτοῖς καὶ προσκυ*|*νεῖν αὐτοῖς.*[k]

Οἶμαι δὲ καὶ ἑτέραν αἰτίαν εἶναι δι' ἣν οὐ πᾶσαν τὴν
70 ἐπηγγελμένην ἐκομίσαντο γῆν. ἔστι δὲ αὕτη· στενωτάτης
ἐδεῖτο γῆς τῆς νομικῆς πολιτείας ἡ φυλακή· τρὶς γὰρ τοῦ
ἔτους ἑορτάζειν ὁ νόμος ἐκέλευσεν εἰς ἓν ἅπαντας χωρίον
συντρέχοντας, ἐν ᾧ τὸν θεῖον νεὼν ἐδομήσαντο. ἐκεῖ καὶ τὰς
ἀπαρχάς, καὶ τὰς δεκάτας, καὶ τὰ τῶν θρεμμάτων πρωτότοκα,
75 καὶ μέντοι καὶ τὰς ἄλλας θυσίας κομίζειν ἐκέλευσεν.[l] εἰκότως
τοίνυν αὐτοὺς σμικρῷ περιώρισε τόπῳ ὥστε ῥαδίως καὶ τοὺς
νωθεῖς εἰς τὸν ἀφιερωμένον νεὼν συναγείρεσθαι.

VIII

Πῶς νοητέον τόδε τὸ χωρίον· *ταῦτα τὰ ἔθνη ἀφῆκεν*
Ἰησοῦς *ὥστε πειρᾶσαι ἐν αὐτοῖς τὸν Ἰσραήλ, πάντας τοὺς μὴ*
ἐγνωκότας . . . τοὺς πολέμους Χανάαν· πλὴν διὰ τὰς γενεὰς
τῶν υἱῶν Ἰσραήλ, τοῦ διδάξαι αὐτοὺς πόλεμον, πλὴν οἱ
5 *ἔμπροσθεν αὐτῶν οὐκ ἔγνωσαν αὐτά;*[a]

(1) Ἰησοῦ τοῦ Ναυῆ στρατηγοῦντος, οὐ κατὰ πολεμικὴν τέχνην
ὁ λαὸς ἐνίκα παραταττόμενος, ἀλλὰ τῆς ἄνωθεν ἀπολαύων
ἐπικουρίας· *ἀποστελῶ,* γὰρ ἔφη, *τὰς σφηκίας ἔμπροσθεν*
ὑμῶν, . . . καὶ ἐξολοθρεύσει . . . τὸν χαναναῖον καὶ τὸν χετταῖον,

---

i. Jgs 2.16   j. Jgs 2.18   k. Jgs 2.19   l. Ex 23.14–17; Dt 16.16f.

VIII A *[32]*, B, C, 7 9 10 31* 35 37 = 20 mss.
a. Jgs 3.1f.

sequent events of sacred history: "The Lord raised up judges, who rescued them from the hands of those who plundered them."[i] "And when he raised up judges for them, the Lord was with the judge and rescued them from the hand of their foes all the days of the judge."[j] And a little later, "When the judge died, they would relapse and become worse than their fathers in following after other gods, serving them, and worshiping them."[k]

I believe there was also another reason for their failure to acquire all the promised land: namely, that observance of life according to the law required a very constricted space. As you recall, three times each year the Law required them all to assemble for the celebration of a festival in that one place where they had built the Temple of God. It was there that he commanded them to bring their first-fruits, their tithes, the firstborn of their animals, and their other offerings.[l] So it was logical to circumscribe them within a small territory, so that even the lazy could easily assemble in the consecrated Temple.

VIII

How are we to understand the passage, "Joshua left these nations so as through them to test Israel, all who had not experienced the wars in Canaan. It was only on account of the generations of the children of Israel, to teach them to fight. Only, those before them did not know about this"?[1a]

(1) When Joshua, son of Nun, was in command, the people were victorious in battle, not through military tactics, but because they received assistance from on high. As God said, "I shall send a swarm of wasps before you, and it will destroy the Canaanite and the Hit-

---

1. Though the MT of Jgs 3.1 says that the Lord left gentile nations in order to test Israel, the Greek translations differ among themselves; the *codex vaticanus* agrees with the Hebrew, but both Theodoret's recension of the LXX and the *codex alexandrinus* make "Joshua" subject of the verb "left" (ἀφῆκεν); *cf.* note 1 to *Q.* 4.

10 καὶ τὰ ἑξῆς.[b] καὶ μέντοι καὶ σκηπτοὺς ἄνωθεν ἀφιεὶς καὶ χάλαζαν
λίθων ἔχουσαν μέτρον, τοὺς πολεμίους ἀνήλισκε.[c] λέγει τοίνυν
ὅτι τούτου χάριν οὐ πάντας ἄρδην διώλεσε τοὺς τὴν γῆν ἐκείνην
οἰκοῦντας, Ἰησοῦ τοῦ Ναυῆ στρατηγοῦντος, ἵνα καὶ οἱ μετ'
ἐκεῖνον τῇ πείρᾳ τὴν τοῦ Θεοῦ διδαχθῶσι κηδεμονίαν καὶ διὰ τὴν
15 πολεμικὴν ἀνάγκην τὸν δεσπότην καλῶσιν εἰς συμμαχίαν. τὸ
μέντοι *πειρᾶσαι* ὁ Σύμμαχος *ἀσκῆσαι* ἡρμήνευσεν· ἀσκῆσαι γὰρ
αὐτοὺς ἠβουλήθη καὶ διδάξαι τοῦ πολέμου τὴν τέχνην.

(2) Καὶ τὸ *πειρᾶσαι* δὲ κατὰ τοὺς ἑβδομήκοντα κείμενον οὐ
τὴν ἄγνοιαν τοῦ Θεοῦ δηλοῖ. οὐδὲ γὰρ τὸν Ἀβραὰμ τούτου
20 χάριν ἐπείραζεν, ἵνα μάθῃ τοῦ Ἀβραὰμ τὴν γνῶσιν· κἀκεῖ γὰρ
ἐδίδαξεν ὅτι ᾔδει ὁ Θεὸς ὅτι συντάξει Ἀβραὰμ τοῖς υἱοῖς
αὐτοῦ καὶ τῷ οἴκῳ αὐτοῦ μετ' αὐτὸν φυλάσσειν πάντα τὰ
κρίματα Κυρίου τοῦ Θεοῦ.[d] οὐχ ἵνα τοίνυν αὐτὸς μάθῃ
πειράζει, ἀλλ' ἵνα τοὺς ἀγνοοῦντας διδάξῃ. ὥσπερ τοίνυν εἰς
25 γυμνασίαν τοῦ λογικοῦ τῷ Ἀδὰμ ἐδεδώκει τὴν ἐντολήν,[e] οὕτω
κἀνταῦθα ἔνια τῶν ἐθνῶν καταλέλοιπεν ὥστε τῶν μὲν δεῖξαι
τὸ εὐσεβές, τῶν δὲ διελέγξαι τὸ δυσσεβές· τοῦτο γὰρ λέγει·
ὥστε πειρᾶσαι ἐν αὐτοῖς τὸν Ἰσραὴλ τοῦ γνῶναι εἰ
ἀκούσονται τὰς ἐντολὰς Κυρίου, ἃς ἐνετείλατο τοῖς πατράσιν
30 *αὐτῶν ἐν χειρὶ Μωϋσῆ.*[f]

Καὶ αὐτὰ δὲ διδάσκει τὰ πράγματα ὡς αὐτοὶ αἴτιοι
γεγένηνται τοῦ μὴ παντάπασιν ἀπαλλαγῆναι τῶν δυσσεβῶν
ἐκείνων ἐθνῶν. ἐννέα γὰρ καὶ εἴκοσι βασιλέας, δίχα τῶν τῆς
Ἰεριχὼ καὶ τῆς Γαῒ στρατηγῶν, ὁ Ἰησοῦς σὺν ταῖς στρατίαις
35 αὐτῶν κατηκόντισε,[g] μὴ πόλιν ἔχων, μὴ ὁρμητήριον, μὴ

ll. 16f. τὸ ... *πειρᾶσαι* ὁ Σύμμαχος *ἀσκῆσαι* ἡρμήνευσεν 5, C[-52], 9 37 :
τὸ ... *πειρᾶσαι* ὁ Σύμμαχος Sir. Sch. F.M.

l. 17 ἀσκῆσαι γὰρ αὐτοὺς ἠβουλήθη 5, c, 37 : ἀσκῆσαι γάρ φησιν
αὐτοὺς ἠβουλήθη c₁ : ἀσκῆσαί φησιν αὐτοὺς ἠβουλήθη Sir. Sch. F.M. :
ἀσκῆσαί φησιν αὐτοὺς ἠβουλήθησαν B[-17]. Elsewhere in the *Quaest. in oct.*
Thdt. reserves the formula γάρ φησιν almost exclusively to set off a citation of
the LXX or a quotation of a scriptural personage; never does he employ it with
reference to Symmachus, Aquila, or Theodotion or their translations.

b. Ex 23.28   c. Cf. Jos 10.11.   d. Gn 22.1–18   e. Gn 2.16f.   f. Jgs 3.4
g. Jos 12.9–24

tite" and so on.[b] Furthermore, he slew the enemy with thunderbolts and hail the size of stones.[c] Yet, he declared that he did not utterly destroy all the inhabitants of that land during Joshua's command, so that future generations would also learn of God's care through their own experience and entreat the Lord's assistance when under pressure of the enemy. Symmachus, however, says that rather than "test," he wanted to "exercise" them and instruct them in the art of war.

(2) The term "test" found in the Septuagint does not suggest ignorance on God's part. It was not to discover his attitude that he "tested" Abraham. In fact, the point of that passage is that God knew that Abraham would instruct his sons and his household after him to observe all the judgments of the Lord God.[d] Thus, God tests, not to learn, but to teach the ignorant. So, as he laid the commandment on Adam to provide exercise for his reason,[e] so here he allowed some of the nations to survive to demonstrate the faithfulness of some Israelites and to convict the faithlessness of others. That is the meaning of "to test Israel through them to find out whether they would heed the commandments of the Lord that he gave their fathers through the hand of Moses."[f]

Now, the bare facts are enough to show that they were themselves responsible for their incomplete deliverance from those pagan nations. Without a city, a base of operations, or troops trained in warfare, Joshua and his forces overthrew twenty-nine kings, not even counting the commanders of Jericho and Ai.[g] In contrast, owing to

στρατιώτας ἐμπειρίαν ἠσκημένους πολεμικήν. οἱ δέ γε μετ'
ἐκεῖνον, καὶ πόλεις ὀχυρὰς ἐσχηκότες, καὶ πλοῦτον ὅτι
μάλιστα πλεῖστον ἐκ τῶν λαφύρων κτησάμενοι, καὶ πανοπλίας
ἔχοντες, καὶ τείχη, καὶ περιβόλους, περιγενέσθαι τῶν
40 ὑπολειφθέντων οὐκ ἴσχυσαν διὰ τὴν οἰκείαν ἀσέβειαν.

IX

Πῶς ὁ Γοθονιὴλ καὶ τοῦ Χαλὲβ ἀδελφὸς καὶ Κενὲζ υἱός;[a] ὁ
γὰρ Χαλὲβ Ἰεφονῆ υἱός.[b]

Εἰκὸς καὶ διώνυμον εἶναι τὸν Ἰεφονῆ καὶ καλεῖσθαι καὶ
Κενέζ. εἰκὸς καὶ ἐκ διαφόρων αὐτοὺς εἶναι πατέρων, μιᾶς δὲ
5 μητρός, καὶ τὸν μὲν Χαλὲβ τὸν Ἰεφονῆ ἐσχηκέναι πατέρα,
μετὰ δὲ τὴν τούτου τελευτήν, γήμασθαι τὴν αὐτοῦ μητέρα τῷ
Κενὲζ καὶ τεκεῖν τὸν Γοθονιήλ.

Ὅτι μέντοι τὴν Ἰεριχὼ πόλιν φοινίκων ὠνόμασε[c] τὰ κατὰ
τὸν Ἐγλὼμ διδάσκει· ἐπορεύθη, γάρ φησιν, Ἐγλώμ, καὶ
10 ἐπάταξε τοὺς υἱοὺς Ἰσραήλ, καὶ ἐκληρονόμησε τὴν πόλιν τῶν
φοινίκων·[d] καὶ μετ' ὀλίγα, καὶ Ἐγλὼμ ἀνέστρεψεν ἀπὸ τῶν
εἰδώλων τῶν ἐν Γαλγάλοις, καὶ εἶπεν Ἀὼδ τῷ Ἐγλώμ, λόγος
μοι κρύφιος πρὸς σέ, βασιλεῦ.[e] ἡ δὲ Γάλγαλα τῇ Ἰεριχὼ
πελάζει.

15 Φλόγα δὲ τὸ σιδήριον τῆς μαχαίρας ὠνόμασε, παραξιφίδα
δὲ τὴν λαβήν· τοῦτο γὰρ λέγει· καὶ ἔλαβε τὴν μάχαιραν αὐτοῦ
ἀπὸ τοῦ μηροῦ αὐτοῦ τοῦ δεξιοῦ, καὶ ἐνέπηξεν αὐτὴν εἰς τὴν
κοιλίαν Ἐγλώμ, καὶ ἐπεισήνεγκεν καὶ ... τὴν λαβὴν ὀπίσω τῆς
φλογός, καὶ ἀπέκλεισε τὸ στέαρ τὴν παραξιφίδα.[f]

ıx A [32], B, C, 7 9 10 31 35 37 = 20 mss.
a. Jgs 1.13; 3.9   b. V., e.g., Nm 13.6.   c. Jgs 1.16   d. Jgs 3.13   e. Jgs 3.19
f. Jgs 3.21f.

their idolatry, his successors, though possessed of fortified cities, of enormous wealth acquired in booty, of armor, walls, and ramparts, could not overcome even the remnants.

IX

How could Othniel be both the brother of Caleb and the son of Kenaz,[a] when Caleb was the son of Jephunneh?[b]

Possibly, Jephunneh had two names and was also called Kenaz. It is also possible that they were sons of different fathers but the same mother. Caleb might have had Jephunneh as father, and after the latter's death, his mother might have married Kenaz and given birth to Othniel.[1]

Furthermore, the story of Eglon provides confirmation for our identification of "the city of palms"[c] as Jericho: "Eglon set out and struck the children of Israel and took possession of the city of palms";[d] and shortly after, "Eglon turned back from the idols in Gilgal, and Ehud said to Eglon, 'I have a secret message for you, Your Majesty.'"[e] Now, Gilgal is near Jericho.

Finally, the iron blade of the knife is called a "flame" and the handle "heft." This is the sense of "He took his knife from his right thigh and thrust it into Eglon's belly and pushed the handle in after the flame, and the fat closed over the heft."[f]

---

1. Here, as in Q. 16 on Nm (10.29), Theodoret has recourse to the suggestion of a double name to eliminate an apparent inconsistency in his scriptural narrative. Like the *codex alexandrinus,* his recension of the LXX at 1.13 and 3.9 apparently identified Othniel as "son of Kenaz and younger brother of Caleb" rather than as "son of Kenaz, the younger brother of Caleb," the reading of the MT. At both these places, the reading of the *codex vaticanus* makes Othniel "son of Kenaz" but applies the adjective "younger" to Othniel rather than to the noun "brother."

X

Τὰ κατὰ τὸν Ἰαβίν, τὸν βασιλέα Ἀσώρ, ἱστορεῖ καὶ ἡ
ἱστορία τοῦ Ἰησοῦ·ᵃ εἰ τοίνυν ἐπ' ἐκείνου ἀνῃρέθη, πῶς μετὰ
πολὺν χρόνον ἐπανέστη τῷ Ἰσραήλ;ᵇ

Ἄλλος ἦν ἐκεῖνος καὶ ἄλλος οὗτος· ὁμώνυμοι δὲ ἦσαν, τὴν
5 αὐτὴν ἐσχηκότες βασιλείαν. εἰκὸς δὲ τοῦτον καὶ υἱὸν ἐκείνου
γενέσθαι· ἔστι γὰρ πολλοὺς εὑρεῖν τὰς τῶν πατέρων
ἐσχηκότας προσηγορίας. αὐτίκα γοῦν Κωνσταντίνου τοῦ
βασιλέως ὁ πρῶτος υἱὸς Κωνσταντῖνος ὠνόμασται.

XI

Ἀλλ' ἡ τοῦ Ἰησοῦ ἱστορία, οὐ μόνον τὸν Ἰαβὶν εἶπεν
ἀνῃρῆσθαι, ἀλλὰ καὶ τὴν Ἀσὼρ ἐμπρησθῆναι.ᵃ

Οὐδὲν ἀπεικὸς καὶ τότε κατασκαφῆναι καὶ αὖθις
οἰκοδομηθῆναι. πλὴν ἐνταῦθα μέμνηται μὲν τῆς Ἀσώρ, οὐ μὴν
5 ἐν αὐτῇ κατοικεῖν αὐτὸν ἔφησεν, ἀλλ' ἐν τῇ Ἀσηρώθ.ᵇ

Ἐπισημαντέον δὲ καὶ τοῦτο, ὅτι *κιναίους* τοὺς ἀπογόνους
τοῦ Ἰοθὼρ καλεῖ.ᶜ

---

x A *[32]*, B, C, 7 9 10 35 37 = 19 mss.

a. Jos 11.1–11   b. Jgs 4.2

---

xi A *[32]*, B, C, 7 9 10 35 37 = 19 mss.

l. 5 ἐν τῇ Ἀσηρώθ C, 9 37 : τῇ Ἀσηρώθ 12, B, 7 10 : τὴν Ἀσηρώθ *Sir.
Sch. F.M.* Thdt. normally uses κατοικεῖν + ἐν + the dative to indicate "to dwell
in" and the accusative for "to colonize," "take over." Furthermore, the switch
from dative to accusative, a harsh inconcinnity, is hardly typical of Thdt., who
prefers parallelism. For the parallelism and the repetition of the preposition,
here presented by the oldest ms. and all the other members of class C, cf. H. rel.
vita 8.6: οὔτε ἐν Ἱεροσολύμοις ἀλλ' ἐν παντὶ τοπῳ.

a. Jos 11.11   b. Jgs 4.2   c. Jgs 4.11

X

The book of Joshua also records the story of Jabin King of Hazor.[a] If he was slain in the time of Joshua, how did he attack Israel long afterwards?[b]

They were two different people, who bore the same name and possessed the same kingdom, one probably son of the other. One could list many examples of men who bear the same name as their fathers. For example, the first son of the emperor Constantine was also called Constantine.[1]

XI

But the book of Joshua says not only that Jabin was slain, but also that Hazor was burned.[a]

There is no improbability in Hazor being destroyed and later rebuilt. Furthermore, while this passage mentions Hazor, it does not say that he lived there, but rather that he lived in Harosheth.[1b]

Moreover, we should note that the descendants of Jethro are called Kenites.[c]

---

1. Previously, to rationalize an apparent contradiction in the scriptural narrative, Theodoret has suggested that one person bore two names (Q. 9 above and Q. 16 on Nm); here he concludes that there were two kings of the same name. He is not willing to see this sort of discrepancy as indicative of the diversity of authorship he had detected in Q. 2.

---

1. Although the *NRSV* (4.2) says, "King Jabin of Canaan . . . reigned in Hazor; the commander of his army was Sisera, who lived in Harosheth-ha-goiim," the phrasing of the LXX is sufficiently ambiguous to allow Theodoret to claim that it was Jabin who lived in Harosheth. In his summary account of his excavations of

XII

Τί δή ποτε γυνὴ προφητεύει;[a]

Ἐπειδὴ ἀνδρῶν καὶ γυναικῶν μία ἡ φύσις· ἐκ γὰρ τοῦ Ἀδὰμ ἡ γυνὴ διεπλάσθη[b] καὶ λόγου μετείληχεν ὡς ἐκεῖνος. διὸ καὶ ὁ ἀπόστολός φησιν, ἐν Χριστῷ Ἰησοῦ... οὐκ ἔνι ἄρσεν καὶ
5 θῆλυ.[c] οὕτω καὶ Μωϋσῆς προφήτης, καὶ Μαριὰμ προφῆτις. οἶμαι δὲ τὴν Δεββώραν εἰς ἔλεγχον τῶν τότε ἀνδρῶν τῆς προφητείας ἀξιωθῆναι· οὐδενὸς γὰρ ἐξ ἐκείνων εὑρεθέντος ἀξίου τῆς χάριτος, αὕτη τῆς τοῦ παναγίου πνεύματος τετύχηκε δωρεᾶς. καὶ οὕτω δήλη ἦν ὅτι τῆς ἄνωθεν ἠξίωτο
10 χάριτος ὡς τὸν Βαρὰκ μὴ τολμῆσαι δίχα ταύτης εἰς τὴν παράταξιν ἐξελθεῖν.[d]

Τοῦτο δὲ καὶ ἐν τῇ ᾠδῇ αὐτῆς ἔφη· ἐξέλιπον οἱ κρατοῦντες ἐν τῷ Ἰσραὴλ... ἕως οὗ ἐξανέστη Δεββώρα... μήτηρ ἐν... Ἰσραήλ.[e] λέγει δὲ καὶ τὴν τῶν ὁμοφύλων ἀσέβειαν·
15 ἠρέτισαν θεοὺς κενοὺς ὡς ἄρτον κρίθινον.[f] τὴν πολλὴν αὐτῶν ἀφροσύνην διὰ τῆς εἰκόνος ἤλεγξεν· ὥσπερ γὰρ ἀνόητος ὁ τῶν πυρίνων ἄρτων προτιμῶν τοὺς κριθίνους, οὕτως ἄγαν ἐμβρόντητος ὁ τοὺς ψευδωνύμους θεοὺς τοῦ ἀληθινοῦ προτιθείς. δηλοῖ δὲ αὐτῆς καὶ τὸ πιστὸν τῆς γνώμης· ἐὰν γὰρ
20 ἴδω, φησί, σειρομαστῶν τεσσαράκοντα χιλιάδας, ἡ καρδία μου ἐπὶ τὰ διατεταγμένα τῷ Ἰσραήλ.[g] ταῦτα δὲ ὁ θεῖος διηγόρευσε νόμος· ἐὰν γὰρ ἴδῃς, φησίν, πλῆθος πολεμίων, καὶ ἅρματα, καὶ ἵππον, μὴ φοβηθῇς,[h] ὅτι Κύριος ὁ Θεός σου

---

xii A [32], B, C, 7 9 10 31 35 37 = 20 mss.

a. Jgs 4.4   b. Gn 2.21f.   c. Gal 3.26, 28   d. Jgs 4.8   e. Jgs 5.7
f. Jgs 5.8   g. Jgs 5.8f.   h. Dt 20.1

Question XII

XII

Why did a woman prophesy?[a]

Because men and women have the same nature. As you know, the woman was formed from Adam[b] and, like him, possessed the faculty of reason. Hence, the apostle says, "In Christ Jesus there is neither male nor female."[1c] Thus, Moses was called a "prophet," and Miriam a "prophetess." It is my view that Deborah was granted the gift of prophecy as a reproof to the men of that time. When none of them was found worthy of this charism, she attained the gift of the most Holy Spirit. And it was so patent that she had been deemed worthy of this heaven-sent charism, that Barak dared not march out to battle without her.[d]

She says as much in her song:[2] "The mighty in Israel were faint-hearted until Deborah arose, a mother in Israel."[e] She speaks also of the idolatry of her own people: "They chose gods as worthless as barley bread."[f] Using a metaphorical image, she censures the enormity of their folly; as only a fool prefers barley, to wheat, bread, so anyone who puts false gods before the one true God is quite deranged. She also indicates her fidelity when she declares "If I should see forty thousand scourges, my heart would be directed to the commands laid on Israel."[g] This was entirely in accordance with the instruction of the divine Law, which says that "If you see a multitude of enemies, chariots and cavalry, do not be afraid,[h] because the

----

Hazor, Y. Yadin concludes (*Hazor*, p. 254f.) that the Canaanite city was destroyed by Joshua in the thirteenth century and that the mention of Jabin in Jgs 4.1 "must have been an editorial interpolation," because in this later period the site was occupied by semi-nomadic Israelites. J. Gray (on 11.1–23) and M.D. Coogan, (on 11.1–15), while accepting Yadin's chronology, hesitate to attribute the destruction of Hazor to Joshua.

1. Theodoret here upholds the equality of the sexes on the basis that both possess a rational nature; *cf.* note 7 to Q. 20 on Gn.

2. As M. O'Connor points out (on 5.1–31), the Song of Deborah "is generally viewed as the most archaic part of the Hebrew Bible and, in keeping with its antiquity, it is among the most obscure Hebrew poems."

πολεμήσει ὑπὲρ σοῦ.[i] *κελεύει δέ, οὐ μόνον τοῖς πένησιν, ἀλλὰ*
25 *καὶ τοῖς ἐπὶ πλούτῳ μέγα φρονοῦσιν ὑμνεῖν τὸν Θεόν· οἱ*
δυνάσται, γάρ φησι, τοῦ λαοῦ εὐλογεῖτε τὸν Κύριον,
ἐπιβεβηκότες ἐπὶ ὑποζυγίων . . . φθέγξασθε φωνὴν
ἀνακρουομένων ἀνὰ μέσον εὐφραινομένων. ἐκεῖ δώσουσι
δικαιοσύνην τῷ Θεῷ.[j] *μοσφαθὲ δὲ ἀγροὶ ἑρμηνεύονται,*[k]
30 *ἀμαδαρὼθ δὲ ἀβλεψία*[l] *τὸ δὲ καὶ ἀρᾶσθαι μαζώρ,*
καταράσασθαι ἐν τῷ κραταιῷ.[m]

Διδασκόμεθα δὲ διὰ τῆς ἱστορίας ὡς, πατρικῇ φιλοστοργίᾳ
κεχρημένος, ὁ δεσπότης Θεὸς καὶ παρανομοῦντα τὸν λαὸν
παρεδίδου τοῖς ἀλλοφύλοις, οἷόν τινι ῥάβδῳ κεχρημένος καὶ
35 *μάστιγι, καί, πάλιν μεταμελόμενος, ἐλέει, καὶ παντοδαπῆς*
ἠξίου κηδεμονίας. αὐτίκα γοῦν, μετὰ τὴν διὰ τῆς Δεββώρας
εὐεργεσίαν, εἰς ἀσέβειαν ἐξοκείλαντα μαδιηναίοις
παρέδωκεν·[n] *εἶτα, μετὰ τὴν παιδείαν, τῆς ἐπικουρίας ἠξίωσε.*
διά τινος δὲ τοῦ προφήτου πρῶτον ἐξήλεγξεν αὐτῶν τὴν
40 *ἀσέβειαν, ἀνέμνησε δὲ καὶ τῶν εὐεργεσιῶν ὧν ἀπήλαυσαν·*[o]
εἶτα, διά τινος ἀγγέλου τὸν Γεδεὼν παραθαρρύνας,
παρατάξασθαι τοῖς πολεμίοις ἐκέλευσεν.[p]

---

ll. 30f. *ἀρᾶσθαι μαζώρ, καταράσασθαι ἐν τῷ κραταιῷ* C, 9 37, Sir. Sch. :
ἀρᾶσθαι ἐν τῷ κραταιῷ F.M. : om. 5, B

i. Dt 3.22   j. Jgs 5.9–11   k. Jgs 5.16   l. Jgs 5.22   m. Jgs 5.23
n. Jgs 6.1   o. Jgs 6.8–10   p. Jgs 6.14

Lord your God will fight for you."[3i] She bids not only the poor, but also those glorying in their wealth, to sing God's praises: "Leaders of the people, bless the Lord; you who ride on asses, cry out in applause amidst those who are rejoicing. There they will pay righteousness to God."[j] "Mosphathe" means "fields,"[k] amadaroth "blindness";[l] "curse Meroz" is equivalent to "curse in power."[4m]

Now, we learn from the sacred history that, when the people sinned, the Lord God, acting with fatherly affection, would deliver them into the power of the gentiles. After applying, as it were, the rod and the whip, he would mercifully repent and bestow on them every kindness. Thus, after conferring this benefaction through Deborah, he surrendered them to the Midianites, when they had drifted into idolatry.[n] Then, after chastising them, he deigned to come to their assistance. But first, through an unnamed prophet he charged them with idolatry and reminded them of the acts of kindness he had performed on their behalf.[o] Then, through the agency of an angel, he stirred up Gideon and commanded him to go into battle against the enemy.[p]

3. Though this exhortation to trust in God may be based on Dt 20.1 and 3.22, Theodoret is not so much quoting, as paraphrasing, Scripture. Here, as often elsewhere, he renders the paraphrase more lively and direct for his audience through the use of pronominal and verb forms of the second person; *cf.* the very similar manner in which he has appended an explanatory and equally dramatic paraphrase ("This is tantamount to saying," *etc.*) to the quotation of Jgs 2.1–3 in *Q.* 7.1.

4. Theodoret's version of the Song of Deborah agrees with the *codex alexandrinus* against the *vaticanus*. Obviously puzzled by the obscurity of the ancient text, the translator(s) had resorted to transliteration of difficult terms in Jgs 5.16, 22f.; Theodoret's proposed Greek equivalents do not convey the sense of the Hebrew. For the relationship between Theodoret's recension of the LXX and *A*, *v.* note 1 to *Q.* 4, and *cf.* note 1 to *Q.* 8 and note 1 to *Q.* 9.

The Questions on Judges

XIII

Τί ἐστι πορεύου ἐν τῇ ἰσχύϊ σου ταύτῃ καὶ σώσεις τὸν Ἰσραὴλ ἐκ χειρὸς Μαδιάμ;[a]

Προτραπεὶς ὑπὸ τοῦ ἀγγέλου στρατηγῆσαι καὶ τοῦ πολέμου καταθαρρῆσαι, ἔφη πρὸς αὐτόν, καὶ εἰ ἔστι Κύριος ἐν ἡμῖν,
5 ἵνα τί εὗρεν ἡμᾶς πάντα τὰ κακὰ ταῦτα; καὶ ποῦ ἐστι . . . τὰ θαυμάσια αὐτοῦ, ὅσα διηγήσαντο ἡμῖν οἱ πατέρες ἡμῶν, λέγοντες, ὅτι ἐξ Αἰγύπτου ἀνήγαγεν ἡμᾶς Κύριος; καὶ νῦν ἀπώσατο ἡμᾶς Κύριος καὶ παρέδωκεν ἡμᾶς εἰς χεῖρας Μαδιάμ.[b] ἐπειδὴ τοίνυν ἔσχε τὴν μνήμην τῆς τοῦ Θεοῦ
10 θαυματουργίας καὶ βεβαίαν ἐκέκτητο τὴν περὶ Θεοῦ δόξαν, ὅτι ῥάδιον αὐτῷ βουληθέντι τῶν κατεχουσῶν αὐτοὺς συμφορῶν ἀπαλλάξαι, ἔφη ὁ ἄγγελος, πορεύου ἐν τῇ ἰσχύϊ σου ταύτῃ καὶ σώσεις τὸν Ἰσραὴλ ἐκ χειρὸς Μαδιὰμ ἀντὶ τοῦ· μετὰ ταύτης παράταξαι τῆς πίστεως καὶ νικήσεις.

15 Μηδεὶς δὲ τοῖς ἑξῆς ἐπιμεμφέσθω· οὐ γάρ, ὡς τῷ Θεῷ ἀπιστῶν, ἔφη, ἡ χιλιάς μου ταπεινοτέρα ἐν Μανασσῇ, καὶ ἐγὼ . . . σμικρὸς ἐν τῷ οἴκῳ τοῦ πατρός μου,[c] ἀλλὰ μετρίῳ κεχρημένος φρονήματι. ὅθεν ὑπολαβὼν ὁ ἄγγελος ἔφη, ὅτι ἔσται Κύριος μετὰ σοῦ, καὶ ἀποκτενεῖς τὴν Μαδιὰμ ὡσεὶ
20 ἄνδρα ἕνα.[d] εὐθὺς γοῦν πιστεύσας, θυσίαν προσήνεγκεν. ὁ δὲ ἄγγελος οὐχ ἥρπασε τὴν θείαν τιμήν, ἀλλ' ἱερέως χρείαν ἐπλήρωσε καί, ῥάβδῳ πατάξας τὴν πέτραν, ὡλοκαύτωσε τὴν θυσίαν παραδόξῳ πυρί.[e]

XIII A [32], 14 17(inc.) 24, C, 7 9 10 35 37 = 19 mss.

a. Jgs 6.14 (LXX B)   b. Jgs 6.13   c. Jgs 6.15   d. Jgs 6.16   e. Jgs 6.19–21

XIII

What is the meaning of "Go in this might of yours, and you will save Israel from the hand of Midian"?[a]

When the angel encouraged him to take the leadership and boldly prepare for battle, Gideon replied, "If the Lord is among us, why have all these troubles befallen us? Where are all his miracles that our ancestors have reported to us, saying, 'The Lord led us out of Egypt.' Now the Lord has rejected us and given us into the hands of Midian."[b] Since Gideon retained the memory of God's wonderworking and had a firm opinion that God, if he so willed, could easily set them free from the calamities besetting them, the angel said, "Go in this might, and you will save Israel from the hand of Midian"; that is, "Advance into battle with this faith, and you will be victorious."

Now, no one should criticize what Gideon said next. It was not out of any lack of trust in God that he replied, "My clan is the weakest in Manasseh, and I am the least in my father's house";[c] this was just modesty. Hence, the angel replied, "The Lord will be with you, and you will smite Midian as though they were one man."[d] Immediately, as a gesture of faith, Gideon offered sacrifice. But the angel, rather than arrogating the divine honor to himself, played the role of priest and, striking the rock with a rod, burned the entire victim in a miraculous blaze.[e]

XIV

Τί δή ποτε τὸν τῷ Βαὰλ τρεφόμενον μόσχον τῷ Θεῷ
προσενεχθῆναι προσέταξε;[a]

Μετατιθεὶς αὐτοὺς ἐκ τῆς πλάνης πρὸς τὴν ἀλήθειαν. διά
τοι τοῦτο καὶ τὸν ἐκείνου βωμὸν κατασκαφῆναι παρηγγύησε,
5 καὶ τὸ ἄλσος ἐκκοπῆναι· ἔδει γὰρ τὸν τῆς τοιαύτης χάριτος
ἀξιωθέντα, μὴ μόνον εὐσεβεῖν, ἀλλὰ καὶ ἄλλων γενέσθαι
διδάσκαλον.

XV

Τίνος σύμβολον ὁ πόκος, ὁ τὴν δρόσον δεξάμενος;[a]

Πρῶτον ᾔτησεν ὁ Γεδεὼν ἐν τῷ πόκῳ γενέσθαι τὴν δρόσον,
πᾶσαν δὲ τὴν γῆν διαμεῖναι ξηράν· μετὰ δὲ ταῦτα τὴν μὲν
γῆν ὑγρανθῆναι, μόνον δὲ τὸν πόκον ἄμοιρον διαμεῖναι τῆς
5 δρόσου. δηλοῖ δὲ ὁ λόγος ὡς πάλαι μὲν ὁ Ἰσραὴλ τῆς θείας
ἀπήλαυσε χάριτος ὡς ὁ πόκος τῆς δρόσου· ὕστερον δὲ πᾶσα
τῶν ἀνθρώπων ἡ φύσις τῶν πνευματικῶν τετύχηκε δωρεῶν,
ἔρημος δὲ τούτων ὁ Ἰσραὴλ γέγονε καθάπερ ὁ πόκος ἐστερήθη
τῆς δρόσου.

xiv A [32], B, C, 7 9 10 35 37 = 19 mss.
a. Jgs 6.25f.

xv A [32], B, C, 7 9 10 31 35 37 = 20 mss.
a. Jgs 6.36–40

XIV

Why did the Lord order that the calf raised for Baal be offered to God?[a]

To turn them from error to truth. That is why he also command-ed that Baal's altar be overturned and his grove cut down. It was God's will that he who had been honored with such wonderful grace should not only practice the true religion himself but become a teacher of others.

XV

What was symbolized by the fleece that absorbed the dew?[a]

Gideon first asked that the dew fall on the fleece and the ground remain completely dry, and later that the ground become wet and only the fleece remain free of dew. This account indicates that, as the fleece received the dew, so in antiquity Israel received the benefit of divine grace; later, when the whole human race had access to spiri-tual gifts, Israel was bereft of these just as the fleece was deprived of the dew.

XVI

Τί δή ποτε τοὺς κυνὶ παραπλησίως πεπωκότας μόνους ἐκέλευσε παρατάξασθαι;[a]

Δεδήλωκε τὴν αἰτίαν αὐτὸς ὁ δεσπότης Θεός· πολύς, γάρ φησιν, ὁ ὄχλος ὁ μετὰ σοῦ ὥστε ... παραδοῦναί με τὴν
5 Μαδιὰμ ἐν χειρὶ αὐτῶν μήποτε καυχήσηται Ἰσραὴλ ἐπ' ἐμὲ λέγων, ἡ χείρ μου ἔσωσέ με.[b] τῶν πλείστων τοίνυν ἀπολυθέντων,[c] τοὺς ὑπολειφθέντας τῷ ποταμῷ προσαχθῆναι προσέταξεν. εἶτα τῶν πλειόνων εἰς γόνυ κλιθέντων καὶ πεπωκότων συντόμως, τῶν δὲ τριακοσίων τοῦτο μὲν δι' ὄκνον
10 οὐ πεποιηκότων, τῇ δὲ χειρὶ τὸ νᾶμα προσενεγκόντων τῷ στόματι, τούτους μόνους ἐκέλευσεν,[d] ὡς ἀργοὺς καὶ νωθεῖς, κατὰ τῶν ἀντιπάλων ὁρμῆσαι ἵνα γένηται δήλη πᾶσιν ἡ θεία ῥοπή.

Οὕτω καὶ διὰ δώδεκα ἁλιέων[e] καὶ τελωνῶν[f] καὶ σκυτοτόμου
15 ἑνὸς[g] τὴν τῶν δαιμόνων κατέλυσε φάλαγγα καὶ τῶν ἀνθρώπων τὴν φύσιν διέσωσε. τούτου χάριν ὁ προφήτης Ἠσαΐας τούτοις ἐκεῖνα παρέβαλλεν καὶ ἔφη, τὴν γὰρ ῥάβδον τῶν ἀπειθούντων διεσκέδασε Κύριος ὡς τῇ ἡμέρᾳ τῇ ἐπὶ Μαδιάμ.[h] ὥσπερ γὰρ ἐνταῦθα γυμνοῖς ἐχρήσατο στρατιώταις, τῇ μὲν λαιᾷ φέρουσι
20 κεκρυμμένας ἐν ἀμφορεῦσι λαμπάδας, τῇ δεξιᾷ δὲ τὰς σάλπιγγας,[i] οὕτω τοὺς ἱεροὺς ἀποστόλους γυμνοὺς εἰς τὴν οἰκουμένην ἀπέστειλε φέροντας τὴν λαμπάδα τῶν θαυμάτων καὶ τὴν σάλπιγγα τῶν κηρυγμάτων.

XVI A [32], B, C, 7 9 10 31 35 37 = 20 mss.

a. Jgs 7.7   b. Jgs 7.2   c. Jgs 7.3   d. Jgs 7.5–7   e. V., e.g., Mk 1.16–20.
f. V., e.g., Mk 2.14.   g. Acts 18.3   h. Is 9.4   i. Jgs 7.20

XVI

Why did he order only those who drank like dogs to go into battle?[a]

The Lord God himself indicated the reason. As he declared, "The force accompanying you is too large for me to give Midian into your hand, lest Israel boast against me and say, 'It was my hand that saved me.'"[b] So when most of the men had been dismissed,[c] he had the remainder brought to the river. Then, while most went down on their knee and drank quickly, three hundred hesitated to do this but brought the water to their mouth with their hand. It was these and only these, lazy and indolent as they were, that he commanded to advance on the enemy,[d] so that the divine intervention would be obvious to everyone.[1]

Just so, he routed the devil's column and rescued the human race with a dozen fishermen[e] and tax collectors[f] and a single leather worker.[g] Thus, the prophet Isaiah compared these modern, to those ancient, events when he declared, "The Lord scattered the rod of the disobedient as on the day of Midian."[h] As, in this passage, he used unarmored soldiers bearing lamps hidden in jars in their left hand and trumpets in their right,[i] so he sent into the world the sacred apostles equipped with nothing more than the lamp of miracles and the trumpet of proclamation.

---

1. In the LXX, as in the MT, verses 7.5f. seem to mean that those who lapped the water as dogs would have remained standing and picked up the water in their hands to raise it to their mouths. While M. O'Connor ("Judges") suggests (*ad loc.*) that these gave evidence of a quality to be desired in a soldier (they would have been "the more alert"), Theodoret interprets their behavior as indicative of an undesirable sloth.

XVII

Τί ἐστιν ἐποίησεν αὐτὰ Γεδεὼν εἰς ἐφοὺδ καὶ ἔστησεν
αὐτὸ ἐν τῇ πόλει αὐτοῦ ἐν Ἐφραθά;[a]

Παράνομον μὲν τὸ γεγονός· τῷ γὰρ ἐφοὺδ μόνοις ἐξῆν
κεχρῆσθαι τοῖς ἱερεῦσι·[b] δι' ἐκείνου γὰρ τὸ πρακτέον
5 ἀπεκαλύπτετο. ὁ μέντοι τοῦ Γεδεὼν σκοπὸς οὐκ εἰς ἀσέβειαν
ἀπέκλινεν, ἀλλ' ὡς ἄρχων καὶ στρατηγὸς ἐβούλετο διὰ τοῦ
ἐφοὺδ τὸ πρακτέον μανθάνειν. τῷ δὲ λαῷ πρόξενον παρανομίας
ἐγένετο· ἐξεπόρνευσε, γάρ φησι, πᾶς Ἰσραὴλ ὀπίσω αὐτοῦ
ἐκεῖ, καὶ ἐγένετο τῷ Γεδεὼν καὶ τῷ οἴκῳ αὐτοῦ εἰς
10 σκάνδαλον.[c]

Τὸ δὲ ἐφοὺδ ἐπωμίδα ἐν τῇ Ἐξόδῳ ἡρμήνευσα, ᾗ τὸ λόγιον
συνήπτετο.[d] δι' ἐκείνου δὲ ἡ ἐν πολέμοις ἐδηλοῦτο νίκη. ἡ δὲ
τῶν Βασιλειῶν ἱστορία σαφέστερον τοῦτο διδάσκει· τῶν γὰρ
ἀλλοφύλων συνηθροισμένων, ἐκέλευσεν ὁ Σαοὺλ ἆραι τὸ ἐφοὺδ
15 τὸν ἱερέα· εἶτα, τεταραγμένους τοὺς πολεμίους ἰδών, καὶ τὴν
νίκην δεδηλωμένην, συνάγαγε, φησί, τὸ ἐφούδ.[e] δῆλον τοίνυν
ὡς ὕφασμα ἦν τοῖς ἱερεῦσι περιτιθέμενον καὶ προμηνύον τὸ
πρακτέον, καὶ ὁ Ἀκύλας δὲ ἐπένδυμα αὐτὸ κέκληκεν.

Τὰ δὲ κατὰ τὸν Ἀβιμέλεχ καὶ τοὺς σικημίτας διδάσκει
20 ἡμᾶς ὡς ἡ πονηρὰ συμφωνία τοῖς χρωμένοις ἐπάγει
πανωλεθρίαν, εἰς διχόνοιαν τελευτῶσα· κοινῇ γὰρ τοῦ Γεδεὼν
ἀνελόντες τοὺς παῖδας, ὑπ' ἀλλήλων διώλοντο.[f]

xvii A [32], 14 17(inc.) 24, C, 7 9 10 35 37 = 19 mss.

a. Jgs 8.27   b. Ex 28.6–14   c. Jgs 8.27   d. Ex 28.28   e. 1Sm 14.18
f. Jgs 9.23–45

XVII

What is the meaning of "Gideon made them into an ephod, and set it up in his city, Ophrah"?[a]

Gideon committed a transgression, since only the priests were permitted the use of the ephod,[b] as it was through this that they received revelation regarding what was to be done. Of course, Gideon had no idolatrous intent. As ruler and general, he wanted to use the ephod to find out what he had to do. For the people, however, it proved to be a cause of transgression. As Scripture says, "All Israel prostituted themselves to it there, and it proved a stumbling block for Gideon and his household."[c]

In Exodus, I explained "ephod" as "shoulder cape"; to this was attached the "oracle,"[d] by means of which victory in battle was revealed. Now, this is quite evident from the narrative of First Samuel. When the Philistines had mustered for battle, Saul commanded the priest to pick up the ephod; then when he saw that the enemy had been routed, and the victory revealed, he said, "Withdraw the ephod."[e] So it was clearly a woven garment worn by the priests, which indicated what had to be done. Aquila called it an "overgarment."[1]

Now, the story of Abimelech and the Shechemites teaches us that any harmony of interests among the wicked will end in discord and bring ruin on its participants. Indeed, after joining forces to slay Gideon's sons, they perished at each other's hand.[f]

---

1. Theodoret has already wrestled with these difficult terms "ephod" and "oracle"; *v.* Q. 60.5 on Ex (ch. 28) and notes 9f. In 1Sm 14.19, where Theodoret's LXX reads "Withdraw the ephod," the MT reads "Withdraw your hand."

XVIII

Τί ἐστιν ἔσπειρεν αὐτὴν ἅλας;[a]

Τὴν ἀκαρπίαν τοῦτο δηλοῖ· οὐδὲν γὰρ ἐξ ἁλῶν φύεται.

'Επισημήνασθαι δὲ δεῖ ὅτι, μικρᾶς ἀνακωχῆς ἀπολαύοντες, εὐθὺς τοῖς εἰδώλοις ἐλάτρευον· προσέθεντο, γάρ φησιν, οἱ υἱοὶ
5 'Ισραὴλ ποιῆσαι τὸ πονηρὸν ἔναντι Κυρίου καὶ ἐλάτρευσαν τοῖς Βααλείμ, καὶ τοῖς 'Ασταρώθ, καὶ τοῖς θεοῖς Σιδῶνος, καὶ τοῖς θεοῖς Μωάβ, καὶ τοῖς θεοῖς . . . 'Αμμών, καὶ τοῖς θεοῖς τῶν ἀλλοφύλων.[b] ἐπειδὴ δὲ ὀργισθεὶς ὁ Θεὸς ἐπέστησεν αὐτοῖς τὸν τῶν ἀμμανιτῶν βασιλέα,[c] ἐβόησαν μὲν πρὸς τὸν σωτῆρα
10 Θεὸν καὶ σφῶν αὐτῶν κατηγόρησαν, ὅτι τὸν εὐεργέτην καταλιπόντες καὶ ἀληθινὸν Θεόν τε καὶ Κύριον, τοῖς ψευδωνύμοις ἐλάτρευσαν. εἶτα διελέγξας αὐτῶν ὁ φιλάνθρωπος Κύριος τὴν ἀχάριστον γνώμην·[d] πολλῆς γὰρ πολλάκις ἀπολαύσαντες κηδεμονίας, τὴν τῶν εἰδώλων προετίμησαν
‖24 15 θεραπείαν·‖ καὶ ἀπειλήσας ὡς οὐδεμιᾶς αὐτοὺς ἀξιώσει κηδεμονίας· οὐ προσθήσω, γάρ φησιν, ἔτι σῶσαι ὑμᾶς. βαδίζετε καὶ βοᾶτε πρὸς τοὺς θεοὺς οὓς ἐξελέξασθε ἑαυτοῖς, καὶ αὐτοὶ σωσάτωσαν ὑμᾶς ἐν καιρῷ θλίψεως ὑμῶν[e]—ἐπειδὴ τοίνυν καὶ τὰς οἰκείας ὡμολόγησαν παρανομίας, καὶ
20 μετέστησαν τοὺς θεοὺς τοὺς ἀλλοτρίους ἐκ μέσου αὐτῶν, καὶ ἐλάτρευσαν Κυρίῳ, τῆς παρ' αὐτοῦ βοηθείας ἀπήλαυσαν.[f]

xviii A [32], 14 17 24(inc.), C, 7 9 10 35 37 = 19 mss.

a. Jgs 9.45   b. Jgs 10.6   c. Jgs 10.7–9   d. Jgs 10.11f.   e. Jgs 10.13f.
f. Jgs 10.15f.

XVIII

What is the meaning of "He sowed the city with salt"?[a]

This indicates infertility, as nothing grows from salt.

Furthermore, we should point out that, while they were enjoying a brief respite, they immediately began to engage in idolatry: "The children of Israel proceeded to do what was evil in the sight of the Lord and worshiped the Baals, the Astartes, the gods of Sidon, the gods of Moab, the gods of Ammon, and the gods of the Philistines."[1b] But when, in his wrath, God brought upon them the king of the Ammonites,[c] they cried out to God their savior and accused themselves of abandoning their benefactor, the true God and Lord, to serve false gods. Then the loving Lord upbraided them for their ingratitude,[d] since, though they had frequently benefited from his generous care, they had still preferred to worship idols, and, threatening that he would no longer deign to assist them, he declared, "I shall no longer rescue you. Go cry to the gods you have chosen for yourselves, and let them save you in your time of trouble."[e] So when they had confessed their sins, removed the foreign gods from their midst, and given worship to the Lord, they received his help.[f]

1. After giving the briefest of answers to this precise question, the commentator feels free to develop the theme uppermost in his mind: the vicissitudes of fortune that accompanied the people's changes in religious allegiance. Here, the question, demanded by the genre, is no more than a formal means to introduce an ethical disquisition.

The Questions on Judges

XIX

Τί ἐστιν εἴπατε δὴ σύνθημα;[a]

Οἱ τῆς Ἐφραῒμ φυλῆς ἐπεστράτευσαν τῷ Ἰεφθάε, χαλεπαίνοντες ὅτι δὴ τῆς κατὰ τῶν ἀμμανιτῶν οὐκ ἐκοινώνησαν νίκης. εἶτα δυσπραγήσαντες ἔφυγον, ἀλλὰ λόχον
5 τινὰ τῶν συστρατευομένων ἀποστείλας, ὁ Ἰεφθάε διαβῆναι τὸν ποταμὸν αὐτοὺς διεκώλυσεν. ἔπειτα πειρωμένους ἐξαπατῆσαι καὶ λέγοντας ἐκ τῶν ἄλλων εἶναι φυλῶν ἐκέλευσεν ἐπερωτᾶσθαί τινα λόγον, ὃς ἐπέφερε διὰ τῆς γλώττης τὸν ἔλεγχον.[b] ὥσπερ γὰρ ὀσροηνοί, καὶ σύροι, καὶ εὐφρατήσιοι,
10 καὶ παλαιστῖνοι, καὶ φοίνικες τῇ σύρων χρῶνται φωνῇ, πολλὴν δὲ ὅμως ἡ διάλεξις ἔχει διαφοράν, οὕτως ἑβραῖοι μὲν ἦσαν αἱ δυοκαίδεκα φυλαί, εἶχον δέ τινα, ὡς εἰκός, ἰδιώματα, ὥσπερ ἀμέλει καὶ αὕτη· ὡς γὰρ ὁ σύρος φησί, τῶν ἄλλων τὸν ἄσταχυν σεμβλὰ καλούντων, οἱ τοῦ Ἐφραῒμ ἔκ τινος
15 συνηθείας σεμβελὼ ἔλεγον. τοῦτο γινώσκων, ὁ Ἰεφθάε λέγειν ἐκέλευσε καὶ διελεγχομένους ἀνῄρει.

XX

Τί δή ποτε συνεχώρησεν ὁ δεσπότης Θεὸς τοῦ Ἰεφθάε σφαγῆναι τὴν θυγατέρα;[a]

(1) Ἀνόητος ἄγαν ἡ τοῦ Ἰεφθάε ὑπόσχεσις·[b] ἔδει γὰρ αὐτὸν συνιδεῖν ὡς εἰκὸς κύνα πρῶτον ἢ ὄνον συναντῆσαι, τὰ
5 κατὰ τὸν νόμον ἀκάθαρτα.[c] παιδεύων τοίνυν δι' ἐκείνου τοὺς ἄλλους, ὁ δεσπότης Θεός, ὥστε μετὰ συνέσεώς τε καὶ

---

xix A [32], B⁻²⁴, C⁻⁵¹, 7 9 10 35 37 = 17 mss.

a. Jgs 12.6   b. Jgs 12.1–6

xx 2c(inc.) 6 [32(inc.)], 5, 12, B⁻²⁴, C⁻⁵¹, 7 9 10 31 35 37 = 17 mss.

a. Jgs 11.39   b. Jgs 11.30f.   c. Lv 11.1–3

XIX

What is the meaning of "Say the password"?[a]

Aggrieved at not sharing in the victory against the Ammonites, the tribe of Ephraim made war on Jephthah. When worsted, they took to flight, but Jephthah sent a band of men to prevent them from crossing the river. When the Ephraimites tried to deceive them by claiming to be from other tribes, he gave orders that they be asked a certain word so they could be unmasked by their pronunciation.[b] You see, as the Osroënians, the Syrians, the people of the Euphrates, the Palestinians, and the Phoenicians all speak Syriac, but with many differences in pronunciation, so, the twelves tribes, while all Hebrews, probably had some individual peculiarities of speech, as, indeed, did this one. According to the Syriac, while the others referred to a stalk of wheat as "sembla," the Ephraimites were in the habit of saying "sembelo." Aware of this, Jephthah commanded them to pronounce the word for "stalk" and killed those betrayed by their speech.[1]

XX

Why did the Lord permit the sacrifice of Jephthah's daughter?[a]

(1) Jephthah's was a very foolish vow.[b] He ought to have realized that, in all likelihood, a dog or an ass, both unclean by Law,[c] would be the first to come out to meet him. So that Jephthah's example would teach others to make their vows with prudence and under-

---

1. Theodoret cites the Syriac version to adduce a case of dialectal variation similar to that found in Hebrew; for his previous references to this translation v. Qq. 60, 62, and 94 on Gn. Here it seems that his Greek and Syriac versions differed. While his Greek recension of the LXX, again in agreement with the *codex alexandrinus* (*cf.* note 4 to Q. 12), read the generic σύνθημα ("password"), his Syriac, in agreement with the *codex vaticanus,* read a word meaning "stalk of wheat." The

γνώσεως ποιεῖσθαι τὰς ὑποσχέσεις, οὐκ ἐκώλυσε τὴν σφαγήν.

ὅτι γὰρ τῶν τοιούτων θυμάτων κατηγορεῖ μάρτυς ὁ μακάριος
Δαβὶδ βοῶν, καὶ ἔθυσαν τοὺς υἱοὺς αὐτῶν καὶ τὰς θυγατέρας

10 αὐτῶν τοῖς δαιμονίοις· καὶ ἐξέχεαν αἷμα ἀθῷον, αἷμα υἱῶν
αὐτῶν καὶ θυγατέρων, ὧν ἔθυσαν τοῖς γλυπτοῖς Χαναάν, καὶ

||2c, 32 ἐφονοκτονήθη ἡ γῆ ἐν τοῖς αἵμασι, καὶ τὰ ἑξῆς.ᵈ|| καὶ αὐτὸς
δὲ ὁ δεσπότης Θεὸς δι' Ἰεζεκιὴλ τοῦ προφήτου φησί, καὶ
ἔλαβες τοὺς υἱούς σου καὶ τὰς θυγατέρας σου, οὓς ἐγέννησάς

15 μοι, καὶ προσήνεγκας αὐτοὺς τοῖς ἐρασταῖς σου·ᵉ τοῦτο παρὰ
πᾶσαν τὴν πορνείαν σου.ᶠ καὶ δεικνὺς τὴν τῆς ἀσεβείας
ὑπερβολήν, προσέθηκεν, ὃ οὐκ ἐνεθυμήθην, οὐδὲ ἀνέβη εἰς τὴν
καρδίαν μου.ᵍ καὶ τοῦ Ἀβραὰμ δὲ γυμνᾶσαι τὸ φιλόθεον
βουληθείς, προσέταξε μὲν τὸν υἱὸν ἱερεῦσαι· δείξας δὲ τοῦ

20 δικαίου τὴν γνώμην, ἐκώλυσε τὴν σφαγήν.ʰ

(2) Δηλοῖ δὲ καὶ τὰ ἑξῆς τοῦ Ἰεφθάε τὸ ἀτελές.
ὑποσχόμενος γὰρ πᾶν πρῶτον ὑπαντῶν εἰς θυσίαν προσοίσειν,
εἶτα τὴν παῖδα τοῦτο δράσασαν θεασάμενος, καὶ τὴν ἐσθῆτα
διέρρηξε, καὶ πικρῶς ὠλοφύρατο, καὶ θρηνῆσαι αὐτῇ

25 συνεχώρησε πρότερον, εἶθ' οὕτω κατέθυσεν.ⁱ ἀμείνων δὲ αὐτοῦ
ἡ θυγάτηρ πολλῷ· εἰ ἐν ἐμοί, γάρ φησιν, ἤνοιξας τὸ στόμα
σου πρὸς Κύριον, ποίει μοι ὃν τρόπον ἐξῆλθεν ἐκ τοῦ
στόματός σου, ἀνθ' ὧν ἐποίησέ σοι Κύριος ἐκδίκησιν ἐκ τῶν
ἐχθρῶν σου, ἐκ τῶν υἱῶν Ἀμμών.ʲ διδάσκων τοίνυν ὁ δεσπότης

30 Θεὸς πῶς δεῖ ποιεῖσθαι τὰς πρὸς αὐτὸν ὑποσχέσεις, οὐκ
ἐκώλυσε τὴν σφαγήν.

Μετὰ ταῦτα διδάσκει ἡμᾶς ἡ ἱστορία τῶν ἀγγέλων τὴν
περὶ τὸν Θεὸν εὔνοιαν. τοῦ Μανωὲ γὰρ ἔριφον αὐτῷ
προσενεγκεῖν ἐθελήσαντος, ἔφη ὁ θεῖος ἄγγελος, ἐὰν

35 παραβιάσῃ με, οὐ φάγομαι τῶν ἄρτων σου, καὶ ἐὰν ποιήσῃς
ὁλοκαύτωμα, τῷ Κυρίῳ ἀνοίσεις αὐτό.ᵏ τροφῆς, φησίν, οὐ

---

d. Ps 106.37f.   e. Ezek 16.20   f. Ezek 16.22   g. Cf. Jer 7.31; 39.35 (LXX).
h. Gn 22.1–13   i. Jgs 11.34–39   j. Jgs 11.36   k. Jgs 13.16

standing, the Lord God did not prevent the sacrifice. Nonetheless, confirming God's condemnation of such sacrifices, the blessed David cries out, "They sacrificed their sons and their daughters to demons; they poured out innocent blood, the blood of their sons and daughters, whom they sacrificed to the idols of Canaan, and the land was polluted with their blood" and so on.[d] And the Lord God himself declared through the prophet Ezekiel, "You took your sons and your daughters, whom you had borne me, and offered them to your lovers;[e] this was worse than all your prostitution."[f] And to bring out the enormity of the idolatry, he added, "Something I never planned, nor did it enter my heart."[g] It is true that, to exercise Abraham's piety, God ordered him to sacrifice his son. But, after bringing to light his righteousness, God prevented the sacrifice.[1h]

(2) What happens next again reveals Jephthah's moral inadequacy. Although he had vowed to offer in sacrifice whatever first came out to meet him, and he saw that his daughter had done just that, he tore his garments, lamented bitterly, and gave her permission to grieve before he immolated her.[i] His daughter was much better than he, for she declared, "If you have opened your mouth to the Lord regarding me, do to me what came from your mouth in return for the Lord's avenging you against your enemies, against the sons of Ammon."[j] So, to impress upon us the proper manner of making vows, the Lord God did not prevent the sacrifice.

The next passage of the sacred history teaches us about the angels' love for God. When Manoah desired to offer him a kid, the holy angel declared, "Even if you try to compel me, I shall not eat your bread. If you offer a holocaust, offer it to the Lord."[k] The angel

---

NRSV simply transliterates the Hebrew "shibboleth," which in this context clearly means "river," though it may also mean "stalk of wheat."

---

1. The commentator feels he must both exonerate God of responsibility for the human sacrifice, condemned by Scripture, and offer a rationale for his failing to prevent it.

δέομαι, θυσίαν οὐ δέχομαι· τοῦτο μὲν γὰρ Θεοῦ, ἐκεῖνο δὲ
τῆς ἀνθρωπίνης φύσεως ἴδιον. ἐγὼ δὲ οὔτε ὡς ἄνθρωπος χρήζω
τροφῆς, οὔτε τὴν θείαν ἁρπάζω τιμήν. καὶ ἐντεῦθεν δῆλον ὡς
40 οἱ ὑπὸ τοῦ Ἀβραὰμ δεξιωθέντες ἑτέρῳ τινι τρόπῳ τὴν
παρατεθεῖσαν τροφὴν κατηνάλωσαν.¹

XXI

Πῶς ὁ Σαμψών, ἐκδεδιητημένως καὶ παρανόμως ζῶν,
πνευματικῆς ἀπήλαυσε χάριτος;ᵃ

Καὶ ἐντεῦθεν δῆλον ὡς καὶ ἀναξίοις ὁ δεσπότης, ἑτέρας
χάριν οἰκονομίας, τῆς θείας μεταδίδωσι δωρεᾶς. τοῦτο καὶ ἐν
5 τοῖς ἱεροῖς εὐαγγελίοις δείκνυσιν ὁ σωτήρ· *πολλοί*, γάρ φησιν,
*ἐλεύσονται ἐν ἐκείνῃ τῇ ἡμέρᾳ καὶ ἐροῦσί μοι, Κύριε, Κύριε,
οὐ τῷ σῷ ὀνόματι προεφητεύσαμεν . . . καὶ τῷ σῷ ὀνόματι
δυνάμεις πολλὰς ἐποιήσαμεν; καὶ ἐρῶ αὐτοῖς, . . . ἀποχωρεῖτε
ἀπ' ἐμοῦ οἱ ἐργαζόμενοι τὴν ἀνομίαν·*ᵇ *οὐκ οἶδα τίνες ἐστέ.*ᶜ
10 τοῦτο καὶ ἐνταῦθα πεποίηκεν ὁ δεσπότης Θεός· τῶν γὰρ
ἀλλοφύλων ἐθελήσας καταλῦσαι τὸ κράτος, διὰ τῆς
πνευματικῆς χάριτος ῥώμην αὐτῷ καὶ δύναμιν ἐδωρήσατο. διά
τοι τοῦτο καὶ συνεχώρησεν αὐτὸν ἀλλόφυλον γῆμαι γυναῖκα.
τοῦτο δὲ καὶ ἡ ἱστορία διδάσκει· *καὶ ὁ πατὴρ αὐτοῦ καὶ ἡ
15 μήτηρ αὐτοῦ οὐκ ἔγνωσαν ὅτι παρὰ Κυρίου ἐστίν, ὅτι
ἀνταπόδομα αὐτὸς ζητεῖ ἀπὸ τῶν ἀλλοφύλων.*ᵈ τὸ δὲ *παρὰ
Κυρίου ἐστίν*, οὐ τὴν ἐνέργειαν τὴν θείαν, ἀλλὰ τὴν
συγχώρησιν τὴν θείαν δηλοῖ.

l. Gn 18.8

xxi *6, 5, 12, B⁻²⁴, C, 7 9 10 31 35 37* = 17 mss.

a. Jgs 14.6, 19; 15.14   b. Mt 7.22f.   c. Lk 13.27   d. Jgs 14.4

meant, "I have no need of food, nor do I accept sacrifice; the latter belongs to God, the former to humanity. I have no need of food like a human being, nor do I grasp at the honor due to God." Thus, this passage provides a further indication that it must have been in some non-human way that Abraham's guests consumed the food he set before them.[21]

XXI

How is it that Samson, who lived a dissolute and sinful life, enjoyed the gift of the Spirit?[a]

This passage offers additional proof that, with other designs in view, the Lord imparts his grace even to the unworthy. The Savior makes the same point in the sacred Gospels: "On that day, many will come and say to me, 'Lord, Lord, did we not prophesy in your name and work great miracles in your name?' And I shall reply to them, 'Depart from me, you workers of iniquity.[b] I do not know who you are.'"[c] This is just what the Lord God did in this case. As it was his will to destroy the dominion of the Philistines, he granted Samson strength and power through the gift of the Spirit.

As the sacred history explains, this is also why he allowed him to marry a Philistine wife: "His father and his mother did not know that this was from the Lord, because he sought retribution from the Philistines."[d] Now, the phrase "was from the Lord" indicates, not God's act, but his permission.

2. *Cf. Q.* 70 on Gn 18.

The Questions on Judges

XXII

Τί δή ποτε, καὶ ναζηραῖος ὢν καὶ ὑπὸ τὸν νόμον τελῶν, ἔφαγε τὰ ἐν τῷ στόματι τοῦ λέοντος, καὶ νεκροῦ ὄντος, κατασκευασθέντα κηρία;[a]

Δηλοῖ καὶ τοῦτο τῶν τοιούτων νόμων οὐ πᾶσιν ἀναγκαίαν
5 τὴν χρείαν· οὐδεὶς γὰρ τῶν τοὺς τοιούτους παραβεβηκότων νόμους εἰσεπράχθη δίκας. εἰ δέ τις ὑπείληφε τοῦτο πεπραχέναι τὸν Σαμψών, ὡς οὐκ ἀκριβῆ φύλακα τοῦ νόμου γεγενημένον, σκοπησάτω πάλιν ὡς διψήσαντι νᾶμα δέδωκεν ὁ Θεός, τὸ κοῖλον τῆς τοῦ ὄνου σιαγῶνος ἀναβλῦσαι κελεύσας.[b]
10 αὕτη δὲ κατὰ τὸν νόμον τριπλῆς μετεῖχεν ἀκαθαρσίας· καὶ γὰρ ζῶν ὁ ὄνος ἀκάθαρτος,[c] καὶ νεκρὸς πάλιν ἀκάθαρτος,[d] καὶ τὸ φονικὸν γενόμενον ὄργανον καὶ χιλίους κατακοντίσαν τῶν ἀλλοφύλων ἄλλην εἶχεν ἀκαθαρσίαν.[e] ἀλλ' ὅμως, ὁ τοῦ νόμου νομοθέτης ἐντεῦθεν αὐτῷ, καὶ οὐκ ἄλλοθεν, παρέσχε τὴν τοῦ
15 ὕδατος χρείαν.

Ἀλλὰ τοῦτον τὸν ἀχείρωτον, τὸν ἀήττητον, ὃν πολλαὶ τῶν ἀλλοφύλων ἔφριξαν μυριάδες, ἑταιρικὸν ἐξηνδραπόδισε γύναιον.[f] τοσοῦτον χαλεπώτερος τῆς ἐν πολέμοις παρατάξεως τῆς ἐπιθυμίας ὁ πόλεμος· τὸν γὰρ οὕτω γενναίως ἠριστευκότα
20 καὶ διὰ τὰς ὑπερφυεῖς ἀνδραγαθίας πολυθρύλλητον γεγενημένον δορυάλωτον ἀπέφηνεν ἡ ἡδονή. αὕτη καὶ τῆς θείας αὐτὸν ἐγύμνωσε χάριτος· ἐξηγέρθη, γάρ φησι, Σαμψὼν ἐκ τοῦ ὕπνου αὐτοῦ καὶ εἶπεν, ἐξελεύσομαι, καὶ ποιήσω καθὼς ἀεί, καὶ ἀποτινάξομαι· καὶ αὐτὸς οὐκ ἔγνω ὅτι ἀπέστη Κύριος
25 ἀπ' αὐτοῦ.[g] οὐ παντελῶς δὲ αὐτὸν καταλέλοιπεν ὁ φιλοικτίρμων Θεός, ἀλλ', ἰδὼν ἐπικερτομούμενον, ᾤκτιρε, καὶ εὐξαμένῳ ἐπήκουσε, καὶ τοσαύτην ἰσχὺν ἐχορήγησεν ὡς μὲν κλονῆσαι τοὺς φέροντος κίονας τὸν τῶν εἰδώλων σηκόν,

---

XXII 6, 5, 12, B⁻²⁴, C, 7 9 10 31 35 37 = 17 mss.

a. Jgs 14.8f.   b. Jgs 15.18f.   c. Lv 11.1–3   d. Lv 17.15
e. Jgs 15.15; Nm 19.13   f. Jgs 16.18–21   g. Jgs 16.20

XXII

Why is it that, though a nazirite subject to the Law, Samson ate the honeycombs that had been built in the mouth of the lion, and a dead one at that?[a]

This passage, among others, indicates that the observance of this kind of law was not universally binding; after all, nobody was ever called to account for breaking them. But if anyone imagines that Samson did this because he was not a careful observer of the Law, he should note as well that, when Samson was thirsty, God commanded the hollow of an ass's jawbone to gush forth water for him.[1b] Now, the ass's jawbone was unclean on three counts. First, even while alive, the ass was unclean;[c] second the ass was doubly unclean because dead;[d] finally, when it was used as an instrument of homicide, the slaying of a thousand Philistines, it acquired yet another uncleanness.[e] Nevertheless, it was from the jawbone, and nowhere else, that the giver of the Law himself met Samson's need for water.

This invincible man, the terror of countless Philistines, was subdued by a mere harlot[f]—the war against lust being much more challenging than any military combat. It was pleasure that captured this courageous champion, so well-known for his remarkable deeds of valor; pleasure even stripped him of divine grace. As Scripture says, "Samson woke from his sleep and said, 'I shall go out and do as ever before and shake myself free,' unaware that the Lord had left him."[g] Nonetheless, God, in his compassion, had not completely abandoned him. Seeing him mocked, God pitied him, hearkened to his prayer, and supplied him with such strength that Samson shook the pillars of that idolatrous shrine, brought down the roof along with

---

1. Missing the reference to the toponym "Lehi" ("Jawbone)," the LXX speaks of God opening up not "the hollow place that is at Lehi," but the hollow of the jawbone (τὸν λάκκον τὸν ἐν τῇ σιαγόνι). Here, Theodoret apparently tries to acquit the leader of Israel of charges of infidelity to the Law by claiming that the cultic prescriptions were not binding; cf. his attempt to defend Gideon from the charge of idolatry in Q. 17.

συγκατενεγκεῖν δὲ τούτοις τὸν ὄροφον, καὶ τρισχιλίους
30 ἄνδρας συγχῶσαι καὶ γυναικῶν πολλαπλασίονα ἀριθμόν.[h]

XXIII

Πόθεν ὁ Σαμψὼν τοσαύτας ἀλώπεκας ἤγρευσεν;[a]

Ὄρος ἐστὶ παρ' αὐτοῖς πολλὰς ἀλώπεκας τρέφον. καὶ
τοῦτο ἡ ἱστορία διδάσκει· *ἤρξατο, γάρ φησιν, ὁ ἀμορραῖος τοῦ*
κατοικεῖν ἐν τῷ ὄρει τοῦ μυρσινῶνος, οὗ οἱ ἄρκοι καὶ αἱ
5 *ἀλώπεκες.*[b]

XXIV

Τί ἐστιν *ἐποίησεν αὐτῷ Μιχὰ ἐφοὺδ καὶ θεραφίν;*[a]

Περὶ τοῦ ἐφοὺδ πολλάκις εἰρήκαμεν, ὅτι ὕφασμα ἦν
ἱερατικόν, καὶ δι' αὐτοῦ ὁ Θεὸς τὸ πρακτέον ἐδήλου. τὸ δὲ
θεραφὶν τοιουτότροπόν τι ἦν εἰδώλοις, ἀλλ' οὐ τῷ Θεῷ,
5 ἀνακείμενον· τοῦτο γὰρ καὶ ἐνταῦθα ἡ ἱστορία διδάσκει·
ἐποίησε, γάρ φησι, . . . γλυπτὸν καὶ χωνευτόν.[b] εἶτα ἐπάγει,
καὶ ἐποίησε Μιχὰ ἐφοὺδ καὶ θεραφίν, καὶ ἔπλησε τὴν χεῖρα
ἑνὸς τῶν υἱῶν αὐτοῦ, καὶ ἐγένετο αὐτῷ εἰς ἱερέα.[c] τῆς δὲ

---

h. Jgs 16.25–30

xxiii 6, 5, 12, B^{-24}, C, 7 9 10 35 37 = 16 mss.

a. Jgs 15.4   b. Jgs 1.35

xxiv 6, 5, 12, B^{-24}, C, 7 9 10 35 37 = 16 mss.

l. 4 θεραφὶν 12, 1 3, 51, 9 10 35 37, *cod. A.* : θαραφιν *cod. B* : θεραφίμ *Sir.*
Sch. F.M. The form θεραφίν appears, apparently without variant, in the
question as well as in *cod. A* (*v.* Rahlfs, Jgs 17.5) with which Thdt.'s text agrees
throughout this book; *cf.* note 1 to Q. 3.
l. 7 θεραφίν 6, 5, B^{-24}, 3, 52, 9 10 37 : θεραφίμ *Sir. Sch. F.M.*

a. Jgs 17.5   b. Jgs 17.4   c. Jgs 17.5

them, and buried three thousand men and a far greater number of women.[2h]

XXIII

Where did Samson catch so many foxes?[a]

In that area, there is a mountain teeming with foxes. According to the sacred history, "The Amorite began to live on the mountain of the myrtle grove, where there were bears and foxes."[1b]

XXIV

What is the meaning of "Micah made himself an ephod and a teraphim"?[a]

As we have often remarked, the ephod was a woven garment worn by the priests, through which God revealed what had to be done. The teraphim was something similar, but dedicated to idols, rather than God. Indeed, this can be deduced from the passage of the sacred history now under consideration: "He made a graven image and an idol of cast metal."[b] Then it adds, "And Micah made an ephod and a teraphim and consecrated one of his sons, who became his priest."[c] Now, he was not a member of the Levitical tribe, but of

---

2. Theodoret's figure of 3,000 men is much closer to that of the *codex alexandrinus*, which speaks of 3,000 men and women, than to that of the *vaticanus* (700 men and women; *cf.* note 1 to *Q.* 19 above), but his misogynistic comment about the number of women seems wholly without textual basis; *cf.* his more favorable remarks on women in *Q.* 12 above.

---

1. In Jgs 1.35 the LXX fails to recognize a series of Hebrew toponyms and speaks of Amorites dwelling on "the mountain of sherds, where there are bears and foxes," rather than, "in Harheres, in Aijalon, and in Shaalbim" (*NRSV;* the last name perhaps signifies "haunt of foxes," *v. BDB ad uoc.*); *cf.* note 1 to *Q.* 22. In yet another demonstration of Antiochene precision, Theodoret recalls this easily overlooked narrative detail and applies it to the elucidation of the Samson saga.

λευιτικῆς οὐκ ἦν οὗτος φυλῆς ἀλλὰ τῆς τοῦ Ἐφραΐμ. ἐδίδαξε
10 δὲ καὶ τὴν αἰτίαν τῆς παρανομίας· *ἐν ταῖς ἡμέραις, γάρ*
φησιν, ἐκείναις οὐκ ἦν βασιλεὺς ἐν Ἰσραήλ· ἀνὴρ ἕκαστος τὸ
ἀρεστὸν ἐν ὀφθαλμοῖς αὐτοῦ ἐποίει.[d] τοσαύτης πρόξενος
βλάβης ἡ ἀναρχία.

XXV

Τὰ ἑξῆς πολλὴν ἔχει ἀμφιβολίαν· *ἦν, γάρ φησι, παιδάριον*
ἐκ Βηθλεὲμ δήμου Ἰούδα ἐκ συγγενείας Ἰούδα, καὶ αὐτὸς
λευίτης, καὶ αὐτὸς παρῴκει ἐκεῖ.[a] εἰ γὰρ λευίτης, πῶς ἐκ
συγγενείας Ἰούδα;
5 *Δῆμον* Ἰούδα τὴν Βηθλεὲμ ὠνόμασεν· ὡς δὲ νομίζω, καὶ
συγγένειαν Ἰούδα τὴν αὐτὴν προσηγόρευσε κώμην. εἰρήκαμεν
δὲ ὡς τοῖς ἱερεῦσι καὶ λευίταις ἴδιον κλῆρον οὐκ ἀφώρισεν ὁ
Θεὸς[b] ἀλλ' ἐν ἁπάσαις αὐτοὺς διέσπειρε ταῖς φυλαῖς[c] ἵν'
ἔχωσιν ἅπαντες τῆς εὐσεβείας τοὺς διδασκάλους. τοιγάρτοι
10 καὶ οὗτος, λευίτης ὤν, ᾤκει τὴν Βηθλεὲμ οὖσαν τοῦ δήμου καὶ
τῆς συγγενείας Ἰούδα. εἰ δέ τις βεβιασμένην ταύτην
ὑπείληφε τὴν ἑρμηνείαν, ἀναμνησθήτω τῶν ἤδη παρ' ἡμῶν
εἰρημένων, ὡς ἐπεμίγησαν ἀλλήλαις αἱ δύο φυλαί, ἥ τε
βασιλικὴ καὶ ἡ ἱερατική. εἰκὸς δὲ τοῦτον λευίτην μὲν εἶναι
15 πατρόθεν, μητέρα δὲ ἐκ τῆς Ἰούδα ἐσχηκέναι φυλῆς.
Πολλὴ μέντοι τοῦ ἀνδρὸς ἡ παρανομία. πρῶτον γὰρ τοῦ

---

d. Jgs 17.6

---

xxv 6, 5, 12, B⁻²⁴, C, 7 9 10 35 37 = 16 mss.
a. Jgs 17.7   b. *V.*, *e.g.*, Dt 18.1f.   c. *V.*, *e.g.*, Nm 35.8.
d. Jos 18.1   e. Jgs 17.4   f. Nm 3.5–10   g. Jgs 18.18–20

Ephraim. This passage also indicates the cause of this transgression. As Scripture says, "In those days there was no king in Israel; each man did what was pleasing in his own eyes."[d] Such is the great harm arising from anarchy.[1]

XXV

The passage that follows contains a notable contradiction: "There was a young man of Bethlehem of the clan of Judah of the tribe of Judah; he was a Levite living there."[a] If he was a Levite, how could he have been a member of the tribe of Judah?

The Scripture attaches Bethlehem to "clan of Judah," and I take it that the phrase "tribe of Judah" is predicated of the same town. As we have explained, God assigned no lot to the priests and the Levites[b] but scattered them among all the tribes[c] so all of these would have teachers of right religion. Thus, this man, though a Levite, lived in Bethlehem, which belonged to the clan and the tribe of Judah. But whoever regards this as a forced interpretation should recall that, as I have previously mentioned, these two tribes, the royal and the priestly, had intermarried with each other.[1] Therefore, it might be that this man was a Levite through his father though his mother had been a member of the tribe of Judah.

His transgressions were certainly numerous. First, though God

1. For previous discussion of the ephod, v. Q. 17 above. As appears from the comparison of the present question with Q. 33 on 1Sm, Theodoret understands both the teraphim and the ephod to be woven garments used in securing oracles from a god, the former associated with pagan deities, the latter with the God of Israel. He does not realize that "teraphim" is a plural Hebrew noun (*N.B.* his τὸ δὲ θεραφὶμ) denoting statuettes of the family gods. Though teraphim noun appears in the MT of Gn 31.19 and 34, a context where the sense is quite clear (*cf.* 31.30, 32), in both those places the LXX offers the translation "idols" (εἴδωλα) rather than a transliteration (as in Jgs 17.5); *cf.* Q. 91 on Gn.

1. *V.* Q. 19.1 on Jos.

Θεοῦ τὴν σκηνὴν ἐν τῇ Σιλὼμ πήξαντος,[d] ἐν ἑτέρῳ παρὰ τὸν
θεῖον νόμον ἐλειτούργει χωρίῳ. ἔπειτα χειροποιήτοις εἰδώλοις·
τοῦτο γὰρ δηλοῖ τὸ γλυπτὸν καὶ τὸ χωνευτόν·[e] τὰς θυσίας
20 προσέφερε. πρὸς δὲ τούτοις καὶ ἄλλην ἐτόλμα παράβασιν·
ἱερᾶσθαι γὰρ τοὺς λευίτας ὁ νόμος ἐκώλυε, τοῖς δὲ ἱερεῦσιν
ἐκέλευσε λειτουργεῖν.[f] τοιγαροῦν καὶ τοῦτον παρέβη τὸν
νόμον, ἱερατεῦσαι τολμήσας. ἀχάριστος δὲ καὶ περὶ τὸν
τεθεραπευκότα γεγένηται· λαβὼν γὰρ τῆς ἀπάτης τὰ ὄργανα,
25 τοῖς ἐκ τῆς Δὰν φυλῆς ἠκολούθησε καὶ τῆς περὶ τὰ εἴδωλα
πλάνης ἐγένετο πρόξενος.[g]

XXVI

Τί ἐστιν *ἐν κοιλάδι ἦν τοῦ οἴκου Ῥηχάβ;*[a]

Παρ' ἐκείνην, ὡς εἰκός, τὴν πόλιν ᾤκησεν ὁ Ῥηχάβ.[b] αὕτη
δὲ πάλαι μὲν Λαϊσὰ προσηγόρευται, πολιορκηθεῖσα δὲ ὑπὸ
τούτων, μετεκλήθη Δάν,[c] νῦν δὲ Πανεὰς ὀνομάζεται.
5 Ἐνταῦθα μέντοι τοῦδε τοῦ λευίτου τὸ γένος σαφῶς
μεμαθήκαμεν· *Ἰωναθάν,* γάρ φησιν, *υἱὸς Μανασσῆ, υἱοῦ
Γηρσώμ, υἱοῦ Μωϋσῆ, αὐτὸς καὶ οἱ υἱοὶ αὐτοῦ ἦσαν ἱερεῖς τῇ
φυλῇ Δὰν ἕως ... τῆς μετοικεσίας τῆς γῆς. καὶ ἔταξεν αὐτοῖς
τὸ γλυπτὸν Μιχὰ ὃ ἐποίησε πάσας τὰς ἡμέρας ὅσας ἦν ὁ
10 οἶκος τοῦ Θεοῦ ἐν Σιλώμ.*[d] παρανόμως τοιγαροῦν ἱεράτευον, οὐ
μόνον εἰδώλοις λατρεύοντες, ἀλλὰ καὶ ἱερατικὸν ἔργον

XXVI 6, 5, 12, B⁻²⁴, C, 7 9 10 35 37 = 16 mss.

a. Jgs 18.28   b. Jer 35   c. Jgs 18.27–29   d. Jgs 18.30f. (LXX var.)

had fixed the tabernacle at Shiloh,[d] he conducted worship in a place other than that sanctioned by God's law. Second, he offered sacrifices to idols made by human hands, for this is the meaning of "a graven image and an idol of cast metal."[e] On top of this, he was guilty of yet another transgression. As you know, the Law forbade Levites to perform priestly functions and committed the conduct of worship to the priests.[f] So, in presuming to take the part of a priest, he broke this law as well.[2] He was even ungrateful to the man who had provided for him, for he stole the instruments of deceit, joined the Danites, and fomented the error of idol worship.[g]

XXVI

What is the meaning of "It was in the valley of the house of Rechab"?[a]

Rechab probably lived near that city.[b] In ancient times it was known as Leshem, but was renamed Dan after its captors,[c] and is now called Paneas.[1]

It is in this passage that we get clear information on the Levite's family, for Scripture says, "Jonathan, son of Manasseh, son of Gershom, son of Moses, he and his sons were priests to the tribe of Dan until their deportation from the land.[2] All the time the house of God was at Shiloh, they set up for themselves Micah's graven image that he had made."[d] They served as priests in defiance of the Law, not only because they worshiped idols but because they presumed

2. As the legal traditions on this point are not univocal, the Levite could have cited Dt 18.6f. against Theodoret; *v.* Blenkinsopp's remarks on Dt 18.1–5 and J.L. McKenzie, *Dict.*, "Levi, Levite."

1. Again, Theodoret mistakenly attempts to link a proper noun to the founder of the famously pious house of Rechab (*cf. Q.* 6 above). In his version, the Hebrew toponym Beth-rehob is translated "house of Rechab" (Ρηχάβ), though the *codex alexandrinus* and the *codex uaticanus* represent the second part of the place name as Roôb (Ροωβ) and Raab (Ρααβ).

2. In Jgs 18.30, the MT reads "Jonathan the son of Gershom, son of Manasseh,"

The Questions on Judges

τολμῶντες πληροῦν· λευῖται γὰρ ἦσαν, οὐχ ἱερεῖς· μόνον γὰρ
τοῦ Ἀαρὼν τὸ γένος ἱερατεύειν ὁ δεσπότης Θεὸς διηγόρευσε.ᵉ

Καὶ νομίζω, διὰ τὸ ἀλλόφυλον ἀγαγέσθαι γυναῖκα τὸν
15 νομοθέτην,ᶠ τοὺς ἐκ τούτου φύντας τοῖς λευίταις
συνταχθῆναι, καὶ οὐ τοῖς ἱερεῦσι, προσέταξεν ἵνα μὴ τὸ
ἱερατικὸν ἀξίωμα καθυβρίζηται, ὀνειδιζόμενον τὴν δυσγένειαν·
εἰ γὰρ ἀδελφὸς καὶ ἀδελφὴ ταύτην τῷ νομοθέτῃ τὴν λοιδορίαν
ἐπήνεγκαν,ᵍ τί οὐκ ἂν ἐτόλμησαν οἱ περὶ τὸ στασιάζειν καὶ
20 τυραννεῖν προχειρότεροι; οἱ γὰρ κατὰ τοῦ Ἀαρὼν
θρασυνόμενοι, ὃς κόρην ἔγημεν ἐκ τῆς βασιλικῆς
βεβλαστηκυῖαν φυλῆς,ʰ τί οὐκ ἂν ἔδρασαν κατὰ τῶν Μωϋσέως
παίδων, ὃς μαδιηναίου καὶ εἰδώλων ἱερέως ἠγάγετο θυγατέρα;ⁱ

XXVII

Τί δή ποτε, ζήλῳ κινηθεὶς ὁ Ἰσραὴλ καὶ τῆς συγγενείας
τὴν εὐσέβειαν προτιμήσας, ἡττήθη;ᵃ
(1) Ὅτι ταῖς ὁμοίαις παρανομίαις ἐκέχρηντο, καὶ τὰς μὲν
τῶν ἄλλων ἀκολασίας ἑώρων, παρεώρων δὲ τὰς οἰκείας. τοῦτο
5 καὶ ὁ θεῖος ἀπόστολος ἔφη, ἐν ᾧ γὰρ κρίνεις τὸν ἕτερον,
σεαυτὸν κατακρίνεις· τὰ γὰρ αὐτὰ πράσσεις ὁ κρίνων·ᵇ καὶ
πάλιν, λογίζῃ δὲ τοῦτο, ὦ ἄνθρωπε, ὁ κρίνων τοὺς τὰ τοιαῦτα
πράσσοντας καὶ ποιῶν αὐτά, ὅτι σὺ ἐκφεύξῃ τὸ κρίμα τοῦ
Θεοῦ; ἢ τοῦ πλούτου τῆς χρηστότητος αὐτοῦ, καὶ τῆς ἀνοχῆς,
10 καὶ τῆς μακροθυμίας καταφρονεῖς, ἀγνοῶν ὅτι τὸ χρηστὸν τοῦ

e. V., e.g., Nm 18.2–7.   f. Ex 2.21f.   g. Nm 12.1   h. Ex 6.23   i. Ex 2.16

xxvii 6, 5, 12, B⁻²⁴, C, 7 9 10 31(inc.) 35 37 = 17 mss.
a. Jgs 20.20f., 24f.   b. Rom 2.1

to perform priestly functions. After all, they were Levites, not priests, and by command of the Lord God only the family of Aaron were to be priests.[e]

I believe it was due to the lawgiver's marriage to a foreign wife[f] that God ordered his offspring to be reckoned among the Levites rather than the priests. His purpose was to forestall any affront to the priestly dignity arising from criticism of low birth. Given that his brother and sister reproached the lawgiver for this very reason,[g] could there have been any limit to the effrontery of those bent on rebellion and tyranny? Indeed, what about those who insolently rose against Aaron, though he had married a maiden born of royal lineage?[h] Imagine how they would have opposed the children of Moses, who had married a daughter of a Midianite and a priest of idols at that![i]

XXVII

Why is it that Israel was defeated, when, motivated by zeal, they put religion ahead of kinship?[a]

(1) Because they engaged in similar transgressions and, while taking note of the licentiousness of others, overlooked their own.[1] The holy apostle himself declared, "In passing judgment on the other person, you condemn yourself, for you the judge engage in the same behavior";[b] and again, "Do you imagine, mortal that you are, that you, who pass judgment on those guilty of such acts yet perform them yourself, will escape the judgment of God? Or do you

---

but in an unpointed consonantal text, the names Moses and Manasseh differ only in that the latter contains the letter nûn (n), which in many mss. is written above the line, *i.e.* in a way that suggests it might be more accurately omitted; *cf. ap. crit.* of the *BHS ad loc.* The *codex alexandrinus* has "Jonathan the son of Gershom, son of Moses," and the *uaticanus* "Jonathan the son of Gershom, son of Manasseh"; in contrast, Theodoret's text contains both Moses and Manasseh.

---

1. Theodoret pointedly declines to describe the crime committed by the Ben-

Θεοῦ εἰς μετάνοιάν σε ἄγει; κατὰ δὲ τὴν σκληρότητά σου καὶ
ἀμετανόητον καρδίαν, θησαυρίζεις σεαυτῷ ὀργὴν ἐν ἡμέρᾳ
ὀργῆς, καὶ ἀποκαλύψεως, καὶ δικαιοκρισίας τοῦ Θεοῦ, ὃς
ἀποδώσει ἑκάστῳ κατὰ τὰ ἔργα αὐτοῦ.ᶜ

15 Τοῦτο καὶ οὗτοι πεπόνθασι. δικαίῳ γὰρ χρησάμενοι κατὰ
τῶν ἐν τῇ Γαβαὼν παρανενομηκότων θυμῷ,ᵈ τὰς τετρακοσίας
ἐξώπλισαν χιλιάδας·ᵉ παιδεῦσαι δὲ αὐτοὺς βουληθεὶς ὁ Θεός,
ὡς τὰ ὅμοια δρῶντας καὶ ἐν ἄλλοις μὲν τὸ κακὸν θεωροῦντας,
ἐν ἑαυτοῖς δὲ τοῦτο ποιεῖν οὐκ ἐθέλοντας, καὶ ἅπαξ καὶ δὶς
20 συνεχώρησεν ἡττηθῆναι καὶ πολλὰς αὐτῶν χιλιάδας
ἀναιρεθῆναι. ἐπειδὴ δὲ εἶδε καὶ τὴν παιδείαν δεξαμένους, καὶ
τῷ δικαίῳ θυμῷ κεχρημένους, καὶ ὀλοφυρομένους, καὶ
ποτνιωμένους, καὶ πολλὰ προχέοντας δάκρυα,ᶠ συνήργησε τῇ
προθυμίᾳ καὶ τὴν παράνομον φυλὴν ἄρδην ἀπώλεσε, πλὴν
25 ὀλίγων ἄγαν εὐαριθμήτων.ᵍ καὶ γὰρ τῶν ἀκολάστων χείρους οἱ
ἐκείνων προκινδυνεύσαντες· ἐξαιτούντων γὰρ τῶν ὁμοφύλων
τοὺς τὴν παρανομίαν τετολμηκότας, οὐ μόνον οὐκ ἐξέδοσαν,
ἀλλὰ καὶ προθύμως αὐτῶν ὑπερήσπισαν.ʰ οὗ δὲ χάριν κοινὸν
ὑπέμειναν ὄλεθρον.

30 (2) Οἶμαι δὲ τοῦτον τὸν πόλεμον πρὸ τῶν ἄλλων
γεγενῆσθαι πολέμων, οὐ μετὰ πολὺν χρόνον τῆς Ἰησοῦ
‖31 τελευτῆς·‖ *Φινεές, γάρ φησιν, υἱὸς Ἐλεαζάρ, υἱοῦ Ἀαρὼν τοῦ*
ἱερέως, παρειστήκει ἐνώπιον τῆς κιβωτοῦ ἐν ταῖς ἡμέραις
*ἐκείναις.*ⁱ ὁ δὲ Ἐλεαζὰρ εὐθὺς μετὰ τὸν Ἰησοῦν τοῦ βίου τὸ
35 τέλος ἐδέξατο, διεδέξατο δὲ τὴν ἱερωσύνην ὁ Φινεές. καὶ
τοῦτο ἡμᾶς ἐδίδαξε τὸ τέλος τῆς Ἰησοῦ τοῦ Ναυῆ
συγγραφῆς.ʲ

Οἶμαι τοίνυν τὸν τήνδε τὴν ἱστορίαν συγγεγραφηκότα οὐχ
ὡς ἔτυχε τάξαι τελευταῖα τὰ πρῶτα γεγενημένα. ἠβουλήθη

---

c. Rom 2.3–6   d. Jgs 19.22–28   e. Jgs 20.2   f. Jgs 20.26
g. Jgs 20.35, 46f.   h. Jgs 20.12–14   i. Jgs 20.28 (LXX var.)   j. Jos 24.33

despise his abundant kindness, forbearance, and long-suffering, in your ignorance that God's kindness leads you to repentance? With your hardness of heart and impenitence, you store up wrath for yourself on the day of the wrath, revelation, and righteous judgment of God, who will pay each according to his deeds."[c]

This was also the experience of these people. In an exercise of righteous indignation against the sinners of Gibeah,[d] they armed four hundred thousand men.[e] But God allowed them to be defeated twice with the loss of many thousands, as it was his will to punish those who engaged in similar conduct and, though seeing the evil in others, were wilfully blind to themselves. But when he saw that, after their chastisement, they were not only possessed of righteous outrage but were also lamenting, wailing, and shedding copious tears,[f] he seconded their zeal and utterly destroyed the sinful tribe, with the exception of a very few.[g] After all, even worse than those guilty of the outrage were those who risked their lives to protect them. When their fellow citizens demanded the surrender of those who had committed the crime, they not only refused to hand them over but eagerly undertook their defense.[h] Thus, they were destroyed along with them.

(2) Now, it is my view that this war took place before the others and not long after the death of Joshua. As you recall, Scripture says, "Phinehas, the son of Eleazar, the son of Aaron, stood by the ark in those days."[i] Now, Eleazar came to the end of his life immediately after Joshua, and Phinehas succeeded him in the priesthood, as we learn at the end of the history of Joshua, the son of Nun.[j]

In my view, the author of this biblical book was not being merely arbitrary in placing the earliest events last. It was his intention first

----
jaminites in Gibeah. Only in the last sentence of his comment does he make mention, in general terms, of the terrible rape of the Levite's concubine related in ch. 19. Instead, he concentrates on an ethical exegesis of the successive defeats of the tribes that wished to exact punishment for the outrage; cf. note 50 to the "Introduction to Theodoret's Life and Works."

40 γὰρ τὰς τῶν κριτῶν ἡμῖν πρότερον ἐπιδεῖξαι διαδοχάς· καὶ
    τίς πρῶτος, τίς δεύτερος, τίς τρίτος ἡγήσατο· εἶθ' οὕτω τὰ
    δύο ταῦτα διηγήματα θεῖναι· τό τε κατὰ τὸν Μιχὰν καὶ τὴν
    Λαϊσὰνᵏ καὶ τὸ κατὰ τὸ γύναιον ὅπερ ἡ μανικὴ τῶν
    ἀκολάστων ἀνεῖλε λαγνεία.ˡ

XXVIII

    Τί δή ποτε προσέταξαν οἱ υἱοὶ Ἰσραὴλ τοῖς διακοσίοις,
    τοῖς ἐκ τοῦ Βενιαμίν,ᵃ ἐκ τῶν ἐν Σιλὼμ χορευουσῶν παρθένων
    ἁρπάσαι τε καὶ γῆμαι;ᵇ
    Αἱ τῆς φυλῆς αὐτῶν γυναῖκες ἅπασαι κατεσφάγησαν·ᶜ
5   αὐτοὶ δὲ ὀμωμόκεισαν μὴ κατεγγυῆσαι αὐτοῖς τὰς ἑαυτῶν
    θυγατέρας.ᵈ ἵνα τοίνυν μή, βιασθέντες ὑπὸ τῆς ἀνάγκης,
    ἀλλοφύλους γυναῖκας ἀγάγωνται, πόρον εὗρον ἐν ἀπόροις καὶ
    τὴν ἁρπαγὴν ἐπενόησαν.

k. Jgs 17f.   l. Jgs 19

xxviii 6, 5, 12, B⁻²⁴, C, 7 9 10 35 37 = 16 mss.

a. Jgs 20.47; 21.12–14   b. Jgs 21.20f.   c. Jgs 20.48   d. Jgs 21.1

to set out for us the succession of the judges—who was the first, who second, who third—and after this, to append these two stories, the first about Micah and Leshem[k] and the second about the woman murdered by the lust of immoral men.[21]

XXVIII

Why did the Israelites order the two hundred men of Benjamin[a] to seize for their wives some of the maidens of Shiloh as they performed the choral dance?[b]

All the women belonging to the tribe of Benjamin had been slaughtered,[c] and the rest of the tribes had sworn an oath not to betroth their daughters to them.[d] Therefore, so the Benjaminites would not be forced to take foreign wives, they excogitated this rape as a way out of the impasse.

2. As in Q. 2, Theodoret shrewdly surveys the structure of the book. Like his modern counterparts, he notes that chapters 17–21 constitute an appendix following the presentation of individual judges. These five chapters, though perhaps quite ancient, are now generally believed to owe their place to post-deuteronomistic scholars. Though Theodoret believes this book to be the work of only one author, it was probably assembled by many hands in several stages; v. M. O'Connor, p. 134.

QUAESTIONES IN RUTH

I

Τί δή ποτε τὸ κατὰ τὴν Ῥοὺθ συνεγράφη διήγημα;

(1) Πρῶτον διὰ τὸν δεσπότην Χριστόν· ἐξ αὐτῆς γὰρ κατὰ σάρκα βεβλάστηκε. διὸ δὴ καὶ ὁ θειότατος Ματθαῖος, τὴν γενεαλογίαν συγγράφων, τὰς μὲν ἐπ' ἀρετῇ πολυθρυλλήτους
5 γυναῖκας κατέλιπε· τὴν Σάρραν, καὶ τὴν Ῥεβέκκαν, καὶ τὰς ἄλλας· τῆς δέ γε Θάμαρ ἐμνημόνευσε, καὶ τῆς Ῥαάβ, καὶ τῆς Ῥούθ, καὶ μέντοι καὶ τῆς τοῦ Οὐρίου,[a] διδάσκων ὡς πάντων ἀνθρώπων χάριν ὁ τοῦ Θεοῦ μονογενὴς ἐνηνθρώπησε· καὶ ἰουδαίων καὶ τῶν ἄλλων ἐθνῶν, καὶ ἁμαρτωλῶν καὶ δικαίων. ἡ
10 μὲν γὰρ Ῥοὺθ μωαβῖτις·[b] ἡ δέ γε Βερσαβεὲ παρανόμως συνήφθη τῷ βασιλεῖ·[c] πόρνη δὲ καὶ ἡ Ῥαάβ[d] ἀλλὰ διὰ πίστεως τῆς σωτηρίας τετύχηκε. καὶ ἡ Θάμαρ δὲ ταύτῃ λαμπρύνεται· οὐ γάρ, ἀκολασίας ἕνεκα, τῷ κηδεστῇ κεκοινώνηκεν ἀλλ', ὁρῶσα μὴ βουλόμενον αὐτῇ συνάψαι τὸν παῖδα, ἔκλεψε τὴν
15 γεωργίαν ἵνα βλαστήσῃ τὴν εὐλογίαν.[e] αὐτίκα γοῦν μετὰ τοῦτον τὸν σπόρον ἄλλον οὐκ ἐδέξατο σπόρον ἀλλὰ τὴν ἀγαμίαν ἠγάπησεν.[f]

Ἴδοι δ' ἄν τις καὶ τὴν Ῥοὺθ διὰ τὴν εὐσέβειαν τοὺς μὲν γεγεννηκότας καταλιποῦσαν, ἀκολουθήσασαν δὲ τῇ πενθερᾷ·
20 εἶπε, γάρ φησιν, ἡ Ῥούθ, μή μοι γένοιτο τοῦ καταλιπεῖν σε ἢ τοῦ ἀποστρέψαι ὄπισθέν σου, ὅτι οὐ ἐὰν πορευθῇς σύ, πορεύσομαι, καὶ οὗ ἐὰν αὐλισθῇς, αὐλισθήσομαι ἐκεῖ, ὅτι ὁ λαός σου λαός μου, καὶ ὁ Θεός σου Θεός μου, καὶ οὗ ἂν

1 6, 5, 12, B, C, 9 10 31 35 37 = 16 mss.

a. Mt 1.3, 5f.   b. Ru 1.4   c. 2Sm 11   d. Jos 2.1   e. Gn 38.13–19
f. Gn 38.25f.

ON RUTH

I

Why was the story of Ruth composed?[1]

(1) First, on account of the Lord Christ, who drew his bodily descent from Ruth. Hence, when he was composing the genealogy, St. Matthew passed over women such as Sarah, Rebekah, and the others, who were celebrated for their virtue, but mentioned Tamar, Rahab, Ruth, and even the wife of Uriah,[a] to teach us that God's only-begotten became man for the sake of all human beings: both Jews and gentiles, sinners and saints. Ruth was a Moabite;[b] Bathsheba was unlawfully joined to the king;[c] Rahab was a prostitute,[d] but gained salvation through faith; and Tamar also distinguished herself by her faith. After all, she did not engage in intercourse with her father-in-law to satisfy her lust, but, as she realized he would not marry his son to her, she filched the planting, so it might blossom into a blessing.[e] Indeed, after that sowing, she received no other, but accepted her widowhood.[f]

Anyone could see that Ruth was also motivated by right religion when she left her parents and followed her mother-in-law. According to Scripture, Ruth declared, "May I never leave you behind or turn back from following you! Wherever you go, I shall go, and wherever you lodge, I shall lodge, because your people are my people, and your God my God, and wherever you die, I shall die and be

1. Theodoret's questions constitute the sole surviving, but not the first, patristic commentary on Ruth. H. Achelis (vol. 2.1, p. 120) printed a testimony to, and a fragment from, a commentary of the third-century Greek author Hippolytus of Rome; *cf. CPG* #1880.8. Thus, Guinot's remark (note 75, p. 778), "En dehors de

ἀποθάνῃς, ἀποθανοῦμαι, καὶ ἐκεῖ ταφήσομαι. τάδε ποιήσαι μοι
25 Κύριος καὶ τάδε προσθείη, ὅτι θάνατος διαστελεῖ ἀνὰ μέσον
ἐμοῦ καὶ σοῦ.[g] καὶ ταῦτα εἴρηκε, πολλάκις ὑπὸ τῆς
κηδεστρίας παρακληθεῖσα πρὸς τοὺς γεγεννηκότας
ἐπανελθεῖν· ἀποστράφητε . . ., γὰρ ἔφη, θυγατέρες μου· καὶ
ἵνα τί πορεύεσθε μετ' ἐμοῦ; μὴ ἔτι μοι υἱοὶ ἐν τῇ κοιλίᾳ μου
30 καὶ ἔσονται ὑμῖν εἰς ἄνδρας; ἀποστράφητε, δὴ θυγατέρες μου,
ὅτι γεγήρακα τοῦ μὴ εἶναι ἀνδρὶ καὶ εἶπον, οὐκ ἔστι μοι
ὑπόστασις τοῦ γενέσθαι με ἀνδρί. καὶ τέξομαι υἱούς, μὴ
αὐτοὺς προσδέξεσθε ἕως οὗ ἀνδρυνθῶσιν; ἢ αὐτοῖς
κατασχεθήσεσθε τοῦ μὴ γενέσθαι ἀνδρί; μὴ δή, θυγατέρες
35 μου, ὅτι ἐπικράνθη μοι ὑπὲρ ὑμᾶς, ὅτι ἐξῆλθεν ἐν ἐμοὶ χεὶρ
Κυρίου.[h] οὔτε, φησίν, ἐγκύμων εἰμὶ ἵνα τοῖς ὑπ' ἐμοῦ
τεχθησομένοις ἀναμείνητε συναφθῆναι, οὔτε ἀνδρί με
γήμασθαι δυνατὸν διὰ τὸ γῆρας ἵνα προσμένητέ μου τὸν
γάμον, καὶ τὴν παιδοποιίαν, καὶ τὴν ἐκείνων ἀναστροφήν· ἐγὼ
40 γὰρ θεήλατον ἐδεξάμην πληγήν.

(2) Ἔδει μὲν οὖν καὶ διὰ τὸν δεσπότην ἀνάγραπτον
γενέσθαι τῆς Ῥοὺθ τὸ διήγημα· ἱκανὴ δὲ ὅμως καὶ αὐτὴ καθ'
αὐτὴν ἡ ἱστορία πᾶσαν προσενεγκεῖν ὠφέλειαν τοῖς τὰ
τοιαῦτα κερδαίνειν ἐπισταμένοις. διδάσκει γὰρ ἡμᾶς καὶ τῆς
45 Νοεμὶν τὰς χαλεπὰς συμφοράς, καὶ τὴν ἐπαινετὴν καρτερίαν,
καὶ τῶν νυμφῶν τὴν σωφροσύνην, καὶ τὴν περὶ τὴν πενθερὰν
φιλοστοργίαν, καὶ διαφερόντως τῆς Ῥούθ, ἢ γεγηρακυῖαν

g. Ru 1.16f.   h. Ru 1.11–13

buried. May the Lord do this and more to me, for only death will come between me and you."[g] Moreover, she made this declaration after her mother-in-law had repeatedly urged her to return to her parents: "Go back, my daughters. Why go with me? Are there any more sons in my womb to be your husbands? Go back, my daughters, because I am too old to be married, and as I said, I have no intention to marry a husband. Even if I should bear sons, surely you would not wait for them to grow up or refrain from marrying a husband for their sakes? No, my daughters, I am sad for you, for the Lord has stretched out his hand against me."[h] What she means to say is "I am not pregnant, so that you should wait to marry any sons I might bear, and, given my age, I cannot be married off to a husband so that you should wait for me to be married, have children, and raise them. I am the victim of a heaven-sent punishment."

(2) Though the story of Ruth had to be recorded for its christological significance, this narrative is sufficient of itself to offer great benefit to those who know how to profit by it.[2] Indeed, it teaches us Naomi's severe misfortunes and commendable patience, the continence of the young wives, and their affection for their mother-in-law, especially Ruth's, who, moved by a pious heart and the remembrance of her partner, honored even more than her parents an

----

Théodoret et de ses *Quaest.*, aucun autre Père ne semble avoir commenté le livre de Ruth," is not quite accurate. Theodoret, who reads the OT as preparatory to the New, finds in Matthew's genealogy the explanation for the inclusion of the book of Ruth in the scriptural canon. He maintains that Ruth, Tamar, Rahab, and Bathsheba figure in the genealogy because, in terms of Israelite law, they would all seem in some way problematic: sinners, gentiles, or both. According to B. Viviano (on 1.2–16), modern commentators on Matthew would focus rather on the "extraordinary or irregular" character of their marriages and the important roles played by these women in God's plan of salvation. It does not occur to Theodoret to ask about the place of Ruth within the Hebrew Bible. Modern discussions of that issue divide according to the date, pre- or post-exilic, assigned to the work; *v.* A. Laffey, "Ruth," pp. 553f.

2. Now, Theodoret identifies a further reason for the inclusion of Ruth in the

γυναῖκα καὶ πενομένην τῶν γεγεννηκότων προὐτίμησε διὰ τὴν
τῆς γνώμης εὐσέβειαν καὶ τὴν τοῦ ὁμοζύγου μνήμην. ἐδίδαξε
50 δὲ ἡμᾶς καὶ τοῦ Βοὸζ τὴν ἀρετήν· οὐ γὰρ μόνον φιλοτίμως τῇ
'Ροὺθ τοῦ καρποῦ μεταδέδωκεν, ἀλλὰ καὶ λόγοις ἐψυχαγώγησε·
μὴ πορευθῇς, γὰρ ἔφη, θύγατερ, ἐν ἀγρῷ ἑτέρῳ
συλλέξαι . . . ἀλλ' ὧδε κολλήθητι μετὰ τῶν κορασίων μου.[i]
κελεύσας δὲ αὐτῇ καὶ συνεσθίειν καὶ συμπίνειν τοῖς
55 θερίζουσιν,[j] ἐπήγαγεν, *ἀπαγγελίᾳ ἀπηγγέλη μοι ὅσα*
πεποίηκας μετὰ τῆς πενθερᾶς σου μετὰ τὸ ἀποθανεῖν τὸν
ἄνδρα σου, καὶ πῶς κατέλιπες τὸν πατέρα σου, καὶ τὴν
μητέρα σου, καὶ τὴν γῆν τῆς γενέσεώς σου, καὶ ἐπορεύθης
πρὸς λαὸν ὃν οὐκ ᾔδεις ἐχθὲς καὶ τρίτης. ἀποτίσαι σοι Κύριος
60 *τὴν ἐργασίαν σου, καὶ γένοιτο ὁ μισθός σου πλήρης παρὰ*
Κυρίου Θεοῦ Ἰσραήλ, πρὸς ὃν ἦλθες πεποιθέναι ὑπὸ τὰς
πτέρυγας αὐτοῦ.[k] καὶ τετύχηκεν ἡ εὐλογία τέλους· ἔλαβε γὰρ
τὸν μισθὸν πλήρη παρὰ Κυρίου, πρόγονος γενομένη τῆς τῶν
ἐθνῶν εὐλογίας. οὐ μόνον δὲ αὐτῇ τροφῆς μεταδέδωκεν, ἀλλὰ
65 καὶ αὐτουργὸς τῆς θεραπείας ἐγένετο· οὐκ ἄλλῳ διακονῆσαι
προστάξας, ἀλλ' αὐτὸς κατασκευάσας τὰ ἄλφιτα καὶ τοὺς
ἄρτους μάλα φιλοτίμως προσενεγκών·[l] κορεσθεῖσα γὰρ
ἀπήνεγκε τὸ περιττεῦσαν τῇ πενθερᾷ.[m] εὐγνωμόνως δὲ καὶ ἡ
κηδέστρια τὸν ἀπόντα εὐεργέτην ταῖς εὐλογίαις ἠμείψατο·
70 ἔφη γάρ, *εἴη ὁ ἐπιγνούς σε εὐλογημένος,*[n] ὅτι ἐχόρτασε ψυχὴν
κενὴν καθὼς ἐποίησε μεθ' οὗ ἐποίησεν· οὐ γὰρ εἰς τὴν σήν,
φησί, πενίαν ἀπέβλεψεν, ἀλλ' εἰς τὸν νομοθέτην, ὃς
διηγόρευσε πᾶσαν ποιεῖσθαι τῶν χηρῶν ἐπιμέλειαν.[o]

i. Ru 2.8   j. Ru 2.9   k. Ru 2.11f.   l. Ru 2.14   m. Ru 2.18   n. Ru 2.19
o. Ru 2.20

elderly woman, and a pauper at that. It also teaches us about the virtue of Boaz, who not only generously shared his crops with Ruth but also encouraged her: "Do not, daughter, go gleaning in another field; instead, attach yourself to my girls here."[i] And after bidding her eat and drink with the reapers,[j] he continued, "A report has reached me of all you did for your mother-in-law after the death of your husband and how you left your father and your mother and the land of your birth and travelled to a people you did not know before. May the Lord repay you for your actions, and may you have a full reward from the Lord, the God of Israel, under whose wings you have come to shelter."[k] This blessing was fulfilled. She received a full reward from the Lord, when she became ancestress of the blessing of the nations. Boaz not only shared his food with her, but himself waited on her. Without ordering someone else to serve her, he personally provided the barley meal and very generously brought her loaves of bread.[l] Then, when she had eaten her fill, she took the leftovers to her mother-in-law.[m] In return the mother-in-law gratefully blessed her absent benefactor with the words, "May he who took notice of you be blessed,[n] for he has satisfied an empty soul through his dealings with you. He had regard, not for your poverty, but for the Lawgiver, who enjoined the especial care of widows."[o]

Scriptures: in addition to its christological bearing, the account is morally edifying. Together these constitute a fair summary of his understanding of the relevance to Christian readers of the Octateuch and the OT in general.

II

Ἐπιμέμφονταί τινες καὶ τῇ Νοεμὶν καὶ τῇ Ῥούθ· τῇ μέν, ὡς ὑποθεμένη, τῇ δέ, ὡς ὑπακουσάσῃ, τε καὶ πραξάσῃ, καὶ παρὰ τοὺς πόδας καθευδησάσῃ τοῦ Βοόζ.[a]

(1) Ἀκούσασα ἡ Ῥοὺθ εἰρηκυίας τῆς πενθερᾶς, ὅτι ἐγγίζει
5 ἡμῖν ὁ ἀνήρ, ἐκ τῶν ἀγχιστευόντων ἡμῖν ἐστι,[b] τῆς πολλῆς ἀνεμνήσθη θεραπείας[c] καὶ ᾠήθη τὸν Βοόζ, ὡς τοῦ ἀνδρὸς συγγενῆ, συναφθῆναι αὐτῇ κατὰ τὸν νόμον ἐθέλειν ὥστε τοῦ τετελευτηκότος φυλάξαι τὴν μνήμην.[d] τοῦτο γὰρ δηλοῖ τὰ ἑξῆς· εἶπε, γάρ φησι, Ῥοὺθ πρὸς τὴν πενθερὰν αὐτῆς,
10 καὶ... ὅτι εἶπε..., μετὰ τῶν κορασίων μου κολλήθητι ἕως ἂν τελέσωσιν ὅλον... τὸν ὑπάρχοντά μοι.[e] τούτων ἀκούσασα τῶν λόγων, ἡ Νοεμὶν ὑποτίθεται αὐτῇ παρὰ τοὺς πόδας καθευδῆσαι τοῦ Βοόζ, οὐχ ἵνα τὴν ὥραν ἀποδῶται· τοὐναντίον γὰρ δηλοῖ τὰ τῆς εἰσηγήσεως ῥήματα· ἐλεύσῃ, γάρ φησι, καὶ
15 ἀποκαλύψεις τὰ πρὸς ποδῶν αὐτοῦ, καὶ κοιμηθήσῃ, καὶ αὐτὸς ἀπαγγελεῖ σοι ἃ ποιήσεις.[f] οὕτως ἐθάρρει τῇ τοῦ ἀνδρὸς καὶ σωφροσύνῃ καὶ δικαιοσύνῃ.

Ἐβεβαίωσαν δὲ τοὺς λόγους αἱ πράξεις· κατὰ γὰρ τὰς ὑποθημοσύνας τῆς πενθερᾶς, πάντων ὕπνῳ κατεχομένων,
20 προσεκλίθη παρὰ τοὺς πόδας τοῦ Βοόζ ἡ Ῥούθ. ὁ δὲ ἤρετο τίς εἴη, ἡ δὲ τῆς τοῦ τετελευτηκότος συγγενείας ἀνέμνησεν.[g] ὁ δὲ τὸ μὲν πραχθὲν ἐπήνεσε, τὴν δὲ σωφροσύνην οὐ προὔδωκεν, ἀλλὰ τῷ νόμῳ τὴν γαμικὴν διετήρησεν ὁμιλίαν· εὐλογημένη, γὰρ ἔφη, σὺ τῷ Κυρίῳ..., θύγατερ, ὅτι ἠγάθυνας τὸν ἔλεόν
25 σου τὸν ἔσχατον ὑπὲρ τὸν πρῶτον τοῦ μὴ πορευθῆναί σε ὀπίσω νεανιῶν, ἤτοι πτωχὸς ἤτοι πλούσιος.[h] δεδήλωκας, φησί, δι' ὧν ἔπραξας ὡς, οὐκ ἐπιθυμίᾳ δουλεύσασα, τοῦτο δέδρακας· ἢ γὰρ ἂν πρὸς τοὺς νέαν ἄγοντας ἡλικίαν ἐφοίτησας, οὐ

II 6, 5, 12, B, C, 9 10 35 37 = 15 mss.

a. Ru 3.4, 7   b. Ru 2.20   c. Ru 2.8–16   d. Dt 25.5f.   e. Ru 2.21
f. Ru 3.4   g. Ru 3.6–9   h. Ru 3.10

11

There are those who find fault with Naomi and Ruth: with the former, for suggesting that Ruth sleep at the feet of Boaz and with the latter, for heeding and doing what Naomi suggested.[1a]

(1) Since Ruth had heard her mother-in-law say, "That man is related to us; he is one of our next-of-kin,"[b] she recalled his close attention[c] and became convinced that, as her husband's kith and kin, Boaz wanted to be united with her to preserve the memory of the deceased, as the Law required.[d] This is borne out by what happened next. According to the Scripture, "Ruth said to her mother-in-law, 'He said, "Attach yourself to my girls until they have finished all the harvest belonging to me."'"[e] Hearing these words, Naomi suggested that she sleep at the feet of Boaz, but not to sell her beauty, since the words in which she couched her proposal indicate the opposite. As she said, "You will go and uncover the place at his feet and lie down, and for his part he will tell you what you are to do."[f] This is how confident she was in the man's continence and righteousness.

His actions confirmed these words. In keeping with her mother-in-law's suggestion, when everyone was fast asleep, Ruth lay down at Boaz's feet. When he asked her who she was, and she reminded him of his relationship to the deceased,[g] he commended her actions, but, without forgetting his continence, in observance of the Law, deferred the marital union. "May you be blessed by the Lord God, daughter," he declared, "for this act of kindness surpasses your first, as you have not pursued young men, whether poor or rich."[h] He means to say, "Through your actions you have shown that you did not take this step in thrall to lust; otherwise you would have sought

1. Guinot wonders (p. 778) which fault-finders Theodoret has in mind: those detractors of Scripture whom he mentions in the preface to the *Quaest. in oct.* or Theodore of Mopsuestia and/or Diodore? If one or both had questioned the canonicity of this book, Theodoret may have wished to demonstrate its ethical value as a way of justifying its use in the Church.

πλοῦτον, οὐ πενίαν, ἀλλὰ μόνην λογιζομένη τῆς ἡδονῆς τὴν
30 ἀπόλαυσιν· ἀλλ' ἐλήλυθας πρὸς ἄνδρα πατρός σου τάξιν
πληροῦντα· τοῦτο γὰρ σημαίνει τὸ *θύγατερ*. καὶ δὶς δὲ αὐτὴν
οὕτω κέκληκε· *καὶ νῦν, θύγατερ, μὴ φοβοῦ· πάντα ὅσα ἂν*
εἴπῃς ποιήσω σοι· οἶδε γὰρ πᾶσα φυλὴ λαοῦ μου ὅτι γυνὴ
δυνάμεως εἶ σύ, καὶ ὅτι ἀληθῶς ἀγχιστεὺς ἐγώ εἰμι.[i] οὐδείς
35 μοι, φησίν, ἐπιμέμψεται· σύ τε γὰρ ἐπαινῇ παρὰ πάντων,
κἀγὼ διὰ τὴν συγγένειαν, οὐ δι' ἀκολασίαν, τὸν γάμον
ποιήσομαι. ἐπειδὴ δέ ἐστιν ἕτερος πλησιαίτερος συγγενής,
ἐκείνῳ με δεῖ πρότερον διαλεχθῆναι ἵνα, εἰ μὲν ἕλοιτο, γήμῃ
κατὰ τὸν νόμον, εἰ δὲ μὴ πείθοιτο κατὰ τὸν νόμον, ἐγὼ δή
40 σοι τότε τὸν γαμικὸν ἐπιθήσω ζυγόν.[j]

(2) Τοσαύτη ἡ τοῦ ἀνδρὸς ἀρετὴ ὅτι, κόρης νέας εὐπρεποῦς
νύκτωρ πρὸς αὐτὸν φοιτησάσης, τὴν σωφροσύνην ἐφύλαξε, καὶ
τῷ νόμῳ τὸ πρᾶγμα τετήρηκε, καὶ οὐδὲ τῷ γάμῳ παρὰ τὸν
νόμον προσέδραμεν, ἀλλὰ τῷ πλησιαιτέρῳ τοὺς περὶ τοῦ
45 γάμου προσενήνοχε λόγους. εἶτα, ἐκείνου παραιτησαμένου τὸν
γάμον, τότε λοιπὸν τῇ ἀξιεπαίνῳ γυναικὶ συνηρμόσθη.[k]

Ἀξιάγαστα δὲ αὐτοῦ καὶ τὰ πρὸς ἐκεῖνον ῥήματα. οὐ γὰρ
πρώτους αὐτῷ τοὺς περὶ τοῦ γάμου προσενήνοχε λόγους ἀλλὰ
περὶ τῆς τῶν ἀγρῶν κτήσεως διελέχθη.[l] ἔπειτα, ἐκείνου τὸ
50 συμβόλαιον ἀσπαστῶς δεξαμένου,[m] τὸν περὶ τοῦ γάμου
προστέθεικεν λόγον, εἰρηκὼς δίκαιον εἶναι τὸν τοῦ
τετελευτηκότος κτώμενον τοὺς ἀγροὺς γῆμαι καὶ τὴν γυναῖκα
καὶ φυλάξαι τῇ παιδοποιίᾳ τοῦ κατοιχομένου τὴν μνήμην.[n]
ἐπειδὴ δὲ διὰ τὸν γάμον καὶ τὸ τῶν ἀγρῶν ἐκεῖνος ἠρνήθη
55 συμβόλαιον, ὑπελύσατο μὲν κατὰ τὸν νόμον καὶ τὸ ὑπόδημα
δέδωκεν·[o] ἠγάγετο δὲ ὁ Βοὸζ τὴν Ῥούθ.

Ὅτι δέ, οὐχ ἡδονῇ δουλεύων, ἠνέσχετο γῆμαι δηλοῖ αὐτοῦ
καὶ τὰ ἀξιέπαινα ῥήματα· *εἶπε*, γάρ φησι, *Βοὸζ τοῖς*

---

i. Ru 3.11f.   j. Ru 3.12f.   k. Ru 4.1–13   l. Ru 4.3f.   m. Ru 4.4
n. Ru 4.5   o. Ru 4.6–8

out young men, with no thought for their wealth or poverty, but only for the enjoyment of pleasure. Instead, you have come to a man who plays the part of your father." Indeed, this is the implication of the word "daughter," a title with which he addressed her a second time: "As it is, daughter, have no fear. I shall do all you ask. All the tribe of my people knows that you are a woman of strength and that I am, in fact, a close relative."[i] What he means to say is "No one will blame me, as you enjoy everyone's good opinion, and I shall undertake this marriage because of kinship rather than lust. Nonetheless, since there is another closer relative, I must first speak with him so that, should he wish, he may marry you as the Law provides. But if he exercises his legal right of refusal, I shall place the yoke of marriage upon you myself."[j]

(2) Such was the man's virtue that though a lovely young lady visited him at night, he maintained his continence and conducted the matter according to the Law. He did not even rush into marriage in defiance of the Law, but addressed the closer relative on the topic of the marriage. When the latter declined the marriage, then, and only then, did he unite himself to that excellent woman.[k]

How admirable his negotiations with that man! He did not begin by raising the question of marriage but first discussed the ownership of the property.[l] Next, when the other gladly accepted the contract,[m] he went on to raise the question of marriage and pointed out that it was only fair for the purchaser of the deceased man's property to marry his wife as well and preserve the memory of the departed by raising children.[n] When, to avoid the marriage, the other man rejected the contract for the property, he undid his sandal and gave it to Boaz as enjoined by the Law.[o] Then Boaz married Ruth.

Moreover, we deduce from his praiseworthy speech that when he agreed to the marriage it was not because he was in thrall to pleas-

πρεσβυτέροις καὶ παντὶ τῷ λαῷ, μάρτυρες ὑμεῖς σήμερον ὅτι
60 κέκτημαι πάντα τὰ τοῦ Ἀβιμέλεχ καὶ πάντα ὅσα ὑπάρχει τῷ
Μααλὼν καὶ τῷ Χελεὼν ἐκ χειρὸς Νοεμίν· καί γε Ῥοὺθ τὴν
μωαβῖτιν τὴν γυναῖκα Μααλὼν κέκτημαι ἐμαυτῷ εἰς γυναῖκα
τοῦ ἀναστῆσαι τὸ ὄνομα τοῦ τεθνηκότος ἐπὶ τῆς κληρονομίας
αὐτοῦ, καὶ οὐκ ἐξολοθρευθήσεται τὸ ὄνομα τοῦ τεθνηκότος ἐκ
65 τῶν ἀδελφῶν αὐτοῦ καὶ ἐκ τῆς φυλῆς αὐτοῦ.[p] ἄξιον θαυμάσαι
τῶν εἰρημένων καὶ τὸ εὐσεβὲς καὶ τὸ ἀκριβές· οὐ παραβαίνω,
γάρ φησι, τὸν νόμον, μωαβῖτιν γυναῖκα λαμβάνων, ἀλλὰ τὸν
θεῖον νόμον πληρῶ, τοῦ τετελευτηκότος ἄσβεστον φυλαχθῆναι
τὴν μνήμην σπουδάζων.

70 (3) Ἐκράτυναν δὲ καὶ οἱ πρεσβύτεροι τῇ εὐλογίᾳ τὸν γάμον·
εἶπον δὲ οὕτως· δῴη Κύριος τὴν γυναῖκά σου, τὴν
εἰσπορευομένην εἰς τὸν οἶκόν σου, ὡς Ῥαχὴλ καὶ . . . Λείαν, αἳ
ᾠκοδόμησαν ἀμφότεραι τὸν οἶκον Ἰσραήλ, καὶ ποιῆσαι δύναμιν
ἐν Ἐφραθά· καὶ ἔσται ὄνομα ἐν Βηθλεὲμ παρὰ πᾶσιν
75 ἀνθρώποις ἀοίδιμον. καὶ γένοιτο ὁ οἶκός σου ὡς . . . οἶκος
Φάρες, ὃν ἔτεκε Θαμὰρ τῷ Ἰούδα, καὶ ἐκ τοῦ σπέρματός σου
δῴη σοι Κύριος ἐκ τῆς παιδίσκης ταύτης.[q] αἰνίττονται τῆς
εὐλογίας οἱ λόγοι καὶ ἑτέραν αὐτὸν ἐσχηκέναι γυναῖκα· διὸ
καὶ τῆς Ῥαχὴλ καὶ τῆς Λείας κατὰ ταὐτὸν ἐμνημόνευσαν καὶ
80 ἐπήγαγον, αἳ ᾠκοδόμησαν ἀμφότεραι τὸν οἶκον Ἰσραήλ.[r] τὸ δὲ
ποιῆσαι δύναμιν ἐν Ἐφραθά· καὶ ἔσται ὄνομα ἐν Βηθλεὲμ παρὰ
πᾶσιν ἀνθρώποις ἀοίδιμον τὸν σωτήριον προθεσπίζει τόκον, δι'
ὃν γέγονεν ἡ Βηθλεὲμ πᾶσιν ἀνθρώποις ἀοίδιμος. τῆς δὲ

ll. 74f. καὶ ἔσται ὄνομα ἐν Βηθλεὲμ παρὰ πᾶσιν ἀνθρώποις ἀοίδιμον
6, 5 : καὶ ἔσται ὄνομα ἐν Βηθλεὲμ παρὰ πᾶσιν ἀοίδιμον ἀνθρώποις Sir.
Sch. : καὶ ἔσται ὄνομα ἐν Βηθλεὲμ F.M. = "'and there will be a name in
Bethlehem.'"
ll. 80–83 τὸ δε . . . ἀοίδιμον τὸν σωτήριον προθεσπίζει τόκον, δι' ὃν
γέγονεν ἡ Βηθλεὲμ πᾶσιν ἀνθρώποις ἀοίδιμος c_1, 37 : τὸ
δε . . . ἀοίδιμον τὸν σωτήριον προθεσπίζει τόκον, δι' ὃν γέγονεν ἡ
Βηθλεὲμ ἀοίδιμος πᾶσιν ἀνθρώποις 1 : τὸ δὲ . . . ἀοίδιμον τὸν σωτήριον
προθεσπίζει τόκον, δι' ὃν γέγονεν ἡ Βηθλεὲμ ἀοίδιμος παρὰ πᾶσιν
ἀνθρώποις 5, Sir. Sch. : τὸ δὲ . . . ἀοίδιμον F.M.

p. Ru 4.9f.   q. Ru 4.11f. (LXX var.)   r. Ru 4.11

ure. As Scripture says, "Boaz declared to the elders and all the people, 'You are witnesses today that I have acquired from the hand of Naomi all the property of Elimelech and everything belonging to Mahlon and Chilion. In addition, I have acquired Ruth the Moabite, the wife of Mahlon, to be my wife so as to raise up the deceased man's name over his inheritance to prevent the deceased man's name from perishing from among his brethren and his tribe.'"[p] The piety and precision of those words deserve admiration. What he means to say is, "In marrying a Moabite woman, I am not breaking, but fulfilling, the divine Law, for it is my goal to rescue from oblivion the memory of the deceased."

(3) The elders endorsed the marriage with the following blessing: "May the Lord make the woman who is coming into your house like Rachel and Leah, who together built the house of Israel, and may he perform mighty deeds in Ephrathah so that there will be in Bethlehem a name famous among all people. May your house be like the house of Perez, whom Tamar bore to Judah, and, through this girl, may the Lord give you offspring from your seed."[q] The words of the blessing imply that he had had another wife; hence, they mention Rachel and Leah at the same time and then continue, "who together built the house of Israel."[r] The subsequent "may he perform mighty deeds in Ephrathah so that there will be in Bethlehem a name famous among all people," foretells the saving birth by which Bethlehem became famous among all people.[2] They mentioned Tamar be-

2. Omitting the final clause, "foretells the saving birth by which Bethlehem became famous among all people" (τὸν σωτήριον . . . ἀνθρώποις), Fernández Marcos and Sáenz-Badillos leave without a verb the preceding subject, *i.e.*, the noun clause, "The subsequent 'may he perform mighty deeds in Ephrathah so that there will be in Bethlehem a name famous among all people'" (τὸ δὲ . . . ἀοίδιμον); *v.* the critical note.

The Questions on Ruth

Θαμὰρ ἐμνημόνευσαν, ἐπειδὴ κἀκείνη, ἀλλόφυλος οὖσα, τὸν
85 Φάρες γεγέννηκεν,ˢ ἐξ οὗ Δαβὶδ ὁ βασιλεὺς κατάγει τὸ γένος,
καὶ ὁ τοῦ Δαβὶδ ἀπόγονος, καὶ δεσπότης, καὶ υἱός, καὶ Κύριος.ᵗ

Ἐκ ταύτης ὁ Ὠβὴδ ἐγεννήθη, τοῦ Ἰεσσαὶ ὁ πατήρ, ὃς
ἔφυσε τὸν Δαβίδ. τοῦτο τὸ βρέφος αἱ γυναῖκες
προσενεγκοῦσαι τῇ Νοεμίν, ἔφασαν, εὐλογητὸς Κύριος, ὃς οὐ
90 κατέλυσέ σοι σήμερον τὸν ἀγχιστεύοντα ... καλέσαι τὸ ὄνομά
σου ἐν Ἰσραήλ. καὶ ἔσται ... εἰς ἐπιστρέφοντα ψυχήν.ᵘ τοῦτο
δέ, κατὰ μὲν τὸ πρόχειρον νόημα, τὴν ἐκείνης ψυχαγωγίαν
δηλοῖ· κατὰ δὲ τὴν ἀλήθειαν, τῆς οἰκουμένης ἐπιστροφήν·
ἐκεῖθεν γὰρ ἤνθησε τῆς οἰκουμένης ἡ σωτηρία.

s. Gn 38.29   t. Ru 4.17–22; Mt 1.3–6   u. Ru 4.14f.

cause, though she was also a foreigner, she gave birth to Perez,[s] from whom King David drew his descent as also David's descendant, master, son, and Lord.[t]

Ruth bore Obed, the father of Jesse, who begat David. Presenting this infant to Naomi, the women declared, "Blessed be the Lord, who today has not allowed you to lack a kinsman so as to proclaim your name in Israel. He will be the one to restore your life."[u] Now, in its superficial meaning, this refers to the consolation of that ancient woman, but in its deeper and true meaning, to the conversion of the world, since the salvation of the world was to blossom from that stock.[3]

3. According to A. Laffey (on 4.18–22), the concluding genealogy is generally regarded as a later addition. Theodoret, who is, of course, oblivious to this source critical issue, looks precisely to these verses for the deeper christological meaning (ἀλήθεια) of the book, which both justifies its position within Scripture and makes it a fitting conclusion to the Octateuch. Perhaps surprisingly, he has made no typological use of the figure of Boaz, the next-of-kin and redeemer; *cf.* Laffey's remarks on 2.19f. and 4.1–3.

INDICES

INDEX SCRIPTURISTICUS

1) Bold-faced numbers indicate direct quotation (*i.e.*, verbal equivalences; *v.* sec. 11 of the "Introduction to Theodoret's Life and Works"); those in normal typeface all other citations, whether paraphrases, allusions, or comparanda.

2) Citations appearing within the *Quaest. in oct.* are listed by question or question and subsection, those appearing in the introductions by the number of the page or footnote. A passage quoted or referred to more than once within a brief compass (*i.e.*, within a question lacking subdivision, a single subsection of a question, or a single explanatory note) is listed only once. If any of these citations is a direct quotation, the number appears in bold face. Thus in the context indicated by a bold-faced number, in addition to the direct quotation, the reader may find references to or paraphrases of the same verse(s). Verses cited in the critical and explanatory notes are listed separately even if they are also cited in the text of the work. Thus, the entry "*Q. in Gen.* **19.1,** 19 n. 2" would indicate that the same biblical passage is quoted in the first subsection of *Q.* 19 on Gn, and referred to in the second explanatory note on this question. The abbreviation c. n. indicates a critical, rather than an explanatory, note.

3) The abbreviation *(Q.)* indicates that the citation occurs in the query introducing the question. This notation is reserved for the longer questions in which the answers have been subdivided. Only in these do the actual queries fall outside a numbered section; *cf.*, *e.g.*, the set-up of *Q.* 1 on Gn with that of *Q.* 7.

4) As there are two introductions, one by R.C. Hill ("Introduction to Theodoret's Life and Works") and the second by J.F.P. ("Introduction to the Greek Text"), and each has its own series of footnotes, an asterisk marks references to the pages and notes of J.F.P.'s essay.

OLD TESTAMENT

Genesis
1: Intro. n. 7*; *Q. in Gen.* 21 n. 1, 22 n. 1; *Q. in Deut.* 1 n. 1
1.1: *Q. in Gen.* 1, **5, 11.1,** 14
1.2: Intro. **n. 28***; *Q. in Gen.* **5f., 8,** 8 n. 1
1.3: Intro. **p. xl;** *Q. in Gen.* 4.2, **9,** 14
1.4: *Q. in Gen.* 1, **10**

1.6: *Q. in Gen.* 4.2, **9, 11.1,** 14
1.7: *Q. in Gen.* 14; *Q. in Ex.* 60.2
1.7f.: *Q. in Gen.* **11.1,** 14
1.9 (LXX): *Q. in Gen.* **12**
1.9–12: *Q. in Gen.* 4.2, 14
1.10: *Q. in Gen.* 1
1.11 (LXX var.): *Q. in Ex.* **72,** 72 n. 1

1.11f.: *Q. in Gen.* 13, 13 n. 1, 16
1.12: *Q. in Gen.* 1, 17
1.14: Intro. p. xl; *Q. in Gen.* 14, **15,** 15 n. 2
1.14f.: *Q. in Gen.* 16
1.14–19: *Q. in Gen.* 4.2
1.16: *Q. in Gen.* 14
1.18: *Q. in Gen.* 1
1.20–25: *Q. in Gen.* 16

379

Index scripturisticus

NEW TESTAMENT

Index scripturisticus

GENERAL INDEX

In both the General Index and the Index of Modern Authors, the order of reference is 1) to the introductions, cited by page then footnote number; 2) to the *Quaest. in oct.*, cited by question or question and subsection; 3) to the critical and explanatory notes on the questions. References to the text and footnotes of R.C. Hill's "Introduction to Theodoret's Life and Works" precede those to the text and footnotes of J.F.P.'s "Introduction to the Greek Text"; in both the General Index and the Index of Modern Authors, an asterisk marks references to the pages and notes of J.F.P.'s essay.

In order to prevent confusion between the numbers of questions and subsections of questions on the one hand and those of the critical and explanatory notes on the other, we have adopted the following conventions. References to noncontiguous explanatory notes are joined by "and." Thus, under the heading "Feasts and Festivals: Passover," the sequence *"Q. in Ex.* 24, 24 nn. 1f. and 4f., 54, 72" makes reference first to *Q.* 24 on Ex, then to notes one, two, four and five on the translation of *Q.* 24, and then to *Q.* 54 (*i.e.,* not to explanatory note 54 on *Q.* 24). The abbreviation c. n. sets off references to notes on the Greek text.

In the General Index, the more complex articles are subdivided. In these, there is usually a collection of general references followed by one or more subheadings, which may be further divided. Capital letters set off the lemmata and those first subheadings that are themselves subdivided or followed by cross-references. The first and subsequent subheadings are arranged by a variety of criteria: alphabetical, chronological, logical. In the effort to facilitate reference we have had to sacrifice complete consistency of presentation.

In cross-references, a colon divides a main-, from a sub-, heading, and a semicolon items listed under separate lemmata. Thus, under "Animals / Irrational Beasts," the cross-references "Ritual Purity and Impurity: clean *vs.* unclean animals; Sacrifice: Animal Sacrifices" direct the reader to one subheading below the lemma "Ritual Purity and Impurity" and to another under "Sacrifice."

General Index

General Index

angels visit Abraham: Intro. p. xxxviii; *Q. in Gen.* 70, 70 n. 1

angel appears to Hagar: *Q. in Gen.* 2, 73

angels appear to Jacob: *Q. in Gen.* 84, 90

angel wrestles with Jacob: *Q. in Gen.* 93, 93 n. 1

angel tries to kill Moses: *Q. in Ex.* 14, 14 n. 1

angel appears to Balaam's ass: *Q. in Num.* 41

angel appears to Joshua: *Q. in Ios.* 5

angel appears to Gideon: *Q. in Iud.* 12f.

angel appears to Manoah: *Q. in Iud.* 20.2

"angel," the second person of the Trinity: *Q. in Gen.* 90; *Q. in Ex.* 5

cult of: Intro. p. xlviii, n. 73; *Q. in Gen.* 2 n. 1; *Q. in Num.* 41 n. 1

guardian angels: *Q. in Gen.* 3; *Q. in Num.* 41 n. 1

v. Gabriel (the archangel); Michael (the archangel); Salvation

Animals / Irrational Beasts: *Q. in Gen.* 7.1, 13, 16–18, 38 n. 1, 50.2, 52, 54f.; *Q. in Ex.* 32, 38, 52; *Q. in Num.* 43, 43 n. 1; *Q. in Deut.* 11 n. 1, 31 n. 1

blood of animal = its soul: *Q. in Leu.* 23; *Q. in Deut.* 11

v. Ritual Purity and Impurity: clean *vs.* unclean animals; Sacrifice: Animal Sacrifices

Anthropos (ἄνθρωπος): *Q. in Gen.* 20 n. 7

Antichrist: *Q. in Gen.* 112; *v.* Dan, Tribe of

Antioch: Intro. pp. xix, xxii, lii; *v.* Bible (Hebrew Scriptures): Ancient Translations: Greek (Septuagint): Antiochene recension; Biblical Interpretation: Patristic (Schools of Interpretation)

Apollinaris: *Q. in Num.* 22.1; *v.* Heretics, Christian

Apollo: *v.* Phoebus; Delphi; Pagan Deities

Aquila: Intro. p. xxvi, n. 24; *Q. in Gen.* 22, 31, 38 n. 1, 41, 47.2, 51, 111 n. 1, 112.6, 112 n. 8; *Q. in Ex.* 1; *Q. in Leu.* 1, 22.2; *Q. in Deut.* 8; *Q. in Ios.* 10; *Q. in Iud.* 8 c. n., 17

Aramaic: Intro. p. xxvi, n. 14; *Q. in Gen.* 60 n. 1

Archangels: *v.* Angels; Gabriel (the archangel); Michael (the archangel)

Arethas of Caesarea: *Q. in Gen.* 34 c. n.

Aristarchus: Intro. n. 62

Aristeas, Letter of: Intro. n. 74

Arius / Arians: *Q. in Ex.* 37, 37 n. 1; *v.* Heretics, Christian

Ark of the Covenant: *Q. in Ex.* 12, 31, 60.2; *Q. in Leu.* 22.1; *Q. in Num.* 3.1, 6, 11.3, 34.1; *Q. in Ios.* 2.4, 7 n. 1; *Q. in Iud.* 27.2

Ark of Noah: *Q. in Gen.* 18.1, 43, 50.2, 50 n. 1, 51f.

Armenia: *Q. in Gen.* 29; *v.* Bible (Hebrew Scriptures): Ancient Translations: Armenian

Asher (son of Jacob): *Q. in Gen.* 88 n. 1

Asher, Tribe of: *Q. in Gen.* 112.5; *Q. in Deut.* 45.2

Assyria / Assyrians: *Q. in Gen.* 59; *Q. in Leu.* 18; *Q. in Num.* 44 n. 2; *Q. in Deut.* 24.1

Astarte: *Q. in Iud.* 7.2, 18; *v.* Pagan Deities

Astrology: *Q. in Gen.* 25

Athens: Intro. p. lxv*; *Q. in Gen.* 11.2

Augustine: Intro. p. xxxiii

Baal: *Q. in Ex.* 44 n. 1; *Q. in Deut.* 4; *Q. in Iud.* 7.2, 14, 18

Baal of Peor: *Q. in Num.* 44.2; 44 n. 3; *Q. in Deut.* 1.3

v. Pagan Deities

Babylon / Babylonians: *Q. in Gen.* 73; *Q. in Leu.* 18, 37.1; *Q. in Num.* 3 n. 3; *Q. in Deut.* 34.2, 41 n. 1; *Q. in Ios.* 2.1; *v.* Tower of Babel

Babylonian Exile: *v.* Exile, Babylonian

Balaam: Intro. pp. xxxix, xlix; *Q. in Num.* 39–42, 44, 44 n. 3; *Q. in Deut.* 1 n. 2; *Q. in Ios.* 19.4

General Index

General Index

General Index

General Index

Decalogue: *v.* Ten Commandments

Delphi: *Q. in Gen.* 11.2; *Q. in Deut.* 13.1; *v.* Phoebus

Demiurge: *Q. in Gen.* 19 n. 1

Demons: *Q. in Gen.* 19.1, 31; *Q. in Ex.* 14 n. 1; 44, 54, 60.1 ; *Q. in Leu.* 1.1, 23, 28f.; *Q. in Deut.* 10, 12, 28
> children sacrificed to demons: *Q. in Gen.* 74; *Q. in Iud.* 20, 20 n. 1
> goat of dispatch not sacrificed to a demon: *Q. in Leu.* 22.2; 22 n. 2
> *v.* Devil; Egypt / Egyptians: type of demons

Devil: Intro. pp. xlii, xlv, n. 63; *Q. in Gen.* 36, 37.1, 112.2; *Q. in Ex.* 34, 69; *Q. in Leu.* 30; *Q. in Deut.* 5, 42.1
> makes use of the serpent: Intro. p. xlii, *Q. in Gen.* 32, 32 n. 1, 33, 35, 37.3, 40, 40 n. 1; *Q. in Leu.* 13
> *v.* Demons; Pharaoh: In the Time of the Exodus

Didymus: *v.* Thomas (Didymus)

Didymus the Blind: Intro. p. xxx, nn. 34, 32*; *Q. in Gen.* 20 n. 5

Dietary Laws: Intro. p. xxxiv; *Q. in Gen.* 93 n. 2

Diodore of Tarsus: Intro. pp. xix, xxii, xxix, xxxif., xxxvii, xli, xlvi, nn. 18, 35, 48, 62, 64, 74, 32*; *Q. in Gen.* 8 n. 1, 20 n. 5, 40 n. 2, 48 n. 1, 59 n. 1, 94 c. n., 94 n. 2, 112 nn. 5 and 9; *Q. in Leu.* 1 n. 6, 14 n. 1, 21 n. 1; *Q. in Ios. pf.* n. 1; *Q. in Ruth* 2 n. 1

Ebed Jesu: *Q. in Ex.* 1 n. 1

Ebla: *Q. in Gen.* 20 nn. 1 and 5

Eden: *v.* Paradise / Garden of Eden

Edom / Idumaeans: *Q. in Gen.* 62, 69, 95; *Q. in Ex.* 3; *Q. in Leu.* 37.2; *Q. in Deut.* 1.2, 26

Egypt / Egyptians: Intro. pp. xxi, xxxix; *Q. in Gen.* 1, 61f., 73, 101, 109, 109 n. 1; *Q. in Ex.* 10f., 14, 40.2, 76; *Q. in Leu.* 37.1; *Q. in Num.* 1, 18.1, 22.1
> benefactors of Israelites: *Q. in Gen.* 78, 96, 101; *Q. in Deut.* 26; *Q. in Ios.* 19.4

circumcised: Intro. p. xxxv; *Q. in Gen.* 69, 111; *Q. in Ex.* 3, 3 n. 1; *Q. in Ios.* 3

despoiled: *Q. in Gen.* 66; *Q. in Ex.* 23, 70

enslave, oppress, pursue the Israelites: Intro. p. xlv; *Q. in Gen.* 67; *Q. in Ex.* 5f., 10, 12.2, 13f., 19, 22f., 24.2, 24.4, 27, 33, 72; *Q. in Leu.* 37.2; *Q. in Deut.* 1.4f., 34.2; *Q. in Ios.* 3f.

idolaters: Intro. p. xl; *Q. in Gen.* 1; *Q. in Ex.* 10, 12.3, 13, 18 n. 1, 19–21, 24.2, 38, 40.2, 55; *Q. in Leu.* 1.1, 1.5, 24

magicians, sorcerers, wizards: *Q. in Ex.* 11, 12.3, 18, 20

nostalgia for Egypt: *Q. in Ex.* 13, 66

punished by God: *Q. in Gen.* 67; *Q. in Ex.* 8, 12.2, 12.5, 18–20, 22, 24.1, 24.4, 24 n. 1; 36, 68; *Q. in Num.* 5, 33

type of demons: Intro. p. xlv; *Q. in Ex.* 27

Egyptian killed by Moses: *Q. in Ex.* 47 n. 1

Egyptian language: Intro. p. lv; *Q. in Gen.* 104 n. 1; *Q. in Ex.* 24 n. 1

Ehud: *Q. in Iud.* 9

Eleazar: *Q. in Leu.* 10, 10 n. 1; *Q. in Num.* 47; *Q. in Ios.* 19.2, 20 n. 1; *Q. in Iud.* 27.2

Elijah: *Q. in Ex.* 44, 44 n. 1

'elohim: Intro. pp. xxv, xlvii; *Q. in Gen.* 1 n. 3, 19 n. 2; *Q. in Ex.* 51 n. 1

Enoch: *Q. in Gen.* 45, 45 n. 1, 47 n. 1, 98

Ephesus, Council of: Intro. p. xx

Ephod: *Q. in Ex.* 60.5, 60 nn. 9f.; *Q. in Iud.* 17, 17 n. 1, 24, 24 n. 1

Ephraim (son of Joseph): *Q. in Gen.* 111; *Q. in Deut.* 34 n. 1, 45.1

Ephraim, Tribe of: Intro. p. xxvi; *Q. in Gen.* 111; *Q. in Deut.* 34, 34 n. 1; *Q. in Iud.* 19, 24

Esau: *Q. in Gen.* 79, 81f., 111; *Q. in Deut.* 33
> ancestor of Job: *Q. in Gen.* 95

General Index

Eschatology: Intro. pp. xliii, li; *Q. in Gen.* 54 n. 1; *Q. in Num.* 44 n. 4; *Q. in Deut.* 11 n. 1, 41 n. 1, 44 n. 1

Ethiopia: *v.* Sheba

Etymologicum gudianum: Q. in Gen. 51 c. n. (κρεοφαγεῖν)

Etymology: *v.* Biblical Interpretation, Patristic (Method / Themes): Etymological Interpretation

Eunomius: *Q. in Ex.* 37; *v.* Heretics, Christian

Euphrates, River: *Q. in Gen.* 29, 62; *Q. in Iud.* 19

> boundary of promised land: *Q. in Ex.* 69; *Q. in Ios.* 2

Eusebius of Ancyra: Intro. n. 4

Eusebius of Caesarea: Intro. n. 13; *Q. in Gen.* 59 c. n. (ᾠκοδομῆσθαι); *Q. in Ios.* 5 n. 1

Eusebius of Emesa: Intro. pp. xxxi, xxxiii; *Q. in Gen.* 59 n. 1; *Q. in Leu.* 21 n. 1

Eustathius of Antioch: Intro. n. 60

Eutyches: Intro. p. xxi; *Q. in Leu.* 1 n. 1; *v.* Heretics, Christian

Eve: Intro. pp. xxxiv, xlix; *Q. in Gen.* 27f., 30, 32, 32 n. 1, 33, 37.2f., 39; *Q. in Ex.* 9

Exile, Babylonian: Intro. p. xxxix; *Q. in Gen.* 49, 49 n. 1; *Q. in Deut.* 1 n. 1, 36 n. 1

Exodus, The: Intro. pp. xxxix, xlii; *Q. in Gen.* 67, 110, 112.3; *Q. in Ex.* 12.5, 14, 24, 33, 40, 44 n. 1, 54, 60.1, 60 n. 10, 70; *Q. in Leu.* 32.2; *Q. in Deut.* 1.1, 15, 43; *Q. in Ios.* 2.2, 8, 19.4; *Q. in Iud.* 7.1, 13; *v.* Egypt / Egyptians: nostalgia for Egypt

Faith: *v.* Virtue: Theological Virtues

Fall, The: Intro. pp. xlix, lif.; *Q. in Gen.* 24, 24 n. 1, 25 n. 1, 26, 28, 33, 37, 37 n. 2, 38–40, 40 n. 2, 43 n. 2, 49 n. 1

Feasts and Festivals: Intro. p. xxix; *Q. in Ex.* 24, 24 n. 2, 54, 72; *Q. in Leu.* 6, 22.4, 32, 32 n. 1; *Q. in Num.* 15, 47; *Q. in Deut.* 1 n. 6, 9f., 13, 33; *Q. in Ios.* 2.4, 4

> Passover: Intro. p. xxv; *Q. in Ex.* 24, 24 nn. 1f. and 4f., 54, 72, 72 n.

1; *Q. in Leu.* 32, 32 n. 1; *Q. in Num.* 14; *Q. in Ios.* 2.4, 2 n. 2, 4, 5

> etymology of the word: *Q. in Ex.* 21, 21 n. 1

> passover lamb: *v.* Sacrifice: Animal Sacrifices

> Pentecost: Intro. p. xxix; *Q. in Ex.* 54; *Q. in Leu.* 32, 32 n. 1

> Feast of Trumpets: *Q. in Leu.* 32.2, 32 n. 1

> Day of Atonement: *Q. in Leu.* 22, 22 n. 1, 32.2, 32 n. 1, 35

> Feast of Tabernacles: Intro. p. xxix; *Q. in Ex.* 54; *Q. in Leu.* 32.2, 32 n. 1; *Q. in Deut.* 1 n. 6

First Fruits, Offering of: *Q. in Ex.* 54, 61, 70; *Q. in Leu.* 1.5, 2; *Q. in Num.* 9, 34.1; *Q. in Deut.* 9, 13 n. 3, 33 n. 1, 44.2, 45.1; *Q. in Ios.* 7

Free Will: Intro. pp. xlix–lii; *Q. in Gen.* 36, 36 n. 1; *Q. in Ex.* 12.2–4, 12 n. 1; *Q. in Num.* 8, 8 n. 1; *Q. in Deut.* 1, 1 n. 1, 22, 29, 37.1, 37 n. 1; *Q. in Iud.* 8.2

Gabriel (the archangel): *Q. in Ex.* 72; *Q. in Deut.* 42.1; *v.* Angels

Gad (son of Jacob): Intro. p. xxxviii; *Q. in Gen.* 88 n. 1

Gad, Tribe of: *Q. in Gen.* 112.5; *Q. in Deut.* 45.2

Giants: *Q. in Gen.* 48, 48 n. 1; *Q. in Num.* 26, 26 n. 1; *Q. in Deut.* 7.1, 18; *Q. in Iud.* 1

Gibeah: *Q. in Iud.* 27.1, 27 n. 1

Gibeon, Gibeonites: *Q. in Gen.* 68; *Q. in Num.* 14, 14 n. 1; *Q. in Ios.* 13, 15 n. 1

Gideon: *Q. in Iud.* 12–17

> not an idolater: Intro. p. xxxiv; *Q. in Gen.* 107 n. 1; *Q. in Iud.* 22 n. 1

> not lacking in trust in God: *Q. in Iud.* 13

Gilgal: *Q. in Ios.* 4, 4 n. 2; *Q. in Iud.* 7.1, 7 n. 1

> etymology of the name: *Q. in Ios.* 4, 4 n. 2

Gnostics: *Q. in Gen.* 19 n. 1; *Q. in Ex.* 23 n. 2; *v.* Heretics, Christian

General Index

God:

His Qualities (without reference to humanity):

eternal: *Q. in Gen.* 1

impassible: *Q. in Ex.* 67

incorporeal: *Q. in Ex.* 62

invisible: *Q. in Ex.* 68; *Q. in Deut.* 1.4

triune: *v.* Christ; Trinity

true God: *Q. in Gen.* 20.2, 109; *Q. in Leu.* 11.2, 33; *Q. in Num.* 39; *Q. in Iud.* 12, 18

uncircumscribed: *Q. in Gen.* 3, 20.1, 20.3; *Q. in Ex.* 60.1; *Q. in Deut.* 1.4

unchanging: *Q. in Gen.* 37.2; *Q. in Num.* 42

His Intervention in History:

Creator: Intro. p. xl, n. 28*; *Q. in Gen.* 1, 4–9, 11, 13f., 16–22, 24f., 35f., 48, 86; *Q. in Ex.* 21, 43, 60.2; *Q. in Deut.* 1.4, 44.1; *Q. in Ios.* 19.4; *v.* Image of God

Lawgiver: *Q. in Gen.* 37; *Q. in Ex.* 60.1; *Q. in Leu.* 32.2; *Q. in Num.* 15; *Q. in Deut.* 1, 1 n. 1, 7.2; *v.* Census; Circumcision; Covenants: God's Covenants with Mankind; Dietary Laws; Feasts and Festivals; First Fruits, Offering of; Image / Idol; Jubilee; Kingship, Israelite; Law of Moses; Leprosy; Liturgy; Marriage; Oaths / Swearing; Oracles; Prayer; Priest / Priesthood; Ritual Purity and Impurity; Sabbath; Sacrifice; Sexuality; Sin; Sinai, Mt.; Tabernacle; Tattoo; Temple; Ten Commandments; Tetragrammaton; Tithes; Virtue; Vows

Guide of History: Intro. pp. xlvi, xlix, n. 55; *Q. in Gen.* 13, 18.1, 19.2, 24, 35f., 37.2f., 48, 50, 52, 55, 63 n. 1, 72, 74, 78, 84, 90, 102, 112.6; *Q. in Ex.* 18, 20, 24.1, 24.4, 28 n. 1; *Q. in Num.* 42, 49; *Q. in Deut.* 6, 6 n. 1, 12, 43, 44.1; *Q. in Iud.* 8; *v.* Astrology; Blessings and Curses; Christ; Covenants; Exile, Babylonian; Exodus, The; Fall, The; Free Will; Grace; Israel, Nation of / Israelite; Jordan, River; Luck; Manna; Oracles; Red Sea, Crossing of; Salvation; Typology; Wandering of Israel / Forty Years in the Wilderness

all-knowing / foreknowing: Intro. pp. xxxiv, xlixf.; *Q. in Gen.* 18, 20.2, 24, 35, 37.2f., 50, 55, 72, 74, 102; *Q. in Ex.* 8, 12.3f., 13, 20, 40.2; *Q. in Num.* 37, 42f.; *Q. in Deut.* 6, 37, 43; *Q. in Iud.* 8.2

all-powerful: *Q. in Ex.* 6, 11, 58; *Q. in Num.* 1; *Q. in Deut.* 1.4

glorious: *Q. in Gen.* 20.2; *Q. in Ex.* 69; *Q. in Num.* 11.3, 22.2, 27, 43; *Q. in Deut.* 42.1; *Q. in Ios.* 2.3

good / loving / merciful: Intro. pp. xxxiv, l, n. 28*; *Q. in Gen.* 18 n. 1, 37–39; *Q. in Ex.* 6, 8, 12.1f., 12.4, 15, 24.2, 40.2, 51, 66–68; *Q. in Leu.* 16, 18, 22.3; *Q. in Num.* 18.1, 42; *Q. in Deut.* 1.3, 6, 22, 38.1, 42.1; *Q. in Ios.* 2.3; *Q. in Iud.* 12, 18, 22, 27.1

jealous: *v.* Israel, Nation of / Israelite: beloved of God

just: Intro. pp. xxxiv, xlix; *Q. in Gen.* 24, 35–37, 42, 50.1, 63f.; *Q. in Ex.* 8, 12, 18, 23, 23 n. 2, 40, 51, 68; *Q. in Leu.* 7, 7 n. 1, 20, 33; *Q. in Num.* 19, 23, 33, 37; *Q. in Deut.* 1.2, 12, 29, 37; *Q. in Ios.* 12, 12 n. 1, 15; *Q. in Iud.* 8.2, 27.1

General Index

God: *(cont.)*
  His Intervention in History:
    (cont.)
    Savior: *v.* Salvation
    v. Christ; *'elohim;* Trinity;
    Yahweh
Goliath: *Q. in Gen.* 48
Grace: Intro. pp. xxviii, xxxii, xliii, xlv, xlixf.; *Pf.* n. 3; *Q. in Gen.* 8, 26, 76, 81, 83, 98, 112.3; *Q. in Ex.* 24.3, 27, 69; *Q. in Leu.* 9, 11.1; *Q. in Num.* 11.3, 18, 21, 36, 47; *Q. in Deut.* 42 n. 1, 43; *Q. in Iud.* 14f., 21f.
Greece / Greeks: Intro. p. xxi; *Q. in Gen.* 3, 61; *Q. in Ex.* 21, 38; *Q. in Leu.* 1.1, 28f.; *Q. in Ios.* 16
Greek language: Intro. p. lxxxiv*; *Q. in Gen.* 11.2, 61f.; *Q. in Leu.* 29
  Greek Terms in this Index: *v.*
    Ainigmata (αἰνίγματα);
    Akribeia (ἀκρίβεια);
    Anthropos (ἄνθρωπος); *Historia*
    (ἱστορία) / *Historiographos*
    (ἱστοριογράφος); Prophet
    (προφήτης); *Skopos* (σκοπός);
    Synkatabasis (συγκατάβασις);
    Sexuality: sexual diseases
    (γονορρυής, γονορρυέω)
Gregory of Nazianzus: *Q. in Gen.* 3 n. 1
Gregory of Nyssa: Intro. p. xxx; *Q. in Gen.* 20 n. 4; *Q. in Ex.* 60.4 c. n.

Hagar: *v.* Angels; Jerusalem: heavenly *vs.* earthly Jerusalem; Sarah
Ham: Intro. n. 28*; *Q. in Gen.* 57f., 111 n. 2
Harosheth: *Q. in Iud.* 11, 11 n. 1
Hazor: *Q. in Ios..* 10f., 11 n. 1
Heaven: Intro. pp. xl, xlv; *Q. in Gen.* 1, 3–8, 11f., 14, 16, 20.1f., 21, 25, 37.2, 75.1, 84, 86, 112.6; *Q. in Ex.* 21, 29, 43, 60.2f.; *Q. in Leu.* 1.3, 22.2, 22.4, 32.1; *Q. in Num.* 6, 18.1, 31, 47; *Q. in Deut.* 1.3f., 7.2, 38.2, 40, 42.1; *Q. in Ios.* 2.2
  Kingdom of Heaven, of God: Intro. p. xlvii; *Q. in Gen.* 24, 38; *Q. in Leu.* 11.2; *Q. in Num.* 6, 27, 35;

Q. in Deut. 34.1, 43; *Q. in Ios. pf.,* 2.2, 2.4, 3
Heber: *Q. in Gen..* 72
Hebrew Language: Intro. pp. xxivf., xxxvf., xli, xlvii, lii, nn. 21, 47, 70; *Q. in Gen.* 1 n. 3, 6 n. 2, 11.2, 11 n. 1, 20 n. 5, 44 n. 1, 47 n. 2, 60 n. 1, 61, 61 n. 1, 62, 62 n. 2, 71 n. 2, 88 n. 1, 89 n. 1, 91 n. 2, 93 n. 2, 94 n. 2, 100 n. 1, 111 n. 1; *Q. in Ex.* 24.1, 24 n. 1, 25 n. 1, 26 n. 1, 30 n. 1, 51 n. 1, 58 n. 1, 60 n. 10, 70 n. 1; *Q. in Leu.* 22 n. 2, 25 n. 2, 35 n. 2; *Q. in Num.* 3 n. 3, 25 n. 1, 35 n. 1, 43 n. 1; *Q. in Deut.* 44.1; *Q. in Ios.* 4 n. 2, 10 n. 2, 11 n. 2; *Q. in Iud.* 3 n. 1, 7.1, 7 n. 1, 19 n. 1, 23 n. 1, 24 n. 1, 26 n. 1; *v.* Bible (Hebrew Scriptures)
Hebron: Intro. p. xxviii; *Q. in Gen.* 66, 110, 110 n. 1; *Q. in Ios.* 17; *Q. in Iud.* 1
Hell: *Q. in Gen.* 20.1, 37.1; *Q. in Ex.* 12.4; *Q. in Num.* 33; *Q. in Deut.* 34.1
Heresy: Intro. pp. xxif., xxxii, nn. 8, 55; *Q. in Gen.* 19.1, 22 n. 1; *Q. in Ex.* 24.3; *Q. in Leu.* 1 n. 1; *Q. in Ios.* 26
Heretics, Christian: *Q. in Gen.* 19.1, 37.1; *Q. in Ex.* 24.3f.; *Q. in Leu.* 1.1, 9, 9 n. 1; *v.* Apollinaris; Arius / Arians; Eunomius; Eutyches; Gnostics; Manicheans; Marcion / Marcionites; Nestorius / Nestorians; Simon Magus
Herod (Agrippa): *Q. in Deut.* 42.2
Herodotus: *Q. on Leu.* 24 n. 1
Hexapla: Intro. pp. xxiiif., nn. 19, 21, 23; *v.* Bible (Hebew Scriptures): Ancient Translations: Greek (Septuagint); Origen
Hippolytus: *Q. in Gen.* 112 n. 9; *Q. in Ruth* 1 n. 1
Historia (ἱστορία) / *Historiographos* (ἱστοριογράφος): *v.* Biblical Interpretation, Patristic (Method / Themes): Historicity of Old Testament Narrative
Hittites: *Q. in Ios.* 16; *Q. in Iud.* 8.1
Hobab: *v.* Jethro
Holy of Holies: *Q. in Ex.* 60.2f.; *Q. in Leu.* 22, 22 n. 4; *Q. in Num.* 11.3

412

General Index

Holy Place: *Q. in Ex.* 60.2; *Q. in Leu.* 10, 22.1

Holy Spirit: *v.* Trinity: Holy Spirit

Homer / Homeric Poems: Intro. p. xxxiii, n. 62

Homeritae: *Q. in Num.* 22.1

Hope: *v.* Virtue: Theological Virtues

Horeb, Mt.: *Q. in Deut.* 1.1, 1.4, 1 n. 1, 35, 35 n. 1; *v.* Sinai, Mt.

Human Being: *v.* Anthropos (ἄνθρωπος)
   composed of soul and body: Intro. pp. xlivf., n. 66; *Q. in Gen.* 112.5; *Q. in Leu.* 11.1, 19
   mortal by nature: Intro. n. 9; *Q. in Gen.* 37.2
   possesses immortal soul: *Q. in Leu.* 23
   has dominion over other creatures: Intro. n. 28*, *Q. in Gen.* 18.2
   tills the earth: Intro. n. 28*
   gains immortality through Christ: *Q. in Gen.* 37.3, 38

Hypatius: Intro. pp. xx, l; *Pf.*, *Pf.* n. 2

Image / Idol: *Q. in Deut.* 1.3f., 1 n. 3, 34.1; *Q. in Iud.* 24–26
   of God: *Q. in Ex.* 6; *Q. in Deut.* 1.3f.
   of other gods: *Q. in Gen.* 31, 74, 87, 91; *Q. in Ex.* 38, 41; *Q. in Leu.* 25, 25 n. 1; *Q. in Num.* 44.2, 44 n. 3; *Q. in Deut.* 34.1; *Q. in Ios.* 2.1; *Q. in Iud.* 9, 18, 20.1, 24, 24 n. 1, 25f.
   of the golden calf: *Q. in Gen.* 2; *Q. in Ex.* 60.1, 66; *Q. in Deut.* 7.2, 43
   of the bronze serpent: *Q. in Num.* 38
   Worship of, Idolatry: Intro. pp. xxxiv, xl, xlii; *Q. in Gen.* 1, 47.3, 55, 72, 88; *Q. in Ex.* 10, 38, 40.2, 44, 59; *Q. in Leu.* 16f., 23, 25; *Q. in Num.* 44.2, 44 n. 2, 48; *Q. in Deut.* 1.3, 7, 10, 12, 26, 43; *Q. in Ios.* 2.1f., 4, 4 n. 2, 19.2f., 20, 20 n. 1; *Q. in Iud.* 6f., 8.2, 12, 17f., 20.1, 22, 22 n. 1, 25f.; *v.* Sexuality: prostitution

Image of God: Intro. pp. xxvii, xlvii, li, n. 28*; *Q. in Gen.* 18.1, 19, 19 n. 2, 20, 20 nn. 1 and 6, 27; *Q. in Ex.* 69

Incorporeal existence: *Q. in Gen.* 36; *v.* Angels; Demons; Devil

Isaac: *Q. in Gen.* 64, 75, 75 n. 1, 78, 98
   Sacrifice of Isaac: *v.* Abraham: tested by God
   blessed by God: *Q. in Gen.* 75, 112.3
   his covenant with God: *Q. in Gen.* 110f., 112.7, *Q. in Ex.* 5, 35; *Q. in Leu.* 37.2
   blesses Jacob: *Q. in Gen.* 79–81, 83
   type of the divinity of Christ: *Q. in Gen.* 74
   Fear of Isaac: *Q. in Gen.* 92

Ishmael: Intro. p. xxxiv; *Q. in Gen.* 69, 73, 111

Ishmaelites: *Q. in Leu.* 37.2, 38

Israel (name given to Jacob): *v.* Jacob

Israel, Nation of / Israelite: Intro. pp. xxi, xxxix, xlviii, n. 63; *Q. in Gen.* 62, 69; *Q. in Ex.* 21, 28, 30, 34, 60.5, 72 n. 1; *Q. in Num.* 18.1, 22.2, 47; *Q. in Deut.* 13 n. 2; *Q. in Iud.* 7.1, 28
   beloved of God: *Q. in Gen.* 74; 112.3; *Q. in Ex.* 39; *Q. in Num.* 42; *Q. in Deut.* 7.2, 44.1, 45.1; *Q. in Iud.* 20.1
   blessed by God: Intro. p. xxxvii; *Q. in Ex.* 54; *Q. in Leu.* 37.2; *Q. in Num.* 45; *Q. in Deut.* 13.2, 43; *Q. in Ios.* 19.3f.
   chosen by God: *Q. in Gen.* 58, 72, 76, 110, 112; *Q. in Ex.* 5f., 22, 35, 39, 58, 65; *Q. in Leu.* 22, 25; *Q. in Num.* 4, 11.3, 22.1, 37, 41 n. 1, 42f., 44 n. 4, 46 n. 1; *Q. in Deut.* 2, 10, 33, 33 n. 1, 44.1, 46; *Q. in Ios.* 2.3, 3, 15f., 20; *Q. in Iud.* 7.2, 18; *Q. in Ruth* 1.2, 2.3
   enslaved to Egypt: *Q. in Gen.* 88; *Q. in Ex.* 12, 22, 72
   guilty of idolatry: Intro. p. xl; *Q. in Gen.* 1, 47.3; *Q. in Ex.* 40.2, 60.1; *Q. in Leu.* 18, 18 n. 1, 25; *Q. in Num.* 44.2, 44 n. 3; *Q. in Deut.*

413

General Index

Israel, Nation of / Israelite: *(cont.)*
  guilty of idolatry: *(cont.)*
    7.2, 26, 28 n. 1, 43; *Q. in Ios.* 20, 20
    n. 1; *Q. in Iud.* 17f., 24, 24 n. 1
  inherits the promised land: Intro.
    pp. xlvii, l; *Q. in Gen.* 58; *Q. in
    Num.* 37; *Q. in Deut.* 1.2, 6 n. 1,
    46; *Q. in Ios.* 8, 12 n. 2, 13, 15f.; *Q.
    in Iud.* 5, 7.2, 8, 8 n. 1, 9f., 11 n. 1,
    12f.
  Religious Rites and Institutions of:
    Intro. pp. xxix, xxxix, xliv; *Q. in
    Leu.* 20 n. 1, 21 n. 1, 27 n. 1, 30 n. 2,
    32 n. 3; *Q. in Num.* 28 n. 1; *Q. in
    Deut.* 9 n. 1, 33 n. 1; *Q. in Iud.* 22
    n. 1; *v.* Altar of Incense; Altar of
    Sacrifice; Ark of the Covenant;
    Circumcision; Dietary Laws;
    Feasts and Festivals; Holy of
    Holies; Holy Place; Jubilee; King-
    ship, Israelite; Law of Moses;
    Liturgy: Jewish; Marriage: levi-
    rate marriage; Mercy Seat; Oaths
    / Swearing; Oracles; Prayer;
    Priest / Priesthood; Ritual Purity
    and Impurity; Sabbath; Sacrifice;
    Tabernacle; Temple; Tithes; Vows
  subject to the Law: Intro. pp.
    xxxviiif.; *Q. in Gen.* 71 n. 1; *Q. in
    Ex.* 12.5, 65, 72; *Q. in Leu.* 1.2, 21,
    22.4, 23, 27 n. 1, 30, 32.2; *Q. in
    Num.* 18.1, 34.1; *Q. in Deut.* 1.3, 2,
    7.2, 10, 33, 35, 38, 44.2; *Q. in Ios.*
    2.1, 13, 19.3; *Q. in Iud.* 8.2, 12, 16,
    22 n. 1, 27; *Q. in Ruth* 1 n. 1
  weights and measures of: Intro.
    p. xxxvi; *Q. in Ex.* 30, 64; *Q. in
    Leu.* 38; *Q. in Num.* 34.1
  v. Jews / Jewish
Issachar, Tribe of: *Q. in Gen.* 112.4; *Q. in
  Deut.* 45.2
Italy: *Q. in Gen.* 61

Jacob: Intro. p. xxxviii; *Q. in Gen.* 84f.,
  90–92, 98, 101, 106, 110; *Q. in Ex.* 10; *Q.
  in Num.* 16; *Q. in Deut.* 40; *Q. in Ios.*
  19.1, 19.4, 20

Jacob's blessing is identical to the
  blessing of Abraham: *Q. in Gen.*
  83f., 112.3
appropriates Esau's blessing: *Q. in
  Gen.* 80–82, 111
Jacob at Bethel: Intro. p. xliii; *Q. in
  Gen.* 84f., 90
Jacob at Penuel: Intro. p. xxxvi;
  Q. in Gen. 93, 93 n. 2; *Q. in Num.*
  16
blesses Ephraim and Manasseh: *Q.
  in Gen.* 111; *Q. in Deut.* 45.1
blesses and curses his sons: *Q. in
  Gen.* 112; *Q. in Num.* 3; *Q. in
  Deut.* 44.1, 45.2, 45 n. 2, 46, 46 n.1
prophesies Christ: *Q. in Gen.* 112.3f.
buried in Hebron: *Q. in Gen.* 110f.
An Exemplary Man:
    did not lie to Isaac: *Q. in Gen.*
      82
    not an idolater: *Q. in Gen.* 85,
      88f.
    not lustful: *Q. in Gen.* 86
    piously rebuked Rachel: *Q. in
      Gen.* 86
his covenant with God: *Q. in Ex.* 5,
  35; *Q. in Leu.* 37.2
type of the God of Jews and gen-
  tiles: *Q. in Gen.* 91
James (brother of Jesus): *Q. in Gen.* 112.3;
  Q. in Num. 11.1; *Q. in Deut.* 42.2
James (son of Zebedee): *Q. in Deut.*
  42.2
Japheth: *v.* Shem, Ham, and Japheth
Jashar, Book of: Intro. p. xli, n. 59; *Q. in
  Ios.* 14 n. 1
Jebus: *v.* Jerusalem
Jehoiada (high priest of Judah): *Q. in
  Ios.* 19.1
Jephthah: Intro. pp. xxvi, xxxiv; *Q. in
  Iud.* 19f.
Jericho: *Q. in Ios.* 7, 11 n. 1; *Q. in Iud.* 5, 5
  n. 1, 8.2, 9
    curse on the rebuilder of Jericho:
      Q. in Ios. 9
Jerome: Intro. pp. xxii, xxv, xxxiii, nn. 21,
  44; *Q. in Gen.* 104 n. 1; *Q. in Ios.* 10 n. 1

General Index

General Index

General Index

Love: *v.* God: His Intervention in History: Guide of History; Virtue: Theological Virtues

Lucian of Antioch: Intro. pp. xxii–iv, nn. 1 and 14; *v.* Bible (Hebrew Scriptures): Ancient Translations: Greek (Septuagint): Lucianic Recension (Vulgate)

Luck: *Q. in Gen.* 88, 88 n. 1, 99

Macedon / Macedonians: *Q. in Leu.* 18; *Q. in Num.* 44.1; *Q. in Deut.* 34.2; *v.* Alexander of Macedon

Magi: *v.* Persia / Persians / Persian Empire

Manasseh (son of Joseph): *Q. in Gen.* 111; *Q. in Deut.* 34 n. 1, 45.1; *Q. in Ios.* 16

Manasseh, Tribe of: *Q. in Deut.* 34.1, 34 n. 1; *Q. in Ios.* 16; *Q. in Iud.* 13

Manicheans: *Q. in Leu.* 22 n. 2; *v.* Heretics, Christian

Manna: Intro. p. xlv; *Q. in Ex.* 27, 29–32, 60.2, 60 n. 1; *Q. in Leu.* 32.1; *Q. in Num.* 18.1; *Q. in Deut.* 6; *Q. in Iud.* 5
  etymology of the word: *Q. in Ex.* 30, 30, n. 1

Manoah: *Q. in Iud.* 20.2

Marcion / Marcionites: Intro. p. xxii; *Q. in Gen.* 37.2; *Q. in Ex.* 23 n. 2; *v.* Heretics, Christian

Mari documents: *Q. in Gen.* 67 n. 1

Marriage: *Q. in Gen.* 30, 37.2, 86f., 90, 110; *Q. in Leu.* 1.6, 20; *Q. in Ruth* 1 n. 1, 2
  intermarriage with foreigners: *Q. in Gen.* 47.3, 50.1, 72, 75.1; *Q. in Deut.* 6; *Q. in Ios.* 19.3; *Q. in Iud.* 7.2, 21, 26
  Intermarriage between Tribes: *Q. in Num.* 51, 51 n. 1
    between Judah and Levi: a type of Christ's royal priesthood: *Q. in Ex.* 16; *Q. in Ios.* 19.1; *Q. in Iud.* 25
  legislation regarding marriage: *Q. in Leu.* 24, 30
  levirate marriage: Intro. p. xxxviii; *Q. in Gen.* 97; *Q. in Deut.* 32; *Q. in Ruth* 1.1

Marriage of Moses: *v.* Moses

marriage of the Benjaminites: *Q. in Gen.* 112.7

marital strife: Intro. p. xx; *Q. in Gen.* 30
  second marriage: *Q. in Leu.* 1.3
  sibling marriage: *Q. in Gen.* 43

Mary: *v.* Virgin Mary, The

Masoretes / the Masoretic Text: *v.* Bible (Hebrew Scriptures)

Matthew: *Q. in Gen.* 98; *Q. in Num.* 16 n. 1; *Q. in Ruth* 1.1, 1 n. 1

Medicine: *v.* Science, Ancient

Melchizedek: *Q. in Gen.* 65f., 98
  blesses Abraham: *Q. in Gen.* 65
  consulted by Rebekah: *Q. in Gen.* 77, 77 n. 1,
  type of the royal priesthood: *Q. in Gen.* 65, 65 n. 1; *Q. in Ex.* 60.3; *Q. in Num.* 50

Mercy Seat: *Q. in Ex.* 60.2, 60 n. 1; *Q. in Leu.* 22.1, 22.3f., 22 n. 1; *Q. in Num.* 11.3

Micah (the Ephraimite): *Q. in Iud.* 24–27

Michael (the archangel): Intro. pp. xlviiif.; *Q. in Gen.* 2, 2 n. 1, 3, 3 n. 3; *Q. in Num.* 41, 41 n. 1; *Q. in Ios.* 5; *v.* Angels

Midian / Midianites: *Q. in Gen.* 47.3; *Q. in Num.* 22.1, 22 n. 1, 44.2, 44 n. 3, 48; *Q. in Iud.* 12f., 16, 26

Miriam: *Q. in Iud.* 12
  Rebels against Moses: *v.* Aaron

Moab / Moabites: Intro. p. xlvi; *Q. in Gen.* 62, 71 n. 1; *Q. in Num.* 44.1; *Q. in Deut.* 1.2, 26; *Q. in Ios.* 20; *Q. in Iud.* 18; *Q. in Ruth* 1.1, 2.2
  worshippers of Chemosh: *Q. in Gen.* 72
  v. Covenants: God's Covenants with Mankind: with Israel

Moloch: *v.* Ammon / Ammonites; Pagan Deities

Moses: Intro. pp. xxviii, xxxivf., xxxviii, xlixf.; *Q. in Gen.* 91, 107 n. 1; *Q. in Ex.* 14 n. 1, 27, 47 n. 1; *Q. in Iud.* 4, 4 n. 1, 12, 26, 26 n. 2

General Index

Origen: Intro. pp. xxiv, xxvii, xxx, xlv, nn. 1, 13, 19, 21, 23, 28, 34, 44, 66; *Q. in Gen.* 3 n. 1, 48 n. 1, 75 n. 2; *Q. in Ex.* 25 n. 1; *Q. in Num.* 43 n. 1; *Q. in Ios.* 5 n. 1; *v.* Hexapla

Osroënians: *Q. in Iud.* 19

Othniel: Intro. n. 80; *Q. in Iud.* 3, 9, 9 n. 1

Pagan Deities: *v.* Astarte; Baal; Chemosh; Kaiwan; Moloch; Phoebus; Rephan

Palestine / Promised Land: Intro. pp. xxiv, l; *Q. in Gen.* 58, 62, 65–67, 69, 78, 84, 110; *Q. in Ex.* 30 n. 1, 44, 54, 59, 60.1; *Q. in Leu.* 22.3, 32.1; *Q. in Num.* 27, 37, 37 n. 1, 45; *Q. in Deut.* 1.1–4, 7, 9, 35, 43, 43 n. 1; *Q. in Ios.* pf., 2–4, 17; *Q. in Iud.* 7f.

Paneas: Intro. p. xxxvi; *Q. in Gen.* 112.4; *Q. in Deut.* 45.2; *Q. in Iud.* 26; *v.* Dan: capture of Leshem

Paradise / Garden of Eden: Intro. n. 28*; *Q. in Gen.* 24f., 25 n. 1, 29, 29 n. 1, 37.3, 40; *Q. in Num.* 50

Passover: *v.* Feasts and Festivals

Pentecost: *v.* Feasts and Festivals

Penuel: *Q. in Gen.* 93 n. 2

Persia / Persians / Persian Empire: *Q. in Gen.* 3, 61; *Q. in Leu.* 24, 24 n. 1; *Q. in Num.* 44.1, 44 n. 2

    magi: Intro. pp. xxf.; *Q. in Leu.* 1.1, 1 n. 1

Peshitto: *v.* Bible (Hebrew Scriptures): Ancient Translations: Syriac

Peter (Simon): *Q. in Leu.* 11.2; *Q. in Num.* 5 n. 1, 16; *Q. in Deut.* 42.1

Pharaoh:

    in the time of Abraham: *Q. in Gen.* 63f., 64 n. 1

    in the time of Joseph: *Q. in Gen.* 101, 109, 109 n. 1

    In the Time of the Exodus: Intro. p. xxxv; *Q. in Gen.* 88, 88 n. 1; *Q. in Ex.* 8f., 17 n. 1, 21f.; *Q. in Deut.* 12

        his heart hardened by God: Intro. p. l; *Q. in Ex.* 12, 12 nn. 1 and 3, 18; *Q. in Deut.* 37.1;

Q. in Ios. 2.2

    type of the devil: Intro. p. xlv; *Q. in Ex.* 27

Philistines: *Q. in Ex.* 12.5, 59, 60.5, 60 n. 10; *Q. in Num.* 44 n. 2; *Q. in Iud.* 17f., 21f.

Philo Iudaeus: Intro. pp. xxv, xxx, xxxiii, n. 34; *Q. in Gen.* 62 c. n. (ὁ περάτης), 75 n. 2; *Q. in Ex.* 23 n. 2, 24.1; *Q. in Leu.* 1 n. 6

Philosophy, Ancient: Intro. p. xxi; *Q. in Gen.* 25 n. 1; *Q. in Leu.* 1 n. 1; *v.* Philo Iudaeus; Plato; Pythagoras; Sophists; Stoics

Phinehas: *Q. in Ios.* 19.2; *Q. in Iud.* 27.2

Photius: Intro. pp. xxxiii, lii, n. 76, p. lx*, n. 14*; *Pf.* c. n.

Phoebus: *Q. in Deut.* 13.1, 13 n. 1; *v.* Delphi; Pagan Deities

Physiology: *v.* Science, Ancient

Plato: *Q. in Gen.* 15, 19.2

Potiphar: Intro. p. xxxv; *Q. in Gen.* 100, 100 n. 1

Prayer: *Q. in Ex.* 53; *Q. in Leu.* 1.6, 10; *Q. in Deut.* 22 n. 1

    of Abraham: *Q. in Gen.* 64

    of Abraham's servant: *Q. in Gen.* 75.2

    of Rebekah: *Q. in Gen.* 77

    of Isaac: *Q. in Gen.* 83

    of Rachel: *Q. in Gen.* 91

    of Jacob: *Q. in Gen.* 112

    of Moses: *Q. in Ex.* 12.3; *Q. in Deut.* 7.2, 44.1

    of Samson: *Q. in Iud.* 22

    in Israelite worship: *Q. in Ex.* 41, 60

Priest / Priesthood:

    Israelite: Intro. pp. xxxiv, xliiif., l; *Q. in Gen.* 112.1, 112.3; *Q. in Ex.* 7, 15f., 16 n. 1, 36, 44, 60, 60 n. 1 and 5, 61, 61 n. 1, 63; *Q. in Leu.* 1.3, 1.5f., 3, 8, 8 n. 1, 10, 10 n. 1, 15, 22, 22 n. 4, 23, 30, 30 n. 1, 38; *Q. in Num.* 3–6, 9–11, 15, 18.2, 23, 32f., 34.1, 47, 50, 50 n. 1, 51, 51 n. 1; *Q. in Deut.* 9f., 13 n. 3, 17, 34.1, 44.2, 44 n. 3, 45.1; *Q. in Ios.* 2.4, 7 n. 1, 19.1; *Q. in Iud.* 17, 24–26, 27.2

General Index

General Index

General Index

General Index

Trumpets, Feast of: *v.* Feasts and Festivals

Typology: *v.* Biblical Interpretation, Patristic (Method / Themes)

Ugarit: *Q. in Gen.* 20 n. 1

Urim and Thummim: *v.* Oracles

Virgin Mary, The: *Q. in Gen.* 19.2, 49.2; *Q. in Ex.* 6; *Q. in Deut.* 24; *Q. in Ios.* 1 n. 1

Virginity: *v.* Sexuality: virginity

Virtue: *Q. in Gen.* 18.1, 37, 51, 69 n. 2; *Q. in Leu.* 11.1

    Characteristics of:

        active in deeds: *Q. in Ex.* 60.6, 61; *Q. in Leu.* 1.6

        voluntary: Intro. p. l; *Q. in Gen.* 36; *Q. in Deut.* 37.1

    Figurative Descriptions:

        adornment of soul: *Q. in Ex.* 60.5

        agonistic imagery:

            athletes of virtue: *Q. in Gen.* 36, 45; *Q. in Ex.* 12.4

            Paradise = the prize of virtue: *Q. in Gen.* 24, 45

        wealth of soul: Intro. p. xxxv; *Q. in Ex.* 53

    Exemplified by:

        biblical saints: Intro. n. 53; *Q. in Gen.* 98

            Abraham: *Q. in Gen.* 69, 73, 78

            Abraham's descendants: *Q. in Gen.* 97

            Boaz: *Q. in Ruth* 1.2, 2.2

            Joseph: *Q. in Gen.* 96; *Q. in Ios.* 19.3

            Moses: *Q. in Ex.* 68; *Q. in Num.* 22

            Noah: *Q. in Gen.* 50.1

            Rebekah: *Q. in Ruth* 1.1

            Sarah: *Q. in Ruth* 1.1

            Seth: *Q. in Gen.* 47

            Seth's descendants: *Q. in Gen.* 50.1

            Shem: *Q. in Gen.* 58

Christians: *Q. in Gen.* 18.1; *Q. in Ex.* 24.3; *Q. in Leu.* 1.6; *Q. in Deut.* 43

    women: *Q. in Gen.* 20 n. 7; *Q. in Ruth* 1.1

Cardinal Virtues:

    courage (fortitude): *Q. in Iud.* 22

    justice: *Q. in Gen.* 58, 97 n. 1, 105, 108; *Q. in Ex.* 23, 51; *Q. in Leu.* 2; *Q. in Num.* 9; *Q. in Deut.* 16, 31

        for the poor and needy: *Q. in Gen.* 47.2; *Q. in Ex.* 51; *Q. in Deut.* 34.1

    prudence: *Q. in Gen.* 31, 31 n. 1; *Q. in Num.* 14, 14 n. 1, 18.1; *Q. in Deut.* 12; *Q. in Iud.* 20.1

    temperance (moderation): *Q. in Ex.* 12.1; *Q. in Leu.* 30, 32.2; *Q. in Deut.* 13.1; *Q. in Ios.* 15, 18; *v.* Sexuality: continence

Theological Virtues:

    faith: *Q. in Gen.* 91, 98, 111; *Q. in Ex.* 68; *Q. in Num.* 22.2; *Q. in Deut.* 28; *Q. in Iud.* 8.1, 13; *Q. in Ruth* 1.1

        of Abraham: *Q. in Gen.* 66, 69, 69 n. 2, 74, 75.1; *v.* Circumcision

        Israel lacking in: *Q. in Ex.* 31, 39; *Q. in Dt.* 1.2

        in Christ: *Q. in Deut.* 42.1

        necessary for salvation: Intro. p. xlii; *Q. in Gen.* 26; *Q. in Ex.* 22; *Q in Num.* 38; *Q. in Ios.* 2.1f.

        must be complemented by works: Intro. p. l; *Q. in Ex.* 60.6, 63; *Q. in Leu.* 11.1

    hope in God: *Q. in Gen.* 6, 47.2, 47 n. 2

        Christ, the hope / expectation of Christians: *Q. in Gen.* 83, 112.3; *Q. in Ex.* 60.3

INDEX OF MODERN AUTHORS

We define as "modern" those scholars active since the invention of the printing press. Figures of the earlier period are identified first by the Latin, and then by the vernacular, version of their names. We have tried to catch all those places where an author's name appears but have not traced all those where he or his work is referred to without name; thus, in the immediate context of those contained in this index, the reader may find additional references to the same or another work by that scholar. In references to the critical notes, we have extracted all names except those of J.F.P. and the editors routinely cited: Sirmond, Schulze, and Fernández Marcos and Sáenz-Badillos. In addition to the introductions and the notes on the text and translation of the *Quaest. in oct.*, this index cites the *Conspectus siglorum* (*Cs*). For other details of organization and abbreviation, *v*. the introduction to the General Index.

Index of Modern Authors

Index of Modern Authors

Support for the
LIBRARY OF EARLY CHRISTIANITY
from the following donors is gratefully acknowledged

The Annenberg Foundation
Ave Maria School of Law
Christopher A. Beeley
The Gladys Krieble Delmas Foundation
Mr. and Mrs. Peter Flanigan/New York Community Trust
Herrick Jackson and Polly Jackson/The Connemara Fund
Rev. Richard T. Lawrence
The National Endowment for the Humanities
Mr. and Mrs. Michael Novak
Dr. and Mrs. Paul S. Russell
Mark Ryland
Sacred Heart School of Theology
The Cynthia L. and William E. Simon Foundation
The Strake Foundation

Michael J. Aquilina Jr.
Rev. William R. Deutsch
Rev. Gerard H. Ettlinger, S.J.
Everett Ferguson
Rose A. Frascello
Michael Gaddis
Craig L. Hanson
Rev. Stanley S. Harakas
Walter Harrelson
Daniel and Ann James
Joel D. Kalvesmaki
Adam Kamesar
Paul R. Kuhn

Henry Ciemniecki Lang, Ph.D.
Johan Leemans
Rev. Joseph T. Lienhard, S.J.
Samuel J. Mikolaski
Michael Mintz
Susan E. Myers
Rev. Karen L. Onesti
Rev. Dr. L. G. Patterson
Claudia Rapp
Michael Slusser
Louis Swift
Dr. Karen Jo Torjesen
Efthalia Makris Walsh, Ph.D.

Robert Wilde